THE FIELD OF HONOR

The Field of Honor

ESSAYS ON SOUTHERN CHARACTER AND AMERICAN IDENTITY

EDITED BY
John Mayfield and Todd Hagstette

FOREWORD BY
Edward L. Ayers

THE UNIVERSITY OF SOUTH CAROLINA PRESS

Published by the University of South Carolina Press
Columbia, South Carolina 29208

www.sc.edu/uscpress

Manufactured in the United States of America

26 25 24 23 22 21 20 19 18 17
10 9 8 7 6 5 4 3 2 1

Library of Congress Cataloging-in-Publication Data

Names: Mayfield, John, 1945– editor. | Hagstette, Todd, editor.
Title: The field of honor : essays on southern character and American identity / edited by John Mayfield and Todd Hagstette ; foreword by Edward L. Ayers.
Description: Columbia, South Carolina : Published by the University of South Carolina Press, [2017] | Includes bibliographical references and index.
Identifiers: LCCN 2016047777 (print) | LCCN 2016048207 (ebook) | ISBN 9781611177282 (hardcover : alk. paper) | ISBN 9781611177299 (ebook)
Subjects: LCSH: Honor—Southern States. | Southern States—Social life and customs—1775–1865. | Southern States—Social life and customs—1865–
Classification: LCC F209 .F54 2017 (print) | LCC F209 (ebook) | DDC 975/.03—dc23
LC record available at https://lccn.loc.gov/2016047777

This book was printed on recycled paper with 30 percent postconsumer waste content.

CONTENTS

Edward L. Ayers

FOREWORD

Honor's Southern Journey

Honor threatened to end my scholarly career before it had properly begun. The encounter occurred just after I had delivered my first conference paper, sketching the outlines of crime and punishment across the South in the nineteenth century, arguing that much of the well-documented homicidal violence in the South had been shaped by and driven by a culture of honor. Previous explanations for the persistent bloodshed in the region's past had focused on dysfunctional conditions such as the frontier, alcohol, militancy, pessimism, and a sense of grievance, so the idea that violence followed a certain kind of perverse logic seemed provocative and perhaps even useful.

After the session ended a genial scholar in a bright plaid jacket and bow tie came up to offer a word of support. I recognized the memorable name on his tag—Bertram Wyatt-Brown—from an article he had published a few years earlier, "The Ideal Typology in Antebellum Southern History." I told him how much I admired that piece and asked him what he was working on now. He cheerfully said that he had just completed the final touches on a book to be called *Southern Honor.* In fact he had been reading the page proofs in his hotel room, and the book would be out in a few months.[1]

I must have done a poor job of disguising my anxiety and disappointment, for he kindly invited me to have a beer with him at the hotel bar, where he described his forthcoming book in detail. I was astounded by its reach and scale but reassured by Wyatt-Brown's generous spirit, reflected in his insistence that I call him Bert. He said he would send me the page proofs as soon as he finished reading them.

A couple of weeks later I studied the many pages with admiration but also with churning stomach as I confronted a proudly idiosyncratic work that combined literary history, gender, law, psychohistory, and more, all in surprising ways. The book explicated honor in lovingly detailed vignettes of violence, disorder, and betrayal. Wyatt-Brown invoked W. J. Cash's *The Mind of the South* as an inspiration, and indeed both books were intoxicating in their confidence. Wyatt-Brown announced in the introduction of *Southern Honor,* moreover, that he would write another book on slavery and honor and yet another on honor's decline—which he saw beginning as early as the time of Thomas Jefferson. In the meantime those aspects of honor would have to wait, for "the task of the moment is to show how honor functioned in the first place." He performed that task with daunting energy and imagination.[2]

Southern Honor was not a fashionable book in 1982; in fact it was boldly iconoclastic, insisting on culture's independence from its social and material foundations. Nevertheless Wyatt-Brown's book, we can see at this distance, embodied several aspects of the intellectual climate of the 1970s and early 1980s. The concept of honor as a coherent culture had recently been defined, elaborated, and theorized by anthropologists and sociologists, who found honor at work in many places throughout the world. Julian Pitt-Rivers, J. G. Peristiany, and others had pioneered the idea in the 1960s and published a series of influential essays and collections over the next decade that brought the topic wide recognition. In its depth and coherence, their portrayal of honor fit comfortably with the work of fellow anthropologist Clifford Geertz; his seminal article on the cultural logic of the Balinese cockfight was becoming one of the most influential works among historians in the 1970s and 1980s.[3]

Powerful new books in southern history at the time also inclined scholars to look for inclusive and coherent cultural interpretations. Eugene Genovese's *Roll, Jordan, Roll* exerted remarkable intellectual hegemony after its publication in 1974, portraying the slave South as a complex society dominated by the relationship between master and slave. Honor corresponded well with such a hierarchical and organic society in which a personalized relationship between master and slave effectively resisted the machinery and values of capitalism. Many historians agreed with Genovese that the South was a place profoundly distinct from the North, with a ruling ethic in sharp contrast to the ethic of industrial capitalism. The dramatic critical rise and fall of the Robert Fogel and Stanley Engerman's *Time on the Cross*, which aimed to demonstrate through econometrics that the slave South was in fact profoundly capitalist, only secured the conviction of many historians that the South was nothing of the kind.[4]

As a graduate student in the late 1970s, consumed by these exciting developments, I was intrigued by another recent book, this one by sociologists Peter Berger, Brigitte Berger, and Hans Kellner: *The Homeless Mind: Modernization and Consciousness*. The Bergers argued that the modern world was tone deaf to the concept of honor. "Honor occupies about the same place in contemporary usage as chastity," they observed. "An individual asserting it hardly invites admiration, and one who claims to have lost it is an object of amusement rather than sympathy." In our own time, the communal and hierarchical concept of honor had been replaced by the individualistic and egalitarian concept of "dignity," tailored to a dynamic capitalist society, for dignity "relates to the intrinsic humanity divested of all socially imposed roles or norms. It pertains to the self as such, to the individual regardless of his position in society."[5]

Elliott Gorn and I read *The Homeless Mind* for an independent reading in the "new social history" in 1977. The book led us in turn to the anthropological literature on honor also influencing Wyatt-Brown in these years. Elliott and I would both adopt honor versus dignity in our work, the binary appearing in my 1980 dissertation and in what would become Elliott's important and influential essay on backcountry fighting in the *American Historical Review* in 1985.[6]

Despite the doors it opened, *The Homeless Mind* presented only a brief excursus on honor. Its real subject was "modernization," a concept that promised to unify economic, cultural, political, and psychological aspects of society. In modernization theory change in one aspect of a society's development comes accompanied with others in a kind of package. As Berger and colleagues put it, "All social reality has an essential component of consciousness."[7] The honor-and-dignity binary easily fit the North-and-South binary. A premodern and communal South, tied only tangentially to the machinery of the market and the state would of course foster honor while a North born modern would of course foster its opposite.

In the midst of these exciting developments, I staked out a dissertation that would try to connect the South's notorious history of crime and punishment across the nineteenth century. Crime was another hot scholarly topic in the 1970s, and honor helped address one of the key questions of such a study, for historians and sociologists had long agreed that the South, since at least the early nineteenth century, had outstripped the rest of a violent nation in its rates of homicide. The South had also sustained a horrible history of chain gangs, lynchings, and mob violence, and perhaps honor would help explain some of these haunting issues as well. I certainly had no problem locating many firsthand accounts of white southerners of all classes acting by the dictates of honor when they shot each other in carefully staged duels or bit off each others' ears while wrestling on a barroom floor, but the same language also marked defenses of lynching and vigilante violence decades later.

As grateful as I was for its organizing power, I adopted the teleological honor-versus-dignity schema with some qualms, qualifying the notion of honor even as I deployed it. The titles of the chapters on honor hedged their bets with puns: "Honor and Its Adversaries" and "The Hurt That Honor Feels." The "adversaries" were not only the men who fought each other but also the forces that increasingly challenged and undermined honor—the evangelical church, the state, and the values of business. The "hurt" that honor felt after the Civil War came in the form of widespread disdain and even ridicule, signaled by the virtual disappearance of the duel within a couple of decades after the collapse of slavery and the Confederacy, even as poor white and poor black men continued to kill one another with relentless regularity for the next century.

No sooner did I set honor up as one explanation for southern violence, in other words, than I questioned its larger implications. I found clear evidence of countervailing power, embodied in the anomaly of the penitentiary in the slave South. According to every historian and theorist of the penitentiary—another scholarly boom of the 1970s—there should have been no penitentiaries in the antebellum South. The penitentiary, Michel Foucault and others told us, was the key modern institution, deploying the power of the state to penetrate inmates' very minds, to focus on the personality rather than the body. And yet every southern state except South Carolina built some of the world's first penitentiaries for white inmates. That expensive and ambitious agenda suggested that the white South could not be simply a premodern, honor-bound society.[8]

When I looked at the prisoners in those penitentiaries, moreover, they looked a lot like the prisoners in the North, sent there in enormous numbers from supposedly inconsequential southern cities that stood at the intersections of the global market that supposedly had no real role in the South. When international economic crises hit, the population of the southern penitentiaries ballooned. The antebellum prisoners were often immigrants, Irishmen who played no role in our understanding of the South, and they had often committed property crimes indistinguishable from the crimes committed in the North. Clearly the state and the economy played roles quite different in the South from those that modernization theory led us to expect.

Other parts of southern society also refused to fit into a vision of a society subsumed by honor. Court records showed that southerners had no qualms about going to court for everything other than offenses against honor, and sometimes for those as well. The trials and exclusions in church records demonstrated that vast numbers of white and black southerners explicitly rejected the claims of honor. Evangelical religion, growing stronger across the entire century even as honor grew weaker, defined itself against honor and its dictates.

These inconvenient anomalies were turning in my mind when Wyatt-Brown's page proofs arrived in the midst of the revision of my dissertation into the book *Vengeance and Justice: Crime and Punishment in the Nineteenth-Century American South*. Frankly I was relieved to see that our arguments diverged at two critical junctures. First, Wyatt-Brown dwelt on honor's ancient roots and its existence before and independent of slavery. I, by contrast, argued that it was only slavery that allowed honor and its manifestations of dueling and other affairs of honor to survive and even flourish in the 1840s and 1850s South, while those kinds of violence were dying in the North. Second, Wyatt-Brown went to considerable lengths to show the ways that honor had infiltrated the entire culture of the white South, including religion and the law. I, on the other hand, put honor in persistent tension and conflict with these other powerful forces in the South. Southern honor, firmly rooted in the social relations fostered by slavery, nevertheless fit the South poorly. The American slave South's central but anomalous position in the emerging world of the capitalistic and state-oriented world of the nineteenth century proved an uncomfortable home for honor.[9]

Wyatt-Brown's vision won out quite handily. Not only did he beat me to the marketplace of ideas with a sizeable lead and a more fully realized vision, but he refused to surround his argument with qualifications and conflicts, banishing enervating aspects in a compelling panorama. I resigned myself to being the perpetual second reference in footnotes about honor when I managed to make an appearance at all, eventually recognizing that had his book never been published my own sketches of honor would not have attracted much attention on their own. Rather than being the habitual runner-up in footnotes I would not have been footnoted at all.

I moved on, not writing about honor again until now, though I did excerpt a piece about the topic for *American Heritage,* explaining how a large portion of present-day violence could be explained by honor among white and black southerners and descendants of southerners. Other people picked up that theme of that cultural appropriation and continuity in ways I did not agree with, and so I did nothing more with that concept. Even in my long book on the post-Reconstruction South that came out in 1992, where I dealt again with lynching and other forms of violence, I made only passing references to honor. Honor, contrary to Wyatt-Brown's subsequent writing, played no role in my explanation of the coming, fighting, and consequences of the Civil War, a project that has preoccupied me for the last two decades.[10]

In fact much of what I have written since *Vengeance and Justice* could be seen as a kind of penance for the pages of modernization theory, cultural homogenization, ahistorical generalization, regional reification, and other multisyllabic transgressions into which the honor/dignity binary seduced me. I have actively rejected those convenient habits of thought ever since and have tried to portray the South in ways that reject them.[11]

With this story of my youthful dalliance with honor buried in the past, therefore, I accepted the writing of this foreword with both eagerness and trepidation. Some of my own doctoral students, such as John C. Willis and Amanda Mushal (represented in this volume) have written on honor in ways that revise my own interpretation, and I was on the dissertation committee of Joanne Freeman, whose book has perhaps done the most to demonstrate that honor was not a uniquely southern affair in the early years of the nation. I was interested to see how the conversation has developed since I last paid close attention.[12]

Several things became clear as I read these fascinating essays. Wyatt-Brown's *Southern Honor* remains the touchstone for every student of the subject, especially for literary and cultural historians, and his definitions continue to define the topic and guide its further exploration. Kenneth Greenberg's *Honor and Slavery* appeared in 1996, and its subtitle—*Lies, Duels, Noses, Masks, Dressing as a Woman, Gifts, Strangers, Humanitarianism, Death, Slave Rebellions, the Pro-slavery Argument, Baseball, Hunting, and Gambling in the Old South*—advertised its affinity with Wyatt-Brown's exuberant portrayal and extended the concept even more fully while grounding it in slavery. Wyatt-Brown's own subsequent writing did the same, steadily expanding honor's reach. The impression created by scholars writing on the topic today seems to be that the concept emerged fully formed, as a kind of school, and is now ready for revisiting and revision with new questions.[13]

The essays in this volume show that the fundamental issue of southern history remains the relationship of the South to the non-South. But there is an important difference now, for in recent decades the distance between the North and South has narrowed and blurred. For one thing we have recovered the role of the northern colonies in the Atlantic slave trade and the patterns of racial exclusion in the North after the Revolution. The distance has narrowed, too, as historians shift the portrayal of slavery from one of timeless plantations to one defined by a churning slave trade and the massive displacement of enslaved people. The relationship between master and slave now seems more a fleeting and brutal transaction than anything that can be disguised as quasi-familial. Historians such as Ira Berlin, Walter Johnson, and Edward Baptist do not picture the market as a force outside of slavery, even opposed to slavery; rather slavery appears as the literal embodiment of the market, feverishly at work across the South, driving railroads and steamboats, taking advantage of sophisticated banking and insurance networks.[14]

For their part, the historians busy recasting the relationship between the slave South and the machinery of capitalism have not had much to say about honor to this point. The implication of their work, however, would seem to be that honor was unlikely to find the kind of bounded, static communities the vision of honor Wyatt-Brown and his successors assumed. If the South was as dislocated and dynamic as the new history of slave capitalism suggests, the very social bases of honor could never have existed in the way that Wyatt-Brown portrayed them. The anthropology of the Mediterranean, the model for his vision of honor in the South, would seem a poor fit.

John Mayfield's helpful essay at the beginning of this volume describes this unfolding scholarship and poses the key problem. If the slave South was as turbulent as it is currently being portrayed, if honor was as prevalent in the early Republic and in the American political system as Joanne Freeman shows, and if southern intellectual life was as modern as Michael O'Brien has demonstrated, an enveloping code of honor would seem unlikely.[15] Today, the slave South appears marbled with the networks and carriers of modernity, and as Lawrence T. McDonnell reminds us in his essay in this collection, the last antebellum decade stood as "a moment of financial, technological, communications, and detective revolution, when telegraphs, daguerreotypes, rotary-press-printed newspapers, railroad travel, prices-current sheets, and professional police forces flooded the South."

The assumptions of the 1970s and 1980s about the South, in other words, have shifted beneath honor's feet. Anyone who would study honor now would have to begin with a South of repeated and profound dislocation, of unstable class relations, of perpetual struggle between enslaved people and those who held them in slavery, of confident and dynamic churches, and with a South that stood at the very center of the world's most sophisticated and powerful markets. The South we imagine today, in other words, looks profoundly different from the South many historians, including Bertram Wyatt-Brown, imagined in 1982.

All the authors in this book point to ways to reconcile honor with this more dynamic South. In her essay on James Chesnut, for example, Anna Koivusalo argues that "rather than an independent, self-evident notion, honor was a tool for finding and expressing appropriate emotions." Precisely because the South was unpredictable, "southerners craved security and stability in their lives. They sought answers and support from code books and manuals." Koivusalo shows that white southerners used honor to "navigate the complex discourse" between raw emotions and emotions they could display to the world. Thus honor was less a dictate or a rigid system, she argues, than a tool for navigating an unsettled social landscape.

This instrumental and delimited understanding of honor appears in other essays here. Timothy Williams argues that "southern men were not always and everywhere fixated on honor. Instead, they drew from a broader Victorian world to understand and articulate who they were and wished to become." Christopher Curtis demonstrates that even elite white men could go to court and emerge with their honor intact. Kathleen Hilliard effectively uses an "absurd and corrosive dispute over ninety-seven bushels of corn in 1824" to show the "deep ambivalences gripping southerners in the midst of extraordinary social and economic change." Amanda Mushal demonstrates that "ideas of honor were invoked in support of the emerging modern business culture," as the credit agency, the very embodiment of a distended market, "re-created the face-to-face world it was in the process of replacing." Matthew Byron documents how the "capitalistic professions" of lawyers, doctors, editors, and merchants accounted for a large share of duels. And David Moltke-Hansen shows that the supposed worship of chivalry in the Old South was an invention of the New South.

Bradley Johnson argues that the duel, rather than an anachronism, was "a calculated means of bridging the gap between republican government and elite control over the varied levels of social class." Todd Hagstette shows that "the written word was as important as the loaded pistol to the southern man of honor." Jeffrey Anderson emphasizes that honor had a "horizontal" as well as "vertical" dimension, working among African Americans as well as among white southerners. Jeff

Forret's detailed research in court records shows that the language of shame, a component of an honor culture, recurred in cases in which enslaved women appeared. Brenda Faverty argues that gossip was as important as dueling in the honor culture of the South. And Robert Levine joins others in the collection in demonstrating that honor was not strictly a southern phenomenon.

The final three essays of this collection bring our understanding of honor to play in the contemporary South. Sarah Gardner shows the concept still troubling the twentieth-century fiction of Andrew Lytle. Edward Crowther argues that even today "in many households in the American South, an honor-based Christian masculinity persists, challenging androgynous and feminist ideas in the same manner that antebellum southern evangelicalism resisted abolitionism." Crowther sees a great continuity across southern history, a continuity that helps explain why the South today remains so politically distinct, unified, and powerful. His portrayal bears the closest resemblance to Wyatt-Brown's original vision of any of the essays in this collection.

Dickson Bruce and Emily Bruce, also writing about the current-day South, take a different approach. They argue that "as the large body of scholarship on honor makes clear, any attempt to fix a universal definition of *honor* not only does violence to its richness but also ignores its central character: the flexibility with which it justifies an array of actions in the social and political arenas." The Bruces show how the language of honor is thrown around with abandon in current political conversations, used to justify whatever combatants think honor will help justify. This honor looks little like the stifling community consensus Wyatt-Brown saw as the key to honor and nothing like the clumsy suit of armor (and clumsy metaphor) I used to describe the rigidity of honor.

So have we come full circle, so that honor, identified so clearly and robustly in the early 1980s, no longer explains very much in particular about the South? Have we found it distributed so profusely in so many times, places, and facets of life that it has lost its explanatory power? If honor appears, in some form, virtually everywhere we look but always in a qualified and bedraggled form, what then does it actually explain?

Honor, it seems to me, is most useful regarding particular facets of social life. Manhood in the South has long struggled, and continues to struggle, with honor. The language of honor appears throughout accounts of shootings and stabbings that still appear in every southern newspaper. The politics of the South, more distinct from the rest of the country today than in 1982, is marked by tough-talking language about independence, manliness, and the strong defense of individual, of state, and of nation, language that echoes the language of secession, redemption, and massive resistance. The language of honor remains tightly bound to the language of race, in profound tension with the dictates of Christianity, and contemptuous of the compromises of the white-collar workplace.

None of this is simple, and none of it is static. As the essays in this collection show, it never has been. Precisely because honor constantly takes new forms and meanings, in fact, honor helps us understand a southern past that has never stood still. Such an understanding marks scholarly progress, a movement toward more supple and more inclusive understanding.

NOTES

1. Wyatt-Brown, "Ideal Typology."
2. Wyatt-Brown, *Southern Honor,* xvi–xvii.
3. Geertz, *Interpretation of Cultures.*
4. Genovese, *Roll, Jordan, Roll;* Fogel and Engerman, *Time on the Cross.*
5. Berger et al., *Homeless Mind,* 83, 89.
6. Gorn, "Gouge and Bite."
7. Berger et al., *Homeless Mind,* 12.
8. Foucault, *Discipline and Punish.*
9. Ayers, *Vengeance and Justice.*
10. Ayers, "Legacy of Violence"; Ayers, *Promise of the New South;* Ayers, *In the Presence of Mine Enemies.*
11. See, in particular, the title essay and "Worrying about the Civil War" in Ayers, *What Caused the Civil War?*
12. John C. Willis, "From the Dictates of Pride"; Freeman, *Affairs of Honor.*
13. Greenberg, *Honor and Slavery.*
14. Berlin, *Generations of Captivity;* W. Johnson, *River of Dark Dreams;* Baptist, *Half Has Never Been Told.*
15. O'Brien, *Conjectures of Order.*

PREFACE

This is a book about something called "honor" and its role in shaping southern and—by extension—American life. It gathers the work of twenty authors who write about what honor is and how it expresses itself, and it does so from their many different, but related, methodologies and interpretive perspectives. There is no simple "thesis" here, nor could there be. Honor is too complicated, as we shall see. What is here is an interdisciplinary discussion of four basic questions: How do we define honor? How does it manifest itself? Was it peculiarly southern? Finally, does honor still have any meaning in modern America?

There is no single response to any of these questions, but there are certain common threads of inquiry. Modern studies of honor draw on the work of Mediterranean anthropologists such as Julian Pitt-Rivers, whose work was broadcast in this country by the historian Bertram Wyatt-Brown. Indeed Wyatt-Brown's influence is evident in virtually any book about southern honor that has been produced in this country for the last thirty years. At its core honor is reputation, and as such it constitutes a code of behavior directed to the public and what we might call an "honor group" of people whose opinion we value. It is a matter of self-esteem, and its darker side is the fear of humiliation. It may manifest itself in elaborate rituals, ranging from genteel courtesies to episodes of violence and even death, and its relation to "manliness" is evident in ways both subtle and gross. It finds its way into identity, sex, law, child rearing, sports, politics, and so on. Wyatt-Brown's work produced a scaffolding on which to hang almost anything southern, and it has been richly provocative.

Yet as these essays show, the idea that honor was a stable "code" needs revisiting, and so does its peculiar southernness. This is a frankly revisionist volume. Rather than as a fixed set of rules, honor appears here as an interpretive tool, for two groups. For southerners, especially antebellum ones, it was an adaptable means by which they—men, women, people of color—could deal with the many contradictions and ambiguities in their world. The South appears here as somewhat less than modern, whatever that term may mean, but certainly not static. For scholars honor becomes an analytical lens that takes a seemingly transparent mode of behavior and refracts it in unexpected patterns. These range from mythmaking to infanticide. All involve reputation, but that is a term with many points of view.

These points of view are grouped here into five general topics, each of which is prefaced by a brief overview and all of which intersect. The first examines honor and its relationship to the marketplace. The study of market behaviors is as appropriate in terms of ritual and behavior as anything honor can offer, and the fact that the market revolution and the rise of southern honor occurred at about the same time needs exploration. These essays set down the guidelines for understanding honor and reinforce the American South's place in the market revolution. The second section addresses law and violence. Honor operated outside the codifications of formal law, yet the boundaries were permeable and thin. Here issues of violence and manhood were critical, as were the social definitions of respectability. That issue evolves naturally into a third question: honor and character. Repute and respectability may or may not be the same thing, but they are intensely related, and each has its standards of ethics and behavior.

The fourth and fifth sections venture into somewhat novel territories. As the fourth section shows, honor was not the province of elite white males alone. White women and African Americans developed their own standards of reputation and their own means of inflicting humiliation. Here the influence of the "honor group" is definitive, and this section challenges scholars to follow through and explore honor's meaning in broader contexts. So does the fifth section, which looks to honor's place in modern, perhaps postmodern, culture. This may seem a futile quest in our culture of celebrity and self-revelation (not to mention drone warfare and data mining) but the essays here reveal honor's persistent influence and remind us again of its utility as an interpretive tool—this time for opening up the American experience, and not just the southern.

Overall honor as a subject of study has received excellent development over the course of several decades, especially among scholars of the American South, and it continues to be an animating and important value in our collective national culture. The essays that follow build on this classic scholarship in an effort to expand traditional understandings of the topic. They explore honor in varying contexts, as practiced by multiple peoples, and through the lenses of divergent disciplinary approaches. They seek to revise and elaborate on existing assumptions or paradigms about the function or limitations of honor in American culture. And they bring a reach and focus that encapsulates the current state of honor studies in the university, offering a wide gaze, while anticipating the study's future. The collected scholarship on display here, we hope, offers much promise for expanding the national dialogue on this much-discussed but little-understood value, its influence on southern character and American identity.

ACKNOWLEDGMENTS

A project of this breadth incurs many debts. As editors our sincerest gratitude goes to the scholars and friends who have contributed to this collection. Individually these pieces provide intriguing glimpses into the strange world of American honor from a host of distinct vantage points; together they become something grand, a more kaleidoscopic tableau of the South and the nation as a whole than previous studies acknowledged. It has been our honor taking this journey together. Thanks especially to David Moltke-Hansen, not only for introducing us but for being an early advocate for this project and an enthusiastic supporter throughout its development. The editorial staff at the University of South Carolina Press, especially Alexander Moore, have been kind and supportive, not to mention knowledgeable and patient. Our thanks also to the anonymous outside reviewers, whose enthusiasm for the project was reassuring and timely. We thank them all for their efforts and advice in bringing this volume to fruition. We are grateful too for financial support of this book provided by the University of South Carolina Aiken and Stanford University.

Each of us has special debts. Todd Hagstette would like to first thank his coeditor, John Mayfield, for his partnership, guidance, and trust. The production of this volume has been a long and at times arduous endeavor, and I have been repeatedly grateful to have your steady hand and level head to get us through it. Many folks at the University of South Carolina deserve recognition. They include the excellent researchers at the South Caroliniana Library, in whose manuscripts reading room the first germ of this project originated; the brilliant members of the Institute for Southern Studies; and my friends and guides in the English department, most significantly my mentor David S. Shields. Finally I would like to thank my family, my wife, Elise, and my son, Davis, for their constant love and support.

From Mayfield: Todd Hagstette is simply fun to work with—smart, organized, literate, and energetic. At times he was Abbott to my Costello; at times the roles changed, and the combination worked with amazing choreography. This project was a delight, chiefly thanks to him. I always rely on Johanna Shields, whose keen insight and cool appraisals are benchmark qualities for a historian. My colleagues at Samford University—especially Jonathan Bass and Jason Wallace—put up with my meanderings with their usual grace, and the librarians there jumped at the chance to help me dig up references. They have true grit. Thanks to them and to Sarah, who calmly read whatever I shoved at her, usually responding with "It's fine, dear. Now press 'Save.'" I need that.

Finally we acknowledge the intellectual and personal legacies of the two superb scholars to whose memory this volume is dedicated. All the contributors to this volume owe a debt to Bertram Wyatt-Brown. His peerless research on the U.S. South and its remarkable customs set the template for all inquiries into elite southern values that followed. Even as the present volume revises some of his conclusions and expands the focus of traditional studies of honor, Wyatt-Brown remains always in the background of our work as the architect of the edifice on which we build.

So does Dickson Davies Bruce Jr., whose work on southern violence and culture anticipated Wyatt-Brown's in subtle but no less compelling ways. Smart, sharp, funny, generous, and utterly unpretentious, he never tried to grab the spotlight, yet his imprint on southern history is inventive, broad in range, and durable. We are saddened that he died shortly after he and his daughter Emily wrote the last essay in this volume. It is predictably smart, sharp, funny, generous, and utterly unpretentious; that is, Dave at his best.

Part I

Challenging Honor—The Marketplace

Honor is defined by reputation. A sense of self-regard and good conduct may be essential to a person's claim to honor, but honor without public recognition is no honor at all. A good name defines the man or woman regardless of time or place. This central truth may give honor a timeless quality, but context and contingency change its meanings constantly, and ambiguities arise. Nowhere is this tension more apparent than in cultures undergoing rapid social change, where defining honor may take on an urgency not felt in smaller, more settled communities. The antebellum South is an example. There notions of mastery—economic, social, sexual, racial—confronted forces of modernity and social mobility to produce an environment where the presentation of self was an enterprise fraught with anxiety and uncertainty.

Much of this tension stemmed from the South's involvement in the market revolution—the rapid spread of commercialism, speculation, and territorial expansion that coincided with the growth of participatory democracy in the decades following independence. Reputation—like a commercial transaction—became a negotiable thing. Ironically, or perhaps predictably, honor became more important than ever. John Mayfield's essay outlines the broad form of this conflict and the historiography surrounding it and suggests that the South's fixation on honor was directly tied to the shifting nature of reputation itself. In that sense, the essay also introduces many of the themes explored in this volume.

David Moltke-Hansen begins this exploration with its most iconic expression, the cavalier. Mark Twain may have blamed the Civil War on southerners' fixation on the cult of chivalry and its romantic self-delusions, but Moltke-Hansen sees a more nuanced possibility. Using the works of the Old South's premier and most prolific writer, William Gilmore Simms, he notes that the cavalier figure—honor personified—was indeed "an assertion of values" but not in Twain's flippant way. The virtues the cavalier embodied were not to be taken literally but to be employed as a civilizing force "against the claims and excesses of the market." If southern culture were not so unsettled, in other words, there would have been no need to idealize such a figure. In time, Moltke-Hansen suggests, the chivalric ideal became a useful phrase in the broader, more complicated, rhetoric of secession, and no one was more articulate in this rephrasing than Simms.

Essays by Kathleen Hilliard and Amanda Mushal focus on the very personal impact the market revolution had on honor and reputation. If honor depended on having a good name, what—literally—were the criteria for measuring worth? Hilliard's engaging study of a planter obsessed with winning a prize for growing the most bushels of corn exposes a paradox: the agricultural society measured worth by output and insisted on precise measurements; the planter insisted on being treated as a honest man by virtue of his reputation alone, never mind that his figures were suspect. Hence a conflict: "The best way to set honor on a firm footing" writes Hilliard, "was to erect a solid foundation that had essentially nothing to do with honor's ethos—and was, in many ways, deeply antagonistic to it."

Mushal shows some of the same impulses at work in assessing credit. Southern businessmen were integrated into a national market for loans and credit (a fact in and of itself indicative of the South's participation in the market revolution). In her analysis of anonymous credit evaluations, honor appears as a means of assessing worth, and all that term implies. Was a borrower's reputation enough to entrust him with a loan? Or should he be, quite literally, discredited? Here the criteria for honor subtly changed. "Commercial honor"—that is, paying one's debts—took precedence over mastery and fearlessness. Ideas of honor were involved—and evolved—in support of the modern business culture. Thus did the ledger become a field of battle and a record of reputation.

John Mayfield

THE MARKETPLACE OF VALUES

Honor and Enterprise in the Old South

In 1977 Bertram Wyatt-Brown was rummaging around a library in Cleveland, Ohio. There he found an 1835 account of a wife murder and the killer's subsequent public shaming in Natchez, which, as he said, puzzled him. The crowd in Natchez had lashed the criminal, tarred him, feathered him, and run him out of town. A simple hanging would have been more merciful and much more economical, but the community seemed to need some kind of public ceremony—some ritual of purgation and contempt—to set things right. Hanging was simply too easy. The town clearly thought that humiliating the offender was the appropriate response. What, Wyatt-Brown thought, was going on there? One thing led to another, and he ended up writing a classic of southern studies, *Southern Honor: Ethics and Behavior in the Old South.*[1]

The title itself is interesting. When we think of honor, we often dismiss it as a kind of self-delusion—a term attached to fate or resignation or an overly inflated ego. It was Wyatt-Brown's rare gift to take the term seriously and to develop it as an architecture of personal identity and conduct. The book set forth certain ways of approaching what can be called "identity," a buzzword no doubt but, pro or con, something to be reckoned with, particularly when applied to a region as self-conscious as the American South. As an ethic honor could be construed variously. Sometimes it meant an Aristotelian sense of virtue—doing what one does well and contributing to the good, a form of citizenship and personal autonomy at once. Honor also meant personal attributes—character, self-worth, reliability, graciousness, valor, style—what Italians call a *bella figura.* As a behavior, however, it meant something more Homeric: to affirm one's worth publicly and to resist, at any cost, threats to that reputation. Often these behaviors were violent, and it is suggestive that the abridged, classroom-ready version of Wyatt-Brown's book was retitled *Honor and Violence in the Old South.*[2] Violent or peaceful or downright bizarre, the connecting thread was the way in which one presented oneself publicly and—perhaps more important—how the community assessed these presentations. Posturing, pretense, and retribution assumed new importance as legitimate terms of historical inquiry; so did ostracism, fame, humiliation, and éclat.[3]

Southern Honor hit a nerve. At a time when historical inquiry was heavy with statistical determinism and literary studies were absorbed with "meaning," this single book seemed to offer a way out of impersonal abstractions and numbing cynicism. Writ large honor provided an interpretive lens for assessing not only

Achilles but Ashley Wilkes—both were self-involved egotists keenly aware of their public personas and doomed by them. Similarly one could take South Carolinian Preston Brooks's caning of Charles Sumner on the Senate floor in 1856 as a legitimate—if monstrous—social mandate rather than as a psychopathic anecdote. The study of honor was relentlessly interdisciplinary: it could be an anthropological expression of *mentalite* or a literary trope or a sociological status marker. Being interdisciplinary it could also be used to study a variety of subjects. Honor—ethics and behavior—opened new avenues for exploring family, recreations, law, class, secessionism, literature, and so on. As a methodology honor often expressed itself in the study of rituals. Steven Stowe and Kenneth Greenberg, for example, issued brilliant studies of what might be called the semiotics of honor, the elaborate exchange of notes, insults, boasts, recriminations, and so forth that marked the dilemmas of being male.[4] In that sense honor also spoke to gender studies.[5] Its behaviors and values were intensely patriarchal. Ideally honor was also paternalistic, defending female virtue and nurturing dependents. Nurturing, however, involved mastering, and honor's imperative to be in control—and show it—was all over southern culture. A man without honor was no man at all.

This was liberating. Suddenly the most peculiar and outlandish examples of southern behavior made sense. "Strictly," Henry Adams had famously written, "the southerner had no mind; he had temperament."[6] Voila. The general edginess of southern men—the in-your-face aggressiveness of a plain man provoked or the haughty sneer of an aristocrat maligned, the patriarchal obsession with female purity and the sense of triumph gained from a sexual conquest, the ready recourse to violence, even the peculiar fascination with tweaking noses—all were sophisticated expressions of identity, not adolescent weirdness. Honor became an actual methodology to confirm Adams and W. J. Cash, whose landmark *The Mind of the South* was a mournful meditation on the South's self-inflicted wounds.[7] In line with Cash's deeply impressionistic view, Wyatt-Brown offered confirmation that "temperament" had legs as an interpretive tool. Dueling, gift giving, chasing down innocent foxes with hounds, these had antecedents that could be proved. But where Cash saw only temperament and wrote accordingly, Wyatt-Brown offered a structuralist framework. Southerners' public posturing and its accompanying ideas were not just so many self-conceits but were powerful social directives that took inchoate expectations and channeled them into action. This was indeed a procrustean bed of social mores where every gesture had to be made to fit, even at the cost of a limb. Temperament became a legitimate field of study, without all the romantic fuzz and fluff. Honor, then, emerged as a kind of historian's paradigm, a set of assumptions on which all kinds of elaborate experiments could be made without destroying the underlying premises.

As Thomas Kuhn has noted, however, paradigms shift. Even as Wyatt-Brown wrote, there were other trends at work.[8] *Southern Honor* appeared at about the same time that the notion of a "market revolution" took hold among historians and even a few literary critics. Here was an American phenomenon in which a continent began to open up to expansion—economic, certainly, but also literary, religious, political, and more. What had been a fairly republican place became a democratic one, in which elites were no longer securely defined and saving face was less important than making a good deal. What the market revolution in fact involved is hotly contested ground, but culturally speaking it seemed to have little in common with arcane versions of honor. To master a railroad or a real estate deal was not the same as mastering fear or staring down a mob. A culture of self-made men had its own concepts of identity and its own rituals.[9]

Questions arise. Were these identities mutually exclusive, or did they overlap, rather like a Venn diagram? On top of that lies a second question: who was the audience for honor's various displays? An ethic grounded in public approval will never satisfy everyone. Which "honor group" held sway over one's claim to honor? To answer that convoluted question brings up a third: how deep did the market revolution, or its concomitant, modernity, extend into the South, and how, if at all, did either or both shape southern honor? It is an unsettling question simply because the South has so long been assigned the role of drag chain in the march of progress. There are no easy answers.

And so a certain friction has set in, and this is a healthy thing for those who would study not only southern but American character. Put crudely, we have the Great Divide between tradition and modernity that polarizes many of our national self-conceptions. As with so much that is called "American," we see these competing values of honor and enterprise in their most distilled form in the South. There issues of race, mastery, patriarchy, law, religion, custom, mobility, nostalgia, ambition, conservatism, liberality, public opinion, hierarchy, and more have come together in what might be called an "emotionology" of postures, raw and noble.[10] Because of his curious place as a self-made man in a hierarchical culture, the white southern man was given to extremes of behavior. Yet at the core was he so different from his peers elsewhere? What of women? What of people of color? These questions are central. If honor is merely categorized as a regional idiosyncrasy, the result is to isolate a thing called "the South" and mark it as somehow apart from the larger American identity. Maybe it is, but the jury is permanently out. In many ways the historiography of the South (and America) has been written on either side of these polarities. Since historiography constantly reinvents itself, it is time to take another sounding.

Defining Honor

For Wyatt-Brown honor was a "cluster of ethical rules, most readily found in societies of small communities, by which judgments of behavior are ratified by community consensus."[11] These ethical rules were, and presumably are, remarkably stable over time and place. Though the precise language of honor might vary, Wyatt-Brown's use of it borrowed freely from cultural anthropologists of the Mediterranean, especially Julian Pitt-Rivers.[12] Honor, as Pitt-Rivers outlined in a seminal essay, has three basic elements. It is at root a sentiment, an internal feeling of self-worth and the *right* to feel that way. As Frank Henderson Stewart has emphasized, honor is a form of self-validation. This right has to be claimed, and that must be done through the second element, conduct: that is, behaviors that can be deemed honorable.[13] Neither self-regard nor conduct means much, however, without public recognition, which in many ways is the key to honor. Honor thus forms itself into a triad. "Honor felt becomes honor claimed," wrote Pitt-Rivers, "and honor claimed becomes honor paid."[14] Honor, reputation, fame, éclat, however the term is refined, is an intensely public thing.

There is no one definition, though, of what this public thing is. As Pitt-Rivers made clear from the start, honor has several meanings, some of them flatly contradictory, depending on the context. Honor could hinge on moral qualities (piety, civic virtue), precedence (rank, status), personal attributes (demeanor, bearing), and so on. These fluctuate. A warrior might achieve precedence in battle, but could he claim it in peace or in the boardroom? That brings up the community in which honor is displayed, what Pitt-Rivers and others call the "honor group." Families, nations, armies, churches, even street gangs or the Mob, all impose criteria as to what is honorable or shameful. "At its simplest," writes James Bowman, "honor is the good opinion of the people who matter to us, and who matter because we regard them as a society of equals who have the power to judge our behavior."[15]

The public quality of honor emphasizes its opposite, shame. If one values one's good name, one had better take care of it. To lose face, to be "given the lie," to be called a wimp or a slut—these are humiliating terms, and the more other-directed a culture is the more the insult stings.[16] It is crucial, therefore, to distinguish between shame and guilt. Shame is by definition public. An honorable man or woman must lay claim to self-respect on his or her honor group's turf. If the penalty for defending honor is death, so be it. Hence Achilles (to take the archetype) must avenge his insults and kill his enemy—though doing so dooms him—because he must have "unfading glory" or, to put it more prosaically, the honor he claims as his due. Conversely a more prudent, some might say cowardly, man or woman has other imperatives. Guilt is private. A pure soul may rejoice in private victories over temptation and sin. God alone is audience to the heart, and while public shame may be painful, it is not definitive of self-worth. Writes Pitt-Rivers, "Those who aspire to no honor cannot be humiliated."[17] Rephrased, shame is for the other-directed.

The display of honor, then, is essentially theatrical. If it is public, it needs an audience, and the venues are many. The most heroic are warfare or the duel, which are supreme tests of honor precisely because of the stakes involved—a defiance of death itself.[18] Nothing is more dramatic. Yet more peaceful arenas abound. For southern men they might include the hunt, the podium or the Senate floor, the racetrack, perhaps the barroom or the faro wheel—any place where manly behaviors can be acted out without regard for the financial expense.[19] For women the options were and may still seem to be more limited but no less compelling. Where chasteness and modest demeanor are honorable traits, gossip can kill; a loose reputation can be devastating. As with all theater, language is crucial. "Sir" and "gentleman" are, or have been, terms that actually mean something; similarly a cad is a cad. To call someone a bastard is actionable in a patriarchal honor group, and to term someone a liar or scoundrel is just as bad, as Charles Sumner discovered to the cost of his health.

This fetishism over words fit well in a society such as the South, where oratory was entertainment and a cutting phrase could elicit whoops and jeers and, hopefully, equally cutting retorts. If the ripostes went too far, the elaborate language of honor translated into the code duello (which was literally a code), and every gesture, word, or nuance took on deadly potential. Language was all-important here, sometimes to absurd lengths. Augustus B. Longstreet, the humorist, mocked the whole scenario with a story about a man, defending a lady's honor, who disagreed over the meaning of the term "it" in an exchange of notes and then shot his opponent through the knees "in due form and according to the latest fashion."[20] It was not a stretch to extend all this to gossip in the drawing room or—if one's tastes run to the bizarre—the ripsnorters who pranced around on court days like the half-alligators they claimed to be, challenging all comers to the privilege of having an ear chewed off, all for the pure show of it.[21] All depended on the honor group and the individual's claim to that group's respect.

Inescapably honor is bound up in questions of class and status. Again Pitt-Rivers's analysis is keen. Acquiring honor is no simple process; it may take generations, or it may come rather quickly. Birth, heredity, and family are essential in the long run, especially when they are accompanied by wealth and influence. These hierarchies can be tough and hard to break, but change does happen, and the criteria for honor can evolve over time and in a place. Certain professions are "honorable" in and of themselves. This has long been true of law and the military, and within the last century or so it has extended to medicine. (The status of college professors is still up in the air.) As Pitt-Rivers forecast there would come a day when previously disrespected pursuits such as acting and athletics would be deemed honorable, perhaps even worthy of a knighthood.[22]

In any case the "honor group" is the referee, and the more complex a society is the more referees there are. One honor group may impose demands on its members that it would not ask of those above or below. It is hard to imagine a judge feeling compelled to get tattooed or a Marine wearing robes, but each profession has its forms of branding. Both robes and tattoos may be badges of honor; the audience is simply different. Still on a broad social scale there are ascending layers of honor, or what Pitt-Rivers called "precedence." Frank Henderson Stewart has simplified this graph into "vertical" honor and "horizontal."[23] Problems, of course, ensue when one tries to cross boundaries. For the upwardly mobile, conduct that elicits respect from one's peers may generate ridicule from the tonier circles one wants to frequent. Benjamin Franklin learned this lesson the hard way when his English superiors mocked him despite the éclat he had won by being a witty and learned colonial. He was still a colonial. What was presumptuous to the English turned out to be charming to the French—a lesson itself in the vagaries of honor.[24]

Wyatt-Brown reduced these complexities into two rubrics—primal honor and genteel honor. The latter is the more easily recognized: it is embodied by the "Christian gentleman" who manages to be simultaneously fiercely independent and genially sociable, aloof but magnanimous, stoic yet quick to take offense, masterful while indulgent, sporting but reserved, pious yet magisterial. In a word he was the consummate southern gentleman, and no one personified him better than Robert E. Lee. There have been subcategories, of course, including the Carolina cavalier, the Hotspur, the fire-eater—any one of which could be found in Shakespeare—and his essential qualities were learning, style, and piety, but above all sociability. Such men were patriarchs in the English fashion, with roots in the Renaissance courtier.

It was primal honor that really engaged Wyatt-Brown. No matter the social rank, one's identity was grounded in securing a reputation for independence, fearlessness, and downright pride. Here lay a potent mix of postures and claims and, more than that, a very means of creating a community of shared values. Family name, valor, physical appearance, hot blood, mastery, an indifference to money—all were more or less given aspects of honor. These he considered stable across time and geography, and they took in virtually every class or subculture—every honor group—the South had. Put together, as Steven Hahn wrote in a review, honor offered "a system of organizing relationships among individuals, groups, and the community: specifically the claims of men to self-worth, prominence, and authority before the public, and the subsequent assessment of those claims by the public."[25] Reworded, it was identity on display, monitored by public opinion.

In effect Wyatt-Brown had come up with a unified field theory of southern ethics and behaviors, and therein lay a problem. Wyatt-Brown's analysis was breathtaking in its sweep, but it tended to merge the South into one honor group. The community is the judge, but honor means one thing to one honor group, something else to another. "Consensus," Pitt-Rivers had warned, "is not easily established in a complex society; individual views differ, and different groups have different standards."[26] Reconciling these differing expectations might be fairly manageable in static or "premodern" societies, especially small communities where privacy is virtually impossible to get or maintain. Wyatt-Brown often treated the antebellum South as such a community, a place where primal and genteel honor trumped all other cards, including class and slavery, in regulating behavior and defining ethics.

But was he right to do so? Granted, some variation of honor is present in all cultures at all times, yet the Old South is the American showcase for its most elaborate expressions. Why should this ethic have come to mark one region so thoroughly that it could be blamed for the Civil War? The simplest explanation is that the South was doomed by slavery to a kind of premodern state that protected and exaggerated "primitive" behaviors such as honor and homogenized the whole region into one honor group. Or maybe, as Wyatt-Brown, James McPherson, and others postulate, Yankees were the odd men out, ahead of the curve in their embrace of liberalism, economic diversification, cities, and alienated individualism.[27] Either way, the Old South was supposedly a cultural laggard, clinging to behaviors that were all the more bizarre for being antique.

It is not clear, however, that the Old South was "old," much less antique. It is easy to pin its obsession with mastery and patriarchal dominance on the presence of slavery; it is also easy to forget that slavery drove southern expansion and was a source of rapid upward mobility for a rather loosely connected bunch of ambitious men, many of whom were born Yankees. They had a big arena for their dreams. By 1845 "the South" was roughly the same size as western Europe. Alabama was not Virginia, and neither was Texas. This was an unsettled place, and the stretch of geography alone might challenge a unified field theory of honor. "The ideal unity of honor is apt to fragment when it strikes the facts," Pitt-Rivers warned, "and the different bases for according it become opposed to one another."[28] The fact is that there was no unified South to act out one version of honor, nor was there an equivalent version of market identity.

In the case of the Old South, this fragmentation struck on two things. One is the very use of the term "Old South," which implies that the region south of the Mason-Dixon Line and the Ohio somehow approached the status of a nineteenth-century nation-state. There are very good arguments that this was so, but there are equally compelling indications that it was not. The very concept of an "old" South stems from the creation of a new one following the defeat of the Confederacy—devotion to which in itself homogenized serious internal divisions. "Patriotism in its modern sense depended on an idea of the whole nation as a single honor group," observes James Bowman.[29] For southerners such a group did not exist before 1861, however much they wanted to believe the opposite.

Second, honor is most visibly displayed through elites, who preferably must be stable and easily identified. Here, as I shall argue below, most of the Old South was so new that stable elites had not had time to settle in. Maybe in Virginia, but Alabama? Moreover, by focusing too much on these wannabes, we miss the presence and peculiar nature of a southern middle class whose concept of honor tended to reflect "character"—a subtle but profound distinction. In the South as in the North, the Victorian idea of the "Christian gentleman" emerged, but he was a delicate hybrid.

Rather than looking at southern honor as the backward antagonist to modernization, then, we might entertain the possibility that southern honor became manifest, visible in stark relief, precisely because the market revolution, and modernization more broadly, were hard at work in the South in complicated and often contradictory forms. If any place was a "complex society" then certainly the Old South qualified. Here were intense conflicts over the meaning of manhood, womanhood, race, class, gentility, and so on. The South's apparent obsession with honor may have been directly tuned to its confusion as to what honor was. "The struggle for honor takes place," wrote Pitt-Rivers, "only where precedence is both of value and in doubt."[30] This struggle in the antebellum South was particularly messy, was often violent, and—in line with Pitt-Rivers's other caution—resulted in fights over differing definitions of honor. The liminal zone between tradition and modernity is where interesting things happen.

The Challenge of the Market

To be fair, Wyatt-Brown was way ahead of his critics. Anticipating most of the objections, he responded to them generously and refined his perspectives, although he never backed off his central thesis.[31] But honor's emphasis on gesture, ritual, poses, and the like, plus its insistence on transparency, all drove the quantifiers mad, particularly since the call of the market revolution was so compelling. Honor seemed to take plain old materialism out of the agenda, and the discovery of agendas, particularly hidden ones, is the very bone of much historical inquiry. Honor may be the measure of how the ancient Greeks or Renaissance courtiers acted, but did it have a real place in the developing United States? If anything the culture of honor seemed to confirm that the South really was an archaic backwater stuck in some kind of neofeudal time warp.

But curiously two things have emerged. One is that the market revolution itself invited anthropological approaches. The market has its own theatricality, its own ritualized expectations, its own language and sense of community and hierarchy. These are the same elements that students of honor pore over, yet they have long been so much a subject of American discourse that we tend to take them for granted. Public opinion is, as Tocqueville observed, the tyranny of the majority in democratic societies, and nothing measures honor more than public opinion.

This is true particularly where a rising middle class is involved. To take an example from colonial history, T. H. Breen's work on the consumer revolution in the eighteenth century is a fine introduction to the shifting standards of status and expectations attached to the very things colonial Americans set their tables with. Teapots and tea, spoons and plates, books: these were the spoils, not of war and heroics, but of an emerging middle class and its need to proclaim itself. They were emphatically "public" displays, made long before Thorstein Veblen placed them into categories of conspicuous consumption.[32] Rhys Isaac's work on the transformation of Virginia details the rituals and presentations of an elite that was rapidly being subsumed into new expressions—and new anxieties—regarding their own status. Everything from pew rents to horseracing to dog breeding can be seen through honor's lens of precedence and condescension, but the line between these pursuits and plain old status seeking is vague.[33]

Pushing down the road, Mary Ryan's splendid study of the middle class in Oneida County, New York, details ways in which the market rearranged space—both physical and social—between classes. Patterns of intimacy between owner and worker (the stop for a quick one after work, for example) fell apart as owners went home to their families in self-conscious displays of middle-class propriety, and the saloon became a target of reform, not a place where interclass community was built and maintained and certainly not a place to show off one's claim to honor.[34] Similarly Nicole Etcheson's work on the Old Northwest suggests that market culture introduced new criteria for honor, namely hard work and success in providing for the family.[35] Is this a version of honor, or mere respectability? What, actually, is the difference? Identity becomes even more problematic.

Literary studies have long recognized this issue. Jean-Christophe Agnew's elegant study of Elizabethan theater, to go back to the basics, aptly describes a wholly honor-bound culture undergoing its own market revolution.[36] The masks, double identities, treacheries, and inward rationalizations of Shakespeare's characters were, to Agnew, staged rehearsals of the changing social relations that were unsettling England as it moved into modernity. "To be or not to be" is not a question that a man secure in his honor would ever ask; neither do the "counterfeit presentments" used by the bard's various connivers, cross-dressers, and seducers make them simple charlatans, because charlatans are notoriously complex creatures. Especially one sees this in Shylock demanding his pound of flesh, or in Iago whispering his lies to a black prince. (Hence did race and religion find their way into the mess.) Shakespeare was in the language of virtually every literate American in the nineteenth century, and so was his imagery. Melville's *Benito Cereno* took up the theme of appearances directly, and his *Bartleby, the Scrivener* moved it into corporate culture. For those studying the presentation of self, the resources are endless.

In the United States, especially beginning about 1800, this obsession with appearances was most evident in the popularity of works on the confidence man.[37] (The actual term was not coined until 1849, but the prototypes were already there.) We tend to associate the type with Mark Twain and the humorists of the Old Southwest who preceded him, but the con artist has had a long and durable spot in our affections. "It is good to be shifty in a new country," said Simon Suggs, the creation of Johnson Jones Hooper of Alabama, in a statement that pretty much says it all.[38] But there's a trace of him in Franklin's *Autobiography*, a handbook for the "self-made man"; so he could be benign as well as scurrilous. Either way he was subject to the same generic needs to forge the right presentation of self, to locate the right community to build (or exploit), and to deploy the right language to mediate the two. Melville's other great book is *The Confidence Man: His Masquerade*—a maddeningly cryptic thing—and it has its protagonist ever asking the same question: "Do I have your confidence?" In terms of honor culture, this is a reformulation of an essential question: "Do I have your respect." The one is all enigma; the other, transparency.[39]

That Melville set his novel on a Mississippi riverboat brings up a second point. Honor's association with the South suggests to some that southerners were outside the loop, culturally speaking. Slavery ossified honor into a set of defensive postures against modernity; the wide gap between planter and poor white and between white and black made "mastery"—a term loaded with racial and class control—absolutely nonnegotiable. Whatever pressures men of the free, presumably market-oriented states may have endured, and whatever masks or strategies they may have employed in negotiating those pressures, the theory goes that southerners were driven by other aims.

Or were they? The trend in southern studies has been to include the slave states in the market revolution at both behavioral and economic levels. This trend, once begun, is certain to continue.[40] The production of cotton is, after all, the first stage in an industrial conveyor belt that has international stretch. It concentrates capital and labor, and it demands risk taking, haggling, and management skill—never mind its moral failings. "In . . . the years before the Civil War," wrote Walter Johnson, "there was no capitalism without slavery. The two were, in many ways, one and the same."[41] Around this core industry a host of ancillary entrepreneurs sprang up, including lawyers, educators, suppliers (of hogs, for example), shippers, and so forth. These activities come together in towns, which may not be cities but are still nerve centers of the market. The South was full of towns even if, outside of the Border States and a few ports, it lacked proper cities. By 1860 Natchez was among the richest such towns in the country. (Natchez, recall, is where honor first suggested itself to Wyatt-Brown.)

It is important not to ascribe this phenomenon to a patriarchal elite of inherited wealth. It is only lately that historians have begun to recognize a rising, acquisitive, reforming middle class in the South, with links intellectual and cultural to the North. The cotton South was an open field to speculators, investors, entrepreneurs, lawyers, cardsharps, and anyone else in search of a fast lane to wealth. All might be grouped as petit bourgeoisie.[42] Possession of slaves (portable, reproductive), not land (static, subject to exhaustion), was the entry card to the middle class and beyond. "The new country seemed to be a reservoir," wrote Alabama lawyer Joseph G. Baldwin, "and every road leading to it a vagrant stream of enterprise and adventure. Money, or what passed for money, was the only cheap thing to be had."[43] It really was good, recalling Simon Suggs, to be shifty in a new country.

It was also good to be pious—or, in honor's terms, to have good character. The evangelical impulse rolled over all the country, and in the eastern South it was strong even in the eighteenth century. The hierarchical, gentrified religion of liturgical denominations such as the Episcopalians did not migrate well into the Old Southwest, but looser, more individualistic ones such as Baptists and Methodists thrived there. Almost every major study of southern religion reveals a crying need to impose order on a disconnected society. Restraining the passions, argues Dickson D. Bruce, was the surest defense against the kind of reflexive violence that the code of honor proposed. A camp meeting is theatrical, for sure, but it is also a venue for confessing weakness, not haughty self-regard. Similarly Jonathan D. Wells has helped reveal a southern middle class full of the same reform impulses that are commonly pegged to New England. These were counterweights to honor's demands in the South, as were the many schools that sprang up in the revivals' wakes. Jennifer Green has shown that the much-honored military schools were places to train accountants and teachers, not mighty warriors. There honor's claim to self-indulgence existed in a nervous tension with the call to develop self-restraint and something called "character."[44]

Then there was the intellectual environment. Wyatt-Brown certainly did not diminish the role of slavery in shaping the southern mind, but he did frankly argue that honor was an equal and longer-lived partner. Honor and slavery were wholly compatible and mutually supportive, he acknowledged, a point driven home by Kenneth Greenberg's *Honor and Slavery* and Orlando Patterson's work on slavery and identity.[45] "Honor came first," nonetheless, and it had a "distinct existence . . . apart from a particular system of labor."[46] This was a remarkable interpretive shift, for it seemed to move the perspective from white/black to white/white, with all the intellectual implications that incurred. The presentation of self among one's peers posed issues that were different from racial mastery.

Again the timing of Wyatt-Brown's book was ironic. While honor seemed to validate Cash's gloomy sense of stagnation, new approaches were portraying the South as a willing, if somewhat hybridized, partner in modernization. It was, at least compared to most of Europe, liberal. The chief architect of this revision was Michael O'Brien, an English scholar. In a string of compelling works, O'Brien did not exactly deny the role of honor in southern thought, but neither did he give it much attention. Honor, class, race, slavery—these were procrustean beds to impose order and community conformity on the South. O'Brien, however, saw a conflicted, internalized, ambivalent South "not premodern but deeply implicated in modernity, though an idiosyncratic version mostly based on slavery." The South was "less than a coherent society, with significant tensions between the world the slaveholders made and the world the non-slaveholders made." Southern intellectuals—and they did exist and exert influence—reflected these tensions, "for their lives mirrored a pattern of instability." Mobile, introspective, they often were migrants to the frontier states of Mississippi and Alabama. Consequently "they knew conflicting identities."[47]

The key words are instability and conflict, and they apply most directly in what Johanna Nicol Shields has called the "rising South"—states on the edge of slavery's expansion and states of mind attuned to doubt and self-rationalization. Shields's own work on Alabama writers reveals a deep strain of ambiguity and very "modern" alienation among what should have been a society most given over to primal honor. This was not simply a Gulf state thing, however; even William Gilmore Simms, the South's premier writer and presumed apologist of the chivalric ideal, has come under scrutiny for his ambivalent and often acid critiques of his honorable peers. Scott Romine's admirable work on southern authors reveals a culture deeply divided over the meaning of community and the role of genteel honor in negotiating harmony. In virtually every area of intellectual endeavor the Old South has emerged as well-read, cosmopolitan in its tastes, and sophisticated about the self-contradictions in its identity.[48]

The list extends in every direction. The charivari, or shivaree, that initially captured Wyatt-Brown's interest has been brilliantly revisited by Joshua Rothman in a study of Mississippians' response to a purported slave insurrection in 1835. This was a community deeply involved in market culture—a wild mass of speculators, in fact. Its members came entirely unglued by rumors of an imminent slave revolt led by (what else?) a gang of thieves, "steam doctors," and gamblers. Con men, quacks, and thimblerigs are the knights-errant of market culture, but their lords are parvenu cotton planters and land speculators. The latter hanged or shot the former. Sometimes, alas, it was *not* good to be shifty in a new country.

Rephrased, honor culture may have been most pronounced in such places as the antebellum South (and, later, the West) because it was under the greatest stress there. In both their personal and social lives, southerners were anxious people. Obsessions over mastery, reputation, legacy, standing, and so on—all the ways by which individuals measure their meaning—these are the dramatic manifestations of personalities under duress, and they command our attention accordingly. The irony is that at a broader, community level, honor may have served as an agency of stability and social equilibrium. Wyatt-Brown, Stowe, Bruce, and Greenberg have all stressed the importance of honor's ritualistic potential for maintaining order and restoring it once it has gotten out of kilter. Joanne Freeman's work on the politics of reputation in the 1790s makes a similar point and puts it right at the core of our founding as a nation. "In essence," she has written, "the code of honor was a remedy for the barely controlled chaos of national public life."[49] The same might be written for the South.

Taking Honor Forward

All of which is to say that the study of southern honor is more important than ever. "Historians are not supposed to think like anthropologists," Wyatt-Brown sighed, and yet we are compelled to do that very thing, even if doing so leads us down unexpected paths.[50] Wyatt-Brown's take on honor was never meant to be static or self-contained, and if we want to know more about ethics and behavior in the Old South—or indeed the new South and even postmodern America—then no single definition of honor can apply. Each component of Pitt-Rivers's triad of honor—sentiment, claim, and recognition—is still useful, but how we approach these elements is elastic and evolving. Sentiment, one's self-assessment, may take on meanings in chaotic, mobile societies that are different from those in stable ones. Terms like "character" cannot be dismissed as "mere" respectability, particularly where a middle class was taking root and a culture of self-improvement was emerging with it. If slaveholding was a means to achieving respectability, then honor became more complicated and in retrospect is more compelling, not less. Once slavery was gone, mastery and honor needed new definitions and required new analysis.

So does the process of claiming honor. It is one thing to be courageous and quick to take offense, another to be process oriented and patient. Law and the court system—to take but one obvious example—are natural predators of primal honor. They rationalize the reflexive. A working legal code means that conflict takes time and is refereed and open to reflection, and it does not reward impulsiveness. The fact that charivaris and duels existed in the South may lay claim to one version of honor. The fact that southerners were hard at work modernizing and codifying their laws may set down another.[51] In effect two different arenas for claiming honor existed, and the postures and rituals of honor changed accordingly. Again the liminal zone between the two is what is interesting.

But honor is still an intensely public thing, and when it is in transition a fundamental question stands out: Who is the audience? More pertinent, who are the audiences? One is either born into an honor group (family, nation, race, sex) or joins one (the military, a social group, a profession). In the American South, as in the country at large, these "horizontal" referees of honor existed and still exist in particular tension with the competitive pull of success in the marketplace. Opportunity accentuates status seeking, which is the quest for vertical honor distilled into upward mobility.

The question is not confined to elite white males. Women, poor whites, and blacks often have been assigned a passive role in the theater of southern honor. This is, gently put, an oversimplification. The theaters of public esteem are many, and so are the variations of honor. As Johanna Shields has observed, "If we want to know more about ethics and behavior in the old South, we will have to go beyond honor and elite white males." Honor may have driven the South's white elite, but its place among the "others" is still fertile ground. "Ethically and behaviorally," Shields later continued, "the millions of people in the Old South who worked farms, hunted squirrels, fished, built and cleaned houses, fed families and raised children, procreated or copulated, worshiped in small churches or camp meetings or homes, privately celebrated and mourned together may *or may not* have been guided by honor."[52] Other instincts, such as the sheer need to protect one's young, abound. A unified field theory of honor is elusive.

Still honor persists. Looming over all these qualifications is honor's place in American identity writ large. In some ways honor may no longer seem relevant as a code of ethics and behavior. Industrialization, mechanized warfare, celebrity culture, and reality television have all taken their toll on honor's terms for personal autonomy and public esteem. (Melville's Bartleby would be right at home in a *Dilbert* cartoon.) So have psychoanalysis and independent women, at least according to conservative critics such as James Bowman. Even to agree with that is not necessarily to agree that America should regain its sense of honor by flexing its muscles internationally, stopping its fixation on rock stars and super athletes, and sending its women back to the kitchen. Rather it is to accept that the terms of honor have changed, not the basic principles underlying them. "The vocabulary of honor has acquired archaic overtones in modern English," wrote Julian Pitt-Rivers, "yet the principles of honor remain" even if they are now "clothed in the idiom of headhunting, social refinement, financial acumen, religious purity, or civic merit."[53]

All these variations were rehearsed, so to speak, in the antebellum South, and they still resonate. If nothing else, a study of southern honor gives us a benchmark for examining who we aspire to be, and that's not an idle task. Moreover the study suggests how demanding the market and modernity have been and continue to be for people concerned about how their behaviors are read. Rather than a bulwark against the market revolution, it seems honor has served as a boat to use in navigating its swirling currents. It still does.

NOTES

1. Wyatt-Brown, *Southern Honor* (25th anniversary edition), vii. (Apart from the prefatory material, pagination in this and the first, 1982, edition are the same.)

2. Wyatt-Brown, *Honor and Violence.*

3. Studies using honor as a reference have proliferated since 1982. In the interests of space and specifics, I have not tried to cover the ground in these notes (nor could I), preferring instead to direct readers to the topical articles in this volume and to the collective bibliography.

4. Stowe, *Intimacy and Power;* Greenberg, *Honor and Slavery.*

5. See, for example, the essays in Friend and Glover, *Southern Manhood;* also Glover, *Southern Sons;* R. Pace, *Halls of Honor.* See also Mayfield, *Counterfeit Gentlemen.*

6. Adams, *Education,* 57.

7. Cash, *Mind of the South.*

8. Kuhn, *Scientific Revolutions.*

9. Historians have made free use of the "market revolution," but systematic analyses of its origins and impact are rather few. One should start with Sellers, *Market Revolution* and the essays in Stokes and Conway, *Market Revolution in America,* and S. Martin, *Cultural Change.* The best and most balanced interpretation is Larson, *Market Revolution in America.*

10. See the essay by Anna Koivusalo in this volume. For an excellent example, see Berry, *All That Makes a Man.*

11. Wyatt-Brown, *Southern Honor* (25th anniversary edition), xxxiv.

12. Pitt-Rivers, "Honor." See also Pitt-Rivers, "Honour and Social Status."

13. Stewart, *Honor,* esp. 21.

14. Pitt-Rivers, "Honor," 503.

15. James Bowman, *Honor,* 5.

16. Greenberg's *Honor and Slavery* is particularly good on the subject. For an expanded view, see W. Miller, *Humiliation.*

17. Pitt-Rivers, "Honor," 504.

18. For expanded notes on the duel and its rituals, see the articles by Hagstette, Levine, and Byron in this volume.

19. See, for example, Nicholas Proctor's imaginative study of hunting, *Bathed in Blood.*

20. Longstreet, "The Ball," in *Georgia Scenes,* 129.

21. See Gorn, "Gouge and Bite, Pull Hair."

22. This was before Mick Jagger became "Sir Mick." See Pitt-Rivers, "Honor," 507.

23. Stewart, *Honor,* 21.

24. Gordon Wood makes the point in *The Americanization of Benjamin Franklin.*

25. Hahn, "Honor and Patriarchy," 146.

26. Pitt-Rivers, "Honor," 504.

27. McPherson, "Antebellum Southern Exceptionalism."

28. Pitt-Rivers, "Honor," 507.

29. James Bowman, *Honor,* 5.

30. Ibid., 508.

31. Wyatt-Brown pursued honor in varying forms in *Yankee Saints and Southern Sinners* (1985); *Shaping of Southern Culture* (2001); and indirectly in *House of Percy* (1994) and *Hearts of Darkness* (2002).

32. Veblen, *Leisure Class*; Breen, *Marketplace of Revolution.*

33. Isaac, *Transformation of Virginia.*

34. Ryan, *Cradle of the Middle Class.*

35. Etcheson, "Manliness and the Political Culture."

36. Agnew, *Worlds Apart.* See also Leverenz, *Manhood in the American Renaissance.*

37. See, for example, Halttunen, *Confidence Men;* Kuhlman, *Knave, Fool, and Genius;* Lenz, *Fast Talk and Flush Times;* Mayfield, *Counterfeit Gentlemen,* ch. 3. Also, Lawrence McDonnell's essay in this volume.

38. J. Hooper, *Adventures of Captain Simon Suggs,* 8.

39. See Karcher, *Shadow over the Promised Land.*

40. See works by Wright, *Political Economy of the Cotton South;* Baptist, *Half Has Never Been Told;* W. Johnson, *River of Dark Dreams.*

41. Walter Johnson, "King Cotton's Long Shadow," *New York Times,* October 30, 2013, 12.

42. See Byrne, *Becoming Bourgeois.*

43. Baldwin, *Flush Times,* 83.

44. See D. Bruce, *Violence and Culture;* Wells, *Origins of the Southern Middle Class;* Elder, "Twice Sacred Circle"; Loveland, *Southern Evangelicals;* Jennifer Green, *Military Education;* Quist, *Restless Visionaries;* Pflugrad-Jackisch, *Brothers of a Vow;* T. Williams, *Intellectual Manhood.*

45. See O. Patterson, *Slavery and Social Death.*

46. Wyatt-Brown, *Southern Honor,* 16, 17.

47. O'Brien, *Conjectures of Order,* 17, 18. See also O'Brien, *Rethinking the South.*

48. See J. Shields, *Freedom in a Slave Society;* Mayfield, "Soul of a Man!"; also the essay by David Moltke-Hansen in this volume. See Romine, *Narrative Forms.*

49. Freeman, *Affairs of Honor,* xvii.

50. Wyatt-Brown, *Southern Honor* (25th anniversary edition), x.

51. They were not, of course, wholly successful at it. See the definitive work, Ayers, *Vengeance and Justice,* and Christopher Curtis's article in this volume, plus his book *Jefferson's Freeholders.*

52. Correspondence with author, August 15, 2014.

53. Pitt-Rivers, "Honor," 510.

David Moltke-Hansen

TO CIVILIZE KING COTTON'S REALM

William Gilmore Simms's Chivalric Quest

What was William Gilmore Simms thinking?[1] Recognized—if not exactly celebrated—by Edgar Allan Poe as the best American novelist of his day, Simms advocated fervently for native subjects and treatments as the proper preoccupation of American writers. Yet from the late 1830s to the mid-1840s he also penned two romances, or novel-length prose epics, set in Spain during the eighth-century Moorish conquest of the Iberian Peninsula: *Pelayo: A Story of the Goth* (1838) and *Count Julian; or, The Last Days of the Goth* (1845). In addition he wrote an 1847 biography of one of the last great medieval knights: *The Life of the Chevalier Bayard; "The Good Knight," "Sans peur et sans reproche"* ("Without Fear and without Reproach").[2]

Simms's was "the first full English language biography . . . , which ma[de] use of multiple sources and attempt[ed] to present Bayard in the larger context of his age." It recounted the career, character, and service of a nobleman devoted to his king and country in an age of mercenary armies and the era of New World conquest by rival European powers. These topics seem far from Simms's home state of South Carolina and the concerns of antebellum America. Yet Simms explicitly juxtaposed them. In *Simms's Monthly Magazine* in August 1845, he included both an article of his entitled "Bayard, the Chevalier," and a portion of a series of lectures he had given entitled "The Epochs and Events of American History, as Suited to the Purposes of Art." What was the connection?[3]

Readers of Mark Twain on southern chivalry have elaborated an interpretation. Twain and they got the story wrong, although they were right that chivalry mattered to southerners. Simms had very different reasons than they understood for writing about the influence and passing of feudalism in Western history, as well as the continuance of the culture of chivalry thereafter. He was not alone in addressing this seeming anachronism. On the eve of the Civil War, for instance, the future president of the South Carolina secession convention, David Flavel Jamison, moved next door to Simms to share conversations and researches on the topic. In these men's and others' eyes, chivalry was not simply a medieval holdover. It had contemporary political, as well as cultural and social, ramifications. Simms did more to explore these consequences than anyone else in the antebellum South.[4]

Like other Victorians, Simms had become fascinated with a question earlier asked by British writers such as Edmund Burke and Walter Scott: could chivalry, given its feudal roots, function in a postfeudal world and in the contexts of emerging centralized states and capitalism? He and Jamison concluded that what had once been a personal code of behavior, defined by fealty, bravery, and courtesy, had become a shared ideology of citizenship, comportment, and allegiance to the nation. It also functioned as a class marker. At the core rules of appropriate conduct still determined behavior. Yet they did so in new environments—in the marketplace, in the hurly burly of republican society, and in America's pursuit of Manifest Destiny. In other words, in the nineteenth century people transferred historically feudal loyalties and behavioral norms to emerging institutions, conditions, and relations.[5]

These new allegiances and their behavioral concomitants proved hellishly expensive. The catastrophic toll in lives lost and fortunes destroyed in the American Civil War provoked Twain's acerbity about southern chivalry. Supporting Twain's reading and the interpretations it fed was the postbellum recalibration of that code, which occupied Simms's last years. Chivalry became a sign of southern difference and a bulwark against capitalism, modernity, and Yankee individualism. These shifts had antebellum roots but took shape after Appomattox. Then they became part of the Lost Cause culture that later framed white southern memory and politics. In that context history no longer was the past left behind, as Simms and Jamison had argued in their medieval explorations before the war. Rather history became a testimony to southern civilization and values affronted by postbellum developments. That argument earned Twain's scorn. Its reverberations have miscast chivalry's role—if not its importance—in King Cotton's domain ever since.

The Twain Error

As Twain knew, Sir Walter Scott published his first English medieval romance, *Ivanhoe,* in 1819. This was just as cotton cultivation began to push west from the South Atlantic seaboard. Forty-one years later South Carolina seceded from the Union, becoming the first state to do so. In Twain's mind those facts were powerfully connected. In typical fashion he simplified a complicated matter in slashing style. He argued that the antebellum southern elite had become besotted with wildly anachronistic, romantic notions of chivalry, knights, and ladies.

That conclusion led Twain to accuse Scott of "having so large a hand in making Southern character" that "he [was] in great measure responsible for the [Civil] war." The irresponsible fantasist, according to W. J. Cash, Rollin G. Osterweis, and others influenced by Twain, prompted his prewar southern readers' absurd medieval tournaments and other "romantic juvenilities." Thus Scott perniciously had encouraged the Old South's children of privilege to embark on faux-chivalric stupidities like dueling and on hypertheatrical gallantries toward ladies that no woman of sense wished to endure.[6]

For Twain and his disciples, this romantic and chivalric mindset had been absent in the Revolutionary generation. Yet, as these writers concurred, it had emerged in full force several generations later, on the eve of the Civil War. This was because antebellum southerners had grown up reading Scott's medieval romances, absorbing their dangerous ideas. The planters had come to consider their African American chattel as loyal serfs. The planters' false expectation was that the slaves would aid their masters and the region's independent yeomanry as they took on the much larger North. In the planters' romance-filled minds, the combination of chivalry, élan, and fealty made their region invincible—more powerful than the North's industrial might and downtrodden free labor.[7]

Although biting, provocative, and widely accepted, Twain's invective against Scott did not reveal the romancer's true influence. His medieval tales played a part, but not in the way Twain and others later would suggest. Famously writing on chivalry for the *Encyclopedia Britannica* the year before publishing *Ivanhoe,* "Scott claimed that chivalry had effected a 'revolution in manners.'" This revolution still retained, in Scott's estimate, "a striking effect" centuries later and "tend[ed] on the whole to the improvement of society." Like Edmund Burke, Scott wondered "whether it was possible to translate the social ameliorating system of chivalric manners into a system of commercial manners," thereby palliating the destructive influences of business and modernity. Despite his recognition that most aspects of feudalism were long and truly moribund, he thought it important to try.[8]

Scott drew this conclusion as he "made the *internal* imperial formation of the modern secular nation state," beginning as far back as the Middle Ages, "his great theme, the canonical topic of history." "While imagining medieval England," he was "simultaneously imagining—'re-presenting'—the modern nation of Great Britain." Historic divisions between Saxons and Normans, like those between Highlanders and Lowlanders, foreshadowed modern ones between the Scots and the English. These latter peoples also would unite in a new identity—the British. Aiding them would be the common values shaping chivalry. Scott's approach appealed to southerners contemplating independence from the Union and ethnogenesis—the becoming of a separate people or ethnicity. Simms read chivalry's value in this context.[9]

Yet the appeal was wider than the South. Readers—and writers—in all regions of the United States liked "Scott's national, local, and characteristic features of . . . life and manners, in terms of both geography and speech." As the modern world moved further and further from the feudal order and worldview, the increasingly alien character of that past became more compelling. The revival of Gothic architecture was one measure of this preoccupation, although less visible in the South than in the Northeast or in Britain. In England the Pre-Raphaelite Brotherhood shared the fascination in their art and literature, starting in 1848. Indeed members used their conception of organic society in the Middle Ages to criticize modern, soulless industrialism.[10]

Simms shared this criticism, while rejecting the Pre-Raphaelites' idealization of the medieval and Catholic past. In part he drew on one of the sources of his *Chevalier Bayard.* Jean Charles Leonard Simonde de Sismondi's *Histoire des Francais* [*History of the French*] appeared in thirty volumes between 1821 and 1844. It reflected the author's anti-Catholic and anticapitalist orientation. Simms drew as well on such other historians of the Middle Ages as the Whiggish Henry Hallam, author of *A View of the State of Europe during the Middle Ages* (1818). Perhaps he, like his friend George Frederick Holmes, however, most admired Jules Michelet, whose concept of the progressive *movement* in history Simms often referenced. In the six volumes of the *History of France* devoted to the Middle Ages and first published between 1833 and 1844, Michelet treated the period as, in Jacques Le Goff's phrase, "the childhood of our society." Those volumes were the ones Simms knew in either French or English translation. As he wrote his *Chevalier Bayard,* they led him to ask two questions: what of the child is there in the adult, and how different is the modern from the medieval world? The answer to both was the same: a great deal.[11]

America's Chivalric Roots

That answer explains Simms's fascination with the Middle Ages and his rejection of its romanticization. Yet the fascination may have begun out of Romantic emulation. Under the guidance of Charlestonian James W. Simmons, a familiar in the British circle around Lord Byron, Simms was among America's early advocates of Romantic poetics. His 1825 verse drama on Count Julian, who had aided the Moors, and Roderick, the last king of the Visigoths, drew inspiration from Robert Southey and Walter Savage Landor, as well as Walter Scott. All three writers had written epically or dramatically on this nadir in Europe's history.[12]

Other developments may have colored Simms's vision as well. In 1822, when Simms turned sixteen, the Chevalier Bayard was reinterred to great fanfare in Grenoble. Then, in 1825, Robert Southey, the British poet laureate, saw through the press a translation by his niece Sara Coleridge of Jacques de Maille's *History of Bayard.* The same year he reviewed it for the *Quarterly Review.* It was then, too, that Simms started writing on the warrior culture of the Middle Ages. By the late 1830s he had concluded that the real legacy of the feudal world was the commitment to honor and rank, courtesy, and care for the weak. These social values were, or should be, fundamental to contemporary civilization. Even though they had originated in the medieval era, they informed the modern, chivalric code. That code continued to play a civilizing role.[13]

John C. Guilds, Simms's literary biographer, determined that, when writing about these medieval subjects, Simms sought to meet the tastes and expectations of polite audiences and did so badly. Guilds judged that Simms had wasted his talent as well on biography—a curious comment for a literary biographer. By anachronistically defining literature as creative writing, Guilds missed an important point. History and biography also were literary pursuits, not just for Simms, but for many others who had grown up reading Scott. So, indeed, was literary criticism. The critic "helped to furnish better notions of what virtue demanded, as well from the citizen as the statesman; and, in the very choice of his topics, he opened the eyes of readers to a more just appreciation of what was required of life."[14]

The man of letters undertook all these genres. Biographical, historical, and critical studies illuminated the human condition and agency and examined the development of civilization. Such writings also helped weigh the essentials of a character, a culture, or a people. Moreover, at least in the 1840s, when new historical romances were selling badly in the wake of the panic of 1837, biographical and critical writing paid, and Simms needed to earn. In these pursuits Scott was a precursor and model as well. Simms read his frequent reviews. Then, in 1827, Scott's nine-volume *The Life of Napoleon Buonaparte, Emperor of the French* became an international best seller.

Simms had another reason, beyond the popularity of biography and the tragic stories of Visigoth leaders, to write on the Chevalier Bayard, Count Julian, and King Roderick. In effect he explained this in an address at the University of Alabama, published as *The Social Principle* in 1843. There he explored the differences in the approaches to American conquest and colonization by the Spanish, the French, and the British. Having fought for God, king, and glory through nearly eight centuries of *Reconquista,* the reconquest of Spain from the Moors, the conquistadors were not looking to become farmers and merchants when they came to the New World. Instead they continued their search for new converts, dominions, and gold. Even more compelling was the chance for fame and recognition in the royal court in Madrid, the warrior's ultimate reward. The French, too, esteemed the honor of battle, the court, and their faith. Bold in exploration, they nevertheless also left a relatively light footprint in the territory they claimed in the future American South. Like the Spanish, they did not settle there in large numbers. They were more interested in conquest than colonization.[15]

The British were different. No less committed to honor, they at the same time were intent on establishing New World provinces where they could build farms and futures while developing centers of commerce, society, and civilization. There were gentry among them, but not many. Instead most British colonists were poor yeomen, sailors, artisans, or laborers and their families. They came to the future South not just to look for the main chance, but to assert "the social principle" through the homes they built and the farms they planted. Joining them were Scots-Irish, Irish, French Huguenots, Sephardic Jews, and Germans fleeing religious persecution or poverty. They too wanted new homes in the New World.[16]

Considering these differences Simms concluded: the shift from feudalism to centralizing monarchies motivated the development of the Spanish and French possessions. Men acted in the name of, and with hope of preferment by, their sovereigns, although they did so out of ambition for martial glory and treasure. The British did not, at least not to the same degree. There were several reasons, which Simms spelled out in different places over time. First, civil war had torn the home country apart in the 1640s. Second, the British crown encouraged settlement through private enterprise. Third, Britain had a parliamentary government. Finally, most colonists in the British sphere were intent on escaping the Old World's bonds in the New World's freedoms and opportunities.[17]

Empowering these settlers was the shift from feudal hierarchy to a patriarchal society of independent proprietors. The habits of local self-government and self-protection that these colonials developed encouraged them to think of themselves as independent in other ways as well. Over time they chafed at the increasing limits imposed on them by the government in Britain. In the revolution that followed, they replaced fealty to the Crown with republicanism and patriotism.[18]

Thus it was that British Americans proved themselves better than either the Spanish or the French at making the transition from Old World inhabitants to New World settlers. As a result Simms expected the former British colonies to continue developing a native civilization. His credo for American letters reflected this ambition: rather than replicate the art of the Old World, Americans should help articulate and reveal the New. "We have our own national mission to perform," he insisted. Furthermore "the true and most valuable inspiration of the poet will be found either in the illustration of the national history, or in the development of the national characteristics."[19]

"To write *from* a people," Simms also maintained, "is to *write* a people—to make them live—to endow them with a life and a name—to preserve them with a history forever." He understood this literary development of America broadly: it did not just allow but compelled examination of the Old World origins of behaviors important in shaping the New. Simms felt impelled, not just permitted, as well to examine the geopolitical contexts out of which the American South of his own day had developed. Therefore he ranged in his writing across Cuba and Puerto Rico, as well as the Isthmus of Panama. This was in addition to his treatments of the Spanish, French, and English possessions in the future South.[20]

Part of Simms's goal was to help people understand aspects of the conquests and conflicts shaping his natal region's emergence. In his mind all these theaters of action had been important. Unlike most Virginia and Maryland writers in his day, Simms was acutely aware that much of his region was newly American. For most of its history, it had been Native American. Then portions became Spanish or French. Not until the annexation of Texas in 1845 did all the South come under the American flag. Located on the international frontier for a century and a half and adjacent to Native American lands until 1838 and the Trail of Tears, South Carolinians understood.[21]

The Chevalier as Model and Symbol

This sweeping, integrative concept of American history notwithstanding, the Chevalier Bayard was not an obvious subject for inclusion by Simms. Yes, the knight's 1524 death by gunshot in Italy, birthplace of the Renaissance, signaled the end of the Middle Ages. Yet in the epoch of the conquistadors and the condottieri, the mercenary commanders against whom Bayard fought, the chivalric world order already was far removed from its feudal roots. According to Simms it had become debased and corrupted almost beyond recognition. That point made, he nevertheless was clear: despite the purer chivalry that the earlier, darker age nurtured, no tears needed to be shed for it or its superstitions and brutality.[22]

At the same time, Simms was emphatic that chivalry, as embodied by the Chevalier Bayard, gave cultural salience to values that should—and often did—appear in societies at very different stages of development. Again and again, from the mid-1820s forward, Simms returned to the theme. He did so especially in his writing on Native Americans. Indians, he judged, had an essential chivalric virtue—honor—as part of their culture. So had the ancient Romans.[23]

In Simms's eyes honor was a universal, not a historically bound, value. Chivalry, the more encompassing behavioral code, was both—a medieval form but one that had continued relevance after the Middle Ages. Honor made men equal at a fundamental level. It reflected nobility and steadfastness of character, commitment to one's people and word, protection of the weak, and willingness to sacrifice everything on behalf of one's reputation and justice. Chivalry, while encompassing all those virtues and others, was more exclusive—the code of an elite, whether of birth or accomplishment, and therefore the mark of social and cultural superiority.

Yet it was not medieval knights who carried forward these transhistorical and hierarchical commitments in the postfeudal world. Gentlemen did. The Chevalier Bayard's nobility of character and death helped inspire this new social being. It also symbolized necessary social order and hierarchy. These, however, were no longer defined by feudal fealties. Rather, Simms contended, in the English-speaking world, such chivalric values had become the responsibility of men in families and of social betters over social inferiors, as measured by character and accomplishment, not rank. As Edmund Burke put it near the end of the eighteenth century, "nothing is more certain, than that our manners, our civilization, and all the good things which are connected with manners, and with civilization, have . . . depended . . . upon two principles . . . the spirit of a gentleman, and the spirit of religion."[24]

The link between gentility and gentlemen led Bertram Wyatt-Brown, in *Southern Honor,* to distinguish between the primal honor influencing everyone in an honor (or shame) culture and the gentility marking the elite. Both supported the pursuit of "power, prestige, and self-esteem." Yet the latter expressed social and cultural status beyond the former. Simms did not want to segregate in this way the martial, heroic, and patriarchal components of authority from elite values. In his conception chivalry had united them and still should. Bayard was a strategic case in support of this argument.[25]

At the same time as the Chevalier represented perduring values, his passing suggested the progress that brought the modern age out of the medieval. In other words, the temporal and cultural distance between Simms's epoch and the Chevalier's was as important as the Chevalier's example. The one made the knight a historical figure; the other made him timeless. The latter illustrated what Americans should admire and pursue. And in time numerous Confederates attested the fact by describing one or another select leader—most often Robert E. Lee—as a "Bayard of the South." Yet the Chevalier's death also marked a transition, one that would make the Middle Ages seem distant, archaic, and barbaric to Simms and Jamison, as well as Walter Scott.[26]

Whither the Chivalric Code?

Clarifying the distance is the book that Jamison dedicated to Simms, *The Life and Times of Bertrand du Guesclin: A History of the Fourteenth Century.* Having contributed to some of the same journals as Simms, Jamison bought Burwood Plantation in 1859, next door to Simms's Woodlands, on the Edisto River. In visits back and forth before Jamison's 1864 death, the two friends talked about the end of feudalism and the emergence of the modern state, beginning in the fourteenth century. "It was the period," Jamison explained, "when the feudal system . . . , with its traditions, its isolation, and real power, was forced to yield to the increasing authority of the prince, the growing influence of the communes and of men acting in masses."[27]

Jamison also discussed with and borrowed from Simms books to research the first life in English of du Guesclin. The Eagle of Brittany was no courtier, full of politesse and social finesse. Instead he was a redoubtable and much-admired soldier and commander. With Joan of Arc, he became an inspiration to the French in the Hundred Years War against England. That protonationalist role also attracted his biographer. It served to suggest how feudal fealty, which, together with honor, was at the core of chivalry, began to be transferred to modern patriotism.

A former state legislator, who had served with Simms, Jamison had almost finished a first draft of the life when public events sidetracked him. His election as president of the South Carolina secession convention was followed by his selection as South Carolina secretary of war. Despite his duties the general returned to his study. There he penned a brief but heartfelt dedicatory letter to Simms that he dated February 1862. The next year he finished the manuscript, including the introduction, while acting as a military judge.[28]

That such prominent figures as Jamison and Simms dwelt on famous medieval knights at the same time as they pursued secession seems odd. It was easy to jump to conclusions about their motivations. Twain was twenty-five when Jamison's directive to the delegates at the secession convention was quoted in newspapers around the South. Even if Twain read it, he may not have remembered the source that Jamison gave—Georges Jacques Danton's famous September 2, 1792, speech before the French Revolutionary Tribunal. In it Danton urged his auditors: "To dare! and again to dare! and without end to dare!" Mindful of the source or not, Twain believed he understood the impulse to dare secession in the fascination with heroic knighthood and chivalry.[29]

While Simms and Jamison certainly admired the knights about whom they wrote, their esteem did not blind them to the distances between themselves and those subjects. Neither did their readers mistake these biographers' intentions or accomplishments. Sufficiently impressed with Jamison's work, Count Jacques Louis Randon, marshal of France and minister of war, had Jamison's book translated from the English in 1866. Clearly his interest in the work did not stem from any putative medieval obsessions of southerners.[30]

Indeed Simms and Jamison had a very different take than the one Twain imputed to Confederates. As Jamison explained, "The institution of chivalry, which had so long exerted its humanizing influences over the individual man, and softened the manners of a barbarous age—with all its romance, its tournaments, and pageant—" had long ago receded. Far from regretting the fact, he and Simms had a different concern: "the progress of mankind in civilization," as Jamison put it in an 1843 review essay. What did a chivalric heritage matter in "the onward movement of society in the improvement of its moral, intellectual and political condition" in a postfeudal age? What was the import of chivalry for civilization in the Victorian era—this in the face of capitalism and the rush to modernity? What past values survived significantly into the authors' present? With what consequences did they survive?[31]

In asking these questions, Simms and Jamison were drawing on a transatlantic discourse that dated back generations. Twain may not have known this background. Yet one should remember that he was perceptive even when erroneous. Like many in Britain and elsewhere, some Confederates did emulate on the battlefield the traditions of chivalry that knights represented. Famously the Crimean War saw such actions in the decade before the Civil War. As Cecil Woodham-Smith noted, the aristocrats who ordered "the charge of the Light Brigade"—celebrated and lamented in Alfred, Lord Tennyson's poem by that name—"glorified courage, called it valour and worshipped it." They "believed battles were won by valour, saw war in terms of valour as the supreme adventure."[32] A later, more deadly conflict even than the Civil War perhaps best expressed the fusion of honor and statism: World War I. Not only a southern development, therefore, it nevertheless clearly emerged as an important element of escalating southern political disaffection in the run-up to the Civil War. Simms's defense of southern patriotism in the American Revolution and his attacks on Yankee dishonor reflect this strain in his and many other southerners' thinking.[33]

Chivalry and Southern Civilization

The relationship of honor and chivalry to patriotism was complex. It was not the simple equation suggested by the fact that in 1847 Simms not only saw his Bayard into print, but also decided to advocate secession from the Union and the creation of an independent southern nation. True, Simms's perception of the distance between southern honor and Yankee interest helped fuel that determination, and he read this divergence within a framework shaped by his understanding of the chivalric code. Yet his reliance on chivalry was broader and deeper. His *The Life of the Chevalier Bayard* provided a cultural compass bearing for him.

The biography also shows aspects of Simms's abiding social concerns and historical preoccupations. For Simms war helped emerging societies and nations supersede their predecessors. When not advancing a people, it at least gave them the chance for honor. This was the case for American Indians, who faced inevitable defeat. To die with honor provided men the opportunity for true—not just birthright—nobility. That commitment was part of the essence of the transhistorical chivalric standard. In the years leading up to the South's secession, the Chevalier Bayard represented it. Indeed the claims of the Chevalier on the American imagination long antedated Simms's biography of him.[34]

Chivalry and honor were directly related in that imagining—not the same but close. Chivalry was the more encompassing. Yet it was restricted to the elite. Honor was an essential expression of chivalry but was also available to people who did not participate in chivalric or elite culture. Neither automatically equated to patriotism, a concept that came long after feudalism.

Chivalry's civilizing role, therefore, was not only anterior to, it was different than, while ultimately important to, patriotism. The point needed emphasis three generations after Sir Edmund Burke's lament in the midst of the French Revolution's overturn of traditional hierarchies: "The age of chivalry is gone.—That of sophists, economists, and calculators has succeeded; and the glory of Europe is extinguished forever." Simms invested in the idea put forward by Scott in 1815: "the revolution in manners" that chivalry had begun in a barbaric age could serve to curb some of the harshness and rudeness of the modern world.[35]

Indeed Simms asked more of the code: it must not only govern individual behavior but direct the development of civilization as a whole. In his region this was because, in the generations after Scott, the restless movement westward of southerners destabilized their society. The progressive, hypercommodification of land and labor in a capitalist economy compounded the problem by undercutting the values of home and community. These perpetually threatened commitments were reflected in Horacian *Georgics,* exemplary lives of the southern founding fathers, and John Taylor of Caroline's pastoral republicanism.[36]

Simms understood the threat personally. His father and uncle were two of those drawn early to the wilderness opportunities of the Mississippi Territory. When visiting in the 1820s, the young Simms was tempted by his father's invitation: leave Charleston, where he had been raised by his grandmother, and come west. Instead the boy returned to his birthplace and, over the next forty-five years, wrote stories and novels about the wild passions, greed, and disorder that southerners had to overcome to build new homes and plant new farms in the West. When speaking at the University of Alabama in 1842, he marveled how rapidly that agenda had transformed much of the state, turning a howling wilderness into a place of rich fields and growing towns.[37]

Without such civilizing progress, Simms insisted early and late, the South could not succeed as a society. Yet there was a tension at the heart of the South's growth. The plantation as an economic enterprise was not the same as the plantation as a center of domestic virtue and life. Agricultural production did not guarantee cultural reproduction and growth. Witness the many plantations abandoned in South Carolina by people moving west to greener pastures. The transformation of agriculture into culture was an effort of will, an assertion of values, an exercise of historical memory, and a matter of commitment.[38]

The priorities informing this choice had to be shared to be meaningful. One could not live and school one's children in isolation. Homes needed neighbors, and they had to have compatible commitments. That said, how did one foster correct choices? After all King Cotton was no medieval monarch. Fealty to him did not bring or reflect the honor of serving a liege lord. Instead it made the market paramount—unless and until one could insure otherwise. The chivalric code helped arm the individual, the community, and the culture against the excesses and claims of the market, of the promiscuous franchise, and of transitory fads in religion, literature, and philosophy. Or so Simms, and some of his compatriots, contended.[39]

Others were not so sure. John Pendleton Kennedy poked fun at the pretensions and incapacities of the Virginia gentry. For that matter Simms also deflated many of the characters in his fiction who did not live up to the standards to which they pretended or with which they had been raised. What he did not do was disparage the standards themselves. Such a critical stance was central also to the understanding of writers from the rising South in Alabama and places farther west. Even when born in the East, those authors faced a different reality than did people in established plantation areas. The rawness of settlements, fluidity of the society, and crudeness of the Old Southwest did not reflect much of chivalry's sway. Yet even near the receding frontier the aspirations to cultural attainment, social status, and graceful living modulated and civilized the grosser aspects of money, power, and social relations.[40]

The chivalric code did not define every aspect of these ambitions. Nevertheless the code was foundational. It served as a rule of life. It elevated certain values and the corresponding conduct. Thereby it instructed the gentleman in the proper attitude toward himself. It also told the gentleman what to do and why when he interacted with others, whether inferiors or equals, white or not, men or women. Following the code meant as well that certain things were not done. It might be advantageous to be shifty in a new country, as humorists of the Old Southwest had their characters say, but a gentleman would never sacrifice the good to the advantageous.

Simms insisted that the code was fundamentally learned at home and through emulation of others, although there were manuals on proper etiquette and behavior. Having elders and betters meant having models. Mimesis was central to cultural reproduction. Yet it was not sufficient to cultural production or leadership. Beyond character and training, one needed vision and discernment, also resolution and drive. Simms's motto, on the crest he designed for himself, conveyed part of this understanding. It read: "*video volans*" or "I see soaring."[41]

Chivalry and Patriotism

The patriot leader was someone with such vision. The loyalty to liege lord of old was not enough any longer. One had to divine the future and work to realize it, bringing along one's fellow citizens. The vessel of that future had become the nation-state—often a new creation sprung from older societal forms. That was why the chivalry of the Chevalier Bayard, as admirable and useful as it was, no longer was sufficient four centuries later. To the constellation of virtues nursed by chivalry one had to add patriotism—commitment to a country and a people. The Chevalier became a symbol of this new virtue aborning but came out of a culture in which it did not matter.[42]

The yoking of chivalry and patriotism transformed the medieval code from the personal virtue and practice of a knight to the collective obligation of a class and a society. The transition is reflected by quotes nearly three centuries apart. Some fifty years after the death of the Chevalier Bayard, Blaise de Monluc, marshal of France, famously declared: "My sword is the King's, my soul God's, my honor mine." While still a Union army officer on the eve of the Civil War, Robert E. Lee crucially replaced king with country. Yet he also gave priority to honor: "there is no sacrifice I am not ready to make for the preservation of the Union," he said, "save that of honour."[43]

By the time Lee wrote, Simms already had long decided that honor did not allow him to remain in the Union. Yet he regarded himself as a patriot. Beyond honor's requirements his commitment was informed principally by two sources.

On the one hand, he embraced republican virtue, drawing on the ancient Roman and more recent English traditions evoked by America's founding fathers. On the other, he resonated with emerging ethnic nationalisms in Europe. That strain of Romanticism also shaped the preoccupations of a New York–centered circle of writers and Democratic politicians in which he participated. It became self-identified as Young America.[44]

The name intentionally evoked European nationalist organizations, such as Young Italy, Young Germany, and Young Ireland. Edgar Allan Poe, Nathaniel Hawthorne, and Herman Melville, as well as George Bancroft, James Fenimore Cooper, and Simms were among the literary members of this circle. John L. O'Sullivan and Evert Augustus Duyckinck recruited them to publish in Young America journals and book series, such as the *United States Magazine and Democratic Review* and Wiley and Putnam's Library of American Books. The group espoused manifest destiny and nationalist revolutions as well as what an Alabama friend of Simms, Alexander B. Meek, called "Americanism in Literature." Generally proslavery, their publications nevertheless occasionally featured even such Whigs and abolitionists as John Greenleaf Whittier.[45]

That inclusiveness reflected a growing fissure in the unifying presuppositions and commitments of not just Young America, but the country. As abolitionism, Transcendentalism, and capitalistic values acquired public resonance in the North, many Americans' definitions of patriotism, Americanism, and progress shifted. Eventually they included opposition to slavery and condemnation of slaveholders even among the founding fathers. Many northerners and most white southerners continued to disagree with this interpretation. Nevertheless by the 1850s sectional antagonism engulfed nearly every discussion of patriotism, honor, and civilization.[46]

The fact was highlighted in a slashing speech that U.S. senator Charles Sumner gave on slavery in Bloody Kansas. Speaking from the floor of the U.S. Senate on May 19 and 20, 1856, he dismissed the South's—especially South Carolina's—patriotism during the Revolution. The massive 1847 study *The American Loyalists* by New Englander Lorenzo Sabine, especially Sabine's "Preliminary Historical Essay," was the authority for Sumner's contention that South Carolina had been home to so many loyalists in the Revolution that New Englanders had been obliged to march south to rescue the patriot cause there. Simms was indignant. Sabine, he argued, was wrong and his conclusions pernicious.[47]

New Englanders had not marched to the aid of their fellow countrymen in large numbers. On the contrary the South was where the great majority of the fighting in the war had occurred. Most New England soldiers were just home patriots, serving in their region. Of necessity local South Carolina paramilitary forces again and again had saved the Continental Army, under the command of New England generals. In doing so they had kept alive the patriot cause. Justice and honor required recognition of the fact.[48]

Hoping to teach this heritage to young South Carolinians, especially his children, Simms published *The History of South Carolina* in Charleston in 1840. It focused on the Revolution. He extended his audience for the topic with his biography of South Carolina militia general Francis Marion, published in New York in 1844. None of his books garnered greater success. Despite its contrarian view of the Revolution, it further elevated the Swamp Fox as a national hero.[49]

This attention came in the months and years after Simms rhetorically asked a July 4, 1844, audience in Aiken, South Carolina: "Do they [the people of the North] not hourly encroach upon our rights, insult our pride and denounce our institutions?" If this were not bad enough, southerners inadvertently fed this growing northern denigration of the South's Revolutionary ardor. This infuriated him. In 1845–46 he attacked (initially, unknowingly) Ann Pamela Cunningham, daughter of a onetime law partner of John C. Calhoun, for her too-indulgent treatment of her loyalist ancestors in South Carolina. He did so first in a review of a volume to which she had anonymously contributed biographies of these men. Then he wrote his own biographical sketches of Bloody Bill Cunningham and others.[50]

Simms did not stop there. He even challenged works by admired friends. For example he excoriated Maryland novelist John Pendleton Kennedy's fictional portrayal of the British occupation of South Carolina in an 1835 novel, *Horse-Shoe Robinson: A Tale of the Tory Ascendency.* Continuing this counteroffensive, in 1853 Simms gathered together several essays under the title *South-Carolina in the Revolutionary War: Being a Reply to Certain Misrepresentations and Mistakes of Recent Writers, in Relation to the Course and Conduct of This State.* Then, in the fall of 1856, he took the campaign north, on a lecture tour. His partisan passion repelled rather than converted his initially packed audiences. Therefore he cut the tour short. This was after concluding that northerners did not understand southern honor or the demands of patriotism. Confounded, he wondered how one could claim to be a patriot and not have, or comprehend the requirements of, honor.[51]

In part the answer was that there was a growing difference in interpretation. Early writers on Revolutionary warriors framed the conflict as a matter of political and moral principle. The rights of freeborn Englishmen in America had been trampled on but were reclaimed through the Revolution. Simms offered a different understanding in his July 4, 1844, oration and elsewhere. The War for Independence "was a revolt of the native mind of the country."[52]

"The educated and wealthy classes," Simms argued, sought to emancipate themselves when they felt able to stand on their own feet. They judged that "the domestic genius [was] eager for employment . . . and restive under the foreign domination." Therefore, despite the indifference or hostility of the lower classes, they led the colonies out of the empire. This was after the British refused to acknowledge their right to self-governance and full citizenship. As a consequence the Revolution was accomplished by gentlemen, men of chivalry. Their honor demanded it. So did their commitment to republicanism, their home colonies, and the country they desired to create.[53]

Simms considered this example of leadership paradigmatic for gentlemen, whether of attainment or birth. He modeled his behavior accordingly, joining the vanguard of the future southern revolution in the summer of 1847. It was then that he started urging, not just predicting, secession. His argument was ethnogenesis: Americans had become a people, although incompletely, through revolution. Now white southerners were becoming one in their turn. Once again "the educated and wealthy classes" had the opportunity to lead and thereby emulate their ancestors. Once again honor and self-respect demanded independence.[54]

Simms began to see his Revolutionary and other regional heroes as representative and epitomic southerners, just as Bayard and du Guesclin had been epitomic knights. Carrying forward this preoccupation with model warriors, he declared war "the greatest element of civilization." It made peoples, men, and manners. Yet, in a review of Elizabeth Ellet's *The Women of the American Revolution,* he also contended that the home, the farm, and daily life were what were at the heart of a people's history. They shaped the culture and transmitted it to the next generation. For gentlemen of aspiration or birth, chivalry was a critical part of that education.[55]

Chivalry after the War

Did the Confederates accept this understanding? Twain thought so. His reasons may have been wrong, but in the end, how wrong was he? Clearly he was in error in ascribing to southerners a deeper or different commitment to chivalry than all others had. Yet that did not mean that chivalry's demands were inconsequential to many of the soldiers who volunteered and fought for the Confederacy. Indeed it was Simms's wish that those demands, modified by the expectations of patriotism, guide men in battle, at home, and, later, in defeat. They were the chief protection men had from the barbarism within and the barbarism without. To die nobly was much better than to live ignobly. No cause was more worthy than defense of hearth and home, family and country.

In his biography of Bertrand du Guesclin, Jamison wrote of someone he regarded as a true defender of his people and place. He did so in the midst of the Confederacy's assertion of nationhood and calls for patriotism. In effect du Guesclin became a patriotic symbol. But he also was more. If Bayard represented the end of the Middle Ages, du Guesclin signaled the beginning of that end. It was during his lifetime, Jamison observed, that "the lance and the battle-axe began to give place to cannon and the matchlock, and when a standing military force came to be substituted for the hasty levies of the feudal militia." It also "was the period when romantic literature disappeared with the songs of the troubadours" and the modern state was born. Shortly after completing his truncated study, Jamison died of yellow fever. Almost immediately upon the end of the Civil War the next year, Simms tried to get the help of old friends in New York to sell copies on behalf of Jamison's destitute widow. So chivalry was honored in defeat.[56]

After the war Simms maintained his antebellum expectations of chivalry except in one regard. He could not be a patriot statist in the land of his conquerors. The identity of country and people had been broken. Consequently he reinscribed the meaning of patriotism to make it tribal rather than territorial. His loyalty was to his people. He recognized his fellow, white southerners by the way they, or the elite among them, used chivalry as their code. In his apocalyptic vision, this set them apart from the Yankees, who had dishonored themselves both by the war they had caused and fought so ignobly and by their conduct in its aftermath.

It was in a speech shortly before his death by cancer in 1870 that Simms told the Ladies Horticultural Society in Charleston that the past was a bulwark against Yankee influences. He urged the importance of the values of that past as a prescription for the future health of southern society and culture, which otherwise would be overwhelmed by soul-stealing capitalism. He did not contend, however, that the past was in any sense ideal. Rather he insisted that it had fostered cultural and moral values that had developed in conscious opposition to materialism and that could protect southerners from national excesses in the future. The ideals he articulated were in part those he regarded as transhistorical, chivalric ones. The true patriot leader would adhere to those ideals in the face of the country's addiction to alien and alienating influences or the forcible imposition of those influences by a victorious enemy.[57]

In making the case, Simms was anticipating the Lost Cause tradition in southern writing. One had to use memory of life before the Civil War, he insisted, to protect against the appalling circumstances of the Reconstruction South. It was looking through this lens to read prewar chivalry that Twain concluded that in the Old South, too, devotion to the code was anachronistic and unreal. His second cousin, Jeremiah Clemens, also a novelist and a former U.S. senator from Alabama, made the same case. His *Tobias Wilson,* published posthumously in 1865, was one of the first novels to identify wooly-headed chivalry as a factor in the coming of the Civil War.[58]

Using "the Sir Walter disease" "as a generalized metaphor for fallen southern ideology," Twain continued to attack "southern notions of gentility." Readers of his 1889 novel, known later by the title *A Connecticut Yankee in King Arthur's Court,* made the point. Yet chivalry had not had the role before the war that Twain ascribed to it—at least not for a Simms or a Jamison. After the war was another matter. Then the South finally became a land of chivalric romance in the fictions of Lost Cause and Moonlight and Magnolias myth writers.[59]

NOTES

1. At points my essay here uses phrasing and analyses from six recent pieces—my critical introduction to Simms, *Views*; my essays "Critical Revolution"; "Southern Literary Horizons"; "Turn Signals," and "When History Failed," as well as my review of Simms's *Life of the Chevalier Bayard.* James Crutchfield, Christopher Curtis, Sarah Gardner, Todd Hagstette, John Mayfield, Alexander Moore, Michael O'Brien, Johanna Shields, and Clyde Wilson prodded me, not always successfully, to clarify my argument and prose.

2. Butterworth and Kibler, *William Gilmore Simms*, 50.

3. J. Rogers, Introduction, xxxvii. W. Simms, "Bayard" and "Epochs."

4. Oliphant et al., "Simms' Circle," 1:cxvii; Meriwether, "Jamison," 9: 604–5.

5. Moltke-Hansen, "Southern," 7–15; cf. Wyatt-Brown, *Southern*, 96.

6. Moltke-Hansen, "Southern," 8; Twain, *Life*, 469, 416; Cash, *Mind of the South*, 65; Osterweis, *Romanticism*, 26, 41–49; R. Watson, *Yeoman*, 70–75. Cf. Hardwig, *Upon*, 38–39; O'Brien, *Rethinking*, 53; Baptist, *Creating*, 247–76.

7. Fox-Genovese and Genovese, *Mind*, 305–8, dismiss this caricature.

8. Diedrick, "Dialogical," 286; Scott, "Essay," 25.

9. Duncan, "Scott's Romance," 370; Diedrick, "Dialogical," 282.

10. Perosa, *American*, 26; Aldrich, *Gothic*; Stanton, *Gothic*; Eastlake, *History*; Barringer, *Reading*; Girouard, *Return*; Moltke-Hansen, "Critical," 198–99; Moltke-Hansen, "Southern," 9–10.

11. Simms, *Life of the Chevalier Bayard*, [vii]; Fox-Genovese and Genovese, *Mind*, 308–11, 372; O'Brien, *All*, 182, 191; Moltke-Hansen, "Ordered," 131, 143; J. Rogers, Introduction, xxx–xxxi; Le Goff, *Time, Work, and Culture*, 6.

12. Kibler and Moltke-Hansen, "Man," 4; Southey, *Roderick*; Landor, *Count Julian*; Scott, *Vision*.

13. Shellabarger, *Chevalier*, 313; [Mailles], *Right*; Southey, "Life." Although Simms did not write about the reinterment of the Chevalier, he used the French biography of Bayard by Jean Cohen, published in 1822: Simms, *Life of the Chevalier Bayard*, v, and also Busick, *Sober*, 38. A widely known portrait medal of the Chevalier also was struck in 1822.

14. Guilds, *Simms*, 1–2, 187; Simms, *Selected*, 273.

15. Simms, *Social*, 8–9. Cf. Pettigrew, *Notes*, 330–32, which insists chivalry resulted from the fusion of Moorish or "oriental" and gothic cultures, spreading from Spain to the rest of Europe. Simms, but especially Jamison, denigrated Moorish influence, instead arguing that chivalry reflected the influence of Christianity on Germanic warrior culture.

16. W. Simms, *Social*, 17–18.

17. See, for instance, Simms, *History*; *Sources*; and *Views*, 1st ser., 63–66, as well as Busick, *Sober*.

18. Simms, *Social*, 17–18. Cf. Greenberg, *Masters*, 3–22.

19. Simms, *Views*, 1st ser., 3, 40.

20. Simms, *Views*, 1st ser., 6. In chronological order by year of publication, the following Simms works treat at least in part the Spanish or French in the Americas before the nineteenth century: *Vision, My Lady, Martin Faber, Damsel, Donna Florida, Lily, Vasconselos, Kiawah*. Many of these and others treat Native Americans: see Simms, *Early and Strong*.

21. Moltke-Hansen, "Critical," 204–8.

22. J. Rogers, Introduction, xxx–xxxi.

23. Hagstette, "Private," 50–51; Simms, *Yemassee*, 10, 132.

24. Burke, *Reflections*, 117.

25. Wyatt-Brown, *Southern*, 16 and 62–115.

26. Cf. Trent, *Lee*, 131; Fox-Genovese and Genovese, *Mind*, 330.

27. Jamison, *Life*, 1:viii.

28. Oliphant et al., "Simms' Circle," *Letters*, 1:cxvii; Meriwether, "Jamison," 9: 618–19.

29. On the Danton quote, see Fox-Genovese and Genovese, *Mind*, 26. The translation there is slightly different than that given by Jamison in South Carolina Secession Convention, *Journal*, 7.

30. Jamison, *Bertrand*.

31. Jamison, Review, 1.

32. P. Anderson, *Blood*, treats the values shaping the actions and the contemporary, as well as later, reading of those deeds of Confederate "knight" Turner Ashby. The quote is in Woodham-Smith, *Reason*, 1.

33. Although stating that "chivalry was born in the court of King Arthur and laid to rest in the trenches of World War I," Frantzen, *Bloody*, 1, concludes that it in fact has continued. Cf. Girouard, *Return*.

34. Hagstette, "Private," 51. "The Chevalier Bayard and the Fair Widow" appeared anonymously in the same issue of the *American Monthly Magazine*, 5, no. 2 (1835), 81–88, as Simms's poem "The Voice of the Streamlet," 95–96; it begins, "All the world has heard, and read, and talked, of the Chevalier Bayard."

35. Burke, *Reflections*, 113; Diedrick, "Dialogical," 286.

36. Tate, *Conservatism*, sketches elements of these concerns. See also Moltke-Hansen, "Between," and "Southern," 9–11.

37. Simms, *Social*, 5–6; J. Shields, *Freedom*, 34–39.

38. A. Smith, *Economic*; T. Rogers, "Great"; James David Miller, *South by Southwest*; C. Morris, *Becoming*; Moltke-Hansen, "Between" and "Ordered."

39. Simms, *Selected*, 294–332; Kibler, Introduction, *Woodcraft*, xxvii, xxxi–xxxiii; Moltke-Hansen, "Southern," 11–13.

40. Mayfield, *Counterfeit*, 1–18; J. Shields, *Freedom*; Tate, *Conservatism*, 71–72, 104–6.

41. Mimesis was central to the poetics of Coleridge and other early Romantics, including Simms. See Burwick, *Mimesis*. On Simms's Coleridgean bent, see Moltke-Hansen, "Critical," 200–202.

42. Moltke-Hansen, "Southern," 13–15; Simms, *Selected*, 217–60, 299–313.

43. On honor in de Monluc (or de Montluc), see, for instance, Knecht, "sword"; Pepper, "Siege," 602–3, and J. Smith, *Culture*, 36–42. The Lee quote is at G. Gallagher, *Becoming*, 19–20.

44. Tate, *Conservatism*, 136–88; Moltke-Hansen, "Southern," 1–13, and Introduction, *Views*, xxiii–xxvii.

45. Simms, *Views*, 1st ser., 1–19. On Young America, see also P. Miller, *Raven*; Widmer, *Young*, and Eyal, *Young*.

46. Moltke-Hansen, "Turn," 174–80, and "When," 6–8.

47. See, for instance, Hoffer, *Caning*; Puelo, *Caning*, and Sinha, "Caning."

48. Sabine, *American*; Simms, *Letters*, 6:328–37; Hagstette, "Private," 52–58.

49. Moltke-Hansen, "Turn," 177–79; S. Smith, "Imagining."

50. Simms, *Sources*; Simms, "Civil"; Moltke-Hansen, "Why."

51. Moltke-Hansen, "When," 9–10; Hagstette, "Private," 52–58; Franklin, "North"; Shillingsburg, "Simms's Failed."

52. Simms, *Sources*, 16–17.

53. Simms, *Sources*, 16–17.

54. Moltke-Hansen, "Fictive"; Wyatt-Brown, *Shaping*, 177–202.

55. Simms, *Selected*, 294–332. See also Simms's orations before college and school audiences—for instance, *Self-Development*.

56. Jamison, *Life*, 1: viii–xi; Moltke-Hansen, "When," 15–16.

57. Moltke-Hansen, "When," 20–30; Georgini, "Angel"; John Miller, "Sense."

58. J. Shields, *Freedom*, 25–54; Hettle, *Peculiar*, 122–41.

59. Bush, *Mark Twain*, 189.

Kathleen M. Hilliard

BUSHELS OF CORN, TUBS OF TROUBLE

Measuring Honor at the Pendleton Farmers' Society, 1823–1824

How often fond and hopeful quests do end in disappointment: so it was for George Reese Jr. Coming home to Chambers County, Alabama, in the summer of 1875, he and his wife, Mary, reviewed the month's travels. The old man had planned a triumphant tour down memory lane, a chance to honor ancestors, share stories, and visit his boyhood home. Seeking comforting confirmation of his family's many contributions back east and recognition of blood ties to kin and community there, the planter and former statesman had rambled through the Carolinas, quite in vain.

In Charlotte few knew the Reese family name. His grandfather, signer of the famed—if contrived—Mecklenburg Declaration of Independence, left no tangible legacy there.[1] His ancestor's grave unmarked, descendants "dead and forgotten," the "old family mansion" long gone, Reese bristled with indignation. "The ingratitude of republics alone is immutable!" he exclaimed. A visit to his childhood home days later brought no redeeming solace. "Everything gone!" he lamented of the family plantation in Pendleton, South Carolina. The farm's old well stood as but a "pool of stagnant water," the "handiwork of my father or the family" lost. As dreams of glory turned to dust, George Reese reassessed his social identity in bitter terms. He was, astonishingly, "a stranger at the place of my birth."[2]

Leaving the "old home place in a buggy, behind an old broken-winded mule," Reese pondered his legacy. Upon return to Alabama, his home for nearly forty years, the old man made certain *his* story would not be forgotten. Now, at eighty years old, George Reese Jr. picked up his pen and began to write. Sentimental and self-deprecating, his memoirs regaled family and friends with tales of Old Pendleton, site of his father's homestead and the place where Reese Jr. grew to manhood. From pranks at the village schoolhouse to prayers at the Old Stone Church, the Pendleton of Reese's childhood emerges as "the old garden of Eden, the healthiest and wealthiest place in all the land."[3]

We might imagine that symbols of honor would mark the pages of Reese's reminiscences. Historian Bertram Wyatt-Brown defines honor as "the cluster of ethical rules . . . by which judgments of behavior are ratified by community consensus." Guided by "family integrity" and "clearly understood hierarchies of leaders and subordinates," communities evaluate behavior and regulate membership as means of maintaining the status of the group writ large. As a son in a rising family in upcountry South Carolina, a precocious state senator representing Pendleton District, a soldier during the Creek War, an elder in his Alabama community during the Civil War, and a respected official during Reconstruction, George Reese Jr. operated in political, social, military and economic spheres where we have come to expect to see honor claimed.[4] But most striking about Reese's memoir is its curious silence about that part of his life in which he would both find his greatest triumph and bring to his family its deepest shame—not the dueling ground or the race course, but in the sandy soil of a Carolina cornfield.

For all the pages of loving detail Reese devotes to the village, careful chroniclers of Pendleton's history must note a glaring oversight. Nineteenth-century travelers' accounts and atlases, reminiscences and memoirs, amateur histories, and contemporary promotional literature all trod similar ground—narrators tout the piety of the town's churches, the good character of its founding families, and, most important, the hardiness of its farmers. Established in 1815 the Pendleton Farmers' Society has come to epitomize the best of Pendleton's past, the hall members built in 1826 a touchstone of the community.[5]

Agricultural societies in the Old South have merited considerable attention from scholars, if not complete agreement on their meaning and importance. Dedicated to wringing the most out of increasingly infertile ground, these organizations loudly lamented farming practices past, deeming them wasteful and unnecessarily exploitative. Agricultural improvement, they argued, was key to both long-term productivity and short-term gain. Historians have struggled to make sense of such rhetoric, given the limited efforts of farmers to implement reformers' prescriptions. On the one hand, scholars view efforts to reform the land as a sign of a modernizing mindset in southern farming communities, pointing to agricultural societies and improvement organizations as evidence of a progressive-minded agricultural class, their efforts thwarted both by war and the hopelessly worn southern soil they aimed to rejuvenate.[6] Not so, argue historians who find reform efforts wanting in the region, and little sincerity behind all that modernization talk. For all their blather about progress and book farming, these scholars say, southern agricultural societies were little more than elite social clubs. Membership merely bolstered the status of men of rank in southern society.[7]

In South Carolina reformers' efforts surged in the 1820s, a period of "economic readjustment" in which Carolinians tried desperately to hang on to economic gains of the cotton boom of the early nineteenth century. Following the catastrophic Panic of 1819, Palmetto farmers fell further and further behind as increasing availability of cheap and fertile western land spurred competition in global cotton markets. Tilling worn soil and bleeding the population as farmers followed fortunes to Alabama and beyond, state agriculturalists and politicians weighed the merits of tools of economic growth. Good times were gone, all signs showed, and few could agree on the best path forward. Debating everything from internal improvements to agricultural reform, Carolinians wondered whether social and political structures their ancestors had created could bear up to the demands of market expansion.[8]

Historians have largely followed suit here, tallying the progress and limits of agricultural reform. In evaluating success in terms of agricultural output meshed with better methods, however, they have neglected to consider whether newfangled farming undermined social and political tradition. This essay examines how tensions between deeply subjective understandings of Old South honor and ostensibly objective calculations of productivity and reform took shape in an absurd and corrosive dispute over ninety-seven bushels of corn in 1824. The story of George Reese Jr.—his desperate search for recognition and status by way of agricultural contest, his ham-handed attempts to save himself when all went wrong, and the Pendleton Farmers' Society's efforts to right itself in the midst of organizational shame and fracture—illustrates the deep ambivalences gripping southerners in the midst of extraordinary social and economic change and offers a fresh point of departure for looking at struggles over honor in the Old South.

Reese's rise, fall, and selective retelling of his time in Pendleton parallels the Pendleton Farmers' Society's emergence as leader among agricultural reform organizations in the South. So it is striking that Reese would fail to mention it in his memoirs. After all, as Reese takes pains to point out, his "parents always said I must be a farmer," going so far as to send the young man on a tour of "model farms" in New England in 1817. His father, George Reese Sr., received one of the society's first prizes in 1816. Awarded for the district's best acre of wheat, the prized silver pitcher had passed from Senior to Junior, along with a portrait of the patriarch, "meek and benevolent," holding a shock of wheat in one hand, denoting him as a planter. His brother Edwin was a member of the organization, as was his brother-in-law David Cherry. Indeed the most prominent men of the town—farmers and lawyers alike—held some role in the group. Membership was a mark of status to which any honorable young man was bound to aspire.[9]

It is clear that the society's importance was not lost on young Reese. Records show that he was granted membership to the organization in 1819. Fresh from his trip north, where he dined with the likes of Judge Richard Peters, founder of the famed Philadelphia Society for Promoting Agriculture and author of endless treatises on soil exhaustion and a recent publication entitled "Notices for a Young Farmer," Reese must have imagined an important role for himself within that group.[10]

Joining this up-and-coming clique of aspiring planters fit well within Reese's broad and ambitious plans for social status. By 1823 he had been elected to the state legislature and was a captain in the local militia. A good marriage could help him further his lofty ambitions. In the summer of 1824, he was set to marry Mary Anne Witherspoon, daughter of Gavin Witherspoon, a local hero who spied for the Swamp Fox, Francis Marion, during the War for Independence. As a budding farmer and upstart politician, there was no doubt that George Reese Jr. was a man on the make. As it turns out, though, such early successes were not enough to sate the young man's grand goals.[11]

Toiling quietly ankle deep in Pendleton's sandy soil could not possibly suit a fellow like Reese, a young man of good family and—as we will see—blind ambition. And so we might imagine Reese beaming with pride in March 1824 when men of mark throughout the state picked up their newspapers and saw the young upstart's name before them: a gold medal awarded for ninety-seven bushels of corn—astonishing numbers from an upcountry farmer working the region's notoriously worn land. The *Charleston Mercury* had published Reese's letter from Pendleton District describing an experiment conducted the year before "on Gourd Seed Corn" made stunningly productive through "highly manuring and close sowing." So impressed was the Agricultural Society of South Carolina with Reese's output that secretary Thomas Condy had hailed it in the state's papers.[12]

But amid the excitement of sudden renown, a new fiancée, and a shining gold medal, we can but wonder—given the turn his fortunes were soon to take—was there uneasiness in Reese's heart as well? This was not the first time he put his crop—*this* crop—and his pride on the line. Five months earlier he had submitted documentation to the Pendleton Farmers' Society for the best "acre of upland corn." But that had gone wrong. "After some contest" with a prominent Pendleton lawyer, planter, and past society president James C. Griffin, the minutes tell us, he lost.[13]

By his own account, and that of his neighbor Henry McCrary, who certified the September 27 harvest, here is what happened: Reese gathered his corn and had McCrary weigh a sample bushel on both the Reese family steelyards and those of fellow society member Colonel Jesse Lewis. There was a discrepancy between the scales, though. Reese's measured a bushel at sixty pounds, Lewis's at fifty-five. McCrary offered to provide a certificate confirming measurement on Reese's scales. Instead Reese submitted documentation to the Pendleton Farmers' Society using the lower weight of fifty-five pounds, claiming that he "distrusted the accuracy of his own" measure. At eighty-nine bushels, his bounty would almost certainly assure victory—or so he thought.[14]

But in his own submission to the society, James Griffin claimed more bushels to the acre and, on that basis, won the first prize medal. Perhaps regretting his decision to submit certification using a lesser weight, Reese now made a wager with Griffin. Whose bushels weighed more? The two men enlisted fellow society member John Benson's scales to find out. Such a bet—and the measurement it required—served two purposes. On the one hand, it promoted an ethic of agricultural reform, clarifying measurement and ensuring the accuracy of reported production. On the other, issuing a wager well suited a circle of men drawn together by honor's ethos. As historian Kenneth Greenberg has shown, gambling allowed men of equal stature to test their mettle, creating moments in which "challenge to a contest was offered and accepted." One might win or lose the game—the transit of money itself was meant to matter not at all—but as long as a debt was paid in the end, gambling worked to diffuse social tension.[15]

Still winning was wonderful, and Griffin won the bet. Though that final measure of corn and men might have smarted in the moment after the steelyards settled, losing fair and square in social terms should have meant no loss at all to Reese. What was supposed to have mattered was that he had contended manfully with his peers, gone through the required motions, and on a different day those peers might have toasted his victory. Either way he would have been deemed worthy of a pat on the back given by the respected leaders of his community, men who understood that the rise and fall of individual fortunes meant nothing compared to the social stability of the group writ large. But Reese never grasped that central point.

Though Reese paid his wager, he felt no sense of satisfaction. Losing stung him sharply. Another man might have licked his wound and let time's passage turn it to a fond badge of honor—a minor tale of half-remembered jovial contest between two planters on a warm autumn day, a memory retrieved to regale aging men of their agricultural jousting. But vaulting recklessly over honor's social promises, Reese would not let matters be. The following day he trucked another portion of his crop to his brother-in-law David Cherry's store to be weighed once again. He sent word to the surely surprised Griffin, urging him to bring another sample for fresh comparison. Per Reese's request, Griffin, sent over another "parcel" but refused to attend himself, declaring "the contest at an end."

Such a response is hardly surprising, as Reese, by that point, was straying onto dangerous ground. Since the wager had been made and lost—and the settling-up seen to by Reese and Griffin's honorable peers—what in the world could possibly be gained by yet another reweighing? Not steelyards, but Reese himself, looked positively unbalanced. Certainly Wyatt-Brown would have winced at such recklessness, explaining that honor is "the moral property of all who belong within the community, one that determines the community's own membership." In traditional societies shared values govern groups and regulate social order, ranking men of property in terms of blood and character, rather than wealth and lands, providing a nonmaterial ethos aimed at modulating social conflict. Contests and games of chance in the Old South served these ends by dampening the sort of self-interest that might atomize the wider community of blood and mastery.

But wagers and bets, horseracing, and duels served to strengthen the circle of honor only if they were approached with the purpose of meeting on a stable middle ground. Clearly Reese was looking for something else: quantified certification of his victory over another man. The facticity of crooked numbers scratched on a sheet of paper would stand objectively triumphant over the honorable opinions of his social peers. That was a bold and potentially shameful claim, fraught with social danger if he could not make that claim stick. But as sociologist Julian Pitt-Rivers reminds us, it is precisely the manly claiming of honor that is the precondition to the social paying of honor. In more than one sense, then, Reese here was looking for a leg up. He got what he was looking for. This time the numbers worked out in Reese's favor, his bushel coming in at fifty-nine pounds, ten ounces. Griffin's bushel weighed "two pounds less," according to both Cherry and Reese's brother Edwin.[16]

Once again a man less rash would have smiled with satisfaction and ended the matter here. Though the numbers confirmed victory among his kin, Reese never claimed public affirmation of his triumph. There is no hint that he asked Griffin for his money back or even sent word of how the numbers finally turned out. Pendleton's farmers did not give Reese a medal and there is no evidence that Griffin acknowledged the results of this fourth weighing. Instead Reese doubled down, wagering his good name recklessly before the whole state. When the call came for competitors for the Agricultural Society of South Carolina's contest for corn culturing, Reese jumped at the chance to compete, trotting out his same marvelous corn bushels once again. He knew a few of these lowcountry fellows from the state legislature—Condy, the society's corresponding secretary, served during the same term—and hoped that budding connections might bloom into the recognition and respect he so desperately desired. He wrote bold words; his claims won the day. With publication of his letter to the society and a gold medal in hand, a woman of pedigree on his arm, and political bona fides secure, Reese claimed his place among the state's most honorable young men.[17]

The Agricultural Society of South Carolina basked in honor's glow too. In a lengthy report published in papers across the state in months preceding the award, the group had touted the importance of agricultural premiums and contests. They were an "encouragement to industry," "serve[d] as an inducement to intelligent enterprize [*sic*]," and, with the publication of prize-winning crop reports, "diffuse[d] the knowledge acquired by the experience of individuals throughout the country." What would encourage the farmer to take a chance on unproven methods, to wager his livelihood, to sacrifice scarce land? "A love of distinction," the committee argued, was "powerful . . . motive" to make the crop—no matter how small the pecuniary prize. But when farmers "abandon the useful guide of former experience, and venture on untrodden ground," the committee knew, certain risks—social, economic, political—came unbidden. Without "sound, enlightened judgment," premiums "will have the effect of ignis fatuus"—the phosphoric haze that arises from rotted organic matter—when the state's goal was to serve as the "polar star" of American agriculture.[18]

How striking that the committee felt the need to defend and promote premiums so stridently. Their careful explanation of risks and benefits—their vivid counterpoint of squibs and stars—reinforced the report's main message and pointed at honorable planters' worst fears. The document explicitly emphasized the insignificance of the society's pecuniary award, noting that a small financial prize might "occasionally be convenient" for farmers who risked so greatly. No man of sense and worth, they implied, would enter a contest simply for money. Indeed, by having contestants provide a "detailed account . . . not only of the product, but of the mode of culture, and cost in money, and labor expended on it," the society would ensure that individual reward might be dispersed among the group writ large. Thus the winning farmer's success would effect "the stimulus of emulation" among others, improving the health of the state's agriculture broadly. All depended, of course, on the "proper management of this auxiliary." All hung, too, on the veracity of honorable farmers' accounts.[19]

Reese's astounding numbers seemed to validate the reformers' big claims. Prompted by just the sort of recognition and, indeed, "distinction" the society offered, Reese had heavily manured his acre and taken the time and expended the labor to plough the earth deep. Robert Mills's 1826 *Statistics of South Carolina* tells us that farmers of that period could expect a yield of ten to twelve bushels per acre in Pendleton District. With proper fertilizing, one might coax the yield up to sixty bushels. A claim of ninety-seven bushels, these duped book farmers would come to understand, was almost all manure.[20]

Careful readers will have noted that the reports Reese gave to the Pendleton Farmers' Society and the Agricultural Society of South Carolina did not match up. At best he had claimed eighty-nine bushels in Pendleton, but to the lowcountry group he now claimed ninety-seven. Someone else must have noticed the discrepancy, too. In May the Pendleton Farmers' Society unsealed a letter from Charleston asking for an explanation. Instantly men understood that the problem focused on much more than eight-odd bushels of corn. Its own credibility silently called into question by association with a member who—at best—could not add, the society took action. Pendleton's farmers promptly formed a three-man investigative committee, charging it with answering the question: "Did Mr. Reese actually raise more corn by seven bushels and eighteen pounds, than the quantity contained in his letter, and Mr. McCrary's certificate to this society?"[21]

The formal character and deep seriousness of this inquiry underlines both the absurdity of this crisis and the real urgency planters felt about the threat it posed. Over the next two months, the committee conducted extensive interviews across the county. They quizzed members of the Reese family and the Pendleton community. They trained their inquiry on the certificates of harvest variously offered by the prizewinning farmer, Reese; by Henry McCrary, the man who measured out the acre of corn and supervised the first weighing; and by assorted kin and neighbors who offered witting and unwitting support. Between eighty-nine and ninety-seven, measurements of acres and tubs and bushels rose and fell as the investigation crept across several long weeks and the committee pursued its verdict.[22]

Any bystander should have seen that, from the standpoint of numerical accuracy, this was bound to be a wild goose chase. Wyatt-Brown argues that northern travelers to the South everywhere noted "irregularity" in southern life and behavior. But this was a mark of honor's strength and flexibility, not a weakness. Rare was the southern planter, he shows, who required the sort of "monetary exactness" preached so stridently by their tight-fisted Yankee brethren. Agricultural improvement, on the other hand, relied on precise measurement and calculation of land costs, fertilizing agents, labor expenditure, and finally the crop itself. Even here, though, all that quantification aimed ultimately at yielding the farmer honorable qualification. Men worked to establish their name, not to gather a pile. Reese tried to play it both ways, though—and backward—deploying the language of reform but playing fast and loose with the numbers in the most egregious and dishonorable way. The committee, too, strove to maintain the front of scientific inquiry, systematically running the figures, searching for a calculation that might exculpate one of the Society's own and restore order once again.[23]

Inquiry focused on—or, more properly, rehashed—a few key problems. First, given measurements had not been standardized in terms of weight or volume. Over the course of the investigation, Reese, his supporters, and the committee compared measurements in pounds, bushels, tubs, and barrels, all of which varied from farmer to farmer. But rejigging old numbers could hardly allay confusion. Reese had revealed as much in his initial documentation for the Pendleton contest. His October 8, 1823, submission to the Society had declared that "the product [was] found to be eighty one bushels and a half, the bushel containing fifty five pounds; making eight nine bushels and a half and seven pounds by the standard measure of this Society." Accompanying that letter Henry McCrary certified that Reese's crop had been "gathered and measured under his [McCrary's] immediate observation, the whole being measured in a barrel which upon calculation amounted to eighty one bushels and an half, the bushel weighing 55 pounds." Reese's submission to the Agricultural Society of South Carolina four months later took a slightly different form. Here he noted that "the product [was] found to be ninety seven bushels . . . the bushels here mentioned weighed only 50 lbs." But now McCrary's letter of support differed substantially, certifying that "the whole [was] measured in a barrel which upon calculation amounted to eighty one tubfulls and an half." Unlike his first letter, the investigative committee noted, McCrary had now eliminated any mention of bushels or weight. Finally Reese included a statement by David Cherry attesting that he had weighed the corn in one of the tubs at fifty-nine pounds and ten ounces, though how big that tub might have been remained uncertain. Just how Reese or McCrary or Cherry or the farmers of Pendleton or the lowcountry might have figured productivity depended on how bushels and weights were measured—which is another way of saying that accurate quantification rested ultimately on an impossibly imprecise social measurement of who was qualified best to make that reading. The problem of Reese's social placement rested on whose word might gain precedence in the company of honorable men.[24]

And that was only the first issue. Numbers aside the corn Reese measured by weight had not necessarily been harvested from the acre of land he had set aside for experiment. His first submission the Pendleton Farmers' Society drew from that acre, he explained, but the bushel of corn submitted for weighing at David Cherry's store had been drawn from corn thrown on top of the crib, the product of harvesting ten days later. That admission redoubled confusion. This was a problem, the committee argued, because "the farina which remains in the grain, and becomes condensed in the process of cureing [*sic*], is of greater specific gravity than the watery particles which escape by evaporation." In other words, corn allowed to stand in the field, exposed to "the influence of the sun and atmosphere," weighed more than that which had been harvested earlier and lay in the crib. Hence Reese's figures overestimated his bushel's true weight.[25]

Finally there was the vexed problem of the steelyards themselves. Reese had weighed his corn on at least four sets of scales. The committee corroborated three of them, finding a difference of only a few ounces in fifty pounds. The "test of the truth," the examiners declared, was in comparing Reese's steelyards to these other three, for it was on his own measurement that his communication to the Agricultural Society of South Carolina was based. If the scales were faulty, the man might be excused. Blaming technology was the only way to salvage Reese's character.[26]

The planter himself must have recognized as much. But here, once again, Reese did not help his case. Not only had he offered a welter of conflicting and confusing testimony and certificates, he proved stubbornly resistant to the committee's inquiries. When asked to provide statements affirming accord between his scales and those of his brother-in-law David Cherry, he stonewalled, only allowing the committee a glimpse of a new certificate by Henry McCrary. This statement now announced that "he (McCrary) had weighed a bushel of Mr. Reese's prize corn . . . by Mr. Reese's Steelyards, that, it weighed 60 pounds. And that he had since compared these Steelyards with Mr. Cherry's scales and the variation was found to be only one pound in 50." But astonishingly Reese "declin[ed] making it evidence . . . nor would he suffer it to remain in [the committee's] hands." "What was the meaning of this?" men must have wondered. When asked to provide his steelyards so that the committee might compare them to the others, Reese sent a note of refusal, huffing that "[the] demand implies something like suspicion." But it was Reese who had initiated the comparison of steelyards many months earlier when he had demanded that Griffin render his up to reassess the outcome of their wager. Now the accuracy that Reese had been so eager to gain against Griffin was transformed into affront to his character when the committee made the same demand. He had been "given the lie," Reese chose to believe, and would allow no set of scales—his own or others—to implicate him in what had morphed into a bizarre affair of honor.[27]

What in the world did Reese think he was doing? And by flashing and then hiding McCrary's note and refusing to render up his steelyards, what choice did he leave the committee? This was the pose of an honorable man wrongly assailed, his behavior protested. But reading events that way put investigators and the broader community in dire social peril. With numbers and measures and stories so various and Reese so unwilling to resolve those ambiguities, the inquisitors were all but compelled to conclude that he had stretched the truth. Worse still it was impossible to tell which part of his fiction was deliberate and which accidental. Not only was George Reese Jr. a man who was sloppy with his figures and reckless in his ambitions, but he treated his own name and the reputation of those around him with shocking carelessness too. In seeking a simple arithmetic solution to the correct measurement of Reese's achievement as agricultural reformer, it turned out, the committee had blundered into a far more desperate crisis. Reese's aim, after all, had never been to claim a medallion for prize corn, but to gain the reputation of a man prime among his honorable peers, worthy of the gentry's acclaim. In that sense agricultural reform had only ever been a modus vivendi for personal honor, and, by failing so badly with his figures and fibbing, Reese surrendered both proximate gains and hopeful desires. Sensible men could not but count his claims spurious. To do otherwise risked rending honor's very fabric.

The committee threw up its hands. Only "morbid sensibility," it was forced to conclude, could have compelled Reese to withhold measurable and exonerating evidence, unless that measurement could not hope to exculpate. Were the steelyards rigged or their reading skewed? After weeks of interviews, on July 10, 1824, the committee offered a reluctant verdict. Independent "of the abstract truth or falsehood of all," they found "much to censure" in Reese's conduct. Bad enough that he "dictated, and received a Certificate which he knew, not to be true." He had "taxed the confidence" of brother-in-law David Cherry, implicated neighbor Henry McCrary in the scheme, and dragged father's and brother's good names through the mud. Worst, he had disgraced the farmers of Pendleton and cast in doubt the society of honor across the state. His calculating behavior brought shame on all.[28]

There was only one way to cleanse this stain. The society enacted a process of expulsion with humiliating formality. Silently a member stood and handed a resolution to the society's president, the revered Revolutionary War hero, prominent planter, and town patron Thomas Pinckney. The room now hummed with debate. Stricken, Reese rose and offered an impassioned and "lengthy" defense: it was too much, too late. By that point there was nothing more he or his few remaining supporters could add to this mess. For the first time, the Pendleton Farmers' Society expelled a member for "ungentlemanly conduct." Culminating social disgrace, the vote was twenty-one to ten. Reese could not count corn, but his neighbors had no better idea in the end on how to measure honor.[29]

Reese left few who knew him unscathed. Though the investigators "disavow[ed] . . . distinctly, any intention of impeaching the character or veracity" of David Cherry, Reese's brother-in-law resigned from the organization minutes after the final vote came down. Henry McCrary chose to remain in the group but faced charges himself for "acting in an ungentlemanlike manner in giving to Mr. George Reese Junior . . . various and contradictory certificates" regarding his prize corn. Unlike Reese, McCrary did his best to comply with a second investigative committee's wishes, humbly promising to provide any information they demanded. Again the committee trained its inquiry on Reese's and Lewis's steelyards. Again Lewis complied. Again the Reese family resisted. At first George Reese Sr. improbably declared that he could not find the scales. Instead four members of the Reese family sent over "certificates," but the committee unsurprisingly deemed them "unsatisfactory . . . in as much as a higher species of evidence might be produced." After inquisitors sent out another request for the steelyards, the Reeses finally relinquished them. Upon comparing these with Lewis's instruments "with all practicable accuracy," the committee finally got its answer: they were "able to make a difference of only 5 ounces in fifty pounds." That number was negligible in terms of measurement of corn, but devastating to McCrary, Reese, and all who supported them. Finding it "wholly out of his power" to reconcile the scales with his certificates, McCrary, too, faced a vote of expulsion. This time the group softened the blow, voting against dismissal but calling McCrary guilty of "uncommonly great negligence" in this contest gone horribly wrong. By the time farmers gathered for their next meeting, the humiliated man had resigned from the club, too.[30]

Having sorted out trouble within their own group, Pendleton farmers still had to face their lowcountry brethren. Immediately upon completion of their investigation and expulsion votes, the society resolved to send a copy of its proceedings to the Agricultural Society of South Carolina in hopes of assuring them that Pendleton had played its part to repair the breach of trust and honor committed by one of its own. Alas that missive served less to soothe than to irritate. "After some debate" the lowcountry organization resolved to send a letter to the Pendleton Farmers' Society "expressing their Indignation at the Conduct practiced by Capt. George Reese, Junr. to obtain the premium awarded to him at the Cattle Show in February 1824."[31] Their anger was understandable. Lowcountry farmers had advocated powerfully and publicly for agricultural prizes as judicious tools of agricultural improvement, their 1823 "Report of the Committee of Premiums" appearing at least a dozen times in the *Charleston Courier* in the fall and early winter of 1823.[32] Moreover they were finalizing publication of an important collection of essays aiming to advance the cause of agricultural improvement in the state. Their

1824 *Original Communications Made to the Agricultural Society of South-Carolina* trumpeted the organization's lofty goals: "to put our Agriculture generally upon the footing on which it ought to stand" both by serving as an "organ of information" and by "giving suitable rewards to those, who shall have been successful, in any department of Agricultural industry." Reese's behavior made a mockery of their efforts, and called into question their standing as honorable men. After all, if one sharper had succeeded so well in fooling this elite, who could say that others did not lurk within their ranks unrecognized. Quite literally George Reese had made fools of them all.[33]

Particularly wounded must have been Thomas Condy, corresponding secretary of the Agricultural Society of South Carolina and colleague of Reese in the state legislature. He had vouched for the Pendleton farmer as a "gentleman of high respectability" to men within the lowcountry group. Compounding that folly he had asked members to forgo their usual requirement of documentation, as Reese's letter and certificates were not "as copious and formal as required by the rules of the Agricultural Society." What a blunder that turned out to be—if, as some must have wondered, blunder it truly was. Men of sense and reputation knew now to steer clear of the Reeses and McCrarys they encountered, but what of those ambiguous Condys who measured corn and notes and honor so errantly?[34]

Over the next several years, we see efforts to ensure that honorable men would not be duped again. The Pendleton Farmers' Society reaffirmed the standard weight of a bushel of corn at fifty pounds and specified how, exactly, an acre should be measured. They required more extensive documentation of both the cultivation and harvesting of contest crops, including certification of "the quantity and quality of land and its product" by two disinterested parties. Further they ordered contestants to give notice of their intention to enter a given contest well before the harvest so that a designated committee from the organization might visit and examine land under cultivation.[35] Trust, they might have said, but verify. For well over a year, they debated whether a premium should take the form of hard cash or less fungible honors.[36] Both Pendleton and lowcountry farmers continued to offer premiums as an impetus to innovation but, surely, were more careful. As these measures show, honorable men tried to tamp down fears about qualitative chaos with quantitative reforms. The best way to set honor on a firm footing, they figured, was to erect a solid foundation that had essentially nothing to do with honor's ethos—and was, in many ways, deeply antagonistic to it. Reform bent and honor fractured, the social, economic, and political goals of southern men clashed here in destructive ways. Their desperate search for order and progress generated crisis with roots deeper and more wide ranging than Reese's prizewinning corn.

And as to George Reese, the jumped-up fellow who caused all the trouble: what might we imagine the future held for him? Lasting dishonor? Odious exile? Merited oblivion? How did he come, fifty years on, to imagine he could return to the scene of so much trouble and turmoil and think he could retrieve an honored standing lost so long ago? As it turns out, although the members of the Pendleton Farmers' Society erased him from their ranks, many must have retained divided opinions about his merits and their own because, within five years' time, they voted him into the legislature to again represent their district. By the mid-1830s he, like many other Pendletonians, gave up on the sandy soil of the upcountry and tried their hand out west. In 1835 he took his immediate family and his budding slave force to West Point, Georgia, and eventually Chambers County, Alabama, where he and other upcountry émigrés tilled the rich earth of the black belt. Over the next four decades, he went on to a profitable and prosperous career as a cotton plantation owner and slave master, a public orator, and a jurist. Why maintain an honorable reputation when it could be resurrected on fresh soil? Ironically enough, in this new community of upright men, he played a leading role in promoting the Bowery Oak Agricultural Society. He died in 1877, an honorable and reform-minded man, like the South itself, a creature of wondrous contradictions.[37]

NOTES

1. McNitt, *Chain of Error.* Though Charlotte Whigs likely met to declare their independence from King George in the wake of the Battles of Lexington and Concord, most historians agree that the written "Mecklenburg Declaration" was a nineteenth-century creation.

2. An extract from George Reese Jr.'s memoirs has been published in a genealogical study of the Reese family. Reese, *Genealogy,* 216–31. For quotations see pp. 217–19.

3. Reese, *Genealogy,* 220, 223.

4. Wyatt-Brown, *Southern Honor,* xxxiv; Reese, *Genealogy,* 216–31; Garrett, *Reminiscences of Public Men in Alabama,* 166–67; Owen, *History of Alabama,* 4:1420–21.

5. See, for example, Mills, *Statistics of South Carolina,* 682–83; Sloan, *Fogy Days,* 54–61; Simpson, *History of Old Pendleton,* 22–24; McFall, *So Lives the Dream,* 9–15; Badders, *Remembering South Carolina's Old Pendleton District,* 47–53.

6. L. Gray, *History of Agriculture,* 2:779–92; Bonner, "Genesis of Agricultural Reform." More recent works include S. Collins, "System," 1–27, and Majewski, *Modernizing,* 22–80.

7. Genovese, *Political Economy,* 124–53; Faust, "Rhetoric." For recent work that attempts to reconcile these positions, see S. Phillips, "Antebellum Agricultural Reform"; Herrington, "Agricultural and Architectural Reform"; Steffen, "Search," 753–802.

8. A. Smith, *Economic Readjustment,* 1–18; Ford, *Origins,* 215–18, 244–77.

9. Reese, *Genealogy,* 222, 225; Pendleton Farmers' Society, *Pendleton,* 125–26, 131. The 1908 publication included the 1820 publication (originally published by Telescope Press in Columbia, S.C.) in its entirety, 120–208.

10. Pendleton Farmers' Society, "Constitution and By-Laws of the Pendleton Farmers' Society," 126; Reese, *Genealogy,* 228; Peters, "Notices," v–lii.

11. *City Gazette and Commercial Daily Advertiser* [Charleston, S.C.], November 26, 1822; Edgar, *Biographical Directory,* 307; A. Moore, *Biographical Directory,* 222; *Miller's Weekly Messenger*

[Pendleton, S.C.], July 12, 1820; *Pendleton (S.C.) Messenger*, June 2, 1824; Reese, *Genealogy*, 234–35.

12. *Southern Chronicle* [Camden, S.C.], March 10, 1824. This article was reprinted from the *Charleston Mercury*.

13. *Pendleton (S.C.) Messenger*, December 17, 1823; Pendleton Farmers' Society [hereafter PFS], Minutes, July 10, 1824.

14. PFS, Minutes, July 10, 1824. Adding to the confusion that would eventually follow, Reese and, indeed, most farmers used nonstandard bushel measures. According the certificate he submitted to the PFS, "the product [was] found to be eighty one bushels and a half, the bushel containing fifty five pounds; making eight nine bushels and a half by the standard measure of the Society."

15. PFS, Minutes, July 10, 1824; Greenberg, *Honor and Slavery*, 138. T. H. Breen makes a similar observation regarding Virginia gentry of the late seventeenth and early eighteenth centuries, arguing that "non-lethal competitive devices . . . were a kind of functional alliance developed by the participants themselves to reduce dangerous, but often inevitable, social tensions." Breen, "Horses," 257.

16. PFS, Minutes, July 10, 1824; Wyatt-Brown, *Southern Honor*, xxxv; Pitt-Rivers, "Honor." For a discussion of one man's attempted rise through "the genteel stratifications" of Old Pendleton, see Friend, "Belles."

17. *Charleston (S.C.) Courier*, July 12, 1823; Edgar, *Biographical Directory*, 1:306–9.

18. *Charleston (S.C.) Courier*, November 19, 1823.

19. *Charleston (S.C.) Courier*, November 19, 1823. For a thoughtful consideration of the use of premiums by the Agricultural Society of South Carolina, see Steffen, "Search," 759–62.

20. Mills, *Statistics of South Carolina*, 674.

21. PFS, Minutes, July 10, 1824.

22. PFS, Minutes, July 10, 1824.

23. Wyatt-Brown, *Southern Honor*, 135.

24. PFS, Minutes, July 10, 1824.

25. PFS, Minutes, July 10, 1824.

26. PFS, Minutes, July 10, 1824.

27. PFS, Minutes, July 10, 1824. As Kenneth Greenberg notes, to "give the lie" was to announce "that [a man's] appearance differed from his true nature," and was considered "an insult of great consequence among men of honor." Greenberg, *Honor and Slavery*, 8–9, 32.

28. PFS, Minutes, July 10, 1824.

29. PFS, Minutes, July 10, 1824.

30. PFS, Minutes, September 9, 1824, October 14, 1824.

31. Agricultural Society of South Carolina, Minutes, Typescript, February 22, 1825.

32. See, for example, *Charleston (S.C.) Courier*: October 6, 1823, November 19, 1823, November 28, 1823, December 2, 1823, December 22, 1823.

33. Agricultural Society of South Carolina, *Original Communications*, iv, vi.

34. PFS, Minutes, July 10, 1824.

35. It is worth noting here that both the Agricultural Society of South Carolina and the Pendleton Farmers' Society had loosely mandated certificates by disinterested parties. In the wake of the Reese affair, Pendleton farmers strengthened these rules.

36. PFS, Minutes: November 11, 1824; August 11, 1825, September 8, 1825.

37. Edgar, *Biographical Directory,* 1:319; A. Moore, *Biographical Directory,* 5:222; 1830 United States Census, Lancaster District, S.C., p. 182, National Archives and Records Administration [hereafter NARA], Microfilm Series: M-19, Roll 173; Garrett, *Reminiscences of Public Men in Alabama,* 166–67; Owen, *History of Alabama,* 4:1420–21; Chattahoochee Valley Historical Society, *Story,* 6–7, 15, 59–60; *Daily Alabama Journal* [Montgomery, Ala.]: January 28, 1852, April 15, 1853.

Amanda R. Mushal

"A VERY HONORABLE MAN IN HIS TRADING"

Honor, Credit Reporting, and the Market Economy in Antebellum Charleston

On December 14, 1858, an anonymous Charleston credit correspondent sat down to assess the creditworthiness of dry goods importers William Ravenel and C. K. Huger. Tucked among hard-nosed intelligence of their net worth, business connections, and length of time in business, he added the more subjective opinion that the two were "highly honorable young men of family."[1] Similarly he had once written of factors A. M. Huger and E. P. Milliken that they were "correct men full of SC honor & SC pride."[2] Known to contemporary subscribers and present-day scholars only as credit correspondent 11007, the writer deployed a language of honor that initially seems incongruous in the modernizing market economy of the nineteenth century. His invocation of honor in these contexts went beyond the kind of reputation connoted by such terms as *mercantile integrity* or *commercial honor,* instead suggesting a more traditional social dimension to these businessmen's reputations. Yet 11007 was also a man of the market. Even as he praised the young men's political loyalties and family connections, he went on to employ what was fast becoming the hallmark of modern commerce—the numerical rating. In hard terms he concluded his report on Ravenel and Huger by estimating their creditworthiness to be "say ab[ou]t 2 ½."[3]

Early credit reporting thus bridged the cultures of the South's traditional social honor and the nineteenth-century market. During this period, as American business expanded and became increasingly depersonalized, businessmen turned to contracts, commodity standardization, credit reporting, and other modern practices to safeguard their interests.[4] Such protections, with their implied distrust among the parties involved, were largely antithetical to the assurances of honor and personal reputation that had historically structured commercial exchange. Yet as this essay will argue, in the antebellum South, ideas of honor were invoked in support of the emerging modern business culture. Disseminating older assessments of honor through new mechanisms for reporting commercial reputation, the new culture allowed creditors to check dishonorable behavior by expanding the community within which businessmen had to guard their reputations.

Although the topic of southern honor has garnered increasing scholarly attention over the past thirty years, few have addressed its significance to the world of nineteenth-century business. Indeed, in his seminal study of southern honor, and his slightly less well-known analysis of antebellum commercial culture, Bertram Wyatt-Brown implicitly distinguished between the concepts of southern honor and commercial honor.[5] Commercial honor, although it included social dimensions, comprised first and foremost a merchant's reputation for repaying his commercial debts. Southern honor, which also had reputation at its core, was the much more all-encompassing culture in which southern white men vied for status and defended their reputations in the eyes of their peers and against the specter of dependency represented by slaves, women, and social inferiors.[6] As slavery increasingly came under attack, elite white southerners lauded this latter culture in a language of chivalry, borrowing from romantic literature to defend a hierarchical society built on racial slavery.[7]

In a separate historiographical vein, scholars of nineteenth-century business history, while exploring the role of commercial honor and reputation in contemporary assessments of creditworthiness, have confined their studies primarily to northern business culture.[8] Scholars of the emerging southern middle class, meanwhile, have argued that members of this commercially oriented class defined themselves against the region's culture of honor.[9]

This essay bridges these historiographies. It argues that even within the increasingly depersonalized world of national credit reporting, southern correspondents often deployed the language, values, and assumptions of southern honor to describe their neighbors' business characters. Correspondents' reports were sprinkled with comments on personal honor, family reputation, and, occasionally, chivalry alongside assessments of "correct" business habits and other virtues of the market. Even as they applied the first numerical credit ratings to their subjects and urged creditors to pursue claims in the courts, correspondents praised businessmen as "upright and honorable" or damned them as scoundrels, rascals, and "worthless dogs." For these correspondents the cultures of southern honor and commercial honor were never entirely distinct, and a reputation for honor or dishonor carried material consequences in the world of business.[10]

This essay focuses on Charleston, South Carolina, the social and commercial capital of a state known for its antebellum political extremism. In South Carolina honor and its violent expressions remained a well-publicized aspect of local political culture and an element of its nascent nationalism.[11] Yet Charleston was also a hub of regional commerce, and the business of its elite merchants and middling shopkeepers kept them closely connected to the developing American and Atlantic economies. It thus provides a useful case study of the ways that ideas about southern honor could not only coexist with, but indeed become a critical tool for engaging with, the contemporary market economy.

Credit and the Correspondents

11007 was one of an army of correspondents recruited by the credit rating agencies of antebellum America. These agencies were established in the wake of the Panic of 1837 to guard against future financial crises. Much of the nation's business was done on credit, with merchants traveling to northeastern commercial centers twice a year to stock their shelves, then returning home to resell goods to individual consumers or smaller retailers. Fraud as well as honest misfortune or national economic downturns could prevent repayment at each step of these transactions. To minimize risk, it became critical for wholesalers, doing business with strangers, to know whom they could most safely credit. By gathering intelligence on businesses throughout the nation, the new credit agencies attempted to provide such information. Prominent among these agencies was the New York–based Mercantile Agency of Lewis Tappan, a predecessor of the present-day Dun and Bradstreet.[12] The agency's ledgers survive today, a testament to the diligence with which Tappan and his successors pursued their investigations.

To provide their semiannual reports, the agency recruited correspondents whose occupations placed them in a position to assess their neighbors' financial standing—their business abilities, their volume of trade, and the value of property available for seizure should they go under. Such correspondents could also report on the more nebulous aspects of a merchant's worth—his reputation within the community, rumors surrounding his personal habits, and other tidbits, often inaccessible to outsiders, that might indicate whether he was a safe credit risk. Often these correspondents were attorneys; like them, from internal evidence it is apparent that 11007—known as "S" until late 1855 or early 1856—had extensive local connections.[13] Because they were so thorough, these reports today provide an unparalleled insight not only into contemporary business practices, but also into the ways that nineteenth-century southerners evaluated their neighbors' business reputations.

It is, of course, difficult to determine how the agency's northern subscribers interpreted correspondents' comments relating to honor. Recent scholarship has found that many antebellum northerners shared understandings of honor with their southern counterparts, so these reports may well have been fully intelligible to readers.[14] What is clear, however, is that southern correspondents believed that they were communicating vital intelligence through the reports. Thus there is much that scholars can learn from the reports about the culture surrounding the correspondents, if not the subscribers.

Correspondents' jobs were of potentially great consequence, for the facts and rumors they reported had the power to destroy their neighbors' commercial reputations and thus materially damage their ability to obtain credit and carry on business.[15] In the world of southern honor, an equivalent slur might be grounds for a caning or a formal challenge. Yet there was little that the subjects of damaging credit reports could do to defend themselves, for only rarely did they know what was being reported about them; in fact it was agency policy to prevent individuals from accessing their own reports.[16] In contrast to the world of southern honor, whose proponents argued that the threat of being held publicly accountable for one's words prevented slander, the new system permitted—indeed, depended on—the possibility of injury without consequence for agency correspondents.

Recognizing the repercussions that correspondents could face should their activities become known, the agency took pains to assure their anonymity.[17] Even in its own ledgers, correspondents were initially identified only by letters, and then, beginning in the mid-1850s, by numeric codes. No key to these codes is known to exist, but information about a few, including 11007, can be gleaned through internal clues. References to collections suits in which 11007 was involved suggest that he faced many of the same challenges as local attorneys. Assumptions he displayed regarding family honor, and the care he took in phrasing certain negative reports, further suggest that he had internalized the ethos of elite southern honor. Although the agency referred to its correspondents only by code, 11007's own reports indicate that his status as a correspondent was known to at least a few members of the Charleston business community.[18]

Commercial Honor and Civic Responsibility

At its most fundamental level, commercial honor entailed a reputation for upholding one's financial obligations. When cotton merchant Rice Dulin failed for a stunning $175,000 in 1848, one agency correspondent reported that he had "compromised honorably." Four years later another correspondent indicated what this compromise had entailed: after his failure Dulin, who had resumed business with a well-heeled partner, had "paid up in full, [and] retained the confidence of his Creditors."[19] When the humbler E. C. Kelting, who sold fancy goods and toys, "left the city, [he] went away honorably after paying off all his debts."[20]

Kelting's and Dulin's behavior stood in stark contrast to that of dry goods merchant James C. Corbett, who managed to transfer most of his assets to his sons in the course of a "dishon[orable] failure," or dry goods importer Andrew McDowall, suspected locally of having "made something" in the course of his bankruptcy.[21] A merchant could profit from a bankruptcy if he could successfully conceal property from his creditors, often by transferring it to family members as Corbett did, then settle with creditors, paying a smaller proportion of his debts than his full assets would have allowed him to do. Such actions were the antithesis of honorable dealing.

A reputation for commercial honor did not necessarily depend on wealth or social status, although it might be augmented by both. It was frequently noted in credit reports alongside honesty, industry, respectability, and other virtues embraced by an emerging northern and southern middle class. Charleston druggist

R. W. Burnham, who had been in business for eight years and had accumulated only a modest $2,000 (correspondents later halved the figure to $1,000), was "called an hon[orab]l[e] man," according to correspondent PHC. Another agreed that Burnham was possessed of "small means but very hon[est]."[22] Peter W. Auten, a clerk admitted to partnership in the firm of T. M. Horsey and Company, had "little or no means" but had served as a clerk for many years and built a reputation for himself as a businessman both "capable and honorable."[23] Grocer Samuel Mills had failed once but reestablished himself in business and one correspondent reported that he was "v[er]y hon[orab]le hon[es]t & ind[ustrious]."[24] And B. Figeroux, who taught French while his wife kept a millinery shop, was "v[ery] honor[able] & correct, attent[ive to business] and close." Although Figeroux had been "in trouble" in the late 1840s, by 1856 he was reported to be "slowly accumulat[in]g a lit[tle], a v[er]y respect[able], hon[ora]bl[e] & steady man" and was considered "no doubt g[oo]d for all his cont[ract]s."[25]

As these usages suggest, contemporaries viewed commercial honor as existing within a spectrum of other business virtues. Like many of these virtues, honor possessed a distinct moral dimension. Credit reports stating that a merchant was honorable might also praise him as *upright, straightforward,* or a man of *integrity.* Wholesale clothing dealer Edwin Bates was recognized as an "honorable" and "straightforw[ar]d upright man," while T. S. and T. G. Budd, a father and son doing a commission business together, were said to be "of first rate char[acter] upright & hon[orab]l[e]" and "straight forward men whose integrity can be relied on."[26] An honorable merchant, contemporaries believed, upheld his obligations because he was driven to do so by an ingrained sense of moral rectitude.

Beyond fiscal reliability and morality, a reputation for commercial honor also connoted a sense of generosity and responsibility to society. Diarist Samuel Wells Leland recalled that deceased moneylender Thomas Heath had been "truthfull" and "strictly honest" in his business dealings, but not generous. "I don[']t suppose he ever did a purely charitable act in the long course of his life," Leland reflected of his friend; tellingly he did not describe Heath as honorable.[27] By contrast Charleston banker James Adger epitomized for many the virtues of the honorable merchant. At the time of his death in 1858, friends remembered the Irish-born Adger as having left "the example of an honest and honorable merchant . . . 'true and just in all his dealings.'"[28] Eulogists recalled his contributions to civic and benevolent associations in Charleston, as well as acts of personal charity to individuals, and perceived that these activities grew out of a sense of patriarchal duty not unlike that claimed by the region's planting elite.[29] Judge Andrew Gordon Magrath, who had himself recently been the subject of a fatal contest of honor, attested that Adger stood "a Patriarch among the merchants of our State," while Columbia bank director Andrew Crawford went a step further, likening Adger to the biblical Job, who "delivered the poor that cried, and the fatherless, and him that had none to help him . . . he caused the widow's heart to sing for joy."[30] In attributing such virtues to him, eulogists identified Adger both with the noblesse oblige of the southern elite, and with the trope of the honorable merchant, an ideal being promulgated through the pages of the New York–based *Hunt's Merchant's Magazine* and other commercial publications.[31]

Family, Status, and Reputation

If even humbler shopkeepers could be recognized as possessing commercial honor, the social reputations of Charleston's elite often reinforced their reputations for honor in business. Contemporaries were quick to attribute honor to the factors and import-export merchants who hailed from Charleston's commercial and social elite. Whereas credit correspondents often struggled to assess the characters of newly arrived shopkeepers, 11007 accounted William Ravenel and C. K. Huger, both members of old-line Huguenot families, as "highly honorable young men of family" shortly after the two commenced business.[32] Likewise he rated Thaddeus Street and Eugene H. West—sons of a "rich" man and a "well off" ship chandler—as "v[er]y honorable" within months of embarking on their general commission business, and presumably before either had had much opportunity to establish an independent commercial reputation.[33] 11007 was not alone in making such attributions. Another correspondent judged that planter's son William Bull Pringle Jr., who had embarked on a factorage business, was "highly hon[ora]ble."[34] And when Pringle's own son commenced business, he and his partner, H. Thirman, were, from the time of their first report, considered "men of good reputation, both in morals & bus[iness]." Indeed, after being in business for only a few years, one correspondent noted that "some of our most caut[iou]s merch[an]ts w[oul]d sell [Thirman and Pringle] any desired am[oun]t without further inq[uiry] into their means, & on the strength of their char[acter] & st[an]d[in]g alone."[35]

Correspondent 11040 provided a clue to this attribution, noting sanguinely that, lacking "any means of their own," the pair would be "supported by their fathers, who will no doubt, back them." The assumption that they would receive such family backing was no doubt a vital part of these younger merchants' reputations, and one whose material significance was revealed when Thirman and Pringle went under. The firm failed badly in the fall of 1858, victim of an ill-timed cotton speculation. At that point one correspondent assured creditors that "their Father endorsed pretty much all they owed, and 'tis now said he will pay up all"—despite the fact that the son's $60,000 loss represented roughly half of the elder Pringle's estimated worth.[36]

If the city's planters and established merchants possessed the means to underwrite their own and their offspring's business ventures, their social and economic position no doubt provided incentive for them to do so. Should family members default on their financial obligations, wary creditors could cut off the credit critical to their businesses, thereby striking at the underpinnings of the family's standing in the community. Members of the commercial elite thus operated within an honor society in its most traditional sense, one in which individual and collective honor were closely interconnected, even as they engaged with the depersonalized institutions of a modernizing economy.[37]

Pragmatically, too, correspondents recognized that the older generation often made a point of imparting its own values to younger family members. Certainly this was a concern regarding less reputable members of the business community. Correspondents fretted that James N. Corbett, whose father had failed dishonorably, "may learn ugly tricks of his Father, James C. who stays with him in the store," while M. McMaster likewise "comes of a bad Stock, has a sm[all] touch of his Fath[er's] rascality."[38] By contrast correspondents no doubt hoped that families who had established honorable reputations for themselves would instill in their sons the same virtues. At the same time, however, correspondents' quickness to attribute honor to the scions of old-line families served to reify the position of the old elite, and to reinforce, in a new venue, the belief that honor was an attribute to which these families held particular claim.

It should be noted, however, that correspondents did not explicitly differentiate among the different shades of honor they invoked. 11007, who was so quick to attribute honor to elite young import-export merchants, in at least one instance applied the term equally reflexively to a nonelite firm. Bakers A. J. Cappell and Brother, he wrote in his first report on them, were "honorable & working men."[39] Nine months later, having gathered additional intelligence on the brothers, he reversed his assessment, but his initial application of the term to ordinary artisans suggests that 11007, whose comments elsewhere indicated that he had internalized both the assumptions and the etiquette of the elite honor culture, believed that at least some of the term's nuances could be applied to humbler citizens without further commentary.

Like honor among the elite, honor among shopkeepers was fundamentally about reputation. Correspondent PHC made this clear when he wrote that the druggist Burnham was "*called* an honorable man."[40] When 11007 reversed his assessment of the Cappell brothers, he did so based on opinions circulating about them in the city, writing that he was "inf[orme]d they have lit[tle] or no mea[ns]. . . . I am told by one of our Comm[ission] M[er]ch[an]ts that he has not confid[ence] enough to trust them."[41] And Peter Auten, the eventual partner in T. M. Horsey and Company, had built his honorable reputation over years of employment as a clerk. Just as elite families had built reputations over the course of generations, so too did individuals' reputations usually reflect a lengthy history of business activity.

Defending Honor in the Marketplace

Concerns for honor not only permeated the credit reports but also had long structured other business transactions between commercial men.[42] Given the stakes involved, businessmen were highly attuned to the nuances of meaning in their interactions with each other. Banker and cotton factor James Adger's early correspondence with planter William Smith suggests that both men recognized that requesting a legal guarantee in business inherently entailed a challenge to a man's honor, a suggestion that his word alone might not be reliable. In a rather involved purchase of Mississippi stock in 1819, Adger agreed, as Smith's agent, to pay the first installment of the purchase price, then "give . . . my obligation to pay the balance" at an agreed-on future date. Since he held Smith's cotton crop, Adger felt no qualms about entering into the first part of the engagement, but he sought to secure the remainder. "I think it would be well for you to send me your Bond . . . for $8000," he suggested. Lest Smith infer that Adger did not trust him entirely, Adger hastened to explain that the legal arrangement "would explain the transaction to others if we both were not living at the time."[43] Given the notorious unhealthiness of the nineteenth-century southern climate, this was not, perhaps, an unreasonable suggestion. Yet Adger's next letter suggests that Smith perceived in the suggestion a thinly veiled challenge, for Adger wrote back quickly, "I expect your letter authorizing the purchase & of this stock is sufficient for me." He repeated his earlier assurance: "I only mentioned a Bond least [*sic*] we might not both be living at the time of payment." Furthermore he assured Smith that he himself had given "Mr. Harper my Bond for the $8,000 and a note for $4,000," thus implying that his request reflected no particular mistrust of Smith—and that he, Adger, had bound himself equally for the obligation. Among men of honor, equality was paramount: slights were felt keenly, and equality was central to the negotiation of honor affairs. With both letters Adger sought to turn the matter into one of business and contract, even as he acknowledged the implications of honor and reputation it entailed. However, with a man like Smith, one could never disregard honor entirely. Thus Adger concluded by adding that he would never trust Smith so little as to *require* legal security of him but instead appealed to the good character Smith believed he had challenged—"I leave this altogether to you, knowing you best know what is right & that you will act accordingly."[44]

11007 was equally adept in this grammar. As carefully worded as Adger's correspondence had been was 11007's response to an inquiry about the medical background of schoolmaster Winfield M. Rivers, who was attempting to establish a drugstore in downtown Charleston. "He says . . . that he had read medicine himself, but tho' I have known him many y[ea]rs I was not aware of that fact & I don[']t think many of his acquaintances are," 11007 told the agency.[45] It was an extraordinarily tactful way of contradicting Rivers's claim, but without giving the "lie direct"—which among men of honor would have demanded a response. And since 11007 also noted that he had "known [Rivers] many years"—well enough to be familiar with the latter's educational background—we may surmise that he viewed the younger man as a peer to whom he would be answerable for his words.

As it turned out, Rivers had at least one loyal protector among the agency's subscribers, someone who could easily have transmitted 11007's report back to him, and in contrast to many of his counterparts, 11007 was a known correspondent of the agency. Whether from a sense of personal honor or a fear of being called out, men like 11007 still guarded their words in the brave new world of credit reporting.

By contrast, in a world that remained highly personal, subjects also occasionally benefited from the direct advocacy of correspondents themselves, who deployed the idea of honor in support of a younger merchant or one whose affairs were on the brink of collapse. Shoe dealer R. A. Pringle, as one correspondent noted, "belongs to an old fam[i]ly wh[ich] was once wealthy, but [is] now somewhat reduc[e]d," and MPS termed him a "high bred gentleman" and a "man of g[oo]d cha[racter] & family."[46] In the fall of 1857, as the entire nation suffered from a second financial panic, Pringle's notes came under protest. 11007 intervened with creditors, arguing that Pringle was merely "eccentric." "I don't believe he was ½ so hard press'd as a great many who h[a]v[e] p[ai]d thro[ugh] thick & thin," 11007 wrote, adding that "he will pay but he is not going to sacrifice 3–4 or 6 ½ [percent interest] to get exchange for anybody."[47] What is critical is that 11007 sought to portray Pringle's nonpayment as a principled protest rather than insolvency, suggesting that Pringle had the means to pay should he wish to do so. In so doing 11007 emphasized Pringle's financial independence, a reassurance to creditors but also a key principle of the South's honor culture. In theory the man of honor—in contrast to slaves and other dependents—boasted a healthy balance of assets to liabilities and was fully the master of his economic fate.[48] Although easy liquidity was a thing of the past in Pringle's case, we can almost hear his defiance through 11007's words. It was the roar of a man of honor caught up in the market but denying his dependency on it, claiming the prerogative to choose the terms under which he would repay his debts. Ironically, of course, Pringle's ability to pay depended on conditions in the very market that he affected to defy.

11007's assurance probably failed to impress creditors whose own businesses might be teetering on the brink of collapse. And 11007's own attitude toward Pringle seemed ambivalent. Having portrayed him as a man of honor in the traditional sense, 11007 added his own estimate that Pringle was worth at least $25,000, all invested in his business—thus providing a more material assurance that Pringle would ultimately be good for his debts. One suspects that 11007 felt a certain admiration for Pringle's defiance, for his refusal to be a slave to the market's fluctuations. Yet we know that 11007 also recognized the centrality of repayment to honor in the commercial arena, his acknowledgement that the "great many who h[a]v[e] p[ai]d thro[ugh] thick & thin" were the standard of honor in business. With his report 11007 recognized the tensions between southern honor and commercial honor, even as he employed the former to reassure creditors that Pringle would ultimately be honorable by the latter's standards as well. A year later another correspondent leapt to Pringle's defense with a similar report, assuring the agency that even as Pringle continued to struggle against slow sales, he was "hon[ora]ble & has correct [cut off] ab[ou]t paying his debts."[49]

11007 would also step in to defend brothers Keating and Sedgwick Simons by deploying references to southern honor. Their earlier enterprise having been brought down through endorsements of a friend's notes, the Simonses struggled to regain their business footing in 1855. Like Pringle, they had been born into the old elite and benefitted from their family's reputation. Moreover their father, uncle, and a cousin had all fought duels (the latter two being shot fatally) in the early nineteenth century, cementing the family's reputation for honor locally.[50] And the cause of the brothers' earlier failure constituted no disgrace among men of honor, for such men were expected to endorse notes for their peers and were bound to each other by a network of interlocking obligations.[51]

As the brothers' commission business faltered, 11007 zealously offered his support, invoking both their family's reputation and the brothers' personal characters as he noted that "they belong to one of our oldest & most respected fam[ilie]s & one which has a chivalrous reputation for honesty."[52] 11007's choice of words here is striking. *Chivalry* was a term far more closely associated with southern honor than with commercial virtues. It had been appropriated by southern writers to defend a society of supposed "cavaliers" against a Yankee abolitionist threat; it was also applied specifically to the practice of dueling, invoked as a point of regional pride by southern apologists or applied sneeringly by northern editors.[53] 11007's use of the term may thus have represented an allusion to the family's dueling history, although subscribers would have been unlikely to recognize the literal reference. Indeed such an invocation would initially seem to have little to do with creditworthiness. Yet insofar as honor constituted a public reputation for private virtue, men of honor viewed a duelist's willingness to face death as evidence of his belief in his own position. It could thus be viewed as a testament to his integrity, a virtue prized in the world of business. For 11007 the Simons family's defense of its "honesty" on the dueling field may have seemed a reliable predictor of their trustworthiness in business.

Whether he referred to the family's propensity for dueling or a more general "chivalrous reputation," 11007 was not alone in trusting the brothers, he assured New York. "Nobody here would doubt th[ei]r integrity for a moment," he wrote, emphasizing the applicability of his comments to business by claiming that he himself "would trust them on th[ei]r char[acter] if I knew they had not a cent in th[ei]r pockets." Yet the firm continued to struggle. Among rumors of failure a year and a half later, 11007 again attempted to shore them up with creditors, lauding the young men as "v[ery] hon[orab]l[e]" even as he admitted, "I fear something wrong is coming." Ultimately the firm would indeed fail. However, the brothers would compromise their debts at the relatively high rate of 85 percent and, by doing so, retain the backing of wealthy friends and a reputation, in another correspondent's words, as "very honorable men, but at the same time very weak."[54]

11007 would likewise turn to the language of chivalry when he was asked to endorse aspiring druggist Winfield Rivers, but this time his recommendation was more guarded. By his own account, 11007 had known Rivers for "many years." Although the younger man was reputed to be a good teacher and "desirous of doing right," 11007 initially could think of very little that would recommend Rivers for shopkeeping. In three lengthy reports, he listed unpaid debts that might still be hanging over Rivers, detailed the somewhat shady lengths that Rivers had gone to obtain stock, and concluded his third report by stating bluntly, "I fear he will not succeed in bus[iness] & cannot recom[men]d cr[edit] to any extent."[55]

Yet the Rivers affair took an extraordinary turn in the lines of the credit ledger, one that underscored the degree to which business remained highly personal, even in the age of national credit agencies, and the ways in which multiple meanings of honor could be deployed in the market. In March 1860 correspondent 1500 advised the agency that they "had better bracket out all prev[ious] rep[or]ts" on Rivers—all of which had been submitted by 11007 and all of which cast doubt on Rivers's commercial abilities—"& give out rep[or]t of Mar 16/60" because a Philadelphia wholesaler "is determined to sell [to] him." Astonishingly the agency did just that, surrounding the previous reports with a heavy bracket that warned clerks not to disseminate the enclosed material to subscribers. In its place the agency substituted the requested report, also penned by 11007. This report omitted all mention of 11007's previous doubts, although a careful creditor might pause over the fact that Rivers had "paid no City tax last year on any p[ro]p[er]ty," a carefully worded indication that he possessed little that a creditor could seize. Otherwise, 11007 wrote, Rivers was "steady—temperate—high-minded—hon[orab]l[e]—chivalrous—educated," and that his firm made their purchases "in Phil[adelphi]a, & their credit is good there."[56] To one familiar with the previous report, the later iteration was a masterpiece of careful phrasing. The Philadelphia wholesaler's demands became one basis of Rivers's rehabilitated creditworthiness. The other included his "high-minded," "honorable," and "chivalrous" nature. Yet these traits had not been sufficient to make him a safe credit risk earlier.

It appears that 11007 invoked chivalry here to compose a favorable report while still cautioning subscribers against extending credit to Rivers. 11007 had earlier conceded that Rivers was "desirous of doing right," and so it seems likely that he was sincere in lauding Rivers as both "honorable" and "high-minded." Yet we know that he considered Rivers a poor credit risk. In contrast to the Simons case, 11007 did not pair his invocation of chivalry—a social virtue—with testimonials to Rivers's commercial integrity. Instead he described Rivers as "educated," another adjective unusual in the credit reports and one whose infrequency of use suggests that it was of minimal interest to the business community. Taken as a whole, 11007's

March report suggests that he sought to send a coded message to subscribers that he described explicitly social, rather than mercantile, virtues—virtues that in fact did *not* amount to an endorsement of Rivers's commercial abilities.

It is, of course, unclear whether subscribers picked up on these nuances. However, a submission by 1500 two months later was the final report for Rivers's drugstore.[57] This fact may suggest that the business folded shortly thereafter, bearing out 11007's assessment of the schoolteacher's business abilities and perhaps indicating that subscribers heeded his coded warning.

The interventions of 11007 and others make sense if we consider that correspondents themselves were deeply enmeshed in their local communities. Although the agency sought accurate intelligence, the men they relied on were not always disinterested observers of their friends and neighbors. Ironically the very familiarity with their subjects that made them valuable sources of information could also lead correspondents to shade their reports according to their own allegiances. In describing their friends and business associates to outsiders, they were aware that their words shaped those associates' reputations and thus had the power to determine their success or failure in business. As credit agents who were simultaneously the friends and confidants of their subjects, men like 11007 had to walk a fine line between providing accurate intelligence and violating their own and their society's sense of honor. Seen in this light, correspondents' intervention becomes the defense of personal acquaintances. Such a defense relied on the same kinds of subjective assessments that, when negative, could destroy a businessman's national reputation.

Failure, Fraud, Recriminations, and Insult

If honor was invoked to defend worthy subjects, it also made its way into the credit reports through the language of personal insult, as reports of *scoundrels, rascals, rogues,* and even *worthless dogs* wended their way north to creditors. All of these terms, which were grave insults among men of honor, denoted a much larger offense than a mere business failure; indeed they were typically applied to explicitly dishonorable actions. After Alfred Bernard had apparently cheated his creditors of property in the course of two failures, his wife purchased real estate and embarked on a millinery business, using (locals believed) the sequestered funds. One correspondent warned wholesalers that "the impress[io]n in the minds of all here is that the whole conc[er]n is a 'rascally' one & that she is the 'biggest rascal' of the bunch."[58] When dry goods dealers John McMaster and Son failed in "swindling operations" that brought down several other Charleston firms, correspondents likewise condemned their "rascally conduct" and judged McMaster's wife—who like Bernard's wife had subsequently set up business in her own name—to be "as g[rea]t [a] rogue as her husband," adding for good measure that she was "a g[rea]t scamp, cheat, &c."[59]

When the subjects whom they had endorsed failed dishonorably, correspondents damned them in terms no less personal than those they had used to laud them. 11007 had once considered grocers E. T. Payne and J. C. Bickley "y[oung] men of g[oo]d char[acter] & of the highest respectability." When they failed two years later, however, he wrote scathingly that "they are totally bankrupt & some of their home cr[e]d[itor]s say great rascals besides."[60] Likewise correspondent JR had once praised Paul F. Villepigue, a cotton factor doing business both in Charleston and in the inland town of Camden, as a man who was "considered honest—very industrious and attentive to business"; a fellow correspondent rated him a "very honourable man in his trading." Although Villepigue had failed once, and his business again appeared to be in trouble, in 1858 JR made an effort to intervene on Villepigue's behalf, noting that he remained "the best judge of cotton in Camden"—a stock in trade that could not be touched by pecuniary losses. Eight months later, however, he dropped his defense of Villepigue, snapping that not only could Villepigue no longer pay his debts, but that he had become extremely disagreeable: "in manners, a 'Mongrel' (between a Bear and a Bull dog)."[61] To call a man a "dog" was affront enough in antebellum America. "Mongrel" bore the added connotations of mixed descent, worthlessness, and bastardy.[62] It was an insult that, if uttered to Villepigue's face, would almost necessarily have provoked a violent response. But in the long-distance world of credit reporting, it seems unlikely that Villepigue ever knew the insult to have been uttered; certainly there is no indication in the agency's ledgers that he demanded redress.

Correspondents' willingness to deploy such insults may perhaps be explained by their own positions when a subject failed. In praising subjects, and particularly in invoking their honor as a defense against default, correspondents were essentially putting their own word on the line, assuring creditors that despite all appearances to the contrary, they judged a particular subject to be a safe credit risk. A failure—particularly a dishonorable one—could call the reliability of the correspondent himself into question.[63]

Honor insults were also deployed in tandem with legal action against dishonest businessmen.[64] A few days after the German-born Baum brothers failed, an attorney called at agency headquarters to relay his suspicions that the Baums "intended to swindle the cr[editor]s & if possible not pay over 25% [of the amount owed]," and the agency transmitted his advice that creditors should begin preparing sworn statements of their claims.[65]

The affair dragged on for the next four years, as the Baums first attempted to settle with their creditors and then were convicted of fraud and jailed. As the Charleston business community awaited their trial, correspondents invoked the language of honor in their reports. "Worthless dogs," wrote 11007, before more pragmatically advising creditors to "sell [to] them for cash only." And as GWB recounted the process of bringing fraud charges on the Baums, he added the opinion that "they are as precious a set of Scoundrels as ever escaped the halter," pessimistically predicting that "they will go thro[ugh] & defeat all Judgments in despite of opposition."[66]

The combination of insult and pragmatic assessment in the correspondents' reports suggests the degree to which honor and business coexisted in the minds of many contemporaries. Even as creditors pursued claims through the courts, and even as correspondents anticipated that news of the cases would serve as a caution to distant subscribers, correspondents nonetheless deployed the language of insult to further damage their subjects. This is perhaps more significant given their cynicism regarding the effectiveness of the courts in checking fraud, revealed in reports that complained of their difficulty in obtaining fraud convictions.[67] While they believed that businessmen could and should turn to the courts to pursue debts (indeed part of the agency's business model depended on their doing so), they also sought an alternate means of crippling dishonest businessmen. Recourse to the language of honor, they evidently believed, provided one such means. By mounting personal attacks on the men whom they perceived as rascals, rogues, dogs, and scoundrels, correspondents sought to damage their reputations within the new, enlarged, community of business peers.

The degree to which such verbal honor assaults resonated with northern subscribers remains an open question. Whether conveying insults or praise of an honorable character, however, correspondents typically couched their words in the context of more specific commentary on subjects' credit histories, characters, and business abilities, information that would have made clear the significance of their honor references. As they invoked the language and grammar of honor, these correspondents penned their reports in the belief that they were conveying vital, and intelligible, information about the creditworthiness of their neighbors and business associates, information that would help safeguard the development of the market economy.

For Charleston's credit correspondents, the ideals of both commercial virtue and southern honor provided standards by which to judge a businessman's creditworthiness. Like a reputation for commercial honor, correspondents believed that a reputation for southern honor provided a degree of assurance that a businessman would at least attempt to do right by his creditors. The language of honor could be used to endorse a struggling businessman; it could also be used to condemn the untrustworthy. In a world where personal acquaintance and long-distance trade, contract and reputation were colliding, honor thus remained a vital element of Charleston's business culture. In many ways the credit agency itself, by collecting and distributing such information, re-created the face-to-face world it was in the process of replacing. This was a larger, more far-flung business community, but one in which personal reputation remained paramount. In this enlarged community, where local ideas about honor factored into assessments of creditworthiness, they assumed new consequences on a national stage.

NOTES

1. South Carolina, vol. 6, p. 204 (Ravenel and Huger), R. G. Dun and Co. Credit Report Volumes, Baker Library, Harvard Business School (hereafter BL); Ferslew, *Directory*, 116–17.

2. South Carolina, vol. 6, p. 94 (Huger and Milliken), R. G. Dun and Co. Credit Report Volumes, BL, emphasis in original.

3. South Carolina, vol. 6, p. 204, R. G. Dun and Co. Credit Report Volumes, BL. On the early development of numeric ratings in the credit reports see Sandage, *Born Losers*, 133–34, 143.

4. Weber, *Economy and Society*, esp. 956–1005; Chandler, *Visible Hand*, 3–12; Cronon, *Nature's Metropolis*, 114–19, 235–47; Sandage, *Born Losers*, esp. 37, 65–66, 112, 132–34.

5. Wyatt-Brown, *Southern Honor;* Wyatt-Brown, "God and Dun and Bradstreet." Other important analyses of southern honor include Ayers, *Vengeance and Justice;* D. Bruce, *Violence and Culture;* Greenberg, *Honor and Slavery;* and Wyatt-Brown, *Shaping of Southern Culture.*

6. Ayers, *Vengeance and Justice*, 13–14, 26; Greenberg, *Honor and Slavery*, 11, 24–43.

7. Osterweis, *Romanticism and Nationalism;* E. Thomas, *Confederate Nation*, 23–25, 28; Wyatt-Brown, *Shaping of Southern Culture*, 181.

8. Balleisen, *Navigating Failure;* Olegario, *Culture of Credit;* Sandage, *Born Losers.*

9. Wells, *Origins of the Southern Middle Class*, 80–86; see also Byrne, *Becoming Bourgeois*, esp. 41–75.

10. T. H. Breen and Joanne Freeman make similar arguments regarding colonial Chesapeake planters and statesmen of the Early Republic. Breen, *Tobacco Culture*, esp. 84–159; Freeman, *Affairs of Honor.*

11. Osterweis, *Romanticism and Nationalism;* LaCroix, "To Gain the Whole World," 551–56. This was part of a larger effort to create a southern cultural nationalism and was influenced by nationalist movements abroad. See McCardell, *Idea of a Southern Nation*, esp. 166–72; Quigley, *Shifting Grounds.*

12. Atherton, *Southern Country Store;* Olegario, *Culture of Credit*, 36–79; Sandage, *Born Losers*, 121–22.

13. On credit agency practices see Atherton, "Problem of Credit Rating," 539–54; Olegario, *Culture of Credit*, 36–118; Sandage, *Born Losers*, 129–58; Wyatt-Brown, "God and Dun and Bradstreet," 435–43. For the identification of 11007 as "S," see reports on A. J. Cappell and Brother, October 25, 1855, and July 18, 1856, South Carolina, vol. 6, p. 125, R. G. Dun and Co. Credit Report Volumes, BL.

14. Foote, *Gentlemen and the Roughs*, esp. 79–117; Wyatt-Brown, *Shaping of Southern Culture*, 192–93; see also Freeman, *Affairs of Honor*, for insights into the shared culture of honor in the early republic.

15. For a nuanced discussion of the impact of the credit reports, see Sandage, *Born Losers*, esp. 153–54, 159–61, 164–84.

16. Olegario, *Culture of Credit*, 58.

17. Atherton, "Problem of Credit Rating," 551; Sandage, *Born Losers* 110–11, 161, 165; Wyatt-Brown, "God and Dun and Bradstreet," 442. So committed was the agency to protecting correspondents' identities that in 1851 partner Benjamin Douglass was jailed for twenty days for refusing to reveal a correspondent's name in the case of *Beardsley v. Tappan*. Olegario, *Culture of*

Credit, 67, 73. The identities of a few prominent correspondents, including Abraham Lincoln and Salmon P. Chase, are known to posterity. Sandage, *Born Losers,* 110, 156.

18. South Carolina, vol. 6, p. 93 (John Caldwell Sen and Son); South Carolina, vol. 6, p. 169 (G. W. Flach); South Carolina, vol. 6, p. 160 (G. W. Williams and Co.); South Carolina, vol. 6, p. 166 (A. N. Cohen Jr.); South Carolina, vol. 7, p. 353 (Albert Longnick); South Carolina, vol. 7, p. 374 (Winfield M. Rivers and Co.), all R. G. Dun and Co. Credit Report Volumes, BL.

19. South Carolina, vol. 6, p. 56 (Sims and Dulin; Rice Dulin), R. G. Dun and Co. Credit Report Volumes, BL.

20. South Carolina, vol. 6, p. 59 (E. C. Kelting), R. G. Dun and Co. Credit Report Volumes, BL.

21. South Carolina, vol. 6, p. 117 (Corbett and Bros.); South Carolina, vol. 6, p. 99 (Andrew McDowall and Co.), both R. G. Dun and Co. Credit Report Volumes, BL.

22. South Carolina, vol. 6, p. 60 (R. W. Burnham), R. G. Dun and Co. Credit Report Volumes, BL.

23. South Carolina, vol. 6, p. 33 (T. M. Horsey and Co.), R. G. Dun and Co. Credit Report Volumes, BL.

24. South Carolina, vol. 6, p. 106 (Dickson and Mills), R. G. Dun and Co. Credit Report Volumes, BL.

25. South Carolina, vol. 6, p. 98 (B. Figeroux), R. G. Dun and Co. Credit Report Volumes, BL.

26. South Carolina, vol. 6, p. 118 (Edwin Bates and Co.); South Carolina, vol. 6, p. 202 (T. S. and T. G. Budd), both R. G. Dun and Co. Credit Report Volumes, BL.

27. Samuel Wells Leland Papers, Journal, vol. 2, 18 December 1854, South Caroliniana Library (hereafter SCL).

28. "Tribute of the Chamber of Commerce to the Late James Adger," *In Memoriam*, South Carolina Historical Society (hereafter SCHS), p. 20.

29. See, for instance, "Death of James Adger, Esq.," *Charleston Courier*, September 25, 1858; "James Adger, Esq.," *New York Herald*, September 1858; "Tribute of the Synod of South Carolina at their Meeting at Sumter, 27th October, 1858," *Southern Presbyterian*, December 18, 1858; "Funeral Sermon of Rev. J. L. Girardeau, 27th November, 1858," all reprinted in *In Memoriam*, SCHS, pp. 9–10; 11; 25; 44–45.

30. "Tribute of Respect, Hibernian Hall, September 25, 1858," and Andrew Crawford, Columbia, to Robert Adger, [Charleston], 4 October 1858, both reprinted in *In Memoriam*, pp. 16, 31. Fought over anonymous attacks on the reputation of Judge Magrath (who was then running for U.S. Congress) published by the *Charleston Mercury*, the Taber-Magrath duel was a complicated honor dispute in which the judge's brother Edward Magrath killed *Mercury* editor William Taber. See James Conner, Papers relating to the Taber-Magrath duel, SCHS.

31. "The Good Merchant," 141.

32. South Carolina, vol. 6, p. 204 (Ravenel and Huger), R. G. Dun and Co. Credit Report Volumes, BL. For examples of the struggles to assess newcomers' creditworthiness, see South Carolina, vol. 6, p. 87 (Stuart Harper and Co), R. G. Dun and Co. Credit Report Volumes, BL; South Carolina, vol. 6, p. 73 (James E. Duryee and Co.), R. G. Dun and Co. Credit Report Volumes, BL.

33. South Carolina, vol. 7, p. 354 (Street and West), R. G. Dun and Co. Credit Report Volumes, BL.

34. South Carolina, vol. 6, p. 56 (W. B. Pringle Jr.), R. G. Dun and Co. Credit Report Volumes, BL.

35. South Carolina, vol. 6, p. 130 (Thirman and Pringle), R. G. Dun and Co. Credit Report Volumes, BL.

36. South Carolina, vol. 6, p. 130 (Thirman and Pringle), R. G. Dun and Co. Credit Report Volumes, BL; South Carolina, vol. 6, p. 56 (W. B. Pringle Jr.), R. G. Dun and Co. Credit Report Volumes, BL.

37. Julian Pitt-Rivers, "Honor," 506.

38. South Carolina, vol. 6, p. 117 (Jas. N. Corbett); South Carolina, vol. 6, p. 138 (M. McMaster), both R. G. Dun and Co. Credit Report Volumes, BL.

39. South Carolina, vol. 6, p. 125 (A. J. Cappell and Bro.), R. G. Dun and Co. Credit Report Volumes, BL.

40. South Carolina, vol. 6, p. 60 (R. W. Burnham), R. G. Dun and Co. Credit Report Volumes, BL, emphasis added.

41. South Carolina, vol. 6, p. 125 (A. J. Cappell and Bro.), R. G. Dun and Co. Credit Report Volumes, BL.

42. Breen, *Tobacco Culture*.

43. James Adger to William Smith, January 20, 1819, James Adger Letterbook, SCL.

44. James Adger to William Smith, February 5, 1819, James Adger Letterbook, SCL.

45. South Carolina, vol. 7, p. 374 (Winfield M. Rivers and Co.), R. G. Dun and Co. Credit Report Volumes, BL.

46. South Carolina, vol. 6, pp. 23, 170 (R. A. Pringle), R. G. Dun and Co. Credit Report Volumes, BL.

47. South Carolina, vol. 7, p. 310 (R. A. Pringle), R. G. Dun and Co. Credit Report Volumes, BL.

48. Breen, *Tobacco Culture,* esp. 124–59.

49. South Carolina, vol. 7, p. 310 (R. A. Pringle), R. G. Dun and Co. Credit Report Volumes, BL.

50. "Geddes-Simons and Wilson-Simons," Fitzsimons, *Hot Words and Hair Triggers*. On the relationship between the commission merchants and their dueling kin, see Simons Family vertical file, SCHS; Salley, "Some Early Simons Records," 145–47.

51. Greenberg, *Honor and Slavery,* 78–80; Faust, *James Henry Hammond,* 111.

52. South Carolina, vol. 6, p. 63 (Simons Bros.), R. G. Dun and Co. Credit Report Volumes, BL.

53. McCardell, *Idea of a Southern Nation*, 147, 166–69; O'Brien, *Conjectures of Order*, esp. 305–22; Osterweis, *Romanticism and Nationalism*, esp. 46; Wyatt-Brown, *Shaping of Southern Culture,* 179–81. *New York Herald* editors mockingly referred to duelists as "the chivalry," whether they hailed from Richmond or Hoboken; see "Affray between Messrs. Wise and Stanley," *Weekly Herald* (New York), May 14, 1842; "The Chase of the Chivalry!," *New York Herald,* January 24, 1845; "The Chivalry of the South," *New York Herald,* October 3, 1856. But southerners too could sneer at each other's chivalric pretensions; see O'Brien, *Conjectures of Order,* 352.

54. South Carolina, vol. 6, pp. 62, 63, 64 (Simons Bros.), R. G. Dun and Co. Credit Report Volumes, BL.

55. South Carolina, vol. 7, p. 374 (Winfield M. Rivers and Co.), R. G. Dun and Co. Credit Report Volumes, BL. In attempting to obtain credit from a local wholesaler, Rivers inexpertly attempted a number of stratagems, all of which failed and, in the process, showed him to be a poor hustler as well as a poor credit risk. He first claimed to be doing business in his sister's name. It was not uncommon for a failed businessmen to use his wife's name to obtain a new line of credit, especially when purchasing from distant wholesalers who might not know who was actually running a business, but this was a ruse that raised warnings for creditors and one that local correspondents attempted to check. In this case, however, Charleston was too small of a business community for such a cover to be effective. Rivers then provided at least one credit reference, evidently hoping that the wholesaler would never bother to contact the man. More savvy than Rivers, the

wholesaler did and was rewarded with the intelligence that the reference "would prefer to sell for cash" to Rivers. Finally, in a supreme vote of no-confidence (in an honor society in which endorsements were expected among friends and family), Rivers's father-in-law refused to endorse for the younger man. Greenberg, *Honor and Slavery*, 78–80. In a desperate bid, Rivers then promised to pay cash if the wholesaler would send him the goods, but when the wholesaler demanded payment in advance it was never forthcoming and the deal fell through.

56. South Carolina, vol. 7, p. 374 (Winfield M. Rivers and Co.), R. G. Dun and Co. Credit Report Volumes, BL.

57. South Carolina, vol. 7, p. 429 (Winfield M. Rivers and Co.), R. G. Dun and Co. Credit Report Volumes, BL.

58. South Carolina, vol. 6, pp. 131, 195 (Mrs. C. H. Bernard, C. H. and A. Bernard), R. G. Dun and Co. Credit Report Volumes, BL, emphasis original.

59. South Carolina, vol. 6, pp. 138, 103, 107 (M. McMaster, John McMaster and Son, Mrs. E. McMaster), R. G. Dun and Co. Credit Report Volumes, BL.

60. South Carolina, vol. 6, p. 115 (Payne and Bickley), R. G. Dun and Co. Credit Report Volumes, BL.

61. South Carolina, vol. 11, p. 58 (Paul F. Villispigue), R. G. Dun and Co. Credit Report Volumes, BL. Although his name appears as "Villispigue" in the agency records, it is spelled "Villepigue" locally, so I have adopted the latter spelling to accord with other sources.

62. "Mongrel," *Oxford English Dictionary*, http://dictionary.oed.com. (Accessed February 16, 2016). In the American South, the term may have more specifically connoted mixed racial descent.

63. Lawyers who provided merchants with references faced similar concerns for their own reputations, as did politicians who promised votes to their allies. Atherton, "Problem of Credit Rating," 536–38; Greenberg, *Honor and Slavery*, 17.

64. In their willingness to deploy both honor and the court system against dishonorable businessmen, correspondents acknowledged both the distance between social honor and the market, and the degree to which market behavior was judged by social standards. On the distinction between appeals to honor and the law in noncommercial venues see Ayers, *Vengeance and Justice*, 18, 31.

65. South Carolina, vol. 6, p. 115 (E. and H. Baum), R. G. Dun and Co. Credit Report Volumes, BL.

66. South Carolina, vol. 6, p. 114 (E. and H. Baum), R. G. Dun and Co. Credit Report Volumes, BL, emphasis in original.

67. South Carolina, vol. 6, p. 154 (William King); South Carolina, vol. 6, p. 114 (E. and H. Baum), both R. G. Dun and Co. Credit Report Volumes, BL.

Part II

Honor, Violence, and the Law

Much of the popular conception of honor centers on the dueling field, a place where defending reputation met its ultimate, horrific expression. Alexander Hamilton's sad fate immediately springs to mind, but so does the elaborate and bloodless settlement between Henry Clay and John Randolph or the fatal exchange between Jonathan Cilley and William Graves (discussed in the next section). Violence, however, was more than settling scores or defying death. It was, as these essays suggest, a means of establishing rank—no small thing in a society changing as rapidly as the antebellum South. The duel was a means of asserting, maintaining, or even creating a reputation as a gentleman of honor and standing.

For this reason the orchestration of a duel was as important as its outcome. Indeed the outcome could be written without a formal exchange of fire. Todd Hagstette's essay shows how "writing" a duel could in and of itself demonstrate mastery and sophistication and—implicitly—identify the superior gentleman simply by the language he employed in resolving conflict. The labyrinthine phrasing of notes and verbal cues may seem profoundly silly to modern eyes, but they were in fact highly nuanced and structured means of preserving reputation in a culture that often was anything but nuanced or structured. Those who were loose with language demonstrated their social ineptness in very public ways, for the affront to honor was certain to enter the public record in published form.

Naturally the law took a dim view of this sort of thing. One could talk and threaten, but gunfire was gunfire and outside the pale, so laws against dueling existed on the books in every state in the Union. The legal system, however, was subject to the same flux and ambiguity as any other institution in this expanding world, and the practical results of stepping over the line were predictably capricious. Matthew Byron's essay demonstrates the fatal union of honor and violence in two ways, personal and institutional. A trio of good-for-naughts arranged a sham duel in frontier Illinois to promote one of their number's gentlemanly aspirations. When the guns went off, however, a respected citizen lay dead, as did the assailant's hope for public esteem. Then the legal system kicked in, and in time the shooter was hanged—the only such execution for murder ever carried out in antebellum America. The story forms a fascinating study of the collision of personal aspirations and a raw political environment that needed to demonstrate its authority in the name of civilization and order—where, arguably, neither existed.

The situation was no less volatile in older regions. Christopher Curtis's essay offers a look at the changing status of the judiciary in Virginia. Judges personified the entwined concepts of law and honor on which social hierarchy was grounded in the lands of the English common law during the nineteenth century. This dualism was made possible because judges not only served as adjudicators of law and justice; they were also responsible for maintaining local governance as "keepers of the peace." Contemporary economic changes and democratic ideals, however, subverted the traditional authority and status of judges, and, by extension, their honor. Law reform during the nineteenth century frequently placed members of the judiciary in perilous professional positions as the sources of their authority were scrutinized. One such call for reform led to the curious case of a judge who physically assaulted one of his critics, who in turn demanded that the judge be removed. The twists and turns of the affair (which produced both a legislative committee review *and* a challenge to a duel) are representative of other cases that arose across the American South as democratic principles and market relations eroded the traditional foundations of judicial status and authority.

After the Civil War, the duel became even more problematic. Was it an expression of noble character or a means of disguising brutality? Bradley Johnson explores the issue as it appeared in the works of writer Thomas Nelson Page. Critics have struggled to make sense of the contradictions in Page's writing about the Old South. While nonfiction works such as *Social Life in Old Virginia before the War* offer an idyllic picture of antebellum southern culture, fictional pieces such as *In Ole Virginia* appear, paradoxically, to both celebrate and subvert southern ideas of honor. Johnson argues that fiction writing allowed Page the rhetorical flexibility to explore, with impunity, the contradictions of southern honor. In particular Page's "Marse Chan" demonstrates the paradoxical actions of gentlemen who enforced standards of behavior by breaking laws against dueling.

Todd Hagstette

WRITING THE DUEL

Rhetorical Negotiation and the Language of Honor in the Nineteenth-Century South

Few archetypes of the South are more inextricably linked to the popular image of the region than the duel. The vision of two men calmly gunning for each other across a misty-dawn field, before a backdrop laden with oaks, magnolias, and moss, dressed as officers or in the arraignment of tony gentlemen, wearing the stoic look of the resigned or the damned: this is the universal picture of elite Old South manhood. So indelible is the association of the South with the duel that even misunderstandings of and outright falsehoods about its history have become iconic in the American imagination. Witness for instance the alternative Hollywood mainstays: two men back-to-back with guns aloft pacing ten steps, spinning, and blasting or the cowboy quick-draw showdown. Both images are fantasy concoctions of the contemporary romantic imagination. Yet the duel is so ingrained in the fabric of southern history that even these invented elements are epitomizing.

Many scholars of the period, in fact, ground their investigations in an assumption of an inextricable link between the South and honor violence.[1] And yet this association of duel and land is not a product exclusively of the modern mind. Dickson D. Bruce has told us that so firmly was southern distinctness symbolized by dueling by the year 1800, that the practice actually grew in popularity as a result of its regional association.[2] Though in its American practice dueling was not limited to the South, consensual agreement both within and outside the region seemed to decree that in its ideology and image there was something pervasively southern about it.

Given the duel's tight association with southern culture, we must ask: what is suggested about regional identity through this association? What does it mean that the violent, at times fatal, expression of honor became a leitmotif for southern identity? What caused men to answer insult with such cool-headed, ritualized performances of vengeance rather than let the heat of the moment and chaos dictate? Perhaps most important of all, how did this communal adherence to ritual in a mostly exclusionary and infrequent behavior actually serve to culturally bind southern society together? The answers to these questions are not to be found on the dueling grounds; instead they reside in the printed, scribal, and oral exchanges that preceded and, more often than not, forestalled the fight of the duelists.[3]

Indeed it was in *writing* the duel, in mastering the language of honor, that the shifting definitions of manners and status related to manhood were defined in the antebellum South. Where social relationships were insecure and status was in doubt, civil discourse was most crucial, and the dueling custom was most prominent. The supposed elite citizens of much of southern society clung to dueling as a symbolic definer of their position, even (perhaps, especially) as the duel's expression turned ever further away from the violent and toward the rhetorical.

Bruce has noted that "one cannot read the letters and diaries of many antebellum Southerners without noticing their great ability to assign universal moral significance to the most trivial events."[4] This tendency is nowhere as apparent as in the interactions of the duelists, where the cost of incivility could be gunfire. The aggrandizement of reality is visible in the seemingly minor incidents that often instigated affairs of honor and in the very nature of the duel itself. Only amid a people accustomed to viewing the world in such grand terms could the remedy for name-calling be couched in so much pomp and theatricality—not to mention blood. The performative nature of dueling and the communications that accompanied it lend high gravity to expressions of honor in the southern mind, for they could potentially cement fundamentally insecure elite status or prove its dearth. Every piece of the duel script—requests for explanation of insult, written challenges, postings, even diary recollections and honor court memoranda—factored into the development of personal honor and group identity in the Old South. The ways that elite southerners expressed themselves, particularly when honor was on the line, marked their status.

This, of course, was doubly so when the expression was put in print. Joanne Freeman has argued that letters sent between honor combatants were far from "spontaneous expressions of thought and feeling," but rather were "artfully contrived performances."[5] Even when intended for an exclusive audience (often for just the eyes of the duel principals and seconds), a duelist's letter had to present in unequivocal terms the sender's credentials as a man of honor. The pubic/private binary broke down, therefore, in relation to honor documents; while these lettered exchanges were cloaked in privacy, they were well known to be public documents and thus exhibited an unacknowledged public-mindedness in their content and tone. When a man signed his name to a private letter of this sort, he knowingly put his whole public persona (and in an honor culture, his whole self-worth) behind it.[6]

The content of these signed communications matched this seriousness and, as Freeman has suggested, reflected some of the most self-conscious writing produced in antebellum America. Reputations hung on nearly every word of a duel communication. In his mastery of the conventions of polite language and usage a gentleman proved his worth and thereby solidified his southern, aristocratic identity. A close look at the details of these documents reveals much about the nature of honor and southern culture as a whole.

The writers of these duel correspondences were clearly aware of the secret/overt dichotomy at work in their communications. As these honor documents affected individual reputation and group identity, they were presented as if private but understood to be anything but. Steven Stowe claimed that a special type of consciousness was at work in the southern elite that "oriented them to showy displays of their beliefs, leading them to find a kind of substance in the show and to rely upon appearances."[7] Dueling was an ostentatious example of this elevation of performance to essence. For this reason the question of reception seemed to be always in the back of the mind of the duelist. His letters, like his performance on the field of battle, would be read and evaluated by his caste at large and judged according to the fluctuating customs of honorable behavior.

The letters, then, spoke to a well-defined and exclusive honor group. In December 1860 Lafayette Strait wrote in a private letter about his approaching duel with Major Thomas J. Dunovant, "In one sense the difficulty I am in is to be deplored. In another it may be considered desirable. But when one party is utterly unblameable and he is sought by a rabble upon whom to centre their party fire, it not only shows his position as a man; but which is still more gratifying, he comes out of the difficulty, with clean hands."[8] Because of this inevitable migration from the personal into the public sphere, a subsection of which would eventually evaluate a participant's accomplishment, the honor culture at large and the dueling class specifically resembled a fraternity of sorts, one that was more tightly woven and consequential than the seemingly covert and violently chaotic dueling custom would suggest.

The dueling subset of honor culture operated in a manner reminiscent of the private societies that David Shields has seen populating the cities of British America. These organizations centered on the popular meeting spots of the day—coffeehouses, clubs, tea tables, and the like—and "formed outside the jurisdiction of the state so that people might share pleasures, promote projects, and fashion new ways of interacting."[9] Though a more loosely organized collective than these clubs, the members of the dueling fraternity also came together contra state sanction and culled society around new, formalized methods of interaction.[10] Their operation differed in some important ways from other private societies too. For example the sense of honor that gave rise to the dueling culture was more of a pervasive aspect of elite society than the more consciously cobbled interests of the private societies, and the actual meetings between duelists, given the official criminality of the practice, were conducted by necessity in liminal spaces.[11] The goals too differed between the dueling culture and the private society. Whereas the latter formed voluntarily around the pursuit of aesthetic and intellectual interests, the former exhibited an almost political form of social control with the participation of its members more or less mandatory.[12]

This social control at work in the honor culture was a rational attempt to subdue an emotional reality. In his treatise on human aggression and dark emotion,

Peter Gay claimed, "humans, pugnacious animals that they are, cultivate their hatreds because they get pleasure from the exercise of their aggressive powers. But the societies in which they live cultivate hatred in precisely the opposite way, by subjecting bareknuckled aggression in most of its forms to stern control; they rein in violence before it destroys everything."[13] Many scholars of the antebellum South see the dueling custom functioning in this way.[14] Recognizing the destructive potential behind savage human emotion, realizing that "no group or society can encourage a fully free indulgence in anger, for no coherent social life could ensue from such indulgence,"[15] the southern elite adopted dueling as a means to control and vent these impulses. Free indulgence in emotion—especially anger, hatred, and aggression—became the mark of ungentlemanly behavior.[16] Social harmony was effected through the codification of violence, and that codification came through the printed component of the duel script.

Shields contended that a private society "depended upon a distinctive manner of discourse for its effective operation. So necessary were these discursive manners to the conduct of these societies that we can speak of [them] as 'discursive institutions'—social entities bound to linguistic formations."[17] In effect the correspondence between duelists operated as a scribal extension of codified discourse, making apparent the discursive manners that ruled the duelists' world. In the written component of the American duel custom, we see how an almost slavish attention to diction and proper linguistic presentation governed the interactions between men of honor. They were fanatically meticulous about rhetoric, seemingly willing to argue indefinitely about the most minor of details.

Stowe has argued that men of honor "wrote with care because letters truly *represented* them in a way that has faded since the late nineteenth century."[18] In the wording of these letters, in other words, was housed the correspondents' honorable reputations. The hallmark of this honor was the tightly controlled emotional response and meticulous adherence to polite discourse contained in the language. Even a letter of the most thinly veiled hostility, for example, invariably concluded with sentiments such as "your obedient servant," "with sentiments of great respect," or "very truly yours, &c." To fail in these formalities was to court dishonor.

This kind of obsessive insistence on decorum may look like the product of well-established elites, but in the American South it may have been, ironically, the offspring of unsettled social status. Scott Romine viewed manners as the glue that binds all communities together. But adoption of these socially sanctioned conventions must be largely universal for effectiveness. He claimed, therefore, that "insofar as it is cohesive, a community will tend to be coercive."[19] The tensions at work in the documents of the dueling community bear out this contention, where such great care was taken in the presentation of the self on paper.

All writers were focused not only on the argument at hand but also, and in some ways more intently, on their linguistic appearance as men worthy of honor.[20]

Again the fixation on proper language stemmed from the very fluidity of the duelist's social status. Alexis de Tocqueville saw America's unique political climate wreaking havoc on the proper exhibition of manners, which would cause much strife amongst the dueling class. He observed, "Genuine dignity of manners consists in always appearing to be in one's place, neither higher nor lower. The peasant can manage this as well as the prince. In democracies, everyone's place is in doubt. Hence manners there are often haughty but seldom dignified."[21] Outside of class and economic concerns (which were important), this appearance of being in one's appropriate social place was effected through proper adherence to the highly structured language of honor for elite members of southern society. Their place may have been shaky or unclear in terms of wealth or inherited position,[22] but through the mannered mechanisms of the honor culture, they could perform the expected behaviors of their rank and thus cement their status.

Conversely, variations in or gaffes against this script had the opposite effect and were problematic for that reason. They revealed a participant's unworthiness in a much clearer light than many of the other social institutions of the day and thereby maintained the membership rosters for honorable society in a practically formal, if ostensibly casual, method.[23] Though not as customarily organized as any of the private societies of the British American landscape, the honor culture, through the duel script, nonetheless exhibited some of the same features in the antebellum South as these more visible predecessors. Furthermore, because of its rather strict discursive controls and dissolute nature, the dueling caste produced that "tyranny of the community" that Bertram Wyatt-Brown claimed "governed Southern society."[24] Dueling was cohesion through coercion.

This coercion was largely a matter of language manipulation. Unlike in European dueling, where "the victor in any competition for honour finds his reputation enhanced by the humiliation of the vanquished,"[25] in the American duel, concerns of martial prowess or marksman's skill were less important than the presentation of honorable determination and mannered membership. It is a historical fallacy that honor could somehow be earned through appeal to the duel in the American South. Honor was upheld or proven (once assumed), but not manifested, through combat.

In the 1852 journal of Samuel Wells Leland, we are told of an altercation between Ned Gunter, "an individual with no business, and no means," and a teacher identified only as Hays. A duel almost ensued, until Hays's friends intervened and informed him that nothing Gunter said could injure his reputation. Leland remarked in conclusion that Gunter for some time had been "endeavoring to get into an <u>affair</u> of <u>honour</u>, with some gentleman, in order to bring himself into notice."[26] Gunter failed because the fight itself would not produce honor in the duelist; the honor had to be assumed to be preexisting. If it was not, then a man would never make it to the dueling grounds in the first place.[27]

Even once on the field, an affair did not determine the quality of a man's honorable reputation, no matter the outcome of the violence. In fact the fight itself could even work the opposite effect. As Frankie Y. Bailey recalled, some duelists "found that the duel did more to harm their status and reputation than to enhance it."[28] Both E. B. C. Cash, after his fatal encounter with William Shannon in 1880, and U.S. vice president Aaron Burr, after killing Alexander Hamilton in 1804, could attest to that eventuality. It was much more common, though, for an honorable persona to be demonstrated, or revealed to be lacking, through rhetoric. The way a man negotiated the complex manners of the duel ritual proved crucial to his aristocratic identity. Those who succeeded in the linguistic challenge either honorably avoided a fight or made their way with full social sanction to the field of honor. Those who failed proved their unworthiness once and for all.

The mannerisms of the duel script can be seen in three examples: identity, provocation, and intent. In an October 3, 1878, letter late in his negotiations for a duel with George Kinloch, George Walker in his anger inadvertently forgot to sign his name. As a result his second, Robert V. Royall, withdrew from the affair, and Kinloch published the correspondence, thus shaming and dishonoring Walker.[29] Such is the gravity of the name attached to a document in the duel script. Defining the issue of provocation came next. Here the duel script became complicated.

Once his second removed himself from the process, Walker sent an exasperated note to Kinloch containing the following: "at 4 P.M. on to morrow, the 8th inst. I shall be at the Oaks Club House, armed with a Colt's pistol, of the kind known as a Peace Maker, (and without other weapon,) and if you appear then and there, armed in like manner, that I shall fire on you three times." Kinloch objected to the "absurd proposition expressed in [Walker's] blurred and almost illegible characters,"[30] because of the audacity of Walker's taking it on himself to select time, place, and weapon for the duel; because of the crass slang he used in referring to his gun; and, because the note was delivered, contrary to duel etiquette, without the aid of a second.[31] In a subsequent note to the public, Kinloch ridiculed Walker for going "through the farce of appearing at the 'Oaks Club Ground'" even though Kinloch had "given no acceptance to his Quixotic proposition."[32] Walker's failures in the rhetorical duel revealed, in the eyes of his peers and his community, his failures as a gentleman. His willingness to risk his life in the pursuit of honor, in the end, was not enough to secure his status. He never got the chance to perform the violent aspect of the honor culture, because he could not perform the linguistic ones.

The altercation had begun on the evening of Friday, August 23, when Kinloch and some friends were socializing at Sullivan's Island, South Carolina; Walker approached the party and demanded to know which of them had called him a "Damned English son of a bitch."[33] As each of Kinloch's party denied uttering the insult, Walker declared to each in turn that he "thought him too much of a gentleman to employ any such language," eventually proclaiming "Mr. Kinloch the *only one* capable of saying so," a charge to which Kinloch responded, "If you charge *me* with, or even mean to insinuate that I used such an expression, you are a damned liar."[34]

Interestingly it was Walker who, two days later, sent a letter demanding an apology for the altercation. This affair of honor was typical for its being instigated through verbal insults and name-calling meant to impugn a man's honor and manhood. To call a man "English" was to accuse him of all the anglophile characteristics antithetical to American machismo, and to accuse a man of lying was to strike at the very heart of his honorable reputation.[35] That it was Walker who issued the first communication in both the oral and scribal moments of this duel, coupled with the fact that Kinloch and Walker's second both eventually disassociated themselves from the affair, suggests that Walker was eager for an honor contest in which he hoped he could prove his masculine and aristocratic worth, neither of which was apparently secure. Throughout the communications that followed over the next several days, Kinloch proved himself to be the more skilled duel rhetorician. He used the proper format of the duel script, of which Walker proved largely ignorant, to manipulate Walker into increasing exasperation until he finally issued his fatal call for redress, the impropriety of which Kinloch used to fully unman him before Charleston society.

Walker started by demanding an apology, to which Kinloch responded by recapping the event in question and flatly refusing to make amends on the grounds that Walker's insinuation was the first insult. He proclaimed, "I cannot reproach myself with the expression I used; and until the cause that produced and justified it is removed, it will have to stand as uttered."[36] To Walker's faux pas, in his reply to this note asking again for an apology, Kinloch wrote back to say that he had nothing to add to his previous communication and would stand ready to accept a challenge should Walker feel so inclined. At that point the Walker camp made a critical error by responding with a request from Robert V. Royall to have a private meeting with Kinloch's second, Constance Rivers. Two aberrations irked the Kinloch camp. First, the indefiniteness of this communication made Walker seem weak and ungentlemanly. A confident challenge was expected, not a squeamish deferral. Second, a face-to-face meeting rather than a written communication was a complete breach of duel etiquette.[37] After the initial confrontation, all negotiations in an affair of honor were required to be bolstered through the legitimacy of writing.

Walker further failed in honor customs when, following his conclusion that Kinloch had not in fact uttered the insulting remark he had originally attributed to him, Walker instructed Royall to make a statement to that effect on his behalf! Kinloch roundly rejected this evasion, writing to Royall, "I shall be ready to return Mr. Walker what in my judgment, will be a proper reply to any note addressed to me by him."[38] In complying with this insistence, Walker placed special emphasis on the fact that it was only "now" that he believed Kinloch innocent of insult. This for Kinloch was the last straw in what he perceived to be clumsy negotiations from an unworthy foe. Taking advantage of the rhetorical opening Walker inadvertently left him, Kinloch replied, "DEAR SIR: Your note of the 25th Sept., 1878, I have received. In it you say that you do not *now* believe that I made use of the expression you attributed to me. The reply I chose to use was to your *then* remarks. Your present acknowledgement consequently suggests that I should not *now* press the reply I then thought proper to employ."[39] In effect, in trying to hedge his mea culpa, Walker validated the very accusation Kinloch laid on him. This fact, combined with the grating manner of its presentation, left Kinloch willing and able to refuse to concede the linguistic battle, and yet still maintain his honorable reputation. He beat Walker in print, causing the meltdown that shamed his adversary before his community. Through Kinloch's mastery of the duel script, honor for one was upheld as honor for the other was stripped away.

This attention to the details of language in the lettered duel was even more stringently applied, though more satisfactorily so, in the settled 1871 affair between Dr. A. H. Davega and Colonel William Johnston. The shifting landscape of social status that Tocqueville described was especially troubling to the members of the professional classes to which Davega and Johnston both belonged. Caught between the aristocratic bent of the planter class and the lowbrow reputations of the less affluent classes, men like these felt it urgent to assert their genteel status in each other's company, especially surrounded as they were by vulgar society. A hint of dishonor provoked incivility, which erupted into a most ungentlemanly altercation, ironically coloring the would-be elites with the taint of common society. The mannered and legalistic discourse of the lengthy ripostes that followed helped to reestablish status and offered a linguistic counterbalance to a dishonorable physical encounter.

The problem between Davega and Johnston began en route to Columbia, South Carolina, aboard a train of the Charlotte, Columbia and Augusta Railroad, of which Johnston was president. Though the men did not know each other personally, they apparently knew each other by reputation, as word had reached Johnston that Davega had previously suggested to mutual acquaintances that Johnston had intentionally mismanaged the railroad to his own personal gain. With this slanderous charge still on his mind, Johnston, after confirming Davega's identity, confronted the doctor. Davega denied the statement, but as he rose from his seat to explain, Johnston assaulted him physically. He punched him in the face, knocked him to the ground, jumped atop his prostrate form, and had to be dragged from his astonished passenger. Affairs of honor that also involved attacks of passion like this were somewhat rare, but not unheard of. Usually a physical attack prior to a duel was inspired by a more egregious affront than a charge of corporate misconduct.

But, with honor on the line, any blight against a man's reputation was potentially volatile.

Rather than issuing an immediate challenge after being attacked, Davega had composure enough to follow honor customs and actually submit a written demand of apology. It is not this measured response, though, that makes this affair noteworthy but rather the kerfuffle that ensued over a single word in his seemingly simple note. Davega wrote to Johnston immediately after the attack, "SIR: Your unprovoked assault upon me to-day requires an apology from you, which I hereby demand." In his lengthy reply, Johnston indicated two reasons for his attack. First, the original verbal altercation that gave rise to the physical one was in response to the insulting claims Davega was reputed to have made about him. Second, and perhaps more significantly, Johnston worried that in rising from his seat, Davega was preparing to strike him, and therefore his own attack was in preemptive self-defense. He concluded, "I therefore think that the right to demand an apology belongs to myself rather than to you, and consequently do not admit that which you characterize as my assault to have been 'unprovoked.'"[40]

It is significant that both parties here attempted to assume the role of the wronged, which is in itself not necessarily uncommon in exchanges over points of honor. This jockeying occurred, though, even in the face of a physical assault, which sets this altercation apart. Both men felt their honor impugned, and thus both felt equal claim to redress. That the affronts were of different characters—Davega was attacked physically while Johnston was disparaged in reputation—and of different visible immediacy did nothing to decide the case. Davega's very public dishonoring and Johnston's more insidious one stood equal in the culture of honor. Honorable reputation and masculine identity were inextricably linked.[41]

This is why that sticky word "unprovoked" from Davega's initial letter proved to be such a focal point for both combatants. Claim to the highroad and thus unstained honor was at stake for both in the meaning of that word. For Davega the attack was unprovoked because Johnston initiated the physical element without warrant; even if the doctor had been guilty of the accusations that irritated the railroad man, there were other, more gentlemanly methods for addressing the charges. For Johnston the libelous claims about his corruption were the provocation for his violence; the initial attack was not made by him against Davega's person, but by Davega against his standing. With each would-be duelist firmly standing his ground on this point throughout nearly three weeks of detailed and heated communications, recourse to pistols seemed all but inevitable. In the end it was averted through the interference of a mutual friend of both men, who used the very problematic diction as the ultimate solution.

Upon reviewing the full correspondence, General W. M. Gary wrote to the two seconds, "I am of the opinion that the affair has proceeded to its present state from a misconception of the technical meaning intended by the word 'unprovoked,' contained in Dr. Davega's first note to Col. Johnston." Later that day Davega received the following letter from Johnston: "SIR: I have just been informed by Gen. M. W. Gary that in your use of the word 'unprovoked,' in your first note to me, you intended a disclaimer of the authenticity of the charge that I had been informed you made against me, also of any intention on your part to make an assault upon me. Such being the facts, I take pleasure in expressing my sincere regret for having inflicted a blow upon you under an erroneous impression and an incorrect inference from your acts; and I hereby cheerfully tender the apology that I feel is due to you for such an indignity."[42] This apology, more magnanimous and gentlemanly than that which George Walker could muster, spawned the equally gentlemanly, if laconic, reply from Davega: "SIR: Your note in which you have made the *amende honorable,* is perfectly satisfactory."[43] Thus a potentially deadly duel was averted by recourse to diction. Though later entries in the paper trail of this affair seem to show that Gary's reading of the word "unprovoked" mischaracterized Davega's original intent, by freeing it from the constraints of mere physicality and defining it as a disavowal of the original insult (with which Davega concurred), Gary allowed Johnston to apologize for his uncouth behavior while preserving his honor. Davega too preserved his reputation by demonstrating graciousness in the face of error. Both men, in other words, were absolved from the appearance of having intentionally dishonored the other—without a single shot fired.

The notion of intentionality formed an additional, vital component of the manners of honor culture. Contrary to popular belief, duelists were not typically hot-blooded and capricious in their interactions. They were not as touchy as we imagine they were, and even when trouble began most altercations were resolved without grand incident.[44] As Edward L. Ayers has written, "Southern violence was triggered only by a limited number of specific cues, particularly insult," but even in response to this eventuality "the insult had to be considered an intentional affront before it would provoke violence."[45] The potential 1831 duel between U.S. diplomat Beaufort Taylor Watts and American minister to Russia Henry Middleton hinged on the perception of intent. Watts, who was secretary of legation under Middleton in St. Petersburg, listed any number of subtle insults under which he suffered at the hands of his superior while serving his post. Most of these transgressions were issues of social etiquette: an invitation to a state dinner that Middleton failed to deliver in a timely manner and Watts's seat placement at other engagements. More problematic was Middleton's insistence that before Watts moved from Russia at the termination of his service, he had to publish his intention to do so, an insistence that in Watts's mind cast aspersions on his honorable endeavors in that country.

John Lyde Wilson, officially acting on behalf of Watts but really more of a mediator for both men than a second for one, negotiated the peaceful settlement to the affair. In his communications with Middleton, he drew out the latter's explanations for all the perceived affronts, and in each case the operative idea was that of intent. Middleton responded to the initial request for reparations by lamenting, "I regret exceedingly the circumstances which have led Col. Watts to conceive himself insulted by me—As soon as I was made acquainted with the offenses he had taken, I was ready to have assured him that it was not intentional on my part, but for this explanation he never would afford me an opportunity."[46] On the minor social issues, Middleton simply pled guilty on the grounds of carelessness. To the charge of his omitting to give Watts his dinner invitation in a timely fashion, Middleton wrote, "I acknowledge that I am totally at a loss at the present time to give precisely <u>the reason</u> for this omission—either it had escaped my recollection—or what is equally probable, I may have concluded from my knowledge of Mr. Watts's feeble health that he would not have accepted an invitation to spend 5 or 6 hours in a crowded assembly where all the discourses delivered were in the Russ, German or French languages, of all which Mr. Watts is ignorant."[47] The important element here was not that he did not commit the offense, but rather that he committed the act without realizing the insulting nature of it. In fact, in some regards, he was even protecting Watts from the execution of a social duty that might have proved onerous to him.

The opposite was true with regards to the insistence that Watts advertise his departure, which though an inconvenient and even ignoble prerequisite was an official requirement nonetheless. "It may be perfectly true, as [Watts] alleges, that in strictness ambassadors and all members of the diplomatic Corps are in some measure exempted from the operation of the common police regulations," conceded Middleton, but the reason he required it of all personnel was "that in case of departure without publication, (which serves as a notice to persons having just claims to present them for settlement) designing persons may subsequently trump up pretended claims against those Diplomatists."

Once again the intention to insult was the issue in question. Whereas Watts perceived this obligation as a slap against his honor, Middleton claimed to view it simply as a practical necessity, one designed to *protect* persons like Watts from illegitimate claims against their honor. Middleton was even able to mitigate his eventual termination of Watts from his position in Russia through claims that insults against the latter's honor were never intended. Rather his dismissal, "which was only a necessary consequence of his own conduct,"[48] was a practical, business matter, the details of which[49] should "satisfy any reasonable being, that no insult was intended."[50] No matter the seriousness or frivolity of the claims against him, Middleton was very careful in the language he employed in answering Watts's objections. Clearly an experienced practitioner of gentlemanly rhetoric, Middleton objectively and systematically leeched the *intent* to dishonor out of his descriptions of all his supposed infractions, thereby rendering them unactionable in terms of duel etiquette.

In his final report back to Watts, Wilson happily reported that "Mr. Middleton has acquitted himself of all intentional wrong, and I have received the enclosed communication which I deem satisfactory. In the negociation [*sic*] which I have had with Mr. Middleton in this unpleasant affair, permit me to add, he has evinced a worthy and commendable desire to do everything consistent with honor."[51] In his command of the language of honor, Middleton placated first Wilson and then Watts and thus avoided the armed conflict that could certainly have arisen. In the end Watts, though still stinging under the perceived injuries to his honor, nonetheless wrote Wilson to announce that he was "pleased to believe, (notwithstanding facts & circumstances) from the assured disavowal of Mr. Middleton, that they were erroneous."[52] The parenthetical portion of this note would seem to suggest that Watts persisted in believing his interpretation of events to be accurate, but in deference to Middleton's rhetorical generosity, aided in no small part by the endorsement of Wilson, the codifier of southern dueling himself, was willing to accept his superior's version of events. It was quite a testament to the power of linguistic adroitness among the antebellum elite.

Bailey, echoing the sentiments of many scholars of this period in American history, declared that in the southern culture of honor, "the possession of honor and manhood were proven by one's willingness to die in defense of them."[53] The duel was the arena for displays of this willingness. But to focus only on the field of battle is to miss the majority of the picture—really it is even to miss the majority of the battle. Before guns were drawn and ground measured, skirmishes between men of honor raged on the printed page. The real duel was the linguistic fracas in which men attempted to perform the trappings of their aristocratic masculine worth through their adherence to the language of polite combat.

In 1838, following the death on the dueling grounds of Maine congressman Jonathan Cilley at the hands of Kentucky congressman William J. Graves, the U.S. Congress organized a fact-finding committee to look into the matter. The premise of the official report stated: "The committee, entertaining the opinion that the cause of the challenge was the cause of the death of Mr. Cilley, have sought for it where it should be found in the most authentic form, in the correspondence of the parties."[54] Besides the remarkable logic of this declaration, logic that all but exonerated Graves (as the challenger) of wrongdoing, this thesis is interesting for the assurance with which it elevated representation as the ultimate arbiter of truth. The most genuine version of the conflict, the committee contended, would be the description presented in the letters in which the duelists expressed their disagreement. What these men wrote to each other defined the legitimacy of the conflict and, thus, the content of their honor. To know the mind of the duelist and how he framed his identity, then, we must look to his letters.

The revelation of these letters in the official congressional inquiry reinforces a facet of these duel communications that bears repeating. Though ostensibly private correspondences in an underground encounter, these letters actually were produced in an environment of blurred distinctions between the private and the public. Particularly when the sensational was involved, as was certainly the case with a duel, there was little hidden from public view. Honor correspondents knew this. An awareness of the possible, even probable, publicity of their letters colored their rhetoric. Freeman has written, "Framed as a private address from one gentleman to another, these public-minded personal letters were in fact intended to be circulated among small numbers of elite readers; endorsed with 'the authority of a name,' a public-minded letter was a sworn statement of fact, the writer staking his honor on its veracity."[55] As a result letter-writing duelists, far from being merely cautious about their tone, used this epistolary culture to their advantage, actively staking out their honorable reputations through mannered linguistic form. Language itself was a performance, a performance of masculine claims to authority and gentlemanly assertions of solid status, isolated from real action.

In an eerily similar analog, anthropologist Clifford Geertz wrote of cockfighting that, because of the vicarious participation of the cock owners and spectators, the sport "renders ordinary, everyday experience comprehensible by presenting it in terms of acts and objects which have had their practical consequences removed and been reduced (or, if you prefer, raised) to the level of sheer appearances, where the meaning can be more powerfully articulated and more exactly perceived."[56] Though the comparison of a duel to a cockfight might be too suggestively metaphoric, for the elite men of antebellum America the written correspondence in an affair of honor performed the same function Geertz described. Giving full vent to the symbolic nature of language, these communications postured for honorable identity wherein appearance became reality. And though at the end of a duel communication there was the potential for practical consequences should the communiques' violent fruition be realized, the meaning of cultural honor was more clearly visible through these writings for their spectacular and ritualistic nature. Aristocratic identity hinged on these "public-minded personal letters."

Understandably, elite men paid rapt attention to the diction and syntax of these communications. As Bailey pointed out, in the duel script, "a settlement negotiated by the seconds was a highly desirable outcome."[57] This kind of settlement was possible, though, only once the combatants had shown themselves to be masterful at mannered discourse. In a time and place where democracy made social status uncertain, honor was always at risk. Because polite dialogue was the hallmark of elite bearing, matters of honor were resolved through the most refined medium available: the written word. Writing the duel was an exercise in civility—evidence of cultivation, breeding, and literacy, all within the larger landscape of a rather uncultivated, crossbred, halfway illiterate world. Men of honor used the public nature of private correspondence to their advantage to prove their elite status in a performance equally significant as, if less spectacular than, the violent clash of the duel itself. They maintained their honor through rhetorical gymnastics as much as by martial readiness. In this way the written word was as important as the loaded pistol to the southern man of honor.

NOTES

1. For writers who make special mention of dueling as a largely southern phenomenon, see Ayers, "Legacy of Violence," 106, and *Vengeance and Justice,* 15; Bailey, "Honor, Class, and White Southern Violence," 331 and 343–45; D. Bruce, *Violence and Culture,* 5; Holland, *Gentlemen's Blood,* 149–50; Nisbett and Cohen, *Culture of Honor,* 1–11; and Spierenburg, "Masculinity, Violence, and Honor," 21–25.

2. D. Bruce, *Violence and Culture,* 42.

3. Dueling offers an interesting and inclusive view of the interplay between various forms of communication. In assessing the common models for approaching print culture, Harold Love cautions as his final word on the subject that scholars should cease to see the world of print "as somehow isolated from the complementary and often actively co-operating media of the oral, the scribal, and the physically performative," "Early Modern Print Culture," 64. A study of dueling in the South all but necessitates just such a view.

4. D. Bruce, *Violence,* 15.

5. Freeman, *Affairs,* 145.

6. For more on the importance of attribution and the problem of anonymity in the print world, see Jackson, "Jedidiah Morse," 8–13. For the particular importance of signing communications in the honor culture, see Freeman's discussion under "The Art of Paper War," especially her contention that "a man who gave information 'with his own signature' staked his reputation on the veracity of his words, thereby giving them weight and power," in *Affairs,* 127.

7. Stowe, *Intimacy,* xviii.

8. Papers of the Gaston, Strait, Wylie, and Baskin Families.

9. D. Shields, *Civil Tongues,* xiv.

10. Andrew Jackson's mother famously impressed on the future president the maxim that "the law affords no remedy that can satisfy the feelings of a true man," qtd. in Ayers, *Vengeance and Justice,* 18. Toward the satisfaction of this shortcoming, dueling established a new means of interaction between gentlemen whereby the code of honor essentially picked up where the law left off. It offered redress for infractions against the intangible aspects of a man, encapsulated in his reputation. At the same time, it helped to codify and control what was formerly a (more) brutal and destructive aspect of human interaction.

11. Popular dueling grounds were typically on state lines where jurisdiction was uncertain, like Sand Bar Ferry, an island in the Savannah River near Augusta, Georgia; remote, like the famous grounds near Bladensburg, Maryland; or in largely inaccessible spots, like the cliffs of Weehawken, New Jersey.

12. In explaining his recent duel with Georgia politician Button Gwinnett in May 1777, General Lachlan McIntosh voiced this feeling of compulsion in the honor culture in a letter to Henry Laurens. Speaking about the dilemma in which Gwinnett placed him considering his antidueling stance, he wrote: "If I refused the Challenge on any pretense, they [his political enemies] would immediately cry out, 'how unworthy he is to hold his commission.'—altho' I have on all Occasions exposed myself more than any Soldier under my Command in defence of the State, which that very Junto often acknowledged.__and if I accepted it & fell, they would get rid of one, who at all

times exposed publickly their designs against the freedom peace and order of the State, or have an opportunity of plaguing me if that should be the fate of my Antagonist," qtd. in D. Chesnutt, *Papers of Henry Laurens*, 342.

13. Gay, *Cultivation*, 9.

14. See D. Bruce, *Violence*, 12 and 28–32; Freeman, *Affairs*, xv–xx; Holland, *Gentlemen's Blood*, 204–5; Stowe, *Intimacy*, 12–13; and Wyatt-Brown, *Southern Honor*, 352–53.

15. C. Stearns and P. Stearns, *Anger*, 12.

16. See E. Anthony Rotundo's three-part theory on the development of American masculinity, where, in the nineteenth century, "a man defined his manhood not by his ability to moderate the passions but by his ability to channel them effectively," *American Manhood*, 3; Stowe's evaluation of Wilson, in which he claims that the "exchange of letters and words became in effect a contest in which the all-important moral advantage lay in the display of controlled resentment. If the insulted man was the most self-controlled, it was a sign of the insult's probable falseness. If the aggressor was, it could be a sign of the seriousness of his charge. Thus, in order for a dispute to ripen into a true affair, it almost paradoxically had to become more and more controlled," *Intimacy*, 12; and C. Stearns and P. Stearns's note that "diaries in the nineteenth century would build abundantly on the sense that anger must be struggled with and conquered," *Anger*, 28.

17. D. Shields, *Civil Tongues*, xiv.

18. Stowe, *Intimacy*, 24.

19. Romine, *Narrative Forms*, 2.

20. This subservience to manner and custom did not come without some problems. The impact on identity could be substantial. John F. Kasson contends, "The rituals of polite behavior and interaction helped to implant a new, more problematic sense of identity—externally cool and controlled, internally anxious and conflicted—and of social relationships," *Rudeness*, 7.

21. Tocqueville, *Democracy*, 711.

22. See Michael O'Brien, *Conjectures*, 366–79.

23. C. Dallett Hemphill contends of customs of behavior like this, "Manners also constitute a mediating level of culture between a society's abstract 'ideals' and the varied behaviors of its individual members. These meaning-laden acts and gestures are the signal flags of an encounter, by which we communicate, often nonverbally, who we are and what we expect of each other," *Bowing*, 4.

24. Wyatt-Brown, *Southern Honor*, 357.

25. Pitt-Rivers, "Honour and Social Status," 24.

26. Samuel Wells Leland Papers (emphasis in original).

27. According to J. Wilson's *Code of Honor*, when inequality is declared, "there should be no fight" because "individuals may well differ in their estimate of an individual's character and standing in society," 93.

28. Bailey, "Honor," 340.

29. Kinloch, *To the Public*, 7–8.

30. Ibid., 9–10.

31. J. Wilson's *Code* advises, "When your second is in full possession of the facts, leave the whole matter to his judgment, and avoid any consultation with him unless he seeks it. He has the custody of your honor, and by obeying him you cannot be compromitted," 91.

32. Kinloch, *To the Public*, 10.

33. Ibid., 2.

34. Ibid., 2 (emphasis in original).

35. For more on insults, especially the accusation of lying, see Baldick, *Duel,* 32–33; Freeman, *Affairs,* 128; Gorn, "Gouge and Bite," 19; Greenberg, *Honor and Slavery*, xiii and 15; and Wyatt-Brown, *Southern Honor*, 360.

36. Kinloch, *To the Public,* 2.

37. J. Wilson's *Code* offers this to seconds: "To the note you carry in writing to the party complained of, you are entitled to a written answer, which will be directed to your principal, and will be delivered to you by his adversary's friend," 92.

38. Kinloch, *To the Public,* 6.

39. Ibid., 7 (emphasis in original).

40. Davega, *Correspondence,* 4–5.

41. J. Wilson's *Code* is less instructive here. He advises, "When blows are given in the first instance and returned, and the person first striking be badly beaten or otherwise, the party first struck is to make the demand, for blows do not satisfy blows," 99. In Davega's case, though, the blows were not returned to the aggressor, at least not in any but a strictly defensive manner. Logic would suggest that Davega, then, has even more cause to make the demand. The fact that this point is muddled here suggests the great importance that was attached to imputations against a man's honesty; otherwise Johnston would have no claim whatsoever as to the rights of the insulted.

42. Davega, *Correspondence,* 22.

43. Ibid., 22 (emphasis in original).

44. "Dangerous as they were, duels too were deliberately deployed at moments of crisis as proof of character; contrary to popular belief, they were not the mere fallout of a slip of the tongue," Freeman, *Affairs,* xxi.

45. Ayers, *Vengeance,* 19.

46. Beaufort Taylor Watts Papers.

47. Ibid. (emphasis in original).

48. Ibid.

49. Middleton submitted an official dispatch to the secretary of state about the matter. The reasons for Watts's dismissal mostly boil down to small failures of duty resulting from absenteeism due to his particularly bad health. Of course glowing from the center of these details is an unshakable sense of the animosity between these two men emanating from their seemingly ongoing personality conflicts, the same ones that underlie these duel correspondences.

50. Beaufort Taylor Watts Papers.

51. Ibid. (emphasis in original).

52. Ibid.

53. Bailey, "Honor," 341.

54. Qtd. in Sabine, *Notes,* 101.

55. Freeman, *Affairs,* 114.

56. Geertz, *Interpretation,* 443.

57. Bailey, "Honor," 340.

Matthew A. Byron

AN HONORABLE DEATH?

The Stuart-Bennett Duel of 1819

On Monday, September 3, 1821, Timothy Bennett stood on a scaffold in Belleville, Illinois.[1] A large crowd, including women and children, stood with anticipation as the state executioner placed a noose around Bennett's neck.[2] In the waning minutes of his life, Bennett cried out to anyone who would listen that he was an innocent man, but to no avail. Minutes later Bennett entered American history: he was the first man convicted of murder in the state of Illinois, a survivor of the only duel fought in that state, and, what is also significant, the first and only man in the nation ever executed for murder while dueling.[3]

Two years prior Timothy Bennett had been living comfortably as a farmer in Belleville when a quarrel over horses and the destruction of property arose with his neighbor, Alonzo Stuart.[4] After the intervention of two so-called friends Jacob Short and Nathan Fike, Bennett and Stuart agreed to settle their affair with a duel. Although designed by the seconds to be a sham duel, things went awry, and Stuart ended up face-down, dead on the ground. After escaping from jail and eluding authorities for nearly two years, Bennett was apprehended. A speedy trial and conviction, followed by the governor's refusal to pardon, led to Bennett's execution in September 1821.

The story of Timothy Bennett and the Stuart-Bennett Duel offers a window into the changing world of honor culture at the beginning of the nineteenth century. Living in an era when Americans struggled to define their position in the post-Revolutionary world and residing in the recently created state of Illinois, where social hierarchy was still very much in flux, aspiring men, such as Bennett, used concepts of honor to define themselves and used rituals of honor, such as the duel, to raise their standing in the community.

During the latter part of the eighteenth century and the early decades of the nineteenth, the United States witnessed the emergence of honor culture's ritualistic practice of dueling on an alarming scale. The sheer quantity of duels between 1800 and 1809 alone nearly eclipsed the total number of recorded duels in American history prior to 1800.[5] This trend continued into the second decade of the nineteenth century.[6] Thus, when Timothy Bennett and Alonzo Stuart took to the field in Belleville, Illinois, in 1819, they participated in a gentleman's ritual well established within the United States.

In response to the increased practice of dueling, especially in the political arena, antidueling factions began pressuring state legislators for a legal remedy to what they perceived as a societal plague. Although these factions were successful in getting dueling laws enacted, the impact of these early laws is difficult to assess. Dueling laws were in existence in the American colonies since the late seventeenth and early eighteenth centuries.[7] During this time the number of duels remained quite low.[8] Yet whether these laws were directly responsible for the low number of duels is unclear. What is clear, however, is that nineteenth-century legislators began enacting dueling laws in direct response to the increased number of duels between 1800 and 1820.[9]

With the number of duels clearly on the rise in open defiance of laws trying to prevent them, in the first two decades of the nineteenth century a new elite class of gentlemen, acting above the law, emerged. Originally honor was confined to the ranks of the landed aristocracy and was "inseparable from hierarchy and entitlement."[10] Yet, as the ideology of the American Revolution crept into the minds of a budding generation, the landed aristocracy was soon joined by the new leaders of society: lawyers, doctors, editors, and merchants. These capitalistic professions encouraged a competitive nature among American men that encouraged social mobility. As Jonathan D. Wells observed, "Middling southerners did consider themselves above the rural yeomen and urban laboring whites, and it appears other southerners recognized the higher status that a career as a doctor, grocer, or teacher might provide."[11] Thus it is not surprising that a large percentage of the duelists between 1800 and 1810 belonged to these capitalistic professions (see table 1).

This burgeoning middle class, therefore, paved the way for middling sorts to stake claim to the exclusive world of honor. This was especially true in the frontier settings found along the Mississippi River Valley during the first quarter of the nineteenth century.[12] Included among those settings was the small town of Belleville, Illinois, where two men of military background, Jacob Short and Nathan Fike, devised a plan to elevate themselves into the elite class of gentlemen.[13]

Jacob Short was not a stranger to the elite class of St. Clair County; however, by 1819 he found himself on the outside of that honorable group of men. Appointed captain to the Illinois militia in 1810, Short was elected to the General Assembly of Illinois Territory in 1812. Seemingly on the rise both militarily and politically, Short resigned his seat in the assembly in 1813 for undisclosed reasons.[14] Then, having "distinguished" himself during the War of 1812, Short was promoted to major of the 2nd Regiment of the Illinois Militia on January 13, 1817.[15] His tenure as major was rather brief. In August of the following year, Short resigned his commission, again for reasons unknown.[16] Thus, by the time of the Stuart-Bennett duel in February 1819, Short had resigned from the army, was out of politics, and, according to one source, had earned a reputation for drinking.[17]

As for Nathan Fike, the record is a little more lacking in terms of his activities prior to the Stuart-Bennett duel. On July 4, 1818, Fike was commissioned a captain in the 2nd Regiment of the Illinois Militia. Whether Fike knew Short prior to 1818 is not clear; however, his service in the 2nd Regiment brought him into direct contact with Short on a daily basis until Short's resignation the following month.[18] For however long Fike and Short knew each other, one thing was clear to their contemporaries; the two men enjoyed drinking together. According to James Affleck, Fike and Short "were a pair of young Bacchanalians, who made their haunt, and hibernated, at Tanehill's tavern," the local drinking establishment.[19]

Although it appears that Short was clearly on the rise socially in 1812, his status had taken a turn for the worse by 1819.[20] As for Fike the only recorded evidence suggests he may have been on the rise after receiving a captain's commission in 1818. Thus Fike and Short were, at best, on the fringe of the elite class of gentlemen in St. Clair County, Illinois, on the eve of the Stuart-Bennett duel. As one historian argues, "Short and Fike believed that a duel with them serving as seconds would elevate their social status and Bennett's in the community."[21] And Fike and Short found their opportunity to do just that in 1819.

That year Timothy Bennett and Alonzo Stuart became entangled in an affair of honor over their property. On numerous occasions a horse belonging to Bennett made its way into Stuart's adjoining field and trampled several rows of crops in addition to knocking down the fence that separated the two properties. Exasperated by Bennett's inability to control his horse, Stuart threatened to shoot the horse if a similar occurrence were to happen again. Days later Stuart made good on his threat, and he shot Bennett's horse. The pepper-loaded cartridge did little harm to the horse besides scaring the beast; Bennett, however, took insult with Stuart's actions. Thus what began as a trifling matter over a wayward horse now blossomed into an affair of honor, the result of which would prove fatal to both.

In the weeks that followed, tales of Stuart shooting Bennett's horse circulated throughout Belleville and became a matter of public discourse at Tannehill's tavern. What began as a personal affair between neighbors now gave way to public gossip. Left to its own devices, this gossip held the potential to ruin the reputations of both men. To stave off potential social discrimination, and encouraged by Fike and Short, Bennett issued a challenge to Stuart.

Already established within the community and seen as a gentleman by the likes of Fike and Short, Stuart possessed all the characteristics of a man of honor.[22] A duel with Bennett, therefore, seemed a natural matter of redress among gentlemen. Yet Stuart's actions suggested that he did not view Bennett as a social equal. The repeated altercations over the trespasses of the horse could have resulted in a challenge to duel from Stuart, but rather than issuing such a challenge to Bennett for failing to maintain control of his horse, Stuart chose to inflict harm on Bennett's property by shooting it. This course of action was reminiscent of a gentleman caning or whipping a man of inferior social status. Stuart's view of Bennett was seemingly in line with the assessment of Bennett by the community at large. In fact, in his contemporary account of the affair, James Affleck noted that Bennett was somewhat of an outcast in Belleville and that "the young men of the village were disposed to tease and plague" him.[23] This characterization has led one historian to argue that "Bennett, who many perceived to be a bully and ruffian, was below Stuart's social station and therefore rightfully deemed unworthy to participate in an affair of honor."[24] Although Stuart may not have viewed Bennett as a social equal, it is clear that Bennett viewed himself as an honorable man and, with Fike and Short supporting his claim, was prepared to confront the community's perception of him.

With his challenge to Stuart, Bennett put his honor in the other man's hands. Accepting the challenge would be tantamount to Stuart acknowledging that Bennett possessed honor, while declining the challenge would question Bennett's claim to honor. In his 1838 *Code of Honor,* John Lyde Wilson advised future duelists on this very point, noting that "when a note is presented to you by an equal, receive it." Implied within Wilson's statement was the notion that a gentleman should refuse a note from someone socially inferior.[25] By all accounts, then, the community's characterization of Bennett provided enough reason for Stuart to decline the challenge. Yet Stuart ultimately chose to accept the challenge.

Was Bennett more honorable than contemporary accounts have led historians to believe? Did Fike and Short convince Stuart that refusing Bennett's challenge would allow the community to question Stuart's own claims to honor? Or was this simply a case of an affair being hijacked by emotion and drunkenness, whereby a refusal to participate could be construed as cowardice? From the evidence only one thing is clear—Stuart was, at the least, reluctant to accept Bennett's challenge.

According to James Affleck, Fike and Short eventually convinced Stuart to accept Bennett's challenge by floating the concept of a sham duel. They suggested that they, acting as seconds, would oversee an affair where "the guns should be loaded with powder only."[26] According to Short and Fike's plan, the sham duel would "unmask" Bennett, the only participant unaware of the deceptive nature of the affair. In the words of honor scholar Kenneth Greenberg, "even men outside the culture of honor understood that the act of unmasking was the worst humiliation one could inflict on a gentleman."[27] This unmasking would ultimately deny Bennett access to the gentleman class, while placing Fike and Short on somewhat equal footing with Stuart as the perpetrators of the rebuke against Bennett.

Agreeing to the sham duel, Stuart met Fike, Short, and Bennett at the courthouse in Belleville. Although it seems quite brazen to conspire to violate the law while standing within the very building designed to uphold the law, the men were, in fact, meeting on the backside of the courthouse, which ironically was the location of their favorite local watering hole, Tannehill's tavern, to arrange the details of the affair.[28] Accordingly, "after the parties had made all the arrangements and were pretty well filled with Tannehill's whiskey," they exited the building and headed for the dueling grounds located "between the Snyder mansion and Main Street." Choosing a location that was considered "vacant . . . with only a few scattered trees," the principals were situated twenty-five steps apart.[29] Upon hearing the word uttered, Bennett discharged his weapon and struck Stuart in the chest. Stuart fell face-forward to the ground and died instantly.[30] As John Reynolds, presiding judge over the trials of Fike, Short, and Bennett, recorded years later in his *Pioneer History of Illinois,* Stuart "experienced an accidental death, that put an end to his usefulness and promise."[31]

Astonished at what had just taken place, Fike approached Stuart's body, turned him over, seized Stuart's gun and discharged it. This seemingly precautionary action of discharging a loaded firearm would cause much controversy in the trials that followed because the jury would be unable to determine if both guns had been loaded with bullets.[32] But for the moment, both seconds were left wondering what exactly had happened.

How was Bennett's gun loaded with a bullet if the rules of dueling had been properly followed? According to traditional practice, the seconds were in charge of the weapons on the field of honor. These men inspected and loaded the weapons and ultimately handed those weapons to their principals. The principals then held their weapons downward and away from their opponent until the word was given. Although some traditional practices (distance apart, how the "word" was given, and so on) were negotiable, the handling of the weapons was not. Yet, according to the testimony of Rachel Tannehill, who was nine or ten years old at the time, Bennett slipped something into his gun as he left the tavern for the dueling grounds. Later, at the trials of Fike and Short, the jury concluded that Rachel had witnessed Bennett loading a bullet into his weapon. This would prove highly unusual and suspicious to anyone familiar with the practice of dueling. To allow the principal to carry his own gun unsupervised before the duel and to not check the gun before giving the word, would have been anathema to dueling protocol. That such was done in this case gives rise to a number of theories. First, Rachel may have been mistaken in what she purportedly saw. Second, Rachel may have been coaxed into lying by someone who desired Bennett's conviction for murder. Or, most likely, the rules of dueling had not been properly followed owing to the inexperience of both Fike and Short in such matters.[33]

Almost immediately after the exchange of shots, Bennett, Fike, and Short were arrested and brought to the St. Clair County jail.[34] Once detained, Fike and Short were released on bond. Bennett, however, remained in custody until a trial could be scheduled, which required the Illinois legislature to call a special session and pass emergency legislation to appoint a judge, prosecutor, and jury for a murder trial in St. Clair County.[35] Securing authorization from the legislature, the newly appointed presiding judge, John Reynolds, began the trial of Fike and Short on June 15, 1819.[36] The court appointed Thomas Hart Benton to defend the two men.[37]

Thomas H. Benton was an interesting selection to serve as defense attorney. Residing at the time in Missouri, and not Illinois, Benton was also no stranger to affairs of honor.[38] In fact Benton had been involved in two duels with Charles Lucas in 1817 that eventually resulted in Lucas's death.[39] Why Benton was chosen to defend the participants of the Stuart-Bennett duel is not clearly known. Arguably his role as a leading lawyer in St. Louis coupled with his reputation for being a gentleman (stemming from the numerous affairs of honor in which he involved himself) convinced the Illinois legislature that he was ably suited to the task.[40]

Following the appointment of Benton as defense for Fike and Short, the court convened. The next morning James and Rachel Tannehill were called to the stand and given $100 each for their testimonies. Rachel's testimony that Timothy Bennett placed something into his weapon on the way to the dueling grounds was enough to convince the jury that Fike and Short were innocent of loading weapons for a duel. However, in an attempt to deny that a duel had ever taken place, Benton focused on a legal technicality found within the men's indictment. Specifically Benton argued that the use of the word "alleged" in referring to the duel between Bennett and Stuart suggested that the duel may not have taken place. Since Fike and Short refused to testify and no other witnesses could confirm that a duel actually occurred (James and Rachel Tannehill testified only to the fact that the men left the tavern carrying weapons), Benton argued that the jury could not convict his clients for an event that did not happen. Within minutes the jury returned acquittals for both Fike and Short, despite Rachel Tannehill's testimony that plainly implied that the four men left Tannehill's Tavern with the goal of fighting.[41] According to historian Dick Steward, "only a vigorous defense by attorney Thomas Hart Benton permitted the seconds to go free."[42] It is plausible that Benton's defense strategy was able to secure an acquittal on a wording technicality, but it seems more likely that the jury exonerated Fike and Short because, in light of Rachel's testimony, it was Bennett who loaded the fateful bullet, not either of the seconds. The short trial and quick acquittal of the seconds gave hope that Benton could also obtain an acquittal for Timothy Bennett; however, things took a dramatic turn.

While the community was enthralled with the trial of Fike and Short, Timothy Bennett plotted his escape. Held in a wooden cell, Bennett managed to acquire an awl, chiseled his way out of confinement, and fled to Arkansas, where he remained for nearly two years. Presuming he was safe from capture, Bennett began corresponding with his wife, who still resided in Illinois. Soon word of this correspondence reached the county authorities, including information that Bennett's wife planned to meet up with Bennett along the Mississippi River just outside of St. Genevieve, Missouri. On the appointed day, the St. Clair County sheriffs followed

Bennett's wife to the rendezvous point on the river, where they arrested Bennett, whom they then returned to stand trial in Belleville, Illinois.[43]

The case of *The State of Illinois v. Timothy Bennett* began on Friday, July 27, 1821. As he had done nearly two years earlier, Thomas H. Benton argued vigorously that the indictment against Bennett should be dismissed based on the use of the word "alleged" when referencing the duel between Bennett and Stuart. This time, however, Benton would not be as fortunate. The following day, July 28, the jury returned a guilty verdict. Judge Reynolds then sentenced Bennett to death by hanging.[44] To the people of Belleville, the verdict and penalty sent a clear message that Bennett's actions were not those of an honorable man.

Not ready to accept defeat, Thomas H. Benton appealed to Illinois governor Shadrach Bond for a pardon. Although it was a long shot—no governor had pardoned a convicted duelist since 1787—Bennett's chances were better than most since the seconds received acquittals and because Governor Bond had been involved in an affair of honor approximately a decade earlier.[45] Despite being a reluctant duelist himself, however, Governor Bond found no sympathy for Bennett's actions.[46] Taking a firm stance in punishing the state's first convicted murderer, Bond refused to issue a pardon, and on September 3, 1821, the State of Illinois executed Bennett.

Timothy Bennett became the first and only recorded duelist in American history to be convicted of murder and executed, which leads to the simple question of why. In an era when the number of duelists killed was on the rise, it would seem plausible that the number of convictions and executions for murder by duel would increase as well. But the evidence contradicts that assumption. Between 1800 and 1819, Americans were involved in 226 known duels, of which 121 (54 percent) proved fatal.[47] Yet, besides Bennett, no other duelist was convicted of murder nor executed in the first two decades of the nineteenth century.[48] In fact the history of the American colonies and United States combined records 1,095 duels, of which 450 (41 percent) proved fatal. Out of those 450 fatal duels, only eleven resulted in convictions—two for murder and nine for manslaughter.[49] As one early nineteenth-century chronicler of South Carolina noted: "It is to be regretted that among the many laws which crowd the statute book of Carolina, there are none that are calculated to suppress the practice of duelling. According to the letter of the law, duellists may be prosecuted for murder; but the uniform verdict of juries for more than thirty years has adjudged the offense to be manslaughter . . . the penalty of that offense, has in every instance been remitted."[50] What, then, made Timothy Bennett so unique? In assessing how honor culture influenced the Bennett case, it is imperative to acknowledge that Reynolds's decision to impose the death penalty was partially influenced by the timing of the case. The Bennett trial was the first murder trial in Illinois. Because the state had only recently been created, officials in Illinois felt it was necessary to enforce the laws to the utmost, lest the state become a haven for criminals. Making an example out of Bennett would send a clear message to those migrating to Illinois that murder, in any form, would not be tolerated. Thus it fell to the jury to find Bennett guilty and to Judge Reynolds to impose the maximum sentence—the death penalty.

As one source noted, "Reynolds had been hesitant in his 1821 murder trial of Timothy Bennett to impose the death penalty. If not for his sworn duty to rid Illinois of duels, he may not have sentenced Bennett to death."[51] Yet it was more than Reynolds's sworn duty to rid Illinois of duels that brought about Bennett's death. Similar to other states, the duel existed in Illinois despite laws prohibiting it. For Judge Reynolds to believe that he alone could excise dueling within Illinois by sentencing one man to death is a bit too optimistic or naïve. And Reynolds was neither. Therefore the jury's guilty verdict and Judge Reynolds's decision to execute Bennett not only rested on their adherence to the laws of Illinois, but also rested on their adherence to the community's concept of honor.

Bennett appeared to fit St. Clair County's definition of honor. He held property and a modicum of wealth, and it is clear that at least Alonzo Stuart recognized, howsoever reluctantly, Bennett's status when he accepted Bennett's challenge. However, Bennett was also an abrasive character who created more animosities than friendships among his neighbors, including Stuart. That Fike and Short would orchestrate an elaborate farce at Bennett's expense demonstrated that both men acknowledged Bennett's honor, but desired to sully it out of spite that Bennett, whom they viewed as a braggart and bully, held honor more securely within their society than did they.[52] If Fike and Short's actions acknowledged Bennett's honor, it appears the court system was reluctant to do the same. In their issuance of an indictment against Bennett, St. Clair County officials listed Bennett as a "laborer," which implied that he did not own his own property and, therefore, worked for someone else.[53] Although technically incorrect (Bennett did own his own farm), the label of "laborer," at least in honor culture terms, was tantamount to calling Bennett a slave. As Greenberg noted, "All insults were equal in the sense that they implied that someone had been reduced to a slavish condition."[54] Thus the indictment itself served as an insult to Bennett's honor and could have influenced the jury's decision.

Bertram Wyatt-Brown highlighted a similar instance when he related the story of Robert Bailey of Virginia, who facilitated gaming and sport for other elite men. Like dueling, gaming was illegal, yet elite men enjoyed the sport, and thus Bailey's services were in high demand—so much so that he gained enough wealth and status to buy a plantation, marry a daughter into the gentry, and almost win a congressional election. However, after insulting a group of women by refusing them the use of a hall, the women publicly labeled him a "gamester." After "the label of 'gamester' was affixed the sporting gentry shunned him; then the authorities felt bold enough to have him arrested for faro dealing," according to Wyatt-Brown. "The labeling process was essential to Bailey's downfall; it clarified at once how the public was to view the fallen gamester."[55] The same was true for Bennett. Once he was labeled a "laborer," what honor he possessed evaporated in the public's eyes.

History also abounds with anecdotal evidence of honorable men who displayed abrasive personalities and yet avoided criminal prosecution for dueling, much less execution for it. For instance Andrew Jackson demonstrated a "touchiness" that produced a surly nature; however, few would publicly deny that he possessed honor, and officials in Tennessee failed to prosecute Jackson for killing a man in 1806.[56] For a jury to convict Bennett solely on his personality, therefore, would seem too simplistic. There had to be more to Bennett's conviction and execution. It is plausible that Bennett's actions following his arrest also influenced the jury's verdict and Judge Reynolds's ultimate decision.

In the wake of his indictment and arrest in 1819, Bennett had to have questioned how an honorable man, as he aspired to be, could find himself in such a predicament. Determined to avoid further dishonor by pining away in jail awaiting trial, Bennett chiseled his way out of jail and began living a fugitive lifestyle in the wilderness of Arkansas and Missouri. While Bennett's actions may have appeared to be dishonorable to some, Bennett may have believed his only recourse as an honorable man was to escape what appeared to be a community's quest to dishonor him. Although Bennett's flight was almost unheard of in legal cases involving duelists, it was not without precedent. In fact the most famous duel in American history provided a model for Bennett to follow.

In 1804 Aaron Burr fled the state of New York to avoid an indictment for the murder of Alexander Hamilton. Realizing that his departure from New York would likely call into question his honor, Burr decided to state his reasoning for leaving. In a letter to his son-in-law, Joseph Alston, Burr proclaimed: "The event of which you have been advised has driven me into a sort of exile, and may terminate in an actual and permanent ostracism. . . . Every sort of persecution is to be exercised against me. A coroner's jury will sit this evening, being the *fourth* time. The object of this unexampled measure is to obtain an inquest of murder. Upon this a warrant will issue to apprehend me, and, if I should be taken, no bail would probably be allowed. You know enough of the temper and principles of the generality of the officers of our state government to form a judgment of my position."[57] Burr was meticulous in blaming his political foes for creating an atmosphere in which justice, according to Burr's definition, could not be properly administered. Sitting in jail without bail was an insult to Burr's honor, and, as a gentleman of honor, Burr would not willingly submit to such treatment. Thus Burr's withdrawal from New York to Pennsylvania and later to South Carolina was a demonstration of his ability to maintain his honor.[58] Was this why Bennett fled to Arkansas in 1819? Unfortunately Bennett never offered an explanation for his escape. This may have allowed the jury in 1821 to construe Bennett's actions as a haphazard flight made by a dishonored man rather than a noble act of a gentleman trying to maintain his honor.

In the case of Aaron Burr, after an initial disappearance into Pennsylvania, Burr openly visited with friends in South Carolina before resuming his role as vice president of the United States in Washington, D.C. Yet the authorities in New York and New Jersey were unable (or unwilling) to forcefully push for Burr's extradition, and eventually Burr was allowed to return to New York unmolested. Unfortunately for Bennett St. Clair County officials were not inclined to give up their pursuit of him. And although they would eventually give up the physical search for Bennett, the county sheriffs kept the investigation open, which ultimately led to Bennett's arrest two and half years later. Thus, if St. Clair County authorities had deemed Bennett's actions as honorable, they almost certainly would have been reluctant to find Bennett and bring him to justice.

Once Bennett's trial began, the events of the duel, as related by the testimonies of several witnesses, provided another reason why Bennett faced a unique punishment—the concept of a fair fight. A fair fight existed when two men voluntarily agreed to follow a community-accepted code of rules. The idea of a fair fight influencing the outcome of a court case was not a novel idea in 1821, when Judge Reynolds prescribed it and Bennett was found guilty by the jury. A decade prior to Bennett's duel with Stuart, David Ramsey recognized the inability of courts to convict duelists who fought in fair fights. In his *History of South Carolina*, Ramsey noted: "The trial of a person who has killed his antagonist in a duel, is now little more than an investigation of the fairness of the procedure. If the rules of duelling have been observed, and no advantage taken, an acquittal as above stated is a matter of course."[59] Even after killing Alexander Hamilton in 1804, Aaron Burr received favorable treatment from a large portion of the United States because the affair had been conducted properly under the code of honor. Accordingly "the Entire West and South accepted the outcome of the Burr-Hamilton duel as honorable to all concerned, and extolled Burr in proportion as the East maligned him."[60]

Thus it was under this concept of a fair fight that the actions of the seconds on the field immediately following Stuart's death were instrumental in determining Bennett's fate. The discharging of Stuart's pistol prevented a proper investigation into whether Stuart's gun had also been loaded. Judge Reynolds noted years later that "many individuals, who were acquainted with the transaction, seem to have doubts that the gun of Stuart was also charged with a ball. [While others] are disposed to believe that the parties, both Bennett and Stuart, had by some means their guns loaded with powder and ball to do execution on one another, or on both."[61] Without evidence and with the seconds refusing to testify, the jury received only Rachel Tannehill's testimony, which implied Bennett had acted dishonorably.

Bennett, though, was unaware that his duel with Stuart was designed as a sham duel. It seems only logical that, upon noticing that he held an unloaded pistol and believing Stuart's pistol was loaded, Bennett would have rectified the situation. Yet the jury thought otherwise. Even Judge Reynolds acknowledged the likelihood that the testimony provided painted Bennett as a dishonorable figure. In his history of Illinois, Reynolds noted, "This unfortunate affair . . . never did assume the character of a regular honorable duel."[62]

"In retrospect," asserted historian Dick Steward, "Bennett's real crime was not murder but the indecorous way he carried it out."[63] Yet it was more than that. Steward's assertion only skimmed the surface of why Bennett was executed. Bennett's death was a result of a number of factors coming together to create the perfect legal storm for a duelist in 1821. In addition to the perception of Bennett's actions on the dueling ground being dishonorable (that is, loading his pistol), there was the alarming rise in the number of fatal duels in the first two decades of the nineteenth century. Furthermore the death of Alexander Hamilton in 1804 created an anti-dueling fervor still being felt in 1821. As one source noted, "Some might say that if not for this 1804 duel [Burr-Hamilton] between these two famous politicians that Timothy Bennett would not have been executed in 1821."[64] Finally the state of Illinois, including Judge Reynolds and Governor Shadrach Bond, desired a clear message be sent to the residents of Illinois that murder would not be tolerated. Yet, even in punishing Bennett to the fullest, Judge Reynolds was forced to acknowledge that neither the law nor the execution of Bennett succeeded in eradicating the practice of dueling in Illinois. In fact Reynolds argued that the Stuart-Bennett affair had "no agency in putting down the barbarous and anti-Christian practice of dueling in this State, but it was the enlightened and Christian tone of public opinion that always banished this blood-thirsty practice of dueling from our borders."[65]

Fike, Short, and Stuart all failed in their attempts to either gain admittance into or remain within the world of honorable gentlemen. Nathan Fike lived a rather uneventful remainder of his life in St. Clair County.[66] Jacob Short, although acquitted of any wrongdoing, left St. Clair County and relocated to Menard County, Illinois, in 1822, where he died three years later.[67] And, of course, Alonzo Stuart, the only participant clearly within the circle of honorable gentlemen, was killed.

Of all the participants, Timothy Bennett was the only man to receive lasting fame. His story, although unique, provided a window into the larger world of honor culture during the early part of the nineteenth century. In its origins the Bennett-Stuart duel highlights how the concept of honor could push men to risk their lives over such a trivial matter as a wayward horse. Furthermore Bennett's arrest and trial were indicative of the growing opposition to dueling found throughout the United States and the legal attempts to eliminate the practice. Overall Bennett's story illustrated that regardless of the changing status of those who considered themselves honorable, society still bestowed honor on men using its own perceived ideas of what was truly honorable. Unfortunately for Bennett, who stood on the scaffold in 1821 defending his actions as those of an honorable man, claiming to be honorable meant nothing if the community believed a person to be otherwise.

TABLE 1. Professional Classification of Duelists between 1800 and 1810[68]

Classification	*Number of duelists*	*Percent of known professions of duelists*	*Percent of total duelists*
Military[69]	77	38%	29%
Lawyers	58	29%	22%
Doctors	17	7%	6%
Merchants	14	6%	5%
Students	13	6%	5%
Editors	9	4.5%	3%

NOTES

1. Early histories of the Stuart-Bennett duel refer to Bennett as William Bennett; however, this essay will use the name found in the Illinois court case of *The People v. Timothy Bennett.* See Sabine, *Notes on Duels and Duelling,* 64; Truman, *Field of Honor,* 78; Baldick, *Duel,* 124.

2. Bateman et al., *Historical Encyclopedia of Illinois,* 704.

3. Bennett was also the first man legally executed in the state of Illinois.

4. History has recorded Stuart's name in numerous ways, including Alfonso C. Stuart, Alphonso C. Stuart, Alfonso C. Stewart, Alphonso C. Stewart. This essay has chosen to follow Missouri dueling historian Dick Steward's use of Alonzo C. Stuart. See Steward, *Duels and the Roots of Violence in Missouri,* 40.

5. Between 1619 and 1799, a total of 140 duels were recorded within the United States (and the British colonies that formed the United States). Between 1800 and 1809, 115 duels were recorded within the United States. All statistics are derived from a database compiled by the author consisting of over one thousand duels. Part of this database is located in Byron, "Crime and Punishment?," appendix.

6. Between 1810 and 1819, a total of ninety-nine duels were recorded within the United States.

7. The following territories and states passed laws specifically addressing the issue of dueling: Pennsylvania (1682); Massachusetts (1719); Massachusetts (1728 revised); Virginia (1776); Massachusetts (1784 revised); Pennsylvania (1785 revised); Kentucky (1799); Tennessee (1801); North Carolina (1802); New York (1803); Mississippi Territory (1803); Pennsylvania (1806 revised); Georgia (1809); Tennessee (1809 revised); Virginia (1810 revised); Illinois Territory (1810); South Carolina (1812); Maryland (1816); New York (1817 revised); Tennessee (1817 revised); Louisiana (1818); Illinois (1819 revised); Arkansas Territory (1820). See respective state and territorial legal codes from each year provided.

8. Between 1619, when the first duel in the American colonies was recorded, and 1774, a total of forty duels were recorded across the American colonies.

9. The enactment of dueling laws on a large scale actually began with the Articles of War issued by the Continental Congress in June of 1775 and carried into the early nineteenth century.

10. Wyatt-Brown, *Southern Honor,* 4.

11. Wells, *Origins of the Southern Middle Class,* 10.

12. One need only look at the number of duels along the Mississippi River valley between 1803 and 1829 to understand the profound power dueling had on the community. During that time period, the number of duels recorded were: Louisiana, seventeen; Missouri, sixteen; Mississippi, sixteen; and Arkansas, four.

13. Official government documents record Fike's first name as Nathan; however, in the contemporary account of the Stuart-Bennett duel, James Affleck notes his first name as Nathaniel. See James, *Territorial Records of Illinois,* 60; *People v. Nathan Fike* indictment in *Transactions of the Illinois State Historical Society for the Year 1901,* 98; Affleck, "Stuart-Bennett Duel," 96.

14. It is highly likely that Short resigned his seat because his duties as an officer in the Illinois militia during the War of 1812 required his absence from the Illinois Territory. James, *Territorial Records of Illinois,* 12, 30, 86; *History of Menard and Mason Counties, Illinois,* 377.

15. Reynolds, *Pioneer History of Illinois,* 406; James, *Territorial Records of Illinois,* 44.

16. James, *Territorial Records of Illinois,* 60.

17. Affleck, "Stuart-Bennett Duel," 96.

18. Jacob Short resigned his commission on August 7, 1818. James, *Territorial Records of Illinois,* 60.

19. Affleck, "Stuart-Bennett Duel," 96.

20. *History of Menard and Mason Counties, Illinois,* 377; Reynolds, *Pioneer History of Illinois,* 368, 406; *Transactions of the Illinois State Historical Society for the Year 1901,* 96.

21. Steward, *Duels and the Roots of Violence in Missouri,* 40.

22. Stuart graduated from Dartmouth College and was licensed to practice law in Pennsylvania in 1812. He established a law practice in Illinois in 1817, where he earned a reputation as a "fine classic scholar and a well-read lawyer." Reynolds, *The Pioneer History of Illinois,* 344.

23. Bateman, *Historical Encyclopedia of Illinois,* 745.

24. Steward, *Duels and the Roots of Violence in Missouri,* 40.

25. J. Wilson, *Code of Honor,* 18.

26. Affleck, "Stuart-Bennett Duel," 96.

27. Greenberg, *Honor and Slavery,* 27.

28. As mentioned earlier Fike and Short were regulars at Tannehill's. For his part Stuart "was more frequent at Tannehill's bar than that of Judge Reynolds." Bateman, *Historical Encyclopedia of Illinois,* 745–46; Affleck, "Stuart-Bennett Duel," 96.

29. The customary distance of a duel involving pistols was ten paces or thirty feet. In this instance the use of "steps" likely refers to feet rather than paces. Thus the distance would be set at an acceptable twenty-five feet apart rather than an unusual seventy-five feet apart.

30. Bateman, *Historical Encyclopedia of Illinois,* 745.

31. Reynolds's use of the word "accidental" refers to Stuart's wrongful death and not to Bennett's innocence. Reynolds, *Pioneer History of Illinois,* 344.

32. Bateman, *Historical Encyclopedia of Illinois,* 745.

33. Ibid. part 2, 745–46.

34. *New England Galaxy,* April 2, 1819.

35. At the time of the Bennett-Stuart duel, St. Clair County lacked the legal ability to conduct a trial. The state legislature needed to pass laws authorizing the appointment of court officials and for sanctioning a trial in such haste. Bateman, *Historical Encyclopedia of Illinois,* 746.

36. After serving as a sergeant in Captain Whiteside's Ranger Company during the War of 1812, for which he would earn the nickname "Old Ranger," Reynolds opened a law office in St. Clair

County in 1814. In 1818 Reynolds was appointed associate justice of the Illinois Supreme Court. Reynolds, *History of Illinois,* 91.

37. Bateman, *Historical Encyclopedia of Illinois,* 705.

38. In 1813 Benton challenged William B. Lewis to a duel; however, Lewis refused to accept the challenge. Later that year Benton was involved in a bar room brawl with Andrew Jackson. McReynolds, *Missouri: A History,* 121.

39. Benton and Lucas were rival lawyers in Missouri. After a bitter campaign of words, the two men met on Bloody Island on August 12, 1817, where Lucas was wounded. Unsatisfied with the result of their first duel, Lucas demanded a second meeting on September 27, 1817. Choosing the same location, Benton mortally wounded Lucas. See Houck, *History of Missouri,* 77–80.

40. In addition to his two duels with Charles Lucas in 1817, Benton was involved in an affair of honor with Andrew Jackson in 1813 while residing in Tennessee. Steward, *Duels and the Roots of Violence in Missouri,* 62; Seitz, *Famous American Duels,* 158–68.

41. The acquittal came on June 17, 1819. *Transactions of the Illinois State Historical Society,* 96; *History of St. Clair County,* 187.

42. Steward, *Duels and the Roots of Violence in Missouri,* 40.

43. Affleck, "The Stuart-Bennett Duel," 96.

44. Ibid., 96.

45. Between 1752 and 1787, three duelists received governor's pardons, and an additional two officers in the Continental Army received reinstatement following their court-martials. See the following duels: Butler-Baker (1752), DeLancey-Haley (1771), Lt. Richardson–Lt. Triplett (1778), Lt. Peter Welch–Cpt. Barnes (1778), and Bradley-Swann (1787). Hendrix, *Down and Dirty,* 89; *Pennsylvania Gazette,* November 21, 1771; *New-York Journal,* November 21, 1771; Henry, *Letters of Patrick Henry,* 248; Sabine, *Notes on Duels and Duelling,* 305; Weeks, *Code in North Carolina,* 446–47; A. Watson, *General Benjamin Smith,* 139–40.

46. In 1808 then Colonel Shadrach Bond fought a bloodless duel with Rice Jones in the Indiana Territory. According to sources, after Rice's pistol misfired, Bond refused to fire his pistol and the affair was settled. Rees, "Bond-Jones Duel," 272–85; Hyde and Conard, *Encyclopedia of the History of Missouri,* 612; *Combined History of Randolph, Monroe, and Perry Counties, Illinois,* 103.

47. All statistics are derived from a database compiled by the author consisting of over one thousand duels. In using such statistics, it must be noted that the percentage of duels that resulted in a fatality are possibly inflated owing to the nature of reporting duels. It can be assumed that nearly, if not all, fatal duels were reported in order to explain the death to the community or family; however, it cannot be assumed that all nonfatal duels were reported. Thus it is likely the 54 percent fatality rate between 1800 and 1819 should be lower.

48. In 1818 a court convicted Malachi P. Varish of manslaughter and sentenced him to ten years imprisonment for killing I. Haney in a duel in New York. Boston *Recorder,* April 24, 1824.

49. Besides Bennett's murder conviction in 1818, Henry Philips was convicted of murder in absentia for killing Benjamin Woodbridge in Massachusetts in 1728. Of the nine duelists convicted of manslaughter, three were pardoned, one was branded on the hand, one was sentenced to ten years imprisonment, and the other four have no record of punishment. *Boston Evening Post,* June 22, 1741, April 22, 1775; *Boston Recorder,* April 24, 1824; *Denton Journal* (Md.), June 26, 1886; *New York Herald,* December 7, 1870; *New York Journal,* November 21, 1771; *New York Times,* September 10, 1852; *Providence Gazette,* April 20, 1765, September 21, 1771; *South Carolina Gazette,* September 20, 1787; Gamble, *Savannah Duels and Duellists,* 2–3; Hendrix, *Down and Dirty,* 89; Meleney,

Public Life of Aedanus Burke, 251; Sabine, *Notes on Duels and Duelling*, 279; Seitz, *Famous American Duels*, 294; Weeks, "Code in North Carolina," 446–47; A. Watson, *General Benjamin Smith*, 139–40.

50. Ramsey, *History of South Carolina*, 216.

51. Meggs, *99 Nooses*, 41.

52. James Affleck suggests that Bennett had become the butt of many jokes at Tannehill's tavern, which resulted in Bennett's incessant need to defend himself through either bragging or action. For example Affleck recounted the story whereby several men were teasing Bennett on his inability to shoot accurately. In response Bennett immediately grabbed his rifle and shot the head off of a chicken in the nearby yard. Bateman, *Historical Encyclopedia of Illinois*, 745.

53. *Papers in Illinois History and Transactions for the Year, 1901*, 99.

54. Greenberg, *Honor and Slavery*, 62.

55. Wyatt-Brown, *Southern Honor*, 346–47.

56. Ibid., 44; Cochran, *Noted American Duels*, 196–207.

57. Aaron Burr to Joseph Alston, July 18, 1804 in A. Burr, *Memoirs of Aaron Burr*, 328.

58. Isenberg, *Fallen Founder*, 268.

59. Ramsey, *History of South Carolina*, 216.[Deletion to match bib entry.]

60. Hulbert, *Ohio River: A Course of Empire*, 290.

61. Reynolds, *History of Illinois*, 140.

62. Ibid., 138–39.

63. Steward, *Duels and the Roots of Violence in Missouri*, 40.

64. Meggs, *99 Nooses*, 37.

65. Reynolds, *History of Illinois*, 140–41.

66. On March 4, 1843, Fike was appointed county commissioner overseeing the construction of a state road in St. Clair County. No record of his death has yet been found. "Act to Locate a State Road from William Brown's, Jr.," 269.

67. *History of Menard and Mason Counties, Illinois*, 284.

68. There were 268 recorded duelists from 1800 through 1810. The professional classification of sixty-six of those duelists is still unknown. Therefore column 3 is calculated based on 202 duelists, while column 4 is calculated based on 268 duelists. In addition to the classifications mentioned in table 1, duelists also belonged to the following classifications (number of duelists in parentheses): land speculators (3); court clerks (2); clergy (2); Indians (2); Negroes (2); farmer (1); teacher (1); and ironmaker (1). All data derived from author's personal database.

69. The classification "Military" refers to any duelist actively serving in the U.S. military and does not include men who would later join the military.

Christopher Michael Curtis

"NOT A JUDICIAL ACT, YET A JUDICIOUS ONE"

Honor, Office, and Democracy

James Gholson was not an aristocrat. At least he would not have been considered so in the measured context of economic influence and power in Virginia's slave-owning society in the 1840s. Neither could he have been mistaken for a "Virginia Cavalier"—that imaginative turn of phrase that Wilbur Cash used to characterize the ruling elite of the Old South. He was, to be sure, a slave owner and, as such, a vested member of that emergent ruling class that would, within two decades time, lead the state into the war to dissolve the Union. But even as a slave owner, Gholson did not meet the minimum standards of entry into the planter class, which, by its example and its insistence, exercised cultural hegemony over the social customs and mores of southern society.[1]

A more accurate depiction might convey instead that he was one of the many men who, given the tumultuous social relations of that period, found himself occasionally on the periphery of power but, more often, in the familiar confines of his locality where he was esteemed and respected. As the oldest son of an established family in Brunswick County he had shown the expected promise as a young man. He attended Princeton University and earned both a bachelor's and a master's degree, which provided him with a scholarly bent and a critical understanding of the classics that distinguished him from most of his peers. Yet upon graduation he followed a well-worn path and returned home to practice law. As was customary for young, ambitious lawyers, he appeared on the political stage of the state legislature to showcase his oratorical skills. As a participant in the famous Virginia debate over slavery in 1832, his zealous criticism of emancipationists' proposals garnered him statewide notoriety and catapulted him into the U.S. House of Representatives the following year. During his sole term in Congress, he aligned himself with the emerging Whig opposition against President Jackson's scheme to remove the federal deposits from the national bank and, in consequence, was defeated by his staunchly Democratic opponent in the next election. Despite these forays Gholson left no legacy of political achievement, and, upon his return home from Washington at the age of thirty-seven, he seemed to have washed his hands of political ambition in preference for the contentment of domestic life and professional practice. He abandoned any pretense of playing the country squire and, along with his brother, moved his family to Petersburg, where the law was more lucrative.[2]

Although he rejected the customary trappings of a southern gentleman, James Gholson was a man of honor. His honor was derived, however, more from the performance of his office than from any sense of class identity or aristocratic conventions. He held office as a judge of the general court from 1841 until his premature death seven years later. With origins in the seventeenth century, the general court was the oldest appellate court in Virginia, although its jurisdiction had been circumscribed following the Revolution. By Gholson's time, the judges of the general court were also assigned to ride circuit to hear all forms of cases on appeal from the county courts as well as some cases that fell under their original jurisdiction. Judge Gholson was given responsibility for the second circuit, which comprised the Southside counties of Norfolk, Dinwiddie, Nottoway, Amelia, Brunswick, Sussex, and Prince George as well as the city of Petersburg. The office was demanding. In one representative year, Gholson traveled 530 miles across the byways of the Tidewater and spent 117 days in session hearing and adjudicating the causes of his people. He decided 745 cases at law, 336 cases in equity, and ninety-six criminal prosecutions, in addition to commencing proceedings on another 1,099 causes.[3]

In donning the mantle of the judicial robe and riding circuit, Gholson performed an ancient rite. The act replicated a ritual of bringing the majesty of the law to the people that, in the lands of *jus commune,* dated back to the twelfth century. In exploring the origins of the English judiciary, Paul Brand has identified Henry II's division of the kingdom into six judicial circuits at the Northampton council, in 1176, as the earliest recorded reference to specifically prescribed judicial functions in Norman England. Three justices were appointed by the king to preside over each circuit, to determine and remedy verdicts, and to mete out justice in accordance with the principles of the realm. Judicial office thus represented a special commissioning by the king to ensure peace through the execution of the royal law and, as such, conveyed the honor of the crown on its officers. The specific manifestations of honor that emanated from judicial office—integrity, impartiality, knowledge, and wisdom—thus stood in contrast to the more familiar conventions of chivalry that had originated in the ancient martial duties of the nobility. Although the sharp social division between the nobility of the robe and the nobility of the sword, familiar in France, was not replicated precisely in Britain, judicial honor still developed distinctively there because it was derived from the performance of office.[4]

It was this particular sense of official honor that motivated Judge Gholson to cross a bustling Petersburg street one winter day in 1847 and assault Robert Ruffin Collier. Collier, a local lawyer, was a familiar occupant of the judge's courtroom, who, most recently, had publicly taken up the cause of legal reform. To that end he had published a pamphlet detailing the problems and abuses of the judicial affairs of Virginia, which he attributed, in sum, to the incompetence and partiality of its circuit court judges. Collier sent a personal copy of the pamphlet to Judge Gholson as well as to the legislative members of the Committee on Courts and Justice. Gholson took umbrage at what he believed to be personal accusations imbedded within a specious call for reform and, with pamphlet in hand, accosted Collier as he was walking down the street in order to confirm his authorship. No serious injuries seemed to have been sustained from the fray by either party—Collier claimed only "slight battery," but he characterized the attack as being delivered "with all the bodily strength of his honour in passion." Both men were escorted to the police office, where the magistrate refrained from arresting either of them once Collier gave his word "that he would not make an attack on Judge Gholson for 30 days."[5]

Judge Gholson immediately petitioned the Virginia House of Delegates to conduct a special investigation into his behavior. In doing so, however, he expressed less concern over the assault than in investigating the charges of malfeasance suggested by Collier's pamphlet. Gholson maintained that he had been indicted by Collier "not only with gross professional ignorance, . . . *but[,] . . . plainly and manifestly, with the specific crime of official partiality in the decision of a particular case.*" Gholson did not contest the facts of the assault. Yet he flatly pronounced all the charges of malfeasance as "absolutely and entirely false" and demanded that if the investigation found him guilty he "be degraded from" the office that he had dishonored and that his "name should be forever erased both from the list of judges and the hearts and memories of those who have heretofore honoured and esteemed [him]."[6]

The House of Delegates heeded Judge Gholson's request, as well as a subsequent petition from Collier demanding Gholson's removal from office. In late January 1847, the House formed a special committee to inquire into the charges. It met over the course of six weeks during February and March. Embracing liberal rules for the admission of evidence, it received depositions and heard testimony from more than one hundred witnesses, allowed cross-examinations and rebuttal witnesses, and even permitted Collier to introduce new evidence into the proceedings. It was an extraordinary episode that probed the standards and expectations of official behavior. In so doing it revealed the parameters of judicial honor and the pressures that democratic reform placed on the ancient conception of office.[7]

The confrontation between James Gholson and Robert Ruffin Collier was an affair of honor. Although it did not culminate in a duel, it conformed to the ritual and conventions of such an affair. The status, behavior, and authority of all the participants were presented for public scrutiny in order to demand a public judgment. In turn each of the participants—as well as those drawn into the conflict through circumstance—responded to these questions through public testimony in order to assert their authority and integrity. The actions of Judge Gholson, both the confrontation and his appeal for satisfaction from the legislature, reflected a formal process by which he asserted the honor of his office. He did so, however, against someone of relative social equality but of clearly unequal official status. Accordingly the affair necessarily departed from the familiar patterns often observed in the study of gentlemanly duels. Gholson's office proved the source of the conflict, but it also dictated the manner of resolution. In this case, therefore, the legislative committee room replaced the secluded meadow as the field of honor, where public satisfaction was determined. Despite this significant distinction, the protocols of language, confrontation, and satisfaction followed convention. Consideration of the affair, then, affords an opportunity to explore a variation on the well-studied contests between the planter elites and provides a different perspective from which to analyze the conceptualization and influence of honor in the Old South.[8]

Studies of honor in the American South have been singularly informed by the scholarship of Bertram Wyatt-Brown. This pathbreaking work resurrected honor as a concept of analysis to evaluate ethics and behavior. Drawing from the anthropological investigations of Julian Pitt-Rivers, Wyatt-Brown identified two distinct strands of honor that enabled the cultural hegemony of the planter class to disseminate across class (but not racial) lines. He posited a strand of primal honor premised on the dictates of evolutionary biology that served as a universal basis for conventions of masculine behavior. In the Old South, however, primal honor operated in correspondence with a code of gentility, which specifically informed the behavior and values of the planter class. Honor thus operated to reaffirm the authority of the master class but did so in a manner that reinforced the gendered conventions of manhood inherent in the lives of Wilbur Cash's plebian "man-at-the-center." The landscape of honor depicted by Wyatt-Brown was essentially syncretic and synchronic, however, and thus did not analyze how the concept changed over time and space; a limitation that he attempted to address more fully in his later work. The southern embrace of liberal democracy, the growth of evangelical Christianity, the increasing acceptance of commercial attitudes and behaviors, and the emergence of racial theory all imposed significant alterations to the inherited conventions of honor. Consequently, by Gholson's time, the chivalric conception of honor that informed the behavioral norms of the eighteenth-century Virginia planter was situated on a precarious perch between ambiguity and nostalgia.[9]

A century earlier Montesquieu had identified honor as the essential badge of aristocracy and the fundamental principle of monarchical governments. For Montesquieu, honor was a prejudice that demanded "preferences and distinctions" and that contrasted sharply with the ideals of equality and virtue characteristic of republican governments. Indeed honor formed the conventional basis of social inequality. Noblesse oblige was not expected of peasants or the bourgeoisie and thus served to define the parameters of the competitive realm in which to distinguish accomplishments among the nobility. In this manner Montesquieu believed that honor could "inspire the finest actions" in the search for aristocratic distinction, which, when "joined with the force of the laws," would foster the ultimate goals of moderated ambition in a monarchical government. Through honor the self-interest of the nobility served the good of the state and the common weal.[10]

William Doyle has contextualized Montesquieu's writings within the landscape of the French political crisis of the eighteenth century and the multiple theoretical efforts to reinvigorate the nobility. Slightly different economic stimuli produced similar efforts to revive an aristocratic political order in Great Britain and in its colonies as well. The exertions of Britain's Robinarchs and of Tidewater planters to reassert aristocratic honor and privileges paralleled the venality of French parvenu financiers during the last decades of the *ancien régime.* These efforts can be considered as calculated responses to what Eric Hobsbawm termed "the land crisis" of the eighteenth century: the political crisis stemming from traditional models of landed ruling classes being challenged by the wealth and influence of merchant capital. And given the specious claims of hereditary entitlement common to each of these groups, the assertion of honor assumed profound significance as a social marker of noble status.[11]

The particular qualities of honor associated with the southern planter class were born of this renewal. As such they developed from the distinct characteristics of the British colonial landscape and were grounded in the reciprocal feudal relations of landed status as articulated by the English common law. The honor of planters, like the chivalry of the nobility, emanated from their real estate. Slavery, or more accurately, the master-slave relation, made the concept of honor in the American South distinctive, but it was not the foundation of honor. The code of gentility performed by the colonial elite mimicked the pretensions of chivalry that informed the conventional behavior of the landed nobility.

These renewal efforts came to naught of course, and this "new nobility" was decapitated—both metaphorically and, in France, literally—by revolutions grounded in the rejection of natural inequality and hereditary right. Republican revolution thus demanded either honor's abandonment or its reconstruction. Montesquieu maintained that it was incompatible with republican government and contrasted the political attributes of honor with the role played by virtue in a republic. Defining virtue as the "love of the republic," he described it as a patriotic civic-mindedness, which he compared to the fond devotion that monks expressed for their order. He believed that virtue would necessarily replace honor in the austere and egalitarian climate of republicanism. Admittedly this substitution was, in his view, the great flaw in republican constitutions.

Thomas Jefferson took a more ambitious tack. Recognizing the ethical vacuum caused by the abolition of nobility, he sought to ground republican virtue in the very status of landholding that had been the source of noblesse oblige. In striking down the hereditary qualities of landholding, however, and replacing tenurial rights with the rights of ownership, Jefferson imbued Virginia's republican citizens with more autonomy than the nobility ever possessed. This autonomy, despite Jefferson's paeans to the "cultivators of the earth," actually subverted virtue and encouraged unfettered self-interest. The spectacular failure of his design became conspicuously evident as his sturdy and independent yeoman farmers fled to the lands of Kentucky, Illinois, Missouri, and Mississippi one step ahead of the sheriff's foreclosure notice.[12]

Expressions of chivalric honor persisted in this murky and transitory environment, however, especially in situations where agricultural success fostered economic inequality. Control over economic resources, most especially arable land and slaves, magnified the importance of planters in their isolated rural localities and allowed them to feign the attitudes of nobility. In the early decades of the nineteenth century, and perhaps a bit longer on the cotton frontier, successful planters could still play the cavalier without subjecting themselves to caricature. Even at that, however, the chivalry of the planter class represented only a faint image of aristocratic noblesse oblige. Wilbur Cash referred to it as a "fundamentally narrow and incomplete" conception of honor, which was ever-grounded on the "brutal individualism" of the frontier and thus never fully comprehended the social obligations of noble birth. Only in contrast with the emergent Yankee capitalist were southern planters allowed to sustain their charade.[13]

The advent of liberal democracy struck hard, however, at these increasingly archaic pretensions of nobility. Liberal personhood, although malleable to definition and discrimination, was essentially egalitarian, unlike real property. Slavery, the sole inequality unaffected by the southern embrace of liberal democracy, correspondingly found justification in Enlightenment theories of race that alleviated the social imperative for honor to govern the behavior of the master class. Furthermore the contemporary surge of evangelical Christianity reconciled postmillennial piety with the bourgeois spirit of improvement and refinement. This combination necessarily brought any and all customs, behaviors, and traditions under the severe scrutiny of social reform.[14]

None of these changes boded well for conventions of honor, particularly the chivalry-based formulations of the planter class. Accordingly James Gholson's alternative assertion of the ancient honor of the judiciary may have been found more acceptable by the middle of the century than the hyperbolic indignation of a besmirched planter. Judicial honor was connected intrinsically to the rule of law and, accordingly, proved to be more amenable to republican reforms than the chivalric model. Laura Edwards has documented the critical role of magistrates in the function of local governance and in keeping the "people's peace" during the initial decades of republican government. Magistrates oftentimes were not legal professionals but, instead, were prominent citizens drawn from the local community. In the performance of their judicial office, however, they typically received deference and honor from a "republicanized" community committed to the rule of law as the basis of local governance. Edwards contrasted the local determination of justice with the more formalistic circuit courts where the noble features of judicial office appeared even more pronounced with all the majestic rituals of court days.[15]

Yet, as the encounter between Gholson and Collier revealed, the judiciary was not immune from the institutional scrutiny arising from the rage for democratic principles. By 1847 judicial offices often appeared as the last vestiges of aristocratic rule in a democratic culture and, as such, were ripe for reform. Reformers called specifically for making state judicial offices subject to popular election. Beginning with the Mississippi Constitution of 1832, and more influentially following the New York law reforms in 1846, measures implementing a popularly elected judiciary spread across the nation. Within eight years, twenty additional states, including Virginia, had recast the foundations and responsibilities of state judicial offices by making them subject to popular election. Certainly there was a democratically infused logic to the reforms: ever since the council of Northampton judges had filled their offices at the behest of the sovereign. Now the sovereign was the popular will, and elections offered a democratic mechanism to divorce judicial office from any lingering pretensions of nobility.[16]

Yet judicial reforms can be attributed only in part to democracy run amok. Other issues of law reform, too, like codification, affected the influence and the authority of the judiciary. Efforts to standardize and formalize law, often expressed as a preference for the positive commands of legislation over adjudicated remedies, tended to diminish the traditional autonomy of the judiciary in preference for a more technocratic and consistent model of judicial review. Judges who did not conform to this new formalist model often found themselves at odds with local legislatures much to their professional peril, and not only in the American South. As John McLaren has illuminated, issues of judicial authority and behavior recurred as significant concerns throughout British settler societies during this golden age of law reform. Judges were no longer tasked with simply keeping the peace by resolving immediate and local issues. Rather they were expected to adjudicate on the basis of national and imperial—and thus ideological—policies designed to create consistency in the administration of the law. Consequently the liberal transformation of the English common law demanded a corresponding reconceptualization of judicial office and its relation to popular authority.[17]

The specific questions of official behavior and propriety arising from the confrontation between Gholson and Collier can thus be considered in this larger context of law reform and the democratic reconstruction of judicial office. Collier's pamphlet, *Some Observations on the Law Affairs in Virginia,* which provoked the assault, was written putatively as a call for legal reform. It was circulated in the midst of public discussion on reform that corresponded with the ongoing codification project being carried out by the legislative-appointed revisers, Conway

Robinson and John Mercer Patton. Collier's exposé, published in January 1847, was actually a compilation of thirteen editorials that had already appeared anonymously in the local newspaper, the Petersburg *Republican,* starting in late October. These pieces covered a broad range of issues and reflected familiarity with the law reform movement in Virginia as well as in other states. Collier attributed most of Virginia's problems, however, to the sheer incompetence and malfeasance of the judiciary, especially those judges serving on the circuit courts who he characterized as "men who derive more respectability from office than they impart to it from their ability and fitness for the service."[18]

Collier drew support from the recent writings by Conway Robinson calling for judicial reform, but he went much further in blaming the problems on the judiciary. He was prone to see significant consequences arising from judicial independence. For Collier the judiciary represented the most dangerous branch of government. Emphasizing the role of the courts in determining property disputes, he noted that "no branch of . . . [government] more intimately" intersects with the "interests [of] its citizens than the Judiciary." Only judges could "infringe those doctrines" of "the rights of person and property, without exciting speedy and resolute resistance" from the citizenry. In part, he argued, this was because "the wheels of other departments are of intermittent action," but the courts were "in constant exercise." Subversion occurred by seldom-read decisions and opinion—hardly attracting the notice of the public. He implored his readers to: "WATCH THE JUDCIARY"—and its power to dispose "the property, liberty, life, and, to some extent, *the honour,* of individuals." In this manner he inverted the traditional honor ascribed to official service and cast it instead as a mere mechanism for power, exploitation, and usurpation.[19]

If Judge Gholson subscribed to the conventions of the ancients to guide his behavior, his adversary embraced the more ambiguous standards of the modern age. Robert Ruffin Collier was not a Virginia Cavalier either. He was, rather, a man of his time. And the times were flush—to borrow the contemporary expression of Judge Joseph Glover Baldwin from his period classic, *The Flush Times in Alabama and Mississippi.* Baldwin referred to the new commercial age as "the Age of Brass" and "the era of the second great experiment in independence," which he characterized as an era "of credit without capital, and enterprise without honesty." Such conditions fostered an environment where men-on-the-make, like Collier, could easily rise above the circumstances of their birth—or, just as easily, fall.[20]

Rise and fall he did. During the course of Collier's professional life he managed to achieve some relative stature and, in 1863, was elected to the Virginia's wartime senate. But it was a long path to this attainment. His ancestry claimed some colonial personages of note, but his direct genealogy ran from a poorer line. His grandfather had settled the family on military bounty land in Kentucky following the Revolution. His father was also a soldier who settled his wife and ten-year-old son in Dinwiddie County before going off to die during the war in 1814. Despite his fatherless condition, a young Robert Collier managed to enroll in the Methodist Ebenezer Academy in Brunswick and excelled sufficiently to gain admission to the University of Virginia. He graduated from there in 1826, married Mary Ann Davis, the daughter of Samuel and Frances Davis, and the following year she gave birth to their first of six surviving children.[21]

Collier was admitted to the Petersburg bar, and his life seemed full of promise. In 1829 he published a book, *Original and Miscellaneous Essays,* which he dedicated to Virginia legal luminary Benjamin Watkins Leigh. The book included sundry essays on legal procedures, scientific observations, an address to the students at Ebenezer Academy, and two self-improvement essays. By 1840 Collier presided over a large household of ten family members and twelve slaves and maintained a consistent law practice. The following year, however, he was presented before a grand jury for his involvement with an illegal faro bank run out of a local hotel. Testimony from the subsequent case revealed that he had faced recurrent problems with gambling and debt during the previous decade.[22]

Collier's gambling debts seemingly served as the source of conflict between him and Judge Gholson. In July 1844 the attorney found himself in the familiar environs of Gholson's Petersburg courtroom, not as a litigator but as litigant in a suit involving a personal debt that he owed to a local bank. The judge's brother, Thomas Saunders Gholson, served as his defense counsel along with A. M. Spooner. Collier's past gambling problems were well known in the community, but he now professed to finding salvation in the local Presbyterian congregation and to reformation. Indeed, in this instance, he explained, he was actually working undercover to expose the particular treacheries of gambling houses to the unknowing public. Court records indicate that he did publish a pamphlet on the evils of gaming, but, despite his extraordinary efforts to promote the public good, the case was decided against him. Judge Gholson ordered him to pay his $17,000 debt. Some witnesses who later testified before the special committee attributed Collier's enmity toward the judge as arising from the ruling.[23]

Collier told a slightly different story about his prior relationship with the judge. In the petition he submitted to the legislature immediately following the assault, he omitted any reference to the ruling against him. He complained, however, that during another trial, while he was serving as defense counsel, Judge Gholson had suddenly interrupted the proceedings to berate him in an inappropriate and unprofessional manner. Collier suggested that a verbal confrontation ensued leading him to recommend to the judge that he be held in contempt if his behavior was truly out of line. He admitted that he hoped to be charged so that a jury might decide who was in the wrong. Gholson did not comply, and his courtroom authority went unchallenged by anyone else. Collier considered this encounter the source of a persistent animus that he suggested the judge had manifested against him leading up to the assault.[24]

A few days later, Collier offered a more complicated and protracted narrative of personal indignation. In another petition to the House of Delegates, he specified five additional charges as indictments against Gholson's judicial conduct. He accused the judge of being either "grossly neglectful of his official duty," or else conniving, in "a breach of trust," to defraud Charles B. Caldwell, an underage heir, who held a $2,000 security bond in a case involving the payment of debts on an estate. Caldwell joined his retainer with a larger bond held by the firm of Thomas Gholson and William Townes after Collier joined the case as counsel for an additional creditor. Judge Gholson, as presiding judge, ordered additional security set aside. Collier suggested a collusive scheme between the judge and his brother to defraud the younger bondholder. He also charged Gholson with sheer incompetence in attempting to determine a probate case in the Prince George Circuit court and further took the judge to task for allowing a commonwealth attorney, who had been convicted of failing to pay out money to his client, to continue to practice at the bar in his circuit. In sum Collier concluded that Gholson had exercised "the powers of his office" with the implicit intent "to cripple some lawyers practicing" in his courts while simultaneously giving "undue aid to others."[25]

The explicit nature of these charges against Gholson undermined Collier's disclaimer that the accusations made in his *Observations* were not defamatory of the judge. When first published in the newspaper, his statements, despite their anonymity, had drawn attention back to Collier and generated speculation about his authorship because of his well-known bias against Gholson. Indeed, a year earlier, Collier had made public claims that he could have impeachment proceedings brought against Gholson. On November 18, 1846, he responded to the speculation, acknowledging that his letters had "excited some talk," and felt compelled to disavow that his proposed reforms reflected any personal animosity. Without explicitly repudiating the claim that they were aimed at Gholson, however, he explained that he "never expressed an opinion derogatory to the integrity of any officer, high or low, in our courts of justice without first having stated such opinion, face to face, to such officer." He continued by protesting that "to suppose that these letters are written with design to reflect on any particular Judge in the circuit courts or Court of Appeals, and not for the sole aim of bringing about some change, is to impute to the writer impulses unworthy of the respect which, he believes, is demanded by the sentiments and suggestions which these letters contain."[26]

Despite this protest of intentions, Collier refrained from taking public responsibility for the letters until January, when he published them in pamphlet form. He gave no explanation for why he initially published the letters anonymously or why he then decided to attach his name to them in pamphlet form. Certainly it was not unusual for the time to publish anonymously or under a pseudonym, and he had published his earlier *Original and Miscellaneous Essays* anonymously—although he did publicly sell them and identified them as his own. Intriguingly, when he took credit for the writings, he did so in a big way and had a copy delivered to Gholson.

Despite previous suspicions it was only when Collier took public responsibility for his comments that Judge Gholson confronted him and assaulted him. Gholson followed the conventions of honor. He did not—as far as can be told—respond to the anonymous innuendo printed in the newspaper. When the assault on his character became personal, that is, when the accusations were attributable to another person, he responded in kind. He defended his honor against a man, not against allegations. From this perspective his assault looks far less rash and impulsive. When Gholson weighed his actions relative to the expected behavior of his office, he concluded that the assault was "not a judicial act, yet a judicious one." And demanding further satisfaction, Gholson immediately petitioned the legislature for an investigation to clear his name.

The House of Delegates moved swiftly to address the issue. On January 26, the day after they received Gholson's petition, they adopted a motion to form the select committee and appointed its members the following day. John W. Syme, the delegate from Petersburg, served as chair of the investigation. Collier's first petition bringing charges against Gholson arrived the day after. The ten-member select committee convened on Saturday, January 30, and, after acknowledging the receipt of Collier's additional charges, passed a resolution authorizing the clerk of the House to issue subpoenas "for such witnesses as may be required either by Judge Gholson or Mr. Collier." More than one hundred names—most of the bar practicing on the Second Judicial Circuit and many members of Petersburg's professional class—were submitted by one or the other party to be called as witnesses.[27]

Things quickly went awry for Collier. Reconvening on February 10, the committee subpoenaed Collier to testify to the charges he had made under oath. Collier refused. The committee ruled him in contempt and, undoubtedly at wit's end, appealed to the full House of Delegates for guidance. The House passed a resolution confirming that Collier was indeed in contempt for refusing to testify but allowed that if he changed his mind it would become inexpedient to prosecute him. Collier then recanted. He composed a letter to the committee explaining that his initial refusal represented a strategy to challenge the authority of the select committee. He believed that the committee did "not sit *in proprio jure*"—a garbling of the Latin phrase meaning "with its own authority"—and therefore could not call its own witnesses. He now acknowledged that the House resolution confirmed the committee's authority, and, lacking any other body to which he could lay further appeal, he acquiesced in their decision.[28]

The committee received the first witness testimony on February 13. Given the large number to be heard, they established a procedure for propounding questions to the witnesses. Once sworn, witnesses were given written questions by the principles to which they were to respond in kind. Cross interrogations were permitted but in the same form. Initially the committee called the witnesses and allowed them to read their own answers to the questions, but as the hearing dragged on over several days, the committee had the two principles read the testimony of their witnesses into the record. The change reflected an inability to keep all the witnesses in town for an extended time, but the effect was to have Gholson and Collier standing together in the room, *mano a mano,* presenting testimony on their own behalf.[29]

The process also encouraged the creation of a standard list of questions to be propounded to most of the witnesses. Collier prepared four questions, which he posed to all his witnesses:[30]

1. Does the late assault and battery on Robert R. Collier by Judge Gholson in the town of Petersburg injure the judge's standing in the estimation of the virtuous portion of that community and detract from his dignity and weight of character in the judgeship? And what is your own opinion?
2. What is the character of R. R. Collier for the observance of the cardinal virtues in his business and intercourse with society, and what is his usual deportment; courteous and respectful or otherwise?
3. Has there not for many years been made by said Collier an attempt to bring about a reform on the subject of gambling at cards, and has he not thereby incurred the hostility of certain citizens of former high standing and influence?
4. Did you think that the letters on the Judiciary recently published in the *Petersburg Republican* were intended to reflect on any particular judge, or that the pamphlet in any part of it was intended to reflect on Judge Gholson except the note on page 26?

The questions naturally revealed more than the answers they provoked. Not surprisingly Collier first inquired about how the assault would affect the judge's professional standing in the community. He sought to demonstrate that Gholson had been dishonored by his behavior and thereby demonstrated himself unfit for office. Unfortunately for Collier even his own witnesses generally failed to consider Judge Gholson to be publicly discredited. The response of G. W. Warren was typical: "I am of the opinion that the character and standing of Judge Gholson will sustain little or no injury in this community, nor will his usefulness as a Judge be impaired." Warren acknowledged that "many of [Gholson's] friends regret the occurrence, and had they been consulted would no doubt have advised against it." George Scott expressed similar sentiments. He professed "that as a christian man I cannot justify anyone in the commencing [of] a street fight, but so far as I can judge of public opinion, Judge Gholson has not lessened himself as a citizen or in his official capacity."[31]

Indeed the framing of Collier's first question undermined his efforts to demonstrate public shaming. Many of the witnesses, like Hugh Nelson, expressed a private opinion that "it does distract from the dignity and weight of character, of any one holding such an office as that of judge to be the assailant in a fight" but offered that he was "unable to say" what the effects of the assault were "on the minds of the virtuous part of this Community." Not everyone parsed the question so exactly, and a few witnesses, like George McNeese and the Reverend E. Sanders, simply presented strong indictments against Gholson's actions. Nonetheless the weight of the testimony proved more ambivalent. Stephen Wells summarized the general consensus: "My own opinion is that conservators of the peace ought not to violate it as readily as other persons, but there are circumstances in which they might be justified in doing so. Not having read the pamphlet, I cannot say whether this would be considered one of the cases that would justify such an assault."[32]

More revealing was the fact that three of the four questions posed by Collier addressed his own reputation in the community. He asked his witness to validate his own character. Overall witnesses offered favorable comments in response to his second and third questions. Descriptions of Collier's character were generally succinct and formulaic. He was a man "respected" in the community and was "courteous" in his relations. Others noted more cryptically that they knew of "no reason" to doubt his conduct was "less than professional." Thomas Gholson and William Townes, however, testifying on behalf of Judge Gholson, offered more damning testimony. Thomas Gholson testified about Collier's gambling problems, and Townes responded in detail to the false allegations of fraud pertaining to the security bond. Indeed even Collier's staunchest supporters necessarily devoted more space to testimony about his own reputation than they did to scrutinizing Judge Gholson's behavior. In this context the committee's demand that Collier provide sworn testimony is telling. His reputation was suitable enough to level charges, but despite the very public nature of the assault, the burden of proof fell on him to prove that Judge Gholson's actions were dishonorable.[33]

By Friday, February 19, Collier had had enough. He requested the committee to "express an opinion" as to whether or not they considered him a "voluntary accuser." The committee confirmed that he volunteered his accusations, and Collier responded with a petition to withdraw his charges against Judge Gholson. He had not regarded himself as a voluntary accuser when he issued his five indictments, he explained, but believed instead that he had been commanded by the committee to do so. He now asked leave, although he promised to provide any additional evidence requested by the committee "compatible with the nature and extent of the investigation." The committee, apparently less than amused with Collier's fickleness, rejected his petition outright and declared "that at this stage of the investigation after a mass of written testimony had been taken . . . it would be [an] injustice to Judge Gholson, to have the proceedings thus arrested."[34]

The committee continued to receive witness testimony for another week before closing down the hearing. They intended to reconvene on Monday, March 1, to hear the direct arguments of Gholson and Collier, but other pressing business in the legislature pushed the meeting back until late in the evening of March 6. Collier delivered a final address on his petition and charges—one might surmise, in a half-hearted fashion. Thomas Gholson replied with the closing argument on behalf of his brother. In the end the select committee declared that the weight of the testimony offered by the witnesses summoned by both parties furnished "a volume of irresistible and conclusive evidence of the eminent ability, mild and courteous demeanor, diligence and inflexible uprightness and integrity of Judge Gholson." As to the charge of assault, the committee "found it unnecessary to express any opinion upon this charge" other than to comment that it was "certainly not deserving the legislative action of this General Assembly."[35]

A stronger exoneration of Judge Gholson could hardly have been delivered. Yet the public confrontation continued for another six weeks. Following the committee's report, Thomas Gholson published a summary of his testimony in order to more publicly restore the reputation of his brother. It also reflected an effort to clear his own name, which Collier had disparaged in the testimony concerning Charles Caldwell. Collier responded a week later renewing his charges against the judge, disputing the integrity of Thomas Gholson, and creatively suggesting that the legislative committee had actually vindicated his claims of judicial impropriety. The language in these publications was deeply personal, openly challenging the honor and character of the respective writers. Both men dismissed the other as a liar and a fraud. After stumbling through a month of sworn proceedings before committee, Collier rediscovered his voice. He published sixty pages of material in two weeks recounting every aspect of the hearings and levying insults at the character of Thomas Gholson. Most notably he relayed the story of Thomas Gholson's own gambling crises when, as a young man, he had lost a portion of his father's fortune at the card table while attending to family business in Mississippi. The personal allegation provoked another published response from the younger Gholson examining the "life and character" of Collier. He characterized the accusations against him and his brother as "vicious" and arising from "mental derangement." Collier naturally responded with an "Appendix" of his own in which he replied to Gholson's charges page by page. He wondered why the Gholsons continued pursuing the matter if their honor had been vindicated by the committee and concluded his diatribe by dismissing "the abuse and vile insinuations" made against him as a "dead body . . . to be interred in the public scorn."[36]

The exchange stopped as abruptly as it began. It is possible that Thomas Gholson realized that his efforts to publicly champion the committee's ruling had backfired, and instead his brother's name was still being dragged through the mud. Yet he also had learned that Collier simply fed off publicity. His previous disgraces had made him immune to the strictures of honorable conduct. Accordingly, in the end, Thomas Gholson simply sought to expose Robert Collier to the public. He made it clear that Collier was not a man of honor; he was not who he pretended to be. Any allegations made by Collier against him or against the judge had no standing among the community. The younger Gholson closed his "Examination" by declaring that he had "torn . . . the veil" from "this pretending reformer," who had for more than fifteen years attempted to fool the community and had been engaged in "the most systematic hypocrisy," as well as the "deepest malignity."[37]

The death of Judge Gholson from pulmonary failure the following year allows for a final consideration of the affair. The existing evidence does not suggest any relation between the disease and the stress of the contest, but it is a fair point for consideration. What is written, however, clearly reveals the full vindication of Gholson's reputation. His honor had been asserted and restored. And it was a manifestation of honor specifically tied to his office. His obituaries testify to this fact by specifically emphasizing his qualities as a judge. The *Petersburg Republican,* the paper in which Collier originally had published his essays, referred to Gholson as "the gifted and the good, the upright Judge and the accomplished scholar, the elegant gentleman and the devoted friend." It characterized his official tenure as having been discharged "with unflagging fidelity, with unwearying industry and with no common ability." The eulogy concluded by noting that few would deny that the judge "commanded an unreserved confidence and the sincerest esteem of those who were associated with him." Thomas Ritchie Jr.'s *Richmond Enquirer,* typically less than effusive in directing any praise to its Whig political rivals, announced the death by proclaiming Gholson as "one of Virginia's purest and best sons," whose "conduct as Judge won the admiration of all who were acquainted with him." No mention was made of the assault or the legislative inquest, not even an oblique reference to any unpleasantness.[38]

In October, when the circuit court convened in Amelia County for its first term following the judge's death, William Booker, the clerk of the court, presented a resolution from the members of the bar mourning the loss of Judge Gholson. It spoke of the public sorrow for the loss of a man "whose ability and longevity as a Judge, and accomplishments as a gentleman, had endeared him to the members of this Bar, and won for him honor." To commemorate that honor, the lawyers of the second circuit vowed to wear a "badge of mourning for thirty days."[39]

The Gholson-Collier affair thus affords a fixed point from which to assess changing conceptualizations of official honor during the heady days of democratic reform in the slaveholding South. It suggests the persistence of recognized conventions of honor for the judiciary, albeit in a manner increasingly divorced from their noble origins and increasingly circumscribed by public opinion. Judges were expected to answer for their behavior and, what is more significant, in a growing number of places where they stood for popular election, for their decisions as well. Gholson was vindicated, even for his daylight assault on Collier—but he had to go to extraordinary lengths to assert his honor against an accuser who lacked either the appropriate class status or even the bourgeois refinement necessary to make any serious pretentions of honor in his own right. Collier already possessed a notorious reputation in the community. In this sense the seriousness with which the select committee pursued its charge stands as a telling measure of the climate.

Neither was Judge Gholson alone among his peers in being subjected to the spectacle of public trial. The highly charged politics of liberal democracy frequently brought the official behavior of judges under public scrutiny. More research remains to be done; but the efforts of Georgia creditors to disqualify Judge Henry Benning and the decade-long effort to impeach Judge John C. Watrous from his seat on the federal bench in Texas offer provocative glimpses into the challenges posed to judicial authority by the political partisanship and commercial associations of the age. Admittedly, public investigations into judicial behavior were often warranted. Judges in the nineteenth-century South routinely involved themselves in political and commercial activities that would have cast aspersion on nobles of the robe a century earlier. Yet these same shifting behavioral conventions for officeholders provide windows on the changing role of official honor in a democratic society. Equally revealing are the very public processes by which these new behaviors were often measured and evaluated by the community.[40]

The form of the Gholson-Collier affair offers insight as well into changing conceptions of judicial honor. There was no challenge to duel, nor could there have been. Virginia's constitution and laws prohibited officeholders from any involvement in a duel. Ironically, then, any effort by Gholson to assert his honor in classic chivalric form would have potentially cost him the honor of his office. Admittedly these laws were breached by southern gentleman on occasion. Certainly both Gholson and Collier would have been familiar with one such local tragedy, when George Dromgoole (Gholson's political rival for congress) killed a close friend in a duel over a drunken slur. The outcome shook the community. But beyond this near experience, Gholson was constrained in the manner by which he sought to defend his honor and the dignity of his office. Clearly his assault on Collier—for that is what it was—reflected an effort to confront publicly his accuser and to project physically his masculinity. Yet he did not do so in a manner that ritually connected him with the martial origins of an aristocratic class. Judges had long ago abandoned the belief in trial by ordeal. Instead he opted to pursue a course by which, through the testimony of his friends and the judgment of his peers, he could preserve the honor and dignity of his office. And, of course, it was that form of official honor that he held most dear and that guided his actions—not some distant image of a rustic cavalier.[41]

NOTES

1. W. J. Cash, *Mind of the South*. In 1840 Gholson owned seven slaves; all but one of them was female. 1840 United States Federal Census. http://search.ancestrylibrary.com/search/db.aspx?dbid=8057 (last accessed December 23, 2013).

2. Fleming, *The South*, 396 (d. reported erroneously as May 3); *Biographical Dictionary*, 1085–86. See also Simms, *The Rise of the Whigs*. The family genealogy can be found in Black, *Families and Descendants*. Gholson married Charlotte Louisa Cary in 1835, and they had two daughters, but one died as a child in 1841.

3. Shepard, "Judges," MS 7:3 JK 3901.81 Sh473:1; Munford, "Abstract from the Reports"; Headlee, "The Virginia"; and Howard, *Commentaries*, 683–701.

4. Brand, "Judges and Judging," 3–36; Muessig, "Superior Courts," 209–33; Doyle, *Venality*.

5. Collier, *Some Observations*; "Petition of Robert R. Collier"; Testimony of John McNeese, Answer #5, Folder 10, and Collier petition requesting inclusion of Judge Gholson's confession into the record," Loose paper, Folder 4, in "Proceedings of the Select Committee Appointed to Investigate the Charges Preferred against Judge James H. Gholson," Library of Virginia, Mss 4461.

6. "Petition of James H. Gholson, January 25, 1847." Italics are from the original.

7. "Proceedings of the Select Committee."

8. Stowe, *Intimacy and Power*, 5–49. Stowe distinguished three forms of experience, albeit always contingent and overlapping, in which specific affairs established, asserted, and served honor. Also see Bruce, *Violence and Culture*.

9. Wyatt-Brown, *Southern Honor and Shaping of Southern Culture*. See Greenberg, *Honor and Slavery*; Gorn, "Gouge and Bite," 18–43; and Mayfield, *Counterfeit Gentleman*, especially his analysis of John Pendleton Kennedy's *Swallow Barn*, 3–24.

10. Montesquieu, *Spirit of the Laws*, book 3, chs. 6, 7, 8; Doyle succinctly summarizes Montesquieu's discussion of honor and its political necessity for the French monarchy in *Aristocracy and Its Enemies*, 18–22.

11. Doyle, *Aristocracy and Venality*; Rozbicki, *Complete Colonial Gentleman*; Hobsbawm, *Age of Revolution*, 149–67; and Weaver, *Great Land Rush*.

12. Montesquieu, *Spirit of the Laws*, book 5, ch. 2. Jefferson, *Notes on the State of Virginia*, query 19.

13. Cash, *Mind of the South*, 74–78.

14. Fox-Genovese and Genovese, *Slavery in White and Black*; Genovese, *Slaveholder's Dilemma*; Fredrickson, *Black Image*; Noll, *America's God*; Bushman, *Refinement of America*; Ford, *Deliver Us from Evil*.

15. Specific commentary on the role of the judiciary in the postcolonial South can be found in Edwards, *People and Their Peace*; Lowe, "Guarding Republican Liberty," 111–33; On the role of law as the modality of rule in the republic, see Tomlins, *Law, Labor, and Ideology*.

16. Hall, "Judiciary on Trial," 337–54; Shugerman, "Economic Crisis," 1063–150; and Hurst, *Growth of American Law*.

17. John McLaren, *Dewigged, Bothered, and Bewildered*. In Virginia the point was particularly salient. Beyond a mechanism for impeachment for judges who did not conform to the "good behavior" of office, the 1830 constitution had also inserted a provision for the removal of judges, without the necessity of due process, by a two-thirds vote in the General Assembly. Howard, *Commentaries on the Constitution of Virginia*, 2:697–98, 760. For contemporary concern about the provision, see Judge Robert Scott's comments in *Ex parte Bouldin*, 6 Leigh 639 (1836).

18. R. Collier, *Some Observations on the Law Affairs*, 18. For context see Christopher M. Curtis, "Codification in Virginia," 140–80.

19. R. Collier, *Some Observations on the Law Affairs*, 21–22.

20. Baldwin, *Flush Times*, 81; on Baldwin and his book, see Mayfield, *Counterfeit Gentleman*, and J. Rothman, *Flush Times*.

21. French, *Biographical Sketches*; Hardy, *Colonial Families*, 152–53.

22. R. Collier, *Original and Miscellaneous Essays*; *Collier v. Robertson*, Circuit Superior Court of Law and Chancery, Second District, Petersburg, July 1844.

23. *Collier v. Robertson*, Circuit Superior Court of Law and Chancery, Second District, Petersburg, July 1844. For a summary see Gholson, *Notice of a Late Pamphlet*, 4–5. Collier's pamphlet on gambling seemingly has eluded historical preservation.

24. "Petition of Robert R. Collier, January 28, 1847," Document 40, *Journal of the Virginia House of Delegates, 1846–1847*.

25. "Charges preferred by R. R. Collier against Judge J. H. Gholson," Document 40, Journal of the Virginia House of Delegates, 1846–1847. Collier's second specification in the petition also pertained to the Caldwell case and an issue of $700 in fees for which Thomas S. Gholson had not, in his mind, provided an adequate account. Collier, himself, was accused of impropriety with a security in another case where it was complained that he released money to creditors prematurely. See Exrs. of Thomas F. Hawthorne v. Bristol, Collier, and Hall, Chancery Causes—047, Petersburg Circuit Court (1846), http://www.lva.virginia.gov/chancery/case_detail.asp?CFN=730-1846-047 (Accessed March 5, 2014). For rebuttal see "Answers to Interrogatories Propounded to William W. Townes by Hon. J. H. Gholson," Folder 5, MS 4461, LVA. Supplement E, Folder 4 refers to Collier's allegation of incompetence in Minge v. Mason.

26. R. Collier, *Some Observations on the Law Affairs*, 23.

27. *Richmond Whig*, January 29, 1847; Journal of the Select Committee in Proceedings, LVA. Members assigned to the select committee were John W. Syme (chair), William O. Goode, Robert E. Scott, Walter D. Leake, James M. Stephenson, Samuel C. Anderson, William S. Goodwin, Charles P. Dorman, Andrew Hunter, and Samuel E. Goodson. Chapman Johnson joined the committee later because of difficulty maintaining a quorum.

28. Journal of the Select Committee, 2–5, 8. Collier introduced three pieces of evidence to support his cause and asked the committee to include Gholson's comment about the assault being "a judicious act" as a confession.

29. Journal of the Select Committee, 6–9.

30. "Proceedings," Folder 10.

31. "Proceedings," Folders 10 and 11.

32. "Proceedings," Folders 10, 11, 12.

33. "Proceedings," Folders 5, 6, 10, 11, and 12. Gholson, *Substance of Remarks*. Searching through the testimony of witnesses one is hard pressed to find anyone who had actually admitted to reading the pamphlet in response to question 4 with the notable exception of Conway Robinson, one of the revisers to Virginia's Code. Robinson's testimony was reprinted in Collier's *A Publication*, 42–43.

34. Journal of the Select Committee, February 19, 1847. Collier subsequently reasserted his desire to prosecute the charge of assault and battery. See the entry for February 26.

35. Journal of the Select Committee, 15–16.

36. Gholson's essays were published as *Substance of Remarks Delivered by Thomas S. Gholson. In Answer to R. R. Collier before the Committee of the House of Delegates in Virginia*; and *Notice of*

a Late Pamphlet issued by R. R. Collier and a Brief Examination of his Life and Character. Collier's responses appeared as *A Publication by R. R. Collier the Occasion Being Made for It by the Circulation of "Substance of Remarks," by T. S. Gholson*, which was followed by *An Appendix to Reply to Gholson's "Substance."* Copies of all these pamphlets are held by the Virginia Historical Society. Collier quotation is from *Appendix to Reply*, 14.

37. T. S. Gholson, *Notice of a Pamphlet*, 31.

38. *Richmond Enquirer*, July 7, 1848. This obituary included the reprint of the original notice published in the *Petersburg Republican*, July 3, 1848, along with additional commentary.

39. *Richmond Whig*, November 10, 1848.

40. Grice, *Georgia Bench and Bar*, 157–59; Hawkins, *Case of John C. Watrous*. For contemporary commentary on the ethical problems of the judiciary see "The Judiciary" *American Law Register* (July 1867): 513–21.

41. Patton and Robinson, *Code of Virginia*, 84–86, 725–26. For discussion of the law, see Patton and Robinson, Reports of the Revisors, 47–48, notes. The revised constitution of 1830 had authorized the legislature to specifically forbid any officeholder from engaging in a duel even to the point of participating as a second or bearing a challenge. The legislature enacted such a law the following year, although evidence suggests that it was not consistently enforced. Indeed the Revised Code of 1849 revised the law to prohibit anyone from office who had not engaged in a duel since March 14, 1848. On the Dromgoole duel, see Lewis, "The Dugger-Dromgoole Duel," 327–45.

Bradley Johnson

THE SUBVERSIVE RHETORIC OF HONOR AND ILLEGALITY IN THOMAS NELSON PAGE'S "MARSE CHAN"

During the late summer of 1880, Thomas Nelson Page, the young lawyer who would eventually gain national fame as the author of "Marse Chan," appeared in court on behalf of one of the elite citizens of Richmond, Virginia: John Sergeant Wise. Wise, a Richmond attorney, veteran of the Civil War, and son of former governor Henry Alexander Wise, was arraigned for preparing to fight a duel with Dr. George Ben Johnston. It was an ugly affair that originated when Wise was blackballed from admission to a Richmond social club and responded by searching out those responsible and publicly insulting them. After identifying Johnston as the principal source of the indignity, Wise instructed a representative that if Johnston, "or any one else, desires a meeting with me, arrange time when and place where fully. I give you *carte blanche*."[1] After producing the correspondence from the affair for the court (one wonders why Page, the attorney, allowed this at an arraignment), Wise denied, quite implausibly, that he had issued any challenge. He posted a $5,000 bond, and the affair, like nearly every other in the history of the American duel, faded out of the legal system.

That Wise chose Thomas Nelson Page to represent him says less about Page's skills as an attorney and more about his personal connections with the Wise family. Two weeks earlier *Lieutenant* Thomas Nelson Page was camped with the Richmond Light Infantry Blues nearly two hundred miles west of Richmond.[2] Although Page had no military experience, his notable descent from the Tidewater Page and Nelson families gained him entrance to the prestigious Virginia company. *Captain* John Sergeant Wise, Page's client, typically led the Blues but was absent from this excursion while he attended to political business and the more pressing issue of his reputation. All this would seem to have little to say about the eventual author of "Marse Chan," except that Page had also been elected by the company to wear the uniform of O. Jennings Wise, half brother of John S. Wise and, as Todd Hagstette has discovered, a probable source for the duel in "Marse Chan."[3] A martyr to the lost cause, Jennings Wise fought a duel in 1859 that primary documents from late nineteenth-century Richmond strongly suggest Page appropriated for his romanticized, yet ambivalent, portrait of Marse Chan. One of the more compelling proofs for this connection is revealed in the fact that Page wore Jennings Wise's old Richmond Blues uniform *and* defended John Sergeant Wise against charges of arranging a duel in the same month that he penned his most famous and most uneasy defense of southern honor before the war.

The affairs of honor of Jennings Wise in 1859 and John Sergeant Wise in 1880 not only serve as sources for Thomas Nelson Page's ambivalent portrait of honor in "Marse Chan"; they also operate as bookends in Page's understanding of the shift from an antebellum tradition of extralegal violence to the Reconstruction emphasis on law. In the late summer of 1880, then, Thomas Nelson Page had in mind two affairs of honor. Both involved lawyers. One was pulled from an already mythic past that Page associated with men like his idealized father, his iconic college president, Robert E. Lee, and so many glorified dead. The other he saw up close. The Wise-Johnston affair was marked by passion, thwarted by law, and denied in court by the principals. "Marse Chan," composed in the midst of events that highlight the tension between the illegal and the legal, the honorable and dishonorable, reveals that Page's subversive representation of honor was defined by historical events and complicated by his professional obligation to the law. Critics have wondered how a writer who seems so unambiguously laudatory in his nonfiction writing about the South could include so many moments of ambiguity in a story like "Marse Chan." Scrutiny of Page's activities in the summer of 1880 help to answer that question by revealing that Page was fully immersed in the complex, historical expressions of southern honor that are fictionalized in "Marse Chan." Moreover the events that inspired an ambivalent portrait of honor in "Marse Chan" also reveal the changing role of the duel, and its parent honor, in a volatile postbellum legal climate.

"Marse Chan" begins with the narrator, probably a northerner, traveling through Tidewater, Virginia, in 1872. He stumbles on a former slave named Sam, who recounts the chivalrous exploits and tragic end of his former master. Sam tells of how, as an eight-year-old boy, he was presented with the infant Channing and told, "You are to be his boy from dis time."[4] When Marse Chan[5] grows older he falls in love with Anne Chamberlain, the daughter of the planter whose property borders the Channing plantation. With the prospect of joining the two properties, the two families get along well until Colonel Chamberlain becomes involved in legal disputes with the elder Master Channing. When his father is blinded in a fire, young Marse Chan takes over management of the plantation and his father's political affairs. Colonel Chamberlain, who has been bested in the legal and political arenas by the Channing family, insults the old master by calling him a cheater and an abolitionist. Young Marse Chan declares Chamberlain a liar, and the two fight a duel in which Marse Chan fires into the air after Chamberlain shoots through Chan's hat. When—in Sam's words—Marse Chan declares, "I mek you a present to yo' fam'ly, seh!,"[6] Anne shares her father's indignation and rejects Marse Chan.

When Virginia secedes from the Union shortly thereafter, Marse Chan enlists as a private in the Confederacy and fights with cavalier bravery and recklessness. After learning that Channing has defended Anne's reputation in camp, Chamberlain allows Anne to express her affection to him. Channing is killed in battle shortly after reading a letter of reconciliation from Anne, and his body is sent back to his family, "wid de fleg wrapped roun' 'im."[7] Anne, old Master Channing, and Marse Chan's mother die in quick succession. When Sam concludes his tale, the narrator gives him "several spare 'eighteen-pences'" for telling such a beautifully tragic story, and Sam returns to tend to his former master's dog.

The long-standing critical challenge of "Marse Chan" is to reconcile what appears to be a sentimental, hyperbolic defense of life in the Old South with several narrative details that subvert that defense. On the one hand is a story so powerfully nostalgic that it reportedly made abolitionists Thomas Wentworth Higginson and Henry Ward Beecher weep when they read it.[8] On the other hand is a narrative controlled by the voice of a former slave who receives money for telling it. Moreover, when the primary narrator first encounters Sam, the latter is chastising Marse Chan's dog for requiring help getting over a fence. Apparently unaware of the white traveler's presence, Sam says, "Jes' like white folks-think 'cuz you's white and I's black, I got to wait on yo' all de time."[9] In another episode Sam says, "Dem wuz good ole times, marster-de bes' Sam ever see! Dey wuz, in fac'! Niggers didn' hed nothin' 't all to do-jes' hed to 'ten to de feedin' an cleanin' de hosses, an' doin what de marster tell 'em to do."[10] Of course the addendum of doing whatever the master says implies potentially incessant work and abuse. It also stands in contrast to an earlier moment when Sam pridefully says that the old master knew his name. In mentioning that there are too many slaves to be remembered by the old master, Page has included a detail he could easily have dispensed with unless he were deliberately subverting the paternalistic model of slavery.

Critics have approached the contradictions of the story in varied ways. Lucinda MacKethan has suggested that "Page never consciously explored the flaws of the Old South" but did depict an "ambiguous paradise which definitely contained the seeds of its own destruction."[11] Scott Romine has argued that Page was aware of the subversions of southern honor in the story but provided "recuperative" terms to overcome them.[12] (For example, if old Master Channing orders one of his slaves into a burning barn to save the horses, he also sacrifices his own sight in order to save the slave who becomes trapped in the fire.) Regardless of whether Page's subversion was consciously or subconsciously devised, most recent critics of the story have struggled to account for why Page would subvert a vision of the Old South that he so unambiguously promoted in his nonfiction as well as in most of his other fiction.

One answer is that the ambiguity of southern honor—a strange blend of unregulated passion and noble self-sacrifice—was already present in the historical precedents with which Page worked. In the figure of O. Jennings Wise—the model for Marse Chan—Page found a source of deep nostalgia whose flaws had been remedied by both time and his sacrifice for the Lost Cause. John Esten Cooke, a writer whom Page admired, represented the contradictions, and their apparent resolutions, in the person of O. Jennings Wise. In his 1867 account of the war, *Wearing of the Gray,* Cooke, after recounting the qualities and perceived flaws of his deceased friend, explained the influence that the end of the southern cause had on the memory of Jennings Wise: "Then came a revulsion. His character was better understood; his faults were forgotten; his virtues recognised. Even his old opponents hastened to express their sympathy and admiration. . . . Dying, he has suffered change; and there is a beauty in the pale, cold face, which it never possessed while living. Traits never suspected come out now, when Death has stamped the countenance with his melancholy seal; and love and pity have quite banished the old scorn and hatred."[13] For Cooke, Wise's martyrdom transformed southern memory of him and shifted focus from his hot-headed recklessness to an eternal ideal of chivalry. That Cooke suggested new traits emerging from Wise's face in death indicates that it is not, in fact, Jennings Wise who was transformed, but our nostalgic vision of him. Cooke, like Page, wrote protracted eulogy. Flaws were incorporated in his account but submerged beneath the larger emphasis on symbolic meaning for the living.

Page used Cooke's account of Jennings Wise directly when he described Marse Chan's body being brought home for burial. Sam recounts that "Miss Anne she tuk de coffin in her arms an' kissed it, an' kissed Marse Chan, an' call 'im by his name, an' her darlin', . . . Well, we burid Marse Chan dyar in de ole grabeyard, wid de fleg wrapped roun' 'im, an he face lookin' like it did dat mornin' down in de low groun's, wid de new sun shinin' on it so peaceful."[14]

In the parallel from John Esten Cooke's account, the body of Jennings Wise was brought to his father, General Henry A. Wise, following the battle of Roanoke Island. Cooke noted that his record of the scene came from a clipping from a Norfolk paper from 1862: "General Wise directed that the coffin containing the remains of his son be opened. Then, I learn from those who were present, a scene transpired that words cannot describe. The old hero bent over the body of his son, on whose pale face the full moon threw its light, kissed the cold brow many times, and exclaimed, in an agony of emotion: 'Oh, my brave boy, you have died for me, you have died for me.' What an epitaph!"[15] Both figures are transfigured by their sacrifice for the cause, and both transfigurations are signified by a pronounced light on their faces: moonlight for Jennings Wise, sunlight for Marse Chan. Whereas Cooke used the transfiguration to indicate that the sacrifice wiped away any moral ambiguity from our memory of Jennings Wise, Page used the transfiguration of Marse Chan as a refrain with which to highlight the incongruities of southern honor. Channing's face bears a similar light when he experiences romantic love (specifically when he reads the letter from Anne), when he emerges from church on Sunday morning, and when he fights the duel against Chamberlain. For Marse Chan each of these moments indicates the magnification of his honor, but each is given equal status. Religious transformation, military sacrifice, romantic love, and haughty behavior on the dueling ground are juxtaposed and thereby called into question by Page.

Thomas Nelson Page applied the same strategy of subversion in his appropriation of the Jennings Wise–P. H. Aylett duel of 1859. That affair began when Patrick Henry Aylett, grandson of his revolutionary namesake, made disparaging remarks about Governor Henry A. Wise. Jennings Wise defended his father in a *Richmond Enquirer* editorial that referred to Aylett as an "Augustus Tomlinson" and as a person "good to lead a retreat, if for nothing else."[16] The Tomlinson sobriquet came from the fictitious author of "Maxims on the Popular Art of Cheating" by George Bulwer Lytton. When Aylett demanded to know whether Wise had intended the terms for "personally offensive reasons," by suggesting that Aylett was a coward and a cheat, Wise refused to retract his statement. Aylett issued a challenge that Wise accepted on condition that they travel over 150 miles to the North Carolina border. The request came, not from fear of prosecution under Virginia law, but from the fact that Wise had "twice consented to a meeting in the State of Virginia. The result was considerable embarrassment to the Governor."[17] Jennings Wise had no concerns about breaking the law; he simply did not wish to allow his father's enemies to claim that the son had broken the laws the father was charged to uphold.

When the duel commenced, P. H. Aylett's shot narrowly missed Wise. Wise then turned away from Aylett and fired into the air. Aylett, moved that Wise had spared his life, approached and told the seconds that he wanted his opponent to know that he "believed the offense offered him by Mr. Wise was the result of a misunderstanding, and wished by-gones to be by-gones."[18] Wise, who had apparently spared Aylett because of the latter's near-sightedness and his large family, responded in less conciliatory terms: "I have just given sufficient evidence that I have no desire for Mr. Aylett's blood, nor do I desire now to use any disrespectful language which may wound his feelings; but Mr. Aylett's relations towards me, and towards another very dear to me, are, in my opinion, such as to preclude any reconciliation between Mr. Aylett and myself. I prefer that we shall meet hereafter only as perfect strangers."[19] During the next two weeks Jennings Wise continued to criticize Aylett in the *Richmond Enquirer* while Aylett continued to write with greater deference toward Wise. What began as a gesture of magnanimity and reconciliation—throwing away his fire—became another way for Wise to demonstrate his power.

Of all the aspects of O. Jennings Wise that Page adopted for his portrait of Marse Chan, this single gesture is the most significant in undermining the notion of southern honor. On the surface it is a gesture that undoes critiques of the duel's violence and selfishness. Ideally refusing to fire at one's opponent can lead to abiding friendship because it acknowledges the public honor of one's antagonist as well as a profound desire not to remove him from the world. As Kenneth Greenberg pointed out, the most prominent "purpose of a duel was not to kill, but to be threatened with death."[20] Throwing away one's fire magnified this facet of the duel, made self-sacrifice and courage more lofty ideals than justice or retribution. Like O. Jennings Wise, however, Marse Chan uses the gesture to demonstrate moral superiority, to emphasize his greater courage and openness to self-sacrifice, and, ultimately, to humiliate his opponent.

Although Marse Chan is canonized by his martyrdom for the Lost Cause, much as Jennings Wise had been, he shows a similar inability to manage the "two contending moral forces, passion and restraint," that Dickson Bruce has defined as the central meaning of the duel.[21] Initially Channing conducts the affair with a measured approach. He refuses to take political insults against himself seriously, and he shows deference toward Chamberlain as his elder. When Chamberlain suggests that Marse Chan's father is an abolitionist and has, incongruently, cheated him out of his slaves, Channing's passion gets the better of him, and Sam reports that Channing says, "an nothin' but yo gray hyars protects you."[22] The insult to his father seems to render Channing incapable of reconciliation with Chamberlain, but filial defensiveness is also the sentiment that magnifies Marse Chan's honor. Matthew A. Byron has suggested that defenses of family honor most often revolved around fathers since their "honor reflected the honor of the family," and duelists who defended the honor of their fathers rarely faced prosecution.[23] Ultimately, however, the passion evoked in defense of his father causes the insulting language that generates many of the other problems in the story. When Channing throws away his fire and proclaims, "I mek you a present to yo' fam'ly, seh!,"[24] he places Chamberlain in the humiliating role of recipient of paternal restraint.

Thomas Nelson Page would have found ample precedent for the passionate, and sometimes dishonorable, defense of the father in the life of O. Jennings Wise. Page's client John Sergeant Wise wrote an 1899 memoir of the Civil War in which he discussed his brother's unhealthy obsession with his father's reputation: "On one occasion, when asked if his heart had not yet been touched by a woman, [Jennings] replied, "'No. My love for father—my desire for his advancement—is the absorbing passion of my life. It leaves no place for other deep affection.' . . . He had resolved that whoever criticised his father should do so at his peril, should be insulted, should be fought if it was so desired, and that to this line of conduct he would adhere until such criticism stopped, or he himself stopped a bullet."[25] John Sergeant Wise further claimed that his "brother Jennings actually fought eight duels in less than two years," all of which were related to defenses of his father's political reputation.[26] Edward Ayers noted that "most duels were not fought between established planters, but between young men in the professions dependent upon the manipulation of language and image: law, journalism and politics."[27] O. Jennings Wise was engaged in all three. After having been trained as a lawyer, Wise became the editor of the *Richmond Enquirer,* a position from which he could most effectively promote his father's political agenda. What Page might have learned about the conflation of honor and illegality as he wore the uniform of Jennings Wise and spoke with John S. Wise during meetings of the Light Infantry Blues is unknown, but the specter of Jennings appears in Marse Chan's defense of paternal honor as well as in his resistance to reconcile with his father's antagonist.

What makes Marse Chan's conduct on the field of honor more disturbing than that of Jennings Wise is his statement to Colonel Chamberlain. Whereas Jennings Wise let the act of throwing away his fire speak for itself, Channing makes Chamberlain acknowledge that his life has been spared. Barbara Holland has suggested that Jennings Wise made a similar statement to Aylett, specifically that "Wise fired into the air, bowed, and said 'Sir, I present you to your wife and children.' It was the perfect thing to say. So gentlemanly, so unbearably patronizing that Aylett must have ground his teeth over it for the rest of his life."[28] There is no suggestion from contemporary sources, however, that Wise ever made such a statement, though several later commentators relate the anecdote. In fact Aylett's second, William Old, published the correspondence and a detailed account of the duel, approved by the principals, a week after it occurred, but he mentions only that Wise threw away his fire and rejected an immediate reconciliation on the field.[29] Other accounts, namely from the brothers of the two principals, are similarly silent about any such dramatic statement and evince a respect for Wise's conduct in the affair.

The most likely source for the story is from a *Richmond Daily Dispatch* column that mentions, in a recounting of the Aylett-Wise duel, a similar gesture and statement in the famous duel between John Randolph of Roanoke and Henry Clay. The reporter suggested that "the course pursued by Mr. Wise, of firing his pistol into the air, is not without precedent in the history of dueling." It is stated that on a similar occasion the celebrated John Randolph of Roanoke fired his pistol in the air, and remarked to his antagonist, the Hon. Henry Clay of Kentucky, that he would make a present of him to his wife and children.[30] Curiously this anecdote was as much a later embellishment to the Randolph-Clay duel as it was to the Aylett-Wise affair. The apparent desire of commentators on the duel to append such statements suggests a compelling interest in the razor's edge of honor and dishonor, passion and restraint, that the duelist walked. To express a concern for family as a reason to withhold fire would engender a gracious response. To state, however, as Marse Chan and the apocryphal John Randolph do, that they "make a present" of their antagonist is to add humiliation to a newly created imbalance of power.

Kenneth Greenberg made a convincing case that gifts in the Old South were loaded with implicit information about power relationships. He argued that gifts "come wrapped in meanings associated with the gift of a master to a slave"[31] and that such an immense gift as Randolph provided Clay, since it could not be reciprocated, created a potential imbalance in power. Such an imbalance was avoidable because Randolph joked, after Clay shot through his coat, that Clay owed him a new one. By trivializing the debt Clay owed him, Randolph allowed Clay to maintain his reputation, to infer that Randolph had acted out of genuine concern for his safety.[32] Had he actually stated that he *made* Clay a present, refashioned him from a man of honor into something dependent on the whim of Randolph, a reconciliation would not have been possible. Page modeled the duel between Marse Chan and Colonel Chamberlain on the Aylett-Wise duel, but he used the precise language popularly attributed to the Randolph/Clay affair in order to exaggerate the ambiguous nature of Channing's honor. Page contextualized the gift exchange earlier in the story when, while on good terms, the Channing and Chamberlain families exchange gifts of ponies in a reciprocal gesture of equality. After the duel and Channing's rhetoric of gift giving, Page included a description of old Master Channing asking Sam for details of the duel and his son's victory on his behalf. When he has recounted the story, Sam says that old Master Channing "gi' me five dollars an' a pyar of breeches."[33] If the reader is uncertain about the nature of the gift exchange that has occurred between Marse Chan and Colonel Chamberlain, Page clarified the shifting power dynamic by demonstrating the significant gift given to Sam, the slave, for being the recorder of Marse Chan's honor.[34]

All this concern with precise postures, words, and procedures indicates that the duel, as an expression of honor, functioned with all the procedural trappings of law. The technical adherence to the *code duello* in "Marse Chan," coupled with subversions of honor, point to an uneasiness in Thomas Nelson Page regarding the relationship between law and honor. Unlike Jennings Wise, who found the practice of law "irksome, and lacking in excitement,"[35] Page was a legal idealist and interested in the overlap between the practice of law and the writer's interpretation of life. Robert Ferguson suggested that the professional merger of law and writing was a common and persistent phenomenon in the South, where rhetoric, particularly oratory, was most highly valued.[36] In a hyperbolic, nostalgic sketch entitled "The Old Virginia Lawyer," Page suggested that, though an archetypal lawyer "never wrote a line, he was a philosopher, a wit, a poet. His knowledge of human nature was profound."[37] Rosewell Page, Thomas Nelson Page's brother and early biographer, suggested that Page's "reverence for law, for age, for womanhood, for genuine piety was a marked characteristic. His father used to describe one of his neighbors as a 'law-abiding' citizen. This the son deemed the highest praise that once could bestow."[38] It is significant that Page, in recalling the composition of "Marse Chan," noted that "the story was written in my law office . . . in Richmond, Virginia in the late summer of 1880."[39] Immersion in the practice of law in defense of John Sergeant Wise during the composition of "Marse Chan" must have summoned up many of the tensions between law and the duel's code of honor, tensions that could find subtle voice in fiction, if not in the society of gentlemen.

Critics tend to overlook the significant role of the law in "Marse Chan." Legal disputes over property and slaves between the Channing and Chamberlain families lead directly to the verbal exchanges that require the duel's extralegal form of conflict resolution. Chamberlain's inability to accept the rulings of the legal system led him to seek a restoration of honor through the calculated insult of Marse Chan and his father. The irony of Chamberlain's anger resides in the fact that one of the lawsuits came about because he was within his legal rights to sell slaves and break apart families. His behavior may have been ungentlemanly, but the law protected his right to it. The lawsuit comes about when Chamberlain will not accept old Master Channing's attempt to make him act as a gentleman and sell Channing the slaves in question. What is most significant, the duel stands in the climactic center of the story as an illegality that at once questions and confirms the principals' status as gentlemen. Young Channing's Randolphian gesture in the duel may mark the height of southern chivalry, but it comes at the expense of a violated law. Also of note is that Marse Chan visits "de big lawyer o' de country" to make his will before facing Chamberlain in the duel.[40] He spends two hours attending to the legal consequences should he die in the illegal defense of honor.

Page's interest in the duel's illegality raises interesting questions about the broad relationship between the duel and the law in the nineteenth-century South. The duel has traditionally been understood as the extralegal attempt by gentlemen to maintain aristocratic power or, conversely, by usurpers attempting to gain the status of gentlemen. While the duel undoubtedly performed both of these social functions to varying degrees, it also operated as a significant movement in the transformation of judicial and punitive power in the nineteenth century. Michel Foucault's analysis of the refashioning of the penal system in the late eighteenth and early nineteenth centuries provides a vocabulary for understanding the duel's contradictory functions of enforcing social conduct and elevating or sustaining elite members of society. In the transition from punishments based on retribution against the body to a system of bodily restraint and spiritual reform, the code of honor provided white southern men with a hybrid form of disciplinary power. The power relationships that develop in conjunction with the duel in "Marse Chan" illustrate both the South's unique responses to penal reform as well as Thomas Nelson Page's ambivalent understanding of the duel as an agent of social control.

In *Discipline and Punish,* Foucault argues that any physical or symbolic structure that regulates the individual and manages power can be classified as a discipline. Disciplinary power is evident in the structures of educational systems, military regulations and drills, even the code duello. Disciplines exist in tension with law because they draw power away from it. Foucault noted, "Whereas the juridical systems define juridical subjects according to universal norms, the disciplines characterize, classify, specialize; they distribute along a scale, around a norm, hierarchize individuals in relation to one another, and, if necessary, disqualify and invalidate. . . . They effect a suspension of law that is never total, but is never annulled either. Regular and institutional as it may be, the discipline, in its mechanism, is a 'counter-law.'"[41]

Foucault suggested that the movement from law to the counter-law of disciplinary control implies not social progress, but merely a shifting dynamic of power.[42]

As a form of disciplinary power, the duel is not simply a holdover of aristocratic power, but a calculated means of bridging the gap between republican government and elite control over the varied levels of social class. As such the code of honor also functions as a hybrid, a transitional form of disciplinary power that is both secretive and public, which both punishes the body and scrutinizes the soul. Whereas the northern penitentiary system could ideally invite the prisoner to reform through reflection, for the southerner, "the deprivation of freedom emerged as the ultimate penalty precisely because freedom stood as the most prized gift of a republican society."[43] Like imprisonment, physical punishments of the body—branding, disfigurement, whipping—were, like restricted freedom, punishments for slaves. Elite white members of society looked to the disciplinary power of the code of honor as an illegality that served as a substitute for threatening forms of judicial and penal control.

The duel, then, provides a hybrid discipline, a balance between the penitentiary's reform of the soul and the old approach to bodily retribution. As Page demonstrated in "Marse Chan," the duelist is at once punisher and victim, engaging directly in the administration of physical punishment while signaling his ability to rise above concern for such base physicality. When Channing stoically accepts the shot from Chamberlain, fires into the air, and makes his statement of ownership, he violates the expectation that the duel will have a redemptive effect on both participants. Colonel Chamberlain, who expected the duel to free him from humiliation, even if it punished him physically, "warn't satisfied, an' wanted to have annur shot." Since the seconds end the duel once Channing has determined not to shoot, Chamberlain cannot establish his superiority or even equality with Channing. As he leaves the dueling ground he appears "like he did de day befo' when all de people laughed at 'im" during the political rally.[44] Chamberlain hoped that the duel would perform its evaluative function as a discipline, that it would confirm his status as a brave, calm man who did not have financial problems and who was unconcerned about a political defeat by a younger adversary. After Channing humiliates him, he desires a second shot to restore his status. By killing or wounding Channing, he hopes to demonstrate a physical superiority to his opponent to compensate for the defeat his honor has suffered.

As a lawyer Thomas Nelson Page's ambivalence about the extralegal nature of the code of honor is apparent in "Marse Chan." Byron noted the remarkable statistic that, out of 734 recorded duels in the United States in the nineteenth century, only one duelist was fully prosecuted.[45] Many hundreds of other affairs of honor must have been resolved by the seconds prior to an exchange of shots, rendering the spectacle of the duel unnecessary. The failure of law to restrain the disciplinary power of the duel was shocking to many law-abiding southerners, as it must have been to Page, the legal idealist. Clayton Cramer noted that legislators generated systems of "double jeopardy" because they lacked faith that jurors would follow the law over the code.[46] Bertram Wyatt-Brown questioned why, when southern lawyers and judges were just as competent in law as their northern counterparts, "was the law so readily manipulated" in the South.[47] Page's own ambivalence toward the concept of honor is emblematic of the general southern crisis of legal and disciplinary power. In *Social Life in Old Virginia before the War,* Page's effusive celebration of antebellum Virginia, he expressed the tensions inherent in elite visions of the social order: "To be a Virginia gentleman was his first duty; it embraced being a Christian and all the virtues. . . . He believed in a democracy, but understood that the absence of a titled aristocracy had to be supplied by a class more virtuous than he supposed any aristocracy to be."[48] Here Page tried to express his confidence in republican government while suggesting that an elite class is required, which transcends the requirements of that government.

How the disciplinary power of the duel could provide elite southerners with a bridge between democracy and aristocracy is a complex question. One answer involves the narrative power of the duel. The duel's secretive nature is, ostensibly, a function of legal proscription, a proscription embraced by the duelist. Nonetheless, while the duel is a private affair, it relies on literary advancement, particularly through what Joanne Freeman termed "public-minded personal letters" that could be "circulated among small numbers of elite readers."[49] Southern duelists also use larger-scale forms of communication—principally newspaper accounts—to transform the duel from a secret event into a public one. The combination of secrecy and eventual publication allow the duel to become myth, to protect its participants from scrutiny, and, most important, to disinvite the masses from public participation, thereby lending a quasi-democratic tone to the proceedings. Marse Chan's resistance to speaking about the duel makes a narrative of the event more valuable, as Sam discovers when he is paid for telling the story. Although the masses are barred from attendance, publication of the event creates the disciplinary control at the center of the duel's power. Since social behavior is shown to have such profound consequences beyond the law, those who hear about the mysterious rites of the duel are brought under its power. They are invited and expected to adhere to the dictates of honor.

Page composed "Marse Chan" at a critical moment in the history of southern honor. By 1880 the enforcement of the civil rights of African Americans by federal troops had come to an end three years earlier, and the white South was reasserting the old hierarchies, though it had not yet fully introduced the Jim Crow laws that would formally undo the major projects of Reconstruction. Reconstruction represented an attempt to forgo the disciplinary structures that elite white southerners had built and replace them with a more rigid system of federal and state law. In the post-Reconstruction South of the 1880s, the question of what southern honor would return to or might eventually become remained unsettled. Such instability in the concept of honor and what it might accomplish in the weakening of law may account for what Byron identified as an "outburst of duels between 1880 and 1883."[50] John Hope Franklin suggestd that by 1880 the planting aristocracy had settled down to habits not unlike those that characterized it in 1860."[51] John Sergeant Wise was at the center of that uneasy reconfiguration, and during that period Wise was involved in what one contemporary referred to critically as "13 bloodless duels."[52]

Although Wise's precise influence on Page's ambivalent portrait of honor is murky, Wise's perception of his personal reconstruction provides a fascinating look at the catastrophic break that the Civil War created in the concept of southern honor. In his memoir of the war, Wise described returning home after, as a young lieutenant, he had delivered some of the final dispatches of the war between Jefferson Davis and Robert E. Lee. Having lost his idealized brother, Jennings, to the conflict and perceiving his father as a defeated general, Wise wrote a bitter last will and testament to account for the crisis of identity he faced. It begins, "I, J. Reb., being of unsound mind and bitter memory, and aware that I am dead, do make, publish, and declare the following to be my political last will and testament." In the first item of the will, he stated that he would "give, devise, and bequeath all my slaves to Harriet Beecher Stowe."[53] As the will continues, however, it takes on a more serious tone: "And now, being dead, having experienced a death to Confederate ideas and a new birth unto allegiance to the Union, I depart, with a vague but not definite hope of a joyful resurrection, upon lines somewhat different from those of the last eighteen years."[54] In the final lines of the memoir, Wise changed to the third person and stated, "In June 1865, a boy named John Sergeant Wise . . . was sent to school."[55]

This refashioning emphasis is particularly fascinating since it foreshadows the fact that, by 1880, John Sergeant Wise would become something of a pariah in Richmond elite society, as his exclusion from the Westmoreland Club suggests. The purpose for the exclusion was his association with the Readjuster movement, an attempt to adjust the Virginia state debt downward. The Readjusters were aligned, at various points, with the Republican Party, particularly African American members of the Republican Party. This alliance was particularly unpopular with white Democrats still smarting from waves of disempowerment during Reconstruction.

Wise's propensity to fight between 1880 and 1883 was, ironically, a product of his awareness of the decline in Republican/Reconstruction imposition of law. The boy who had been so terrified when his older brother disappeared to fight a duel, and the reconstructed adult who increasingly aligned himself with the rule of law, became almost rabid in his defenses of personal honor.

During the composition of "Marse Chan," Page saw, in dramatic fashion, how much had changed in the legal status of the duel. Following the Aylett-Wise affair in 1859, one of the seconds, William Old, published an account of the duel as well as all the preliminary correspondence that generated it. He did this with the full consent of both principals, though doing so provided clear evidence that they had all violated the Virginia statute that forbade dueling in or out of the state. Old clearly presents the account to demonstrate that, as he concluded, "both parties acted throughout as men of honor and courage."[56] By contrast the correspondence of the Johnston-Wise affair of 1880 was presented as part of an arraignment hearing. Of perhaps greater significance is the reporter's statement at the end of the article: "Mr. Wise stated in conclusion that he considered the whole matter a farce, and that he had given the length, breadth, depth, and thickness of it; that he had neither sent nor accepted a challenge, and did not anticipate doing so."[57] Wise's denial suggests a fear of prosecution that was absent in 1859 as well as a repudiation of honor. Clearly Wise intended to fight a duel, but his rhetoric treats the affair as a comical game. If Page did not sense that the Civil War and Reconstruction had significantly damaged the duel's defense of elite honor, he must have known it following the Wise-Johnston affair.

In a significant historical coincidence, during the same week that Page defended John Sergeant Wise, a eulogistic portrait of Patrick Henry Aylett, complete with an account of his duel with Jennings Wise, appeared in the *Virginia Law Journal.* The almost bizarre confluence of sources related to the duels of the Wise family provided Page with a powerful blend of nostalgia and ambiguity regarding southern honor as embodied in the duel. Indeed, given the sources before him in September of 1880, it would be surprising if Page had not written a story based, at least in part, on the exploits of the Wise family. Written by P. H. Aylett's brother, William Aylett, the portrait compares him, in a few pages, to Robert E. Lee, George Washington, Ivanhoe, and "Richard of the Lion-Heart." William Aylett's nostalgic, hagiographic portrait is understandable since his brother died a decade earlier in the "Capitol Disaster," when a floor in the capitol building at Richmond collapsed, killing dozens of people. John Mayfield suggested that, following the Civil War, southern literature's "subversive voice gave way to a more nostalgic one,"[58] a fact that is evident especially in the fiction and nonfiction that treats issues of southern honor. William Aylett's nostalgic portrait is most fascinating in references to Jennings Wise, whose "brilliant genius shone with meteoric splendor."[59] Between the stories told in person about Jennings Wise, the compelling account of his life by

John Esten Cooke, and the hyperbolic description of the honor of the Jennings-Wise affair, Page's sources were deeply nostalgic. In fact one hears in Sam's nostalgic recounting of Marse Chan's life the echoes of brothers and friends who had suffered from their own losses and speak uncritically of the dead.

In "Marse Chan" Page balances competing influences in his depiction of the Old South. His nostalgic side, the side that witnessed his father's face in his hands after returning in defeat from the war,[60] exists in tension with his legal side, the one that searched for facts above feeling. This stands in contrast with the general career of Thomas Nelson Page, where one finds characters and plots that promote a retrospective, white supremacist ideology. In those texts Page routinely utilizes nostalgia as a white gentleman's connection to past white gentlemen of honor, a vehicle for paying them respect and preserving the value system they presumably espoused. In "Marse Chan," however, Page finds that pure nostalgia is fraught with contradictions and ambiguities. Since subversion inhabits so little of Page's fiction and nonfiction, the source and context of Page's finest story suggest a motivation for Page's break with convention. The historical ambiguities of his sources, particularly the Wise affairs of 1859 and 1880, allow the fiction writer to escape, however briefly, from the nostalgia he feels to express the subversions he knows.

NOTES

1. *Richmond Dispatch,* September 2, 1880, 1.
2. *Richmond Dispatch,* August 19, 1880, 1.
3. Hagstette, "Dueling and Identity," 144.
4. Page, "Marse Chan," 6.
5. "Marse Chan" is Sam's rendering of "Master Channing."
6. Ibid., 21. Here, as elsewhere in the story, Channing's speech is recorded through the dialect of Sam's narrative voice.
7. Ibid., 37.
8. Hubbell, *South in American Literature,* 801.
9. Page, "Marse Chan," 3
10. Ibid., 11.
11. MacKethan, *Dream of Arcady,* 59, 55.
12. Romine, *Narrative Forms,* 94.
13. Cooke, *Wearing of the Gray,* 151–52.
14. Page, "Marse Chan," 37.
15. Cooke, *Wearing of the Gray,* 148.
16. *Richmond Enquirer,* July 27, 1859, 1.
17. Ibid.
18. Ibid.
19. Ibid.
20. Greenberg, *Honor and Slavery,* 74.
21. D. Bruce, *Violence and Culture,* 31.
22. Page, "Marse Chan," 17.

23. Byron, "Crime and Punishment," 11
24. Page, "Marse Chan," 21.
25. Wise, *End of an Era,* 94–95.
26. Ibid., 95–96.
27. Ayers, *Vengeance and Justice,* 17.
28. Holland, *Gentlemen's Blood,* 188
29. *Richmond Dispatch,* July 27, 1859, 1.
30. Qtd. in the *New York Tribune,* July 20, 1859, 5.
31. Greenberg, *Honor and Slavery,* 70.
32. Ibid.
33. Page, "Marse Chan," 21.
34. B. Johnson, "Succinct and Formal Violence," 193.
35. Wise, *End of an Era,* 89.
36. Ferguson, *Law and Letters,* 291.
37. Page, "Old Virginia Lawyer," 293.
38. Rosewell Page, *Thomas Nelson Page,* 192.
39. Roberson, "Manuscript of Page's 'Marse Chan,'" 259.
40. Page, "Marse Chan," 18.
41. Foucault, *Discipline and Punish,* 223.
42. Hunt and Wickham, *Foucault and Law,* 35.
43. Ayers, *Vengeance and Justice,* 45.
44. Page, "Marse Chan," 21.
45. Byron, *Crime and Punishment,* 6. See also Byron's essay in the present volume.
46. Cramer, *Concealed Weapon Laws,* 115–16.
47. Wyatt-Brown, *Southern Honor,* 363.
48. Page, *Social Life,* 45.
49. Freeman, *Affairs of Honor,* 114.
50. Byron, "Crime and Punishment," 173
51. Franklin, *Reconstruction after the Civil War,* 212.
52. McCarty, "Mssrs.," 2.
53. Wise, *End of an Era,* 461.
54. Ibid., 462.
55. Ibid., 463.
56. *Richmond Dispatch,* July 27, 1859, 1.
57. *Richmond Dispatch,* September 2, 1880, 1.
58. Mayfield, *Counterfeit Gentlemen,* 126.
59. Aylett, "Patrick Henry Aylett," 522.
60. T. Gross, *Thomas Nelson Page,* 111.

Part III

Defining the Man—Honor and Character

At some point an essential question must be asked: What is the difference between honor and respectability? Both terms display "character," but that word is itself elusive. Honor seems most apparent in small communities headed by stable elites, yet in a modernizing culture with a rising middle class, new standards and definitions of respectability may emerge. The essays in this section address the issue in four of its expressions: regional identity, public repute, personal probity, and emotional stability.

Robert Levine's fine study of the Cilley-Graves duel explores regional definitions of honor, particularly as they came under the critical eye of Nathaniel Hawthorne. Graves, a Kentuckian, could easily be made to embody honor as individualistic and self-absorbed. Cilley was from Maine and just as easily was made a martyr to a New England tradition of defending the community, or a "disinterested nationalism." The one was personal; the other, part of a collective heritage founded in the Revolution. Hawthorne's obituary of Cilley (a former classmate at Bowdoin) could have simply echoed this dichotomy, but—as Levine shows—he hedged. Male rivalries are crucial to much of Hawthorne's fiction, and his rendering of the duel presses us to think more seriously about the importance of sectionalism, masculine codes of honor, fraternalism, and Bowdoin College itself in Hawthorne's career. What is interesting is Hawthorne's ambivalence. The ritual of defending honor was the same for Cilley as for Graves, a fact that Hawthorne could not ignore. It implied that a "shared value system" over how to confront insults may have blurred the distinctions between northern and southern standards of honor and character.

The blending of honor and character is also evident in Timothy Williams's piece on students at the University of North Carolina at Chapel Hill. As Hawthorne knew from his experience at Bowdoin, honor was deeply entwined with manhood, yet "becoming a man" when honor itself was deeply in flux produced tensions that afflicted men—particularly young men—in acute ways. Honor, with its connotations of personal courage and reckless display, should have been the default position, and southern students dueled, drank, and fornicated with almost competitive resolve. Yet this was not the whole story. Most, as Williams reveals, were not radically different from the emerging bourgeoisie elsewhere. They valued propriety, sobriety, self-restraint, learning, all of which they classified as "character," and their oratorical and debating societies were intellectual fields of honor. These boys, as men, staffed the officer corps of the Confederacy.

At the other extreme stood David Hines, the subject of Lawrence McDonnell's spirited essay on the confidence man. Long a beloved figure in American humor and fiction, the con artist occupies a liminal place in the spectrum of our ideals. He is both self-made man and whatever we make him. Hines was perhaps the most brazen of them all (he may be the inspiration for Herman Melville's cryptic masterpiece *The Confidence Man*). Hines used the postures of honor to gain reputation, and he took his show on the road, traveling and swindling his way all over the South. Southerners may have condemned him and imprisoned him, but as McDonnell's essay argues, he reflected their ambivalence with the demands of a "market-driven ethos of respectability" with competing notions of chivalry and invincibility. At some point southerners had to choose.

Anna Koivusalo takes this ambivalence deep into the emotional life of one representative man, James Chesnut. The husband of famed diarist Mary Boykin Chesnut, he was in 1860 the newly elected senator from South Carolina and the first to resign his seat in the wake of Lincoln's election. That, plus the fact that he ordered the first shots at Fort Sumter, should have made him the perfect man of honor—fiercely independent, indifferent to the threat of death, cool, and self-assured. He was not. Koivusalo portrays a man whose emotions and aspirations "created an ever-changing platform on which to enact honor." Rephrased, honor was contingent and changeable, not deterministic and stable, and that made even the most vigorous defenders of southern character impulsive and erratic. "Honor," Koivusalo explains, "was a tool to hide the world of raw emotions and replace them with nobler versions." Southern honor, she concludes, "was not a stable, invariable concept."

Robert S. Levine

"THE HONOR OF NEW ENGLAND"

Nathaniel Hawthorne and the Cilley-Graves Duel of 1838

On February 24, 1838, in a Maryland town several miles north of Washington, D.C., Jonathan Cilley, a first-term Democratic congressman from Maine, fought a duel with William Graves, a Whig congressman from Kentucky. At the third exchange of fire, Cilley was killed by Graves, and from Maine to Washington there was an outpouring of anger and grief over the loss of the popular young Maine politician. The duel had its origins in remarks Cilley had made on the House floor three weeks earlier about the dubious ethics of the Whig New York newspaper editor James Webb, with Graves and other Whigs quickly coming to Webb's defense. Though the duel in crucial respects centered on a New York editor's anger at a Maine congressman, it was nonetheless regarded by northerners as an instance of hot-headed southerners, in the name of an honor culture obsessed with individual reputation, using bully tactics to kill off one of their opponents. That sectional interpretation took special hold in New England, where many prided themselves on an honor culture that they felt disinterestedly served the larger interests of the nation. Accordingly Cilley came to be celebrated as a fallen New England hero in the tradition of the American Revolutionaries. In a biographical sketch published in the September 1838 issue of John L. O'Sullivan's *United States Magazine and Democratic Review,* one of Cilley's friends made just that case, declaring that Cilley, like his patriotic grandfather, had fought for "the honor of New-England."[1] That sketch was authored by Nathaniel Hawthorne, who had first met Cilley in 1821 when they were undergraduates at Bowdoin College.

Hawthorne scholars have generally neglected the Cilley-Graves duel, which had a larger impact on Hawthorne's politics and art than is usually allowed. The duel presses us to think more seriously about the importance of sectionalism, masculine codes of honor, Jacksonian violence, fraternalism, and Bowdoin College itself to Hawthorne's developing career. It is worth noting that Hawthorne's first published novel, *Fanshawe* (1828), focuses on a college very much like Bowdoin and includes a duel scene. Male rivalries are central to much of Hawthorne's fiction, particularly the novels that he wrote after being fired from his Salem custom-house job in 1849. And of course the idea of "the honor of New-England" is absolutely central to his fictions about the American Revolutionary spirit published during the 1830s. In tales like "My Kinsman, Major Molineaux" (1832), "The Gray Champion"

(1835), and "Endicott and the Red Cross" (1838), Hawthorne depicts New England resistance to British authority in the seventeenth and early eighteenth centuries as having paved the way for the Revolution itself. As he wrote memorably at the conclusion of "The Gray Champion" (which portrays New England resistance during the 1690s): "should domestic tyranny oppress us, or the invader's step pollute our soil, still may the Gray Champion come; for he is the type of New-England's hereditary spirit; and his shadowy march, on the eve of danger, must ever be the pledge, that New-England's sons will vindicate their ancestry."[2]

For Daniel Webster and other northern writers and politicians, the nation came into being because of the long history of New England honor, and Hawthorne drew on such beliefs for his fiction. But however much Hawthorne trafficked in such beliefs, he often did so ironically, regularly raising questions about regional self-righteousness and self-glorification while pointing to the ways that honor was deployed by New Englanders in the service of power. Hawthorne's use of "shadowy" in his celebration of the Gray Champion hints at something dark about New England power, which is conveyed even more ominously at the conclusion of "My Kinsman, Major Molineaux," where New England resistance to British authority in the early 1730s is depicted as a "contagion" or "senseless uproar" that leads to a sadistic "trampling . . . on an old man's heart."[3] There is a degree of irony about New England honor even in Hawthorne's sketch-biography of Cilley, which will become apparent when we read it in relation to John O'Sullivan's, which straightforwardly presents Cilley as a martyr. O'Sullivan in his piece locates true American honor in New England; Hawthorne, by contrast, implicitly raises the question of whether honor culture in New England differs in any meaningful way from southern honor culture, as both cultures (in his presentation) are about personal reputation, ambition, and power. Where O'Sullivan, Hawthorne, and other northern writers seem to agree is that by the late 1830s, honor culture, however it is defined, had become overly linked with political violence. The events surrounding the Cilley-Graves duel would suggest that they were right.

Before turning to the duel itself, it would be useful to consider Hawthorne's friendship with Cilley and others at Bowdoin College. In the summer and fall of 1821, Hawthorne met his classmates Jonathan Cilley, Horatio Bridge, and Franklin Pierce, who would all become Jacksonian partisans; he remained lifelong friends with Bridge and Pierce, writing Pierce's presidential campaign biography in 1852. During his time at Bowdoin, Hawthorne was especially close with Cilley, who wrote his sister on several occasions about their friendship. In a letter of May 1824, for example, Cilley recounted how "last evening after tea Hathorne [*sic*] and myself went down to the Adroscoggin and caught between forty and fifty fish apiece, perch, chubs and anglings. . . . We breakfasted on them this morning and are to have some more for dinner." Around six months after this fishing expedition, and indicative of their fraternal closeness, Cilley and Hawthorne made a friendly bet in which whoever remained a bachelor the longest would win a barrel of Madeira wine. Bridge held onto the note of wager, and, as it turned out, Hawthorne won the bet but failed to collect.[4] After graduation Hawthorne met regularly with Pierce and Bridge in the Boston area, but he lost touch with Cilley, who remained in Maine to pursue a career in law and then in politics. It was not until 1837 that Bridge contacted Cilley, in part to let him know that Hawthorne had won the bet, which led Cilley to set up a July 1837 reunion with his old college friend. That reunion was significant in all sorts of ways, bringing Hawthorne into contact with John O'Sullivan, who would become the main publisher of Hawthorne's tales and sketches from 1838 to 1845, eventually helping Hawthorne to obtain a political patronage job as well.[5]

The reunion came about when Bridge in March 1837 sent a just-published copy of Hawthorne's *Twice-Told Tales* to Cilley, who had a wife and children in Maine but at the time, like many congressmen, was living in a boardinghouse in Washington. Perhaps as requested by Bridge, Cilley tried to use his influence to find Hawthorne a patronage job. After proposing Hawthorne for a position as historian for the American Exploring Expedition to the South Seas, he contacted the Democratic editor O'Sullivan, whom he had met in Washington, to recommend Hawthorne as a possible contributor to his new periodical, the *United States Magazine and Democratic Review*.[6] O'Sullivan followed Cilley's recommendation, and Hawthorne would eventually publish over twenty tales and sketches in the Democratic journal. We know that Hawthorne met with Cilley in Augusta, Maine, in July 1837, and that he met O'Sullivan around the same time. The chronology then gets a little fuzzy. Although Hawthorne would later speak out against the Cilley-Graves duel, he himself may have challenged O'Sullivan to an earlier duel, and that possible challenge may have had an influence on Cilley's decision to accept the challenge from Graves. At least that is the story told by Hawthorne's son Julian in his 1884 *Nathaniel Hawthorne and His Wife*.

According to Julian Hawthorne, right around the time that Hawthorne renewed his friendship with Cilley and met O'Sullivan, he fell in love with Mary Silsbee of Salem, whose father was a congressman. By coincidence Mary Silsbee had met O'Sullivan in Washington, and he, too, was attracted to her. In Julian's telling, Silsbee was "a creature of unbounded selfishness" who "at times seemed to be possessed by a sort of moral insanity." Drawing on the tropes of the seduction novel, Julian depicts Silsbee as the dark seductress who attempts to add Hawthorne "to her museum of victims" by telling him that O'Sullivan had made sexual advances that besmirched her female honor. In this way, Julian wrote, she hoped to bring about the "prospect of seeing two men, who had always been dear and cordial friends, engage in a duel on her account." As Julian described events of January 1838, Hawthorne challenged O'Sullivan to a duel in order to redeem Mary's honor. O'Sullivan quickly refused the challenge, explained the deception to Hawthorne, and "claimed the renewal of Hawthorne's friendship"—but not before it was too late. For it was during this time that Cilley received a challenge from Graves. According to Julian, Cilley initially hesitated until an unnamed friend declared: "If Hawthorne was so ready to fight a duel without stopping to ask questions, you certainly need not hesitate." So Cilley in this telling accepted the challenge because of Hawthorne, and Julian went on to report that after Cilley was killed, Hawthorne learned of his role and felt he was "almost as much responsible for his friend's death as was the man who shot him."[7] Though Julian clearly believed that Silsbee was ultimately to blame, he depicted his father as secretly brooding on his guilt for years, and accordingly used the Cilley-Graves duel to explain why the figure of the tragically sad, haunted man pervades Hawthorne's fiction (even though Hawthorne conceived of many such figures, including Young Goodman Brown, well before the Cilley-Graves duel).

In all likelihood Julian's story is apocryphal, having its sources in the storytelling of Elizabeth Peabody, the older and surviving sister of Hawthorne's eventual wife, Sophia Peabody Hawthorne, who died in 1871 (seven years after her husband). In his 1893 *Personal Recollections of Nathaniel Hawthorne,* Horatio Bridge rejected the story, declaring that "I never heard, at that time nor afterwards, that Cilley was in any way influenced by Hawthorne's example. . . . Nor did Hawthorne himself ever intimate to me, by word or letter, that he considered himself at all responsible for Cilley's course in accepting Graves's challenge."[8] Of course Bridge's possible ignorance of the details surrounding the Cilley-Graves duel does not mean that Hawthorne did not challenge O'Sullivan, and modern Hawthorne biographers James Mellow and Edwin Haviland Miller, along with O'Sullivan biographer Robert D. Sampson, have suggested that Julian told a true story.[9] However, Hawthorne's best recent biographer, Brenda Wineapple, is skeptical, noting the lack of corroborating evidence and Hawthorne's own antidueling sentiments, as evidenced in his 1838 sketch of Cilley and his mocking account in *Fanshawe* of the dueler manqué Edward Walcott. When drunk, Walcott challenges a man to a duel for purportedly besmirching the honor of a young woman, and he wakes up the next day so hung over that he "was inclined to believe, that the duel had actually taken place, and had been fatal to him."[10]

Whatever the actual facts of the putative Hawthorne-O'Sullivan duel, Julian Hawthorne clearly understood that Hawthorne, O'Sullivan, and Cilley were entangled in many ways even before the Cilley-Graves duel. He understood as well the "increasingly violent masculinist culture embodied by [Andrew] Jackson," as David Greven terms it, along with the importance to that culture of long-standing traditions of honor.[11] As Julian suggested in his account of his father's challenge to O'Sullivan, a recourse to a duel as an affair of honor was clearly still an option in the late 1830s, even for a shy New England writer like Hawthorne. But how honorable were such affairs of honor? And what does the Cilley-Graves duel indicate about the standing of honor culture at that time? To answer these questions, we need to consider the duel in more detail.

Most commentators agree that the duel was initiated on the House floor early February 1838 when Cilley made acerbic remarks about New York newspaper editor James Watson Webb. Webb was the editor of the *Courier and Enquirer,* a newspaper that had started out in the late 1820s as solidly Jacksonian, but in 1832 had abruptly become an oppositional and soon to be Whig paper, perhaps because Webb felt he was not being taken seriously by the Albany Regency (the New York State Democratic machine), though more likely because he had received a loan of approximately fifty thousand dollars from the Second Bank of the United States at a time when Jackson was attempting to strip it of its charter. In a column in the February 7, 1838 issue of Webb's *Courier and Enquirer,* Matthew L. Davis, who wrote as "The Spy in Washington," claimed that an unnamed Democratic congressman was improperly using his position to secure funds from government contractors. As an emerging leader in the Democratic Party, Cilley took it on himself to respond to the column, asking rhetorically on the House floor on February 12 if the charges were being made by a columnist in the service of "the same editor who once made grave charges against an institution of this country, and afterwards was said to have received facilities to the amount of $52,000 from the same institution, and gave it his hearty support."[12] Though Cilley did not mention Webb by name, Webb was incensed by remarks that he knew readers would recognize as about him when widely printed in the *Congressional Globe.*

According to his biographer, Webb was "a firm believer in the code duello," though one could just as readily say that Webb was a sociopath who took advantage of the code duello to legitimate his recurrent turns to violence.[13] During the 1830s he challenged several people to duels (which never transpired) and three times assaulted his newspaper-editor rival James Gordon Bennett on the streets of New York City. In 1842 he actually fought a duel with Kentucky congressman Thomas F. Marshall that left him with an injured hip and a prison sentence (which was commuted by New York's governor). A man who brooked no criticism, Webb upon hearing of Cilley's remarks immediately traveled to Washington and got the Kentucky Whig congressman William Graves to serve as his intermediary (a sort of second), sending him to the floor of the House with a letter for Cilley in which he demanded an "explanation which the character of your remarks renders necessary."[14] The letter, and all subsequent requests by Graves and others to acknowledge Webb, either as an editor or gentleman, went unanswered by Cilley, who believed that he had the right to speak his mind on the House floor without having to account to anyone other than his fellow congressmen. In refusing to respond to Webb, Cilley also held true to the aristocratic foundations of honor culture during the early national period, which saw editors as unworthy of the response of a gentleman.[15] What ensued from Cilley's refusals was unusual but not unprecedented. Graves, who in his role as the potential second should have done everything he could to prevent a duel, instead took Cilley's refusal to acknowledge Webb as a personal affront and decided to challenge Cilley himself. Graves then lined up as his second the Virginia congressman Henry A. Wise, who for many northerners became the villain of the affair, and whose participation revealed its sectional dimension as well.

With Graves's introduction into the conflict, the duel seemed just a bit more about sectionalism, but still its main impetus had to do with Webb's anger at having been accused of taking a bribe (the loan) from the Second Bank of the United States. But when Wise became Graves's second, sectionalism was undeniable, for Wise, unlike Graves, had been harboring personal anger at Cilley during ongoing debates on slavery and expansionism. Approximately two weeks before Cilley had insulted Webb on the House floor, the Maine congressman had insulted Wise by claiming that his opposition to Van Buren's handling of the Seminole War suggested his lack of sympathy for his "white brethren."[16] Webb may have made the initial demand of an apology from Cilley, and Graves may have made the actual challenge, but many northerners came to believe that lurking behind the aggressiveness of Webb and Cilley was a vengeful Wise, who appeared to do everything he could to make sure Cilley was shot dead by Graves.

On the day of the duel, Cilley and Graves traveled north to a field in Bladensburg, Maryland, where, at Cilley's request, the principles used rifles at eighty yards, perhaps because Cilley believed that with such rules no one would be killed. After each of their initial two exchanges of fire, Cilley declared that he had no animus against Graves, while rejecting demands to acknowledge Webb as a man of honor or gentleman. When Wise refused to declare an end to the duel after the second exchange, Cilley, according to at least one report, turned to his friend Colonel Shaumberg and exclaimed, "They thirst for my blood."[17] And blood is what Graves and Wise got on the third exchange of fire when Graves's shot hit Cilley in the stomach. Cilley fell into the arms of Shaumberg and died within five minutes, leaving behind a grieving widow and three children, including a newborn he had never seen.

In the immediate wake of the duel, memorial services were held in Maine, Massachusetts, New Hampshire, Washington, and elsewhere. The funeral service in Washington was attended by President Martin Van Buren, Vice President Richard M. Johnson, and numerous members of Congress. An effort was made to expel Graves from the House; that motion failed, and instead he was censured by a vote of 102 to 76.[18] Congress set up a commission to investigate the duel and also took up the matter of dueling itself, which led to an 1839 ban on the practice in the District of Columbia (which would not have affected the Cilley-Graves duel). Meanwhile commentators expressed incredulity that congressmen were actually fighting to the death with no legal repercussions, and, particularly in the North, there was considerable questioning of the honor code itself. The prominent

Unitarian minister Henry Ware Jr., for example, in a sermon on the duel delivered at the chapel of Harvard University on May 4, 1838, declared that the "Inquisition was not more inexorable to its victims, than is the court of Honor to him who stands within its jurisdiction."[19] Writings about the duel, which may have been the largest outpouring of antiduel sentiment in the nation's history, ranged from poetic elegies for Cilley to petitions against dueling, funeral orations, and essays in newspapers and journals, including a vociferous attack on Cilley's killers by O'Sullivan and a biographical sketch of Cilley by Hawthorne, both published in O'Sullivan's *United States Magazine and Democratic Review.*[20] O'Sullivan wrote his essay within weeks of Cilley's death; he commissioned Hawthorne's biographical sketch at the same time, and Hawthorne submitted it in April. Both writers addressed honor culture head-on.

As is clear from the title of his essay, "The Martyrdom of Cilley," O'Sullivan saw honor as having little to do with the Cilley-Graves duel, which he regarded as a clear case of "homicide." In O'Sullivan's view Whigs and southerners, "thirsting for human blood," conspired to take the life of a northern Democrat by deploying what they mockingly call the "'Code of Honor.'" Consistent with his reading of the duel as more about sectionalism than partisanship, O'Sullivan made the villain not Webb or Graves but the Virginian Wise, whom he presented as a vicious southerner intent on killing a New Englander. Thus O'Sullivan claimed that the origins of the duel lay not in Cilley's disparaging remarks about Webb, but in the January 1838 speech Cilley gave in Congress castigating Wise for "oppos[ing] the appropriation before the House for the expenses of the Seminole War, in an animated tirade of general attack upon the Administration." Without mentioning that Cilley challenged Wise's sympathies for whites, O'Sullivan proclaimed that Cilley's response to the southern congressman was "one of the most admirable speeches ever heard in that body."[21] Here Cilley is presented as Jacksonian to the core, embracing the genocidal expansionism that O'Sullivan himself, the inventor of the term "Manifest Destiny," would come to champion. The irony is that expansionism served the interests of the southern slave power, and that O'Sullivan himself, so angry at a southerner in this 1838 account, would eventually embrace the southern position on slavery. In the early 1840s he would even exonerate Wise and assert that it was the Whig Henry Clay (whose presidential bid he opposed) who had authored Graves's challenge to Cilley. But at this particular moment, O'Sullivan focused on Wise as "the wretched individual who has enacted the principal part in this drama of death," and who did so by violating his own southern code of honor.[22]

Though O'Sullivan probably had not read John Lyde Wilson's widely influential *The Code of Honor; or, Rules for the Government of Principals and Seconds in Duelling,* published in South Carolina the same year as the Cilley-Graves duel, he was well aware of the increasing belief that the rules surrounding a duel, as Wilson himself emphasized in his text, were intended to keep duelists from actually killing each other. Wilson urged seconds to "sooth and tranquilize your principal" in order to circumvent the need for a duel, and remarked that if a challenge actually led to a duel, then "seconds are bound to attempt a reconciliation . . . after sufficient firing or hits, as specified."[23] From O'Sullivan's perspective Wise did just the opposite, acting dishonorably from beginning to end. Moreover the true principal should have been Wise, given that he was "*already at enmity with Cilley, and having already made an almost openly avowed attempt to force him to a duel.*" Whether or not Wise actually made such an attempt, O'Sullivan argued that by "no other or higher light than by the principles of the 'Code of Honor,' it is as clear as sunlight at noonday" that Cilley was not obligated to fight a duel with Graves. Given Wise's manipulation and violation of the code duello, O'Sullivan at the conclusion of his piece refered to the "miserable fallacy, designated as 'the code of honor,'" while terming Wise a "wilful and deliberate assassin."[24]

If honor cannot be found in what O'Sullivan depicts as the corrupt southern honor code, then where can it be located? The simple and clear answer is in Jonathan Cilley as an exemplar of the honor of New England. O'Sullivan's presentation of Cilley may well have had its sources in his reading of the Revolutionary stories of Hawthorne's recently published *Twice-Told Tales,* which emphasize the important role of New England in battling against British tyranny. Throughout his piece O'Sullivan underscores that Cilley was "a New Englander, of remarkably mild and amiable character" who, like Hawthorne's Gray Champion, revealed his strength when under attack. In O'Sullivan's view, the duel was about competing sectional definitions of honor: southerners had narrowly regional and personal conceptions of honor focusing on reputation; New Englanders were disinterested U.S. nationalists who resembled the disinterested patriots of the Revolutionary generation. Thus O'Sullivan insisted that Cilley chose to fight in a duel that violated the code of honor because he "could not let the name of his grandfather be dishonored, nor his native New England to be trampled upon." O'Sullivan and, later, Hawthorne supported this interpretation by quoting Cilley's own remarks. As O'Sullivan recounted, on the morning of the duel, Cilley reportedly said to friends: "'NEW ENGLAND MUST NOT BE TRAMPLED ON,' my name must not be disgraced, and I go to this field sustained by as high a motive of patriotism as ever led my grandfather or my brother to battle, as an unhappy duty not to be shrunk from, to my honor, my principles, and my country."[25] Cilley's grandfather had fought the British in the Revolutionary War; Cilley in 1838 chose to take on analogous forms of tyranny.

O'Sullivan was not alone in figuring Cilley as the embodiment of New England honor. Congressman John Fairfield of Maine declared that Cilley "partook largely . . . of that fearless patriotism of his ancestors, which made them 'pour out their blood like water' in the war of the Revolution." When Senator Reuel Williams of Maine announced on the Senate floor that Cilley "is now a lifeless corpse," he, too, invoked Cilley's grandfather in declaring that for this "native of New Hampshire . . . patriotism and bravery were his inheritance." Franklin Pierce wrote to Cilley's brother-in-law Hezekiah Prince Jr. on March 17, 1838 with additional information about how Cilley located his actions in the great tradition of New England honor. As Pierce wrote in the letter, which he may well have shared with Hawthorne, "He [Cilley] stated to me, the morning before he went out, that he believed he should go activated by as high motives of patriotism as ever led his grandfather or his brother to the field of battle." Pierce later described how, when he received broken pieces of Cilley's rifle, he proclaimed to those assembled at his Washington, D.C., boarding house (where Cilley had been boarding as well): "I will keep the broken arms, with which our friend defended the honor of New England."[26] New England honor would become both the structuring principle and subject of Hawthorne's biographical sketch of Cilley, which appeared in the September 1838 issue of the *United States Magazine and Democratic Review.*

O'Sullivan had commissioned Hawthorne to write a sketch of Cilley for his ongoing series "Political Portraits with Pen and Pencil." (Hawthorne's essay would be the ninth "portrait" in the series.) Hawthorne found the job "painful,"[27] in part because he was grieving for Cilley, and in part because he had mixed feelings about his friend. Though Hawthorne would write positively about Cilley in his public pronouncements, privately he expressed concerns about a man who may not have been all that honorable in his actions, or, to put this differently, was just another politician. For example, when at Cilley's instigation they met on July 28, 1837, in Augusta, Maine, Hawthorne described Cilley in his journal as "shrewd, crafty, insinuating," a man given to "concealing like a murder-secret, anything that is not good for him to have known." Somewhat enigmatically, when Hawthorne submitted his sketch-biography to O'Sullivan, he told him that he had a mixed response to his March piece: "What an article that was of yours—the Martyrdom of Cilley! Most eloquent and admirable, but I cannot altogether coincide with your view of the affair."[28] The editors of the Ohio State edition of Hawthorne's letters claim that Hawthorne was skeptical of O'Sullivan's political approach to the duel, but there's no clear warrant for such a reading.[29] It may be that Hawthorne did not want to blame Wise in the way O'Sullivan did, or it may be that Hawthorne was skeptical of the idea that the "shrewd, crafty" Cilley was some sort of martyr.

Hawthorne began his sketch by asserting that he would eschew the "narrower sympathy" of the political partisan, declaring that "not merely a party nor a section, but our collective country, has lost a man who had the heart and ability to serve her well." Thus he enjoined readers of the *United States Magazine and Democratic Review* (and arguably O'Sullivan himself): "May not bitterness of party prejudices influence him who writes, nor those, of whatever political opinions, who may read!" Hawthorne then launched into a biographical overview intended to demonstrate Cilley's "thoroughly New England character," which is hardly an apolitical approach at a time of increasing sectional tension. Born in New Hampshire, Cilley was the grandson of Colonel Joseph Cilley, who "commanded a New Hampshire regiment during the Revolutionary War, and established a character for energy and intrepidity of which more than one of his descendants have proved themselves the inheritors." Like the Gray Champion and other of Hawthorne's Revolutionary and proto-Revolutionary heroes, Joseph Cilley fought to establish the country and passed along his legacy to his children and grandchildren, such as Cilley's brother, who fought in the War of 1812. But in a postheroic age, Cilley enrolled not in the army but at Bowdoin College, where he became "a popular leader," a person who "had a power of sympathy which enabled him to understand every character, and hold communion with human nature in all its varieties." In his private notebook entry of July 1837, Hawthorne presented Cilley as devious and unnerving; here, unwilling to directly criticize the dead Cilley, Hawthorne presented even the political side of Cilley as part of his New England character, by which Hawthorne ostensibly meant a disinterested commitment to the nation in the tradition of Cilley's grandfather. Thus, despite his mixed feelings about Cilley, he remarked about the man he knew at Bowdoin and then reconnected with in 1837: "I thought him as true a representative of the people as ever theory could portray."[30]

And yet even as he celebrated Cilley as a man of the people, Hawthorne spent considerable time discussing a leader who recurrently came into conflict with various people, in large part because of his political ambition. He described Cilley's conflict with John Ruggles, the Maine lawyer who initially hired him in the late 1820s and then came to see him as a threat to his own political ambition, and he showed that as Cilley emerged as an important leader in the Maine state legislature, and then in Congress, he tended to alienate his political opposition. Hawthorne asserted somewhat paradoxically that Cilley "loved to subdue his foes; but no man could use a triumph more generously than he." That generosity, which Hawthorne presented as part of Cilley's disinterested nationalism, is linked to the fierceness of his character. Hawthorne asserted that Cilley "possessed iron resolution, indomitable perseverance, and an almost terrible energy" (he presented the proto-Revolutionary John Endicott in similar terms in "Endicott and the Red Cross" as "stern and resolute"), while asserting that "these features had imparted no hardness to his character." Unlike the stereotypical hot-headed southerner, then, Cilley was something like an Arthurian knight, displaying "the same chivalrous sentiment which impels hostile warriors to shake hands in the intervals of battle."[31]

With his invocation of chivalry and battle, Hawthorne set the stage for the duel itself. Hawthorne provided virtually no background about what instigated it, stating that he would spare himself and his readers "the details of the awful catastrophe." He did note that immediately after his election to Congress, Cilley was "found in the vanguard of many a Democratic victory," with the implication that he would therefore have to deal with a number of vanquished foes. Hawthorne emphasized that Cilley attempted to maintain working relations with all his congressional colleagues and to continue the legacy of his forefathers by conceiving of his political work as in the larger service to the nation. Nevertheless, only a year and a few months after his election, "he would be stretched in his own blood—slain for an almost impalpable punctilio!"[32] It is here where Hawthorne shed his "objectivity" and seemed as political as O'Sullivan in locating the source of evil not in a conflict between two northerners—the Maine Democrat Cilley and the New York Whig editor Webb (whom Hawthorne never named)—but between a New Englander and a southerner. And at this point, as implied by his use of the word "punctilio," Hawthorne showed that he was as well informed on the honor culture surrounding the duel as any southerner. Like O'Sullivan, he saw Graves's and Wise's failure to follow their own code of honor as contributing to what O'Sullivan termed and Hawthorne suggested was the *assassination* of Cilley, though Hawthorne much more than O'Sullivan pointed to Cilley's complicity.

Hawthorne wrote a single long paragraph on the duel. His description raised questions about the procedures of the duel, such as the circumstance in which the person who should have been the second—Graves, who had initially represented Webb's grievances—had become the principal. As Hawthorne explained, the challenge from Graves, which was delivered by Wise, "was grounded on Mr. Cilley's refusal to receive a message, of which Mr. Graves had been the bearer, from a person of disputed respectability; although no exception to that person's character had been expressed by Mr. Cilley; nor need such an inference have been drawn, unless Mr. Graves were conscious that public opinion held his friend in doubtful light."[33] Arguably Hawthorne was being disingenuous here, for it was clear that Cilley had insulted Webb in the halls of Congress. Still, that the Kentucky Congressman Graves would serve as an intermediary for the New Yorker Webb, and that the Virginian Wise would then encourage Graves by serving as his second, indicated to Hawthorne, O'Sullivan, and others that there was a plot among southern Whigs to use the code of honor to rid themselves of Cilley.[34]

Hawthorne underscored this interpretation when he described the actual duel. Like O'Sullivan, Hawthorne noted that one or at most two rounds of fire should have been enough to bring the duel to a nonbloody end. As reported by Hawthorne and most other commentators on the duel, Cilley repeatedly offered "generous avowals of respect and kindly feeling . . . towards his antagonist, but without avail." Cilley was then killed by Graves's third shot, and though a House Committee of Investigation was working on its report as Hawthorne drafted his sketch, Hawthorne stated that no such report was needed, for public opinion (at least in the North) and Hawthorne's own opinion was this: "A challenge was never given on a more shadowy pretext; a duel was never pressed to a fatal close in the face of such open kindness as was expressed by Mr. Cilley; and the conclusion is inevitable, that Mr. Graves, and his principal second, Mr. Wise, have gone farther than their own dreadful code will warrant them, and overstepped the imaginary distinction, which, on their own principles, separates manslaughter from murder."[35] Arguably, by further sullying Webb's reputation and then accusing Graves and Wise of murder, Hawthorne put himself at risk of receiving a challenge or cudgeling from one of these three men. That said, by the terms of honor culture, a mere writer of tales and sketches would hardly be worthy of the attention of gentlemen.

In Hawthorne's account, then, as in O'Sullivan's, the honor code ultimately served the ends of murderers. So we can ask the same question of Hawthorne's sketch that we asked of Sullivan's: where is honor to be found in such a lamentable episode? All along, Hawthorne seems to suggest, it can be found in the way that Cilley chose to represent the honor of New England in a duel that was less about a conflict between Whigs and Democrats than between northerners and southerners. In this way the duel, and the "dreadful" southern-based honor code surrounding it, can be seen as indicative of the increasing role of sectionalism in U.S. politics. As in O'Sullivan and in Hawthorne's contemporaneous Revolutionary tales, Cilley can also be placed in the great tradition of the New England heroes who stood up against authoritarian power—in this case bullying southerners who fetishize reputation—in the service of the nation.

And yet the presentation of honor in Hawthorne's sketch is not as clear-cut as in O'Sullivan's, and in the concluding paragraphs Hawthorne seemed to have been simply frustrated by his friend, wondering why the promising New England Democrat "threw away such a life in so miserable a cause." Even as he celebrated Cilley, Hawthorne raised questions about his behavior: "Why, as he [Cilley] was true to the Northern character in all things else, did he swerve from his Northern principles in this final scene!" And he offered this response: "But his error was a generous one; since he fought for what he deemed the honor of New England; and now that death has paid the forfeit, the most rigid may forgive him."[36]

This is a startling, revelatory moment in the sketch, which in crucial ways raises questions about all that has come before. Hawthorne, who always chose his words carefully, juxtaposed "what he deemed" with "the honor of New England" and in this way archly undercut the exceptionalist foundations of the very idea of New England honor. The "what he deemed" makes the honor of New England a matter of subjective perception, suggesting that even as Hawthorne proffered such a reading of Cilley's life in relation to a historical genealogy of New England honor, he had come to regard Cilley, who, as mentioned, invoked New England honor as his own justification for fighting Graves, as somewhat delusional or self-serving, given that there is nothing in the sketch to suggest that Graves and Wise were anything like the British enemy that New England revolutionaries faced in the seventeenth and eighteenth centuries. The "what he deemed" looks forward to Hawthorne's equally ironic account of Dimmesdale's reading of his own and New England's destiny in "meteoric appearances" in the sky, a practice that Hawthorne in his 1850 *The Scarlet Letter* says could be taken as "the symptom of a highly disordered mental state."[37] Was Cilley similarly disordered in invoking the honor of New England with respect to region, nation, and personal genealogy? Is New England honor ultimately a mirror image of that which it opposes?

Hawthorne's answers to these questions would appear to be yes. For as he presented Cilley at the end of the sketch, the man who incarnated New England-ness ultimately swerved from northern principles, ironically enough, in the name of "the honor of New England." In choosing to proceed with a senseless duel, Cilley had in effect gone southern and thus, as Hawthorne said, was in need of forgiveness from his northern friends. But maybe more important is that Hawthorne's account of such swerving worked to undercut the very idea of the large differences between North and South, as he depicted all concerned in the duel as implicated in a shared value system in which northern and southern honor culture were moving in the same direction.[38] By the end of the essay, and implicit throughout, Cilley seems just as concerned about his personal reputation in a community of gentlemen as Webb, Graves, or Wise, and therefore just as implicated in the honor culture typically linked to the South but that here seems integral to the male fraternalism (and violence) of the Jacksonian period. In the context of the overall sketch, the duel is just another of the many battles that Cilley both precipitated and participated in from the moment he entered the political world. Hawthorne used New England honor to structure his sketch, but he remained at a critical distance from his combative friend and the ideals that contributed to his death.

And yet if Hawthorne was skeptical about Cilley's claims to have fought (and died) in the name of New England honor, his readers did not seem to have noticed. In fact, because Hawthorne was seen as a firm supporter of Cilley, his tribute had a positive impact on his career. A few months after its publication, the historian George Bancroft, a partisan Democrat who was the new Democratic collector of Boston, appointed Hawthorne to the position of measurer, calling him the "biographer of Cilley" in a January 1839 letter he sent about the appointment to Levi Woodbury, secretary of the treasury.[39] And just as the essay helped to get Hawthorne a job, it also lost him a job, for after the Whigs' victory in the 1848 presidential election, Hawthorne was purged from his position by Massachusetts Whigs who accused him of having written political articles, such as the biographical portrait of Cilley. In a letter to his Whig friend George Stillman Hillard, Hawthorne expressed his astonishment at this accusation, asserting that his piece on Cilley shows just "what sort of politician I am." Though he told Hillard he wrote it in the "very midst of my grief," he claimed that "it is, though very sad, as calm as if it had been written a hundred years after the event; and, so far as I recollect it, it might as well have been written by a Whig as by a Democrat. Look at it, and see. It cannot be called a political article; and, with that single exception, I have never, in all my life, written one word that had reference to politics."[40] To some extent that is true, if by "politics" is meant something explicit about a particular election or policy. What Hawthorne conveniently forgot is that he did write about politics in his piece on Cilley, though perhaps more through the lens of sectionalism than partisanship. But by raising tough questions at the end of his sketch about the code of honor, which for decades had been linked to southern notions of regional exceptionalism, Hawthorne was being political in the way of a northern sectionalist. And by linking Cilley, with all his self-deluding notions of what he "deemed" New England honor, to practices of southern honor, and by presenting him as anything but a martyr, he was being political by refusing to be as political as O'Sullivan.

After losing his surveyor job at the Salem Custom House, Hawthorne became more explicitly political in his novels of the 1850s, which he called "romances" in part to obfuscate their political implications. Still Hawthorne's "The Custom-House" preface to *The Scarlet Letter* (1850), in which he presented himself as a metaphorically guillotined martyr to Whig politicians, was seen as scandalously political, as was his lightly veiled attack on Massachusetts Whig leaders in *The House of the Seven Gables* (1851). Working in a partisan mode, Hawthorne in the latter novel depicted the Whig businessman and aspiring candidate for governor, Judge Pyncheon, as the direct heir of the Puritan and Revolutionary leaders who helped to make Salem what it was in the 1850s: a soulless marketplace in which those with money had considerable power over the democratic masses. Hawthorne said of the current-day Pyncheon: "Judge Pyncheon was unquestionably an honor to his race." The ironic "unquestionably" is meant to raise doubts about his honor, and the use of "race" links Pyncheon to a New England genealogy that is more a source of embarrassment than pride, given that the founding patriarch Colonel Pyncheon gained his wealth by killing the plebeian Matthew Maule. As it turns out, the Maules had been plotting to regain their place in Salem, not through a recourse to pistols but through their mesmerical eyes. As was rumored among the Salem populace, the Maules' "family eye was said to possess strange power."[41] That eye, of course, is linked to Hawthorne the romancer, who, like Holgrave-Maule, the romancer of the novel, asserts a retributive power through what could be termed ironic surveyance. In the figure of Holgrave, whose family history (or "race") is just as long as Judge Pyncheon's, and just as grounded in New England history, Hawthorne redefined New England honor away from violence, aristocracy, and reputation, and toward more generous interactions with a range of the citizenry in the here and now. In Holgrave, then, Hawthorne celebrated the quietly off-stage, demystifying, democratic, and truly honorable sensibility of the New England romancer. The Cilley-Graves duel had pointed him in that direction.

NOTES

1. Hawthorne, "Biographical Sketch of Jonathan Cilley," 75. Jonathan Cilley's grandfather on his father's side, Joseph Cilley (1734–99), was a general and New Hampshire state senator. For more on Joseph Cilley, see the discussion of Hawthorne's biographical sketch later in the essay.

2. Hawthorne, *Selected Tales and Sketches*, 132.

3. Ibid., 49, 50.

4. Jonathan Cilley to Deborah Cilley, letter of May 25, 1824, in E. Anderson, *Breach of Privilege*, 15. Anderson's volume, which collects the Cilley family papers and numerous documents related to the Cilley-Graves duel, is an invaluable resource. On the wager between Hawthorne and Cilley, see Mellow, *Nathaniel Hawthorne in His Times*, 65–66, 76.

5. On Hawthorne's literary friendship with O'Sullivan, see Levine, *Dislocating Race and Nation*, 122–25.

6. On Cilley's efforts to get Hawthorne a job and a larger readership, see Mellow, *Nathaniel Hawthorne in His Times*, 84–86; and the editors' commentary in Hawthorne, *Miscellaneous Prose*, 583–85.

7. Julian Hawthorne, *Nathaniel Hawthorne and His Wife*, 1:169, 170, 172, 173, 174.

8. Bridge, *Personal Recollections*, 21–22.

9. See Mellow, *Nathaniel Hawthorne in His Times*, 102–7; E. Miller, *Salem Is My Dwelling Place*, 145–54; and Sampson, *John L. O'Sullivan*, 52–54.

10. Hawthorne, *Fanshawe*, 407–8; see also Wineapple, *Hawthorne*, 104–5.

11. Greven, "Fear of *Fanshawe*," 15.

12. Cilley's questioning of Webb, which appeared in the *Congressional Globe*, 25th Congress, 2nd session, is cited in Hay, "Compromise or Conspirator?," 58. For my understanding of the facts of the duel, here and elsewhere in the essay, I am indebted to E. Anderson, *Breach of Privilege*; Crouthamel, *James Watson Webb*; Seitz, *Famous American Duels*; Hay, "Compromiser or Conspirator?"; "Death of Mr. Cilley—Duel" and *Funeral Oration* are also crucially important sources.

13. Crouthamel, *James Watson Webb*, 73.

14. J. Watson Webb to Hon. Jonathan Cilley, letter of February 21, 1838, rpt. in "Death of Mr. Cilley—Duel."

15. As Freeman writes, "Honor culture was an aristocratic holdover premised on social distinctions. Only equals could duel" (*Affairs of Honor*, xxii). Chamberlain noted that editors simply were not regarded as gentlemen in the early republic (*Pistols, Politics and the Press*, 19) for his discussion of Webb's role in the Cilley-Graves duel, see 56–61). However, Ayers notes that by the 1830s these aristocratic ideals were giving way to a new reality, and that duels were increasingly fought "between young men in the professions dependent upon the manipulation of language and image: law, journalism, and politics" *Vengeance and Justice*, 25.

16. "Speech of Mr. Cilley, in the House of Representatives, January 23, 1838," rpt. in *Funeral Oration*, 38.

17. Franklin Pierce to Hezekiah Prince Jr., letter of March 17, 1838, in E. Anderson, *Breach of Privilege*, 175.

18. Seitz, *Famous American Duels*, 278. According to Seitz, John Quincy Adams remarked that Graves, upon his return, "came to the House with his hands and face dripping with blood" (278).

19. Ware, *Law of Honor*, 14.

20. The American Antiquarian Society holds a considerable archive of poems, broadsides, and other writings about the Cilley-Graves duel.

21. O'Sullivan, "Martyrdom of Cilley," 495, 493, 501, 495.

22. Ibid., 493. On O'Sullivan's change of mind on Wise, see Hay, "Compromiser or Conspirator?"; and Sampson, *John L. O'Sullivan,* 137. In 1845 O'Sullivan famously declared that it was the United States' "manifest destiny to overspread the continent allotted by Providence for the free development of our yearly multiplying millions" ("Annexation," 5).

23. J. Wilson, *Code of Honor*, 92, 103, 1838 edition. On dueling and the southern honor code during this time, see also Hagstette, "Dueling and Identity."

24. O'Sullivan, "Martyrdom of Cilley," 501, 506, 504.

25. Ibid. 498, 502.

26. See E. Anderson, *Breach of Privilege*, 163, 164, 192.

27. Hawthorne to O'Sullivan, letter of April 19, 1838, *Letters, 1813–1843*, 272.

28. Hawthorne, *American Notebooks*, 61, 62; Hawthorne to O'Sullivan, letter of April 19, 1838, *Letters, 1813–1843*, 272.

29. See the editors' commentary in Hawthorne, *Letters: 1813–1843*, 273.

30. Hawthorne, "Biographical Sketch of Jonathan Cilley," 69, 74, 69, 70, 73.

31. Ibid., 72, 73; Hawthorne, *Selected Tales and Sketches*, 217; Hawthorne, "Biographical Sketch of Jonathan Cilley," 73, 71–72. On transsectional notions of connections between chivalry and patriotism, see David Moltke-Hansen's essay in this volume.

32. Hawthorne, "Biographical Sketch of Jonathan Cilley," 74.

33. Ibid., 75.

34. Writing after the Civil War, and drawing on his father's account of the duel, Julian Hawthorne, who conflated Graves and Wise, maintained that "Cilley belonged to a knot of young Northern men who had resolved to put down the tyranny of the fire-eating Southerners" (*Nathaniel Hawthorne and His Wife*, 1:173). Here Cilley becomes aligned less with the Revolutionary heroes of 1776 than with the triumphant Union army.

35. Hawthorne, "Biographical Sketch," 75.

36. Ibid., 75.

37. Hawthorne, *Scarlet Letter*, 174.

38. For a discussion of similar issues in the writings of William Gilmore Simms, see Molke-Hansen's essay in this volume.

39. See the editors' commentary on Hawthorne's Cilley sketch, which quotes from Bancroft's letter to Woodbury of January 17, 1849, in Hawthorne, *Miscellaneous Prose and Verse*, 586.

40. Hawthorne to George S. Hillard, letter of June 12, 1849, *Letters, 1843–1853*, 277.

41. Hawthorne, *House of the Seven Gables*, 19, 21.

Timothy J. Williams

PURSUITS OF CHARACTER

Rethinking Honor among Antebellum Southern College Students

In the spring of 1799, Archibald Lytle, a sophomore at the University of North Carolina, faced a serious dilemma. His classmate Thomas Benton stood at his dormitory door holding a cocked pistol, demanding that Lytle fight him in a duel. Lytle had called Benton a "D[amne]d rascal" when he heard that his classmate attacked his nephew just days before, and Benton wished to vindicate his character. Lytle agreed to fight, but only in the woods where they would not violate university prohibitions on physical violence. Benton, however, was determined to fight on campus. He pointed his pistol, "primed and loaded with powder and ball," at Lytle, who then made a surprising decision. He declined Benton's invitation to duel because "he had come a great way to school and did not wish to be expelled or fall into disgrace."[1]

For readers familiar with Henry Adams's classic criticism of his Harvard classmates from Virginia, this scene is not surprising. Writing in his famous autobiography that "strictly the southerner had no mind, he had temperament," Adams created a distinctive prototype that has stood the test of time: the rowdy southern collegian, lurking around corners, drunk from bourbon, waiting to exact revenge.[2] Of course male collegians everywhere in the antebellum United States enjoyed their fair share of dissipation, as they gambled, swore, drank, fought, and caroused their way through college. This was why so many moralists composed sermons, lectures, and conduct books specifically for college-aged young men.[3] But was the misbehavior of southern collegians a deviation from a national norm? Historians have tended to think so, arguing that, as the nineteenth century rolled along, southern collegians held onto a code of ethics based on honor that northerners had abandoned for a quintessentially bourgeois Protestant work ethic. Indeed the literature has often only elaborated Bertram Wyatt-Brown's generalization that southern boys' "entry into young manhood took more social forms" than that of their more individualistic and introspective northern counterparts.[4] As a result histories involving collegians have focused more on *misbehavior* than *behavior*—on group socialization rather than individual identity formation.[5] Robert F. Pace and Christopher Bjornsen have argued, in fact, that for southern collegians, "honor was the framework that gave shape to the natural ambivalence of adolescence." They created a student culture that "focused on their peer groups and involved a peer-designed code of honor" that influenced everything from town-gown shenanigans to daily academic life.[6] The focus, in other words, has been on *affairs* of honor, which were specific rites and rituals, rather than *matters* of honor, which ultimately came to encompass a variety of regional and mainstream cultural values by the antebellum period.

Fortunately a great deal of work is being done more generally on southern men's moral, emotional, and intellectual lives, which provides much needed nuance to this reified caricature. Using gender as a category of analysis, for example, recent scholarship has shown that southern men were not always and everywhere fixated on honor. Instead they drew from a broader Victorian world to understand and articulate who they were and wished to become.[7] In this essay I build on this scholarship by focusing on one of the most important ideals in antebellum America—character—and its relation to southern honor culture as it has traditionally been defined. From the vantage point of southern college life, we can see that character operated alongside traditional "southern" attitudes about honor, mixed with them, and shaped young men's experiences of maturation. Achieving what contemporaries called a "manly character" led to honor and, ultimately, transcended it as the sine qua non of manhood. Thus thinking about honor in terms not limited only to misbehavior reveals the greater complexity of this highly important southern value.

This argument is premised on change over time that often goes overlooked in studies of southern manhood.[8] It is significant, after all, that Archibald Lytle and Henry Adams's Americas were vastly different. In the North as well as the South, forces in the early nineteenth century's intellectual culture gradually eroded the gentry's longtime honor ethic and brought new values front and center. Industrialization and commercialization created a national bourgeoisie that expounded notions of a Protestant work ethic, industry, discipline, and temperance. A well-balanced character comprised these many values. Increasingly historians argue that this was a *national* bourgeoisie. Works by Jonathan D. Wells, Jennifer Green, and John Mayfield, as well as myself, have shown that the culture of the "market revolution" jolted southern culture and southern men's self-articulation, challenging traditional notions of "honor" among the southern well-to-do. In particular John Mayfield has shown that southern humorists poked fun at the honor ideal in their fictional works. The *idea* of the honorable gentleman was always there, he shows, but it was a malleable idea and subject to inflection or even negation. At the same time as the market revolution transformed southern culture, evangelicalism spread throughout the South, bringing with it added attention to the individual—his character and perfectibility. Evangelical demands for temperance, chastity, and restraint—all in the name of conversion—played a significant role in diminishing the salience of the eighteenth-century gentry's commitment to traditional codes of honor within well-off white male communities.[9]

This essay turns to the arena of higher education to explore these transformations and their effects on the meanings and practices of southern honor in the antebellum period. Using sources of student life—not only faculty records but also student writing—this essay first explores the gradual diminution of honor culture at antebellum southern colleges in the late eighteenth and early nineteenth century. It then turns to the structures of college life that conveyed mainstream values of the American bourgeoisie, especially those related to character, which shaped and complicated earlier definitions of honor. Here southern collegians showed a surprisingly introspective quality not usually ascribed to men of honor; this introspection focused on character rather than éclat. In order to show how this worked within college life, the essay concludes with the story of one young man, William Sidney Mullins, and his pursuits of character.

Traditional affairs of honor abounded in college settings in the early national era. We see this particularly well in many acts of student resistance against faculty authority. In efforts to claim individual rights as men in the aftermath of the Revolution, students rioted at Harvard, Princeton, the University of North Carolina, and South Carolina College, as they sought to emphasize independence from authority.[10] There was a weeklong student rebellion against the University of North Carolina's faculty in 1799, with students protesting excessive punishments and expulsions of students. Six years later, in 1805, North Carolina's students left the university en masse in a "great secession," protesting new rules that increased supervision and therefore diminished their own independence. In each case students had to sign a pledge to obey university rules in order to be readmitted to college. After this large-scale student revolt, the university implemented stronger rules to curb misbehavior.[11]

Quotidian misbehavior at this time was often met with this sort of public shaming, which wounded young southern men's honor. Faculty records for the University of North Carolina, for example, document several instances of "violence and disorder," particularly drinking and fighting, which required public confessions of guilt and repentance. Take young Richard Armistead for example. He was called before the university faculty on March 8, 1802, on charges of drunkenness and disorder late at night. His punishment was to issue the following public confession: "I confess that I have been guilty of the facts recited in charge against me—that I see and am now convinced of their unlawfulness and pernicious tendency; and I publickly [*sic*] declare that I will be more faithful hereafter in my obedience to the laws."[12] This public shaming likely brought attention to Armistead. Later that year, for instance, one of Armistead's classmates, Anthony Foster, wrote a "filthy piece of composition which he . . . stuck up on the doors of college for the purpose of insulting Richard Armistead." It is unclear whether the composition directly referenced Armistead's shame earlier in the year, but the piece was insulting enough to provoke a quarrel between the two. Foster, after admitting to writing the composition and provoking a fight, was "directed . . . to retire from college," and "he retired accordingly." This time Armistead was only reprimanded and allowed to continue his studies.[13]

Dueling was not uncommon among early national collegians, as the Lytle-Benton affair illustrates. University of North Carolina faculty minutes document quarrels and "scuffles" involving pistols and swords. Other evidence exists in the laws that southern colleges created to deal with armed conflict generally and dueling particularly. The University of Georgia forbade students from dueling on campus, even though the state had no such law in the early national period. Indeed anything that might lead to an affair of honor was prohibited on campus. Accordingly students were prohibited to "strike, or insult" one another, a faculty member, or a townsperson. Moreover they were not "allowed to keep any gun, pistol, Dagger, Dirk sword cane or any other offensive weapon in his room in College or elsewhere."[14]

Although examples of affairs of honor exist in the antebellum period's historical record, they are inflected with more mainstream cultural values, particularly those of the American bourgeoisie. Between 1820 and 1865, young men went to college in order to grow up, which meant to acquire intellectual, social, and moral maturity, or "manhood" that would set them apart as leaders in their communities, their states, and the republic.[15] Their hope was to win the approval of their parents and communities, for sure, but also to create a foundation for *individual* success and even social mobility. They hoped to please their families by entering "honorable" professions such as law and medicine, as well as Christian ministry, education, and business, which would confer social regard and status. Even if a young man attended college and returned home only to run his family's farm or store, higher education laid the foundation for what contemporaries called a "manly character," or a "well-balanced character."

According to Daniel Walker Howe, a "well-balanced character" was the "dominant model for what was considered a wisely constructed self" in antebellum America.[16] Individual character reflected strong intellectual, social, and moral development. As a result schools were the main arena for character development, but it could also occur in more private settings. Studying clerks in antebellum New York, Thomas Augst has shown how young men created space for character development in their everyday work and private lives. Augst argued that character is associated with middle-class culture and Protestant work ethic of northerners. He defines character as comprising "industry, piety, and temperance," and thus serving as a "form of moral life for an emerging middle class." "Character," he wrote, "provided both a method for development of the self and a standard for social presentation."[17] Similarly Scott Casper's probing work on biographical culture in the antebellum United States has shown how these pursuits of character were embedded within American reading culture, as young readers, especially, looked to the lives of heroic as well as tragic figures to develop character.[18] These ideas about a "well-balanced character" and how to achieve it were central to the educational culture of southern colleges and universities. For collegians and college-aged male youth in the antebellum era, values of a "well-balanced character" were compatible with honor culture of an earlier era.

Character is an idea that often appears in formal addresses to students. These addresses were delivered at various points in the semester, especially before a college or university's two literary societies. Literary society members took pride in finding prestigious alumni for this purpose and, following the delivery of an address, often requested addresses for publication. These speakers focused on ways individual character development complemented higher education's goals of turning boys into men and preparing them for successful lives as adults. In an 1840 address to the University of Alabama's Erosophic Society, for instance, Isaac W. Hayne went to great lengths to explain the nature of character. "Each man, wherever found, has in himself 'the elements combined' as to give individuality to his separate being, making him clearly distinguishable from any and every other man, who has existed since time began. It is this modification of moral being, that gives to each man his individuality, which we call CHARACTER."[19] Students learned that character complemented professional aspirations, as well. Speaking before an audience at the University of Alabama in 1845, one visiting speaker reminded students that distinction in an "honorable profession" required character. "You must never forget that the secret of personal influence is the force of personal character," he explained. "Strive, therefore to be perfect within yourselves."[20] Not surprisingly speakers emphasized that character was work; it required consistent practice and habits in daily life. This is the core message that Isaac W. Hayne imparted to Alabama students in 1840: "As well might one attempt to make an expert swordsman, by the study of *books* alone, as to form *character* by simply convincing the understanding. There must be *habits* formed. The individual must not only think rightly, but he must form a *habit* of acting rightly, and feeling rightly."[21]

All agreed, therefore, that character required work. Formal university life, though sometimes undermined by immature behavior, generally produced an ambience suitable for the honorable pursuit of character. Calvin Jones's 1833 address before students at the University of Alabama drives home this message that knowledge must be met with moral improvement through religion in order to be honorable knowledge. "It is learning, only when imbued with the fear of god,—it is science, when chastened and elevated by religion, which constitutes that *knowledge,* which is truly desirable, invariably beneficial, and ever enduring," he wrote.[22] University authorities across the South did everything they could to establish a religious culture on campus that inculcated ideas about individual character development. At the University of North Carolina, which was not even a denominational college, students were required to attend daily prayers, weekly chapel services, and weekly Bible recitations. Their attendance at these required meetings were recorded and included in regular reports to parents, alongside deportment and class attendance. At these times students often heard sermons about deportment in which professors and clergy advised against swearing, intemperance, vice, and dissipation.[23]

Take, for instance, an address that William Hooper, an Episcopal-turned-Baptist minister and professor of Latin, delivered to University of North Carolina students in 1830. Intended as a "discourse on education" primarily, Hooper's address offered students a broad construction of what education really meant. He explained that higher education tends to elevate genius to the level of God, but students should not forget about the development of their moral character. He urged students to avoid dissipation, which turns a promising youth into a "pampered son" living in such a state that "whenever his passions are solicited, he yields to their sway."[24] "Are you taking all pains, by a course of moral discipline, to prevent so disastrous a defeat of all your early toils and promises?" he asked his audience before launching into a long list of sins to avoid: "hatred, and envy, and cunning, and lust, and impiety." For Hooper this was an active process, requiring students to take the reins of their own maturation and education. In an effort to get students to examine their consciences and work on the self, he used verbs such as "crush," "labour," "eradicate," and "pluck."[25] This character formation business was no easy thing. It required a great deal of work.

Every aspect of formal education catered to young men's maturation, including their mental and moral development. Students derived from antebellum higher education ideals and tools about individuality or personal character that they carried into social peer groups. The prevailing educational philosophy, based as it was on "faculty psychology," held that proper learning not only conveyed knowledge but also promoted moral health. The University of North Carolina's antebellum Latin professor explained the philosophy to students like this: "Our constitution may be said to consist of three parts, the animal, the intellectual, and the moral, to each of which a judicious education will pay a careful regard."[26] Thus the main pedagogy of the era—recitation—was not always a spectacle of young men vying with professors to avoid public ridicule, as some scholars have held; it was a means of moral improvement because it encouraged a sturdy work ethic, industry, and discipline. One antebellum student therefore encouraged his classmates to study. "Let no one pride himself upon the preposition of brilliant talents or eminent abilities, let him not harbour the pleasing but delusive idea that he can make himself master of any branch of literature or science without diligence & industry."[27]

The classical liberal arts curriculum also catered to young men's character development. Ancient authors such as the Greek philosopher Xenophon and the Roman orator Cicero conveyed messages about the importance of elevating mind over temperament and virtue over vice. Students noted in particular Cicero's call for temperance and sobriety in his works on old age and friendship.[28] Similarly mathematics and science courses complemented this character education. Joseph Caldwell, an early president of the University of North Carolina, explained, for instance, that studying geometry could "sway the understanding in its deductions concerning the rules of human conduct."[29] In 1858 one University of North Carolina student from Alabama noted that scientific study had certain "moral effects" on students. "Our hearts are purified, our moral nature refined, and our minds exalted. Such are the benefits flowing from the study of the natural sciences."[30] Finally the capstone course on moral philosophy brought these values together in a synthetic approach to young men's moral development. In this class college seniors throughout the South learned to be men of character, who valued sobriety, chastity, temperance, and discipline. The course almost always dealt with the religious imperative to develop a strong moral foundation in college.

At the same time as mainstream values influenced the formal pedagogy and curriculum, they sometimes met with resistance when it came to the code of southern honor. This was especially the case when it came to awarding students with merit-based distinctions. An early antebellum development, distinctions promoted emulation and catered to the competitiveness of the growing American bourgeoisie. Some southern students were on board with this, but others were not. Soon after distinctions were implemented at the University of North Carolina, for instance, students began to debate their value. When Edmund Covington received a less-than-generous academic report in 1842, he feared a besmirched reputation. "A youth of my age and character sets a high value on a reputation for qualities whether of the head or heart. My fellow students know that I have studied—they know my report and altho' they may tell me that the faculty are unjust, they will rejoice at that injustice in secret."[31] For these reasons cheating was often common at antebellum colleges in the North and the South, where young men would rather maintain the appearance of control than expose the reality of any ignorance.[32]

It is inaccurate, however, to depict student engagement with academics as a question of students' honor versus a curriculum that celebrated individualism, diligence, achievement, and competitiveness. These mainstream cultural values also carried salience within many aspects of antebellum students' informal life, or what we might identify as "student life" today. The rhythm of the school day allowed for some degree of flexibility and downtime. For recreations students walked around campus, or retired to their dormitories to read, write letters, study, or socialize; they gathered in public spaces such as the post office to converse with townsfolk as they awaited the day's mail; they sat around campus socializing, smoking pipes and cigars, and playing card games. In the antebellum period, there were no organized collegiate sports, and fraternities had not yet become popular in southern universities. The only official institutions of student life in the antebellum period were student literary societies. Every college and university in the antebellum United

States supported two literary societies, which were entirely student organized and student centered and usually bore some sort of Hellenized name such as the Dialectic and Philanthropic societies at the University of North Carolina or the Euprhadian and Clariosophic societies at South Carolina College.[33] These societies maintained their own chambers and libraries, where students attended meetings but also mingled informally when societies were not in session.

It is significant that students pursued moral improvement in literary societies, providing a different view on southern male peer groups. These organizations met students' intellectual, social, and moral needs. At South Carolina College, students gathered "in order through letters, to obtain a knowledge of Science in general but more particularly to improve in Oratory."[34] Similarly North Carolina's Dialectic Society pledged to "cultivate a lasting Friendship with each other and to promote useful knowledge."[35] In these societies southern collegians collected books, maintained libraries, performed weekly debates, practiced declamation, and learned parliamentary procedure.

Character development was at the heart of all these activities. Students urged one another to study, work hard, strive for excellence, and develop character.[36] In his 1833 address to Alabama's Philomathic Society, Calvin Jones underscored the pervasive understanding that these organizations were institutions for intellectual and moral character development: "To adorn and ennoble the character of youth, to sweeten your literary attainments, by uniting the charms of friendship, to draw into one harmonious sphere of mutual action and mutual profit . . . these are some of the inducements, which have promoted you to form your literary associations." Not only did these efforts nurture a well-balanced character, but they also conferred honor. "Thus to unite is wise," explained Jones; "it is *honorable*. Such associations for mutual improvement, as yours, gentlemen of the Erosophic Society, have been co-eval with our most honored seats of learning, and have been productive of immense and lasting advantage."[37] At colleges and universities throughout the South, societies commonly competed with one another for the highest honors and the most representatives to speak at the annual commencement. Students considered this sort of rivalry healthy and compatible with core bourgeois values inherent in the intellectual culture of antebellum higher education.

These societies were intellectual safe havens for students to interrogate history, current affairs, ancient literature, and philosophy, as well as quintessentially "southern" topics such as dueling and honor. Between 1795 and 1859, the members of the University of North Carolina's Dialectic Society debated dueling thirteen times. Most of these debates questioned, "Is duelling ever justifiable." Some evidence reveals that not all students of this period were as quick to duel as historians have commonly granted. In 1804, for instance, Daniel Forney, a student at the University of North Carolina, critiqued dueling in a speech before his fellow classmates. After outlining the historical precedent of the custom in early modern

Europe, Forney claimed that dueling was a pernicious custom that undermined individual rights and social order. "Duelling has already become odious & despicable in the eyes of every great and good man, but they are forced by the shackles of custom to participate in this inhuman & unchristian practice or forfeit their fortitude & bravery," he explained. "How miserably interpreted by the promoters of duelling!—Does not experience convince us it by no means tries the courage of a man, for the most cowardly person may be induced to fight a duel. A person of great erudition says, he is a man of the greatest resolution & fortitude who declines the combat, for he has not only to defend his character from the reproach of cowardice but also to overcome the prejudicial sentiments of the times."[38]

Sentiments such as Forney's critique of dueling were in no way representative of student thought as a whole in the early national period, but they do suggest that early national students did not uniformly embrace the ethical code that sanctioned violence. Of significance is that there were always students who voted against dueling. Moreover students' resolutions to these debates reflect a clear chronological split in the answer. Until 1805 students voted that dueling was justifiable, but afterward students of later generations consistently argued that it was an unjustifiable practice. Indeed in 1859 students ultimately decided that a man who killed another in a duel should be "punished as a murderer."[39]

Of course literary societies served other purposes than debate, including maintaining extensive libraries, encouraging reading, and promoting emulation. As intellectual forums, they especially encouraged students' character formation through reading biography. In 1865 one North Carolina student explained to his classmates, "This is the province of Biography, by clear and faithful delineations of character, by commemorating the deeds of their Country's great names, to arouse in young generations a lofty, and generous ambition to perform services, and to achieve deeds as high and lofty." Sentiments such as these corroborate Scott Casper's argument that biography was a popular cultural phenomenon in the antebellum period and played an important role in identity formation of its readers.[40] At universities like North Carolina, students borrowed countless biographies from their literary society libraries and engaged in numerous debates about figures from the past, especially European monarchs and central figures in the narrative of early American history such as Christopher Columbus and George Washington.[41] This collective work of studying and pursuing biography brought individual characters front and center in students' intellectual culture and with it, mainstream American values and practices associated with character development that coexisted with traditional codes of southern honor.

These are the outlines of the influence of character on students' understanding of themselves in the antebellum period. But just how did these ideals bear out in students' experiences on college campuses? Consider the case of William Sidney Mullins, a student at the University of North Carolina, whose daily life unfolded in this particular cultural context, and who displayed a surprising capacity for self-reflection.

Mullins was a grocer's son from Fayetteville, North Carolina, who dreamed of becoming a scholar and lawyer. After attending the Donaldson Academy in his hometown, Mullins matriculated at the University of North Carolina in 1839. There he soon became immersed in an altogether new and conflicting college life, where he struggled for reputation, honor, and character.[42] As a freshman he showed great enthusiasm for schoolwork and sought the approval of prominent members of the Philanthropic Society. His reputation soon came into question, however, when he befriended "the three most dissipated students in college," Sheppard K. Nash, Alfred M. Taylor, and Lucius J. Johnson.[43] Mullins joined these campus misfits as they drank, gambled, and swore their way through the school year. In his own words, Mullins "unconsciously received a tinge from their character, and ere I knew what I was doing, became a rowdy."[44] Although scholars have argued that southern collegians prided themselves on this sort of behavior, Mullins found that misbehavior tarnished his reputation among many distinguished members of the Philanthropic Society, including a longtime friend. Although things looked more promising for Mullins at the start of his junior year, as his dissipated friends had either been expelled or (barely) graduated, the struggling grocer's son instigated a campus-wide prank that further diminished his popularity and called to question the meaning of southern honor.

In the fall of 1840, Mullins and some friends made all the arrangements necessary for a "sham duel," which promised to be a funny joke until word spread around campus. Freshmen in the Dialectic Society were "frightened nearly to death" at the prospect of open violence on campus, and rumors ran wild until Mullins and company admitted that everything was a ruse. There would be no duel on campus that October. Once again Mullins found himself estranged from his fellow "Phis," who viewed the hoax as a dishonor to their literary society. His classmates bullied Mullins, "Hero of the Sham Duel," causing him to threaten anyone who ridiculed him to a *real* duel. "I wish to have no trouble, but if they force me to an encounter," he confessed in his diary, "I shall not shrink from carrying it to extremes, even if it involves one of their lives."[45] Indeed Mullins carried his pistol with him on campus, though he never instigated a duel, real or otherwise.[46]

Stories of collegians often stop here, with the misbehavior reported and cited as an example of pampered collegians raising a ruckus on campus. But if we dig deeper into Mullins's own reflections, we see the very real interaction between codes of honor and mainstream values associated with character, and a striking capacity for self-analysis and self-improvement wholly at odds with the popular notion of southern college life. Indeed Mullins wrote in his diary that he learned "several important lessons" from the hoax that reveal this complicated cultural web: that he and his friends should have quickly demonstrated that the duel was fabricated; that the way they handled the prank was "not sufficiently prudent"; and that juvenile pranks "can do no good—they *may* do much harm." Regarding this final lesson, Mullins added, "Those who are hoaxed are apt to be offended: and those not, raise a laugh that is rather annoying. They do not produce a favourable impression of an individual's steadiness or gravity and are well adapted to diminish respect."[47] The affair was not just dishonorable; it was also immature. As "Hero of the Sham Duel," Mullins acted outside of the bounds of character as well as honor. Mullins's efforts to recover from his miserable first years of college indeed help to shed light on the more personal dimensions of this culture in which honor and character mixed and shaped students' understandings of themselves.

Perhaps the "sham duel" made Mullins hyperaware of the important work that had to go into character formation during his college years. His daily journal writing suggests that this was the case. When he began his journal in 1840, for example, Mullins wrote about the necessity of self-improvement: "He [a young man] should carefully gather from his past history, wisdom for his future conduct. He must ultimately learn the great truth that his purest happiness is connected inseparably with the constant exercise of virtue. . . . To become acquainted with the abundant proofs of these, which are afforded in my own life, is the object of the Journal."[48] Within his diary Mullins turned a critical eye not only on himself but also on his classmates, writing about each member of his class. "The task I undertake shall be *frankly* performed and I will dare to write fully my thoughts," wrote Mullins. "When I have done, I shall recur to these pages with deep solicitude. My opinion of them then, shall likewise be given here, and I will sit in judgment on myself as well as others. I feel that *may* make the exercise I am commencing now, most useful to me through life, and my character *can* now be vastly improved, while my knowledge *must* be . . . increased."[49] Mullins also noted character flaws. In writing about John Davis Hawkins, for example, Mullins wrote, "He loved pleasure, and he pursued it in College, giving to that pursuit the time which of right belonged to self-improvement. Alas. He was not singular in this respect."[50]

In an effort to create a well-balanced character, Mullins developed daily reading habits. Reading, as students saw it, promoted a slew of values associated with individual character—mental discipline, emulation, industry, perseverance, and so on. In the antebellum period, therefore, students consistently encouraged one another to read "useful" literature, especially history and biography, which related directly to individual character development.[51] In just under two years, Mullins visited the Philanthropic Society library at least fifty-five times and borrowed 112 titles, or approximately 148 volumes at a rate of about 9 volumes per month. Library records suggest that Mullins favored fiction, but also read a good bit of periodical literature, philosophy, drama, history, and biography. He recorded his impressions of the works he read, which sometimes involved introspection. After reading James Mackintosh's *The Life of Sir Thomas More* (1830), Mullins enumerated many attributes of More's character: "unceasing industry," honor, honesty, and "love of virtue." These "distinguishing characteristics," Mullins concluded, "points the mind to excellence and glory in any trial. . . . May he [More] be my polar star!"[52] Mullins revealed a similar ambition in a response to a biography of Cardinal Wolsey in Lardner's *Encyclopedia.* "I will . . . aim high; my goal shall be noble, and if I fail to reach it, I shall not be utterly without consolation. As I look back on past years, I shall see what I strove to be and shall stand at least a monument of good intentions," he wrote.[53] In each case biography compelled Mullins to turn inward and assess his own character formation and the work he needed to put into it in order to achieve the success he desired.[54]

And that's exactly what Mullins did; he worked hard. He tackled his own character flaws head-on, recording in his diary efforts to end and forestall bad habits like drinking, swearing, and masturbating. Cultivating personal piety through devotional life was central to these efforts. Church was an important part of Mullins's self-improvement plan, and he often attended Sunday services at the local Episcopal church in addition to the required university services. "For the poor, trembling sinner," he wrote in his diary, "there is no better time to turn from the evil of his way." In particular Mullins noted in his diary that he benefited from hearing Professor William Mercer Green deliver a sermon on "the proper means to be pursued by one who desired the conversion of his soul." Green taught that "prayer, diligent perusal of the Bible, and meditation" were the only "means by which an erring sinner might obtain pardon."[55]

Accordingly Mullins incorporated daily devotional life into his own plan for moral improvement, often writing prayers in his journal. The "dissipation and shameful wickedness" of his first two and a half years at college, for instance, promoted Mullins to write the following prayer: "Oh! Lord!" he begged, "have mercy on me. Wicked as I have been, I am not too vile for the Saviour's blood to cleanse me, and through the merits of that blood, I implore thee to subdue my heart and transform it. Oh! Holy Spirit, visit me and abide with me continually, and by thy agency, let me be numbered among the just made perfect."[56] Mullins also believed he needed to do more than pray; he had to adopt a daily devotional life common to evangelicalism. He promised to pursue "sound practical piety," and "adopt" Christianity "as the rule of my life, the charter of my hopes, the god of my life."[57] In particular Mullins set nighttime aside for "solemn reflection" and private religious practices, which included reading the Bible before he "retire[d] to bed." He hoped that this practice would "have a beneficial effect on my conduct, and will give a healthy, religious tone to all my thoughts and feelings."[58] Even though students were required to attend daily prayer services and weekly Bible recitations and worship services, they carved out space for devotional practices to facilitate self-improvement.[59]

In many ways Mullins is quite typical of young men of his era and social background who tackled the work of growing up head-on. He took to heart many of the lessons about mental and moral improvement that permeated formal and informal life at North Carolina. He recognized that the passionate impulses of youth, sexual or otherwise, did not make the man. Instead he wanted to strengthen his mind and morals. His system for moral self-formation fit perfectly into the expectations for antebellum self-fashioning—he went to church, read the Bible, prayed, stopped drinking, and maybe even quit his so-called deadly vice. We will never know whether Mullins reached the heroic potential he imagined for himself. If he continued to write in journals as an adult, we have no record of it. Nevertheless Mullins reveals the complex ways in which seemingly disparate cultural values shaped young men's experiences of education and maturation in the antebellum period.

Since the publication more than thirty years ago of Bertram Wyatt-Brown's groundbreaking book *Southern Honor: Ethics and Behavior in the Old South,* few studies of southern culture have *not* included the phrase "southern honor." Honor has shaped how we understand topics as sprawling as education, slavery, family, gender, politics, law, religion, baseball, hunting, lynching, secession, and the Civil War. For historians of southern men in particular, honor has explained what made southern men of all types *southern,* which always seems to mean different or exceptional from a national or transatlantic normative type. By focusing on how attitudes about character circulated within antebellum southern colleges and universities in the antebellum period, this essay suggests that honor was more complicated among young southern men than is commonly granted. These men-in-the-making worked hard to shape and define honor in the context of a southern middle class.

Perhaps the most profound ways in which southern honor manifested at antebellum colleges was in the continued reliance on all-male peer groups for validation and approval of young men's actions as well as their characters. Recent literature on the problem of southern honor has emphasized this enduring quality, particularly in its simultaneous ability to exclude others. Students did not consider women and college slaves, for instance, active agents in the processes of mental and moral improvement, or character formation, during their college years. As historians such as Edward Baptist, Jennifer Green, and Ami Pflugrad-Jackish have argued, this enduring manifestation of southern honor in the antebellum period contributed to the exclusivity of white male society.[60]

Students' male culture, however, was not immune to broader social and cultural transformations occurring in the South during the era of the Market Revolution. Advances in print and communication described in the work of Daniel Walker Howe connected southern students to northern culture. In particular emerging bourgeois ideals of a well-balanced character appeared front and center in college life. Students did not hesitate to integrate these values within the honor ethic that lingered in various forms from the eighteenth century. Indeed students came to recognize the pursuit and achievement of character as a matter of maturity—manhood—and therefore an honorable pursuit. Students incorporated mainstream values such as industry, perseverance, sobriety, and piety into their development individually and collectively. In the end the work of character that many young southerners undertook in the antebellum period erodes our strict understanding of southern culture as exceptional based on honor as a defining cultural idiom.

NOTES

1. "Faculty Minutes Including the Testimony on the Duel between Thomas H. Benton and Archibald Lytle, 1799," vol. 1:1, Minutes of the General Faculty and of the Faculty Council, University Archives, University of North Carolina at Chapel Hill (hereafter UA). See also Peterkin, "Lux, Libertas, and Learning," iv.

2. Adams, *Education of Henry Adams,* 57–58.

3. There is excellent scholarship on advice to young men and moral reform in the antebellum period. See, for example, Horlick, *Country Boys and Merchant Princes;* P. Johnson, *Shopkeepers' Millennium;* Hessinger, *Seduced, Abandoned, and Reborn;* B. Dorsey, *Reforming Men and Women;* Abzug, *Cosmos Crumbling;* Horwitz, *Rereading Sex;* Nissenbaum, *Sex, Diet, and Debility.*

4. Wyatt-Brown, *Southern Honor,* 164. Wyatt-Brown overemphasizes this point about the regionalism of male youth culture. Joseph Kett and E. Anthony Rotundo make similar arguments in *Rites of Passage* and *American Manhood,* respectively.

5. See, for example, Glover, *Southern Sons,* 37–82. Many interpretations focus on college men and honor: R. Pace, *Halls of Honor;* Drinkwater, "Honor and Student Misconduct in Southern Antebellum Colleges"; Wagoner, "Honor and Dishonor at Mr. Jefferson's University"; Wall, "Students and Student Life at the University of Virginia"; Tomlinson and Windham, "Northern Piety and Southern Honor"; Wakelyn, "Antebellum College Life and the Relations between Fathers and Sons."

6. Pace and Bjornsen, "Adolescent Honor," 12. Pace further explores this thesis in *Halls of Honor,* which was the first reinterpretation of southern college life to reappear since E. Merton Coulter published *College Life in the Old South* in 1928. My recent book *Intellectual Manhood* offers a corrective to Pace's work and is the first to examine the intellectual culture of higher education as a culturally meaningful process for students and their professors.

7. For another overview of scholarship on southern manhood, particularly the relationships among honor, mastery, and manhood, see Friend and Glover, *Southern Manhood,* vii–xvii. Important works on manhood from the perspective of gender include Cashin, *Family Venture;* Stowe, *Intimacy and Power;* Baptist, *Creating an Old South;* Glover, *Southern Sons;* and Jabour, "Male Friendship and Masculinity" and "Masculinity and Adolescence." Two exceptional works on the antebellum period are Mayfield, *Counterfeit Gentlemen,* and Pflugrad-Jackisch, *Brothers of a Vow.* On the Civil War era, see Berry, *All That Makes a Man* and *Princes of Cotton;* Carmichael, *Last Generation.*

8. Here I echo Stephen Berry's suggestion to better underscore how southern manhood changed over time. See *Princes of Cotton,* x–xi.

9. In particular see Heyrman, *Southern Cross;* Lindman, "Acting the Manly Christian"; Carney, *Ministers and Masters.* Carney acknowledges the complexity of masculinity in the antebellum period but nevertheless seems to view traditional southern masculinity and religious masculinity as difficult to reconcile.

10. On disorder in early national colleges, see Kett, *Rites of Passage;* Novak, *Rights of Youth;* Jackson, "Rights of Man and the Rites of Youth," 46–79.

11. Snider, *Light on the Hill,* 43.

12. Richard Armistead in Faculty Report, March 8,1802, vol. 1:1, Minutes of Faculty Meetings, 1799–1814, UA.

13. Faculty Report, October 18, 1802, vol. 1:1, Minutes of Faculty meetings, 1799–1814, UA.

14. E. Coulter, *College Life in the Old South,* 60.

15. For greater elaboration of these issues see T. Williams, *Intellectual Manhood.*

16. Howe, *Making the American Self,* 5.

17. Augst, *Clerk's Tale,* 1–2, 4.

18. Casper, *Constructing American Lives.*

19. Hayne, *Anniversary Address,* 1.

20. Huntington, "Individuality," 24. Emphasis in original.

21. Hayne, "Anniversary Address," 9–10. Emphasis in original.

22. Calvin Jones, "Address Delivered before the Philomathic Society," 16.

23. Dusenbery, August 7, 1841, Diary, Folder 1, James Lawrence Dusenbery Diary and Clipping, Southern Historical Collection, Wilson Library, University of North Carolina, Chapel Hill, North Carolina (hereinafter SHC). Mullins, August 1, 1841, William Sidney Mullins Diary, SHC.

24. W. Hooper, "Discipline of the Heart," 11.

25. Ibid., 19–20.

26. W. Hooper, "Discipline of the Heart," 1.

27. James Henderson Dickson, Inaugural Address, August 23, 1822, Dialectic Society Records, UA.

28. On Xenephon see Elam Alexander, Address, February 1825, and James Alfred Patton, Inaugural Address, July 24, 1850, Dialectic Society Records, UA; on Cicero see Robert Williams Henry, Inaugural Address, 1835, Dialectic Society Records, UA; Thomas Miles Garrett, August 21, 1849, Diary, Typed Transcript, SHC.

29. Caldwell, "A New System of Geometry," 1806, Folder 4, vol. 2, 14–15, Joseph Caldwell Papers, SHC.

30. Foster, "Speech of W. F. Foster of Ala[bama]," Junior Debate for 1858, Dialectic Society Records, UA.

31. Edmund Covington, October 6, 1842, Diary, SHC. On merit-based distinctions and the emerging American bourgeoisie, see Hessinger, *Seduced, Abandoned, and Reborn,* 94–95. For varying positions among antebellum students, see Richmond Nicolas Pearson, [Junior] Oration [ca. 1840], Robert Duncan Dickson, [Junior] Oration [ca. 1840], Charles Phillips, "[On College Distinctions]," [ca. 1840], all in Senior and Junior Orations, North Carolina Collection, Wilson Library, University of North Carolina, Chapel Hill, North Carolina (hereinafter NCC).

32. R. Pace maintains that honor was not the cause of cheating, though it "weigh[ed] heavily in the background." See *Halls of Honor,* 28.

33. On the history of literary societies, see Horowitz, *Campus Life,* 25; Potter, "Literary Society," 238–40; Robson, *Educating Republicans,* 186.

34. Euprhadian Society Constitution, 1806, vol. 1, Euphradian Society Records, 1806–1908, Microfilm Roll #1, South Caroliniana Collection, Columbia, South Carolina.

35. Membership pledge of the Dialectic Society, Dialectic Society Minutes, vol. 3, Dialectic Society Records, UA.

36. Thomas Pleasant Hall, Oration, [1825–27], Series 2.1, Dialectic Society Records, UA. See also John James Reese, March 11, 1843, "Presidential Address," Dialectic Society Records.

37. Calvin Jones, "Address Delivered before the Philomathic Society," 3, 15.

38. Daniel Forney, "Is Duelling Justifiable," August 29, 1804, Dialectic Society Records, UA.

39. Dialectic Society Minutes, July 9, 1795, September 7, 1797, May 24, 1804, February 9, 1805, October 6, 1808, February 21, 1811, March 5, 1816, September 17, 1823, August 11, 1824, November 12, 1834, August 17, 1838, September 25, 1838, September 30, 1859, Dialectic Records, UA.

40. Casper, *Constructing American Lives*; Jesse Hargrave, Composition, August 23, 1856, Dialectic Society Records, UNC. Also see Bedford Brown, "Address" (1839), and Edmund Gregory Prout, "The Life and Writings of Sallust," Senior Oration, October 1, 1865, Dialectic Society Records, UA.

41. This was common throughout the antebellum United States. See the appendixes to Harding, *College Literary Societies*. On Washington and Columbus, see, for example, Philanthropic Society Minutes, October 13, 1807, February 21, 1809, July 31, 1801, March 31, 1812, March 19, 1828, July 2, 1840, October 2, 1841, August 21, 1857, Philanthropic Society Records, UA.

42. Mullins, November 4, 1840, William Sidney Mullins Diary, SHC. Ishkanian, "Religion and Honor at Chapel Hill," 57–66.

43. Mullins, November 15, 1840, William Sidney Mullins Diary, SHC; Ishkanian, "Religion and Honor at Chapel Hill," 74.

44. Mullins, November 15, 1840, William Sidney Mullins Diary, SHC; Ishkanian, "Religion and Honor at Chapel Hill," 73.

45. Mullins, November 15, 1840, William Sidney Mullins Diary, SHC.

46. Ishkanian, "Religion and Honor at Chapel Hill," 72–76. Additional discussions of the "sham duel" can be found in R. Pace, *Halls of Honor*, 96; Pace and Bjornsen, "Adolescent Honor," 21–24.

47. Mullins, October 28, 1840, William Sidney Mullins Diary, SHC. Emphasis in original. The lessons Mullins learned in the sham duel confirm Kenneth Greenberg's argument that duels were supposed to elevate honesty above all else. See *Honor and Slavery*, 8, 25, 49, 135.

48. Mullins, October 27, 1840, William Sidney Mullins Diary, SHC.

49. Mullins, June 14, 1841. Emphasis in original.

50. Mullins, August 26, 1841, William Sidney Mullins Diary, SHC. Mullins was not the only southern student to write about classmates' characters. See, for example, Edmund Covington, undated, Edmund DeBerry Covington Diary, SHC.

51. Two good examples are Iveson L. Brookes, Inaugural Address, September 1818, and John Madison Stedman, Inaugural Address, February 25, 1830, Dialectic Society Records, SHC.

52. Mullins, January 26, 1841,

53. Mullins, February 11, 1841, William Sidney Mullins Diary, SHC.

54. Mullins's engagement with biography was not uncommon. See Garrett, September 4, 1849, October 15, 1849, Diary, Typed Transcript, 114, SHC.

55. Mullins, February 7, February 21, July 18, 1841, William Sidney Mullins Diary, SHC.

56. Mullins, August 8. 1841, William Sidney Mullins Diary, SHC.

57. Mullins, August 8. 1841, William Sidney Mullins Diary, SHC.

58. Dusenbery, August 7, 1841, Diary, Folder 1, James Lawrence Dusenbery Diary and Clipping, SHC. Also see Thompson, 1851, George N. Thompson Diary, SHC. Benson Field Cole, Diary,

1852–56, MS 269, Benson Field Cole Papers, Z. Smith Reynolds Library, Wake Forest University, Winston-Salem, North Carolina. On young southern evangelicals, see Causey, "Character of a Gentleman"; Young, "Religious Coming of Age among Students at Antebellum Georgia's Evangelical Colleges."

59. Mullins, March 7 and February 14, 1841, William Sidney Mullins Diary, SHC.

60. Baptist, "Me and Southern Honor," 14; J. R. Green, *Military Education;* Pflugrad-Jackish, *Brothers of a Vow,* 2.

Lawrence T. McDonnell

"THE DECEIVINGEST FELLOW"

Honor, Respectability, and the Crisis of Character in the Old South

Across the 1850s a crisis of character swept over the slave South, intersecting with political turmoil and impelling men toward the disaster of disunion.[1] With mounting anxiety newspapers, pamphlets, and periodicals scrutinized the social deportment and personal characteristics of southern gentlemen. The more writers wrote, the more their depictions of manly character diverged, clashed, and soared out of reach. At street level, as religious evangelism competed with a boom in secular voluntarism, an eccentric, aggressive cult of chivalry, and other forms of hypermasculinity, men strove to portray themselves as worthy, potent, even heroic. New styles of dress, social celebrations and rituals, and interpersonal customs vied for dominance. Inevitably these uncoordinated, ad hoc innovations sparked both a resurgence of dueling and a powerful backlash that denounced the code of honor's rule as lawless, ungodly, and barbaric. By the hour of Lincoln's election, just how southern men were supposed to conduct themselves, how to evaluate that conduct, and how to justify that evaluation was much in doubt.

No one so perfectly personified this crisis as David Theophilus Hines. Dave was an American celebrity, striding across the pages of newspapers from New York to New Orleans to California, arousing anger, dismay, jollity, and admiration. He hobnobbed with the powerful, the fashionable, and the famous. His name pops up in public records all over the country. Two popular memoirs glorify his character and career. Everywhere he went Hines was seen as the acme of southern honor, a model for youngsters looking for a leg up in the world. But Dave, alas, was not at all what he seemed, as men and women found out again and again to their consternation. Quite forgotten today, Hines was a confidence man—perhaps *The Confidence Man*—the most famous liar of his age.[2] From notorious to nothing is quite a come-down, especially for a fellow who faked his way across states and thresholds, decades and situations, Br'er Rabbiting into and out of one adventure after another. Dave's story is worth telling for the pure knee-slapping fun of it. But what he called fun others called crisis.[3]

Dave dead makes trouble for historians just as disturbingly as he did for contemporaries who tried to read his identity, motives, and character. Reckoning the truth of a professional liar's life is deep play: Hines's hoaxing aimed at seamlessness, avoiding the sort of uproar P. T. Barnum's humbug thrived on.[4] And smooth he was, even in the tightest squeeze. "It is a pity that Dave is such a rascal," Charleston's Peter Porcher declared in 1839, for he seemed altogether honorable, "generous and disinterested"—exactly what a gentleman was supposed to be. The trouble was his every word and gesture was a sham, the all-too-realistic performance of "the deceivingest fellow you ever did see."[5] His biography had no beginning, his tricks no end.

Dave seemed to come out of nowhere—which was almost true. Dressed sharp, parading faultless manners, portraying an attractively cool, manly demeanor on the day they met at a Tennessee mountain resort, "Doctor" Hines was worlds away from his humble origin as an overseer's son on Porcher's uncle's plantation, near a lowcountry crossroads appropriately called Scuffletown. Born about 1809, Hines was apprenticed to a Charleston druggist where—somehow—the young nobody went wrong.[6] Perhaps it was the gap between poverty and wealth he saw, the juxtaposition of legitimate and illegitimate social behavior in the marvelously wicked Holy City. Certainly his access to and knowledge of opiates and abortifacients and his connections with those in search of shady substances cannot have nurtured a sense of propriety in the lad. Undeniably Dave envied those of lesser ability who held higher status because of name or wealth. Given a chance he knew he could strut with the best of them.

In 1831 Hines constructed that chance, in the form of a banknote endorsed to him by a wealthy neighbor. When the sheriff hunted him down for forgery, Dave drew down with a pistol, furious that his honor was questioned. Suppose that *someone* had counterfeited the note: why blame him for the misdeed? Why should the law doubt his standing as a gentleman when the merchant who cashed the check had not? Posing the question thus transformed petty crime into social crisis: just what, Hines implicitly asked, was the true foundation of southern honor?

Like jesting Pilate, Dave did not stay for an answer. His flight from justice offers the first good glimpse we have of him: a man of "small stature" and "pale complexion," riding "a fine bay mare of great fleetness" away from his home in St. Stephen's Parish, his "short brown coat" and "drab pantaloons" flapping in the breeze. Others constructed this scene as a "well-known" rogue's flight from punishment; Dave called it a decisive moment in a heroic quest to realize personal ambition and win the honor "evil forces" had long denied him. Locals figured he was headed to Alabama or Mississippi—still mostly wild west and up for grabs—but soon he sailed straight up north, trading his "leather cap" for a beaver hat. The game was on.[7]

From 1831 to 1864, Hines ranged all over the eastern United States, from Galveston, Mobile, and New Orleans to St. Louis, Cincinnati, and Saratoga Springs, pulsing steadily between Charleston and New York—and a variety of prisons and penitentiaries in between. By 1833 he was back home, having avoided jail on a technicality, bankrupt, and seeking a new start.[8] Three years more found him in

Manhattan, perfecting his southern gentleman persona and trying on a variety of aliases. Next he went west, deploying alternate identities in Kentucky and Tennessee. Everywhere suave manners, cool confidence, and good clothes opened doors. Henry Clay took him for a gentleman, as did Andrew Jackson, and all those ranging down the social order. They all doffed their hats to him, and Dave laughed into his in reply.

What sort of gentleman could not tell a gentleman from a rogue? Why was it that men who claimed a place within the circle of honor were so easily bamboozled by one who only pretended to that rank? Just about everyone in America knew Dave, or thought they did. Yet almost no one saw him coming. Some few suffered for that error in a financial sense. Many more railed against his casual misappropriation of friendship, propinquity, identity, honor. But the fault in such cases, Hines insisted indignantly, rested entirely with the flimflammed. All Americans on the eve of the Civil War knew to scan any social situation, reading action as melodrama and penetrating to the heart of falsehood.[9] The careless got flummoxed and fleeced and started over again, a little wiser, perhaps. Ranking reputations within a stable community was not difficult: according to honor's scale, one did as had been done, mostly. Calculating by the competing yardstick of respectability was only as risky as figuring which way the wind blew, and reckoning whether and when it was likely to turn about. But few antebellum communities were stable, and fortunes changed relentlessly.[10] No wonder Dave hoodwinked men great and small, honorable and respectable. Who could have expected a landless young fellow deep in debt in rural South Carolina to reinvent himself a thousand miles away as a gentleman of culture and sophistication—without improving his purse or social standing one whit?[11] According to honor's code, a man could no more transform personal identity than he could change the nose on his face.[12] The leap from Scuffletown to high society was too vast to imagine. The failure of honorable men to pick out a villain in their midst was too terrible to contemplate.

Hines looked like a southern gentleman, "fine looking, . . . well set, middle height, of good address," dandified but never flash. He acted as any planter, editor, or politician plausibly would, displaying credentials of merit, wealth, and standing. He portrayed the height of politesse—splendid manners, impeccable dress, and a frank, independent bearing that personified grace. Others called him the "shade of Beau Brummel."[13] He called himself many names—Colonel Allston, Lieutenant Pringle, Major Middleton, Doctor Haynes, Professor Porcher, Reverend Baker, and dozens more, even impersonating James Hamilton, former governor of South Carolina, the "Bayard of the South."[14] David T. Hines was no Dandy Jim Hamilton. But if the antithesis of honor could be mistaken for the acme of honor by men who called themselves honorable gentlemen, what did that slip portend?

Long before he fled Charleston, Dave made himself infamous, swindling cash and running wild in bordellos and "gambling hells." Locals learned to steer clear.

After 1831, though, Hines found his stride, focusing on smaller communities where unknown gents landed up for a short week or so before streaming through, or big cities where men who mattered recognized each other by outward details of social class and declarative clues to personal character. Dave thrived on the pervasive incompetence of honor's devotees to read those signs aright: grifting and counterfeiting; stealing slaves, horses, and carriages; conning men and women, high and low, out of just about anything that might be turned to cash. He masqueraded in the company of the great and powerful, fooling John J. Crittenden in Kentucky, James Gordon Bennett of New York, and countless others who only aspired to honor or respectability. He made common cause with notorious rogues and ne'er-do-wells.[15] He haunted barrooms, whorehouses, and theaters, peddling drugs, extorting and swindling fools, performing abortions. He married and quit a string of women nonsequentially, seduced a dozen more, assaulted at least one, and may have been a serial rapist. By the time things came crashing down in 1839—a stolen slave, a recklessly bold denial of fault, a guilty verdict—Dave earned fourteen years in a Baton Rouge penitentiary. Doctor Hines's celebrity carried a steep price tag.

Yet, at just this moment, Dave determined to make his plight pay.[16] Rather than repenting his sins, he published them in book form, dragging all manner of well-known men into his "life of action, enterprise, and ingenuity," fit subjects for mockery and mirth. True, there was "scarcely any portion of the country which he ha[d] not visited . . . uniformly swindl[ing] every man who . . . put it in his power to do so."[17] But Hines was merely one of those *"chevaliers d'industrie"*—an entrepreneur—"whose researches and appropriations extend to all communities and to every variety of movables." Call him a villain, and what could one make of that vast tribe who preached the gospel of merchant capital, buying cheap and selling dear? Until recently historians have considered the categories of visionary, entrepreneur, financier, trader, shyster, and fraud analytically distinct, yet such boundaries were not nearly so clear in the antebellum era. Nor was it yet obvious just which parts of the emerging capitalist economy should be deemed legitimate and which consigned underground. This was a well-fertilized terrain of political struggle scholars are only beginning to explore, and David Hines, by his own lights, just one mushroom among millions, seeking sun and sustenance.

If, as a "Professor of Appropriation," Dave's experiments had momentarily failed, that hardly meant that he had learned—or should learn—any lesson, beyond Wordsworth's "good old rule": "the simple plan, / That they should take, who have the power, / And they should keep, who can." That dog-eat-dog ethos had suited the "dauntless heart" of Rob Roy and Robin Hood; so it served a thief as "wise and brave" as Dave—and might prove profitable to those who emulated his example.[18]

For pure cheek, though, anyone would be hard pressed to match Hines. As much as the Doctor had once been reviled and feared, the incarcerated Dave was "celebrated" as "a smart, active fellow," "a second *Paul Clifford*," the chivalrous fictional highwayman who operated famously on “a dark and stormy night.”[19] Sorting true from false in his book became a kind of parlor game. As with other famous fakeries of the age—Sam Slick’s Yankee clocks, Johann Maelzel’s Automaton Chess Player, Barnum’s Fiji Mermaid, the crooked cons, trouser-wearing women, and effeminate “foo-foos” who confronted Mose the Bowery B’hoy—readers delighted in the battle of wits between Dave and his foes, spying out the clues to identity his victims missed, hanging on the suspense of character so nearly, nakedly revealed.[20] It was an age of melodrama, when success in daily life depended on an instant, accurate reading of and precisely modulated response to a host of characters, real and pretended, in a world of personages and strangers, rising and falling, coming and going as never before in American lived experience. Emerson spoke of skating expertly on surfaces, but Melville knew that life was more like bobbing alone in shark-filled seas, clinging gladly to another man’s coffin. No wonder men cheered a free swimmer like Dave, and delighted when he bit down hard. His was a freedom, a craft, an acuity of vision they hungered for, the stuff that made men famous and rich.[21]

Soon second-string Daves began popping up in jails around the South, petty thieves and con men aspiring to the life, the fame, even the name of Doctor Hines. That the real Dave tried to break jail twice after sentencing only increased uncertainty about imposters who washed up in the hands of the law: was this fellow or that a failed performance of the celebrated scoundrel, or was it all quite the reverse?[22] In a moment of financial, technological, communications, and detective revolution, when telegraphs, daguerreotypes, rotary-press-printed newspapers, railroad travel, prices-current sheets, and professional police forces flooded the South, men asked whether Dave—supervillain or superhero—had outrun them all. As years passed and Hines rotted in prison, the question changed: could time and reflection reform the rogue? “There is a ‘balm in Gilead,’” optimists preached. “Amen!” shouted the host of doctors, lawyers, colonels, preachers, and more, all from within the confines of a single cell.[23]

In 1852 Louisiana’s governor pardoned Hines for good behavior.[24] Dave had always known how to behave, and how to wait. What difference did twelve years of boot making and bad meals make? By summer, a book-length, tell-all memoir had landed in stores across the country. Hines might have stopped there and gone on the stump like any number of famous men, lecturing and performing for cash. Instead, just as quickly, the Doctor was on the run once more. In August he broke jail in Georgia, where he had been lodged for unspecified crimes. Word said they caught him in Macon, quite “behind the age” for a man of his sagacity.[25] The 1850s went mostly like that for the “rare chap”: his fame preceded him, capture was increasingly easy, and perhaps he enjoyed the attention. Or maybe someone else did. One Baltimore report from 1852 described a typical mix-up: the Hines in Savannah jail was really Jesse Quantrill; the Quantrill in a Kentucky penitentiary was really

Dr. B. J. Hayne; Dave, one way or another, was out roaming. Eventually, right or wrong, catching up with the Colonel, or Doctor, or Reverend, came to seem like shooting fish in a barrel. There were just a whole lot of fish, big and little, fast and loose, as Melville would have said.[26]

Increasingly it was hard not to hit something that squeaked out the name Doctor Hines. By 1853 President Pierce had joined in the sport, pardoning Dave for stealing from the federal mails. In many communities he was arrested on sight, pushed onto a train or carriage, and sent packing. As long as he got a decent dinner and a measure of deference, Dave no longer seemed to mind. He was "polite and gentlemanly," ingratiating in "ten thousand" ways, famed for his "rascalities" from Maine to San Francisco.[27] And so respectable society achieved a rough, negotiated settlement with the South's most shameless citizen.

Honorable men had a tougher time of it. Frederick A. Porcher, professor of political economy at the College of Charleston, seethed when he thought of Hines. The rascal had been a rider thrown at the Pineville races in his youth, he recalled, then given a job as cow minder from plain sympathy. A poor boy worthy of honor? Porcher would not countenance the claim. Hines's career was "proof of the extreme gullibility of the American people," nothing more. Though he stole "the best names in the State," Porcher railed, Dave lacked "the manners, the address, or even the external appearance of a gentleman." Indeed his only qualification as a proper rogue, the professor thought, was "matchless effrontery."[28]

That was manifestly untrue. Hines was abundantly qualified, skilled, and successful—to a point. Hardly any criminal in antebellum America could match his fame, his range, or his run. His memoirs detail how Dave transformed himself into Doctor Hines, a process requiring cool brains, keen vision, ready wit, and nerves of steel. Like the best of actors, he had to inhabit the character he portrayed—"any number of abused names and titles"—yet stand apart from it, examining his impersonation and recalibrating his performance at every moment.[29] An arduous, nearly impossible task that sounds, yet the code of honor required it of every man within its circle at every moment in the Old South.[30] Surely that was what so vexed Porcher: Dave was so much better at perceiving and portraying honor than most anyone else, splendidly, shamelessly so. That was the true source of all the trouble he caused.

But why did he bother? By the 1850s Hines's impersonations were increasingly outwitted, deflected, or bought out as he revisited old stomping grounds. Once he had raided and plundered those too dim to tell a gentleman from a fake. Now communities saw Doctor Hines as a social type to be watched out for and hurried along. Subverting honor was seldom in the cards for Dave now, though taxing a community for dinner, a bed, a bit of joshing, and passage onward became his modus operandi. The honorable thief became an almost respectable celebrity. This was a bloodless, yet quite worrisome sort of *chevauchée*.

By his own lights, Dave presented himself as a true gentleman, standing for "gallant chivalry" and "honorable distinction" against "that class of persons who dislike the excellence of others because they never can attain it themselves."[31] And however odd it must have seemed to see Hines—of all men—portraying the social culmination of the southern elite, we should not doubt his sincerity. To an earlier age, honor had meant privilege, leisure, and license too, not moral uplift.[32] That paternalism conferred responsibilities on the gentry, as well as customary rights, had been easily forgotten. Before 1820 none had imagined portraying slavery as a positive good or planter society as the sine qua non of conservative civilization.[33] That chattel bondage allowed masters to get rich quick and wield political power to their liking was ethic enough. Certainly that attitude continued to thrive in the salons of many mansions in Charleston or New Orleans even after midcentury. But by 1850 honor's culture was besieged in the South—and most of the Western world—and chivalry's choices had come down to self-reform or self-destruction.[34] Doctor Hines summed up perfectly why the drive for social transformation was bound to fail.

The trouble was, though honor embraced all men, it reserved its richest prizes for the upper ranks, barring entrance to all but a handful pushing up from below. That was its political purpose. For men of superior ambition but lesser means, the only alternative was to embrace a potentially parallel status system. On the eve of Lincoln's election, honor's position as the dominant measure of personal attainment across much of the South was threatened by the market-driven ethos of respectability.[35]

The culture of respectability took root first among the urban middle class of England and the United States in the early Victorian period as a buttress against hedonistic excesses pinching bourgeois society from above and below.[36] Like honor, respectability structured reputation in terms of outward appearance and behavior, not inward consciousness: the feelings of the heart were too easily misapprehended or mimicked by those seeking to gull the unwary. Among men of honor, private emotions and intentions were simply irrelevant in calculating social standing. Likewise, for devotees of respectability, purity of heart was a goal to be prayed and striven for, but only the outward evidence of praying and striving could be calculated with any sort of assurance. Under honor's regime a man was the sum of his social relations, no more or less. For advocates of respectability, though, this led inevitably to a hypocritical "flunkeyism." Society here became a system of "toadyism organized—base Man-and-Mammon worship, instituted by command of law."[37] Respectable folk, rather, scrutinized outward demeanor to glimpse signs of the inner man. In this view men and women were stubbornly individual, defined by self-actuated behavior and discrete temperaments. Identities were irremediably singular.

Under each system hallmarks of personal worth were publicly demonstrated and not easily disguised. The qualities respectability venerated, though, clashed directly with those honor's code upheld. Piety, thrift, diligence, candor, propriety, temperance, and other like virtues were not fit topics of discussion among men of honor. Indeed a too-close inquiry might be positively dangerous. For respectable men these were clues, foundations of character that a man might strive to cultivate or ignore at his peril.[38] They were peculiarly reflexive, not relational qualities by which he would be measured and held responsible.

The achievement of the honorable man was always gauged with an eye toward what had been: reputation flowed from the past, real or imagined, to the present and was fixed by an imprecise equation of the two. But that was the attitude of a snob, respectable men held, one "who meanly admires mean things," transferring merit from a dubious source to an undeserving object. In the culture of respectability, attention was directed toward the future. "You must scorn delights," William Gilmore Simms warned southern youth; "you must live laborious days. You are not to think of pleasure, or wealth, or even fame, except as the humblest incidents and tributaries in the prosecution of duty. This duty is life, and life is self-development."[39] What a man was today was the surest sign of what he might become tomorrow. It was this individual journey of self-development and its destination that counted. Not that a man might not suddenly change course: the whole evangelical and reform movement of the age was based on just such an allowance. But there were definite paths to be followed with progressive steps of reward or punishment. All began innocent in the cradle, but while some climbed up to a home in heaven, others descended through sin to a place in hell. It was simply a matter of will, as Dave's career proved in spades.

Central to the power of this ideology was the way it discounted the fitness and permanence of honor's elite. High birth or property offered no advantage in the quest for respectability, advice manuals promised: "the man of iron will may safely pursue his way to success and competence." "We may still keep alive the artificial distinctions of birth and ancestry," Columbia lawyer David McCord allowed, "but let us give to that man of humble condition the opportunity to cultivate his mind . . . and he will soon turn into withering contempt and ridicule our secret and select assemblies; he will soon and easily level to the earth our threatening barricades, even were they of the height and dimensions of the Chinese Wall, and he will march directly and boldly into the very citadel of society, and share its pleasures, its counsels and its honors, in common with the proudest and most wealthy in the land." "Riches and rank have no necessary connexion with genuine gentlemanly qualities," British exhorter Samuel Smiles agreed. "The poor man may be a true gentleman—in spirit and in daily life. He may be honest, truthful, upright, polite, temperate, courageous, self-respecting, self-helping—that is, be a true gentleman."

By that standard the closed circle of elite clubs like Charleston's St. Cecilia Society was as likely to be ill-bred as overbred. Respectability announced a superior pedigree. So did Dave, "the man with the hundred names."[40]

Across the Victorian era, a flood of books, articles, lectures, and sermons cascaded down on Anglo-Americans, declaring the importance and particulars of being respectable. Anyone might put on a show of one or another of the manly virtues, but few were fooled. "No man can be properly called virtuous who is not habitually so," the Presbyterian divine James Henley Thornwell explained. The respectable man demonstrated integrity of character in the most theatrical sense: the various aspects of the role he performed hung together seamlessly. His position in the terrain of virtue and vice, considered as a map or stage, could be plotted precisely. Nothing could have been more discomfiting to honor's champions.[41]

Fear of social subversion in all its forms—snobbery, hypocrisy, denial of merit—drove respectability forward, and with it the ideal of the self-made man. In contrast to the man of action honor paraded, self-made men were notable especially as bearers of character, not doers of deeds. They were, by no accident, remarkably staid and retiring fellows—quite unlike the good Doctor. Passivity gave the purest proof of self-control. The problem, as literary historian Nina Auerbach has explained, was that as Victorians sought to realize their "best selves," their efforts too often trailed off into performance, trapping the self behind a mask. "To do, is to act," Auerbach quoted Melville; "so all doers are actors."[42] Dave could not have said it better himself.

The suspicion that equation aroused struck to the core of honor's ethos. Theatricality was the stock-in-trade of the swindler, the false-hearted harlot, the counterfeit gentleman. Who was safe when fakery invaded the public realm, the "calculating selfishness of the demagogue," and the "charlatancy of political empirics" masquerading as statesmanship? Lurking fears that ordinary men and women might slide into the same devices—or, worse, that they enacted multiple selves in the routine of daily life—were too troubling to contemplate for long. But how could identity escape from behind the mask? "It is scarcely possible to be ourselves without acting ourselves," Auerbach admited, "but to be sincere we must not act."[43]

Or, more precisely, Victorians could not be seen as acting. Either the observer's gaze had to be outrun—by fragmenting the world into various "spheres," for example—or the division between actor and audience transcended. In nineteenth-century theater, this imperative led to the triumph of melodrama, a mode of performance rooted in a "complex but infallibly readable system of coded gestures." As, in the grammar of cultural analysis, Martin Meisel has said of "realisation," the meaning of action here was revealed by connecting clues. The first step in this comforting decoding was the delimitation of a performance space—a market, a political rally, a parlor, a parade—and the common affirmation that within this liminal sphere actors were not merely acting. In Victorian society, as stages of action multiplied and overlapped, the willing suspension of disbelief became a precondition, yielded uneasily and sometimes faithlessly, of daily life under respectability's regime. Men and women came—or claimed—to have confidence in one another.[44]

Respectability was portrayed visually in melodramatic style: through one's features, clothing, manners, and gait; through one's household, possessions, and associates; through geographic situation and a careful balance between self-assertion and self-control. Shiny sleeves, reddened eyes, a choleric temper, forward manners, an impulsive streak: each offered warnings that a man fell short in one way or another. Yet it was dangerous to judge too hastily. A fellow might be down-at-the-heels, but with diligence, honesty, good companions, and patience he would surely rise. The Charleston furniture dealer E. R. Cowperthwait had only a small capital, credit reporters noted in 1848, yet he was "hon[est], Indus[trious] & saving," well on the way to becoming a "Snug man" with a "fair bus[iness]." "When you see a young man diligent in his calling, industrious in all his habits, and assiduously devoting himself to business," E. P. Rogers explained, "you at once have confidence in his character."[45] The French summed it up in the phrase *comme il faut:* a respectable man did respectable things in respectable places among respectable people. The link with—and threat to—honor's shape-shifting code became explicit in that truism.

There were any number of ways for honorable or respectable men to demonstrate worthiness, but the conflict between these perspectives and its social implications are best understood by focusing on the central tendency of each. The man of honor did his duty. The respectable man met his obligations. How vast the gulf between those imperatives: duty was an amorphous quality, socially defined; obligation a precise quantity, contractually delimited, calculated finally in dollars and cents. The honorable man gained reputation. The respectable man earned credit. "The whole composition of our society is arithmetical," one contemporary noted, "each gentleman ranking according to the numerical index of his property." That new math filled honor's votaries with horror.[46]

There was, to begin with, an astonishing apathy toward history among respectable men. Neither the pedigree of blood and kin honorable men based their claims of social worth on, nor the often bloody origins of the wealth on which respectability raised its mudsill, attracted much interest. Whether by hard work, sharp trading, sleight of hand, or simple violence, respectable men had acquired the coin that embodied power and identity both. And by that standard, the honorable man—worth a lick—might not yet be worth a loan. Among respectable men Charleston lawyer Isaac Hayne warned, "MONEY, with its attendant rank and influence, is . . . openly proclaimed to be all in all, and VIRTUE ridiculed as the dream of the enthusiast, or the catch word of the knave." Across the 1840s and 1850s, conservative southerners sneered at the emerging power of capital, damning its zero-sum ruthlessness and rejecting its sweeping, snooping redefinition of value.[47]

Though respectable folk ranked peers according to their deserts—for safety's sake, if no other reason—the true apostles of this rising regime were the credit agencies and life insurance companies that sprang up in these years, transferring calculation of property values to the estimation of human worth. Its chief historians were the army of clerks, bookkeepers, and accountants who recorded the measure of respectability to be accorded each man, be they of the "deserving" poor or the merchant "as sound as a dollar." Respectability went hand in hand with possessive individualism and all the social alienation that came in its train. Zalmon "Wildman will never set an ocean on fire," went one typical valuation, "but will always pay his debts pro[mptly]." That made the Charleston hatter "good" in the most meaningful sense. In America Alexis de Tocqueville affirmed, "the first of all distinctions is money."[48] No maxim better summed up the central tenet of emerging bourgeois society or measured the tide turning against honor's order in the Old South.

A host of hoaxers, real, fictional, and somewhere in between, had made that political point by 1860, skewering respectability and exploding honor's ethos at the same time. Herman Melville's shocking novel *The Confidence Man* (1857) only culminated efforts extending back through Barnum to the character of Jeremy Diddler and European imposters before him.[49] Unable to change a world that shut them out or drew their contempt, these "escapologists" changed themselves to appear to fit the categories that seemed most meritorious. Some few had higher motives—performing false identities for the benefit of others. Most adopted imposture for the same selfish, lazy reasons moderns embrace lifestyles rather than building lives. But the most dangerous of all was Dave.

Across three decades and more, curbing, corralling, changing David Hines proved impossible. Prison did not tame him, nor did public censure slow him down. He was in no way dispirited by defeat, or daunted by any obstacle. Indeed it would be difficult to find a better model in antebellum America for a truly heroic character—except that Dave was pure fake. But so, too, when it came down to it, were the ethical regimes of honor and respectability his conduct skewered. When Dave went strolling as a gentleman, from one end of the South to the other, how could honor's advocates answer him? Not only were they unable to outwit his dupery, but when they looked toward punishment, they could imagine nothing within the code of honor to set him straight—certainly not dueling—and so turned toward respectability's formal law. Imprisoning a rogue for impersonating a gentleman, though, could do nothing to vindicate honor's social hegemony. Likewise, declaring Hines at fault for forging a note, stealing a slave, or failing to pay a bill as promised was quite fruitless: however guilty the law adjudged him to be, Hines considered his standing as an honorable gentleman unblemished: he was utterly shameless. In this way a single man elaborated the differences between and called into question the central purposes of the competing regimes of honor and respectability on the eve of disunion. The crisis he caused rippled outward.

Dave saw things more clearly than most respectable men liked, and nearly any honorable men dared. His career pointed out how hopelessly flawed southern society was, and where its contradictions led. Was it any accident that David Hines became Dorsett Hamilton, or his supposed kinsman James? Jim Dandy had fallen from the pinnacle of southern honor in the 1830s and 1840s, piling up stacks of unpaid bills, dragging his friends' names through the mud, and perishing (however gallantly) on a foolish mission to rescue his ruined fortunes by peddling dubious Texan bonds. Yet through all the years of decline, no southerner dared speak a word against that soul of chivalry, much less haul him to court—unlike poor Dave. Likewise the proud Hamptons in the 1850s were a half million dollars in debt, at wit's end, and begging British middlemen for mercy, yet they remained heroes and kingmakers publicly. More than this their slaves were notoriously mistreated. Privately Fred Porcher berated himself as "a bad judge of men's characters . . . a bad manager of money . . . a bad planter, a bad master, a bad manager," hoodwinked by overseers and slaves alike, "faithless" to the task of manhood he faced—a total flop. There were thousands like him. Every month at every courthouse, especially in chivalrous South Carolina, slaves clustered around a bellowing sheriff, waiting to be sold from some humiliated fellow who had proven unable to meet old obligations to some preening bravo eager to create new ones. By the 1850s suits for debt across the state and further afield had blown sky high.[50]

Politically, too, hypocrisy reigned. John C. Calhoun was perennially penniless, anything but the titan of republican virtue history made him out to be. Still his leadership went unquestioned. Though he railed against "spoilsmen" who infected statesmanship, his political longevity owed precisely to his ability to reward allies and punish enemies in material terms. In spite of all their protestations of disinterest in political office, it was just those men who protested loudest who got elected most often—thanks in no little part to the barbecue and booze their friends ladled out, or the dollars and favors they waved around.[51] And what of the fire-eating leaders of the South who strove to claim Calhoun's mantle after 1850—mostly Carolinians, once again, like Dave himself—the Wigfalls, Yanceys, Keitts, and Yulees, angry, unreasonable men so unlike the model of political virtue they claimed to admire? The moderates like Preston Brooks they drew on to disaster? Or local politicos and editors who doubled down on vitriol because that won votes and sold papers?

Should we be surprised, then, that on the eve of secession, the planter elite embraced a craze for staging medieval jousting tournaments, dressing up as the Knight of This and the Lord of That, and performing their parts sincerely? That South Carolina steadfastly refused to grant a divorce to anyone under any conditions? Or that a fear of itinerant peddlers, foreign tradesmen and mechanics, or northern-born travelers and commercial men suffused the South? Or that honorable men blasted each other to kingdom come on the dueling ground at an increasingly rapid rate, especially in chivalrous South Carolina? At a time when vast estates like "Kensington" stood alongside "Poverty Hall," when grass widows, philandering galore, laudanum addiction, and "mulatto" babies multiplied, when honorable men could not tell the difference between a plain gentleman and a raving abolitionist like James Redpath when he walked into their drawing rooms, what gall it took—or strict class allegiance—to call David Hines an imposter.[52]

Such social contradictions we might multiply ad infinitum. And yet, come 1860, all that double-mindedness seemed to vanish instantly as southerners united in a common shout for secession and finally got what they said they wanted. And here we are humbugged once more by their performance, imagining that they were sincere, united, and truly aiming toward the thing they ultimately hit. One would suppose that the story of Dave—or just about any other instance of historical causation—would urge caution, to say the least. But as Doctor Hines proved again and again, men and women will see what they want to see, and talk themselves into believing it. We need to look closer, deeper, more carefully into the history of Dave and the Old South both if we mean to understand that crisis. There was more than a little con in Confederate nationalism.

As to David Hines, he was too wise to get caught up in the higher nonsense of disunion and civil war. On the eve of secession, "the venerable gentleman" still "maintain[ed] his respectability and dignity," roaming the region as the purported "traveling correspondent of a newspaper in South Carolina," landing in various jail cells, and merrily scamming the unwary. After three decades, it is fair to say, he knew no other life than to keep running, and it did help to keep supper on his plate, whether by scamming or serving time. As it happened, in 1860 he ran straight into a Tennessee prison on a three-year term for swindling.[53] The dream of somehow winning honor and wealth surely died hard, as it does for most men. But, immortal as Doctor Hines was, he probably saw that death only dimly, as it disappeared far behind, twirling in a cloud of dust as he sped on toward his next destination and better times. Any idiot knew better. This was a world of winners and losers. Dave's time was running out.

In 1863 he got out of jail in Memphis and went on the grift once more. Shortly after he was released by a Confederate court for crossing illicitly between the lines of Blue and Gray—he had strayed through liminal territory all his life—a teenager with a shotgun emptied both barrels into him down in St. Stephen's Parish in January 1865. The newspapers said that Doctor Hines died "almost immediately."[54] The story sounds implausible: how did one as clever as he so misread the clues that led to sudden doom? But we might say the same about the Old South as well. Imposters, sooner or later, are all found out.

NOTES

1. This argument is elaborated in McDonnell, "Elizabethan Dreams"; McDonnell, "Politics, Chess, Hats," chs. 4, 7–12.

2. Melville scholars seeking the identity of the "Confidence Man" have focused on Kentucky-born counterfeiter Monroe Edwards, but contemporaries noted that he "has been likened to Dr. Hines," a far more famous, wide-ranging, and (shall we say) well-rounded scoundrel. That James Gordon Bennett drew the contrast so, and not the other way round, weakens the Edwards-as-"Confidence-Man" argument. And Edwards was ten years dead when Melville's book appeared, while Hines was still going strong. Melville, *Confidence-Man; New York Herald,* November 6, 1841. Cf. Dillingham, *Melville's Short Fiction,* 51–52. A prime example of how Hines has given scholars the slip appears in Patricia Cohen's fine study of the murder of New York prostitute Helen Jewett. Cohen wondered about the identity of her victim's lover-doctor, who was surely Hines. Although she explored the case with care, she overlooked evidence linking Jewett to Edwards, Hines's sometime confederate. So she altogether missed Hines's account of Jewett's three-month excursion to Charleston, just before her death in 1836. Cohen, *Murder of Helen Jewett,* 105–8; *Life . . . of . . . Monroe Edwards; Life . . . of . . . Hines.*

3. Hines was famous throughout the nation, "well-known" in the South Carolina lowcountry by 1831, and referred to as "notorious" in nearly every account of his antics by decade's end. (Columbia, S.C.) *Southern Times and State Gazette,* May 28, 1831; (Philadelphia) *Pennsylvania Inquirer and Daily Courier,* November 23, 1839.

4. Cook, *Arts of Deception;* Geertz, *Interpretation of Cultures,* 412–53.

5. Peter C. Porcher to Elizabeth S. Porcher, April 29, May 12, 1839, Peter Cordes Porcher Papers.

6. This summary of Dave's career is based on *Life . . . of . . . Hines.*

7. *Southern Times and State Gazette,* May 18, 1831; (Philadelphia) *National Gazette,* May 28, 1831; *Charleston City Gazette,* May 18, 1831.

8. Petition of David T. Hines, October 16, 1833, Petitions and Schedules of Insolvent Debtors, Records of the Court of Common Pleas, Charleston County, South Carolina Department of Archives and History.

9. Halttunen, *Confidence Men;* Auerbach, *Private Theatricals;* Voskuil, *Acting Naturally.*

10. Cf. Balleisen, *Navigating Failure.*

11. *Columbia (S.C.) Telescope,* May 27, 1831.

12. Cf. Lukasik, *Discerning Characters.*

13. Dandyism implied precision of personal style, not overly elaborate costume. Moers, *Dandy.* By 1860, though, a different view was emerging. "A dandy is a chap who would be a lady if he could," opined one newspaper, "but as he can't, does all he can to show the world he is not a man." *Charleston Courier,* June 16, 1840, May 22, 1858; *Natchez (Miss.) Courier,* July 23, 1840.

14. That Hines passed himself off as "a fop, a decided fop," made it all the easier to impersonate the original "Jim Dandy." *New York Spectator,* August 3, 1840. But there may be more to this still. At various points, while he was in police custody, newspaper reports mocked Hines for a distinctive speech defect. (Philadelphia) *North American and Daily Advertiser,* October 23, 1840. Was this an attempt to portray Hines, the ultimate outlier, as homosexual?

15. *Charleston Courier,* June 16, 1840.

16. Quite possibly Hines was impelled by the initially negative press coverage of his arrest and trial. *Charleston Courier,* June 16, 1840; (Hartford, Conn.) *New England Weekly Review,* June 20, 1840.

17. *Camden (S.C.) Journal,* June 20, 1840.

18. This was, in effect, the tag line selling his memoir. *Charleston Courier,* July 30, 1840.

19. *Camden Journal,* June 20, 1840; *Pennsylvania Inquirer and Daily Courier,* June 22, 1840; *Niles' National Register,* 58 (1840): 263.

20. Haliburton, *Clockmaker;* Standage, *Turk;* Sue, *Mysteries of Charleston;* Baker, *Glance at New York.*

21. Davies, *Mirror of Nature;* McConachie, *Melodramatic Formations.*

22. (New York) *Morning Herald,* August 17, 1840; *Edgefield (S.C.) Advertiser,* October 8, 1840; *Mississippi Free Trader and Natchez Daily Gazette,* January 19, 1841; *New York Spectator,* February 3, 1841; (Charlestown) *Virginia Free Press,* February 4, 1841; *Greenville (S.C.) Mountaineer,* August 12, 1842.

23. (New Orleans) *Times-Picayune,* September 1, 1840; (Columbia) *South Carolina Temperance Advocate,* September 3, 1840; *Greenville Mountaineer,* October 23, 1840.

24. *New York Daily Tribune,* February 25, 1852.

25. (Savannah) *Daily Morning News,* August 18, 1852; (Richmond) *Daily Dispatch,* August 23, 1852. Mid-decade, the "well-known" Dr. Hines did offer "a lecture on Penitentiaries, their discipline, their abuse of the labor system and their cruelties" in New Orleans. (Augusta, Ga.) *Daily Chronicle and Sentinel,* January 11, 1855. Three months later he was arrested at Louisville for impersonating "Col. Hamilton." *Bangor (Maine) Daily Whig and Courier,* April 19, 1855.

26. *Edgefield Advertiser,* November 7, 1855; (Columbia) *Daily South Carolinian,* May 1, 1855; *Baltimore Sun,* August 27, 1852; Melville, *Moby-Dick,* ch. 89.

27. *Daily Cleveland Herald,* July 16, 1853; *Sumterville (S.C.) Banner,* September 7, 1853; (Savannah) *Daily Morning News,* October 28, 1853; *Nashville Union and American,* February 18, 1859; (Montgomery, Ala.) *Daily Confederation,* February 15, 1859; (San Francisco) *Daily Evening Bulletin,* March 18, 1859.

28. [Porcher], "Historical and Social Sketch of Craven County," 421.

29. *Charleston Courier,* June 14, 1859.

30. Pitt-Rivers, "Honor."

31. *Life . . . of . . . Hines,* 9, 21.

32. Calhoun, *Witness to Sorrow,* 59–64; entry of November 28, 1832, Samuel Cram Jackson Diary; Charles Fraser to Hugh S. Legare, April 4, 1832, Charles Fraser Papers.

33. Tise, *Proslavery,* 97–123.

34. Cf. Chaussinand-Nogaret, *French Nobility.*

35. This argument pits honor against respectability—for they were deadly foes—yet some southerners, unsurprisingly, tried to bridge the gap between these ideals. See W. Simms, *Life of the Chevalier Bayard;* Simms, *Self-Development.*

36. Cf. Minton, "Culture of Respectability." Recent literature on the growth of an antebellum southern middle class mostly fails to consider respectability as a social ethos challenging the world of honor. See, e.g., Wells, *Origins of the Southern Middle Class;* Wells and Green, *Southern Middle Class.*

37. Thackeray, *Book of Snobs,* 15.

38. Cf. Ginzburg, "Clues."

39. Simms, *Self-Development,* 42. Note that though Simms here speaks of duty—as other advocates of respectability frequently did—he does not describe it as honor's votaries commonly did, as deriving from the past and describing socially generated expectations.

40. J. Bowman, *Address to Mechanics,* 7; [McCord], "Popular Education," 185–86; Perkin, *Origins of Modern English Society,* 278; *Charleston Mercury,* June 14, 1859.

41. Thackeray, *Book of Snobs,* 12; "Novels," undated manuscript, James Henley Thornwell Papers; E. P. Rogers, *Earnest Words.*

42. Auerbach, *Private Theatricals,* 4; Melville, *Confidence-Man,* 41.

43. Halttunen, *Confidence Men;* Cook, *Arts of Deception;* Moragne, *Address on the Character,* 3; Auerbach, *Private Theatricals,* 4.

44. de Certeau, *Practice of Everyday Life,* 91–110, 115–30; Kasson, *Rudeness and Civility,* 112–81; Auerbach, *Private Theatricals,* 32–34; Meisel, *Realisations,* esp. 29–57.

45. Credit Ledgers, South Carolina, 6:79, R. G. Dun and Company Collection; E. P. Rogers, *Earnest Words,* 274.

46. Grund, *Aristocracy in America,* 84; Robert F. W. Allston to Adele P. Allston, April 24, 1858, Robert Francis Withers Allston Papers. On creditworthiness as the core value of respectability, see (Philadelphia) *Mechanics' Free Press,* October 2, 1830; *Boston Investigator,* December 18, 1839, February 14, 1844, October 22, 1845; *South-Carolina Temperance Advocate,* February 13, 1840; (Columbus) *Daily Ohio Statesman,* January 8, 1841, January 28, 1850; *Pensacola Gazette,* April 2, 1842; *Jonesborough (Tenn.) Whig,* April 20, 1842, January 11, 1843; *Boston Courier,* June 13, 1842; (Montpelier) *Vermont Watchman and State Journal,* June 4, 1846; (Salt Lake City) *Deseret News,* August 10, 1854; *Fayetteville (N.C.) Observer,* 1858.

47. Hayne, *Anniversary Address,* 12; Grayson, *Hireling and the Slave;* Porcher, "Conflict of Capital and Labour."

48. Credit Ledgers, South Carolina, 6:34, R. G. Dun and Company Collection; Persons, *Decline of American Gentility,* 20.

49. Pollin, "Poe's 'Diddling,'" esp. 110. Although scholars note multiple sources for Poe's essay, "Diddling Considered as One of the Exact Sciences," they have overlooked the obvious link to David Hines. Whalen, "Poe's 'Diddling.'"

50. Freehling, *Prelude to Civil War,* 149–52; Stuart, *Three Years,* 2: 71; Stoney, "Memoirs of Frederick Augustus Porcher," 83; McDonnell, "Politics, Chess, Hats," ch. 11.

51. Wiltse, *John C. Calhoun,* 3: 429–33; Freehling, "Spoilsmen and Interests"; Greenberg, *Masters and Statesmen,* 3–22.

52. McDonnell, "Elizabethan Dreams"; Redpath, *Roving Editor,* 50.

53. *Charleston Mercury,* January 28, 1859; *Charleston Courier,* June 14, 1859; *New York Herald,* April 9, 1860.

54. *Memphis Daily Appeal,* May 5, 1863; (Savannah) *Daily Morning News,* May 23, 1863; *Natchez Daily Courier,* June 25, 1863; *Daily South Carolinian,* January 24, 1865.

Anna Koivusalo

"HE ORDERED THE FIRST GUN FIRED & HE RESIGNED FIRST"

James Chesnut, Southern Honor, and Emotion

On the evening before the presidential election of 1860, James Chesnut Jr. addressed hundreds of cheering South Carolinians, urging them to secede from the Union. In the extremely heated atmosphere, the U.S. senator asserted that "a line of enemies" was closing around them. He encouraged his hearers to separate state action, saying that it was their only safety in a world ruled by "blind consciences and crazy brains." For himself, he stated, the answer was simple: he would "determine to live and die as became our glorious ancestors, and ring the clarion notes of defiance in the ears of an insolent foe."[1]

Given the increasing level of agitation and anxiety that reigned over the South, these fierce words were, by no means, unusual. Yet, until that very day, Chesnut had been known for his moderate politics. As a senator he had seen himself as a conciliator and had been worried that the volatility of both northerners and southerners would cause the "cracking [of] every timber in the good old ship, dashing her to pieces."[2] And now, curiously, he was among the first to disrupt the Union: four days after Lincoln's election, Chesnut left his seat in the U.S. Senate, becoming the first southern senator to resign. A few months later, he ordered the first shots of the Civil War to be fired at Fort Sumter.

The broader significance of James Chesnut's conversion can be understood by combining two traditions of analysis that of honor culture and that of the history of emotions. Chesnut serves as an archetype of honor because he, clearly, understood its importance. An experienced duel mediator, he had often headed negotiations to resolve disputes concerning violations of honor. Yet he recognized that honor was needed not only to negotiate the external procedures, but also to ease the internal adjustments. He knew how to channel the raw rage, arising from an ill-placed word, to the controlled expression of noble passion in duels. Indeed, Chesnut's adept skill in applying honor became yet more useful in 1860–61.

The period resulted in extreme intensification of the role of honor in the life of James Chesnut and his fellow southerners. Rather than an independent, self-evident notion, honor was a tool for finding and expressing appropriate emotions. James Chesnut's actions can be read as responses to prevailing emotion rules. His use of emotion demonstrates honor's function as a guiding principle in southern society.

As historians have shown, honor was an inseparable part of southern culture; its effect on both southern society and on individuals was fundamental. Historians such as Bertram Wyatt-Brown, Edward L. Ayers, Kenneth S. Greenberg, Steven M. Stowe, Dickson D. Bruce, and Christopher J. Olsen have contributed much to our understanding of southern honor. Wyatt-Brown and Greenberg, for example, have concluded that honor, with all its variations, was interwoven in everyday life and belonged to all members of society. They, along with Olsen, have also discussed the importance of honor for political thought in the antebellum South. Elliott J. Gorn, in turn, has observed that backwoods fighting among white lower-class men was an honor-bound phenomenon.[3] As a notion, however, honor has not been unequivocal. Some scholars have seen it as a set of cultural values or a certain behavioral pattern. Most have agreed that honor polarized with shame: not acting in accordance with common norms—failing to meet expectations of honor—was shameful.[4] Another concept, manhood, is often mentioned in the same context. It has usually been seen as a cultural value or construction that is closely connected, or even synonymous, with honor.[5]

Southern society was unpredictable, and southerners craved security and stability in their lives. They sought answers and support from code books and manuals. Honor rules—or rather "acceptable options . . . strategies and . . . priorities," as Bertram Wyatt-Brown stresses—gradually became necessary signposts in society.[6] Codes and manuals, nonetheless, left much room for interpretation. Stephen W. Berry has concluded that "all Southerners had to determine what [honor] meant to them, and they did so with considerable variety and finesse."[7] Adding to that I suggest that southern honor was a combination of individual notions of honor (and related cultural norms, such as manhood) that were shaped by individual emotions and aspirations. Put together these created an ever-changing platform on which to enact honor. Ironically, rather than increasing safety, honor contributed to southerners' uncertainty, no matter how determinedly they attempted to maintain the illusion of stability.

Honor has often been treated as a code of dictated behavior that masked individual emotions. Yet, I suggest, rather than hiding emotion, honor helped to create and express it. Emotions were allowed, expected, and encouraged when they were carefully planned and channeled through honor. Honor and emotions, therefore, are closely connected. Indeed, Julian Pitt-Rivers, in his classic interpretation, argued that honor *is* a sentiment.[8] Not fully agreeing I nonetheless suggest that the methods of the history of emotions can help us understand better the interpretations and functions of honor.

Historians of emotions assume that emotions can be learned and shaped by a culture and that social norms and rules have effects on individuals.[9] Carol and Peter Stearns have concluded that external behavior is not necessarily an expression of an actual emotion but more like an acceptable presentation of emotion.

William M. Reddy has suggested that emotions are not unchangeable but can be "navigated"—managed, changed, and corrected. According to Joanne B. Freeman, emotions, as responses to outside requirements, represent beliefs and values of a society.[10]

Southerners subscribed to narrow and homogenous emotional models. Instead of displaying the *raw* emotions of the private sphere, one was expected to evince their *noble* counterparts, the emotions of the public sphere. C. Dallett Hemphill has argued that the method that conduct books offered allowed one to hide one's "actual inner state" by covering it with a "certain emotional pose."[11] That would suggest, however, that there were strictly prescribed emotions from which deviation was only possible if it was concealed. Yet the system was more flexible than that. Noble emotions were not only intended to cover and mask raw emotion; they could also be more refined versions of raw emotions.[12]

Honor helped southerners to navigate the complex discourse between raw and noble emotions. Rather than a code or a value, honor was a cultural resource, a tool to satisfy values or meet goals in society. The variation in honor "code"—as determined by individual southerners themselves—allowed them to change their priorities and goals. Indeed, instead of speaking of "following the honor code," we should perhaps speak of "applying honor."

Secession and the Civil War intensified and altered the complex goals in southern society and the use of honor to achieve them. The transformation that James Chesnut went through, as sudden and peculiar as it seems to later onlookers, represents well the shift in the attitude of most white, moderate southerners in 1860–61.

James Chesnut was a lawyer and legislator and the husband of the well-known Civil War diarist Mary Boykin Chesnut.[13] He was born in 1815 as the second son of a wealthy planter family. His family was staunchly Unionist. He, too, began his career as a long-time member of the South Carolina legislature as a Unionist and later became a moderate cooperationist. By constant guidance from his parents, he learned that certain emotional expressions were not accepted, whereas others were expected and encouraged.[14] Honor, as understood by the Chesnut family, bore a strong resemblance to the concept of conscience: one's principles and internal sense of right and wrong were as important as external reputation and avoiding shame.[15]

Chesnut did not discuss his notion of honor in detail, but neither did he question its existence. It was there, as he clearly indicated on many occasions. His understanding of honor affected how he managed and expressed his emotions in order to meet his goals. For the most part, they were consistent with the goals of southern white men in general: he sought good reputation for his family and himself, the enactment and support of ideals of manhood, success both for his family and his state, and a happy marriage.

The fluctuating nature of honor and the shifts in the weight he gave these different goals resulted in apparent uncertainty. It seemed even to his wife that "he is always decided by accidents & does not object to changing his mind twenty times in an hour."[16] It was not, however, a question of chance: Chesnut merely tried to balance different goals and requirements. In what follows, I will argue that he always sought to produce emotions that were not only publicly acceptable, but also consonant with his personal notion of honor. Simultaneously he needed to adjust his own idea of honor to meet the ever-escaping vague idea of a general honor code.

"The Apotheosis of Pusillanimity and Meanness": Anger/Indignation, May 1860

In 1860 the slaveholding and the free states were on the verge of disunion. As a newly elected U.S. senator, James Chesnut was disconcerted by the conflict between his loyalty to the Union and his loyalty to the South. He hoped that the disintegration of the Union could be prevented by those few men who were "pure, able, elevated, & courageous." Yet, he lamented, "old fashioned patriotism is as much out of date & fashion as a cocked hat & knee breeches . . . [and] would stand in equal chance of being laughed at in our Capitol."[17] Indeed, some South Carolinians were so disappointed in Chesnut's moderate politics that they demanded that he "answer fully for [his] remarkably reserved demeanor" and state whether he was in favor of secession or not.[18]

Against this background his peculiar attack against Senator Charles Sumner of Massachusetts, in the spring of 1860, attracted wide publicity in the press. Sumner had recently returned to his senate seat from Europe, where he had been recuperating from injuries suffered when South Carolina congressman Preston Brooks had caned him on the Senate floor.[19] After Sumner's speech "The Barbarism of Slavery," Chesnut rose immediately. Instead of answering Sumner's arguments, he merely scorned that "slanderer of States and men." In his opinion Sumner, who "had felt . . . the consequences of a former insolence," should have become "wiser, if not better, by experience." Instead, Chesnut insisted, his fellow senator was nothing but "the incarnation of malice, mendacity, and cowardice."[20]

Though some thought that Chesnut's dedication to the southern cause was admirable, his speech made others uneasy. Clearly this conservative and reserved senator had shown a side that was previously unknown. An appalled acquaintance "could not help wondering whether [Chesnut] was indeed identical with the courteous & accomplished gentleman" he knew. "Southern feeling," he continued, "expressed in your *extraordinary language* in reply to the speech of a gentleman & a scholar . . . this feeling is *marvellously* [*sic*] mistaken."[21] Others agreed. In the northern press, Chesnut's speech was described as an "additional illustration of the barbarism of slavery," and, more imaginatively, a "venting of [Chesnut's] impotent spleen" and a "shriek of the demoniac among the tombs."[22]

Earlier Chesnut's beautifully arranged, calmly delivered speeches had merely mirrored his sense of duty as a southerner rather than violent zeal. Thus the transformation from the conservative, quiet senator to this agitated and seemingly rude man seemed strange. If one looks more closely, however, one can see how Chesnut used honor for a twofold purpose. His first goal was to prevent the escalation of the debate into a new violent confrontation that would have further tarnished southerners' reputation. It was necessary to show the world that Sumner, not they, was a barbarian. "We do not intend to be guilty of aiding in the apotheosis of pusillanimity and meanness," Chesnut explained. "We do not intend to contribute, by any conduct on our part, to increase the devotees at the shrine of this new idol."[23] By his short reply, then, Senator Chesnut had "administered a reproof that the brute must have recognized . . . for [Sumner's] face became blanched, and he was so taken down that he could not relieve himself of the embarrassment," wrote the Washington correspondent of the *Charleston Mercury* gleefully, although perhaps not quite truthfully.[24]

What is more important, because Sumner had maliciously scorned southerners, honor prompted Chesnut to express particular emotion in his reply. His deliberate expression of indignation belonged to the acceptable range of emotions in the South. Pure anger, to be sure, was an emotion that antebellum Americans tried to control and defeat. Yet, as Michael E. Woods has noted, indignation was a commonplace emotion in antebellum politics and social life. While anger was seen merely as an expression of rage and blinded reason, indignation "promoted justice, not petty revenge."[25] For example, Preston Brooks's attack on Sumner was seen as an act of uncontrolled anger and senseless violence in the North. Yet Brooks had calmly deliberated and prepared his punishment for three days before delivering it. In southerners' minds, then, it had merely appeared as a noble, justified expression of indignation. Chesnut's verbal lashing mirrored the caning—without actual violence, but with equal feeling. Indeed, his display of emotion, intended to insult the dishonorable northerner, was embraced joyously, while Sumner was depicted as a "whipped hound."[26] With his speech Chesnut attempted to warn northerners of the impending crisis and assure southerners of his loyalty.

"A Heart That Falters Now, Let Him Tear It Out": Fear/Courage, November 1860

As the presidential election of 1860 approached, it became evident that Americans would vote not only for president, but also for slavery and secession. For a U.S. senator to dodge questions about his stand on the matter was increasingly difficult. Yet James Chesnut refrained from saying anything in public before he took time to contemplate the matter in private. It was not merely a question of saving external reputation, but one of private honor and ethics. He was convinced that the states had a constitutional right to secede.[27] Still perhaps southerners should just wait and see, instead of rushing headlong into the unknown.

It was too late, however, to slow down the process that had already begun. Soon the news of Chesnut's hesitation spread like wildfire over South Carolina. Apparently, while on summer vacation in Virginia, he had told someone that he did not regard Lincoln's election as a cause for secession—or so claimed the *Philadelphia Press.* Prosecession newspapers eagerly grabbed the opportunity to declare him an opponent of secession.[28] The *Camden Journal* came to the defense of the town's own statesman: "Our Senator is not given to loose talk with vagabond free-soilers, and such ilk. We know [the rumor] to be untrue, and therefore put the ear mark of falsity on the extract."[29] Rather than a rebuke for the press, however, the piece was intended to show Chesnut what his community expected of him. The doubts about his trustworthiness had been raised, and he could dispel them only by making his stand clear. If not, he would be "burning his fingers," as the secessionist Lawrence M. Keitt advised.[30]

It was obvious that Chesnut could not keep silent much longer. On October 17 he wrote to his fellow senator from South Carolina, James Henry Hammond: "[People from other slave states] urged that South Carolina ought to lead off . . . & that, individually, they would come to us & bring their friends. . . . The question is too momentous to be left to the urgency & decision of . . . States, whose people have decided or will decide not to withdraw. There was somewhat of cool impudence in these suggestions. . . . I think it the most probable thing in the world that Lincoln will be elected & we must soon begin to consider our course."[31] Hammond, also publicly keeping quiet, answered: "The wildest fire-eaters . . . seem to have paused & hold their breath . . . the times are ticklish, & men are to be made responsible for what they say & forced to act it out. . . . I think every sensible man must see how [the election] goes . . . before he can make up his programme definitely. . . . And I would under *all circumstances* prefer to remain in the Union."[32]

Chesnut answered saying that he very much agreed with his colleague. Nevertheless, he wrote, "my mind is daily inclining to the necessity of trying the idea of secession, & the doctrine of coercion. Even by the solitary movement of the State." At the same time, he wished to consult with Hammond before he fully decided.[33] Consultation, however, was impossible. Hammond claimed to be too ill to come to Columbia, where the legislature was getting ready for the presidential election.

There, on November 5, Chesnut was called on to speak and was greeted with multiple enthusiastic interjections and thunderous applause. As in his answer to Sumner, the usually calm and restrained Chesnut expressed himself vehemently in order to create and strengthen desirable emotion in his audience as well as himself.[34] In answering the cries for his participation in the secession movement, he worked himself up to the heat of his fire-eating colleagues. At the same time, Chesnut was trying to justify his actions. In the end the decision was quite simple: both paths were difficult, but only one was honorable: "We have two ways before us. . . . In both lie dangers, difficulties, and troubles . . . but they are not equal in magnitude. . . . One is beset with humiliation, dishonor, *émeutes,* rebellions with submission . . . and confiscation and slavery in the end. . . . The other, it is true, has its difficulties and trials, but no disgrace. Hope, duty, and honor shine along the path."[35] He wanted to stress that he "had never before spoken with so deep a sense of obligations pressing upon him." And he was not the only one. Secession was the duty, and only safety, of all southerners. Justice would stand by their side, he concluded.[36] Caught between two choices, he looked for moral support. It was provided by the language of honor, which southerners used for "uniting with one another to safeguard their families, neighborhoods, and, ultimately, their regional way of life," as Christopher Olsen has phrased it.[37] Deployed in this way, honor proved one's manhood, while protecting the South from insults.

The next day, upon receiving the news of Lincoln's election, the legislature passed a bill calling for a secession convention to meet on December 17. Nevertheless, James Chesnut still hesitated to take the final step. He knew that some South Carolina federal officers had already resigned from their posts, and that the same was expected of him. After delaying the decision for three days, he finally gave the legislature his resignation from the Senate on November 10.[38] The House resolved immediately and unanimously to accept the resignation and stressed that "what under other circumstances would have been regarded as a matter of regret" was now "recognized as an act of loyalty and devotion to the Sovereignty of South Carolina."[39] Hammond sent in his resignation two days later. Privately he was not positive whether this was wise: "I heard yesterday that Chesnut & Toombs had resigned—why I know not . . . all those fellows are great asses for resigning & I have done it myself. It is an epidemic and very foolish. It reminds me of the Japanese who when insulted rip up their own bowels. . . . People are wild."[40] Hammond's view of the events around him was insightful. South Carolinians now had a compulsive need to manifest their allegiance to their home state and secession. The time for rejecting not only the Union, but also political lukewarmness, had come. "The public mind . . . is in a state of great excitement, & I am persuaded that I can do more good here than in Washington," Chesnut explained. Without the support of his colleague, he resigned, "upon consultation of many friends."[41] Yet Chesnut did not indicate that he merely resigned himself to the loud clamors for his participation.

The fear of dishonor played a great role in many southerners' minds. It was painfully apparent to Chesnut, too, that both his personal reputation and that of his home state and the South were at stake. And yet it was absolutely out of the question to show fear.[42] The only appropriate emotion, when facing confusion, chaos, or war, was courage. Hence James Chesnut, usually so cautious and conciliatory in his words, roused the crowds with cries that sounded uncharacteristic in their bellicosity: "If there be a man in South Carolina who has a heart that falters now, let him tear it out; for it is cur's flesh and deserves not to pulsate in the bosom of a freeman!"[43]

By giving up his seat in the Senate, Chesnut believed, he had fully expressed his loyalty to his home state. This eased his decision and the adjustment of his personal sense of honor. Indeed, realizing that secession could not be avoided, he committed himself to it—as fully as possible. The next day Mary Chesnut, upon learning that her husband "had burned the ships behind him," wrote: "No hope now—he was in bitter earnest."[44]

"He Made Himself Eminently Absurd": Jealousy/Romantic Love, April 1861

During the weeks after Lincoln's election, James Chesnut toured South Carolina, giving speeches that echoed the dramatic tones of his earlier declaration of independence. At the same time, he tried to convince southerners of the necessity of peaceful secession. His wholehearted dedication bore fruit: he attended the South Carolina secession convention and was involved in drafting the ordinance of secession. Later he was sent as a representative of his state to the secession convention in Montgomery. There the southern states reorganized themselves as the Confederate States of America, passing a constitution that Chesnut helped to draft.

After the Montgomery convention adjourned at the end of March, the Chesnuts traveled to Charleston, where the secession convention reconvened. There U.S. Army troops, under Major Robert Anderson, were holding Fort Sumter, keeping Charlestonians in suspense. Meanwhile, as if the turbulent political situation were not enough, Mary Chesnut caused a domestic upheaval. Flirtatious by nature, she had always loved the attention given her by numerous admirers. Now her flirtation with Governor John Manning, "the handsomest man alive,"[45] tested the limits of James Chesnut's tolerance.

The flirtation flared up quickly, from a joke that Manning played on Chesnut on the train to Charleston. He came on board, requesting that Mary save a seat for a young lady under his charge. "*Place aux dames,*" Chesnut said politely and left. The young lady proved to be Manning himself, who "threw himself cheerfully down in the vacant place." Thereafter, during the week following their arrival in Charleston, Mary and Manning spent much time together. They breakfasted and had dinner tête-à-tête in the boarding house dining room. He whispered in her ear at the dinner table and brought her a bunch of violets. One day Mary found him at her door, "pretending he thought it was [someone else's]."[46]

Even though Chesnut was very busy with his duties, he did not fail to notice the ongoing flirtation. He was "restive" and "enraged" and "made himself eminently absurd by accusing [Mary] of flirting with John Manning." Mary was amused: "I wonder whether Mr. C will keep [illegible] this John Manning. Is it not too funny & he is so *prosy.*"[47] The straw that apparently broke the camel's back was a letter from Manning's wife, in which she requested Chesnut's picture in order to have a flirtation with him.[48] The letter, light in tone, worked as Mrs. Manning had intended. Thinking that Mary compromised their reputation, Chesnut reprimanded his wife severely.[49]

Whereas Mary and Manning saw the flirtation as a sort of harmless entertainment, Chesnut apparently thought that making advances to a married woman was highly improper. As Bertram Wyatt-Brown has noted, women's behavior could damage or destroy male reputation. If a wife behaved in an indiscreet way, it was a husband's duty to put matters right.[50] Nonetheless, Chesnut seems not to have expressed his disapproval directly to Manning. Because of his conciliatory nature, Chesnut usually avoided open conflicts, especially with his circle of acquaintances. Yet Chesnut did not scold his wife merely to maintain his external reputation and manhood: he was jealous.

Torn between his jealousy and his desire to keep Mary happy, Chesnut was constantly on his toes. Usually he was attentive to his wife and let her enjoy herself. Sometimes, in his opinion, Mary's behavior exceeded the limits of propriety. When Mary had accompanied a male friend, she "received orders that I was not to walk any more with men on the Battery." Once Chesnut locked Mary in their room to prevent her from attending to the errands of the South Carolina politician William Trescot, who had taken a fancy to her.[51] His jealousy, however, was not unwelcome: it is apparent that Mrs. Chesnut enjoyed the attention, even if it was expressed in this way. Indeed, after the incident with Manning, she wrote of her husband in affectionate, even passionate terms. Her later references to Manning, on the other hand, are devoid of intimacy.

Jealousy, as an emotion, was not universally frowned on in the South, where it had a traditional role in protecting one's honor and that of one's family. The Southerners believed that men were right to defend their mastery and ownership to protect their reputation. However, Chesnut's attempts to limit his display of jealousy were also convergent with the emotion patterns that emerged outside the South in the antebellum period. As romantic love became more important in marriage, marital jealousy also gained more strength. Victorian Americans, however, saw jealousy as a threat to love and believed that self-control was required to keep it at bay.[52] James Chesnut balanced between these two notions, Victorian self-control and southern manifestation of emotion. Honor, then, served as a tool for expressing jealousy, but it was also needed to channel it to a nobler emotion, romantic love.

This incident shows us that good marriage, like many other important goals, was about expressing appropriate emotion. Even if jealousy was not entirely disapproved in the South, marital jealousy could reflect unsuccessful mastery of one's marriage. Indeed, the few surviving references to his feelings toward his wife tell us that the emotion James Chesnut linked with marriage, above all, was romantic love—an idealized, even intimate, emotion that excluded everyone but the lovers themselves.[53] But for the more passionate Mary Chesnut, the infrequent demonstrations of affection were not always enough. On the occasions he did express affection, she was touched: "I feel he is my all & I should go mad without him."[54]

"If Anything, More Unruffled Than Usual": Anxiety/Determination, April 1861

James Chesnut's struggle between internal moderation and the external demands of his status were reflected in his behavior—not only in the boarding house, but also not at larger events, as the tension in Charleston harbor escalated.

Hearing the rumor that the Union would shortly declare war, Chesnut accepted a position on General P. G. T. Beauregard's staff.[55] Beauregard, recently appointed as general of the brand new Confederate Army, had come to Charleston to keep an eye on Fort Sumter.[56] As professional soldiers were still thin on the ground in the South, he leaned on amateurs. Chesnut, well-known for his political accomplishments and skills as a conciliator, was quickly assigned responsibilities.

The Union had started preparations to supply the starving fort, and Beauregard could not leave U.S. Major Anderson to continue his preparations undisturbed.[57] Hence, on April 11, Colonel James Chesnut, Captain Stephen D. Lee, and Lieutenant Colonel A. R. Chisolm were sent to carry a message to Anderson, demanding the surrender of the fort.[58] Anderson's reply was unsatisfactory. While Chesnut and his colleagues had a quick supper, Beauregard telegraphed the secretary of war, who gave him ambiguous instructions to "reduce the fort as [his] judgment decides to be most practicable," unless Anderson would promise to evacuate. Beauregard knew that the troops in the fort could not hold out much longer without fresh supplies. He also knew, however, that a Union supply ship would reach the fort soon. With time running short, Beauregard sent his aides promptly back to Fort Sumter. Chesnut and the others boarded a small row boat at 11 P.M., armed with verbal, unclear instructions to evaluate the situation and act without further consultation.[59]

In the fort, the Confederates waited in an empty casemate for hours. Finally Anderson arrived, stating his terms: he would evacuate on the 15th, provided that he did not receive new instructions or fresh supplies. Chesnut understood that Anderson was playing for time. The aides conferred and agreed on the answer: Anderson's terms were "manifestly futile" and "not within the scope of instructions verbally given to us." As the senior officer, Chesnut presented their decision in the form of a letter dictated to Lee:[60] "SIR: By authority of Brigadier-General Beauregard . . . we have the honor to notify you that he will open the fire of his batteries on Fort Sumter in one hour from this time. We have the honor to be, very respectfully, your obedient servants. / James Chesnut, Jr., Aide-de-Camp / Stephen D. Lee, Captain, C.S. Army, Aide-de-Camp."[61] In these courteous words Chesnut interpreted his instructions from Beauregard and thus established his authority to decide of the fate of Anderson and his men. They said goodbye to each other, bowing and shaking hands. The Confederates then rowed to James Island, where their main batteries were situated. There Chesnut gave the battery commander orders to start firing on Fort Sumter at 4:30 A.M. Then the weary aides once again got in their boat and rowed into the harbor in the thickening fog and drizzle. About halfway to shore they were startled by the booming of the Confederate guns. They let the boat drift for a short while, watching the bright semicircles in the sky that the shells made before exploding over Fort Sumter.[62] James Chesnut had just started the Civil War.

The declaration of the war had happened according to the strictest rules of courtesy. In fact, the exchange of letters greatly resembled the procedure preceding duels.[63] James Chesnut, an experienced mediator, made sure that everything was in writing and that the parties knew the state of affairs. Later he spoke only of his delight in the gentlemanly nature of the exchange of words. He felt for Anderson and was especially moved by the major's graceful wish: "If we do not meet again on Earth, I hope we may meet in heaven." Although this would have been a perfect occasion for it, Chesnut did not express the blood-thirsty sentiments that many southerners now cherished. On the contrary, he took the outbreak of the war "quietly enough—if anything, more unruffled than usual in his serenity."[64]

It is not known what James Chesnut's exact thoughts were on the eve of the Civil War. Nonetheless, it seems likely that what he most felt, even more than anger or fear, was anxiety. Following his usual, methodical approach, he no doubt went over the possibilities countless times. He could have withdrawn from the fortress island, stating that the Confederates should wait for Anderson to evacuate, or that they should try to acquire the command of the fort by negotiations. Why would he jump headfirst into unknown waters, allowing—ordering—the use of force that he usually avoided? "If there be no war," Mary Chesnut had written a month earlier, "how triumphant Mr. Chesnut will be—he is the only man who has persisted from the first that this would be a *peaceful* resolution."[65]

Years later Chesnut wrote his only known account of the events at Fort Sumter. Even then he still tried to reassure himself that the decision he and his countrymen had made in 1861 was the right one despite the outcome:

> I would like . . . to correct a grave popular error . . . that South Carolina began the war. . . . [Anderson's taking over Fort Sumter] was an armed & hostile invasion of a State at peace with [the U.S.] Government. . . . It was the beginning of that Great Struggle we sought persistently to avoid. . . . Without the invasion a peaceful solution . . . might have been attained. . . . [We were notified] of a purpose . . . to subjugate the State [that] the manhood of [South Carolina], supported by conscious right, could not longer forbear. Honor & safety forbade it. . . . To avoid unnecessary bloodshed, and proposing terms most courteous & honorable time & again, we demanded the surrender of the fort. Still all in vain . . . there was nothing left for us but pusilanimously [*sic*] to surrender up the State & city without a blow or to attack the Fort. . . . Rightly, I think, we chose the latter.[66]

"He ordered the first gun fired & he resigned first," wrote the shaken but "jubilant" Mary Chesnut after learning of her husband's role.[67] Indeed, this was the second time that her husband made a sudden, dramatic decision that made him an important figure in the secession movement.

Did Chesnut, then, base his decision making on a wish to keep his political authority? To be sure, all southern men struggled to maintain their intact status as men. Politicians especially found that the failure to appear manly could seriously damage their standing.[68] But, more than a practical political decision, the commencement of the firing was, as in the case of secession, a question of honor. Perhaps James Chesnut saw himself only as an "envoy," a message bearer between two duelists—the North and the South. Yet there was not the slightest possibility of the aides withdrawing from the fort without advancement. Not to risk one's life to defend one's family, home, or country would indeed have been pusillanimous—it would have indicated a failure of manhood. The "manly imperative," as Christopher Olsen has called it, was more important to Chesnut and his fellow southerners than the Union was.[69]

The same way Chesnut had sprung to the defense of his personal reputation and manhood at the boarding house, he tried to protect the reputation and pride of South Carolina by ordering the use of force at Fort Sumter. Yet, although under extreme emotional stress, he could not show open anxiety. Rather, he proceeded toward secession with calm determination. If he was not certain that this course of action was the best, he at least knew it to be honorable.[70]

Conclusion

Mary Chesnut was occasionally annoyed, even infuriated, by her husband's reserved behavior. "If there ever was a man who could control every expression of his emotion, who can play stoic or an Indian chief, it is Colonel Chesnut," she complained.[71] Nonetheless, she never indicated that her husband did not *have* emotions, only that he did not display them openly: "Mr. Chesnut, thinking himself an open, frank, confiding person, asked me if he *was not.* Truth required me to say that I knew no more what Mr. C thought or felt on any subject now than I did twenty years ago. Sometimes I *feel* that we understand each other a little—then up goes the Iron Wall once more. Not that for a moment he ever gives you the impression of an *insincere* or even a cold person—*reticent*—& like the Indian too proud to let the world know he feels."[72] This account shows that James Chesnut understood perfectly the need to limit certain emotions to the private sphere. What is more important, it also reveals that his behavior does not suggest insincerity or pretence. Mary Chesnut merely felt that she should have been included in her husband's private sphere, behind "the Iron Wall."

James Chesnut did occasionally express strong emotion, also in public. Nonetheless, the emotions he displayed were carefully summoned and remolded into appropriate versions. For a gentleman, a public appearance above reproach was essential to earn respect. Yet, more than a façade, or a code of appropriate conduct, honor was a tool for hiding raw emotions and replacing them with nobler versions. Indeed, Mary Chesnut herself stated that displaying noble emotions (such as grief) was required in public: "It is expected of all to howl [at funerals]. If you don't 'show feeling,' indignation awaits the delinquent."[73]

Whereas some emotions were discouraged, others were encouraged, even necessary. Honor was a guiding principle that helped southerners in managing their emotions. It helped them not only to cover emotions, but also to generate and channel them. What complicated this, however, was that southern honor was not a stable, invariable concept. Rather than being carved in stone, the "code" varied extensively and caused the constant, unsettling feeling of uncertainty. Therefore, from time to time, southerners needed to recalibrate their personal notion of honor to make it consistent with other notions.[74] By trying to follow the variable concept of honor they, in turn, contributed to the support and sustenance of this illusion of a stable code. It was in this way that the individual's experience became part of the collective notion of honor.

The year between the springs of 1860 and 1861 was loaded with intense emotional stress for all southerners. In an uncertain world, they leaned on the illusion of an unchanging, static code that would always instruct and direct them. Instead of giving them safety and comfort, however, honor pushed them to secession and a civil war.

NOTES

An earlier version of this article was presented at the 2012 Annual Meeting of the South Carolina Historical Association. The author would like to thank Martha M. Daniels, Elliott J. Gorn, Markku Peltonen, Mark M. Smith, and especially Michael E. Woods and David Moltke-Hansen for comments, sources, and encouragement.

1. See, for example, the *Charleston Mercury* and the *Charleston Daily Courier*, November 6, 1860.

2. James Chesnut [hereafter JC] to W. D. Porter, March 31, 1859 (copy). Williams-Chesnut-Manning Collection, South Caroliniana Library, University of South Carolina, Columbia (hereafter W-C-M Collection, SCL).

3. Wyatt-Brown, *Southern Honor;* Wyatt-Brown, *Yankee Saints and Southern Sinners;* Wyatt-Brown, *Shaping of Southern Culture;* D. Bruce, *Violence and Culture in the Antebellum South;* Ayers, *Vengeance and Justice;* Gorn, "Gouge and Bite, Pull Hair and Scratch"; Stowe, *Intimacy and Power in the Old South;* Greenberg, *Honor and Slavery;* Olsen, *Political Culture and Secession.* My article concentrates on the honor notion of white males.

4. See, for example, Pitt-Rivers, "Honor"; Stewart, *Honor;* Frevert, *Men of Honour;* Peltonen, *Duel in Early Modern England.*

5. For manhood and masculinity, see, for example, Mangan and Walvin, *Manliness and Morality;* Carnes and Griffen, *Meanings for Manhood;* Gilmore, *Manhood in the Making;* Ownby,

Subduing Satan; Rotundo, *American Manhood;* Kimmel, *Manhood in America;* Hoganson, *Fighting for American Manhood;* Friend and Glover, *Southern Manhood;* Glover, *Southern Sons.*

6. Wyatt-Brown, *Southern Honor,* 114. For written codes and manuals, see also Kasson, *Rudeness and Civility;* Bushman, *Refinement of America;* C. Hemphill, *Bowing to Necessities;* Freeman, *Affairs of Honor.* For a contemporary classic in southern honor rules, see J. Wilson, *Code of Honor.*

7. Berry, *All That Makes a Man,* 20.

8. Pitt-Rivers, "Honor," 503. Also Frank Henderson Stewart and Ute Frevert have studied how honor can be defined in connection to emotion. Stewart, *Honor;* Frevert, *Emotions in History.*

9. Central works in emotions history include: C. Stearns and P. Stearns, "Emotionology"; Reddy, *Navigation of Feeling;* Rosenwein, "Worrying about Emotions in History"; Rosenwein, *Emotional Communities;* Oatley, *Emotions.* Recent works in the American emotions history include: Lystra, *Searching the Heart;* P. Stearns and Lewis, *Emotional History of the United States;* Berry, *All That Makes a Man;* Coontz, *Marriage, a History;* Eustace, *Passion Is the Gale.*

10. C. Stearns and P. Stearns, "Emotionology"; Reddy, *Navigation of Feeling,* 122; Freeman, *Affairs of Honor,* 289.

11. Hemphill, "Class, Gender, and the Regulation of Emotional Expression," 37. It can be argued that the line between the public and private spheres in the antebellum South was so blurred that we cannot speak of spheres at all. See, for example, Wyatt-Brown, *Southern Honor,* 33–34. Nonetheless the very existence of conduct books and the constant struggle for self-mastery show that individuals sought to define public behavior and separate it from private thoughts and emotions.

12. I do not mean to suggest that the division between raw and noble emotions is a division between negative and positive emotions; some of the "noble" (that is, acceptable) emotions can certainly be seen as negative. I do not engage here in a long discussion about the definition of each emotion, as they can vary widely in different contexts and cultures.

13. There is no extensive research on JC based on primary sources. He is briefly discussed in studies on Mary Chesnut. See Muhlenfeld, *Mary Boykin Chesnut;* Fox-Genovese, *Within the Plantation Household;* DeCredico, *Mary Boykin Chesnut;* Stern, *Mary Chesnut's Civil War Epic.* For JC's politics before the Civil War, see Cauthen, *South Carolina Goes to War;* Schultz, *Nationalism and Sectionalism in South Carolina;* Freehling, *The Road to Discussion,* vol. 2.

14. Lorri Glover mentions that southern parents expected their sons to cultivate a certain list of behavior, including emotions. Glover, *Southern Sons,* 97 and 104. This indicates that emotions were seen as something that could be practiced.

15. See also Wyatt-Brown's discussion on northern evangelical concept of conscience and southern internalized honor. Wyatt-Brown, *Southern Honor,* ch. 5.

16. December 8, 1861. Chesnut, *Private Mary Chesnut,* 217.

17. JC to W. D. Porter, March 31, 1859 (copy). W-C-M Collection, SCL.

18. *Charleston Mercury,* September 1, 1859. A public letter to JC, asking him to "make known . . . your views and sentiments on these momentous questions," was signed by many of his acquaintances.

19. In 1856 Sumner had made a speech in which he mocked southerners, slavery, and Brooks's near relative. In retaliation Brooks had caned Sumner with his walking stick.

20. U.S. Congress, "Congressional Globe," 36th Cong., 1st Sess., 1860, 2603.

21. G. Putnam to JC, June 8, 1860. W-C-M Collection, SCL. Emphasis in original.

22. *Salem (Mass.) Register,* June 21, 1860; *Springfield (Mass.) Republican,* June 6, 1860; *Lowell (Mass.) Daily Citizen and News,* June 6, 1860. Sumner's speech, however, had been so hateful that

many northerners, too, felt that he went too far. His speech was heavily criticized in some northern newspapers. Donald, *Charles Sumner,* 353–60.

23. U.S. Congress, "Congressional Globe," 36th Cong., 1st Sess., 1860, 2603.

24. *Charleston Mercury,* June 8, 1860.

25. C. Stearns and P. Stearns, *Anger,* 36; Woods, "Indignation of Freedom-Loving People," quotation p. 692.

26. *Newberry Conservatist,* June 10, 1860.

27. JC stressed this point in his speeches. *Charleston Mercury,* November 6, 1860; *Anderson Intelligencer,* November 29, 1860; *Yorkville Enquirer,* December 6, 1860.

28. *Charleston Mercury,* October 2, 1860; *Newberry Conservatist,* October 30, 1860.

29. *Camden Journal,* October 9, 1860.

30. Lawrence M. Keitt to J. H. Hammond, August 4, 1860. James Henry Hammond Papers.

31. JC to J. H. Hammond, October 17, 1860. James Henry Hammond Papers.

32. J. H. Hammond to JC, October 23, 1860. W-C-M Collection, SCL. Emphasis in original.

33. JC to J. H. Hammond, October 27, 1860, James Henry Hammond Papers.

34. Orators were expected to combine strong, even violent emotional expressions with cool reasoning to be regarded as efficient. D. Bruce, *Violence and Culture in the Antebellum South,* 180–81.

35. *Charleston Courier,* November 6, 1860.

36. *Charleston Mercury,* November 6, 1860. The speech is reported with variable choice of words in different papers. The *Camden Journal,* for example, used the words "bold, manly resistance" and "tame, dishonorable submission" to describe JC's two paths. November 13, 1860.

37. Olsen, *Political Culture and Secession,* 9.

38. JC to the House, November 10, 1860. South Carolina Department of Archives and History (SCDAH). When the U.S. Senate reconvened on December 3, JC was listed among "senators absent." U.S. Congress, "Congressional Globe," 36th Cong., 2nd Sess., 1860, 1. He was, along with nine other southern senators, later expelled in absentia. Congress, "Senate Journal," 37th Cong., 1st Sess., July 11, 1861.

39. South Carolina General Assembly. House. Resolution no. 54/1860, November 10, 1860. SCDAH.

40. J. H. Hammond to M. C. M. Hammond, November 12, 1860. James Henry Hammond Papers.

41. JC to J. H. Hammond. November 10, 1860. James Henry Hammond Papers.

42. For the importance of maintaining one's honor for aspiring politicians, see Olsen, *Political Culture and Secession;* Freeman, *Affairs of Honor.* For the fear of dishonor as a motivation for secession, see, for example, Wyatt-Brown, *Shaping of Southern Culture,* esp. 166 and 201.

43. *Yorkville Enquirer,* December 6, 1860.

44. Chesnut, *Private Mary Chesnut,* 3 and 5.

45. John Laurence Manning was an extremely wealthy planter, a former governor of South Carolina, and a member of the South Carolina legislature and the secession convention. He had attended Princeton with JC and been a close friend throughout JC's youth. Chesnut, *Mary Chesnut's Civil War,* 35.

46. March 26, March 31, April 3, 1861. Chesnut, *Mary Chesnut's Civil War,* 35, 39, and 40–41; April 1, 1861. Chesnut, *Private Mary Chesnut,* 52.

47. March 29, March 30, April 1, and April 2, 1861. Chesnut, *Private Mary Chesnut,* 49–53. Emphasis in original.

48. April 7, 1861. Chesnut, *Private Mary Chesnut,* 55. Rumors of the flirtation had already reached Mrs. Manning on their plantation. Manning had written to her, explaining that he attended Mrs. Chesnut only because she gave him a good seat on the train. John L. Manning to Sally Bland Manning, April 3, 1861. W-C-M Collection, SCL.

49. The entry under April 8, 1861, is ambiguous. "[Manning?] & [illegible words] with a hand held. He had to be dreadfully scolded when I came to my room. I was merely mad. . . . That husband scold made me melancholy last night." A week later, upon her cousin's complaint that she would not give him her undivided attention, Mary Boykin Chesnut (hereafter MBC) wrote: "That I will never do more to anyone even if it is lamentable be." Chesnut, *Private Mary Chesnut,* 56 and 60–61.

50. Wyatt-Brown, *Southern Honor,* 52–54.

51. March 28, 1861. Chesnut, *Private Mary Chesnut,* 48; July 22, 1861. Chesnut, *Mary Chesnut's Civil War,* 121.

52. P. Stearns, *Jealousy,* 26–27 and 31; Woods, "Heart of the Sectional Conflict," 126–29 and 36–39; Keetley, "From Anger to Jealousy."

53. For the emergence of romantic love in the nineteenth century marriage, see, for example, E. Rothman, *Hands and Hearts;* Lystra, *Searching the Heart;* Coontz, *Marriage, a History,* esp. chs. 9 and 10.

54. April 6 and 8, 1861. Chesnut, *Mary Chesnut's Civil War,* 42; Chesnut, *Private Mary Chesnut,* 56.

55. April 6, 1861. Chesnut, *Mary Chesnut's Civil War,* 43–44; April 9, 1861. Chesnut, *Private Mary Chesnut,* 56–57. MBC mentions that JC's role was that of a "peace negotiator—or envoy." April 12, 1861. Chesnut, *Mary Chesnut's Civil War,* 45.

56. See, for example, Cauthen, *South Carolina Goes to War,* 124.

57. Ibid., 129–30.

58. Lee was a captain in the newly founded Confederate Army, and Chisolm was the South Carolina governor's aide-de-camp.

59. U.S. Government, *OR,* series 1, vol. 1, 13–14, 30–31, and 60. April 12, 1861. Chesnut, *Mary Chesnut's Civil War,* 45–46.

60. U.S. Government, *OR,* series 1, vol. 1, 60; Chisolm, "Notes on the Surrender of Fort Sumter," 82; Lee, "First Step in the War," 75–76.

61. U.S. Government, *OR,* series 1, vol. 1, 14.

62. Lee, "First Step in the War," 76–77. *Charleston Mercury,* April 13, 1861.

63. I would like to thank Todd Hagstette for drawing my attention to this fact. He also advised me of JC's role as a noted duel mediator. See Hagstette, "Dueling and Identity," 48, 54, and 92.

64. April 27 and April 15, 1861. Chesnut, *Mary Chesnut's Civil War,* 55 and 49.

65. March 12, 1861. Chesnut, *Private Mary Chesnut,* 35. Emphasis in original.

66. Undated sketch for a speech given on Memorial Day in 1878, W-C-M Collection, SCL. (The final version was published in the *Camden Journal* on May 21, 1878, with a slightly different wording.) It is noteworthy that JC never uses first-person singular, thus making an impression that the decision was made by some faceless entity rather than him and the others present in Fort Sumter.

67. April 12, 1861. Chesnut, *Private Mary Chesnut,* 59–60. Curiously most works on Fort Sumter leave it unmentioned that it was JC who ordered the first shot to be fired.

68. Olsen, *Political Culture and Secession,* 175; see also Hoganson, *Fighting for American Manhood.*

69. Olsen, *Political Culture and Secession*, 9. A good discussion on the relation of the words *manhood, honor,* and *courage* and their use in politics can be found in Hoganson, *Fighting for American Manhood*, esp. 70–71.

70. During the Civil War, JC served in many military and political posts. After the war he was an active Democrat until his death in 1885.

71. June 3, 1862. Chesnut, *Mary Chesnut's Civil War,* 356.

72. March 11, 1861. Chesnut, *Private Mary Chesnut,* 32. Emphasis in original.

73. June 10, 1861. Chesnut, *Mary Chesnut's Civil War,* 78.

74. Another well-known example of navigating with honor is General Robert E. Lee, who also transferred his loyalty from the Union to the South and later back. After the war he wrote: "True patriotism sometimes requires of men to act exactly contrary, at one period, to that which it does at another, and the motive that impels them—the desire to do right—is the same." Qtd. in J. Jones, *Personal Reminiscences, Anecdotes, and Letters of Robert E. Lee,* 208.

Part IV

Defining the Other—Honor and Shame

As most of the essays in this volume attest, honor studies have largely focused on elite white males, or those who aspired to join the elite. As Julian Pitt-Rivers and others have shown, however, societies encompass many "honor groups." These exist horizontally—among those linked by sex, race, social status, profession, and so on—and they may be grouped vertically, usually by economic or political power or tradition and class. Often the categories overlap. Whatever the honor group, its demands center on reputation, either laudable or shameful.

The three essays in this section explore how honor operated in both vertical and horizontal dimensions. Jeff Forret's study uses the unusual example of infanticide among African American slave women to argue that bondwomen formed a distinct honor group and dearly prized their reputations within that group. Like white women, they valued sexual purity and possession of a good name; they also fought back against humiliation. Subject to rape and exploitation, some chose to kill their offspring rather than endure the shame of unwed motherhood. In a society where black codes did not acknowledge slave marriages, infanticide was an extreme statement of honor; it restored the mother's self-worth among her peers and deprived the white man of his investment. Killing a child also spared it the dishonor of growing up as a slave. White juries, ironically, seldom imposed the death penalty for such crimes, as if tacitly accepting the slave woman's need to protect her reputation—even at such a cost.

The urge to protect virtue was a given among white women as well, who left little margin for error and indiscretion. As Brenda Faverty's study notes, elite white women were deeply sensitive to their social position (no surprise) and intensely Victorian in their standards of propriety, especially sexual propriety. Shame and humiliation were ever on their minds, and the tools of humiliation were gossip and, in extreme cases, social ostracism. Gossip served as a "device of social control," as Faverty demonstrates in selected case studies. Ostracism was the honor group's equivalent of a duel in its impact, as the case of James Henry Hammond and his nieces famously illustrates.

Jeffrey Anderson's essay on hoodoo and conjurers addresses issues of both vertical and horizontal honor within the black community in the century after Reconstruction. African American aspirations for equality took on what Anderson calls an "accommodationist" position, which blended a desire for economic mobility with respectability and self-discipline. That position involved adopting mainstream, mostly Protestant and white, standards of character. An embarrassment to these accommodationists, however, was the conjurer—a man or woman greatly esteemed under slavery and stubbornly persistent in African American culture. Black preachers and intellectuals may have driven hoodoo itself into the shadows, but the conjurer nonetheless offered a distinct alternative to "mastering" both the physical and spiritual worlds. The accommodationists' frustrations with this situation reveal tensions within the black community that still persist.

Jeff Forret

"THE PRISONER . . . THINKS A GREAT DEAL OF HER VIRTUE"

Enslaved Female Honor, Shame, and Infanticide in Antebellum Virginia

Sociologist Orlando Patterson has famously defined the slave as a "person without honor."[1] Whether he is right or not is an open question. In fairness Patterson's observation is easy to understand. Slaveholders routinely dishonored bondpersons in their daily lives. Commodified slave bodies were hired out without regard to slaves' own preferences, mortgaged as collateral for loans, insured like other valuable goods, and regularly bought and sold in a thriving domestic slave trade. Purveyors of human flesh stripped bondpersons publicly for intrusive inspections at slave auctions, and masters and overseers inflicted whippings in full view of spouses, children, and friends. The disfiguring marks of the lash left constant, visible reminders of slaves' subordination in southern society.[2]

Enslaved women were dishonored in additional ways unique to their sex, often as the victims of rape and sexual exploitation. According to southern whites, bondwomen occupied a cultural space entirely outside the boundaries of respectable womanhood because whites accepted the widespread stereotype of female slaves as promiscuous Jezebels. Whites detected and frequently criticized the rampant moral depravity they perceived among bondwomen, who were presumed to be pathologically addicted to sex, and no women of such reputedly loose morals could lay successful claim to honor. That it was often masters, overseers, and other white men who made enslaved women prematurely knowledgeable of sexual matters made no difference; the irony garnered the polite silence of the southern white masses.[3]

Despite antebellum southern whites' claims to the contrary, enslaved women adhered to notions of honor—and its inverse, shame—that would have been familiar to white women of the Old South. In the culture of southern honor, white women were significant in that they not only judged male performances of honor but also possessed the ability to shame spouses and disgrace families and kin. White female power expressed itself most forcefully in the sexual arena. Honorable women maintained their chastity and preserved their virtue. The young woman who gave birth out of wedlock "ruined" herself by her shame, the adulterous woman who cuckolded her husband dishonored him, and the promiscuous woman besmirched the family name. Social convention held that fathers, husbands, and brothers act as guardians of female virtue; hence white women's sexual misconduct demonstrated that the men in the family ineffectually exercised patriarchal authority over their households and exposed them to public opprobrium. The potential ramifications of female behavior thus reached far beyond the individual: white women of the Old South might either validate or undercut male pretensions to honor. The ethic of honor inextricably bound the sexes together.[4]

That the institution of slavery circumscribed enslaved men's ability to protect enslaved female honor and rendered enslaved women sexually vulnerable should not suggest that slaves felt neither honor nor shame. In denying honor to slaves, most scholars have unwittingly adopted the master's perspective.[5] Yet close attention must be paid to the distinction between vertical and horizontal honor. Antebellum southern whites emphasized the vertical dimension of honor, in which inferiors granted respect to those who outranked them in the social hierarchy. In this vertical dimension of honor, whites expected deference from their slaves, whom they regarded as both subordinate and dishonorable. In contrast to whites, slaves better understood honor's horizontal component, in which respect was distributed among equals. Individuals achieved horizontal honor by earning it from their peer group. Whites' refusal to grant honor to slaves was irrelevant because, for slaves, the pertinent audience of reference was black, however degraded they were in wider southern society. Meritorious behavior and demonstrations of desirable traits brought respect, and no single race or class could stake a monopoly to it. In this context, Bertram Wyatt-Brown observed, "male honor was richly prized" among slaves, albeit "confined to the slave quarters."[6] Female slaves, too, valued honor. Despite the obstacles they faced, bondwomen upheld notions of sexual honor that, inasmuch as was possible under slavery, coincided with those of respectable women in southern white society.

Enslaved female sexual honor expressed itself most shockingly in criminal cases of infanticide and child murder. Although such incidents were rare, the resulting trials produced documented evidence of female slaves' notions of sexual honor. Both court records of the bondwomen found guilty of infanticide and the gubernatorial petitions filed by masters and other neighborhood whites on female convicts' behalf prove instructive. In Virginia at least twenty-three enslaved women and one enslaved man were convicted of no fewer than twenty-eight cases of infanticide or child murder from 1799 to 1860. This figure surely does not account for all homicides committed by slaves on their progeny over that six-decade period, but even the small number of sample cases available supplies telling, verbatim testimony of enslaved witnesses, unravels at least some of the tangled motivations lurking behind the alleged murders committed by enslaved mothers, and explains why those bondwomen found guilty of infanticide deserved clemency from the governor. The resulting glimpse into enslaved women's values and their perceptions of themselves and their place as women within the quarters hints at the significance of honor and shame in their lives in defiance of the degradation of slavery. Bondwomen's deadly alleged assaults on slave infants provide an unconventional avenue through which to explore the construction of enslaved femininity and female slaves' conceptions of honor, but through them it becomes clear that enslaved women laid claim to sexual honor despite the many obstacles the institution of slavery erected in fulfilling their preferred vision of womanhood.[7]

Several historians have depicted infanticide as a form of resistance to the system of slavery. For decades scholars defined "resistance" narrowly, referring to slave runaways and rebels, the vast majority of whom were male. More recently historians have examined the theme of slave resistance through a consciously gendered lens. Stephanie M. H. Camp, Jennifer L. Morgan, and others have indicated the ways in which enslaved women challenged the terms and conditions of bondage. In such studies female reproduction emerges as contested terrain, a form of gendered resistance rooted in the enslaved female body. In addition to bondwomen regulating their own fertility or inducing abortion, infanticide, some scholars have proposed, may be understood within this same conceptual framework.[8]

Infanticide as a form of "gynecological resistance" represented for enslaved women a covert exercise of bodily autonomy, albeit ironically in that the life destroyed was not, as in the case of suicide, their own but rather their child's. Through infanticide or child murder, female slaves staked ownership of their offspring, trumping masters' claims. When they killed their children they wreaked vengeance on slaveholders by depriving them of the next generation of bound labor. In this way infanticide marked an egregious infringement on the master's property rights. On the other hand, the destructive act of infanticide might be construed as an act of love and maternal affection warped by bondage. Of course only a minute fraction of all enslaved mothers preferred that their children die than live in slavery, but for those few the horrors of the institution—whippings, rapes, separation, and sale among them—distorted protective maternal instincts. Convinced that the best means available to safeguard their offspring was murder, some enslaved mothers achieved liberation for their children through death, sparing them the torment and suffering of slavery and a lifetime of abuse.[9]

Motivations of resistance were evident in the most widely publicized case of an enslaved mother murdering her child in the antebellum era. Margaret Garner, the real-life inspiration for the character Sethe in Toni Morrison's novel *Beloved*, was a runaway slave trapped by slave catchers with her fugitive family in a Cincinnati, Ohio, cabin in 1856. Frantic, desperate, and vowing to "kill herself and her children before she would return to bondage," Garner slashed her three-year-old daughter's throat with a butcher knife to prevent the girl's recapture and return to slavery. She attempted to take the lives of her other three children as well but was restrained before accomplishing her object. After her apprehension and return to

Kentucky, Garner was sold to Mississippi. En route to the Deep South, the boat she was aboard collided with another vessel on the Ohio River. Either the force of the impact threw Garner and an infant daughter into the water, or Garner took advantage of the chaotic moment to throw the girl in before making her own suicidal plunge. A black cook aboard one of the boats plucked Garner from the river, but her baby girl drowned. Garner was ecstatic that death had liberated a second of her children. For a few enslaved mothers such as Garner, the institution of slavery turned protective maternal instincts on their head. For them dying represented the best protection from bondage.[10] But while infanticide and child murder may be placed within the resistance paradigm, scholars have observed that the practice was neither "an ordinary form of 'resistance'" employed by female slaves, nor did it pose a serious threat to slavery's survival. Virtually all enslaved mothers loved their children too much to sacrifice them for the sake of making a political statement.[11]

Records from antebellum Virginia suggest that shame, grounded in enslaved women's own sense of gendered identity, provided another possible motivation for infanticide and child murder. In early America infanticide was almost exclusively a female crime, with far more documented cases among whites than blacks. Courts typically prosecuted for infanticide unmarried white women accused of murdering their newborns. Recent research suggests that, among white women of the poor and laboring class, poverty motivated a substantial portion of all infanticides. Short on both time and money, working-class white women unable to afford or care for a baby destroyed it at birth. But as Georgia's Reverend Charles Colcock Jones argued, for female slaves, the institution of slavery removed the economic inducement to infanticide prevalent among poor white women. "The crime of *Infanticide*," he wrote, is "restrained in good measure" within the slave community in part because bondwomen could count on their owners' financial support for their offspring. Moreover, he added, the punishments meted out for infanticide and child murder offered a sufficient deterrent to the crime.[12]

Informed by southern whites' understanding of honor's vertical distribution, Jones also posited that infanticide was so rare among slaves because the innate "moral degradation of the people . . . takes away the disgrace of bastardy."[13] American society often presumed that white women committed infanticide in a desperate attempt to hide the shame of an illegitimate birth, and some certainly did. Respectable society demanded the careful guardianship of white female chastity. In contrast southern whites commonly accepted a contradictory image for enslaved women, the Jezebel stereotype of unrestrained passion and promiscuity. The white popular imagination alleged that female slaves lacked virtue and therefore could not suffer the shame associated with certain pregnancies that might prompt a white woman to murder her offspring. But in one exception to the general rule, petitioners on behalf of the Prince Edward County, Virginia, bondwoman Martha asserted "that the injuries done [her infant] were inflicted . . . to conceal the shame of b[e]aring a child" out of wedlock.[14]

Martha's white petitioners made a curious argument since slaves could not lawfully marry. In chastising a perceived lack of sexual ethics among slave women, Jones and other whites frequently overlooked the structural fact that southern legal codes' refusal to recognize slave marriages made bastards of *all* enslaved newborns. That bastardy was the legal norm for births among bondwomen might have reduced their feelings of dishonor associated with bearing children out of wedlock. But in defiance of legal statute, slave marriages proved so deeply entrenched and widely recognized by custom throughout the South that some female slaves indeed expressed the shame attached to childbirth in the absence of a husband. A Culpeper County, Virginia, court believed that the slave Suckey murdered her baby girl "not from any feelings of malice but from a sense of shame & pride of character."[15] Suckey's master testified during his slave's trial that "she had been married a good many years ago to a slave belonging to a neighbor . . . and by him had two children." Unfortunately for Suckey "her husband had been carried off to the South several years ago," a victim of the internal slave trade. Ever since her domestic arrangements had been irreversibly altered, her master continued, Suckey "had maintained a good character in all respects," a remark implying her fidelity to an absent spouse. Therefore, when her owner "suspected from her appearance and other symptoms that she was pregnant," he sent for a physician from Alexandria, who concurred that Suckey "was *probably* pregnant." Suckey, however, "protested with great earnestness that she was not."[16] We cannot know the precise source or sources of her objections. They perhaps stemmed from fears that her master would someday separate her from her child. If among the minority of all slaves exposed to Christian religious teachings, she may have suffered from a heightened sense of guilt over the extramarital sex that resulted in her pregnancy. Or she may have fretted over a loss of horizontal honor among her fellow slaves after moving on from her prior marital commitment.[17]

In scattered infanticide cases from Virginia, bondwomen clearly indicated that white paternity was a source of shame. Even though many slaveholders across the South exercised sexual mastery in the quarters, extorting sexual favors from enslaved women or blatantly forcing themselves on them against their will, assaults held ramifications for female slaves' sense of horizontal honor. Scholars have noted that bondwomen felt "the dishonor of rape" by masters or other white men, and inevitably some of these encounters resulted in pregnancy. It makes abundant sense that some enslaved women might have wished to abort or kill the by-products of sexual coercion and rape. Under such conditions infanticidal violence became a means to terminate an unwanted pregnancy that was itself the result of violence.[18] Although we usually cannot know the specific context in which conception took place, Brooke County, Virginia, slave Letty, convicted of infanticide, said "that if the child had been one of her own color she would not have done as she had done."[19] If Letty intended only to damage the economic interests of her master in an act of resistance, the infant's particular hue was irrelevant. Her remark raises the prospect that a mixed-race child proved an embarrassment for some black mothers in the quarters, a living reminder of sexual coercion and exploitation and an affront to enslaved husbands. Under this scenario killing the newborn destroyed the evidence of an unwanted encounter while it simultaneously—if the father was the owner—spited the master by denying him her offspring. It may have been no accident that the runaway bondwoman Margaret Garner, the infamous child murderer, slit the throat of her daughter just as her master burst into the room where her family was sheltered. According to reports, "The murdered child was almost white, and was a little girl of rare beauty." Gazing on the horrific scene, Garner's distraught master—and probable father of the child—took up the small corpse, clutched it close, and refused to surrender it to white authorities.[20]

Masters who found sexual pleasure in the quarters augmented their property holdings when their dalliances produced children, but not all white fathers welcomed the arrival of enslaved progeny. Petitioners for Letty stated that the unidentified father of her "illegitimate child" was a married "free white man" who "may have moved her to the commission of the crime" of infanticide, perhaps to conceal his sexual indiscretions from his wife, family, or larger community.[21] In a similar case, "the Common report" about Lucy, an "unhappy Black girl" in Lewis County, Virginia, was "that her Child was by a Whight Man," and according to the slave, "her life was threaten[e]d if she . . . should ever let her case be known." The abandonment and subsequent death of her child reportedly "was actuated by fear, occasioned by threats of the consequences, in case she should have another Molatto child," as she had "had one some time before."[22] White fathers may have forced Letty and Lucy to kill their infants or perhaps played an even more direct, insidious role in their deaths.

Regardless of a child's paternity, convicted bondwomen's sense of shame pulsates through many of the court records and governor's petitions documenting their turmoil. Enslaved women charged with infanticide frequently expressed intense anxiety over their characters and reputations in the quarters. Fanny, of Albemarle County, denied strangling her full-term baby girl, explained her owner, because "the prisoner is a woman of great pride, and thinks a great deal of her virtue." After finally admitting that she had given birth, Fanny begged either the master or the doctor who examined her "to conceal the fact and not expose her" because she dreaded other slaves learning of either her pregnancy or her crime.[23] When the Henrico County bondwoman Kesiah gave birth in 1834, she covered the infant's mouth with her hand to muffle the cries that might draw attention to her, she "being very much ashamed at her having had a child."[24] Both of these accounts suggest a form of sexual virtue present among bondwomen that would not have been unfamiliar to their female counterparts in respectable, nineteenth-century white society. Their sense of horizontal honor impugned, enslaved women strove to conceal births that they feared could wreck their hard-earned reputations.

White petitioners to the governor on Kesiah's behalf suggested that the slave's age—"not more than seventeen years old"—may have contributed to her shame.[25] Studies have shown that the typical bondwoman did not bear her first child until she reached her very late teens or early twenties, so Kesiah did deliver her baby somewhat earlier than was typical.[26] Penitentiary and court records from Virginia supply the specific ages of nine enslaved women convicted of infanticide or child murder. The average age fell close to twenty, but seven of the nine found guilty of infanticide were teenagers. For such young bondwomen, barely removed from childhood themselves, bearing a child may have brought with it a certain stigma within the quarters, however pleasing their proven fecundity usually was for their masters.[27]

The white signers of memorials to the governor on convicted bondwomen's behalf cited most frequently the youthful age and heretofore "excellent character" of the convicted.[28] In one petition to Virginia's governor, the five magistrates who presided over the trial as well as a physician shifted blame for an infanticide from a teenaged slave to her mother. The signers described "Maria the Mother of Lucy," the convict, as "more guilty than Lucy. Lucy was under her control, almost constantly under her eye, slept in the same room with her, and could not have committed the act without her knowledge." Suspicion was strong that Maria had helped keep Lucy's pregnancy secret, cut the umbilical cord during delivery, and concealed the infant's death. "We . . . do not think," the memorialists concluded, "that the thought of murdering the child originated with [Lucy]." They therefore appealed to the governor for mercy.[29]

Southern courts—and whites in general—were prepared to accept evidence of enslaved women as bad mothers. One master in the Virginia Tidewater expressed disbelief "that a Mother should be the murderer of her own offspring . . . at the moment of its birth." It "seems . . . improbable," he continued, a "monstrous and unnatural . . . deed."[30] But this commentator was in the minority. For the masses of southern white contemporaries, slave infanticides and child murders merely confirmed widespread assumptions about bondwomen's maternal negligence and innate incompetence. More typically another Virginian blamed the death of an enslaved infant on the "barbarous cruelty" and "unnatural neglect of his infamous mother."[31] To believe the rhetoric, antebellum black women habitually killed their offspring (most often by smothering them), ignored their basic needs, and treated them without the love and care expected of good, responsible mothers.[32]

Nevertheless the Virginia courts that adjudicated the trials of convicted female slaves regularly urged gubernatorial clemency. After finding the bondwoman Ally guilty of infanticide in 1833, "three of the Justices . . . recommend[ed] the said Ally to the Executive as a fit subject to be transported." One favored an outright pardon.[33] In those few instances in which Virginia courts shared their rationale for supporting a mitigation of sentence for a convicted slave woman, they mirrored the reasons offered in the petitions of owners and other concerned residents of the bondwoman's local community. In 1818 one court pleaded for "the mercy of the Executive" in the case of Buckingham County bondwoman Polly "on account of her youth, and former good character."[34] Another court "earnestly recommend[ed] to the Executive to commute the punishment of . . . slave Lucy," sentenced to death for infanticide in 1852, "to sale and transportation, because of her youth and the excellent character which she has borne up to the time of this crime."[35]

If petitions in convicted bondwomen's favor may be read as something more than merely a projection of white values onto female slaves, young or unmarried slave mothers, much like white women who proved careless with their virtue, at times did feel stigmatized in the quarters when they violated social convention. At least some female slaves who gave birth either out of wedlock, to a mixed-race child, or at a young age believed that the delivery impugned the good character they possessed and labored to maintain. The inevitable question is whether the "shame" Virginia whites found so apparent within bondwomen such as Suckey, Fanny, or Kesiah was imagined, genuine, or a clever performance calculated to extract sympathy in a time of personal desperation by exploiting commonly held white assumptions. We cannot know with absolute certainty. Although it is possible that white observers detected and magnified issues of sexual honor in slave infanticide cases because they were culturally predisposed to see them, bondwomen themselves voiced expressions of concern over horizontal honor, reputations, and shame. If their stated anxieties were somehow not legitimate, at the very least female slaves betrayed a remarkably acute understanding of gendered notions of sexual honor and nineteenth-century conventions of proper female sexual comportment.

Isolated cases of slave suicide reinforce the pattern of enslaved female honor evident in so many episodes of infanticide. Ex-slave H. C. Bruce's autobiography confirms the significance that many female slaves attached to childbirth within the confines of marriage and the centrality of legitimate births to female slaves' horizontal honor. Bruce related the story of a "very good-looking" slave girl in Missouri who drowned herself in 1858 to avoid the "dishonor and loss of character" associated with giving birth outside the bonds of matrimony.[36] As a few southern whites realized, this was distinctly not the moral code of the Jezebel. The white Elizabeth Lyle Saxon reminisced decades after the Civil War that her hired slave Nellie and Nellie's sister Clara each "felt the disgrace" of Nellie prematurely becoming a mother "so keenly [that] they attempted suicide."[37]

Most southern whites were not quick to acknowledge slaves' honor, but when criminal convictions put bondwomen's lives at stake, the language of honor infused the petitions and court recommendations directed to Virginia's governors. Thus aided in their decision-making process by testimonials that emphasized female slaves' worthy character, executives in the Old Dominion routinely granted clemency to those enslaved women convicted of infanticide. Of the twenty-three Virginia bondwomen found guilty of that crime between 1799 and 1860, fifteen were condemned to "suffer death for Child murder" and eight to sale and transportation out of the United States. Almost assuredly, however, bondwomen escaped execution, with only two of the twenty-three (9 percent) meeting their fate at the gallows. Nineteen (83 percent) were sold and transported; the remaining two were condemned to the public works.[38]

Enslaved women garnered far more petitions to the governor on their behalf than did the typical male slave found guilty of murder. Governors always needed to weigh the social, economic, and political costs and benefits of executing a convicted slave, but they generally looked more favorably on appeals to spare bondwomen rather than bondmen. Male slaves with violent proclivities posed the greater physical threat to slaveholding society. The pattern of gubernatorial clemency also suggested some possible gender-based squeamishness about executing female slaves, whose procreative power replicated the institution of slavery. Governors' intervention was most forthcoming, and reductions of sentences most generously dispensed, in cases of infanticide or child murder. Though tragic, the deaths of unproductive slave infants and children affected slaveholder profits in the distant future and were not as immediately detrimental to masters' economic interests as the loss of adult slave men and women. Nevertheless no enslaved woman found guilty of infanticide or child murder in Virginia received a full pardon. To excuse such crimes altogether set too dangerous an example in a slaveholding society.

The court records and gubernatorial petitions generated by slave infanticide cases reveal not simply white attitudes about a specific form of slave criminality but the moral assessments made by enslaved women themselves. Though rare, Virginia's documented slave infanticide cases, whether real or imagined, are tantalizingly suggestive. They provide an unexpected avenue for aiding in the recovery of the meanings of black femininity and enslaved female honor in the American South. Although southern whites generally dismissed the slave quarters as sites of sexual license, debauchery, and moral bankruptcy, the language of shame present in court records' and governors' petitions' descriptions of bondwomen convicted of infanticide belie the Jezebel stereotype and in fact suggest the contrary: an enslaved female code of sexual honor. Shame cannot be felt in the absence of honor; both functioned in tandem in the slave quarters. The degradation and denial of vertical honor in white society served only to enhance the horizontal honor felt among slaves themselves. Largely hidden from the historical record, slaves' honor code is difficult to access, but, much as with southern whites, it is episodes of violence that permit the best glimpses of it. Refracted through the lens of violence, a picture of enslaved femininity emerges that was fundamentally at variance with contemporary whites' characterizations of unrestrained black female sexuality. The records generated by infanticide cases reveal bondwomen's values and the priorities of enslaved femininity. Though held in bondage and denied the privileges of white womanhood, female slaves nonetheless possessed a gendered identity that embraced notions of female sexual honor and shame.[39]

NOTES

1. O. Patterson, *Slavery and Social Death,* 12. On honor in the Old South, see Wyatt-Brown, *Southern Honor;* Ayers, *Vengeance and Justice;* Greenberg, *Honor and Slavery;* and Wyatt-Brown, *Shaping of Southern Culture.*

2. John Charles Willis, "Behind 'Their Black Masks,'" 19; Desch Obi, *Fighting for Honor,* 111; A. Gross, *Double Character,* 51–52.

3. Millward, "As Cool as I Now Am," 9; Gray White, *Ar'n't I a Woman?,* 29–46. Although the slave quarters did foster a sense of sexual morality sometimes at odds with that of white society, including more liberal attitudes toward premarital sex than those prevalent among whites, female slaves were not generally the wanton creatures of white imaginations. Whether because of the moral instruction and influence of the slave family or the more formal efforts of southern churches, some bondwomen courageously refused to submit meekly to unwanted sexual advances. As Harriet Jacobs's autobiography and a number of other female slave narratives show, enslaved women struggled valiantly to elude rape and sexual exploitation by masters, overseers, and other white men. Female slaves also resisted masters' attempts to select conjugal partners for them. Most famously Rose Williams, a sixteen-year-old slave girl in Bell County, Texas, fought off the "bully" Rufus, the bondman her master had chosen to father her children. When Rufus attempted to share her bed, Williams "give him a shove" onto the floor and beat him over the head with a "poker." See Gutman, *Black Family,* 70; Jacobs, *Incidents in the Life of a Slave Girl.* See also McLaurin, *Celia, a Slave,* and Rawick, *American Slave: A Composite Autobiography,* vol. 5, pt. 4, 176–77.

4. McNair, "Justice Bound," 230, observed that "women were not thought to possess honor." Pitt-Rivers, "Postscript," 226; Wyatt-Brown, *Southern Honor,* 39, 52, 40, 54, 233, 294, 253; Wyatt-Brown, *Shaping of Southern Culture,* 75. On the significance of female sexual restraint in the Mediterranean context, see Peristiany, *Honour and Shame,* 45, 146, 182.

5. See, for example, Ayers, *Vengeance and Justice,* 13, 26; West, "From Yeoman to Redneck," 161. The historiography of southern honor focuses almost exclusively on whites, to the neglect of the Old South's slave population. John Charles Willis and Bertram Wyatt-Brown excepted, southern historians have been much slower than their counterparts studying Latin America to recognize any code of honor among slaves. On honor among slaves, see John Charles Willis, "Behind 'Their Black Masks'"; John C. Willis, "From the Dictates of Pride"; Wyatt-Brown, "Mask of Obedience"; Forret, "Slave–Poor White Violence," 144–46; Forret, "Conflict and the 'Slave Community,'" 576–86; Desch Obi, *Fighting for Honor,* 111–21; and the following works on Latin America: Graham, "Honor among Slaves"; Boyer, "Honor among Plebeians," 161–64; and L. Johnson, "Dangerous Words," 130, 141.

6. Wyatt-Brown, "Mask of Obedience," 1249 (both quotations); Wyatt-Brown, *Shaping of Southern Culture,* 3, 303; John Charles Willis, "Behind 'Their Black Masks,'" 4, 16, 17; McNair, "Justice Bound," 126; Peristiany and Pitt-Rivers, "Introduction," 4. On vertical and horizontal honor,

see Iliffe, *Honour in African History,* 4, 119–20, 123; and Desch Obi, *Fighting for Honor,* 213, 239n98. Under certain circumstances white men may have acknowledged that enslaved men had honor with respect to one another, but not relative to any white man. See J. Rothman, *Notorious in the Neighborhood,* 161.

7. C. Morris, "Within the Slave Cabin," 272. The frequency of infanticide is impossible to quantify with any precision. Masters typically handled infanticide cases privately on the plantation, determining for themselves the appropriate number of lashes for punishment. Another interpretive challenge for historians is distinguishing genuine infanticides and child murders from other causes of death. Cases labeled infanticides may actually have been late-term abortions, stillbirths, miscarriages, or botched deliveries.

Three female slaves in the Virginia sample were found guilty of killing more than one child. Seventeen of the twenty-eight total deaths (61 percent) were neonaticides, or murders of newborns less than a day old; the remaining eleven deaths (39 percent) qualified as filicides, or murders of children older than one day. The twenty-eight known infanticide and child murder cases in the sixty-one years from 1799 to 1860—a rate of one approximately every two years—represent, by modern standards, a remarkably low tally in a state with a slave population that grew from less than 350,000 in 1800 to almost half a million by 1860. Historical Census Browser, University of Virginia, Geospatial and Statistical Data Center, 2004, http://fisher.lib.virginia.edu/collections/stats/histcensus/index.html (accessed January 17, 2012). According to official Federal Bureau of Investigation statistics, the rate of infanticides in 2005 stood at 2.2 per year per 100,000 whites and 6.6 per year per 100,000 blacks. If these rates had been true for Virginia slaves, approximately thirty slaves would have been infanticide victims in 1860 alone. Indeed K. Black, "Creating Infanticide," 20, has suggested "that infanticide occurred more often than suggested by recent scholarship."

In the modern United States, men commit a majority of all infanticides. For infanticide data compiled from FBI Supplementary Homicide Reports, 1976–2005, see James Alan Fox and Marianne W. Zawitz, "Homicide Trends in the United States," http://www.bjs.gov/index.cfm?ty=pbdetail&iid=966 (accessed December 27, 2013).

Fraser, *Courtship and Love,* 47, hints that there was sexual honor among enslaved women. For a detailed study of an infanticide case in the Spanish context, see Landers, "In Consideration of Her Enormous Crime."

8. Camp, *Closer to Freedom;* Morgan, *Laboring Women,* ch. 6.

9. Neely, "Dat's One Chile of Mine You Ain't Never Gonna Sell," 55–62; K. Black, "Creating Infanticide," 43, 49; Millward, "As Cool as I Now Am," vi, 7, 9, 39, 41.

Infanticidal slave mothers do not appear to have disproportionately targeted children of one sex or the other. Many enslaved girls and women suffered the sexual abuse and exploitation of masters, overseers, and other white men. Possibly acquainted with the hazards peculiar to their sex, enslaved mothers might have employed infanticide more frequently against daughters than sons as a possible means of sparing them a future of sexual violence with which many bondwomen were all too familiar. In the documented cases from antebellum Virginia, however, daughters proved no more likely to be victims of infanticide than sons; indeed, in the eighteen cases for which the sex of the victim is known, there were an equal number of male and female victims. Infanticides and child murders terminated the lives and denied masters the future labor of at least nine girls and at least nine boys born in bondage, with the sex of ten victims unknown (see table 1). Infanticide marked less a gender-specific assault on slaveholders' claims of mastery over enslaved sexuality than a broad rejection of the institution of slavery altogether.

TABLE 1. Virginia Infanticide and Child Murder Victims by Sex and Age, 1799–1860

Sex	*Infants**	*Children*	*Total*
Male	4	5	9
Female	5	4	9
Unknown	8	2	10
Totals	17	11	28**

*Infant here is defined as a newborn only. In one case a six-week-old is counted as a child.

**Only one of the total of twenty-eight, a child of unknown sex, was killed by an enslaved man.

10. Lerner, *Black Women in White America,* 61; Yanuck, "Garner Fugitive Slave Case." See also K. Black, "Creating Infanticide," 22, 50–51; Millward, "As Cool as I Now Am," 2–3; and Weisenburger, *Modern Medea,* 222–25.

11. Gray White, *Ar'n't I a Woman?,* 87, 88; Genovese, *Roll, Jordan, Roll,* 497. Quantitative historians Robert William Fogel and Stanley L. Engerman disputed the notion of infanticide as a form of resistance. If conditions under slavery were "so unbearable," they argued, the suicide rate among slaves should have been dramatically higher than it was. As it stood slaves committed suicide at a rate only one-third as high as that among whites. See Fogel and Engerman, *Time on the Cross,* 124.

12. K. Hemphill, "Driven to the Commission of This Crime," 438; Charles Jones, *Religious Instruction of the Negroes,* 135.

13. Charles Jones, *Religious Instruction of the Negroes,* 135.

14. K. Hemphill, "Driven to the Commission of This Crime," 437; M. Smith, "Unnatural Mothers," 177, 173; Gray White, *Ar'n't I a Woman?,* 29–46; Executive Papers, William B. Giles, May 1827, Box 1, Folder 7, Library of Virginia (hereafter LVA).

15. Charles Jones, *Religious Instruction of the Negroes,* 135; Culpeper County, Minute Book 23, 1853–58, Reel 47, LVA.

16. Executive Papers, Henry A. Wise, Misc. Reel 4202, Box 8, Folder 3, Frames 527–32, LVA. Like Suckey, female slaves suspected of infanticide often vehemently denied their pregnancies. When in doubt about a bondwoman's condition, owners often summoned a local physician to complete an invasive gynecological exam over the spoken or silent objections of the female slave. If a bondwoman confessed her pregnancy, she often claimed her child had been stillborn rather than murdered. Doctors discounted slave mothers' claims of stillbirth in all known antebellum Virginia cases, most frequently determining instead that strangulation terminated the life of a living child. On the invasive white doctors who practiced in the antebellum South, much to the displeasure of female slaves who preferred enslaved healers and midwives, see Fett, *Working Cures.*

17. Fountain, *Slavery, Civil War, and Salvation,* ch. 1; Forret, "Slaves, Sex and Sin."

18. Desch Obi, *Fighting for Honor,* 115 (quotation); Deyle, *Carry Me Back,* 232; K. Black, "Creating Infanticide," 44, 56; Millward, "As Cool as I Now Am," 28.

19. Executive Papers, Thomas Mann Randolph, August 1822, Box 7, Folder 3, LVA.

20. Lerner, *Black Women,* 61; Weisenburger, *Modern Medea,* 47–48, 76. Historian Leslie A. Schwalm has documented that, after the Civil war, freedwomen expressed shame for the mixed-race children resulting from masters' rapes. See Schwalm, *Hard Fight for We,* 248.

21. Executive Papers, Thomas Mann Randolph, August 1822, Box 7, Folder 3, LVA.

22. Executive Papers, James Patton Preston, November 1819, Box 9, Folder 3, LVA.

23. Executive Papers, Joseph Johnson, August–October 1852, Box 413, Folder October 1–12, 1852, LVA.

24. Henrico County, Minute Book 1833–35, Reel 81, LVA.

25. Ibid.

26. M. Schwartz, *Born in Bondage,* 189; Trussel and Steckel, "Age of Slaves at Menarche."

27. Penitentiary records, Auditor of Public Accounts, Condemned Blacks Executed or Transported, Records—Condemned Slaves, Court Orders, and Valuations, 1858–65, Misc. Reel 2555, Frames 997–98, LVA; Executive Papers, James McDowell, February 1844, Box 3, Folder 4, LVA; Executive Papers, Joseph Johnson, February–April 1852, Box 411, Folder April 1852, LVA; Executive Papers, Joseph Johnson, March–May 1855, Box 426, Folder April 1855, LVA; Executive Papers, John Letcher, Misc. Reel 4714, Box 5, Folder 4, Frames 187–91, LVA.

TABLE 2. Ages of Female Slaves in Virginia Convicted of Infanticide or Child Murder

Year	*County*	*Name*	*Age*
1818	Buckingham	Polly	18
1819	Surry	Liza/Lizza	17/18
1822	Brooke	Letitia/Letty	28
1824	Louisa	Mildred/Milly	30
1827	Prince Edward	Martha	18
1833	Fairfax	Ally/Alley	19
1834	Henrico	Kesiah	17/18
1855	Richmond City	Lucy	16/18
1860	Amherst	Mary	18

28. On the respectability of petitioners or the force of popular sentiment in the community, see, for example, Executive Papers, James Patton Preston, November 1819, Box 9, Folder 3, LVA; Executive Papers, Thomas Mann Randolph, August 1822, Box 7, Folder 3, LVA; and Executive Papers, Joseph Johnson, March–May 1854, Box 424, Folder March 1854, LVA. On youth and good character, see, for example, Executive Papers, James Patton Preston, December 1819, Box 9, Folder 4, LVA; Auditor of Public Accounts, Condemned Blacks Executed or Transported, Records—Condemned Slaves, Court Orders, and Valuations, 1846–57, Misc. Reel 2554, LVA; and Executive Papers, Joseph Johnson, August–September 1854, Box 422, Folder September 1854, LVA.

29. Executive Papers, Joseph Johnson, March–May 1855, Box 426, Folder April 1855, LVA.

30. Executive Papers, James Patton Preston, December 1819, Box 9, Folder 4, LVA.

31. Quoted in Stampp, *Peculiar Institution,* 346.

32. According to a widely held belief among whites, female slaves frequently rolled over onto their offspring as they co-slept, resulting in the suffocations of countless infants and children. To be sure, for enslaved mothers seeking to destroy an infant, suffocation was clean, bloodless, and relatively nonviolent. Deaths by smothering appeared natural and might be attributed to other causes, thereby deflecting suspicion away from the mother. Probably more often overlaying deaths could be attributed to maternal exhaustion. New mothers, already residually tired from the physical ordeals of pregnancy and childbirth and now with added parental responsibilities, often returned to their customary work routines within a short month or so. Little surprise, then, that one former Mississippi field slave openly admitted that she fell asleep "nussin'" her infant son "and rolled over on him and smothered him to death." Between 1790 and 1860, more than sixty thousand slave infants were allegedly smothered. In 1850 alone slaves accounted for 82 percent of the more than nine hundred suffocation deaths in the United States. Of all enslaved infants who died that year, 9.3 percent had supposedly suffocated, compared to 1.2 percent of white infants. Michael P. Johnson's study of infanticide in the slave South concluded, however, that enslaved

women neither intentionally nor accidentally smothered their children, as white contemporaries so often assumed. His study showed, rather, that slave infants suffered from an unusually high incidence of Sudden Infant Death Syndrome (SIDS). Gross disregard for proper prenatal care, female slaves' grueling work regimens late into their pregnancies, and nutritional deficiencies in their diet conspired to make SIDS more prevalent among slave than white infants. Those same factors could have contributed to the delivery of stillborn babies. See King, "'Mad' Enough to Kill," 43; K. Black, "Creating Infanticide," 10; Gray White, *Ar'n't I a Woman?*, 89, 88; M. Schwartz, *Born in Bondage*, 55–58; King, *Stolen Childhood*, 11; Rawick, *American Slave: A Composite Autobiography, Supplement, Series 1*, vol. 6, pt. 1, 3–4 (quotation); Fogel and Engerman, *Time on the Cross*, 125; M. Johnson, "Smothered Slave Infants," esp. 495, 494. On SIDS see also Savitt, *Medicine and Slavery*, 122–27. The scholarship of both Gray White and King is sympathetic to the SIDS thesis. Even with changes in the work routines of black women after the Civil War, suffocations among black infants continued. For an analysis of the role of slave infanticide in antislavery fiction, see Roth, "Blade Was in My Own Breast."

33. Executive Papers, John Floyd, February 1833, Box 9, Folder 4, LVA.

34. Auditor of Public Accounts, Condemned Blacks Executed or Transported Records—Condemned Slaves, Court Orders, and Valuations, 1810–22, Misc. Reel 2551, LVA.

35. Auditor of Public Accounts, Condemned Blacks Executed or Transported, Records—Condemned Slaves, Court Orders, and Valuations, 1846–57, Misc. Reel 2554, Frame 516, LVA.

36. H. C. Bruce, *Twenty-Nine Years a Slave*, 75.

37. Saxon, *Southern Woman's War Time Reminiscences*, 30–31.

38.

TABLE 3. Punishments and Sentences of Bondwomen Convicted of Infanticide or Child Murder in Virginia, 1799–1860

Punishments	*Sentence*	*Actual*
Execution	15 (65%)	2 (9%)
Sale and transportation	8 (35%)	19 (83%)
Public works	0 (0%)	2 (9%)
Total	23	23

39. John Iliffe's work on honor in African societies shows that female honor in Africa was less contingent on sexual conduct than it was in the American South. Iliffe, *Honour in African History*, 80, 115–16, 262–63.

Brenda Faverty

"TATTLING IS FAR MORE COMMON HERE"

Gossip, Ostracism, and Reputation in the Old South

Reputation and honor were fundamental elements of the antebellum South's society. Part of the foundation of social status, they were fervently guarded by individuals and families. Community image depended on loyalty to societal standards and was the duty of the entire family. The shame and humiliation that resulted from the failure meant communal expectations extended from the guilty individual to his or her family. This familial connection to reputation made it necessary for women, as well as men, to protect their honor. While men had the extreme option of the duel to defend their good name, women used more subtle means. Southern women used gossip and ostracism to guard reputation and honor.

This was particularly true of elite women in the antebellum South, where the community's gender standards connected women's actions to their families' reputation and social position. Women who remained within the communal ideals of proper female behavior helped their families attain status and power. Conversely women who failed to acquiescence to common socially conferred gender doctrine challenged the social order and threatened their families' image and honor. Their shame brought dishonor to themselves, their families, and their communities. To eliminate threats to the social order, members of the plantation society employed gossip and ostracism as essential tools to make sure that women complied with the ideals of proper behavior.[1]

Gossip and ostracism, though, are not interchangeable terms. Gossip was a means of gauging reputation; ostracism was the penalty for having failed the test. Both were structured and ritualized even when subtle and indirect. Gossip was an important element in the functions of reputation and honor. The connection between the actions of women and familial image, honor, and social status created the necessity for some form of penalty for misbehavior. Thus community members paid close attention to the events of their neighborhood and severely chastised those who did not stay within the bounds of accepted principles. As deterrents gossip and ostracism worked to maintain communal gender values. They also served as guides that told the community who to associate with and who to avoid. Their severe impact led to the conformity that was vital to planter society, for elite southern women knew that their failure to adhere to the standards was quickly known by their neighbors and led to their societal isolation.[2]

As devices to safeguard honor, gossip and ostracism could carry nearly as much significance for the South's plantation society as did the practice of dueling. All three of these customs were used to protect the reputation of men and women who depended on their communal image to achieve power and status. If a man's reputation, or that of a female family member, was tarnished because of insult or scandal, power and social standing were lost. In the case of men, their loss could often be forestalled or even reversed and their honor restored through dueling. However it was rare for women who lost their good image to regain their honor. This is what made gossip and exclusion so important. They both protected women from guilt by association and helped to preclude damage to their reputation and honor. Gossip provided the community with the identity of women who violated southern gender principles and judged their association as dangerous. Exclusion, both a penalty and a safeguard, punished misbehaving women and shielded proper women from the influence of those who might lead them astray.

The scandals of antebellum author and socialite Susan Petigru King were typical examples of the function of gossip in regulating female southern honor. Born into the prominent Petigru family of Charleston, South Carolina, in 1824, King grew up within the confines of the regimented values that defined the behavior of proper ladies. At the same time, she was quick-tempered and adventurous, traits that made her presumptuous and indiscreet and continually placed her under the public's censure. King's improper friendships with men, associations with inappropriate women, and habit of publicizing the lives of her neighbors violated the gender standards of the time—which insisted on piety, purity, submission, and domesticity—and placed community members in the public eye. King's failure to meet the principles prescribed by her southern society affected not only her own reputation and honor, but that of her family and her community as well. As a result King was shamed by the gossip of her community, which declared her "too wicked" for association.[3] This ostracized King and protected the reputations of those in her sphere who otherwise would have risked their own reputations by commingling with her.

King's impetuous nature made her coquettish and frequently led to flirtations with young men, which in turn led to gossip and scandal. One of the more serious incidents that was noted by her community involved Arthur Hayne, the son of South Carolina's renowned senator and governor Robert Hayne. A friend and admirer of King, the younger Hayne might have even flirted with her, but his romantic attention ultimately turned to the actress Julia Dean. Once Hayne married Dean, King became the gossiper as she began to vehemently criticize his choice for his spouse and vociferously denounced the actress as an unsuitable wife for the son of the great Robert Hayne. King's participation in the ritual of scandal worked against her, though, when the intensity of her disapproval led her associates to conclude that the King-Hayne relationship was more than a casual flirtation and caused rumors of infidelity to emerge.[4]

King caused further damage to her reputation when she attended a costume ball wearing jewelry that was loaned to her by Sara Felix, an actress and the sister of a well-known brothel madam. Condemned by association with her, local society castigated King for her connection to the women and declared her immoral. To make matters worse, King wrote a full report of the ball for publication in the *Charleston Courier.* When the sponsors of the ball heard that the commentary was going to appear in the newspaper, they demanded its suppression. They argued that the article violated society's standards and placed the women who were present in the public light. Regardless of their protest, the *Courier* printed the piece. When her community denounced her for her actions, King claimed that her description of the ball was a private letter that was published without her permission; that claim was not widely believed. Since King commonly used Charleston residents and events from their lives as models for her fiction, it was difficult for Charlestonians to believe her story.[5]

Sally Baxter Hampton, a member of the renowned Hampton family, declared that King was "too wicked" for them to maintain a connection. King was so notorious that the criticism of her behavior spread well beyond her native Charleston. Ella Gertrude Clanton Thomas of Augusta, Georgia, recorded gossip about King in her journal, repeating a rumor in which the English novelist William Makepeace Thackeray pronounced King "a fast lady." Thomas supposed that this depiction must be true because her neighbor, Mrs. Harris, told her that King was "indeed a fast woman" and that "her reputation [was] anything but unblemished."[6]

King's example illustrates how gossip was a useful social tool in the protection of reputation and honor. Public scrutiny and the circulation of its conclusions aided the communal preservation of the societal standards that maintained the plantation and upper-class urban way of life, thereby binding the community together. The importance of antebellum gossip was evident in the frequency with which it appeared in letters, diaries, journals, newspapers, and travel logs. Northerner Lucius V. Bierce confirmed this in the travel journal he kept during his 1822 journey through the South. During this trip he covered more ground than most visitors to the region and recorded his views of the southern customs. He addressed gossiping by stating, "Tattling is far more common here than in those places at the North where I have lived. Although all countries are in a greater or less degree productive of those pests of society which raise their own character by the fall of others, yet a Southern clime appears to be as particularly favorable to the production of these as to that of other reptiles." A similar sentiment was found in a letter that Charlotte Porcher received from her cousin, who wrote, "I know of nothing new or interesting to tell. The good people are all taking the best care of their neighbors [*sic*] business and their own as they can."[7]

Even the evangelical religious ban on gossip revealed its ties to the protection of reputation and honor. In a recent article, Robert Elder looked at church punishments for gossip and found that while men were tried in greater frequency than women, the women faced heavier penalties than men. Women who gossiped had the ability to threaten men's honor and were deemed to be more dangerous than men. This partially resulted from men's inability to violently defend their reputations against the statements of women, but more important, it also came from the connection between women and moral virtue. Since antebellum society considered women to be the exemplars of morality, their statements about reputation and honor carried credibility and were more readily believed than those made by men. Therefore the gossip spread by women was a more precarious threat than that circulated by men.[8]

Though for many the word gossip connotes malicious tales that expose people's personal lives and secrets, recently scholars have begun to regard gossip as a more constructive, culturally binding facet of society. Robert F. Goodman, for instance, has claimed that gossip "promotes friendship and group cohesion, helps to sustain group norms, and often serves to effectively communicate important information." Rather than an impulse to negatively interfere in the lives of others, gossip can be a useful tool that helps to form the values of various groups and to define the limitations of the groups' membership. By revealing the individuals who broke the group's rules, gossip establishes grounds for the exclusion of those who do not observe the same values as the other members. Thus gossip becomes the information that helps to protect groups from those who do not meet their social standards and, thereby, a device of social control.[9] Scholar Catherine Allgor has demonstrated how gossip helped to shape society and created ties between those who participated in the gossiping. Charlene Lewis explained that gossip played an important role in ranking visitors at Virginia springs. She showed that the guests established their places among the springs' society by whispering, snubbing, and watching "for a breach of etiquette or something even more scandalous."[10]

This same social control was evident in the gossip that had the ability to devastate southern women's lives and to lead to their exclusion from society. Susan Petigru King's actions caused stories to circulate and led proper women such as Sally Hampton to shun her. It was gossip's power to destroy lives that led some southerners to denounce the practice of spreading rumors. In 1843 one journal editor reported receiving letters that declared that gossip indicated a "weakness of character" in those who engaged in the habit. In her work *Letters on Female Character* Virginia Cary avowed that "female gossip is the source of one half the mischief that is done in society" and instructed young ladies to "go into company prepared to aid the common cause of morality and religion" instead of causing harm to others. In his collection of lectures for young ladies, James M. Garnett depicted those who gossiped as meddlesome, indiscreet, untrustworthy, and insensitive toward others.[11]

The rumors and tales that circulated in the South encompassed minor and major infractions of proper behavior; still any breach of propriety was a serious matter for society women. In a letter to Charlotte Hannah, Mary Barksdale relayed her sister's account of a woman who wore "face paint." The use of makeup was a fairly significant offense in the antebellum plantation society; in fact Barksdale saw it as a severe transgression. She instructed Hannah to do all that was in her power to prevent her son Willie from "seeing [the woman] and never, no never invite them to your house together." Caroline Merrick also addressed appearances in a letter to a friend when she described a neighbor's daughter as "very bright and lovely to look upon." Yet she looked beyond beauty to the young lady's temperament and stated, "I see no material out of which the solid virtues which are necessary to the character of the true woman are to be formed."[12] Barksdale and Merrick wrote about issues that were easily apparent, but gossip regarding less obvious subject matter was even more important.

The revelation of secrets and their distribution throughout the neighborhood was vital to the societal evaluation of individual image and reputation. It created a mechanism that conserved or destroyed status and character. The elite women who suffered the destruction of their personal reputations, those who did not strictly adhere to community standards, were subsequently excluded from society. The shunning of these social pariahs was a fundamental part of the regulation of social position and prestige and the undeniable consequence of the continual flow of gossip. Julia Gardiner Tyler, the second wife of President John Tyler, expressed this notion when she wrote that a woman's actions could "cast a doubt upon her fidelity . . . [and would] excite against her the odium of the community, and, in great measure, to dethrone her from her high position." One of James Garnett's lectures for young ladies noted that those who did not conform found "neglect, and degradation, and scorn, and avoidance must inevitably be [their] portion, as well as the just reward of [their] contempt of publick [*sic*] opinion."[13]

The most important aspect of female honor, of course, was a woman's purity. As a result, marriage and a woman's fidelity to the institution were prime subjects for gossip, both benign and malicious. Since a woman's indiscretions threatened family honor as well as her own, communities placed women under particular scrutiny as they searched for any violation of the marital values. Exposed infractions of these ideals quickly spread throughout the public and threatened the offender's social status. Mary Chesnut of South Carolina offered examples of the importance of purity as she resolutely recorded the distress of fallen women in her diary. For example, her mother-in-law once asked her about the marital status of an acquaintance who was an unwed mother. Moved by pity the mother-in-law was unable to think of the other woman as "a bad girl." Chesnut, however, had no such qualms and asserted that "an unmarried girl with two children was necessarily not a good woman." A few years later, Chesnut held similar views of her mother's ex-protégé Fanny, who fell from a high social status to the lower classes. The young woman was infatuated with a young doctor, who later refused to marry her. She became pregnant and was "turned out-of-doors" by her strict parents. Eventually Fanny began a relationship with a working-class man and gave birth to six children. As the unwed mother of so many children, Fanny was completely separated from the elite world she formerly occupied. One day she approached Chesnut's mother and, with tears in her eyes, exclaimed, "Woman! he has married me." The long overdue wedding did not restore Fanny's reputation, but that her former mentor knew of it gave Fanny some comfort.[14]

Similarly elopement was a grave social transgression that could lead to ostracism. It challenged the patriarch's authority, the observance of gender conventions, and the communal honor. When a young woman disregarded her father's wishes to marry the man of her choosing, she disturbed familial stability and publicly violated the obedience that was essential to the South's gendered hierarchy. She also left her family's reputation open to questions of worthiness.[15] The guardians of Sally Canty, a South Carolina heiress, exhibited similar sentiments when they learned of her secret marriage. Canty's elopement with Lieutenant Phil Augustus Stockton, a northern naval officer, generated gossip that quickly spread across the plantation community. After the couple was married by a magistrate in Philadelphia, Canty returned to Mrs. Greeland's boarding school until it was time for her and her new husband to travel to her home in Camden, South Carolina. When the newlyweds arrived in the South, "they were received with a cold, stately, and faultless politeness, which made them feel as if they had been sheep-stealing." Upon Canty's confession of her elopement, her guardians decided that it was best to keep "her name from all gossip or publicity" by keeping things quiet and acknowledging the union. They did, however, assure the legality of the marriage by calling for a parson to perform a second ceremony.[16]

But the damage had been done, and gossip evolved quickly into ostracism. There were members of the community who remained critical of the marriage. In a letter addressed to her daughter Marion Singleton, R. T. Singleton expressed her dismay over the Stockton-Canty elopement by referring to Canty's conduct as "truly criminal." She opined that "any man capable of pursueing [*sic*] the course Stockton has done to lead a school girl astray, deserves the epithet bestowed on him . . . 'a base scoundrel.'" Singleton encapsulated the wider communal sentiment when she wrote that Sally's "friends are very outrageous and indeed some of them talk of shooting Stockton."[17] A month later R. T. Singleton was still articulating her shock in letters to her daughters.

The gossip that resulted from the Stockton-Canty affair led some of the couple's neighbors to socially exclude them. R. T. Singleton issued staunch warnings to her daughters. Since Marion and Angelica Singleton also attended Mrs. Greeland's school in Philadelphia, they were warned not to follow Canty's path and were counseled to sever their acquaintance with her. Singleton cautioned her girls to "remember that you would not have the same excuse that Sallie Canty has—she has never known the care of a mother" and was "intrusted to the management of servants and no doubt imbibed many of their low principles." Despite the justification allowed to Canty for her misconduct, the Singletons instructed Marion and Angelica "to withdraw entirely from the acquaintance of Mrs. Stockton, as you must be in a greater or less degree contaminated by such an association." A neighbor, Mrs. Sumpter, also communicated concern for the reputation of the Singleton daughters when she advised their mother to "write to Mrs. Greeland to keep your daughters close in school as they do in France, and not let them visit—girls are not 'to be trusted.'" The support of Canty's guardian, Colonel Deas, helped the Stocktons to weather the storm, and they were, at least partially, accepted back into society. Of course the revelation that Stockton was the son of a signer of the Declaration of Independence made it a little easier for the community to offer him forgiveness.[18] Nevertheless most women who violated the southern social standards never experienced such leniency.

At its extreme, the ostracism that resulted from gossip and the loss of a woman's reputation generally left her unmarriageable and consigned her to a life of maidenly spinsterhood. During the 1840s the James S. Smith family of Hillsboro, North Carolina, experienced the effects of gossip and exclusion. The Smiths began the decade as one of the county's leading families and ended it as a family mired in scandal. Their disgrace began when both of their sons, Francis and Sidney, fathered children with a beautiful slave named Harriett and intensified with the family's indiscreet handling of the situation. Gossip developed because rather than concealing the relationship, as the slave society dictated, Sidney joyfully received his daughter Cornelia and boasted of her openly. His sister Mary made matters worse when she refused to relegate her nieces to the slave quarters. She never admitted to any of their neighbors that Harriet's daughters were Smith offspring, but she took Sidney's and Francis's daughters into the Smith home and raised them in a world that resided somewhere between slavery and freedom. By candidly acknowledging kinship with Harriet's daughters, the Smiths defied the accepted principles that maintained the slave system.[19]

The Smith family eventually moved to Chapel Hill, North Carolina, to escape the scandal that resulted from their children's behavior. But the Smiths did not avoid further gossip and exclusion by moving. Harriet's children still resided within their home, and Francis still sustained a relationship with her. Mary regularly took her four nieces to church with her and was confronted with stares from the people who saw them. The community "nudged one another and said, 'There goes Miss Mary Smith and her girls.'" While the celebrated family ties and illustrious social standing that the Smiths originally enjoyed should have ensured outstanding marriages for their children, the communal criticism that remained with the family assured that Mary remained single throughout her life.[20]

The scandal and exclusion that Mary Smith endured were similarly experienced by the daughters of one of South Carolina's most prominent families, the Hamptons. The gossip that touched the lives of Harriet, Catherine, Ann, and Caroline Hampton began when their community learned that they had each had physical relationships with their uncle, James Henry Hammond. The rumors eventually rendered the four Hampton sisters unsuitable for marriage and for the association of respectable women. The scandal reveals the important connection between the reputation of individuals and the honor of the family. The girls' father, Wade Hampton II, ultimately sacrificed his daughters' futures to protect the family's honor, status, and power. By disclosing the events of his daughters' downfall to key men in the community, Hampton labeled Hammond as a man without honor, and the Hampton family as his victims. Despite their position as victims, the girls' exclusion from society was ensured.

Since he was married to their mother's sister Catherine, James Henry Hammond was in frequent contact with the Hampton sisters, particularly after the death of their mother in 1833. After the loss of their mother, the girls looked to their Aunt Catherine for motherly attention and visited her often. In approximately 1839 the two families "became gradually more & more intimate" when the Hammonds purchased a new home and moved to Columbia, South Carolina, where they were "thrown into constant communication with all [the Hampton] children." The two oldest Hampton girls, Harriet and Catherine, even helped Hammond decorate the new house while his wife was in confinement following the birth of her sixth child. Hammond wrote that he "found all of these young ladies extremely affectionate" and that they "profess[ed] great love for [him]." He later blamed the fondness expressed by his nieces for their indiscretions.[21]

The relationship between Harriet, Catherine, Ann, and Caroline Hampton and their planter uncle James Henry Hammond became intimate around 1841, when the girls were nineteen, seventeen, fifteen, and thirteen respectively. By this time the Hampton girls were already subjects of gossip for hosting unchaperoned parties. However, the community largely attributed this infraction to the lack of a mother's instruction and supervision. Neighbors believed that the loss of their mother left the sisters without a complete indoctrination into the South's gender conventions and led to their failure to comprehend the importance of safeguarding their personal and family image. Yet, when further scandal broke and their relationship with their uncle was exposed, the focus of the community's comments about the sisters became more serious and alleged that the girls exhibited "loose morals" and "ardent temperaments." It did not matter that Hammond took advantage of his young nieces; the Hampton sisters had engaged in inappropriate behavior, and planter society deemed them unworthy of their association.[22]

The only firsthand account of the liaisons between Hammond and the Hampton girls came from Hammond's diary, where he confessed that his transgressions included "every thing short of direct sexual intercourse." The December 9, 1846, journal entry gave Hammond's explanation of the entire situation with the four sisters and the consequences of his actions. He stated that his nieces were "lavish of their kisses and embraces . . . and not only permitting but promptly responding to every species of dalliance which circumstances brought about between us . . . each contending for my love, claiming the greater share of it as due to her superior devotion to me, all of them rushing on every occasion into my arms and covering me with kisses, lolling on my lap, pressing their bodies almost into mine, wreathing their limbs with mine, encountering warmly every portion of my frame, and permitting my hands to stray unchecked over every part of them and to rest without the slightest shrinking from it, and all this for a period of more than two years continuously." Hammond also claimed that the sisters tempted him beyond his resistance and that anyone who could condemn him had a "virtue of the closet, removed from temptation, incapable of realizing the extent of those by which I was beset."[23]

Hammond ceased his relations with the Hampton daughters in April 1843, when Catherine Hampton "took offence at a familiarity." Hammond maintained that, in an attempt to protect both his nieces and his wife, he resorted to "profound and utter secrecy" about his indiscretions. Yet the power and influence of gossip reached his life nonetheless. On November 1, 1843, Hammond received a letter from Wade Hampton II that addressed the incident of April 13, 1843, and "denounce[ed] [him] in the coarsest terms." At the time Hammond did not know how much he knew but believed that Hampton was convinced that he "made a gross attempt to seduce perhaps to force his daughter Catherine." Owing to his position as the governor of South Carolina and Hampton's supposed fatherly desire to protect his daughters, Hammond did not consider a challenge to a duel to be imminent. Still it quickly became apparent that his breach with Hampton was known within the legislature. Hammond's diary noted that he recognized that "their desire was to black ball me and to mortify me and mine by keeping us out of Society and respectable persons from coming to our House." Hampton continued his campaign of revenge in 1846 when he sought to ruin Hammond's political career, at the expense of his daughters' reputations.[24]

In 1846 Wade Hampton II exacted further retribution on James Henry Hammond and destroyed the reputation and social position of his daughters in the process. Hampton used the family secret to block Hammond's election to the United

States Senate. He revealed Hammond's mistreatment of the girls to key members of the South Carolina legislature, who insured Hammond's defeat. As one of the state's most influential men, Hampton made it patently clear that support for Hammond would be interpreted as a challenge to Hampton's own social and political status. By painting Hammond as a man without honor, Hampton protected his own individual and familial honor. His machinations successfully damaged Hammond's political career, but they also caused the downfall of his own daughters as they suffered "indelible disgrace." For plantation society chastity was an essential element of female honor, and the loss of virtue signaled a woman's unsuitability for association with respectable members of the community. Despite their positions as Hammond's victims, the sisters failed to meet their duty by observing the social values that they were taught, and this made it impossible for them to recover from the resulting gossip. One state legislator concisely illustrated their new social station when he asserted that "after all the fuss made no man who valued his standing could marry one of the Hampton girls." Following the scandal Harriet, Catherine, Ann, and Caroline Hampton were excluded from plantation society. In order to avoid being tainted by association, their neighbors severed all ties with the Hampton sisters. This social exclusion protected the reputations and honor of the community itself. [25]

The South's plantation society did not always consider duels, gossip, and ostracism to be socially beneficial, but the devices were significant elements in the defense of reputation and honor. The letters and diaries of antebellum plantation women illustrate the existence of gossip within southern society and demonstrate its positive quality within the roles of reputation and honor. When women failed to exhibit the qualities displayed by proper ladies or to behave in a manner that upheld social principles, they became a danger to the cohesion of the region and had to be removed from society before they caused the onset of instability. They also threatened the existence of individual and familial honor and social status. Thus it was necessary to monitor the activities of planter women. Gossip, scandal, and ostracism were the tools that were used to ensure the observance of communal conventions. They revealed misbehavior and led to the loss of reputation and honor, which resulted in exclusion from society.

NOTES

1. Stevenson, *Life in Black and White,* 5, 116, 142; Fox-Genovese, *Within the Plantation Household,* 38–39; Clinton, *Plantation Mistress,* 87–109; Bynum, *Unruly Women,* 45; Wyatt-Brown, *Southern Honor,* 53–54.

2. Clinton, *Plantation Mistress,* 112; Kierner, *Scandal at Bizarre,* 69; Allgor, *Parlor Politics,* 216; Wyatt-Brown, *Southern Honor,* 446.

3. Pease and Pease, *Family of Women,* 15; Hampton, *Divided Heart,* 6.

4. Pease and Pease, *Family of Women,* 79.

5. Ibid., 80–82.

6. Hampton, *Divided Heart,* 6; V. Burr, *Secret Eye,* 143.

7. Allgor, *Parlor Politics,* 216–17; Knepper, *Travels in the Southland,* 79; Stevenson, *Life in Black and White,* 58; Wyatt-Brown, *Southern Honor,* 446–47; Barksdale to Hannah, March 21, ca. 1850, Hannah-Barksdale Family Papers

8. Elder, "Twice Sacred Circle," 590, 596–97.

9. Goodman and Ben-Ze'ev, *Good Gossip,* 3, 13.

10. Allgor, *Parlor Politics,* 216–17; C. Lewis, *Ladies and Gentlemen on Display,* 170.

11. A Lady of South Carolina, "Female Education," 62; Cary, *Letters on Female Character,* 160; Garnett, *Lectures on Female Education,* 357–58.

12. Barksdale to Hannah, March 21, ca. 1850; Merrick to Friend, May 23, 1857, Caroline E. Merrick Letters.

13. Julia Gardiner Tyler, "To the Duchess of Sutherland," 120; Garnett, *Lectures on Female Education,* 241.

14. Woodward, *Mary Chesnut's Civil War,* 200, 831–32.

15. Stowe, *Intimacy and Power,* 100; Stevenson, *Life in Black and White,* 59; V. Burr, *Secret Eye,* 140.

16. I. Martin and Avary, *Diary from Dixie,* 120–21.

17. Singleton to Singleton, May 16, 1830, Singleton-Deveaux Family Papers.

18. Singleton to Singleton, June 15, 1830; I. Martin and Avary, *Diary from Dixie,* 120–22.

19. P. Murray, *Proud Shoes,* 35–37, 45–46, 53–54; Bynum, *Unruly Women,* 38. The story of the Smith family was related to Murray by her grandmother, the daughter of Sidney Smith and the slave, Harriet. Since it is the reiteration of childhood memories during the later years of life, the facts may lead to some questions about their validity and the capacity of memory. However it is the perception of the memories that is important here. Even if there are some deviations from the strict relation of the facts, their meaning remains the same. The significance of the continued support for the rules that maintained the slave system is still evident. Murray's grandmother was still able to grasp that violations of society's regulations led to ostracism and the loss of honor.

20. P. Murray, *Proud Shoes,* 47, 53–54.

21. Bleser, *Hammonds of Redcliffe,* 9; Faust, *James Henry Hammond and the Old South,* 241; Bleser, *Secret and Sacred,* 174.

22. Bleser, *Hammonds of Redcliffe,* 9, Faust, *James Henry Hammond and the Old South,* 241–42, Bleser, *Secret and Sacred,* 171.

23. Ibid., 171, 173; Faust, *James Henry Hammond and the Old South,* 242.

24. Bleser, *Secret and Sacred,* 120, 169–71, 175–76; Faust, *James Henry Hammond and the Old South,* 243–44.

25. Bleser, *Hammons of Redcliffe,* 10, 33; Bleser, *Secret and Sacred,* 170, 290.

Jeffrey E. Anderson

"EARLY-ACQUIRED SUPERSTITION"

Conjure and the Attempted Redefinition of Racial Honor

Societal perspectives define honor, and there is no reason to think that different social classes and races should share definitions. At the turn of the twentieth century, many African American intellectuals attempted to undermine racism by proving the black race was eligible to participate in the white-defined code of honor—which the intelligentsia assumed to be universal and not confined to any one race. Standing in the way of this project were features of African American culture that responded to a different code of honor, one defined by blacks. Not least among these cultural characteristics was a form of magic known as conjure or hoodoo. Throughout the nineteenth century, professional conjurers provided services, to a largely black clientele, that ranged from herbal medicine to divination to magical assistance in matters of luck, love, legal matters, revenge, and virtually anything else one could envision. Many whites, on the other hand, considered conjure a marker of black inferiority, an idea they were not shy of expressing in newspapers, academic studies, and works of fiction.[1] In response the accommodation-minded black intelligentsia argued that unless African Americans embraced whites' rejection of hoodoo as a legitimate part of spirituality, blacks could never enter the ranks of honorable respectability. Conjure had to be erased from black culture. The individual honor acquired by professional hoodoo practitioners worked against such racial uplift, however, by keeping them respected members of their communities in the face of the best efforts of the intelligentsia and despite the ethically ambiguous nature of the conjuring profession. The failure of accommodationists to persuade African Americans as a race to conform to a white-defined code of respectability opened new fractures within black society, making honor a source of division rather than the unifying force for equality so ardently sought by those pursuing racial uplift.[2]

As a race black Americans were denied honor within southern society during the nineteenth century. After emancipation and the instability of Reconstruction, however, many African Americans felt capable of eliminating the racist thinking that barred them from an honorable place in American society. African American author Charles Chesnutt stated a popular view of the situation when he opined, "The instinct of antagonism—the prejudice—will disappear just as characteristics that called it into play are modified. In other words, as the structure was built up, beam by beam, stone by stone, so it must be torn down, stone by stone, beam by beam."[3] The structure of racism, argued Chesnutt, was a mere "accumulation of superficial differences" between the races. Eliminating prejudice would take time, he believed, but its accomplishment would depend on the disappearance of dissimilarities between whites and blacks.[4]

Among a series of distinctions between the races that Chesnutt proclaimed as largely erased involved religious difference. Significantly, though Chesnutt proclaimed that African Americans had abandoned their heathenism to become Christians as devout as whites, he nevertheless recognized that "the quality of Negro religion is much decried."[5] Context indicates that Chesnutt was thinking primarily in terms of morality, but just as important to his audience was the existence of non-Christian beliefs among black Americans.[6]

Chesnutt and others like him were responding to writings such as an 1872 article by Mrs. M. P. Handy—a white writer—that appeared in *Appleton's Journal.* "All over the South, wherever the African has been settled," she wrote, "he has carried with him the belief in and practice of the necromancy known in Africa as *obi,* and throughout the Southern States as voodooism, or 'tricking.'" Handy went on to lament, "In vain have religion and the white man waged war against this relic of barbarism."[7] Philip A. Bruce, also white, took much the same tack in his 1889 book *The Plantation Negro as a Freedman.* According to Bruce, who drew a sharp distinction between religion and supernaturalism, the latter had a greater impact on African Americans' conduct than any other force. He offered the assessments that blacks' supposedly inherent imaginativeness and intellectual deficiencies had made them more "superstitious" than any other race and that conjurers, or "trick doctors" as he knew them, were more important to their communities than preachers. According to such writings, this African American spiritual distinction was clearly an important one.[8]

In the eyes of Chesnutt and the African American intelligentsia of his day, the existence of such supernaturalism was a particularly shameful blot that barred African Americans as a race from acquiring respect in American society. To those for whom slavery was a living memory and the rise of Jim Crow an ongoing development, the concept of honor was very much linked with the reality of inequality. White society, as demonstrated by the writings of Handy and Bruce, proclaimed that what Chesnutt judged to be merely superficial differences were profound barriers to whites' acceptance of blacks as their peers. In effect supernaturalism made buffoons of African Americans, thereby shaming them and excluding them from participation in the broader American society.

Unlike W. E. B. Du Bois, who forcefully proclaimed that "a straightforward, honorable treatment of black men according to their desert and achievement" on the part of southern whites would solve the nation's racial issues, many other blacks adopted an accommodationist approach, concluding that African Americans would have to first prove their equality as a race by achieving a version of racial honor that can be roughly defined as eligibility to achieve bourgeois respectability in the eyes of whites.[9] The years surrounding the turn of the twentieth century were imbued with the spirit of racial uplift. Booker T. Washington and others urged African Americans to improve themselves through personal effort, most notably industrial education and economic achievement, which he believed would demonstrate that blacks were worthy of white regard. Chesnutt's argument that racism should be torn down by removing the differences between the races was part of the same mindset. The respectability—and thereby racial honor—Washington, Chesnutt, and those like them sought was simply a recognition on the part of whites that blacks were not *inherently* dishonorable.[10] Part of establishing the honorable standing of blacks and thus their potential for respectability was eliminating sources of shame, such as conjure.

The honor at issue here took two forms, vertical and horizontal. Social scientists describe the sort of respect pursued by accommodationists as a form of vertical honor, or the right to respect by those who are superior in rank, power, or status. Of course all honor is in one sense vertical, since gaining respect is the key to public approval. But the concept is complicated by the "honor group." According to anthropologist Frank Henderson Stewart, an honor group is "a set of people who follow the same code of honor and who recognize each other as doing so."[11] Within such a population, abiding by the rules wins one horizontal honor, "a right to respect . . . of the kind that is due an equal."[12] In the case at hand, whites made up the honor group that defined the respectability sought by the intelligentsia for their race, yet blacks were still excluded. Acceptance by the white middle class was an upward move. In order to achieve it, the accommodationists felt they needed to persuade African Americans to embrace practices and values esteemed by whites while rejecting those that whites denigrated. They were, in effect, seeking to integrate their race into a broader American honor group by proving that, as a race, blacks lived according to white values. Those individuals who indeed lived according to white standards, they believed, would earn respect from whites.[13]

On the other hand, race itself is an honor group—a horizontal one of equals—in which a wholly different set of criteria could come into play. The "right to respect" among newly emancipated blacks was complicated, and the position occupied by conjurers was a point of conflict within the black community. Were conjurers honorable? Was conjure itself presentable in the quest for acceptance by the larger, biracial honor group of middle-class America? This delicate interplay between aspirations reveals honor's complicating role in African Americans' sense of identity.

African Americans who adhered to the prevailing uplift ideology of their day easily accepted that conjure—understood by the majority of white society as a sign of blacks' backwardness—was a blot on their religion and thus their respectability. For example the anonymous editor of a collection of letters about conjure published in 1878 by the school newspaper of Virginia's Hampton Normal and

Agricultural Institute, *Southern Workman,* encouraged its readers to eradicate what he or she called "early-acquired superstition." Conjure, the editor argued, was a serious impediment not just to the civilization of African Americans but a threat to their very survival. Though this commentator was probably a white member of the school's faculty, the letters themselves make it clear that a great many of the contributors had absorbed their professors' outlook. Despite what the editor described as a "natural hesitation—partly fear, and partly shame" to sharing their views on hoodoo, the letter writers had no reluctance proclaiming conjure "superstitious folly" and a "horrible feature of ignorance and vice."[14] According to them, individuals who practiced or believed in conjure as well as the race to which they belonged were tarred with a shameful mark, but it was not, the editor proclaimed, an indelible one. In light of the use of such uplift ideology, it should come as no surprise that Booker T. Washington himself was a Hampton Institute alumnus.[15]

The faculty and students of the Hampton Institute were certainly not alone in their attempt to erase conjure from black culture—or at least from public perceptions of it. William Wells Brown, a former slave, treated conjure as a feature of a bygone age, relegating it to the "ignorant days of slavery" in an 1880 autobiography entitled *My Southern Home.* He followed a brief description of what he termed "voodooism, goopherism, and fortune-telling" by recounting stories that poked fun at practitioners and the antebellum African American culture to which Brown implied they had been confined.[16] Another former slave who participated in the engineering project was Louis Hughes. He had once been a believer in the power of conjure bags to prevent whippings from cruel masters. By the time he published his autobiography in 1897, however, he had become convinced that it had been "one of the superstitions of a barbarous ancestry." Throughout the passage addressing the use of charms, Hughes invariably spoke of them in the past tense, indicating that readers should no longer consider hoodoo a part of blacks' worldview or see it as reflecting on their honor as a race.[17] Even the notorious critic of uplift ideology, W. E. B. Du Bois, participated in the attempt to unshackle African Americans from associations with what he termed "Obi worship." In his 1903 work *The Souls of Black Folk,* he described conjure as "barbarous rites, spells, and blood sacrifice" that had once placed the "witch-woman and the voodoo priest" at the center of black life. Like his contemporaries at the Hampton Institute, however, Du Bois admitted that aspects of these practices still existed in his day among what he called "the unlettered Negro."[18]

Chesnutt and his ilk adopted the approach they did because of their position in history. Only a generation before their heyday, war and a series of constitutional amendments had supposedly transformed blacks into free American citizens with legal and political rights equal to those of whites. As the black intelligentsia readily understood, the legal sea change had not altered the culture of whites to the degree that most would accept ex-slaves and their children as equals. These same upheavals left many aspects of black culture equally unchanged. The existence of supernaturalism was itself a prime example. Just as pertinent to the issue of racial honor, the intelligentsia found itself intellectually trapped within assumptions that defined white culture and its notions of honor and respectability as superior to those of African Americans. The accommodationists believed that their best hope of demonstrating to whites the honorable standing of the black race was by proving its members could live according to white-defined mores of respectability.

One monumental problem facing the intelligentsia was that according to the honor code of the upper-class antebellum South, which continued to inform concepts of race for decades after the Civil War, blacks could never be honorable. Among the many qualities planters had defined as honorable were gentility, public repute, civic responsibility, chivalry, military courage, hierarchical position, autonomy, aggression, wisdom, and refined manners, all of which had been either explicitly denied slaves or assumed by the broader society to be unobtainable for bondpersons. Even whites who were not from among the ranks of the elite nevertheless accepted planters' definition of the honorable. As Craig Thompson Friend and Lorri Glover succinctly put it, "In the eyes of whites, black men were the antithesis of honor and mastery—dependent, acquiescent, externally controlled."[19] In light of the fact that public perception conferred honor, one can confidently say that the manifestation of southern honor constructed by whites and with which the accommodationists engaged was not fully obtainable by blacks under the conditions that prevailed during the nineteenth and early twentieth centuries.[20]

African Americans certainly recognized that they, as a race, did not fit into whites' parameters of the honorable, but this acknowledgement in no way prevented them from seeking to prove their worthiness to the dominant race. After all, at its heart, honor is a value awarded—albeit usually to individuals—by communities. Moreover whites like Handy and Bruce were the ones who initially claimed that aspects of black culture, such as conjure, set blacks apart from white America. Careful excising of offensive cultural material should, according to theory, lessen or even remove the racist assumptions that kept blacks outside of the sphere of honorable respectability.[21]

Even though whites had long defined the black race as categorically dishonorable, routes to limited honor had always existed for individual blacks. These served as examples the accommodationists attempted to follow. Under slavery the surest path to the bounded honor available to blacks was accepting one's situation, working hard within it to please whites, and embracing white cultural norms. To be sure, slaves had no hope of acquiring an honorable standing that would place them in the same social orbit as whites, but that fact in no way barred them from acquiring regard on the part of whites that would elevate them above their fellow. An excellent example was the case of Caesar or Cesar, a slave healer whom the colonial Assembly of South Carolina freed in gratitude for his reputed discovery of a cure for poison. In addition to his freedom, he was to receive a one hundred pound annuity in recognition of his services. By working within the system, he found himself with the honor of a free man that made him the social superior of bondpersons, at least in the eyes of whites.[22]

An even clearer example of a slave who acquired limited honor from whites by accepting the system was April Ellison, also of South Carolina. As a young man, Ellison learned the art of gin making and repair and was later freed by his master, William Ellison. Through hard work, meticulous business dealings, purchases of slaves, careful protection of his reputation, and a legal change of his given name to William, he distanced himself from his past and the racial assumptions that went with it, gaining a limited measure of respect in the eyes of whites by living according to their standards. The most potent symbol of his place within southern society was his successful effort to persuade Stateburg's Holy Cross Episcopal Church to allow him and his family to leave the gallery, which was reserved for slaves and free people of color, to worship on the main floor.[23]

Accommodationists understandably relied on experience to determine their approach to the problem of racial barriers to honor, but the keep-your-head-down-and-do-your-job approach had its limitations. For one, while many slaves gained a modicum of honor through hard work, notable achievements, or simple manumission, few attained the relative heights of Caesar or William Ellison. Just as important, even Ellison and Caesar found themselves sharply restricted in just how far they could advance in the estimation of whites. Ellison may have gained a seat on the floor of Holy Cross, but the church leadership confined him to a bench at the back of the sanctuary, under an organ loft. In the case of Caesar, other than frequent mentions of his name in connection with herbal remedies, he slipped out of the public eye. There is no evidence that any whites ever accepted him as their peer.[24]

Despite its limitations this model for the pursuit of honor had proven functional, and by the late nineteenth century it was a pervasive feature of literature and public life in the image of the faithful slave. A prime example was the enormously popular Uncle Remus character from the folkloric writings of Joel Chandler Harris. Throughout the seven books in which Remus is a major character, he acts as a kindly and respected dispenser of wisdom who rarely seems to feel the weight of bondage. The short stories of Thomas Nelson Page frequently include ex-slave narrators who embrace their service to masters, thereby accruing reflected honor for themselves. The image of the docile, nonoffensive bondman was embraced in public life as well. Following the death of Jefferson Davis, former president of the Confederacy, organizers of funerary ceremonies held several discussions of how to include African Americans. An *Atlanta Constitution* article reportedly noted that Confederate veterans wanted to include former slaves in one procession to show their respect for "the faithful of Southern darkies."[25] The path to limited honor followed by antebellum blacks had served individuals well and continued to resonate in white society. Could it not serve the race—the larger honor group—equally well?

The reason for the African American intelligentsia's embrace of accommodation makes sense in context, but why was it that conjure became such a focal point? Part of the answer is simple. The Christian faith of the majority of whites and a rapidly growing number of blacks from the early eighteenth century forward included numerous pronouncements against the practice of magic, including Deuteronomy 18:10–14, which called it "abhorrent to the LORD." Some African Americans—but by no means all—saw hoodoo opposed to Christianity, an increasingly definitive aspect of African Americans' understanding of all aspects of life, including honor. The much-quoted antebellum hymn "You Must Be Pure and Holy" memorably proclaimed, "The devil am a liar and conjurer, too. . . . If you don't look out, he'll conjure you."[26] In this understanding hoodoo was not just outside of Christianity. It was a tool of Christ's enemy. Ann Bishop, a former slave from Livingstone, Alabama, expressed much the same sentiment when she described the nature of hoodoo and Voodoo to Federal Writers' Project workers during the Great Depression. Bishop stated her belief in "voodoo an' hoodoo an' sper'ts." She bluntly criticized the profession of conjurer as "nothin' but a lot of folk's outten Christ."[27]

Still scripture and the Christian faith based on it do not explain why the accommodationists identified conjure as so shameful that it needed erasure from black society. For one, many conjurers avoided condemnation by fellow African Americans by identifying the source of their power as Christ, claiming a role similar to that of Old Testament prophets rather than disreputable sorcerers.[28] An even more important key to understanding the suppression of conjure was that despite biblical condemnations and whites' reference to hoodoo in their belittlement of blacks, most nineteenth-century black southerners and a large but gradually declining population thereafter considered conjurers honorable men and women.[29]

In a society in which whites defined African Americans as not just dishonorable but in all other ways inferior, the supposed power to manipulate the spirit world and openly defy masters placed conjurers on a social level with or even above whites—at least in the eyes of some blacks. In effect conjure created an alternate and potentially rebellious form of what Julian Pitt-Rivers has called "sacred honor," by which one "stands in a preferential relation to the deity."[30] The most recognizable form of sacred honor is the oath, which invokes the Deity and binds the actions of the swearer. The flip side of this is the curse, which can be used against one's enemies and is an agent of shame and humiliation. Conjure, therefore, competed with Christianity for divine authority, and the conjurer stood as an alternative to the minister.

Unfortunately for the late nineteenth- and early twentieth-century black intelligentsia, the conjurer was usually the only one to benefit within this framework, and a certain strange honor attached to him that defied anything acceptable to the aspiring black middle class. While individual hoodoo practitioners could claim places of respect and even fear in black society—as well as the broader American society according to folklore—the black intelligentsia recognized that the image of the conjurer had become a tool used by whites to denigrate the entire African American race. So as long as a blacks conferred honor on hoodoo practitioners, the African American race could not hope to enter an honor group defined by whites.[31] Accommodationists, then, hoped to discredit a small group of individuals in an effort to win respectability for an entire race.

Discrediting conjurers was a step in redefining black perceptions of honor, and leading African Americans were not the first to attempt to alter their society's perceptions of honor for the betterment of society. A notable parallel was the antidueling movement among antebellum whites. Both dueling and conjure centered around the performance of ritual, the practice of which could be combated. Duels were often elaborate affairs, the carrying out of which demonstrated one's public standing. Conjuring required equally elaborate rituals to make charms and work spells, which likewise won esteem for their performers. Foreshadowing the later struggle to suppress hoodoo, the fight to eliminate dueling emanated not from the general public but from a relatively small group of ministers, journalists, and members of the gentry. Moreover opponents of both dueling and hoodoo saw what they opposed as barbaric rituals unworthy of a Christian society. The cases were far from identical, however. Antidueling activists sought to change their honor group's code of conduct. The accommodationists, on the other hand, sought to incorporate their race into an honor group operating under rules developed by whites. Furthermore the two engineering projects differed in that antebellum whites had access to the political machinery that allowed them to outlaw dueling, while African Americans had little recourse other than persuasion, hence the attention conjure received from accommodationists.[32]

On the other hand, it might seem odd that the black intelligentsia would see the prevailing black viewpoint on hoodoo as open to attack. Working alongside the perceived need to conform to white culture was the recognition that African American believers in conjure drew a distinction between practitioners and their profession. While they accorded successful conjure men and women substantial respect, they often thought of the profession of hoodoo as something ambiguous, disreputable, or even dangerous. Hoodoo provided practitioners with the means of doing harm, and there was no guarantee that they would refrain from using it against members of their own race. In other words, the command of the supernatural that built individual conjurers' reputations also made them suspect as a class.

At play in the seeming paradox of conjurers who win honor through the disreputable practice of hoodoo were independent—and clashing—vertical and horizontal understandings of honor. African Americans' growing attachment to Christian values and conjure's potential for social disruption meant that hoodoo could never be an acceptable part of a system that rested on adherence to values that bind an honor group together. This fact was just as true within the black community as it was among whites. African Americans nevertheless honored individual practitioners because conjurers' supposed powers raised them above fellow blacks and, in the eyes of many believers, elevated them even beyond many whites.

Marie Laveau's fame, for example, was such that she appeared frequently in white-owned newspapers, and those who remembered her told impressive stories about her doings during the late nineteenth century. When asked about Laveau by Federal Writers' Project workers in 1940, for instance, New Orleans resident Marie Brown stated that "she walked lak' she owned the city an' ev'rythin'. . . . She said she could call sperets outer your house—She could make pictures come off the wall—She could do ennythin' she wanted." Though Laveau was viewed with a kind of fear-based respect by her African American community, Brown voiced the conclusion of many that Laveau was likely "a-burnin' for her sins," a declaration that suggested Laveau, despite her rumored power, did not live up to the values that would have won her enduring respectability.[33] Other informants gave considerable detail on what Laveau's sins entailed. According to Marie Dede, who claimed to have known her, the Voodoo Queen would acquire dead babies from an abortionist and fellow hoodoo worker named Mamie Hughes. The corpses were what Laveau supposedly fed to snakes she used in Voodoo rituals. Though tales of murdered children fed to serpents in the pursuit of spiritual power were probably nothing more than rumor-turned-folklore, the fact that Dede and others like her believed the stories testifies to the burden of shame borne by a profession associated with such brutality. Laveau's manipulation of the spirit world might have brought the Voodoo Queen a kind of grudging honor among her community, but her profession relied on emphatically dishonorable deeds.[34]

The place of conjure and conjurers illustrates a truth not fully recognized or engaged by the accommodationists: African American culture often admired blacks who existed outside the white honor paradigm and whose standing within African American society was independent of white approval. In some cases black-defined honor could resemble the version constructed by the antebellum planter class. For example, in the book *All God's Children: The Bosket Family and the American Tradition of Violence,* journalist Fox Butterfield persuasively argued that some slaves and their descendants adopted the aggressive aspects of the antebellum white code of honor, manifesting them in brutal, often immediate violence toward those who questioned their worth. Conjure, meanwhile, did not replicate the aspects of honor defined by antebellum whites; it was not civic-minded or genteel. Instead it was predominantly about personal power that raised successful practitioners above their peers. According to widespread belief, such power was not confined to operation only within black society but could effectively protect African Americans from whites or even strike down offending members of the dominant race. Whether or not they fully understood conjure's place within the African American community, the black intelligentsia would have been compelled to suppress hoodoo to have any hope of successfully integrating their race into the white-defined honor group. Members of the dominant race were unlikely to accept a race that honored those considered a threat to whites' power.[35]

In light of African Americans' experience of the pursuit of honor in the face of profound racism as well as the success of earlier cultural engineering projects, the African American intelligentsia saw their project as promising. The conflicting forces of individual honor and professional shame may have made conjure a seemingly easy target for cultural engineering, but stripping hoodoo practitioners of their honor was not as easy as Chesnutt and the editors of the *Southern Workman* seemed to think it would be. Unsurprisingly, despite the accommodationist intelligentsia's attempt to eliminate the honor associated with conjure men through the power of racial uplift, conjure refused to disappear. Their efforts did little to erase the divide between black and white and instead created fault lines within African American society.

The engineering project emphatically failed to demonstrate to the satisfaction of whites that African Americans were worthy of respect. One could easily argue that the divide between the races grew wider rather than narrower. The late nineteenth and early twentieth centuries, after all, saw frequent lynchings and the implementation of Jim Crow. White writers remained as dismissive of African Americans as ever and continued to use hoodoo as a justification for their attitudes until the days of the civil rights movement. Despite the success of the so-called Second Reconstruction, conjure has largely retained its negative connotations among whites, who tend to associate it with crime, death, zombies, and curses.[36]

In addition the very idea that black culture should have been altered was itself a recognition of the existence of a population, an honor group, that would likely resist the change. That the intelligentsia was still working to suppress hoodoo a generation after the editors of the *Southern Workman* helped begin the project was a telling sign that the task would not be easy. Journalists recorded sensationalist tales of the respect given conjure throughout the early twentieth century. Ruth Bass, for instance, recounted the death of an aged practitioner named Old Divinity on March 28, 1935. Despite the man's death, Bass clearly depicted conjure as a living tradition that had simply lost one of its more eminent adepts. Many dozens of newspaper articles from New Orleans alone testify to hoodoo and Voodoo practitioners' standing between 1900 and 1940.[37]

It is tempting to dismiss the work of journalists as racial propaganda, but while many of their accounts should be treated with caution, more reliable sources also testify to the widespread survival of honor associated with conjurers throughout the late nineteenth century and first half of the twentieth century. Sociologist and folklorist Newbell Niles Puckett worked with both published accounts and practitioners to compile his 1926 work *Folk Beliefs of the Southern Negro.* His informants indirectly testified to their regard for hoodoo practitioners by describing exorbitant sums of up to $500 they were willing to pay for magical assistance. In 1931 Zora Neale Hurston published "Hoodoo in America," an account of conjurers in Louisiana, Florida, and Alabama. Alongside records of well-known current practitioners, she recounted tales of deceased conjurers whose names and stories had survived them. Her article and a later book partially based on it read very much like celebrations of hoodoo and its honored practitioners rather than simple collections of folklore. Harry Middleton Hyatt's *Hoodoo-Conjuration-Witchcraft-Rootwork,* a five-volume compilation of oral histories collected from believers in and practitioners of hoodoo mostly during the 1940s, lacks Hurston's celebration, but it nonetheless testifies to the respected position that conjurers maintained in black society.[38]

Revealing, albeit indirect, evidence of the continued awe accorded conjurers by many black Americans were the plentiful newspaper advertisements for magical supplies that flooded African American periodicals during the late nineteenth and early twentieth centuries. By 1898, for instance, the *Alabama Time-Piece* had begun to carry notices of the sale of rods to locate buried treasure, one of conjurers' professional services. The *Chicago Defender,* the nation's most prominent African American periodical, followed suit as the Great Migration rapidly increased the Windy City's population beginning in the 1910s.[39] So strong was the demand for hoodoo-related products that the newspaper often carried multiple ads per page. A single page of the July 3, 1926, edition of the *Defender* offered opportunities to order Luck Star Incense, a Little Imp wishing ring, love drawing perfume, a selection of magical handbooks, and information on how to find buried treasure. Doubtless many of these products made their way into the hands of do-it-yourself amateurs, but the very fact that the newspaper had taken on the role of conjurer testifies to the continued esteem its practitioners retained.[40]

The failure of the engineering project as well as the intra–African American cultural division it created can be seen in Hamilton Bims's "Can You *Believe* It . . . Superstition Lives!," which appeared in *Ebony* in July 1976. Bims opened his piece by presenting supernaturalism of any sort as something the average reader under fifty years of age—assumed to be African American—would have been unlikely to encounter. Somewhat contradictorily the article went on to examine what its author saw as a lamentable and unsettling rise in the number of believers in "superstitions" like Voodoo and hoodoo. Without rejecting the accommodationists' basic contention that conjure brought shame on the black race, Bims effectively conceded the failure of their engineering effort, seeking to deflect the disrepute he obviously felt conjure entailed by arguing that superstition was not confined to an economic class or race.[41]

Even today the rifts opened by the cultural engineering project remain visible. A recent doctoral dissertation by Kodi Roberts indicates just how powerful the accommodationists' vision has been. In this fascinating work, Roberts argued that rather than defining conjure and Voodoo as African American practices, scholars should think of them as "religious, magic, and business practices created and re-created in the image of the city and nation in which they were practiced," a viewpoint reminiscent of Hamilton Bims's *Ebony* article in its dissociation of hoodoo from black society.[42] On the other end of the spectrum are those who argue that the efforts of the accommodationists should be emphatically rejected. One notable examples is Katrina Hazzard-Donald's *Mojo Workin': The Old African American Hoodoo System,* which contends that conjure should be embraced as an honorable part of African American culture in both the vertical and horizontal senses. In a move that would have bemused Charles Chesnutt, she is even critical of whites who practice it, implying that legitimate practice is for blacks alone.[43]

African American proponents of cultural change dreamt that merging their honor with that of whites would allow individual blacks to overcome racism through achievement of respectability—a vertical step up—but they had little hope of success. In the end the accommodationists failed to eliminate conjurers' literal ability to inspire awe, which they believed stood in the way of respectability and, thus, equality. In the eyes of the black intelligentsia, average African Americans' reluctance to abandon their culture's notions of the honorable kept the race bound to inequality by preventing it from lifting itself out of oppression. Honor proved to be something less than the unifying force that they hoped it would be. Rather than providing the racism-free social cohesion the accommodationists desired, the search for honor proved to be a source of division, opening rifts that remain to this day. To be fair, however, the search for equality through respectability was a fool's errand. No effort at uplift was likely to succeed during a time that witnessed the entrenchment of white supremacy, itself a form of vertical honor through which whites claimed a place of privilege in American society.

NOTES

1. J. Anderson, *Conjure in African American Society,* 1–9.

2. Wyatt-Brown, *Southern Honor,* xiii–xiv, xxx–xxxiii, 313, 315–16, 424. For discussion of the extent of belief in conjure among whites, see J. Anderson, *Conjure in African American Society,* 78.

3. C. Chesnutt, "Race Prejudice," 219.

4. Ibid., 218.

5. Ibid., 220–22, 236.

6. The precise relationship between conjure, hoodoo, and Voodoo is a subject of some contention among scholars, but for purposes of this essay, they fill the same position in relation to

African American honor and shame. While the terms are not used interchangeably, they have been the object of the same cultural engineering projects.

7. Handy, "Witchcraft among the Negroes," 666.

8. P. Bruce, *Plantation Negro as a Freedman*, 111, 115. For a full discussion of the ways in which whites used hoodoo and Voodoo to justify the subjection of blacks, see J. Anderson, *Conjure in African American Society*, 1–24.

9. Washington and Du Bois, *Negro in the South*, 182–84, quote from 183.

10. Ibid., 61–68, 70–75; C. Chesnutt, "Race Prejudice," 219.

11. Stewart, *Honor*, 54.

12. Ibid.

13. Ibid., 54–59.

14. R., L., G., and A., "Conjure Doctors," 30.

15. Washington, *Up from Slavery*, 45–73.

16. W. Brown, *My Southern Home*, 68–82.

17. Hughes, *Thirty Years a Slave*, 108.

18. Du Bois, *Souls of Black Folk*, 203.

19. Friend and Glover, *Southern Manhood*, xi.

20. Wyatt-Brown, *Southern Honor*, xv, xvi, 4, 14; Friend and Glover, *Southern Manhood*, viii–xi.

21. Friend and Glover, *Southern Manhood*, viii–xi.

22. "Negro Cesar's Cure."

23. M. Johnson and Roark, *Black Masters*, 3–29.

24. Fett, *Working Cures*, 64, 68–69; M. Johnson and Roark, *Black Masters*, 26.

25. Harris, *Complete Tales of Uncle Remus*; Page, *In Ole Virginia*; *Atlanta Constitution* qtd. in D. Collins, *Death and Resurrection*, 108.

26. Allen, Ware, and Garrison, *Slave Songs*, 108.

27. Bishop, "Gabr'el Blow Sof! Gabr'el Blow Loud!," 6: 36–37, quote from 37.

28. J. Anderson, *Conjure in African American Society*, 35–36.

29. In an unpublished draft of a book chapter on slave honor, Bertram Wyatt-Brown briefly addressed the honor that bondpersons accorded hoodoo doctors during the nineteenth century. According to Wyatt-Brown a conjurer could typically claim "a position of honor and awe in their communities." Other scholars have come to the same conclusion. In 1979 John W. Blassingame made the same argument in *The Slave Community*, stating, "Often the most powerful and significant individual on the plantation was the conjurer." Sharla Fett seconded Blassingame and provided a plethora of support from primary sources in her own extensive study of slave healing practices, *Working Cures*. The list of scholars in agreement with Wyatt-Brown, Blassingame, and Fett is lengthy. See Wyatt-Brown, e-mail message to author, August 22, 2011; Blassingame, *Slave Community*, 109; Fett, *Working Cures*, 97.

30. Pitt-Rivers, "Honor," 506.

31. W. Brown, *Narrative*, 414–15, quote from 414; Breaux and Villere, "Marie Laveau: Her Tomb and Descendants"; Hyatt, *Hoodoo-Conjuration-Witchcraft-Rootwork*, 1:923–29; Steiner, "Observations of the Practice of Conjuring."

32. J. Williams, *Dueling in the Old South*, 60–71; Wyatt-Brown, *Southern Honor*, 351–53.

33. M. Brown, "Negro (Marie Laveau)."

34. Dede, "Marie Laveau."

35. Butterfield, *All God's Children*, especially 3–67. According to Butterfield, particular objects of African American ire were any structures or institutions that they thought of as representing

authority, often envisioned as embodying white oppression. Believers in conjure often employed it to the same ends, especially during the antebellum era.

36. For examples of the trend, see Rice, *Feast of All Saints,* in which the author links Voodoo with prostitution and rape. See also Preston and Child, *Cemetery Dance,* in which adherents of an African creole religion are the apparent source of a series of supernatural assaults. It is notable that Preston and Child concluded their novel by depicting the apparent aggressors as having been framed.

37. Bass, "Little Man"; B. Morrison, *Guide to Voodoo,* 47–59.

38. Puckett, *Folk Beliefs,* 167–310; Hurston, "Hoodoo in America"; Hurston, *Mules and Men,* 183–286; Hyatt, *Hoodoo-Conjuration-Witchcraft-Rootwork.* Hurston's accuracy has been questioned in recent years. See, for instance, J. Anderson, "Voodoo in Black and White," and Long, *Spiritual Merchants,* 277n67. Whether or not the details of her accounts can be trusted, the honor Hurston sought to give to hoodoo speaks volumes as does the embrace of her viewpoint over the last few decades.

39. "Rods"; Long, *Spiritual Merchants,* 130.

40. The page in question was section 2, page 3.

41. Bims, "Would You *Believe* It." During some of my previous research, I frequently encountered similar aversion to having hoodoo depicted as an African American practice. Of course practitioners—who remain numerous—have no qualms about embracing their practice.

42. K. Roberts, "Promise of Power," iii.

43. Hazzard-Donald, *Mojo Workin,'* 1–18, 179–85, quotes from 165. For other scholars who embrace aspects of Hazzard-Donald's viewpoint, see Boyd, *Wrapped in Rainbows,* 436–37; T. Smith, *Conjuring Culture,* 3; Chireau, *Black Magic,* 1–5. For popular authors along the same lines, see Walker, *Third Life;* T. Morrison, *Sula;* Naylor, *Mama Day;* Reed, *Conjure: Selected Poems, 1963–1970;* Rhodes, *Voodoo Dreams.*

Part V

The Persistence of Honor

Where is honor's relevance today? Mechanized warfare has negated whatever mastery the duel offered for self-definition; celebrity culture has trivialized the image of the lady or gentleman; personal therapy has replaced public esteem. The presentation of self in mass society frequently manifests itself in narcissistic careerism and consumerism—both counterweighted by inner-directed quests for simplicity and holistic meaning. Honor's assessment of good repute and shameful humiliation may seem hopelessly dated and quaint.

Or not. The military still makes much of honor, as it should and must. So, sadly, do street gangs and organized crime, both fetishized by a film industry in search of an audience. (*The Godfather* and *The Sopranos* expertly mixed old-fashioned honor with the demands of market culture.) We seem to like heroes who spike their honor with a bit of roguishness. In that spirit honor's appeal meshes with our very human and perennial longing for the past and its supposedly clearer, cleaner, simpler codes of right and wrong. Who needs ambiguity?

At no time was the question more pertinent than during the Great Depression, when the market revolution seemed to be in collapse. In a world signified by John Steinbeck's Okies or Raymond Chandler's alienated Philip Marlowe, Margaret Mitchell offered *Gone with The Wind,* a lost Eden of gentlemen and ladies whose enactments of honor were so stylized as to be definitive. Granted, Rhett Butler was a rogue and Scarlett O'Hara was vulnerable to gossip, but that merely proved the point. As Sarah Gardner's essay on Andrew Lytle shows, however, honor was still capable of being interpreted as something destabilizing and destructive. Lytle's alternate vision of honor in his novel *The Long Night* may have been a needed antidote to Mitchell's more successful offering, but its story, its creation, and its marketing history suggest that even in the literary world—perhaps especially there—honor retains its power to complicate and divide.

By contrast honor can still be invoked as an agent of solidarity. Two essays on the contemporary right illustrate this. As Edward Crowther argues, the kind of role-playing and mastery encoded in honor resonates in religious life, especially among evangelicals and self-identified biblical literalists. This pairing of honor and religious imperatives converges on gender roles—"divinely mandated gendered essentialism"—which inscribes clear boundaries of authority and guardianship between the sexes. "Complementarianism," as Crowther writes, defines the roles of man and woman in paternalistic terms taken straight from the language of honor.

This language is essential to contemporary political conservatism, as argued by Emily S. Bruce and Dickson D. Bruce Jr. An essential part of claiming honor has been the presumed independence of the honorable man, who feared nothing more than being regarded as a "dependent." This could be interpreted in a social, physical, economic, or racial sense—all harking back to the Old South. The duality has been present in political discourse since colonial times and is put to use (with differing emphases) by both left and right—progressive and conservative—right up to the present. Family values, military preparedness, the free market, and race—the four legs of modern political stances—all echo the vocabulary of honor.

Sarah E. Gardner

"THE SECRET OF VENGEANCE"

Honor and Revenge in Andrew Lytle's *The Long Night*

In 1931 literary critic Edmund Wilson published his wonderfully acerbic profile of the Nashville Agrarians in the *New Republic.* Suggesting that the "neo-Confederates" failed—philosophically and financially—in the world's intellectual centers, Wilson maintained that they returned home to "think tenderly of the South." Because they had "no common ideal or religion," he explained, they made one of ancestor worship—and churned out Civil War novels and biographies of Confederate generals.[1] Of all those books written by the Agrarians and their compatriots, Andrew Lytle's 1936 novel *The Long Night* mounted the most significant challenge to the sentimental and romantic reading of the Confederate cause, made famous by the likes of Thomas Nelson Page, Thomas Dixon, and, of course, Margaret Mitchell.

The Long Night's creation, publishing history, and reception illuminate the persistence of southern honor in three overlapping arenas. It is, of itself, a harshly revisionist look at the nature of antebellum southern honor—a bleak record of vengeance and violence, not nobility and sacrifice. This must be set next to a sentimentalized version of honor made popular by the almost simultaneous release of *Gone with the Wind,* a phenomenon that defined honor in romantic terms for a generation or more. In between these competing public expressions was a very private, highly personal affair of honor between two men—Lytle and Frank Owsley—over authorship and recognition. The language used in the exchange between these men is almost a study in honor itself.

The novel tells a gruesome tale of a young man's efforts to avenge his father's murder at the hands of the Lovell Gang, a roving band of horse thieves and slave stealers that terrorized the Alabama backcountry during the early decades of the nineteenth century. Pleasant McIvor was monomaniacal in his pursuit of gang members, their kin, and members of the corrupt legal system that had failed to convict Lovell and his crew for their crimes. Indeed Pleasant enlists in the Confederate Army not to defend hearth and home from invading Yankees but to better his chances of killing those associated with his father's murder. By the novel's end, Pleasant McIvor had killed fifteen men, but not before recognizing fully the enormity of his actions. Isolated from humanity, Pleasant learns that the price of vengeance is steep.

The southwestern frontier of Lytle's literary imagination was a brutal place, where "archaic" forms of honor, to borrow a formulation from historian Bertram Wyatt-Brown, persisted, "kept alive by the exigencies of an inhospitable and dangerous world." In particular the society imagined by Lytle valorized a strain of honor that demanded revenge against "familial and community enemies." Again Wyatt-Brown's explication proves instructive here. Citing Moses I. Finley's observation about the ancient Greeks, he noted that the conviction that "'one's kin were indistinguishable from oneself'" held equally true in the honor-bound, heroic South. Wyatt Brown elaborated: "The personal and familial were wholly united with the fate of the . . . kin-related community, whose defense was brave men's obligation." Lytle's protagonist thus fulfills his filial obligation to avenge a wrong and to remove the family's shame secure in the knowledge that his vengeance was just.[2]

Lytle had originally collaborated with his fellow Agrarian Frank Owsley on a fictionalized account of Owsley's "Uncle Dink," whose intimate knowledge of the Murrell Gang—the historical inspiration for Lytle's Lovell Gang—deeply informed the novel's plot.[3] Lytle responded enthusiastically to Owsley's invitation to work on this project, noting that he had immediately conceived of the novel's narrative arc and recommended writing it as an "Aeschylean tragedy." Richard Holway's study of Greek honor culture suggests that *The Long Night* owes as much to the Homeric epic as it does to the Oresteia, however. Holway's reading of the *Iliad* reveals the consequences of reproducing "heroic culture," which Holway defined as "highly competitive, honor-based, strife- and violence-prone." In many ways, in the wake of the slaughter of World War I, Lytle saw the Old South's frontier as "heroic" and Pleasant McIvor as that culture's victim.[4]

As Lytle drafted his novel, having long since abandoned Owsley, his publisher worried that *The Long Night* would not conform to readers' expectations. The in-house readers' reports, bordering on the euphoric, praised Lytle for his consummate technical skill and for his ability to create suspense. But they sounded cautionary notes that highlighted the iconoclasm of Lytle's imagined Civil War. Bobbs-Merrill thus faced difficulties in marketing this alternative narrative, designing an ill-fated campaign that highlighted its almost nonexistent similarities with *Gone with the Wind*, which had appeared two months earlier. Indeed, as Lytle reviewed page proofs for *The Long Night* in the late summer of 1936, he lamented: "What a shame that Georgia woman and her *Gone with the Wind* had to come out at this time. I heard she had been at it ten years[.] Why in God's name couldn't she have waited another year and added several more hundred pages."[5] Yet even as he fretted about *The Long Night*'s potential sales, he stood steadfastly by his narrative vision. Decrying both sentimentalists and realists for distorting the southern past, Lytle maintained he alone had employed "the right philosophical approach" to the Civil War.[6] Whether readers were prepared to accept a version that resembled the House of Atreus, and not the O'Haras' Tara, remained to be seen.

Andrew Lytle's Heroic South

Although Lytle acknowledged the classical antecedents of his tale, he also understood the novel's form and content—a revenge tale handed down from one generation to the next—as organically tied to the rural south. Moreover the novel's structure simultaneously underscored the primacy of oral tradition in honor-bound societies. *The Long Night* opens with an old and reclusive Pleasant McIvor sending for his nephew Lawrence in order to unburden his soul. "What I have to say is not a thing I can tell my wife and children," he explained. "But it is a thing that must be told." At once rapt and terrified, Lawrence listened spellbound to Pleasant's tale of revenge. In turn Lawrence narrates Pleasant's tale to the novel's readers.[7]

Pleasant's story begins with the family's forced migration from Georgia westward. "You're too young to remember militia musters," Pleasant tells his young nephew, "but in my boyhood they were mighty fine gatherings. . . . A man didn't care what happened," he elaborated, "so long as he could feel his strength or try his skill." Much to Pleasant's disappointment, his father, Cameron, refused to participate, claiming he was getting too old to fight. The Caruthers brothers, insulted by Cameron's refusal, sought out the McIvor patriarch the following day, determined to provoke a contest. The elder brother attacked first, but Cameron quickly seized the advantage and hurled the young man over a fence, "where he lay with his arm broken in three places and a pole jabbed in his head." Humiliated at the older brother's defeat, the younger brother planned his revenge. Once the elder brother had recovered, the two returned, to "borrow" two of Cameron's prized colts. They returned the horses, "dripping wet with sweat and wind broke. They were a pitiful sight to see." Outraged, Cameron shot both men. The elder brother died instantly; the younger survived, bringing charges against Cameron, who sat in jail for two years as the case wended its way through the courts. Cameron was finally released, but he had to sell his farmstead and his slaves to pay his legal fees. Now ruined, the family set out to Texas, accompanied by an assortment of kinfolk. "In this way," Pleasant explained, "they proposed to show their loyalty to the family head and their disgust with the way of justice which allowed an innocent man to suffer while defending himself against premeditated injury."[8] In this opening scene, Lytle established the novel's central theme: the obligation to maintain and protect honor rested with family and not with the state.

In their travels west, the McIvors run into the Lovell gang, setting off a series of skirmishes and standoffs, ultimately leading Cameron to appeal to the courts for redress. Given Pleasant's accounting of the McIvors' past history with the courts, Pleasant's nephew, and Lytle's readers, had little reason to expect this encounter would end satisfactorily. The U.S. district attorney, who was in Lovell's pocket, dismissed McIvor's accusations. In the meantime Lovell had sworn a bench warrant—"Dead or Alive"—against McIvor, effectively outlawing him. With a price on his head, Cameron's days were numbered. One evening, three men broke into his room; the Wilton brothers held him down, Pleasant recalled, "while a man by the name of Fox shot his head off."[9]

Lytle established Pleasant's fated role in this revenge drama early in the novel, even before he had detailed the McIvors' run-in with the Lovell Gang. Pleasant had been Cameron's favorite son. His older brother, William, "didn't take after any of our people," Pleasant recounts to his nephew. "He didn't look like any of our kin."[10] Singled out for Cameron's "especial confidence and affection," Pleasant not surprisingly feels immediately the full weight of his father's murder.[11] Locking himself in his room, he fell into a delirium of grief, intoning "strange and awful prayers," his "rapid tongue growing more violent and distraught." Eventually his frantic incantations ceased and Pleasant's praying assumed "a more conversational tone." William, with his ear pressed to Pleasant's door, explains to their mother, "He thinks he's talking to pa. He thinks pa is telling him who the murderers are." Suddenly the prayers stopped altogether. As he emerged from his room, his mother sensed that he had been transformed. "He was young, but his youth seemed gone," Lytle wrote. "In its place there was a terrible patience and a terrible purpose, and at once she knew this younger son, grown so wonderfully strange, would take their shame away."[12]

Honor-bound, Cameron's brothers and his sons spread out through Georgia and Kentucky to inform extended kin of Cameron's murder. Two weeks later the family gathers to plot its revenge. William speaks first: "Nothing will bring my father back. As the oldest son I claim the right to try the courts first. Then, if we can't get justice, we'll make our own." The clan is stunned and appalled by William's suggestion. Lovell's acquittal had already signaled a break down in the social order. These men had come to exact blood vengeance, not to appeal to a broken legal system to adjudicate a matter of personal and familial honor. One elder threatens to leave: "It's plain that what's wanted here is lawing, and lawing is out of my line." Another tries to reason with William: "you mustn't forget we all share this dishonor." Eventually a third turns to Pleasant, who initially feigns deference to his older brother but then reminds his kinfolk that the men William wants to stand trial "an't the only ones. . . . They ain't even the chief ones. Fox and the Wiltons killed pa, but others had him killed." Lest anyone misinterpret his point, Pleasant declares, "The Wiltons who held him, Fox who killed him, every one that had anything to do with it are going to die."[13]

Vengeance would not come swiftly or easily. Removing himself from the company of kith and kin, Pleasant steals away and trains in the art of killing. Although he missed his family, he knew that his "feelings had changed, that the thing he had to do had crowded everything else from his heart."[14] He becomes quite accomplished, hunting down Lovell's associates one by one in gruesome fashion. He chokes Lovell's overseer with his bare hands, his victim's "flipper arms . . . wav[ing] aimlessly upon the air . . . while his legs tramped the floor, first desperately, then weakly, then not at all." For good measure he sets the house on fire, but not before stabbing his victim "under the ribs near the heart."[15] Pleasant took an almost instant satisfaction in his work. "To be at ease in the dark. To know what the long night meant. That was the secret of vengeance. All at once he felt a great pity for the weakness of those men who would fall by his hand."[16] Rumors of the killings spread, heightening Pleasant's delight at imagining his future victims squirming in fear.

Pleasant's need to avenge his father's murder was so consuming that he had not heard of secession, the formation of the Confederacy, or the buildup to war. Only when he tracks down the gang's leader, shortly after the fall of Fort Sumter, does he learn of the impending crisis. Lovell assumes correctly that Pleasant had come to kill him, "saving [him] until the last." Pleasant, however, seizes on new opportunities opened up by war. He explains: "I'm not going to kill you now, Tyson Lovell. But I'll return. . . . I'll comb every company in the army. When I come back, you'll know all the others are dead but you. It may be months, it may be years, but every day of those years, you will think of death."[17]

McIvor made good on his promise. He found five of his father's murderers stationed with Albert Sidney Johnston's men at Corinth. Volunteering for duty Pleasant spent two months earning the men's trust. No one had recognized Pleasant. Five years had passed since Cameron's execution, and as Pleasant later explained, "Daylight men don't see beneath the skin." Still his plan called on becoming friendly with his victims. When he and the five men were assigned outpost duty in the thick bare woods, Pleasant grabbed his six-shooter, one bullet for each of his father's murders, and one for the sergeant in charge. He shot Sergeant Beatty first, making the other men bear witness. "The man leaped high in the air with a shout," Lytle wrote, "spread-eagled his arms and legs, and fell against a gun stack. After the clatter there was no other sound. The bullet had found his heart." The murder had the desired effect on the other men. Dropping to their knees, some begged. Others cursed. One professed his innocence. "Don't argue," Pleasant warned. "I'm not justice. But I'm going to send you where'll you'll get justice." Then he opened fire. Positioning the bodies to appear as if they had died at the hands of the enemy, he fired their guns, wiped his shoes, and headed back to camp. Johnston, who listened to McIvor deliver a falsified report—complete with details of his picking off Yankees and forcing a retreat—congratulates McIvor, noting that "General Bragg trains good soldiers. . . . Always do your duty," he advised, "with as much intelligence."[18]

This scene prompted literary scholar Richard Gray to ask, "Just what is Pleasant's 'duty'": "Is it to his family or to his community, the McIvors or the South?" Pleasant asked the same question of himself, for he sensed that war had changed him. The Confederate cause became his cause: "He realized with a shock that he had not been watching for his blood enemies." The five-way vengeance killing had been his last. Instead his thoughts had turned to the army and his desire that it might finally engage the enemy and drive them out of the country. He is reminded of his quest when he witnesses his cousin Armistead, now a colonel in the Confederate Army, reprimand a young deserter who had left camp to visit his ailing mother. Although the punishment Armistead exacted was light—a cord of wood chopped and a promise to kill two Yankees in the next battle—his parting words resonated with Pleasant. "Public duty," he instructed the wayward soldier, "when your country is in peril, comes before private." Gray thus read Pleasant as a "divided man" who does not know "whether he should avenge his father or defend the South."[19]

At some level Gray's reading works. Still much had transpired between Cameron McIvor's execution and Pleasant's stint in the Confederate Army. Wyatt-Brown has explained that "transformations" modified honor's "starkest elements. Loyalty to family," he wrote "was transformed into duty to country. . . . Virtuous revenge gave way to more abstract concepts of justice." Armistead, who was of Cameron's generation, weathered the transition seemingly effortlessly. As Cameron's "double first cousin," Armistead had participated in the family's blood vengeance. As he explained to Pleasant shortly after the funeral, "I'd go mighty far and wait a long time to deal with the people who have killed your pa." Indeed he murders one of Cameron's executioners before Pleasant had completed his "training" as an expert killer. By the time of the Civil War, however, Armistead's loyalties had shifted.[20]

For Pleasant, who was a teenager at the time of his father's murder, the transition was more difficult. Pleasant tries to regain the purpose to which he had dedicated his life, but ultimately he cannot. That he struggled to reach this moment does not gainsay his changed priorities. As Lytle explained to his editor at Bobbs-Merrill, Pleasant "could not remain unmoved by the high drama of four years of war." Not since Shiloh, Lytle wrote near the end of the novel, had Pleasant "attended to what he had to do. For months he had held his hand, had let his father lie uneasy in his grave. All that time his father's blood enemies skulked in the army." He told himself that he could return to his pursuit after the war. Now all men, even his father's murderers, were needed for the cause. Yet once Pleasant was forced to admit that he had developed other loyalties, that he did, in fact, have more to lose, he knew his vengeance was gone. Disturbed by this epiphany, he sets out one last time to track down one of his father's murderers. Detained, he fails to return to camp in time to deliver crucial information about a Union attack. His private vengeance had cost a comrade, a friend, his life, and Pleasant believed "He had killed him as certainly has if he had pressed the cold blade into his heart."[21] At last Pleasant finally understood the consequences of his private war.

This knowledge is devastating. Pleasant is unable to return to society at the novel's end. "Suddenly he had known what he had done," Lytle wrote in the novel's final scene. Leaving camp, he sets out for the hills of Alabama. "It was not such a long journey to a man who knew the way, who had lost every other way. There he would go," the novel concludes. "There in the secret coves, far away from the world and vengeance, a deserter might hide forever."[22]

The novel's conclusion suggests a different fate for Pleasant McIvor than the one sketched out in the novel's prologue. The soldier, shattered by vengeance's price, bears little resemblance to the family man who summons his nephew to hear his tale. This narrative flaw did not escape attentive readers' attention. An in-house reader expressed concern during the summer of 1936. Summarizing the novel as a "brilliant hodgepodge on which much talent has been carelessly spent," the reader cited Lytle's failure to "tie up" the prologue with the end as the contributive factor for the novel's ultimate failure. Frank Owsley offered a fuller criticism, noting "that the old man who commands his nephew to come to see him on his way from college cannot possibly be the young Pleasant who deserts and goes to hide in the hills." Because the prologue is enigmatic, Owsley claimed, the reader is forced to conclude that the old Pleasant called his nephew to carry on the bloody revenge. The novel fails to reconcile the old Pleasant, who had according to the prologue "accomplished great things," with the young soldier who "went off to hide, having lost interest in both the private war and the Civil War." Owsley feared these issues, unless resolved, would damage "a really great book."[23]

As the manuscript moved its way to production, Lytle's editor tried to minimize the narrative's inconsistency. "I was not so struck as you have been by the change in the character of Pleasant McIvor as he appears in the prelude to THE LONG NIGHT, and as we leave him at the end of the story," he told Owsley. Perhaps more an expression of hope than a statement of fact, D. L. Chambers surmised that readers would likely forget the initial narrator "in the compelling interest of the narrative."[24] Chambers had reason to dismiss these concerns. By the summer of 1936, the novel's illogical ending was the least of his worries.

Honor among Friends

If Lytle sought to explain a variant of honor as it operated on the southwestern frontier, his compatriots wondered if he behaved dishonorably with one of their own. What began as a collaborative effort between friends ended with recriminations and hurt feelings.[25] Because Owsley had spoken of the novel as a joint project, he felt embarrassed when it was published under Lytle's name, with no acknowledgment of his contribution to its crafting. Owsley accused Lytle of rendering him a liar, sending letters to their mutual friends and to Chambers. Although the two eventually mended their friendship, the episode illuminates the ways in which personal affairs of honor interrupted its theoretical exploration. Lytle might have claimed to understand how honor functioned in the Old Southwest, but he failed to see how his actions dishonored his friend.

Lytle had originally agreed to Owsley's proposed partnership. "You write it down in narrative form," he suggested, "then I can tackle it; then we can talk it over, and both of us fix and bring to bear two critical attitudes."[26] The two continued to work together throughout 1934–35, Owsley sending Lytle information about his great uncle and Lytle mulling the story in his mind.

By the end of 1935, however, the strains in their working relationship emerged. Lytle's rendering of the story increasingly frustrated Owsley, who wrote polite but pointed and detailed criticisms of the drafts. To be sure, he was quick to praise what he thought worked well. The opening scenes were "perfect," he wrote. "Almost anything that you might do to that section would be injurious." Even so Owsley registered concern about the novel's tone, fearing that Lytle's penchant for comedy would "burlesque the whole book before you know it." That Owsley continued to comment suggests that he still thought he had a voice in the shaping of the novel. More to the point, he forwarded drafts of scenes that he had penned, noting "I do not know whether any of these will aid you." Owsley soon discovered that he faced far more serious concerns.[27]

Lytle thanked Owsley for his "able criticism," explaining that "it's just the sort of thing I want." He responded fully to Owsley's concerns, noting when they helped to clarify his thinking and when he disagreed. Conceding that vision does not always equal execution, he asked Owsley for his continued help. "What I have had in mind to do and what I have done may not be apparent on paper, and that's what I want you to do—pick out these flaws and I will try to get rid of them the best I can," he promised. Lytle thus encouraged Owsley to believe that he still played a vital role in the manuscript's drafting.[28]

Indeed Owsley was gratified that Lytle took his comments in the spirit with which they were offered, having feared that he had been "so sharp and impersonal . . . that you might have gained the impression that I thought less highly of the novel . . . than I actually do." Owsley also reminded Lytle that he had already drafted two novelettes based on this material. He sensed immediately that both efforts "flopped." The first, told from Uncle Dink's point of view, "merely pictured a mass murderer." In the second, told from the community's point of view, Uncle Dink "ceased to be a person and became a shadow or a dark spirit without any real interest." This narrative conundrum in part fueled Owsley's asking Lytle to "take the lead in writing the story." Owsley was satisfied with the way in which Lytle resolved this narrative dilemma, reassuring him that "under no circumstances do I want to cramp your style." Encouraging Lytle to hammer away at his draft, he professed his confidence: "If you can stave the publishers off until you have really completed the book your future is made."[29]

Owsley's correspondence with Lytle's editor, however, suggests that he was less sanguine about his relationship with Lytle. To Chambers's request for comments on the novel's page proofs, Owsley reiterated his point that the novel's ending was both illogical and unsatisfying. More to the point, he took the opportunity to unleash on what he considered to be Lytle's betrayal, cataloguing in painstaking detail the ways in which Lytle had abrogated their partnership. From the moment Owsley had first told Lytle the story of his Uncle Dink, he explained, he had imagined a collaborative project, proposing the two become "joint authors." Owsley made clear that there were parts of the narrative he wished to write, "parts which [Lytle] did not know as well as I, but he was always to have the right of final revision and final phrasing: this was my own suggestion, not his—this final revisory power." Owsley emphasized that he took the first stab at drafting the narrative; Lytle did not pen a word for more than a year. Only in the summer of 1935 did Lytle start writing in earnest. At this point "the book was still a joint undertaking," Owsley clarified, noting that he had "carried Andrew to the country where the crimes were committed and to let him study at first hand the physical setting." By the fall of 1935, Lytle had "casually mentioned that 'we' had a contract," but he never offered to show it to Owsley. "Then the book began to be Andrew's by some imperceptible process," Owsley recalled. "I never have understood it, and I never shall, I suppose." He confessed to being "greatly embarrassed and very much upset" by the turn of events for he considered Lytle one of his closest friends. He closed by suggesting to Chambers that Lytle was still "quite a young man just coming into his own, a person of transcendent gifts . . . and there might arise an occasion, later, when your more mature judgment could be brought to focus upon his muddled code of ethics which might be of great benefit to him."[30]

Owsley's version of events shocked Chambers. Chambers knew that the story was based loosely on Owsley's family history and that Lytle had strayed from the facts in order to achieve his artistic vision. Nonetheless Owsley's accusations surprised Chambers, who defended Lytle, finding it difficult to believe that his author had intentionally or maliciously misled Owsley. Fending off any potential legal entanglement, Chambers made clear that Lytle had assured Bobbs-Merrill of "complete ownership of all rights and warranted us against the invasion of any other's literary property, as is customary in publishing contracts." Although he understood Owsley's "peculiar" interest in *The Long Night,* he was "bound by the author's determination of his copy." In other words, Owsley's concerns, particularly about the novel's ending, were irrelevant. Perhaps to assuage Owsley, Chambers closed by registering his interest in "his study of upcountry people" and in a political history of the Confederacy.[31]

Owsley reiterated his sense of embarrassment in a letter to Lytle written shortly after the novel's publication. "During the time the book has been in mind and in progress," he explained, "I . . . spoke of the book that <u>we</u> were going to get out together, and since the book came out our friends, their friends, and certainly our enemies have plied me with unanswerable questions." Owsley found this position untenable. "I have lied until it became revolting, then I referred them to you or maybe swore pretty loudly." That Lytle could see the interplay between appearance and reality, deceit and truthfulness as it functioned in the old Southwest but not in his personal life stunned Owsley. Still Owsley could not bring himself to believe that Lytle would engage deliberately in a "dishonorable or unethical act." He confessed that he had always imagined Lytle to be generous, modest, and a man of honor.[32] His sense of betrayal was acute.

Lytle defended his actions by admitting that he had lost control of his narrative during a critical stage of the drafting process. Owsley had perceived the shift in the narrative well before Lytle. "What I was saying and did not completely understand," Lytle explained, "was that the true story of your Uncle Dink could not be treated as fiction. . . . I didn't understand the implications of my remarks because I hadn't admitted to myself that the biography of your Uncle Dink and [the] novel I was doing had turned out to be different things." He attributed his blindness to his long-standing friendship with Owsley and the pleasure derived from thinking "that together we would present this great figure . . . in a heroic light. There are moments when friends become almost one in thought," he confessed, "and if the novelist has betrayed the friend, in this instance the emotion of the friendship betrayed the novelist's aesthetics." For the embarrassment he caused, Lytle apologized profusely, claiming it had "taken all the pleasure out of the book." By claiming his actions were unintentional, Lytle argued that he had not affronted Owsley's honor. After all a challenge had to be recognized by both parties. Subtlety and obliqueness had no place in honor culture. Acknowledging that he could not have written the book without Owsley, he promised to make restitutions and implored Owsley to forgive him. Owsley accepted, perhaps because by doing so his reputation had remained intact. A threat to his honor had now been reinterpreted as a misunderstanding.[33] Lytle thus saved a straining friendship and Chambers staved off a potential lawsuit. The fate of the novel now rested with critics and general readers.

The Marketing Campaign

Much to the delight of Lytle and his editor, the manuscript received wildly enthusiastic readers' reports. "Unless I'm led by wishful thinking, we have the biggest novel we've had on our list for years," one report read. "One minute in my elation I would nearly tear the typewriter to pieces trying to beat out all the superlatives that crowded my brain. The next," the reader continued, "I would be in despair because I could not write as I wanted to about it—all I could do was 'feel.'" Other readers concurred, prophesying tremendous sales and a spot at the top of the 1936 best-sellers lists. "I know that words are thinned by that injudicious use of them by critics and blurb-writers," a second reviewer recognized, "but the book has a sweep, a scope, an indefinable power to it that obliterates the real world around the reader, and makes him feel he's had a wholly new and almost god-like experience of reality."[34]

Despite these glowing reports, the in-house readers did sound cautionary notes. Even Chambers had doubts. In many ways these reservations foretold the problems Bobbs-Merrill would have in marketing Lytle's counternarrative of the war. With only an incomplete draft in hand, Chambers wondered about the novel's intended audience. Perhaps prompted by an in-house reader who summarized the novel as "a man's book," Chambers asked Lytle outright whether *The Long Night* was "aimed at an audience of men? Will some woman assume a role of importance? Is there room for a love story?"[35] These were not idle considerations. During the 1930s book industry insiders sought to determine America's book-buying habits.[36] These findings confirmed what years of experience in the publishing business had taught Chambers, namely, that women buy books, and he reiterated this point in a letter to Lytle: "I want to remind you that most novels are bought by women, and it is always wise therefore to keep the feminine interest in mind."[37]

The second point raised by the in-house readers centered on the novel's explicit and orgiastic violence. Chambers reported the concern raised by one of the readers to Lytle: "I wish the author wouldn't make it such a chamber of horrors," the reader confessed. "It doesn't appeal to me but," she added, "I'm not a Faulkner or Caldwell fan."[38] This last admission is telling, for both writers had earned, by 1936, the reputations as "purveyors of the grotesque."[39] That *The Long Night* conjured up Faulkner and Caldwell, and not Stark Young and Thomas Nelson Page, was, from a marketing standpoint, troubling.

The dilemma faced by Bobbs-Merrill, then, was one of strategy: how to market a novel that inspired effusive readers' reports but also raised important questions about popular reception. Readers do not encounter texts in a vacuum, and Chambers was well aware of the kinds of problems that *The Long Night* might face. The publication of Margaret Mitchell's *Gone with the Wind* presented Bobbs-Merrill a problem of a different magnitude, however. By September 5, the week *The Long Night* was released, *Gone with the Wind* had sold more than 330,000 copies.[40]

Chambers had to act quickly. He originally imagined leveraging the success of *Gone with the Wind* to Lytle's advantage. "Ought it not make people want to read another book of much the same time and place—provided it is an entirely different kind of story," he wondered. Lytle appreciated Chambers's efforts to "cash in" on Mitchell's popularity but nevertheless sensed that "the Georgia woman [was] going to hurt" his novel's sales. Lytle's doubts aside, Bobbs-Merrill embarked on an innovative marketing strategy that offered incentives to those who *sold* the book. "*The Long Night* is a book which the booksellers must be forced in some way to read," the marketing department determined. "It must be read to be sold effectively because no description of plot, locale, the writer's ability can possibly do justice to the effect created by the consummate skill in which Lytle handles this story." Salesmen were thus directed to offer to booksellers free titles if they signed the "accompanying pledge," which required them to compel their staff to read *The Long Night* by October 12, "to mention the book in every sales interview during the week of October 12," and to display the book prominently in their stores. It also developed "A Plan for Keeping Active the Huge Book Market Created by *Gone with the*

Wind," which included a direct-market campaign to booksellers that asked them to appeal to their customers who had bought *Gone with the Wind*. Their strategy questioned, "Why wouldn't it be profitable to phone those scores of people who have bought and enjoyed Miss Mitchell's magnificent novel and tell them of [this] other fine southern book. If your customers liked *Gone with the Wind*—and who didn't—they will also like *The Long Night*."[41]

Lytle understood that his work bore little resemblance to *Gone with the Wind*. Mitchell had written a sentimental and nostalgic novel of the war that emphasized a more genteel strain of southern honor, which, according to Wyatt-Brown, coupled moral uprightness with high social position. Lytle found little in Mitchell's novel that spoke to the conditions in the Confederacy's backcountry. Chivalry played no part in Lytle's narrative, and Pleasant McIvor was no Ashley Wilkes. That McIvor had not heard of the firing on Sumter until he met up with Lovell suggests how utterly unconcerned McIvor had been about purported infringements on the nascent Confederacy's honor. Mitchell might have offered a more romantic account of the Confederate cause, but hardly one that was truthful. Not surprisingly Bobbs-Merrill's publicity department soon discerned that comparisons to *Gone with the Wind* did not necessarily work to *The Long Night*'s advantage. A memo directed at booksellers titled "How to Sell More Copies: *The Long Night*" acknowledged that a change in strategy was in order: "We haven't been calling it a thriller or a mystery. But the fact is that it is a SUPER-THRILLER. . . . When people come into the store looking for a mystery or detective story," the memo directed, "why not suggest to them *The Long Night*, [which] packs more thrills than any such ten books of the ordinary rank. This is the simple truth."[42]

Most reviewers concurred and stressed the novel's action, fast pace, and violence. To be sure, comparisons with *Gone with the Wind* were inevitable, but they tended to be cursory: "Another first novel laid in the old and deep South, following in the wake of 'Gone with the Wind,' which, like its predecessor, 'So Red the Rose,' quickly reached the top of the bestseller lists, makes its bid for recognition." Thus reads the first line of Fred T. Marsh's review in the *New York Times Book Review*. It also marks the only mention of the novel by "that Georgia woman." In fact Marsh thought Lytle's novel had more in common with older, Gothic tales: "The opening chords are ones of mystery and terror as we arrive at a kind of *House of Usher* or *Wuthering Heights* where, as in the Brontë novel, our dark tale of the past is unfolded, here in the course of a long night." Hamilton Basso, who reviewed *The Long Night* for the *New Republic*, did not even mention Margaret Mitchell. He did, however, reference Balzac, Dostoyevsky, and Dumas. Lytle's novel, Basso explained, "is simply a very good story about a man who sets out to avenge the murder of his father, and the One! Two! Three! of the way the murderers fall is more like 'The Count of Monte Cristo' than anything else: except, along the way, . . . you get a very well done picture of life in the American South around 1860. And that," he concluded, "is a lot to get in one book."[43]

At least from the standpoint of reviewers, then, *The Long Night* demonstrates an expansive literary market, perhaps one more expansive than general readers were willing to accept. Critics, it seems, welcomed a southern narrative of the Civil War that rejected the plantation legend of "the big white-columned house sleeping under its trees among the cotton fields; the band of faithful retainers, . . . the white-haired massa bathing in mint juleps, . . . and the magnolia-colored moonlight."[44] Lytle's literary friends concurred. Caroline Gordon, who had published *Penhally* in 1931 and was working on a second Civil War novel when *The Long Night* was released delighted in reading a novel that recognized "the South is . . . full of violence." Stark Young, Lytle's fellow Nashville Agrarian and author of the hugely popular 1934 Civil War novel *So Red the Rose,* congratulated Lytle for the novel's "masculine effect." Recent trends in literature had worried Young: "I had thought perhaps that balls had vanished from literature." For these "professional" readers, then, *The Long Night* proved a welcomed tonic.[45]

General readers, however, were not buying it. Despite mountains of anecdotal and empirical evidence collected by publishing firms, booksellers, journals of opinion that linked positive reviews, advertising campaigns, and increased sales, *The Long Night* could not challenge the enormous popularity of *Gone with the Wind.* Of course it is impossible to know whether the novel would have enjoyed healthier sales in the absence of *Gone with the Wind.* To be sure, *The Long Night* was not a publishing failure; it sold more than nine thousand copies in its first five months of publication. (Then again, *Gone with the Wind* sold more than thirty-seven thousand copies one random day in September 1936.) Lytle's novel hardly achieved the success promised by Chambers's enthusiastic predictions or anticipated by Bobbs-Merrill's aggressive advertising campaign, however. It flirted briefly with best-sellers lists, appearing twice on the *New York Herald Tribune Books*' "What America Is Reading" roundup and once on *Publishers' Weekly*'s list of best sellers for October 1936.[46] Lytle and Chambers had hoped for more.

The Long Night serves as a corrective, reminding us that alternative visions of the Old South circulated in 1930s America. Unfortunately for Lytle, however, the public remained largely unsold. This is not to say that Mitchell's evocation of honor in the Old South was the deciding factor for readers. It was not. It is to say, however, that Mitchell's romantic and sentimental reading the South's past resonated with Depression-era readers in ways that Lytle's violent and dark novel did not. Indeed *Gone with the Wind* was a scorched-earth text that, for a time, wiped away all other imaginary versions of the South. Bobbs-Merrill scrambled to market Lytle's novel, which offered a decidedly unromantic and inglorious view of the Old South, to an audience hopelessly captivated by images of Tara.

NOTES

1. E. Wilson, "Tennessee Agrarians."

2. Wyatt-Brown, *Southern Honor,* 34–36; 42; D. Bruce, *Violence and Culture,* 5, 92–101; Cash, *Mind of the South,* 42–44; 70–74; and J. Rothman, *Flush Times,* 1–13.

3. On the legend of John Murrell, see Penick, *Great Western Land Pirate,* 1–31; 55–81; J. Rothman, *Flush Times,* 51–87.

4. Andrew N. Lytle to Frank L. Owsley, Guntersville, Ala., n.d., in the Frank L. Owsley Papers, Special Collections and University Archives, Jean and Alexander Heard Library, Vanderbilt University (hereafter VU); Holway, *Becoming Achilles,* 3.

5. Andrew N. Lytle to Robert Penn Warren, Mufreesboro, Tenn., July 22, 1936, in the Robert Penn Warren Papers, BL.

6. Lytle, "Life in the Cotton Belt."

7. Wyatt-Brown, *Southern Honor,* 27, 47; Lytle, *Long Night,* 50–51.

8. Lytle, *Long Night,* 23, 27–28.

9. Ibid., 53–54.

10. Ibid., 32–33.

11. Ibid., 32–33.

12. Ibid., 57–60.

13. Ibid., 64–69; D. Bruce, *Violence and Culture,* 80, 82; Wyatt-Brown, *Southern Honor,* 35, 42. As Wyatt-Brown has explained, in the Old South, as in ancient times, "it was important to have kinfolks who needed valorous protection and who could undertake justifiable revenge when the hero was himself slain. Without relatives one was helpless, and shorn of a major reason to exist."

14. Lytle, *Long Night,* 103.

15. Ibid., 138–39.

16. Ibid., 106.

17. Ibid., 188–89.

18. Ibid., 189, 199.

19. R. Gray, *Southern Aberrations,* 141–43; Lytle, *Long Night,* 207–9.

20. Wyatt-Brown, *Southern Honor,* 59; Lytle, *Long Night,* 71, 97.

21. Andrew Lytle to D. Laurance Chambers, Romar Beach, Ala., June 30, 1936, in the Bobbs-Merrill Records, Lilly Library, Indiana University (hereafter, IU); Lytle, *Long Night,* 316, 329–30.

22. Lytle, *Long Night,* 330–31.

23. Miriam Solar Lyman, [Reader's Report for *The Long Night*], n.d., in the Bobbs-Merrill Records, IU. For Lytle's dismissal of the report, see Andrew N. Lytle to D. L. Chambers, Foley Beach, Ala., June 30, 1936, in the Bobbs-Merrill Records, IU; Frank L. Owsley to D. L. Chambers, Miami Beach, Fla., July 19, 1936, in the Frank L. Owsley Papers, VU.

24. D. L. Chambers to Frank L. Owsley, Indianapolis, Ind., July 24, 1936, in the Frank L. Owsley Papers, VU.

25. See, for example, Donald Davidson to Frank L. Owsley, Bread Loaf, Vt., August 3, 1936, in the Frank L. Owsley Papers; Allen Tate to Andrew N. Lytle, Monteagle, Tenn., September 13, 1936, in the Andrew N. Lytle Papers, VU.

26. Andrew N. Lytle to Frank Owsley, Guntersville, Ala., n.d., in the Frank Owsley Papers, VU.

27. Frank Owsley to Andrew Lytle, n.p., November 25, 1935, in the Andrew Lytle Papers, VU.

28. Andrew N. Lytle to Frank L. Owsley, Monteagle, Tenn., n.d., in the Frank L. Owsley Papers, VU.

29. Frank L. Owsley to Andrew N. Lytle, [Nashville, Tenn.], November 27, 1925, in the Frank L. Owsley Papers, VU.

30. Frank L. Owsley to D. Laurance Chambers, Miami Beach, Fla., July 19, 1936, in the Frank L. Owsley Papers, VU.

31. D. Laurance Chambers to Frank L. Owsley, Indianapolis, Ind., July 24, 1936, in the Frank L. Owsley Papers, VU.

32. Frank L. Owsley to Andrew N. Lytle, Nashville, Tenn., October 3, 1936, in the Andrew N. Lytle Papers, VU.

33. Andrew N. Lytle to Frank L. Owsley, Monteagle, Tenn., n.d., in the Frank L. Owsley Papers, VU; Frank L. Owlsey to Andrew N. Lytle, Nashville, Tenn., November 3, 1936, in the Andrew N. Lytle Papers, VU.

34. TSS, Readers' Reports of Andrew Lytle's *The Long Night,* Jessica Mannon, John H. Johnson, Eleanor Carroll Chilton, n.d., in the Bobbs-Merrill Records, IU.

35. [D. L. Chambers] to Andrew N. Lytle, Indianapolis, Ind., December 7, 1935; TS, ["Reader's Report of Andrew Lytle's *The Long Night,*" John H. Johnson, in the Bobbs-Merrill Records, IU.

36. See, for example, Daniels, "Zero Times Zero"; Canby, "Charged Books"; DeVoto, "Snow White."

37. D. Laurance Chambers to Andrew N. Lytle, [Indianapolis, Ind.], May 3, 1935, in the Bobbs-Merrill Records, IU. Indeed Malcolm Cowley attributed the success of *Gone with the Wind,* in part, to meeting the "specialized demands of the book-buying public." Mitchell's novel, he explained in his review, "is written from the woman's point of view, and most book-buyers are women." See Cowley, "Going with the Wind," 161.

38. D. Laurance Chambers to Andrew N. Lytle, [Indianapolis, Ind.], April 24, 1935, in the Bobbs-Merrill records, IU.

39. See, for example, Glasgow, "Heroes and Monsters"; Wade, "Sweet Are the Uses of Degeneracy"; L. Schwartz, *Creating Faulkner's Reputation;* Duck, *Nation's Region.*

40. See "The Best Sellers List," *Publishers' Weekly* 130 (September 5, 1936): 836.

41. D. Laurance Chambers to Andrew N. Lytle, [Indianapolis, Ind.], August 3, 1936, in the Bobbs-Merrill Records, IU; Andrew N. Lytle to Frank L. Owsley, Monteagle, Tenn., August 17, 1936, in the Andrew Lytle Papers, VU; Bobbs-Merrill, "Market for this Book," n.d.; Bobbs-Merrill Memo, "Directed at Salesmen to make offer to Booksellers," n.d.; TS, mock-up of pamphlet, "A Plan for Keeping Active the Huge Book Market Created by Gone with the Wind," n.d.; D. A. Cameron to "booksellers," [New York, N.Y.], October 1, 1936, in the Bobbs-Merrill Records, IU.

42. Bobbs-Merrill, Memo "How to Sell More Copies of The Long Night," New York, n.d., in the Bobbs-Merrill Records, IU.

43. Marsh, "Mystery and Terror"; Basso, "Orestes in Alabama."

44. Cowley, "Going with the Wind," 161.

45. Caroline Gordon quoted in TS, "From the Publicity Department, Bobbs-Merrill," Indianapolis, Ind., [October 1936], in the Bobbs-Merrill Records, IU; Stark Young to Andrew N. Lytle, New York, N.Y., 1936, in the Andrew Lytle Papers, VU.

46. Bobbs-Merrill Financial Ledgers, Royalty Records July 1936–June 1937 (A–Z), "Andrew Lytle—*The Long Night* (published September 2, 1936)," for period ending February 27, 1937; for information on sales figures for *Gone with the Wind,* see "The Best Sellers List," 1425; *New York Herald Tribune Books,* "What America Is Reading," October 18 and 25, 1936; Memo, "Best Selling Books during October 1936," n.d., in Bobbs-Merrill Records, IU.

Edward R. Crowther

IRON CHESTS

Honor and Manhood in Southern Evangelicalism

Masculine honor has typically taken the form of courage in the face of a threat, commonly in protecting one's reputation, property, and dependents against harm or loss. Consistent displays of fortitude are the hallmark of an honorable man, one who will meet force with force. With the coming of Christianity in Western civilization, honor competed with notions of meekness—"turning the other cheek"—but by the time of the Crusades, and consistently thereafter, honor and Christianity could and did fuse into a hybrid type of manliness. The Christian gentleman is a notable example. This man fought for the true faith, tempered his passions, triumphed over worldly temptations, and governed his household. As James Bowman has argued, masculine honor has served as an organizing principle in a welter of human societies, competing with Christianity, democracy, the emergence of the nation-state, and—in his treatment—mechanized warfare, feminism, and psychoanalytic alienation in the twentieth century.[1]

Still the Christian gentleman endures, especially in the American South, where concepts of manly honor have contended and, over time, melded with evangelical Christianity. From the end of the American Revolution to the beginnings of the twenty-first century, evangelicalism has sought to redirect masculinity toward socially beneficial expressions—temperance, for example—and to define the household as a Christian patriarchy. In this context consistent biblical principles that emphasize male leadership govern the fundamental domestic relations between men and women, husbands and wives, parents and children. And whereas Bowman posits a post-honor United States, in many households in the American South, an honor-based Christian masculinity persists, challenging androgynous and feminist ideas in the same manner that antebellum southern evangelicalism resisted abolitionism. Publicly this Christian masculinity fights against gay marriage and evolution, but—as this essay argues—its core battle is for the primacy of evangelical masculinity in the home.

Evangelical sermons often become paeans to Christian manliness, urging men to take charge of their homes. Consider the words of Pastor Greg Gibson, who has urged his male parishioners to embrace and embody the demands of Christian patriarchy, direct his home, continue the "daring pursuit of his wife," and exhibit a Christ-centered spirituality, despite, in his view, the socially acceptable message encouraging male passivity: "It is no secret that we find a high view of wimpy husbandry alive and well today, in culture and all-too-often in the church, as well. C. S. Lewis might call them 'men without chests.' I tend to agree. And, I hate it. There should always be the highest standard in place for how we pursue our calling as husbands. The next generation is watching. If it is true that we pass down manhood—the good and bad—to the next generation, then we need to model it for them."[2] As a southern minister currently serving in eastern Tennessee, former athlete, and outdoor enthusiast, Gibson has urged men to practice a "biblical manhood . . . to be a leader in your home and workplace . . . developing the character of courage and quick decision making." In an era, he believes, when masculinity and male virtue face withering attacks both by actual inappropriate male behavior and by a media culture that celebrates male lassitude, he has urged a masculine revival: "Become a man with an iron chest."[3]

Ministerial language routinely urges improved behaviors, the assumption of a particular set of Christian attributes. Theologically a minister might speak of congregants' shortcomings in the language of sin, "falling short of the mark," defined in the Bible. But as a member of a series of interconnected communities comprising his congregation, town, state, and region, and their shared beliefs about proper masculine behavior, Gibson is also carrying out a long-standing southern tradition of policing honor-based religious behaviors.

This tradition of evangelical honor has a long lineage. It first expressed itself when evangelicalism encountered older traditions of male behavior in the early South and antebellum era; it shaped southern male prerogatives as husbands, slaveholders, and soldiers during the Civil War and Reconstruction. It resonated in the twentieth century, as evangelical honor confronted Darwinism, the civil rights movements, and recent challenges to gender roles and sexuality. For over two centuries, this sense of evangelical honor has enjoyed great normative power in southern culture and has found itself besieged by external changes and internal failures to live up to the behaviors it prescribes. Its exponents have consistently believed it worth fighting for, sometimes physically, at the ballot box, and rhetorically in defending their way of life.

As Bertram Wyatt-Brown has demonstrated, "honor is essentially the cluster of ethical rules, most readily found in societies of small communities by which judgments of behavior are ratified by community consensus." He argued that a social ethic of honor defined and shaped masculine behavioral ideals in the old South. Wyatt-Brown's definition of honor consists of three interconnected components: an "inner conviction of self-worth," which is placed before the community for its adjudication (the claim to honor), and the community's acceptance or rejection of that claim. A man had to assert his honor and receive societal affirmation that he was an honorable man. In the early South, this honor expressed itself most often in martial terms: a man defended what was his and guarded what he owned. More succinctly "honor is reputation," which orders one's standing in the society and the home.[4]

In his splendid delineations of the sources and expressions of the community-based timocracy that regulated antebellum southern male behavior, Wyatt-Brown's honor-driven men grappled with their relationship to other impulses. Modernizing trends and market-driven forces challenged earlier male atavisms; moral concepts such as evangelical Christianity offered another source to modify honorable male behavior. Some scholars have attempted to reconcile the persistence of a southern masculinity rooted in what Wyatt-Brown termed the "Indo-European" and the "Stoic-Christian" with the growth of denominational religion and its ties to an emergent evangelicalism, which superficially appeared to have been a haven only for clergy and women. One early effort detected an emergence of "Holy Honor" based on biblical ideas about the duty of males to exercise proper authority over their wives, children, and slaves. Drawing on a literal reading of Ephesians 5 and 6, an honorable man was the "head" of the wife, who submitted to her husband. Children obeyed their parents, and slaves obeyed their masters. Archaic and biblical senses of honor affirmed this cultural norm. Indeed Stephanie McCurry has explained that nonslaveholding whites supported secession precisely because they interpreted Lincoln's election as a threat to their personal honor: the power they enjoyed as males to the "command of dependents, and the public prerogatives manhood conferred."[5] Manhood and honor were not the same things, of course, but to enjoy the public status of an honorable man with a favorable reputation, a man had to appear to assert effective moral and material control over his household. And he had to defend that reputation from assault.

Stephen R. Haynes has provided compelling evidence of how southern concepts of honor shaped the way southern white men used the Bible: Noah's curse on Canaan, son of Ham, in Genesis 9 shows how the culture of honor shaped, reinforced, and was reinforced by how white southerners interpreted Ham's uncovering of his father's nakedness, after Noah became drunk in a postdiluvian bender. Rather than focus on Noah's intemperance, or as more recent exegetes have done, the possible homoerotic nature of Ham's indiscretion, southern antebellum divines and laymen focused on Ham's public shaming of his father: he, in effect, told the community that Noah was naked and drunk in his tent. Instead of defending the reputation of the family and its patriarch, Ham subjected it to public ridicule, the antithesis of honorable male behavior. It was unseemly by secular community standard and a clear violation of God's law to "honor thy father." To loosely paraphrase Kenneth Greenberg, rather than clad his nakedness, the first thing Noah did upon awakening was eternally condemn his progeny to perpetual slavery for impudent and dishonorable behavior.[6]

The consilience between honor and Christianity consistently manifested itself in the antebellum South. Parsons routinely couched their appeal to serve God in language that appealed to honor. Ministers such as Presbyterian preacher William Jessup Armstrong explained the necessity of the crucifixion as expiation for humanity's violation of God's commands: "When a law is transgressed, its honor is stained, its authority is destroyed," he intoned, and only such a sacrifice could again make the laws of God "honorable." Similarly notions of Christian and regional honor infused how white southern males thought about slavery, abolitionism, and secession. Southern evangelical justifications of slavery included injunctions to view African Americans as part of the human family and to treat them humanely but consistently asserted that God had ordained slavery, Jesus had never condemned it, and the Apostle Paul crafted rules to regulate it. Hence abolitionism not only lacked scriptural warrant, but abolitionist claims that southern slaveholders were immoral imposed an external community's judgment of moral humiliation and shame on slaveholders who, as Wyatt-Brown has shown, "believed . . . that they conducted their lives by the highest ethical standards." Hence southern evangelicals broke their denominational ties with northern congregants prior to the Civil War and denounced how the latter allegedly misused the Bible. Similarly abolitionists' depictions of the slaveholder "as a pirate, a kidnapper, a murderer, a demon fit only for hell," while sporting cotton clothing produced with slave labor, made southern men dishonorable hypocrites.[7]

Honor-based morality undergirded two vital decisions by white antebellum southern men: secession and civil war. Leading clergymen such as Benjamin Morgan Palmer of New Orleans and James Henley Thornwell thought it dishonorable to submit to Lincoln's election and supported disunion. In the upper South, evangelicals had counseled patience following Lincoln's election, but when the president appeared willing to compel the lower South to remain in the Union by force in the wake of the shelling of Fort Sumter, evangelicals endorsed secession as an honorable remedy to unwarranted coercion. And no one could mistake the intent of Palmer's use of Psalm 144 in a sermon to the Washington artillery: "Blessed be the Lord my strength, which teacheth my hands to war and my fingers to fight."[8]

During the four long years of bloodshed, honor-based evangelicalism helped sustain the morale of Confederate troops and reaffirm that theirs was a holy cause. Even defeats such as Gettysburg, in the wake of victories at Fredericksburg and Chancellorsville, were explained by evangelical honor. Alabama Baptist chaplain John Jefferson Deyampert Renfroe reminded the members of Cadmus Wilcox's brigade that their successes at Fredericksburg and Chancellorsville were due to their honorable subordination to God; conversely their hubris in believing it was they and General Robert E. Lee who were in charge had led to the defeat at

Gettysburg. Godly men enjoyed dominion over the secular world but owed their martial glory to God alone.[9]

Yet Lee's surrender after the collapse of Confederate lines surrounding Petersburg slowed but did not still southern martial ardor or its understanding of moral order. Ex-Confederates waged a largely successful guerilla and political war to reclaim white supremacy in the wake of the Thirteenth Amendment and African American attempts to forge political and economic equality. As Timothy L. Wesley has observed, the Civil War preserved southern ministers in their antebellum role as moral arbiters and shapers of southern memory in a society that quickly embraced the "Lost Cause," a deification of an idealized Confederacy and a sanctification of its heroic generals and indefatigable soldiers and the core of a revitalized southern civil religion. And as Charles Reagan Wilson has shown, this religion was about reforging a southern identity in the wake of a military defeat that could be viewed as a humiliation for southern white males. As a countermeasure, preachers extolled the virtue of southern white womanhood, re-created the common soldier as a medieval knight errant, and, through the works of minister-chaplains like John William Jones, exalted Robert E. Lee and Stonewall Jackson into exemplars of patriarchal piety and humble honor.[10]

But the Lost Cause, as it evolved, complicated as much as it comforted the collapsed white Confederacy. Not only had southern white men failed to protect the homes and hearths of white women, it was the women themselves who took the lead in creating the rituals of the Lost Cause, including the creation of Confederate cemeteries that sometimes involved the reinternment of slain Confederates in sacred southern soil from far-off shallow graves. Women thus justified their own wartime sacrifices for slavery and independence. To defend their men from shame, they readily adopted the idea that the Confederacy had not a chance to win against the teeming Yankee hordes, but southern men had fought valiantly anyway, against impossible odds, rather than to whimper before throngs of northern aggressors. Finding room to maneuver in the gender roles of the Victorian era, southern white women portrayed their deeds as neither traitorous nor as usurpations of masculine prerogative; rather, in the words of Caroline Janney, their deeds were the expressions of "sentiment, emotion, and devotion to one's menfolk."[11]

Scores of women and men worked in the years after the war to enshrine the Lost Cause into school curricula and, with the success of films such as *Birth of a Nation,* into the national consciousness. Indeed, until recent years, when revisionist films such as *Glory* resurrected the link between African American participation in the Civil War and emancipation, national media and culture either affirmed or was at least sympathetic to the idea that the Confederacy had fought honorably against long odds to protect its benign way of life, as if antebellum divines and other proslavery apologists were still writing the scripts. In the same way that John Leadly Dagg had written *Elements of Moral Science* in 1860 to battle northern authors who challenged slavery (and by extension impugned the moral honor of southern slaveholders) postbellum southern writers consistently promoted southern ideals as honorable and ethical.[12]

While white men and women shared the goals of vindicating the Confederate South, postbellum southern white laymen continued to test the boundaries between evangelical piety and their secular activities, especially male-only recreation. Although the saloon and the pool hall were taboo, hunting was an activity where masculine evangelical honor could express itself. This activity mixed masculine recreation, sport, and the notion of the male provider, but, unlike gambling or drinking, hunting did no violence to the ecclesiastical values shared by southern white men and women. Revival meetings permitted those men who fell into temptation to repent. Over time urban reforms, from prohibition to game laws, began to pervade the rural landscape of its manly rituals and morally marginalized demonstrations of secular masculine honor—drinking, fighting, and cavorting.

Ted Ownby has shown how evangelical culture and secular male culture competed for dominance in the rural south well into the twentieth century.[13] His analysis of the decline of church discipline illustrates how evangelicalism changed community identification from the local congregation, which expelled unrepentant sinners for their conduct, to the larger southern society, in which ungodly public expressions of male behavior—"drunken staggering, loud swearing, fighting on the streets"—placed men not just outside the pale of the sacred community of the congregation, but outside the bounds of honorable, law-abiding citizenry. What Ownby termed the South's "semi-official morality" policed by the congregation became the official regional morality, enforced by state authority, even though the tension between evangelical Christianity and the "culture of the largely masculine sinfulness" persisted. As the South modernized, voters imposed evangelically sanctioned rules governing male behavior, suggesting that honorable men behaved in ways acceptable to church and state.[14]

This evangelical effort to direct masculinity in a modernizing South resonated with other shifts in the southern mind, especially white southern identification with their historical tragedy—the only white Americans who had known military defeat. It also offered a sense of divine election, as defeat was a sign that God was preparing the South for a greater work, one that would ultimately provide a moral counterweight to secular materialism. The South constituted a faithful remnant devoted more to God and less to mammon. The belief in a chastened but righteous South took contradictory expressions, including denunciation of Darwinism, which culminated in the *Scopes* trial and laws prohibiting the teaching of anything other than the Genesis account of human origin. There were other voices, however, and they became more vocal as time passed. By the end of World War II, the evangelical few who embraced both the social gospel and the ironic and tragic elements in American and human history called for an end to segregation.[15] Some of these latter men, such as Duncan Gray, rector of St. Peter's Church in Oxford, Mississippi, counseled parishioners to support the admission of James Meredith in 1962, suggesting that Oxford's Christian men had an opportunity to show how Christian brotherhood could produce a better world.

But Gray was in a decided minority, as most white southern evangelicals believed that scripture supported segregation. In their minds the only duty of churches was to counsel individuals to salvation, a position not unlike the proslavery defenses a century earlier. Evangelical ministers and laymen played a central role in the White Citizen's Councils, which incited resistance to the *Brown* decision and considered the racial hierarchy to be "God-given." As had been true in the antebellum debate with abolitionists, southern whites linked the defense of white supremacy with a literal biblical hermeneutic, which made nineteenth-century critics of slavery and twentieth-century crusaders for racial equality little more than dishonorable atheists in the minds of many southern evangelicals. And as they had done earlier in the century to combat booze and evolution, white evangelicals used the power of the state and the church to defend their segregated communities from attack by outside forces. In Mississippi, for example, the legislature authorized the revocation of the tax-exempt status of churches that permitted integration, a major reversal on the tradition of church-state separation. At the same time, the Mississippi Association of Methodist Ministers and Laymen used the power of their churches and their roles as members and supporters of the White Citizen's Council to expunge Mississippi Methodism of integrationist teachings.[16]

All these efforts were linked to the status of manhood. Steve Estes has demonstrated that beneath the ideology espoused by the Citizen's Councils lay a perceived threat to white male authority to defend their homes and institutions according to their own beliefs about what was morally and socially correct. These ideas simultaneously linked the defense of segregation to the opposition to communism, twin threats to home and community. To mobilize support for its crusade against integration, "white southern leaders in the Citizen's Councils demonized black men's sexuality and galvanized southern white men with ideals of whiteness, honor, and manhood." Estes concludes that this strategy led to serious violence, including the October 1, 1962, riot at the University of Mississippi. In the long run, these appeals for white men to protect their home and hearth led to interventions and legislation at the federal level, which ultimately dismantled de jure white supremacy. But in the short run, Mississippi's evangelicals largely portrayed themselves as victims of an external secular threat, fired the few ministers who supported integration, dissolved ecclesiastical ties with denominations supporting desegregation, and reaffirmed their traditional rights to defend their segregated life from outsiders. And, in the end, and not unlike the era of Reconstruction, the national sentiment and efforts by the national government to support African American rights yielded to fatigue and white southern (and, in this case, much white nonsouthern) backlash.[17]

The complex changes and continuities related to the destruction of legal white supremacy in the South worked hand in hand with the outcomes of evangelical honor's embrace of massive resistance. Schools desegregated and then resegregated, following white flight, the creation of segregation academies and the nascent home school movement. The ecclesiastical focus on missions and conversion, espoused by many southern evangelicals, allowed for a convenient amnesia about the vital role played by evangelical males in the name of local and regional honor in resisting desegregation. Over time, however, southern evangelical whites made an odd peace with the racial tumult of the 1950s and 1960s and the longer history of white evangelical support for slavery and racism. In 1995 the Southern Baptist Convention's messengers apologized for both slavery and racism. External forces had not compelled their core institutions—home and congregation—to desegregate; such real and remembered circumstances permitted white evangelical men to sidestep race, including their own and their elders' efforts to block civil rights. Simultaneously these circumstances allowed them to maintain the idea that anti-biblical cultural liberalism was both the cause of moral ills and the biggest threat to male honor, which was increasingly defined in terms of a divinely mandated gendered essentialism: men have a duty to lead the home, the church, and the community to carry out God's rules for human behavior. Women nurture.[18]

Thus entered complementarianism, a refined emphasis on male authority and the conviction that men and women are not the same and their domestic roles are not fungible. Complementarianism undergirded efforts by contemporary godly male warriors to wage a battle for eternal truth and the fulfillment of their own masculinity. It was drawn from the deep well of southern evangelical honor but especially focused on the cultural issues from the 1970s onward (premarital sex, divorce, abortion, and open homosexuality). In some ways this contemporary articulation of the Christian male was simply part of a larger, national Christian movement addressing the exigencies of the postmodern, postindustrial world. Christian men are to become what Charles Lippy called the "faithful leader" or what W. Bradford Wilcox has termed "Soft Patriarchs," modeling behaviors rooted in a modern variation of muscular Christianity and the newer concept of "servant leadership." The various iterations of men's movements are national, such as the 1990s phenomenon of the Promise Keepers; but in the white south and where southern white evangelical culture has spread its roots, this movement has a southern accent, perceives its challenges and opportunities from the perspective of southern history—especially religious history—and relies heavily of mythopoeic southern male codes of behavior.[19]

Consider the case of the Southern Baptist Convention, whose long missionary arms reach to Africa and Asia, but whose heart and mind is deep in Dixie. In the 1970s much of its male leadership believed its hegemonic position was besieged by cultural relativism and that relativism stemmed from a loss of certainty in the infallible truth, indeed the inerrant words, of the Bible. Moving to stem the tides of moral change, conservative leaders disrupted an earlier denominational arrangement, one that emphasized the right of individual believers to determine what the Bible meant and the local doctrinal autonomy of congregations that had permitted a range of Baptist beliefs on a number of issues, including abortion. This was "soul freedom." In its place, as Seth Dowland has shown, biblical inerrancy became a new litmus test for those guiding the denomination, its seminaries, state conventions, and colleges, resulting in a successful effort by biblical inerrantists to assume control of the convention between 1979 and 1990. Their control had gendered meaning because it simultaneously brought an end to denominational experimentation with women in formal church leadership roles (especially that of pastor), signaled Southern Baptist opposition to external challenges to the traditional social patriarchy, and affirmed traditional Southern Baptist hermeneutics. Dowland noted that Baptists had long contrasted their own biblical literalism with textual liberalism, which they considered effeminate and unmanly. Yet now "defenders of the new patriarchy read the Bible in particularly 'masculine' ways, promoting verses that ascribed authority to men and interpreting scripture in the most direct manner possible." No longer able to stem changes to racial and gendered norms outside the denomination and congregation, evangelical men (and many women) waged a battle to protect their sacred communities, the congregations and denomination, from cultural norms they viewed as unscriptural.[20]

This hermeneutic reinforced male evangelical honor—biblical texts define an honorable male as head of the house and spiritual shepherd in the church—and helped Baptists identify a two-headed dragon of feminism and homosexuality, as the latest cultural and moral threat to the South, just as desegregation and abolition had menaced earlier white evangelical Souths. Tactics to slay the two-headed monster took a variety of forms: celebrating wives and stay-at-home moms, which the convention did via resolution in 1987, and affirming a clear doctrine of separate, noninterchangeable, but complementary roles for men and women. Through a variety of federated means, many Southern Baptists endorsed the 1987 Danvers Statement, a conservative evangelical articulation of the different roles that God had assigned to men and women.

The Danvers Statement was the work of the then-nascent Council on Biblical Manhood and Womanhood (CBMW), whose mission and work many Southern Baptists also consistently affirmed. An ecumenical group of conservative evangelicals, the CBMW emerged following a session on the biblical roles of men and women at a 1986 meeting of the Evangelical Theological Society. Its membership consisted of many conservative evangelicals, including Al Mohler, president of the Southern Baptist Theological Seminary, which housed the council in the 1990s. Currently six members of its board hold appointments at Southern Baptist seminaries. The council promotes the "teachings of the Bible about the complementary differences between men and women, created equally in the image of God, because these teachings are essential for obedience to Scripture and for the health of the family and the church." The council likewise considers the Southern Baptist Convention firmly supportive of its ideas.[21]

The Danvers Statement laments "the widespread uncertainty and confusion in our culture regarding the complementary differences between masculinity and femininity," which threatens traditional marriage as defined in scripture. At risk is "the glad harmony portrayed in Scripture between the loving, humble leadership of redeemed husbands and the intelligent, willing support of that leadership by redeemed wives." It links the challenges faced by contemporary families to expressions of sexual promiscuity, domestic abuse and violence, and androgynous church leadership structures, which are all symptomatic of faulty interpretations of the Bible. This, in turn, threatens its status (the honor the Bible enjoys as the cultural authority affirmed in the larger society).[22]

In a manner reminiscent of antebellum defenses of slavery—in which earthly subordination of slaves to owners competed with the image of slaves and masters as equal before God—the Danvers Statement affirms separate gender roles as "ordained by God" as part of the created order, but equality of men and women "before God as persons and distinct in their manhood and womanhood," a view often termed complementarian. This term contains two ideas: men and women support one another but do not have the same roles, and, while both men and women are equally valuable in God's eyes, God has ordained men to lead the church and the home. The Edenic Fall introduced sin into the primordial relationship so that "the husband's loving, humble headship tends to be replaced by domination or passivity; the wife's intelligent, willing submission tends to be replaced by usurpation or servility. . . . In the church, sin inclines men toward a worldly love of power or an abdication of spiritual responsibility, and inclines women to resist limitations on their roles or to neglect the use of their gifts in appropriate ministries." Conversion to Christ by non-believers and rededication to God's eternal truths by believers would restore the proper relations between men and women, between individuals and God, and prevent the "increasingly destructive consequences in our families, our churches, and the culture at large."[23]

As in earlier expressions of evangelical honor, especially those debates between southern and northern evangelicals over the morality of slavery, the duty of the godly man was to choose submission to the supernatural authority by acting in accordance with the Bible's unchanging rules for male and female behavior in the face of secular agendas that emphasize human freedom to live as one chooses. Pastor John Piper and Professor Wayne Gundem, cofounders of the Council of Biblical Manhood and Womanhood, consider the core threats of feminism and androgyny to be violations of the plain words of scripture defining the divergent duties of men and women in the church and the home. If the dictates of contemporary culture trump the Bible's basic teachings, then the Bible loses its authority everywhere. In short, they say, "If we can wrest egalitarianism from the Bible, we can pervert it to say anything we wish."[24]

Assertions of God-ordained gendered essentialism, alongside the dire consequences of failing to honor its implications, occupy prominent places in the publications of the CBMW, denominational literature, and the plethora of Christian books penned by southern complementarians. The CBMW posits a slippery slope of moral evils that attend androgynous behaviors. By abandoning their biblically prescribed roles, men and women may then affirm abortion, turn to pornography, or embrace homosexuality.[25]Appealing to the authority of scripture, complementarians remind those people who desire to alter church and home life to reflect more contemporary gendered behaviors that "wives are several times in the New Testament told to be subject to their husbands . . . , [but] the situation is never reversed: husbands are never told to be subject to their wives."[26]

As in the antebellum debates with abolitionists, contemporary evangelical complementarians have multiple reasons for relying heavily both on scripture and their literal hermeneutic. Clearly, where an authoritative text and a commonsense reading of it enjoy cultural authority, an appeal to the Bible supposedly settles the argument. But some evangelical Christians have long espoused a more egalitarian reading of biblical texts, and, since the early 1970s, feminist scholars have offered alternative interpretations of key essentialist texts and highlighted other passages to make their case for an inclusive and even feminist Christianity. From the time it appeared in 1974, Letha Scanzoni's and Elizabeth Hardesty's *All That We're Meant to Be: A Biblical Approach to Women's Liberation* threatened the traditional southern biblical hermeneutic, even though, as Seth Dowland has shown, evangelical conservatives at the time conceded that women had endured mistreatment at the hands of men and the church. But evangelical honor has not conceded an alternative hermeneutic.[27]

Professor Chad Brown of North Greenville University, a Baptist institution in South Carolina, notes that egalitarians and feminist scholars have looked for a different reading to core essentialist texts like Ephesians 5:22 through 6:4. "The newer, revisionist camp defends the dual principles of equality and mutuality," he explains. "By this revisionists mean that men and women are equal and carry responsibilities in both the home and church which are mutual or interchangeable between the sexes. There is no doubt that this concept of mutuality or interchangeability arises from feminist ideology, which claims that, 'Physical differences apart, men and women are the same.'" Other than "obvious biological distinctions," women and men are exactly the same, a position complementarians consider anathema.[28]

For Brown and the Southern Baptist Convention the hermeneutics matter and not just for the purpose of privileging one point of view over another in debates about gender roles at the end of the twentieth century. According to the study committee authorized by the SBC in 1997 to consider revising the *Baptist Faith and Message,* improper hermeneutics not only threaten gender roles; they fundamentally distort the means and ends of biblical revelation: "Doctrine and practice, whether in the home or the church, are not to be determined according to modern cultural, sociological, and ecclesiastical trends or according to personal emotional whims; rather, Scripture is to be the final authority in all matters of faith and conduct (2 Tim. 3:16–17; Heb. 4:12; 2 Pet. 1:20–21). God chose to reveal Himself to His people through family language: He used the metaphor of the home to describe the heavenly dwelling where believers will join Him for eternity. He selected the analogy of family relationships (husband/wife and parent/child) to illustrate how believers are to relate to Him: God is the Father; Jesus is the Son; the Church is the Bride of Christ; believers are His children."[29]

For evangelical essentialists the implications of the debate are dire and imminent. In a 2013 issue of the *Journal of Biblical Manhood and Womanhood,* discussing the valedictory of Pope Benedict's final address to the Curia, Southern Baptist pastor, professor, and editor Denny Burk concluded that the stakes between egalitarians and complementarians were nothing less than the survival of civilization itself: "Our culture has given up on the idea that men and women are different and that they are so by God's design." He continued, "This secular narrative defines this discussion exclusively in terms of the march of human progress and equality. It is able to do that because it has already accepted—perhaps uncritically—the notion that gender is something you learn, not something that you are." In the end, he warned, "If those assumptions about gender turn out to be false—and Scripture tells us that they are indeed false—then the narrative of equality that is built upon them crumbles. Those advancing the 'equality' narrative may not realize this, but they have built their entire house on shifting sand. That house will be washed away in due time."[30]

For evangelical traditionalists the debate not only portends perdition of the soul and Western civilization; egalitarians and feminists wish to undo "a beautiful portrait of complementarity between the sexes, with both men and women charged to reflect God's glory in a distinct way. Thus, there are very real distinctions that mark the difference between masculinity and femininity, male and female." And the fault is within the evangelical community, which allowed contemporary ideas about gender to challenge the eternal word of God, as well as from outside the church, where secularists placed human artifice above divine revelation. Paige Patterson, president of Southwestern Baptist Seminary, blamed "the feminization not only of the social order in general but also of the local church in particular [which] has pushed men increasingly away from the center." For David Jones, then assistant professor of Christian Ethics at Southeastern Baptist Theological Seminary, well-meaning egalitarians had been duped by worldly forces: "The main reason why some advocates of egalitarianism have been led to endorse homosexuality is that feminist-type arguments so minimize gender identity that once biblical feminism is embraced, it is but a small logical step to accept homosexuality."[31]

Greg Gibson has told his readers about the antidote: "Men, we must distinguish ourselves from that which is feminine in our culture. We must not blur the lines . . . [and] we must teach our children what biblical femininity and masculinity are." Rather than looking "to what the culture says a man is . . . the Bible alone says what a man must be." Gibson's own understanding of that masculinity includes husband, protector, and father: "As men, we are called to be protectors. We are also called to be risk-taking warriors. By default, a gospel-centered husband is a courageous man. He is courageous in the pursuit of his wife; in his lifestyle at work (everyone knows he loves his wife the most); in his speech; and in his goals for his marriage and family."[32]

Evangelical complementarians consistently call for a revitalized biblical manhood to resurrect a masculinity with "a kind of courage, toughness, and self-sacrifice" to deal with the problems of a changing world. Sometimes echoing that famous language of Pastor Tony Evans at the 1994 Promise Keeper rally for men not merely to ask for but to "take back" their role as head of the household, and often urging a more masculine rearing of young boys, the rhetoric of evangelical honor continues to assert itself in none-too-subtle codes. Paige Patterson, the Baptist seminary president, extolled the three things every boy needs: "First every boy in this country needs a big dog—and not a little yapper. Give him the responsibilities associated with having a dog. . . . Number two, every boy needs a gun—not a play gun; those are dangerous. He'll just learn to point them at people and say 'Bang! Bang!' which is a bad habit. Give him a real one. Third, every little boy needs a dad in the home to help him face an unsure world with courage and without undue fear. Daddy, he needs you."[33]

Evangelical honor similarly confronted homosexuality beginning in the 1970s. Like attacks on feminism, early denunciations suggested that the apparent upsurge in openly homosexual behavior and nascent crusades for gay rights was a harbinger of the decline of American civilization. Evangelical spokespersons such as Jerry Falwell and Anita Bryant linked homosexuality to pedophilia; since gays and lesbians do not reproduce, so their reasoning went, older gays and lesbians would have to recruit and convert the young to continue their movement. Children's safety was at stake as well as core elements of male identity, procreator, and defender of children. As Seth Dowland has pointed out, initially evangelical opposition did not rely on biblical injunctions to prove homosexuality was a sin but rather marshaled opposition to homosexuality by the alleged threat such behavior implicitly had on children and the future of the family. A timocratic reading of scripture, affirming male headship of a heterosexual household, to denounce homosexuals and their defenders came later.[34]

Southern evangelical conservatives continued to hold themselves up as following the dictates of God's word rather than yielding to what many increasingly termed "the homosexual agenda." Their beliefs made compromising essentialism to more fluid concepts of gender unscriptural and toleration of others' homosexuality impossible. It dishonored God and portended a range of human depravity. Indeed conservative evangelicals linked the breakdown of traditional marriage roles as defined in scripture to toleration of abortion and growing acceptance of homosexuality.[35]

As evidence mounted of greater acceptance of homosexuality around the world, within the United States, and even among younger people raised in evangelical households, the response was to see this new apparent tolerance as a current manifestation of the age-old problem of sin, of rejecting the clear teachings of scripture. Referencing an increase in lesbian relationships in England, the CBMW *News* reminded its readers: "Paul decries this abominable behavior in the first century: 'their women exchanged the natural function for that which is unnatural'" (Rom. 1:26). Apparently people have not changed. The natural man—2,000 years later—still rejects God's perfect design for men and women that he might indulge in the "passing pleasures of sin" (Heb. 11:25). The media increasingly portrayed homosexuality, apart from sin, as healthy and normal, and, as the *News* reminded its readers, the decision by the American Psychiatric Association to remove homosexuality from its lists of disorders gave it the authority of humanistic science.[36]

By the early 2000s complementarians were suggesting that religious toleration of homosexuality was likely the logical result of egalitarian readings of scripture, which did not honor biblical gender distinctions and roles. In a lengthy article, Wayne Grudem, an author of the Danvers Statement, argued that the contemporary movement toward gender-neutral language in translating the Bible for contemporary readers was not simply an exercise in inclusiveness. Rather it represented a rejection of scriptural authority and likely would "be used again and again by those who advocate the moral legitimacy of homosexuality."[37]

Honorable evangelical men are not only warriors for truth, they are "dangerous." According to Rick Johnson, the Bible requires men to use their authority for the good of their families and for others, citing Job 29, a scripture that "speak[s] powerfully to a man's heart." Here the text referred to a godly man who aided the destitute, cared for the orphan, supported a widow, aided the blind and crippled, and rescued "victims" from wicked men. He concludes with a paean to evangelical honor: "When you see a man who does this, you are looking authentic masculinity in the eye."[38]

Beneath the warrior and hunter-gatherer rhetoric in today's evangelical honor, a timocratic reading of scripture undergirds its contemporary expression among complementarians who see the authority for their place in what they consider

God's created order once again under assault from external forces, both from secular ideas and within the larger Christian community. While the specific social context is new and fluid, evangelical honor and its use of scripture is not. It began with evangelical men staking out positions of what they saw as biblically defined moral responsibility in the early Republic and antebellum eras. It persisted through the travail of Civil War and the racial disruptions and challenges to their masculinity from Reconstruction, twentieth-century modernism, and the civil rights revolution. In continues today with modern essentialist evangelicals defending their understanding of their place at the head in the home and in the church and the ancient, unchanging text of the Bible.

NOTES

1. James Bowman, *Honor,* 4–8, 50–51, 69–70, 321–24.

2. Gibson, *Gospel Centered Husband.*

3. Gibson, *Reformational Manhood,* 13.

4. Wyatt-Brown, *Southern Honor,* xv, 14.

5. Crowther, "Holy Honor," esp. 629–33; McCurry, *Masters of Small Worlds,* 304.

6. Haynes, *Noah's Curse,* 78–85. Greenberg wrote: "when the man of honor is told that he smells, he does not draw a bath—he draws his pistol. The man of honor does not care if he stinks, but he does care that someone has accused him of stinking"; in Greenberg, *Honor and Slavery,* 14.

7. Calhoon, *Evangelicals and Conservatives,* 145, 171; Wyatt-Brown, *Southern Honor,* 3; Crowther, "According to Scripture," 299–300; Crowther, *Southern Evangelicals,* 162–65.

8. Rable, *God's Almost Chosen People,* 35, 38; Crowther, *Southern Evangelicals,* 204–11, 217; Wesley, *Politics of Faith,* 123–25.

9. Renfroe, *"Battle Is God's"*; G. Gallagher, *Confederate War,* 51–52.

10. Wesley, *Politics of Faith,* 197–99; C. Wilson, *Baptized in Blood,* 12–15, 37–57.

11. Janney, *Remembering the Civil War,* 9, 86–87, 96–97.

12. McPherson, "Long-Legged Yankee Lies," 64–76; G. Gallagher, *Causes Won, Lost, and Forgotten,* 43–50; Crowther, "According to Scripture," 294–95.

13. Ownby, *Subduing Satan,* esp. 210–12.

14. Ibid., 208–9, 212.

15. C. Wilson, "God's Project," 19, 21, 28–31.

16. Eagles, *Price of Defiance,* 299–300; DuPont, *Mississippi Praying,* 2–14, 72–73, 92–100.

17. Estes, "Question of Honor," 100–101, 106–8, 116; DuPont, *Mississippi Praying,* 142–50; Crespino, *In Search of Another Country,* 63–74.

18. Crespino, *In Search of Another Country,* 239; *Resolutions on Racial Reconciliation;* Wilcox, *Soft Patriarchs,* 20–21; See generally Kruse, *White Flight.* Evangelical emphasis on individualism and skepticism toward collective and state action, as well as secular culture, spawned a pervasive "*religiously informed antiliberalism,*" which colored how evangelicals approached post-1960s social change. See S. Miller, "Persistence of Antiliberalism," 83.

19. Lippy, *Do Real Men Pray?,* 175–97; Wilcox, *Soft Patriarchs,* 20, 97.

20. Dowland, "New Kind of Patriarchy," 252–53.

21. Ibid., 254, 259; Southern Baptist endorsement of the Danvers essentialism comes in a variety of ways. Al Mohler, president of SBC Seminary in Louisville, Kentucky, helped house the

Council of Biblical Manhood and Womanhood on his campus, and Southwestern Baptist Theological Seminary endorsed the Danvers statement in 2009. Baptist Women for Equality Newsletter. See Akin, "Role of Men and Women in the Church," 6–9. "CBMW's Roll Call of Churches on Ministerial/Household Roles." Dowland's "Family Values" wisely makes a three-headed dragon for evangelicals to slay: feminism, gay rights, and abortion. My two-headed construct is simply a function of how evangelical honor-speak approaches abortion to male audiences: in much of the discourse targeting men, abortion is depicted as a fruit of feminism that denies men any control (deprives them of honor) over the fate of their unborn children by empowering women and their physicians control over pregnancy-termination decisions. See P. Patterson, "Toward a Theology of Manhood."

22. "Danvers Statement."

23. Ibid.

24. Piper and Grudem, *Recovering Biblical Manhood and Womanhood,* xi–xii.

25. *CBMW News* 1, no. 3 (June 1996): 10.

26. *CBMW News* 1, no. 4 (October 1996): 3. A key area of dispute in interpreting Ephesians 5:23: "For the husband is the head of the wife, even as Christ is the head of the church." The meaning of *kephale* (κεφαλη), "head" in the King James Version, figures prominently in this debate. Feminists and many egalitarians argue that it really means "source," but complimentarians insist on "head." See appendix 1 in Piper and Grudem, *Recovering Biblical Manhood,* 424, for the complimentarian view. See Mickelsen and Mickelsen, "Head of the Epistles," 20–23 for an egalitarian view.

27. Dowland, "Family Values," 618–19.

28. C. Brown, "Building a Christ Centered Marriage," 8.

29. Ibid., 12

30. Burk, "Pope Benedict's Final Address," 3. In recent years the cover of the *Journal* features Genesis 2:23: "And Adam said, 'This is now bone of my bones, and flesh of my flesh: she shall be called Woman, because she was taken out of Man.'"

31. P. Patterson, "Letter from the President"; D. Jones, "Egalitarianism and Homosexuality," 13.

32. Gibson, *Reformational Manhood,* 12–13. Gibson, *Gospel Centered Husband.* Similar themes appear in Cole, *Maximized Manhood,* and Cole, Strong *Men in Tough Times.*

33. P. Patterson, "Letter from the President"; K. Collier, "3 Things Every Boy Needs."

34. Dowland, "Family Values," 624–27.

35. *CBMW News* 1, no. 3 (June 1996): 10; *CBMW News* 1, no. 4 (October 1996), 2.

36. *CBMW News* 5, no. 2 (Fall 2000) 2, 18; Jones, "Egalitarianism and Homosexuality," 11–12

37. Grudem, "Is Evangelical Feminism," 76.

38. R. Johnson, "Noble and Dangerous Man."

Dickson D. Bruce Jr. and Emily S. Bruce

HONOR AND THE RHETORIC OF CONSERVATISM IN TWENTY-FIRST-CENTURY AMERICA

Traditions of honor have done much to inform and give foundation to American conservatism, both historically and in our own time. Honor's imperatives have provided and continue to provide a deep cultural background that shapes and gives resonance to some of the main themes of conservative thought and some of the main features of conservative authenticity. This essay will explore the strong interconnections between honor and American conservatism and will suggest how, taken together, the key characteristics of contemporary conservative thinking do much to show the continuing significance of honor in American political culture. At the same time, it will indicate how honor's key traditions do much to illuminate the continuing appeal of conservatism itself.

As the large body of scholarship on honor makes clear, any attempt to fix a universal definition of *honor* not only does violence to its richness but also ignores its central character: the flexibility with which it justifies an array of actions in the social and political arenas. Still several things stand out in a fairly general consideration of honor, at least in its American context. One, certainly, is the great concern for reputation, a concern with both internal and external dimensions. Externally honor entails a drive to be recognized by one's community—and especially one's peers—as (in traditional American terms) a "man of honor." Internally it entails a strong component of self-assessment, a nearly constant effort to make sure that one is living up to what are seen as honor's imperatives.

Within American traditions those imperatives have been fairly clearly defined and have included a reputation for integrity (to be accused of lying is the strongest charge that can be leveled at one who claims to live up to honor's demands), courage, and coolness under fire.[1] American honor takes for granted that not everyone can heed such imperatives. Indeed hierarchy has historically been critical to honor. In the antebellum American South, where an ethic of honor received its fullest American expression, whether one was capable of honor was a measure of one's place in the social order, defining a class-, gender-, and race-based hierarchy that dominated the social and political order, and would continue to do so, with more or less subtlety, into our own time.

Finally—and crucially—the imperatives of honor rest on a view of the world as on the edge of disorder. In its internal and external dimensions alike, honor is seen as a fragile quality, difficult to gain and easy to lose. The fear of dishonor is an important driver in any honor-based community. More deeply, however, honor tends to be founded on a deep distrust of self and others, drawing on strong traditions of pessimism about human abilities to live up to society's demands, and a still deeper understanding of human nature as essentially given to those negative impulses that stand as honor's obverse—to cowardice, for example, or to misrepresentation. This was certainly the case in the antebellum South, where such concerns drove a heavy reliance on systems and codes of etiquette designed to encourage the appearance of self-mastery and address the power of such impulses in the social realm.[2] It was embedded in a sense that it takes both courage and vigilance to live in such a world—embodied most vividly in those southern traditions of dueling, where men displayed their willingness to risk their lives, coolly and openly, in defense of their claims to status and respect and, as they saw it, of their social order, as well.

Conservatism in the United States has deep connections to American ideas of honor. Such pioneering theorists of traditional conservatism as Clinton Rossiter or Russell Kirk, for example, identified essential conservative principles that had significant overlap with basic notions of honor. Kirk, for instance, noted the belief that "civilized society requires orders and classes," based on a recognition of the inevitability of human imperfection and the need for a leadership dedicated to maintaining both social order and self-control.[3] Rossiter paid special attention to conservatism's awareness of the problems of human nature that also inform honor's fragile underlying foundation—"innate human qualities" said to include "irrationality, selfishness, laziness, depravity, corruptibility, and cruelty"—as well as to an assumption that people are "grossly unequal" in "talent, taste, appearance, intelligence, and virtue."[4]

To be sure, American conservatism has hardly comprised a static tradition. Within conservative history scholars have identified a number of major shifts. Rossiter, for example, has seen the rise of a business-oriented, "laissez faire" conservatism in the late nineteenth century as the beginning of a departure of conservatism, as a movement, from older conservative traditions.[5] Others have assigned similar significance to, among other things, reaction to the New Deal, opposition to the civil rights movement of the 1950s and 1960s, the same era's anticommunist crusade, Barry Goldwater's 1964 presidential campaign, and even, intellectually, William F. Buckley's 1955 founding of the *National Review* as the chief outlet for serious conservative thought.

Nor has contemporary conservatism been anything like a monolithic movement. Among contemporary conservatives there have been strong and significant disagreements among those who, nevertheless, identify themselves as conservatives. There are powerful splits between those who consider themselves libertarians and those who identify as social conservatives.[6] There are divisions, increasingly contentious, between those who see themselves as "traditional conservatives," seeking to preserve many of the ideas delineated by Kirk and Rossiter, and those Americans for whom "freedom," itself variously defined, represents the ultimate goal of social policy and the very essence of a conservative faith.[7] There are differences between those one might think of as *New York Times* conservatives, such as David Brooks, and those who dominate the schedule of Fox News: one may note Fox contributor David Limbaugh's characterization of Brooks as a "reputedly conservative" columnist.[8] There are major differences—exacerbated by the October 2013 government shutdown and its aftermath—between those who see themselves as part of the American political mainstream and those, such as some Tea Party members, who adopt more radical stances toward what they see as an overwhelmingly liberal hegemony.[9]

Still, and despite such disagreements, there is much to indicate that it is reasonable to talk about a conservative movement in the contemporary United States, and the label itself has great resonance in American political life. Political scientists Christopher Ellis and James A. Stimson have reported that it is the most common American political "self-descriptor,"[10] and conservative writers themselves have felt confident in claiming a unity that underlies more specific differences. The *National Review*'s Jonah Goldberg described a "conservative culture," in ways that evoke not only the existence of a conservative community but of a structure of quasi-moral codes: values, ideas, and even modes of behavior that set conservatives off from their contemporaries.[11] Conservatism, Ellis and Stimson have documented, is viewed by many of its adherents as a way of life, a way of being, and a distinct identity within the larger framework of American political culture.[12] Honor plays an important role in providing the unifying assumptions and ideas for conservatives of every stripe and helps to give the label its appeal and its meaning.

Like conservatism, honor has undergone processes of adaptation and redefinition that have moved it away from its purest antebellum southern expressions into new but nonetheless recognizable forms. These have ranged from what some scholars have seen as an honor-based background to later traditions of American violence and personal resentment[13] to a general American admiration for the heroic individual who can understand the necessity of confronting both a corrupt world and a craven society.[14] Within the framework of contemporary conservatism, however, perhaps the key adaptation is that embodied in the distinction drawn by Dinesh D'Souza between honor and such "liberal" notions as self-esteem or dignity. Both dignity and self-esteem are said to represent a demand for respect that is due every human being, simply by virtue of his or her humanity, and thus to contrast sharply with honor. "Unlike honor," D'Souza has written, dignity and self-esteem do not "have to be earned," a distinction he sees as crucial.[15]

The notion of earned honor is critical to contemporary conservative thought. As scholars such as Sharon Krause have noted, it represents an adaptation from its early American incarnations. In the South, for example, honor was closely connected to land ownership and, more tenuously, to family background—a process that began during the antebellum period outside the South, and, arguably, within the South, as well.[16] As she and others have noted, there was a "democratization" of honor beginning during the first half of the nineteenth century, focusing less on matters of background and more on merit-based notions of status.[17] Honor was something that could be achieved, and achievement itself came to be seen as the measure of one's claim to honor in a natural, merit-based social and economic hierarchy.

The moral dimension of achievement is critical to conservative literature, and its basis in traditions of honor is recognizable in two key, related ideas. There is, first, an element of courage evoked in definitions of achievement, usually expressed by citing a willingness to take risk in what is said to be a competitive environment. Arguing that "self-respect must be earned," for example, the conservative sociologist Charles Murray has written that "the only way to earn anything is to achieve it in the face of the possibility of failing."[18] But an honor-based celebration of achievement is no less visible in what might be described as a related but distinct aspect of contemporary conservative writing, a critique of egalitarianism connected to a pervasive dialectic of independence and dependence. Egalitarianism, especially where it is attached to public efforts to overcome "natural" inequalities, is said to foster a culture of dependence.[19] If, as Rossiter suggested, the innate tendencies of human nature include laziness as well as such classic, honor-defined failings as cowardice or dishonesty, then the essence of an achievement-focused honor will include, as well, the assertion of a self-mastery evidenced by a life embodying self-determination and personal responsibility. It is along these lines that conservatives have decried what they describe as a liberal rhetoric of "victimization" or "victimology," a rhetoric asserting that individuals' problems are caused by, say, hostile institutions or historical traditions. "Ideologies of victimhood and grievance," as scholar and commentator Ruth R. Wisse has described them,[20] minimize not only individual agency but also individual, moral obligations to take control of one's own fate.

Within the framework of contemporary conservatism, this view of honor's moral imperatives gives particular prominence to individual obligations. Thus, as in regard to older honor traditions, a newer conservative rhetoric suggests, as the critic David Leverenz has argued, that it is honorable to take on the burden of having dependents (typically family members) but never to be dependent oneself, and this has come to play a major role in conservative ideology.[21] Certainly it is a view that serves as a background to fairly common laments regarding, to use economist Nicholas Eberstadt's words, "the collapse of the nation's family structure."[22]

As usually conceived, this collapse has been engendered by several factors, including undesirable cultural changes with regard to family norms and to gender. But it chiefly grows from political and ideological trends that have undermined family-based obligations, especially, as Charles Murray has explained, government programs and institutions that have encouraged an unhealthy dependence on external supports rather than internal duties.[23] This is the point commentator Laura Ingraham made when she suggested that President Barack Obama is given to using what she called his "out-of-control spending" to encourage irresponsibility among American fathers.[24]

But this dialectic of dependence and independence goes beyond family obligations, interacting, for example, with ideals of risk taking, pointing toward a condemnation of dependence as an evasion of risk, and a healthy self-reliance. Again, when individuals know they can rely on outsiders for help, especially when they can rely on the government to protect them from failure, this creates a moral deficit in the social order tantamount to ignoring the shame, the dishonor, that any acceptance of dependence entails.

Such an understanding of dependence underlies one of the more prominent distinctions within the framework of conservative literature, that which Mitt Romney evoked in his infamous remarks at a Florida fundraiser during the 2012 presidential campaign indicting the "47 percent" of Americans who would vote against him "no matter what," because they are "dependent upon government" and "believe that they are victims."[25] It underlies the moral critique of contemporary America articulated by Rick Santelli of CNBC, who is widely credited with launching the Tea Party movement with his February 2009 televised rant against people who—in his view—thoughtlessly took on too much mortgage debt and then asked the government to rescue them from the consequences of their actions.[26]

Within the rubric of honor, such a critique takes on special force. As philosopher Kwame Anthony Appiah has suggested, to be dependent should be a cause of shame. One who is not ashamed falls outside the boundaries of honor culture.[27] Such a view of dishonor may help to explain Charles Murray's lament that bankruptcy has become devoid of moral stigma in contemporary America, that it stands as a measure of declining personal morality—a morality that he himself describes in terms of traditional concerns about honor.[28] Many conservative commentators draw a strong distinction between such public benefits as Medicare and Social Security—which they see as earned—and those that go to undeserving freeloaders who eschew the demands of self-reliance and both demand and expect continuing support at public expense.[29]

It is difficult not to follow David Leverenz in seeing a racial dimension to such an honor-framed understanding of the virtue of independence, since dependence, dishonor, and race have been closely linked in traditions of honor since the antebellum period.[30] Within the contemporary rhetoric of conservatism, as Theda Skocpol and Vanessa Williamson have noted, they have continued to be so. Skocpol and Williamson have found that conservatives often assume African Americans have depended on government largesse—or at least government support—for whatever they have been able to achieve.[31] Oklahoma senator Tom Coburn's 2010 characterization of Barack Obama is a case in point. Offering a kind of backhanded defense of Obama's character, Coburn asserted that one of Obama's major goals as president was to "create dependency because it worked so well for him." Coburn went on to say of Obama that, as an African American male, "coming through the progress of everything he experienced, he got tremendous benefit through a lot of these programs."[32] Similar equations of race with an acceptance of dependence were to become common in the aftermath of the strong nonwhite vote for Obama in the 2012 presidential election, epitomized, perhaps, by Fox commentator Bill O'Reilly's argument that minority voters supported Obama because they "want stuff"—echoing Dinesh D'Souza's 2002 comment that African Americans tend to vote Democratic because Democrats give them "goodies"—a charge that takes on resonance within a more general framework of independence and dependence, undergirded by deeper, racially linked notions of honor.[33]

With its undergirding of racial implications, this view of dishonor emphasizes, still further, the importance of the distinction between earned public benefits and those given to freeloaders. To deny the distinction is to enter the world of the dishonored. It may also help to explain the vociferousness of at least some conservative opposition to Obamacare, a program said not only to reward the undeserving but, because it is designed to be universal, to ignore that distinction altogether. Overriding, conservatives often claim, individual choice and self-reliance in regard to health care,[34] it also in effect turns all its beneficiaries into recipients of federal largesse, lowering those who see themselves as independent into the realm of dependence, imposing on them the involuntary shame of a place among the dishonored.

Many of these same considerations carry forward into yet another component of conservative concerns about honor, those focusing on the question of national honor. These are concerns that draw on the conservative rejection of egalitarianism in favor of natural hierarchy, as well as on notions of independence and, too, on those of honor's fragility. In parallel with the natural hierarchy of individuals, conservatives posit a natural, merit-based hierarchy of nations, with the United States earning the top spot. Sarah Palin, for example, asserted that a "belief that America is the best country on earth" represents a bedrock conservative principle.[35] But such a view is still more closely linked to honor by one of the more striking motifs in the literature, an overwhelming concern for America's reputation in the eyes of other nations.[36] Certainly this has been a key theme in conservative attacks on the Obama administration's approach to foreign affairs. It is an administration that, in the words of former George W. Bush attorney general Michael Mukasey, "explicitly shuns the notion of American exceptionalism,"[37] but, worse, has brought shame to America by emphasizing multilateral efforts and showing excessive regard for international sensibilities. Conservative journalist James Bowman has directly connected such thinking to notions of national honor, which, he said, elevates "pride as jealousy for reputation and credibility as the respect a country or a military unit is able to command" over "democracy or freedom or religious tolerance or multiculturalism." He argued that "there can be no accommodation between honor and the kind of liberal internationalism that sees national identities and therefore national honor as obsolescent."[38]

Within this framework most conservatives see among the bedrock principles of conservatism not only American exceptionalism but also the need for a strong national defense. Certainly there are liberals who are also defense oriented, not to mention strong believers in American exceptionalism, Bowman to the contrary notwithstanding. Few contemporary liberals, however, would suggest that such a stance represents one of the "pillars" of liberalism—as conservative publisher Arthur Regnery, for example, defined it as one of the "pillars" of contemporary conservatism.[39]

But there is an important basis for the conservative concern for national and communal honor that is no less critical to stress. At the international level, this dimension entails a characterization of the world as a dangerous place. A strong national defense is required because other nations cannot be "hugged into submission," as Michael Gallagher emphasized.[40] Nor, as Elliott Abrams said, can it be said to be so "benign" that "we hardly need an army."[41]

It would, of course, be foolish to deny that the world is a dangerous place, but, within an honor-based framework, it is also important to note that danger can be interpreted in a variety of ways. Within conservatism the understanding of the world's hostility tends to be tied to that negative view of human nature that, as Kirk, Rossiter, and others have stressed, is a critical component of the conservative tradition and that remains vital today. As Abrams indicates, there is a strong tendency in conservatism to take a hostile world as a given, and it is a given because nations, like individuals, may be assumed to be driven by base purposes. Honor among them is not to be taken for granted.

This sense of a hostile world applies not only in the sphere of foreign policy. Focusing particularly on what they describe as "Sam's Club" voters, conservative writers Ross Douthat and Reihan Salam have noted a general sense of anxiety among such voters, a general sense of what they describe as "public disorder, family disintegration, cultural fragmentation, and civic and religious disaffection."[42] But anxiety about the state of American society and culture is a leitmotif in conservative writing, as is a lack of confidence in the existing leadership to address the sources of anxiety. There are many reasons for this. Fundamentally both the sources of anxiety and the failures of leadership rest on the same kind of pessimism about human nature that has long informed ideas of honor and traditions of conservatism as well.

Such a view of human nature and society informs one of the more influential books within the contemporary conservative canon, Thomas Sowell's *A Conflict of Visions,* in which he contrasted a conservative vision that recognizes human imperfection and human limitations with a liberal optimism about human moral potential that is, Sowell said, ultimately delusional.[43] Sarah Palin cited Sowell's book directly in a summary statement of her own principles for shaping her recognition that "man is fallen" must be the foundation for her approach to politics and policy.[44]

As Sowell's ideas indicate, conservative writers also tend to offer their assessment of human nature as more realistic than that of liberals and present themselves as more realistic judges of government and politics. From this point of view, liberals and progressives are trying to create utopian schemes doomed to failure by their unrealistic assessment of what human beings are like. Such schemes—affirmative action, for example, or large-scale interventions into the American economy—are problematic for an array of reasons, wrote Hillsdale College president Larry Arnn, not least in the extent to which they entail "the overturning of human nature."[45]

For contemporary conservatives, however, it is not enough to suggest that utopian liberals are wrong in their approach to government and society. Consistent with what Bertram Wyatt-Brown saw as an antebellum southern honor-based suspicion of government and the elites who run it,[46] there are strong tendencies in conservative writing to suggest that progressive utopian schemes have to do not only with a delusive desire to remake society but also with personal ambitions, with a desire for personal gain at the expense of the nation and its people. Arnn made this point, as did talk-show host Mark Levin in his 2012 book *Ameritopia.* "Utopian" schemes, whatever their claims may be, are ultimately about an illegitimate exercise of power in the guise of modern, enlightened leadership.[47] Assumptions not simply of bad ideas but, more, of bad motives underlie much of the rhetoric of twenty-first-century conservatism, rendered credible by the more general notions of human perversity.[48]

Looking back to an honor-based political rhetoric in the early American republic—a politics, as Joanne Freeman has documented, focused on "obtaining, maintaining, and attacking reputations"[49]—it is a rhetoric dominated by charges of dishonesty, excessive partisanship, and power hunger. It is a rhetoric that was critical to the honor-dominated politics of the antebellum South, and today's conservative rhetoric maintains that tradition.

Thus one of the more striking aspects of contemporary conservative rhetoric is its focus on the dishonorable character of contemporary liberal leaders. In 2010 Newt Gingrich, for example, asserted that his "leftist" opponents "hate accurate language about their goals," because it would expose their own self-seeking purposes. The "secular-socialist left," he says, "has to lie."[50] Ann Coulter, in her 2002 book *Slander,* described the "sheer joy liberals take in telling lies," characterizing her antagonists as "savagely cruel bigots who hate ordinary Americans and lie for sport."[51]

Since 2008 much of this kind of language has focused on Barack Obama and his "efforts to destroy all that is best in our country," as Dick Morris and Eileen McGann put it.[52] Fox News contributor David Limbaugh described Obama as "one of the most fundamentally dishonest chief executives in our history."[53] But lying is only one sign of Obama's dishonor. He has also been condemned for, among other things, excessive partisanship, stoking class envy, and purposefully—and falsely—"demonizing" his opponents, rather than seeking to work with them.[54] Historian Wilfred McClay, in an essay for *Commentary*'s postmortem on the 2012 election, described the Obama campaign as one based mainly on "pandering and identity politics."[55]

McClay's essay does not go in this direction, but his comments point to what truly is one of the more crucial and complex confrontations with race in contemporary conservatism, brought to the fore by Barack Obama's presence in the White House.[56] Beyond the issue of race and dependence, attitudes toward race, as such, have come to form a critical part of contemporary conservative writing, relating directly to an honor-based politics with honesty and reputation at its core.

Part of the reason for the prominence of concerns about race is that there have been strong tendencies among outsiders to charge conservatives with racism, and to use attitudes toward Obama as what conservative commentator Michael Gallagher called "a living Rorschach test" for the "race-obsessed Left."[57] As the conservative legal scholar Elizabeth Foley has said, those accused of racism have come to resent what they see as a liberal use of the "race card" to subvert genuine conservative objections to Democratic policies.[58]

Recent conservative writers, like Gallagher and Foley, have gone out of their way to protest charges of racism. Such protests are reinforced by a minor tradition of inclusiveness, especially in regard to those who exemplify such core American values as freedom, courage, and achievement. Sarah Palin, for example, has remarked on the influence Harriett Tubman's career had on her own.[59] Laura Ingraham, decrying the relativism of contemporary education, has evoked an earlier time when young people learned of the heroism of such figures as John Adams and Frederick Douglass. She grouped Rosa Parks with the patriots of the American Revolution.[60]

Accompanying its strong rejection of accusations of conservative racism, there is a pervasive tendency in the literature to charge that Obama—like others on the left—is himself dedicated to exacerbating racial discord to further his own ambitions, and in a way that stresses his own dishonor as a political actor. To some extent the charge is connected to other symptoms of pandering and partisanship. But it is still more fully connected to an indictment of what are said to be Obama's own racist attitudes. Obama, Glenn Beck famously asserted in 2009, shows a "deep-seated hatred for white people or the white culture."[61]

Such charges create a framework within which other writers have gone deeper into Obama's motives for wanting to destroy America. Savage has seen in Obama's policies a desire for retribution for America's past sins.[62] Jerome Corsi described how Obama, earlier in life, internalized a black rage that led in the direction of leftist and anti-American politics. A number of commentators, including Corsi, have focused on Michelle Obama's 2008 remark, in response to her husband's early primary victories, that, "for the first time in my adult lifetime, I am really proud of my country." As Corsi concluded, these words were symptomatic of "an angry black woman who was not proud of America."[63]

Conservatives often explain their discomfort with black anger in terms of their rejection of unsettling rifts in what ought to be a national community with a coherent understanding of honor and virtue.[64] But there are significant historical dimensions to this combination of race and rage. It is central to, for example, Thomas Jefferson's fearful predictions in the *Notes on the State of Virginia* of a vengeance-fueled race war should the slaves be given their freedom.[65] It became central to the proslavery argument.[66] It occupied white southern ideologues through the Jim Crow era and, as a number of historians have documented, contributed to conservative growth beginning in the mid-1960s.[67]

What gives that fear such significance, however, are attitudes toward black rage that are, themselves, closely related to honor. In Jefferson's time, and later, what made black rage seem such a potent force—and enhanced connections between race and dishonor—was a sense that, unlike men of honor, blacks were incapable of the self-command that controlled that rage (just as, similarly, they were incapable of that self-command that produced an independent character).[68] Once given vent that unregulated rage would create a truly fearsome prospect. Such views underlay Jefferson's fearful predictions, and they are apparent in the language of figures like Savage and Corsi. But they also look outward from race to point to one of the more salient connections among honor, a larger conservative tradition, and a contemporary conservatism no less founded on distrust and anxiety about human nature and politics.

A language connecting rage and dishonor looks back to a kind of early psychological theory that informed ideas of both honor and conservatism in the nineteenth century,[69] and that continues to play a role in conservative thought in the twenty-first. A critical component in early American forms of honor was the understanding of the passions, the emotions, as drivers of human action. Although there was an understanding of the necessity of passion as an element in human motivation, there was also a profound distrust of the passions in human interactions. Again looking to older traditions, keeping the passions restrained was critical to the self-command so deeply bound up with honor's conventions, even as a fear of their strength helped to illuminate honor's role in the preservation of the social and political order.[70]

Similar expressions play a role in contemporary conservative language. Conservatives most commonly cite power madness, overweening ambition, and greed as passions out of control, but there is a variety of quotidian but no less critical examples that figure strongly in the rhetoric. Michelle Malkin, for example, has written about "liberals who've lost their grip on sanity and reality"; she described them as "unhinged" and argued that they dominate liberal politics and institutions in general.[71] Michael Knox Beran is one among many who have decried what they see as liberals' emotional attachment to Barack Obama, prompted by what he called a "need to adore" that inhibits all critical thinking about him—and that Obama himself is fully prepared to exploit.[72]

This focus on passions is important. Counterposed to reason, as in these examples from Malkin and Beran, it serves to contrast still more delusional liberals with more grounded conservatives. But, within the framework of honor, concern about passion has additional significance as a key justification for adherence to defined codes of behavior, codes that serve as both guides to honor and as protection against dishonor. Such a framework was epitomized in southern traditions, not only in the notorious "Code of Honor," with its very precise rules for dueling, but also in the kind of unwritten social code demanding careful attention to manners, and to language, that was intended to prevent duel-worthy behavior in the first place.[73]

Within the literature of contemporary conservatism, such an attention to codes constitutes a major motif. It appears, for example, in David Brooks's response to the National Security Agency "leaker," Edward Snowden, who, Brooks wrote, "is violating the honor codes of all those who enabled him to rise."[74] This orientation toward codes also helps to explain at least some aspects of conservative discussions of religion, at least in regard to relations among religion, society, and the state, where there is a general tendency to stress religion's essential role in helping to provide those rules that privilege the maintenance of social bonds and social institutions over any other needs faith might fulfill.[75]

Politically, however, the attention to codes is most obvious in the celebration of the American Constitution, a celebration viewed as one of the cardinal tenets of conservatism itself. "Conservatives," wrote the commentator Hugh Hewitt, "are, first and chiefly, charged with protecting the Constitution."[76] It is "our holiest scripture," in the words of the conservative legal scholar Lino A. Graglia.[77] More crucial, however, is the general orientation toward the American Constitution. From the conservative perspective, the Constitution is a text, legitimated by its historical origins, to be taken literally and in terms of the "original intent" of its framers. Its provisions are seen to be both timeless and transparent and to set clear limits on the actions of those who govern. For Michael Savage such an approach stands in clear contrast to, for example, Barack Obama's "shameless disregard for that precious document and the procedures for governing it outlines."[78]

Honor-framed themes of independence, courage, and integrity thus form a basis for much in contemporary conservative rhetoric, but in no place do they come together more vividly than in conservative approaches to the debate over gun control, self-defense, and the nature of violence in American life. Conservative supporters of a broad right to possess and carry firearms invoke what they characterize as the original intent of the Second Amendment to the U.S. Constitution, as well as what they describe as a literal reading of the amendment's language, both of which are said to support individual gun ownership. It is an attitude reflected in National Rifle Association spokesman Wayne LaPierre's comment, in response to gun control proposals, that the amendment's "clearly defined absolutes" are not to be subordinated to more impressionistically defined "principles." The Constitution, he added, "becomes a blank slate for anyone's graffiti" when impressions triumph over absolutes.[79]

But constitutional arguments are augmented, significantly, by arguments for the moral responsibility of self-defense that look straight back to honor's more traditional imperatives. The NRA's lobbying, outreach, and media efforts have created powerful links between the Second Amendment as a necessary component of conservative constitutionalism and defending the American way of life in a world in which even other Americans are motivated by a desire for its destruction. "The possession of arms by the people is the ultimate warrant that government governs only with the consent of the governed," conservative lawyer Jeffrey Snyder wrote, widespread gun ownership being the best guarantee of liberty, he said, and the best defense against tyranny.[80]

The idea of violent self-defense as a moral act also figures strongly in links between conservative arguments for gun ownership and honor's demands for independence and self-determination. It was evoked by Jeffrey Snyder, for example, when he made explicit connections between gun ownership and issues of dependency, arguing that we become "a nation of cowards and shirkers" when we refuse to take responsibility for our own personal defense—including when we depend on the police to keep us safe.[81] Dave Kopel, of the Independent Institute, concludes that "telling the population that they are incapable of owning a tool that can be dangerous means you are creating a population that loses its self-reliance and increasingly sees itself as wards of the state."[82]

The moral implications of self-defense, in the context of honor, feature still more strongly in public debate over so-called Stand Your Ground laws. The first of these laws, promoted by NRA activist Marion Hammer, was enacted in Florida in 2005.[83] The law permits any person, in any place where they have a legal right to be, to "meet force with force, including deadly force," provided they reasonably believe that they or another person is at risk of great bodily harm.[84] Its sponsor in the Florida House of Representatives, Dennis Baxley, described the law as a way to "empower people" to "do the right thing" by meeting violence with violence.[85]

The Stand Your Ground laws have had real consequences. Most notably Stand Your Ground was the law invoked by the police when they initially released the Neighborhood Watch volunteer George Zimmerman in a much-publicized 2012 homicide case. Ignoring instructions from a police dispatcher that he stay put, Zimmerman followed and shot unarmed African American teenager Trayvon Martin in a gated Florida condominium complex. Zimmerman ultimately was acquitted on the theory that Martin rather than he may have been the aggressor.[86]

The case has clear associations with traditional notions of race and honor, with a fear of black rage that has haunted commentators from Jefferson to Corsi. But it is also important to note here that Zimmerman's compulsion to act despite police instructions not to follow Martin is consistent with the conservative, honor-based approach to self-defense—what legal scholar Janine Young Kim has described as "the belief that the social condition is one of violent disorder."[87] Benjamin Domenech, arguing against gun control, echoed this, suggesting that "the law itself has little power to protect us in the moment when darkness knocks," and argued that being prepared to "face evil unflinchingly" is essential. "In a world of darkness and insanity," he wrote, "we may not be able to do more—but we can do no less."[88]

Although many of the key links between honor and conservatism exist at what might be called a foundational level, providing unspoken but critical support for conservative rhetoric, at least some contemporary conservatives have in fact sought to assert more direct links between honor and conservative ideals—though they have tended to take a highly selective view of honor and conservatism alike. In one of the more elaborate conservative efforts to discuss such links, the journalist James Bowman, who essentially equated honor with chivalry, called for a revival of honor in what he described as a Western civilization crippled by "honor skepticism." He called for the "revival" of a kind of "warrior spirit" in the West to counteract what he has seen as the triumph of antihonor intellectual and cultural trends.[89]

To a great extent, Bowman's lament builds on a larger tendency among conservatives to see themselves, individually and collectively, as occupying an essential oppositional space within American culture and politics, whatever the popularity of "conservative" as a label of choice in American politics. As James Piereson has observed, conservatives "no longer exercise much influence within the major professions or the leading cultural and educational institutions in the country," and, although Piereson expressed hope that the situation will change "when liberals run the system aground," his lament echoes much conservative writing—as does his belief, expressed here, that conservatives are standing for the right in a society and political order headed for the wrong.[90]

As honor plays a role in conservative assessments of this situation, it points toward the elements of courage and risk evoked more generally in conservative definitions of independence. To a great degree, conservatives have lost the major American culture wars,[91] and conservatives often argue that such a situation demands courage in response. "Bravery," Newt Gingrich has said, "is a student challenging his teachers when they propagandize factually incorrect accounts of U.S. history." It is, he said, "a conservative faculty member risking the loss of tenure and even the loss of her job by standing firm for her beliefs."[92] Conservatives, the writer Todd Seavey has said, are risk takers in a hostile world that demands risk taking.[93]

To take risks, to stand against the tide, to resist manipulation by others, these have become key attributes for a model conservative identity. Sarah Palin evoked them frequently in her 2009 autobiography, tellingly entitled *Going Rogue,* stressing her independence from party-line politics, her outsider status in Alaska—and American—politics, her resistance to the demands of others, including the national Republican organization, where her convictions were concerned. She is "out-of-the-box," she said, bringing only her courage and conservative principles to a hostile political world.[94] Along these lines, it is useful to note Tevi Troy's tribute to what he calls "Ronald Reagan's gift": "Reagan made clear," Troy wrote, "that his views were those of conservatism, and he did not allow other voices on the left, the right, or in the mainstream media to define conservatism for him."[95]

The shadow of William F. Buckley looms large in such conservative thinking. As Grace Elizabeth Hale has written, Buckley's brand of conservatism was "uncompromising" and rebellious in style.[96] Conservative journalist Helen Rittelmeyer's celebration of young conservatives at Yale (Buckley's alma mater) during the first decade of the twenty-first century captures Buckley's influence, even as it provides a useful summary of the appeal of an honor-based identity as it is understood in modern conservative thought. Rittelmeyer—who also has seen the potential of violence to be "an important and admirable expression" of a "moral system"—described the Yale conservatives as a rowdy bunch, given to violating bureaucratic dictates for the sake of violating bureaucratic dictates, drawing strong connections between morality and resistance. Theirs was, she wrote, "a culture of honor"—standing in defiance to an otherwise hegemonic liberal milieu.[97]

The stance outlined here may help to reveal both the source of conservatism's appeal and, as even many conservatives suggest, the source of its greatest dilemmas. On the one hand, honor's chief imperatives have and continue to supply an important foundation for a political rhetoric that stresses independence, self-reliance, even agency in a difficult, demanding world. Kept alive not only by political discussion and debate, but also by the myriad forms of popular culture that have adapted, readapted, and strengthened honor's traditions for the last two centuries, plus, those same traditions lend continuing credibility to ideas and ideals that continue to make "conservative" such a popular self-descriptor in American social and cultural life.

At the same time, there is much in an honor-based conservative rhetoric to urge conservatives themselves into a posture that is almost purely oppositional,[98] in which the virtue of "fighting the good fight," for its own sake, becomes the test of conservative purity, as many claimed in the aftermath of the October 2013 shutdown events.[99] Fox talk-show host Sean Hannity offered a related, honor-based justification for such a stance when he urged Republicans in Congress to avoid working with Barack Obama because Obama is a liar, and it is wrong to compromise with liars.[100] But such a view is implicit in a rhetoric that sees opposition leaders as not only wrong but also perversely corrupt. Deliberately placing themselves outside what they see as a liberal political, social, and cultural arena, conservatives may also find themselves engaged in a politics of nay-saying that will continually undermine their efforts to shape an American political agenda.

Nevertheless, because much about honor is fundamental to notions of both moral and cultural status among those who call themselves conservatives, its continuing force will likely help to maintain the life of the movement—despite such apparent setbacks as Barack Obama's 2012 reelection to the presidency—for some time to come.

NOTES

1. Greenberg, *Honor and Slavery,* 9–12; D. Bruce, *Violence and Culture,* 38–39.
2. D. Bruce, *Violence and Culture,* e.g., 32; Appiah, *Honor Code,* e.g., 177.
3. Kirk, *Conservative Mind,* 8–9.
4. Rossiter, *Conservatism in America,* 22, 24.
5. Ibid., 131–32.
6. D'Souza, *Letters to a Young Conservative,* 11–12.
7. In "What Is the Future," 19.
8. Limbaugh, *Crimes against Liberty,* 47; see Kabaservice, *Rule and Ruin,* 401.
9. Seavey, "Conservatism for Punks," 196, 201.
10. Ellis and Stimson, *Ideology in America,* 16.
11. Jonah Goldberg, *Proud to Be Right,* xx.
12. Ellis and Stimson, *Ideology in America,* 14.
13. McKanna, "Seeds of Destruction," 71–72, 82–83; Butterfield, *All God's Children.*
14. D. Bruce, *Kentucky Tragedy,* 102, 147–48; McClay, *Masterless,* 265. See also Douthat and Salam, *Grand New Party,* 29, 31.
15. D'Souza, *Letters to a Young Conservative,* 163; see Appiah, *Honor Code,* e.g., 131.
16. See Mayfield, *Counterfeit Gentlemen,* e.g., xvii–xviii.
17. Krause, *Liberalism with Honor,* 28–31.
18. C. Murray, *Coming Apart,* 281; Horwitz, *America's Right,* 45.

19. Leverenz, *Honor Bound,* 52.
20. In "What Is the Future," 52.
21. Leverenz, *Honor Bound,* 58; Wyatt-Brown, *Southern Honor,* e.g. 35.
22. In "What Is the Future," 22.
23. C. Murray, *Coming Apart,* 282.
24. Ingraham, *Obama Diaries,* 59.
25. Qtd. in Horwitz, *America's Right,* 179.
26. Formisano, *Tea Party,* 26–27.
27. Appiah, *Honor Code,* 177.
28. C. Murray, *Coming Apart,* 198–99.
29. Skocpol and Williamson, *Tea Party,* 59–60, 64–67.
30. Leverenz, *Honor Bound,* 28; Greenberg, *Honor and Slavery,* 66–67.
31. Skocpol and Williamson, *Tea Party,* e.g., 69.
32. Sargent, "What Coburn Really Said."
33. D. Edwards, "O'Reilly"; D'Souza, *Letters to a Young Conservative,* 216.
34. Foley, *Tea Party,* 34.
35. Palin, *Going Rogue,* 45.
36. Wyatt-Brown, *Warring Nation,* 10.
37. In "What Is the Future," 35.
38. James Bowman, *Honor,* 308.
39. Regnery, "Pillars of Conservatism," loc. 725.
40. M. Gallagher, *That's No Angry Mob,* 17.
41. In "What Is the Future," 14.
42. Douthat and Salam, *Grand New Party,* 8.
43. Sowell, *Conflict of Visions,* 12–15, 17–19.
44. Palin, *Going Rogue,* 385.
45. In "What Is the Future," 16.
46. Wyatt-Brown, *Southern Honor,* 71.
47. Levin, *Ameritopia,* 203, 212.
48. See Horwitz, *America's Right,* 9.
49. Freeman, *Affairs of Honor,* 59.
50. Gingrich, *To Save America,* 46.
51. A. Coulter, *Slander,* 27, 57, 205.
52. Morris and McGann, *2010,* 244.
53. Limbaugh, *Crimes against Liberty,* 5.
54. See, e.g., Ingraham, *Obama Diaries,* e.g., 298–99.
55. In "What Is the Future," 36.
56. See Parker and Barreto, *Change,* 35, 86; Skocpol and Williamson, *Tea Party,* 77–78.
57. M. Gallagher, *That's No Angry Mob,* 172.
58. Foley, *Tea Party,* 11.
59. Palin, *Going Rogue,* 13.
60. Ingraham, *Obama Diaries,* 17, 28.
61. "Glenn Beck."
62. Savage, *Trickle Up Poverty,* 257.
63. Corsi, *Obama Nation,* 69, 231, 233.
64. See, e.g., James Bowman, *Honor,* ch. 11.

65. [Jefferson], *Portable Thomas Jefferson,* 186.
66. D. Bruce, "Racial Fear."
67. Critchlow, *Conservative Ascendancy,* 82, 84.
68. D. Bruce, *Violence and Culture,* 126–28.
69. D. Bruce, *Rhetoric of Conservatism,* 163; Rossiter, *Conservatism in America,* 22, 183.
70. D. Bruce, *Violence and Culture,* e.g., 40–41.
71. Malkin, *Unhinged,* 8.
72. Beran, "Falls the Shadow," 36.
73. D. Bruce, *Violence and Culture,* 32, 25.
74. Brooks, "Solitary Leaker," A23.
75. Bork, *"A Country I Do Not Recognize,"* xxvii.
76. In "What Is the Future," 27; Honderich, *Conservatism,* 174; Skocpol and Williamson, *Tea Party,* 48–49.
77. Graglia, "Constitutional Law," 48.
78. Savage, *Trickle Up Poverty,* 302.
79. Shear, "N.R.A. Leader," A15.
80. Snyder, "Nation of Cowards," 258–59.
81. Ibid., 250–51.
82. In Jeffrey Goldberg, "Case for More Guns," 78.
83. O'Neill, "NRA's Marion Hammer."
84. Fla. Stat. §776.013.
85. Schorsch, "Five Questions."
86. Alvarez, "Lawyers for Zimmerman."
87. Kim, "Rhetoric of Self-Defense," 276.
88. Domenech, "Truth about Mass Shootings," 29.
89. James Bowman, *Honor,* e.g., 88, 307.
90. In "What Is the Future," 38.
91. See, e.g., Courtwright, *No Right Turn.*
92. Gingrich, *To Save America,* 323, 324.
93. Seavey, "Conservatism for Punks," 201.
94. Palin, *Going Rogue,* e.g., 85, 232, 223.
95. In "What Is the Future," 49.
96. Hale, *Nation of Outsiders,* 140–41.
97. Rittelmeyer, "Smoker's Code," 175, 177.
98. For a good discussion, see Douthat and Salam, *Grand New Party.*
99. For a useful account, see Joshua Green, "Why Ted Cruz."
100. *Hannity,* Fox News, February 20, 2013.

BIBLIOGRAPHY

1840 United States Federal Census. June 1, 1840. http://search.ancestrylibrary.com/search/db.aspx?dbid=8057 (accessed December 23, 2013).

Abzug, Robert H. *Cosmos Crumbling: American Reform and the Religious Imagination.* New York: Oxford University Press, 1994.

Acts Passed at the First Session of the Fourth General Assembly of the State of Tennessee, Begun and Held at Knoxville, on Monday, the 21st Day of September 1801. Knoxville, Ky.: George Roulstone, 1801.

Acts Passed at the First Session of the Twentieth General Assembly for the Commonwealth of Kentucky. Frankfort, Ky.: W. Gerard, 1812.

An Act to Locate a State Road from William Brown's, Jr., in St. Clair County, to Nashville, in Washington County, *Laws of the State of Illinois.* Springfield: Walters and Weber, 1843.

Adams, Henry. *The Education of Henry Adams.* Edited by Ernest Samuels. Boston: Houghton Mifflin, 1973.

Affleck, James. "The Stuart-Bennett Duel: The First Duel Fought in Illinois, at Belleville, in St. Clair County, on February 8, 1819." In *Publications of the Illinois State Historical Library,* 96–100. Springfield, IL: Phillips Bros., State Printers, 1901.

Agnew, Jean-Christophe. *Worlds Apart: The Market and the Theater in Anglo-American Thought, 1550–1750.* Cambridge: Cambridge University Press, 1986.

Agricultural Society of South Carolina, Minutes, Typescript, 1825–60. South Carolina Historical Society, Charleston, South Carolina.

Agricultural Society of South Carolina. *Original Communications Made to the Agricultural Society of South-Carolina; and Extracts from Select Authors on Agriculture.* Charleston, S.C.: A. E. Miller, 1824.

Akin, Daniel L. "The Role of Men and Women in the Church." *Southern Seminary Magazine* 71 (Winter 2003): 6–9.

Aldrich, Megan. *Gothic Revival.* London: Phaidon, 1994.

Allen, William B. *Kentucky Officer's Guide and Legal Hand-Book.* Louisville, Ky.: John P. Morton, 1860.

Allen, William Francis, Charles Pickard Ware, and Lucy McKim Garrison. *Slave Songs of the United States.* New York: A. Simpson, 1867. Retrieved from Documenting the American South, University Library, University of North Carolina at Chapel Hill, 2000. http://docsouth.unc.edu/church/allen/allen.html (accessed August 22, 2013).

Allgor, Catherine. *Parlor Politics: In Which the Ladies of Washington Help Build a City and a Government.* Charlottesville: University Press of Virginia, 2000. Reprint, 2001.

Alvarez, Lizette. "Lawyers for Zimmerman Rest Their Case without Calling Him to the Stand." *New York Times,* July 11, 2013, A15.

Anderson, Eve. *A Breach of Privilege: Cilley Family Letters, 1820–1867.* Spruce Head, Maine: Seven Coin, 2002.

Anderson, Jeffrey E. *Conjure in African American Society.* Baton Rouge: Louisiana State University Press, 2005.

———. "Voodoo in Black and White." In *Southern Character: Essays in Honor of Bertram Wyatt Brown,* ed. Lisa Tendrich Frank and Daniel Kilbride, 143–59. Gainesville: University Press of Florida, 2011.

Anderson, Paul C. *Blood Image: Turner Ashby in the Civil War and the Southern Mind.* Baton Rouge: Louisiana State University Press, 2002.

Appiah, Kwame Anthony. *The Honor Code: How Moral Revolutions Happen.* New York: Norton, 2010.

Atherton, Lewis. "The Problem of Credit Rating in the Ante-bellum South." *Journal of Southern History* 12, no. 4 (November 1946): 534–56.

———. *The Southern Country Store, 1800–1860.* Baton Rouge: Louisiana State University Press, 1949.

Auditor of Public Accounts, Condemned Blacks Executed or Transported, Records—Condemned Slaves, Court Orders, and Valuations, Library of Virginia, Richmond.

Auerbach, Nina. *Private Theatricals: The Lives of the Victorians.* Cambridge, Mass.: Harvard University Press, 1990.

Augst, Thomas. *The Clerk's Tale: Young Men and Moral Life in Nineteenth-Century America.* Chicago: University of Chicago Press, 2003.

Ayers, Edward L. *In the Presence of Mine Enemies: Civil War in the Heart of America.* New York: W. W. Norton, 2003.

———. "Legacy of Violence." *American Heritage* 42, no. 6 (October 1991): 102–9.

———. *The Promise of the New South: Life after Reconstruction.* New York: Oxford University Press, 1992.

———. *Vengeance and Justice: Crime and Punishment in the Nineteenth-Century American South.* New York: Oxford University Press, 1984.

———. *What Caused the Civil War? Reflections on the South and Southern History.* New York: W. W. Norton, 2005.

Aylett, W. R. "Patrick Henry Aylett." *Virginia Law Journal* 4 (September 1880): 517–30.

Bache, Richard. *The Manual of a Pennsylvania Justice of the Peace, Containing Principally the Laws, Adjudications, and Process, for the Exercise of His Jurisdiction in Criminal Cases.* Philadelphia: John Binns, 1814.

Backus, Joseph. *The Justice of the Peace.* Hartford: B. and J. Russell, 1816.

Badders, Hurley E. *Remembering South Carolina's Old Pendleton District.* Charleston, S.C.: History Press, 2006.

Bailey, Frankie Y. "Honor, Class, and White Southern Violence: A Historical Perspective." In *Violent Crime: Assessing Race and Ethnic Differences,* edited by Darnell F. Hawkins, 331–53. Cambridge: Cambridge University Press, 2003.

Baker, Benjamin A. *A Glance at New York: A Local Drama in Two Acts.* New York: Samuel French, 1848.

Baldick, Robert. *The Duel: A History.* New York: Barnes and Noble Books, 1965.

Baldwin, Joseph Glover. *The Flush Times of Alabama and Mississippi.* D. Appleton, 1858.

Balleisen, Edward J. *Navigating Failure: Bankruptcy and Commercial Society in Antebellum America.* Chapel Hill: University of North Carolina Press, 2001.

Baltimore Sun [Md.].

Bangor Daily Whig and Courier [Maine].

Baptist, Edward E. *Creating an Old South: Middle Florida's Plantation Frontier before the Civil War.* Chapel Hill: University of North Carolina Press, 2002.

———. *The Half Has Never Been Told: Slavery and the Making of American Capitalism.* New York: Basic Books, 2014.

———. "Me and Southern Honor." *Historically Speaking* 9 (August 2008): 13–14.

Baptist Women for Equality Newsletter. February 2010. http://www.bwebaptist.com/files/Jackboots_of_the_Southern_Baptist_Convention.pdf (retrieved June 1, 2012).

Barbour, Oliver Lorenzo. *A Treatise on the Criminal Law of the State of New-York.* Albany: Gould, Banks, 1852.

Barringer, Tim. *Reading the Pre-Raphaelites.* New Haven, Conn.: Yale University Press, 1999.

Bass, Ruth. "The Little Man." *Scribner's Magazine* 97 (1935): 120–23.

———. "Mojo." In *Mother Wit from the Laughing Barrel: Readings in the Interpretation of Afro-American Folklore,* edited by Alan Dundes, 380–87. Jackson: University Press of Mississippi, 1990.

Basso, Hamilton. "Orestes in Alabama." *New Republic* 88 (September 30, 1936): 231.

Bateman, Newton, et al. *Historical Encyclopedia of Illinois.* Part 2. Chicago: Munsell, 1907.

Beaufort Taylor Watts Papers, South Caroliniana Library, University of South Carolina, Columbia.

Belleville News Democrat [Ill.].

Benson Field Cole Diary, University Archives, Z. Smith Reynolds Library, Wake Forest University.

Beran, Michael Knox. "Falls the Shadow." *National Review,* November 12, 2012, 35–38.

Berger, Peter, Brigitte Berger, and Hans Kellner. *The Homeless Mind: Modernization and Consciounsess.* New York: Random House, 1973.

Berlin, Ira. *Generations of Captivity: A History of African-American Slaves.* Cambridge, MA: Belknap Press of Harvard University Press, 2004.

Berry, Stephen W. *All That Makes a Man: Love and Ambition in the Civil War South.* New York: Oxford University Press, 2003.

———, ed. *Princes of Cotton: Four Diaries of Young Men in the South, 1848–1860.* Athens: University of Georgia Press, 2007.

Bims, Hamilton. "Would You Believe It . . . Superstition Lives!" *Ebony,* July 1976, 118–22.

Biographical Dictionary of the American Congress, 1774–1996. Alexandria, Va.: CQ Staff Directories, 1997.

Biographical Directory of the United States Congress, 1774–2005: The Continental Congress, September 5, 1774 to October 21, 1788, and the Congress of the United States, from the First through the One Hundred Eighth Congresses, March 4, 1789, to January 3, 2005, inclusive. Washington D.C.: U.S. Government Printing Office, 2005.

Bishop, Ann. "Gabr'el Blow Sof! Gabr'el Blow Loud!" Interview by Ruby Pickens Tartt. In *The American Slave: A Composite Autobiography,* 2nd rpt. ed., vol. 6, edited by George P. Rawick, 35–38. Westport, Conn.: Greenwood, 1972.

Black, James M. *Families and Descendants in America of Golsan, Golson, Gholson, Gholston Also Goldston, Golston, etc.* Salt Lake City: J. M. Black, 1959.

Black, Kelli M. "Creating Infanticide: A Comparative Study of Early Modern British Servant and Antebellum American Slave Women." M.A. thesis, San Diego State University, 2003.

Blassingame, John. *The Slave Community: Plantation Life in the Antebellum South.* 2nd ed. New York: Oxford University Press, 1979.

Bleser, Carol, ed. *The Hammonds of Redcliffe.* New York: Oxford University Press, 1981.

———, ed. *Secret and Sacred: The Diaries of James Henry Hammond, a Southern Slaveholder.* New York: Oxford University Press, 1988.

Bonner, James C. "The Genesis of Agricultural Reform in the Cotton Belt." *Journal of Southern History* 9 (1943): 475–500.

Bork, Robert, ed. "A Country I Do Not Recognize": *The Legal Assault on American Values.* Stanford: Hoover Institution Press, 2005.

Boston Courier [Mass.].

Boston Evening Post [Mass.].

Boston Investigator [Mass.].

Boston Recorder [Mass.].

Bouvier, John. *Institutes of American Law.* Vol. I. Philadelphia: Robert E. Peterson, 1851.

Bowman, J. *Address to Mechanics on Temperance.* Nashville: E. Stevenson and F. A. Owen, 1855.

Bowman, James. *Honor: A History.* New York: Encounter Books, 2006.

Boyd, Valerie. *Wrapped in Rainbows: The Life of Zora Neale Hurston.* New York: Scribner, 2003.

Boyer, Richard. "Honor among Plebeians." In *The Faces of Honor: Sex, Shame, and Violence in Colonial Latin America,* edited by Lyman L. Johnson and Sonya Lipsett-Rivera, 152–78. Albuquerque: University of New Mexico Press, 1998.

Brand, Paul. "Judges and Judging 1176–1307." In *Judges and Judging in the History of the Common Law and Civil Law,* edited by Paul Brand and Joshua Getzler, 3–36. Cambridge: Cambridge University Press, 2012.

Breaux and Villere. "Marie Laveau: Her Tomb and Descendants." Louisiana Writers' Project, box 3-C-1, folder 25. Federal Writers Project, 1935–43. Cammie G. Henry Research Center, Watson Memorial Library, Northwestern State University of Louisiana.

Breen, T. H. "Horses and Gentlemen: The Cultural Significance of Gambling among the Gentry of Virginia." *William and Mary Quarterly* 34 (1977): 239–57.

———. *The Marketplace of Revolution: How Consumer Politics Shaped American Independence.* New York: Oxford University Press, 2004.

———. *Tobacco Culture: The Mentality of the Great Tidewater Planters on the Eve of Revolution.* Princeton, N.J.: Princeton University Press, 1985.

Bridge, Horatio. *Personal Recollections of Nathaniel Hawthorne.* 1893. New York: Haskell House, 1968.

Brooks, David. "The Solitary Leaker." *New York Times,* July 10, 2013, A23.

Brown, Chad. "Building a Christ Centered Marriage: How Husbands and Wives Can Complement One Another in Marriage." *Journal of Biblical Manhood and Womanhood* 3, no. 2 (Summer 1998): 8–9, 14.

Brown, Marie. "Negro (Marie Laveau)." Interview by Posey. Louisiana Writers' Project, box 3-C-1, folder 25, 4. Federal Writers Project, 1935–43. Cammie G. Henry Research Center, Watson Memorial Library, Northwestern State University of Louisiana.

Brown, William Wells. *My Southern Home: or, The South and Its People.* A. G. Brown, 1880. Reprint, Upper Saddle River, N.J.: Gregg, 1968.

———. *Narrative of William W. Brown, a Fugitive Slave.* In *Slave Narratives,* ed. William L. Andrews and Henry Louis Gates Jr., 369–424 New York: Library of America, 2000.

Bruce, Dickson D., Jr. *The Kentucky Tragedy: A Story of Conflict and Change in Antebellum America.* Baton Rouge: Louisiana State University Press, 2006.

———. "Racial Fear and the Proslavery Argument: A Rhetorical Approach." *Mississippi Quarterly* 33 (1980): 461–78.

———. *The Rhetoric of Conservatism: The Virginia Convention of 1829–30 and the Conservative Tradition in the South.* San Marino, CA: Huntington Library, 1982.

———. *Violence and Culture in the Antebellum South.* Austin: University of Texas Press, 1979.

Bruce, H. C. *Twenty-Nine Years a Slave, Twenty-Nine Years a Free Man: Recollections of H. C. Bruce.* York, Pa.: Anstadt and Sons, 1895.

Bruce, Philip A. *The Plantation Negro as a Freedman: Observations on His Character, Condition, and Prospects in Virginia.* New York: G. P. Putnam's Sons, 1889.

Burk, Denny. "Pope Benedict's Final Address to the Roman Curia and the Decline of Western Civilization." *Journal of Biblical Manhood and Womanhood* 18, no. 1 (Summer 2013): 2–3.

Burke, Edmund. *Reflections on the Revolution in France. . . .* 2nd ed. London: J. Dodsley, 1790.

Burr, Aaron. *Memoirs of Aaron Burr: With Miscellaneous Selections from His Correspondence.* Edited by Matthew L. Davis. Vol. 2. New York: Harper and Brothers, 1837.

Burr, Virginia Ingraham, ed. *The Secret Eye: The Journal of Ella Gertrude Clanton Thomas, 1848–1889.* With an introduction by Nell Irvin Painter. Chapel Hill: University of North Carolina Press, 1990.

Burwell, Letitia. *A Girl's Life in Virginia before the War.* New York: Frederick A. Stokes, 1895.

Burwick, Frederick. *Mimesis and Its Romantic Reflections.* University Park: Pennsylvania State University Press, 2000.

Bush, Harold K. *Mark Twain and the Spiritual Crisis of the Age.* Tuscaloosa: University of Alabama Press, 2007.

Bushman, Richard L. *The Refinement of America: Persons, Houses, Cities.* New York: Alfred A. Knopf, 1992.

Busick, Sean R. *A Sober Desire for History: William Gilmore Simms as Historian.* Columbia: University of South Carolina Press, 2005.

Butterfield, Fox. *All God's Children: The Bosket Family and the American Tradition of Violence.* New York: Alfred A. Knopf, 1995.

Butterworth, Keen, and James E. Kibler Jr. *William Gilmore Simms: A Reference Guide.* Boston: G. K. Hall, 1980.

Bynum, Victoria E. *Unruly Women: The Politics of Social and Sexual Control in the Old South.* Chapel Hill: University of North Carolina Press, 1992.

Byrne, Frank J. *Becoming Bourgeois: Merchant Culture in the South, 1820–1865.* Lexington: University Press of Kentucky, 2006.

Byron, Matthew A. "Crime and Punishment? The Impotency of Dueling Laws in the United States." Ph.D. diss., University of Arkansas, 2009.

Caldwell, Joshua W. *Studies in the Constitutional History of Tennessee.* Cincinnati, Ohio: Robert Clarke, 1895.

Calhoon, Robert M. *Evangelicals and Conservatives in the Early South, 1740–1861.* Columbia: University of South Carolina Press, 1988.

Calhoun, Richard J., ed. *Witness to Sorrow: The Antebellum Autobiography of William J. Grayson.* Columbia: University of South Carolina Press, 1990.

Camden Journal [S.C.].

Camp, Stephanie M. H. *Closer to Freedom: Enslaved Women and Everyday Resistance in the Plantation South.* Chapel Hill: University of North Carolina Press, 2004.

Canby, Henry Seidel. "Charged Books." *Saturday Review of Literature* 17 (April 1938): 8.

Carmichael, Peter S. *The Last Generation: Young Virginians in Peace, War, and Reunion.* Chapel Hill: University of North Carolina Press, 2005.

Carnes, Mark C., and Clyde Griffen. *Meanings for Manhood: Constructions of Masculinity in Victorian America.* Chicago: University of Chicago Press, 1990.

Carney, Charity R. *Ministers and Masters: Methodism, Manhood, and Honor in the Old South.* Baton Rouge: Louisiana State University Press, 2011.

Caroline E. Merrick Letters. Special Collections, Hill Memorial Library, Louisiana State University, Baton Rouge.

Carter, Clarence Edwin. *The Territorial Papers of the United States.* Washington: U.S. Government Printing Office, 1934.

Cary, Virginia. *Letters on Female Character Addressed to a Young Lady on the Death of Her Mother.* Richmond, VA: A. Works, 1828.

Cash, W. J. *The Mind of the South.* With a new introduction by Bertram Wyatt-Brown. New York: Vintage Books, 1991. First published 1941.

Cashin, Joan E. *A Family Venture: Men and Women on the Southern Frontier.* New York: Oxford University Press, 1991.

Casper, Scott E. *Constructing American Lives: Biography & Culture in Nineteenth-Century America.* Chapel Hill: University of North Carolina Press, 1999.

Causey, Evelyn D. "The Character of a Gentleman: Deportment, Piety, and Morality in Southern Colleges and Universities, 1820–1860." Ph.D. diss., University of Delaware, 2006.

Cauthen, Charles Edward. *South Carolina Goes to War, 1860–1865.* Chapel Hill: University of North Carolina Press, 1950.

"CBMW's Roll Call of Churches on Ministerial/Household Roles." *Council of Biblical Manhood and Womanhood News* 1, no. 1 (August 1995): 6.

Chamberlain, Ryan. *Pistols, Politics and the Press: Dueling in 19th Century American Journalism.* Jefferson, N.C.: McFarland, 2009.

Chandler, Alfred D., Jr. *The Visible Hand: The Managerial Revolution in American Business.* Cambridge, Mass.: Belknap Press of Harvard University Press, 1977.

Charles Fraser Papers, South Caroliniana Library, University of South Carolina, Columbia.

Charleston City Gazette [S.C.].

Charleston Courier [S.C.].

Charleston Mercury [S.C.].

Charters and General Laws of the Colony and Province of Massachusetts Bay. Boston: T. B. Wait, 1814.

Chattahoochee Valley Historical Society. *The Story of Bluffton-Lanett Alabama.* Salt Lake City: Paragon, 1971.

Chaussinand-Nogaret, Guy. *The French Nobility in the Eighteenth Century: From Feudalism to Enlightenment.* Cambridge: Cambridge University Press, 1985.

Chesnut, Mary Boykin. *Mary Chesnut's Civil War.* Edited by C. Vann Woodward. New Haven, Conn.: Yale University Press, 1981.

———. *The Private Mary Chesnut: The Unpublished Civil War Diaries.* Edited by C. Vann Woodward and Elisabeth Muhlenfeld. New York: Oxford University Press, 1984.

Chesnutt, Charles W. "Race Prejudice: Its Causes and Cures; Speech to the Boston Literary and Historical Association, Boston, Mass., 25 June 1905." In *Charles W. Chesnutt: Essays and*

Speeches, edited by Joseph R. McElrath Jr., Robert C. Leitz III, and Jesse S. Crisler, 214–38. Stanford, Calif.: Stanford University Press, 1999. Retrieved from EBSCOhost (Accession 6685).

Chesnutt, David R., et al., eds. *The Papers of Henry Laurens*. Vol. 11, *Jan. 5, 1776–Nov. 1, 1777*. Columbia, S.C.: University of South Carolina Press, 1968.

"The Chevalier Bayard and the Fair Widow." *American Monthly Magazine* 5, no. 2 (1835): 81–88.

Chireau, Yvonne. *Black Magic: Religion and the African American Conjuring Tradition*. Berkeley: University of California Press, 2003.

Chisolm, A. R. "Notes on the Surrender of Fort Sumter." In *Battles and Leaders of the Civil War: Being for the Most Part Contributions by Union and Confederate Officers*, edited by Robert Underwood Johnson and Clarence Clough Buel, 82–83. New York: T. Yoseloff, 1956.

City Gazette and Commercial Daily Advertiser [Charleston, S.C.].

Clinton, Catherine. *The Other Civil War: American Women in the Nineteenth Century*. New York: Hill and Wang, 1984. Reprint, 1999.

———. *The Plantation Mistress: Woman's World in the Old South*. New York: Pantheon Books, 1982.

———. *Tara Revisited: Women, War, and the Plantation Legend*. New York: Abbeville, 1995.

Cochran, Hamilton. *Noted American Duels and Hostile Encounters*. New York: Chilton Books, 1963.

The Code of Virginia. Richmond, Va.: William F. Ritchie, 1849.

Cohen, Patricia C. *The Murder of Helen Jewett: The Life and Death of a Prostitute in Nineteenth-Century New York*. New York: Oxford University Press, 1998.

Cole, Edwin Louis. *Maximized Manhood: A Guide to Family Survival*. Rev. ed. New Kinsington, Pa.: Whitaker House, 2001.

———. *Strong Men in Tough Times: Exercising Manhood in an Age That Demands Heroes*. Southlake, Tex.: Watercolor Books, 1993.

Coleridge, Samuel Taylor. *Biographia Literaria*. Vol. 1. Edited by James Engell and W. Jackson Bates. Princeton, N. J.: Princeton University Press, 1983.

Collier, Keith. "3 Things Every Boy Needs." *Southwestern News* 69 (Winter 2011): 16–17.

Collier, Robert Ruffin. *Original and Miscellaneous Essays*. Richmond: T. H. White, 1829.

———. *A Publication by R. R. Collier, the Occasion Being Made for It by the Circulation of "Substance of Remarks" by T. S. Gholson*. Richmond, VA: R. R. Collier, 1847.

———. *Some Observations on the Law Affairs of Virginia*. Petersburg, VA: N.p., 1847.

Collier v. Robertson. Circuit Superior Court of Law and Chancery, Second District of Virginia, July 1844.

Collins, Donald E. *The Death and Resurrection of Jefferson Davis*. Lanham, Md.: Rowman and Littlefield, 2005.

Collins, Steven G. "System, Organization, and Agricultural Reform in the Antebellum South, 1840–1860." *Journal of Southern History* 75 (2001): 1–27.

Columbia Telescope [S.C.].

Combined History of Randolph, Monroe, and Perry Counties, Illinois. Philadelphia: J. L. McDonough, 1883.

Compendium of the Common Law in Force in Kentucky. Lexington, Ky.: William Gibbs Hunt, 1822.

Congress, U.S. "Senate Journal."

Cook, James W. *The Arts of Deception: Playing with Fraud in the Age of Barnum*. Cambridge, Mass.: Harvard University Press, 2001.

Cooke, John Esten. *Wearing of the Gray: Being Personal Portraits, Scenes, and Adventures of the War.* New York: E. B. Treat, 1867.

Coontz, Stephanie. *Marriage, a History: From Obedience to Intimacy; or, How Love Conquered Marriage.* New York: Viking, 2005.

Cooper, Thomas. *The Statutes at Large of South Carolina.* Vol. 5. Columbia, S.C.: A. S. Johnston, 1839.

Corsi, Jerome. *The Obama Nation: Leftist Politics and the Cult of Personality.* New York: Threshold Editions, 2008.

Coulter, Ann. *Slander: Liberal Lies about the American Right.* New York: Crown, 2002.

Coulter, E. Merton. *College Life in the Old South.* New York: Macmillan, 1928.

Council of Biblical Manhood and Womanhood News. 1995–97.

Court Records, Culpeper County, Minute Book, Library of Virginia, Richmond.

Courtwright, David T. *No Right Turn: Conservative Politics in Liberal America.* Cambridge, Mass.: Harvard University Press, 2010.

Cowley, Malcolm. "Going with the Wind," *New Republic* 88 (September 16, 1936): 161–63.

Cramer, Clayton E. *Concealed Weapon Laws of the Early Republic.* Westport, Conn.: Greenwood, 1999.

Crespino, Joseph. *In Search of Another Country: Mississippi and the Conservative Counterrevolution.* Princeton, N.J.: Princeton University Press, 2007.

Critchlow, Donald T. *The Conservative Ascendancy: How the GOP Right Made Political History.* 2nd ed. Lawrence: University Press of Kansas, 2011.

Cronon, William. *Nature's Metropolis: Chicago and the Great West.* New York: W. W. Norton, 1991.

Crouthamel, James L. *James Watson Webb: A Biography.* Middletown, Conn.: Wesleyan University Press, 1969.

Crowther, Edward R. "'According to Scripture': Antebellum Southern Baptists and the Use of Biblical Texts." *American Baptist Quarterly* 14 (September 1995): 288–305.

———. "Holy Honor: Sacred and Secular in the Old South." *Journal of Southern History* 58 (November 1992): 619–36.

———. *Southern Evangelicals and the Coming of the Civil War.* Lewiston, N.Y.: Edward Mellen, 2000.

Curtis, Christopher Michael. "Codification in Virginia: Conway Robinson, John Mercer Patton and the Politics of Law Reform." *Virginia Magazine of History and Biography* 117 (2009): 140–80.

———. *Jefferson's Freeholders and the Politics of Ownership in the Old Dominion.* New York: Cambridge University Press, 2012.

Daily Alabama Journal [Montgomery, Ala.].

Daily Chronicle and Sentinel [Augusta, Ga.].

Daily Cleveland Herald [Ohio].

Daily Confederation [Montgomery, Ala.].

Daily Evening Bulletin [San Francisco, Calif.].

Daily Ohio Statesman [Columbus, Ohio].

Daily South Carolinian [Columbia, S.C.].

Daniels, Jonathan. "Zero Times Zero Equals Zero." *Publishers' Weekly* 134 (October 15, 1938): 1430–32.

"Danvers Statement." http://cbmw.org/core-beliefs/ (accessed March 30, 2013).

Davega, A. H. *Correspondence between Dr. A. H. Davega and Col. Wm. Johnston,* South Caroliniana Library, University of South Carolina, Columbia.

Davies, Robertson. *The Mirror of Nature*. Toronto: University of Toronto Press, 1983.

Davis, Rebecca Harding. *Bits of Gossip*. Boston: Houghton, Mifflin, 1904.

Dawson, William C. *Compilation of the Laws of the State of Georgia*. Milledgeville, GA: Grantland and Orme, 1831.

"Death of Mr. Cilley—Duel." U.S. House Report No. 825, *Congressional Globe*, 25th Congress, 2nd Session, 1838: 1–182.

de Certeau, Michel. *The Practice of Everyday Life*. Berkeley: University of California Press, 1984.

DeCredico, Mary A. *Mary Boykin Chesnut: A Confederate Woman's Life*. Lanham: Rowman and Littlefield, 1998.

Dede, Marie. "Marie Laveau." Interview by McKinney. Louisiana Writers' Project, box 3-C-1, folder 25, 4. Federal Writers Project, 1935–43. Cammie G. Henry Research Center, Watson Memorial Library, Northwestern State University of Louisiana.

Denton Journal [Md.].

Desch Obi, T. J. *Fighting for Honor: The History of African Martial Art Traditions in the Atlantic World*. Columbia: University of South Carolina Press, 2008.

Deseret News [Salt Lake City, Utah].

DeVoto, Bernard. "Snow White and the Seven Dreads." *Harper's* 177 (November 1938): 669–72.

Deyle, Steven. *Carry Me Back: The Domestic Slave Trade in American Life*. New York: Oxford University Press, 2005.

Diedrick, James. "Dialogical History in *Ivanhoe*." In *Scott in Carnival: Selected Papers from the Fourth International Scott Conference*, edited by J. H. Alexander and David Hewitt, 280–93. Aberdeen: Association for Scottish Literary Studies, 1993.

Dillingham, William B. *Melville's Short Fiction, 1853–1856*. Athens: University of Georgia Press, 2008.

Domenech, Benjamin. "The Truth about Mass Shootings and Gun Control." *Commentary*, February 2013, 25–29.

Donald, David Herbert. *Charles Sumner and the Coming of the Civil War*. Chicago: University of Chicago Press, 1961.

Dorsey, Bruce. *Reforming Men and Women: Gender in the Antebellum City*. Ithaca, N.Y.: Cornell University Press, 2002.

Dorsey, Clement. *The General Public Statutory Law and Public Local Law of the State of Maryland*. Baltimore: J. D. Troy, 1840.

Douthat, Ross, and Reihan Salam. *Grand New Party: How Republicans Can Win the Working Class and Save the American Dream*. New York: Doubleday, 2008.

Dowland, Seth. "'Family Values' and the Formation of a Christian Right Agenda." *Church History* 78 (September 2009): 606–31.

———. "A New Kind of Patriarchy: Inerrancy and Masculinity in the Southern Baptist Convention." In *Southern Masculinity: New Perspectives on Manhood in the South Since Reconstruction*, edited by Craig Thompson Friend, 246–68. Athens: University of Georgia Press, 2009.

Doyle, William. *Aristocracy and Its Enemies in the Age of Revolution*. New York: Oxford Univeristy Press, 2009.

———. *Venality: The Sale of Offices in Eighteenth-Century France*. New York: Oxford University Press, 1997.

Drinkwater, L. Ray. "Honor and Student Misconduct in Southern Antebellum Colleges." *Southern Humanities Review* 27 (Fall 1993): 323–44.

D'Souza, Dinesh. *Letters to a Young Conservative*. New York: Basic, 2002.

Du Bois, William Edward Burghardt. *The Souls of Black Folk.* In *The Oxford W. E. B. Du Bois Reader,* ed. Eric J. Sundquist. Oxford: Oxford University Press, 1996.

Duck, Leigh Ann. *The Nation's Region: Southern Modernism, Segregation, and U.S. Nationalism.* Athens: University of Georgia Press, 2006.

Duer, John. *The Revised Statutes of the State of New-York.* Albany, N.Y.: Packard and Van Benthuysen, 1829.

Duncan, Ian. "Scott's Romance of Empire: *The Tales of the Crusaders.*" *Scott in Carnival: Selected Papers from the Fourth International Scott Conference,* edited by J. H. Alexander and David Hewitt, 370–79. Aberdeen: Association for Scottish Literary Studies, 1993.

DuPont, Carolyn Renee. *Mississippi Praying: Southern White Evangelicals and the Civil Rights Movement, 1945–1975.* New York: New York University Press, 2013.

Eagles, Charles W. *The Price of Defiance: James Meredith and the Integration of Ole Miss.* Chapel Hill: University of North Carolina Press, 2009.

Eastlake, Charles. *A History of Gothic Revival.* London: Longmans, Green, 1872.

Eaton, Margaret. *The Autobiography of Peggy Eaton.* With a preface by Charles F. Deems. New York: Charles Scribner's Sons, 1932.

Edgar, Walter B., ed. *Biographical Directory of the South Carolina House of Representatives.* Vol. 1, *Session Lists 1692–1973.* Columbia: University of South Carolina Press, 1974.

Edgefield Advertiser [S.C.].

Edmund DeBerry Covington Diary, Southern Historical Collection, Manuscripts Department, University of North Carolina at Chapel Hill.

Edwards, David. "O'Reilly: Minorities and Women Voting Obama Because They 'Want Stuff.'" *Raw Story,* November 6, 2012. http://www.rawstory.com/rs/2012/11/06/oreilly-minorities-and-women-voting-Obama-because-they-want-stuff/ (accessed August 9, 2013).

Edwards, Laura F. *The People and Their Peace: Legal Culture and the Transformation of Inequality in the Post-Revolutionary South.* Chapel Hill: University of North Carolina Press, 2009.

Elder, Robert. "A Twice Sacred Circle: Women, Evangelicalism, and Honor in the Deep South, 1784–1860." *Journal of Southern History* 78, no. 3 (August 2012): 579–614.

Ellis, Christopher, and James A. Stimson. *Ideology in America.* New York: Cambridge University Press, 2012.

Estes, Steve. "A Question of Honor: Masculinity and Massive Resistance to Integration." In *White Masculinity in the Recent South,* edited by Trent Watts, 99–120. Baton Rouge: Louisiana State University Press, 2008.

Etcheson, Nicole. "Manliness and the Political Culture of the Old Northwest, 1790–1860." *Journal of the Early Republic* 15 (Spring, 1995): 60–77.

Euprhadian Society Records, South Caroliniana Collection, University of South Carolina, Columbia.

Eustace, Nicole. *Passion Is the Gale: Emotion, Power, and the Coming of the American Revolution.* Chapel Hill: University of North Carolina Press, 2008.

Executive Papers, James Patton Preston, Thomas Mann Randolph, William B. Giles, John Floyd, *Exrs. of Thomas F. Hawthornes v. Bristol, Collier, and Hall.* 047. Circuit Superior Court of Law and Chancery, Second District of Virginia, 1846.

Eyal, Yonatan. *The Young America Movement and the Transformation of the Democratic Party, 1828–1861.* New York: Cambridge University Press, 2007.

Faust, Drew Gilpin. *James Henry Hammond and the Old South: A Design for Mastery.* Baton Rouge: Louisiana State University Press, 1982.

———. "The Rhetoric and Ritual of Agriculture in Antebellum South Carolina." *Journal of Southern History* 45 (1979): 541–68.

Fayetteville Observer [N.C.].

Ferguson, Robert A. *Law and Letters in American Culture.* Cambridge, Mass.: Harvard University Press, 1984.

Ferslew, W. Eugene. *Directory of the City of Charleston, to Which is Added a Business Directory, 1860.* Volume I. Savannah, GA: John M. Cooper & Co., book and job printers, 1860.

Fett, Sharla. *Working Cures: Healing, Health, and Power on Southern Slave Plantations.* Chapel Hill: University of North Carolina Press, 2002.

Fitzsimons, Mabel Trott. *Hot Words and Hair Triggers.* Unpublished typescript, available on microfiche. Original in the collections of the Charleston Library Society, Charleston, SC.

Fleming, W. L., ed. *The South in the Building of the Nation.* Vol. 11. Richmond, VA: Southern Historical Publication Society, 1909.

Florida Statute §776.013. http://www.state.fl.us/statutes/indes.cfm?App_mode=Display_Statute&URL=0700-0799/Sections/0776.html (accessed August 9, 2013).

Fogel, Robert William, and Stanley L. Engerman. *Time on the Cross: The Economics of American Negro Slavery.* 1974. Reprint, New York: W. W. Norton, 1995.

Foley, Elizabeth Price. *The Tea Party: Three Principles.* New York: Cambridge University Press, 2012.

Foote, Lorien. *The Gentlemen and the Roughs: Violence, Honor, and Manhood in the Union Army.* New York: New York University Press, 2010.

Ford, Lacy K. *Deliver Us from Evil: The Slavery Question in the Old South.* New York: Oxford University Press, 2009.

———. *Origins of Southern Radicalism: The South Carolina Upcountry, 1800–1860.* New York: Oxford University Press, 1988.

Formisano, Ronald P. *The Tea Party: A Brief History.* Baltimore: Johns Hopkins University Press, 2012.

Forret, Jeff. "Conflict and the 'Slave Community': Violence among Slaves in Upcountry South Carolina." *Journal of Southern History* 74 (August 2008): 551–88.

———. "Slave–Poor White Violence in the Antebellum Carolinas." *North Carolina Historical Review* 81 (April 2004): 139–67.

———. "Slaves, Sex and Sin: Adultery, Forced Separation and Baptist Church Discipline in Middle Georgia." *Slavery and Abolition* 33 (September 2012): 337–58.

Foucault, Michel. *Discipline and Punish: The Birth of the Prison.* 1975. Translated by Alan Sheridan. New York: Vintage, 1979.

Fountain, Daniel L. *Slavery, Civil War, and Salvation: African American Slaves and Christianity, 1830–1870.* Baton Rouge: Louisiana State University Press, 2010.

Fox, James Alan, and Marianne W. Zawitz. "Homicide Trends in the United States." http://www.bjs.gov/index.cfm?ty=pbdetail&iid=966 (accessed December 27, 2013).

Fox-Genovese, Elizabeth. *Within the Plantation Household: Black and White Women of the Old South.* Chapel Hill: University of North Carolina Press, 1988.

Fox-Genovese, Elizabeth, and Eugene D. Genovese. *The Mind of the Master Class: History and Faith in the Southern Slaveholders' Worldview.* New York: Cambridge University Press, 2005.

———. *Slavery in White and Black: Class and Race in the Southern Slaveholders' New World Order.* Cambridge: Cambridge University Press, 2008.

Frances Jane Bestor Robertson Diary, *American Women's Dairies: Southern Women.* Microfilm.

Franklin, John Hope. "The North, the South, and the American Revolution." *Journal of American History* 62, no. 1 (1975): 5–23.

———. *Reconstruction after the Civil War.* 1961. Reprint, Chicago: University of Chicago Press, 2013.

Frantzen, Allen J. *Bloody Good: Chivalry, Sacrifice, and the Great War.* Chicago: University of Chicago Press, 2003.

Fraser, Rebecca J. *Courtship and Love among the Enslaved in North Carolina.* Jackson: University Press of Mississippi, 2007.

Fredrickson, George. *The Black Image in the White Mind: The Debate on Afro-American Character and Destiny, 1817–1914.* New York: Harper and Row, 1971.

Freehling, William W. *Prelude to Civil War: The Nullification Controversy in South Carolina, 1816–1836.* New York: Harper and Row, 1966.

———. *The Road to Disunion.* Vol. 2, *Secessionists Triumphant, 1854–1861.* New York: Oxford University Press, 2007.

———. "Spoilsmen and Interests in the Thought and Career of John C. Calhoun." *Journal of American History* 52 (1965): 25–42.

Freeman, Joanne B. *Affairs of Honor: National Politics in the New Republic.* New Haven, Conn.: Yale University Press, 2001.

French, Samuel Bassett. "Biographical Sketches, Entry 531." *Library of Virginia Digital Archives.* http://image.lva.virginia.gov/cgi-bin/GetBF.pl?dir=0061/C0039&card=28 (accessed March 18, 2014).

Frevert, Ute. *Emotions in History: Lost and Found.* Budapest: Central European University Press, 2011.

———. *Men of Honour: A Social and Cultural History of the Duel.* Cambridge, UK: Polity, 1995.

Friend, Craig Thompson. "Belles, Benefactors, and the Blacksmith's Son: Cyrus Stuart and the Enigma of Southern Gentlemanliness." In *Southern Manhood: Perspectives on Masculinity in the Old South,* edited by Craig Thompson Friend and Lorri Glover. Athens: University of Georgia Press, 2004, 92–112.

Friend, Craig Thompson, and Lorri Glover, eds. *Southern Manhood: Perspectives on Masculinity in the Old South.* Athens: University of Georgia Press, 2004.

Funeral Oration Delivered at the Capitol in Washington over the Body of Hon. Jonathan Cilley, with a Full Account of the Late Duel, Comprising Many Facts Never before Published. New York: Wiley and Putnam, 1838.

Gallagher, Gary W. *Becoming Confederates: Paths to a New National Loyalty.* Athens: University of Georgia Press, 2013.

———. *Causes Won, Lost, and Forgotten: How Hollywood and Popular Art Shape What We Know about the Civil War.* Chapel Hill: University of North Carolina Press, 2008.

———. *The Confederate War: How Popular Will, Nationalism, and Military Strategy Could Not Stave Off Defeat.* Cambridge, Mass.: Harvard University Press, 1997.

Gallagher, Michael. *That's No Angry Mob, That's My Mom: Team Obama's Assault on Tea-Party, Talk-Radio Americans.* Washington, D.C.: Regnery, 2010.

Gamble, Thomas. *Savannah Duels and Duellists, 1733–1877.* Savannah, Ga.: Review Publishing and Printing, 1923. Reprint, Savannah, Ga.: Oglethorpe, 1997.

Garnett, James M. *Lectures on Female Education, Comprising the First and Second Series of a Course Delivered to Mrs. Garnett's Pupils, at Elm-wood, Essex County, Virginia by James M. Garnett, to Which Is Annexed, The Gossip's Manual.* Richmond, Va.: Thomas W. White, 1825.

Garrett, William. *Reminiscences of Public Men in Alabama, for Thirty Years* (Atlanta: Plantation Publishing, 1872.

Gay, Peter. *The Cultivation of Hatred.* New York: W. W. Norton, 1993.

Geertz, Clifford. *The Interpretation of Cultures: Selected Essays.* New York: Basic Books, 1973.

General Faculty and Faculty Council of the University of North Carolina at Chapel Hill Records. University Archives, Manuscripts Department, Wilson Library, University of North Carolina at Chapel Hill.

General Statutes of the Commonwealth of Massachusetts. Boston: William White, 1860.

Genovese, Eugene D. *The Political Economy of Slavery: Studies in the Economy and Society of the Slave South.* 2nd ed. Boston: Wesleyan University Press, 1989.

———. *Roll, Jordan, Roll: The World the Slaves Made.* New York: Random House, 1974.

———. *The Slaveholder's Dilemma: Freedom and Progress in Southern Conservative Thought, 1820–1860.* Columbia: University of South Carolina Press, 1992.

George N. Thompson Diary. Southern Historical Collection, Manuscripts Department, University of North Carolina at Chapel Hill.

Georgini, Sara. "The Angel and the Animal." In *William Gilmore Simms's Unfinished Civil War: Consequences for a Southern Man of Letters,* edited by David Moltke-Hansen, 212–23. Columbia: University of South Carolina Press, 2013.

Gholson, Thomas S. *A Notice of a Late Pamphlet Issued by R. R. Collier and a Brief Examination of his Life and Character.* Richmond, VA: 1847.

———. *Substance of Remarks Delivered by Thomas S. Gholson.* Richmond, VA: 1847.

Gibson, Greg. *The Gospel Centered Husband.* http://cbmw.org/men/manhood/the-gospel-centered-husband (accessed December 10, 2013).

———. *Reformational Manhood: Creating a Culture of Gospel-Centered Warriors.* Mountain Home, Ariz.: BorderStone, 2012.

Gilmore, David D. *Manhood in the Making: Cultural Concepts of Masculinity.* New Haven, Conn.: Yale University Press, 1990.

Gingrich, Newt. *To Save America: Stopping Obama's Secular-Socialist Machine.* Washington, D.C.: Regnery, 2010.

Ginzburg, Carlo. "Clues: Morelli, Freud, and Sherlock Holmes." In *The Sign of Three: Dupin, Holmes, Pierce,* edited by Umberto Eco and Thomas A. Sebeok, 81–118. Bloomington: Indiana University Press, 1983.

Girouard, Mark. *The Return to Camelot: Chivalry and the English Gentleman.* New Haven, Conn.: Yale University Press, 1981.

Glasgow, Ellen. "Heroes and Monsters." *Saturday Review of Literature* 12 (May 4, 1935): 3–4.

"Glenn Beck: 'Obama Has a Deep-Seated Hatred for White People.'" July 28, 2009. http://www.youtube.com/watch?=MIZDnpPafaA (accessed August 9, 2013).

Glover, Lorri. *Southern Sons: Becoming Men in the New Nation.* Baltimore: Johns Hopkins University Press, 2007.

Goldberg, Jeffrey. "The Case for More Guns (and More Gun Control)." *Atlantic,* December 2012, 68–78.

Goldberg, Jonah, ed. *Proud to Be Right: Voices of the Next Conservative Generation.* New York: Harper, 2010.

Goodman, Robert F., and Aaron Ben-Ze'ev, eds. *Good Gossip.* Lawrence: University Press of Kansas, 1994.

"The Good Merchant—William Parsons." *Merchants' Magazine and Commercial Review* 1, no. 2 (August 1839): 137–42.

Gorn, Elliott J. "'Gouge and Bite, Pull Hair and Scratch': The Social Significance of Fighting in the Southern Backcountry." *American Historical Review* 90, no. 1 (February 1985): 18–43.

Graglia, Lino A. "Constitutional Law without the Constitution: The Supreme Court's Remaking of America." In *"A Country I Do Not Recognize": The Legal Assault on American Values,* edited by Robert Bork, 1–55. Stanford, CA: Hoover Institution Press, 2005.

Graham, Sandra Lauderdale. "Honor among Slaves." In *The Faces of Honor: Sex, Shame, and Violence in Colonial Latin America,* edited by Lyman L. Johnson and Sonya Lipsett-Rivera, 201–28. Albuquerque: University of New Mexico Press, 1998.

Gray, Lewis C. *History of Agriculture in the Southern States to 1860.* Vol. 2. Washington, D.C.: Carnegie Institution of Washington, 1933.

Gray, Richard. *Southern Aberrations: Writes of the American South and the Problems of Regionalism.* Baton Rouge: Louisiana State University Press, 2000.

Grayson, William J. *The Hireling and the Slave, Chicora, and Other Poems.* Charleston: J. J. McCarter, 1856.

Gray White, Deborah. *Ar'n't I a Woman? Female Slaves in the Plantation South.* Rev. ed. New York: Norton, 1999.

Green, Jennifer R. *Military Education and the Emerging Middle Class in the Old South.* New York: Cambridge University Press, 2008.

Green, Joshua. "Why Ted Cruz Might *Still* Try to Force a Default." *Bloomberg Businessweek,* October 16, 2003. http://www.businessweek.com/articles/2013-10-16/why-ted-cruz-might-still-try-to-force-a-default (accessed October 21, 2013).

Greenberg, Kenneth S. *Honor and Slavery: Lies, Duels, Noses, Masks, Dressing as a Woman, Gifts, Strangers, Humanitarianism, Death, Slave Rebellions, the Pro-slavery Argument, Baseball, Hunting, and Gambling in the Old South.* Princeton, N.J.: Princeton University Press, 1996.

———. *Masters and Statesmen: The Political Culture of American Slavery.* Baltimore: Johns Hopkins University Press, 1985.

Greenville Mountaineer [S.C.].

Greven, David. "Fear of *Fanshawe:* Intransigence, Desire, and Scholarship in Hawthorne's First Published Novel." *Nathaniel Hawthorne Review* 29, no. 2 (2003): 1–37.

Grice, Warren. *The Georgia Bench and Bar.* Vol. 1, *The Development of Georgia's Judicial System.* Macon, Ga.: J. W. Burke, 1931.

Gross, Ariela J. *Double Character: Slavery and Mastery in the Antebellum Southern Courtroom.* Princeton, N.J.: Princeton University Press, 2000.

Gross, Theodore L. *Thomas Nelson Page.* New York: Twayne, 1967.

Grudem, Wayne. "Is Evangelical Feminism the New Path to Liberalism: Some Disturbing Warning Signs." *Journal of Biblical Manhood and Womanhood* 9, no. 1 (Spring 2004): 35–84.

Grund, Francis J. *Aristocracy in America: From the Sketch-Book of a German Nobleman.* New York: Harper, 1959.

Guilds, John Caldwell. *Simms: A Literary Life.* Fayetteville: University of Arkansas Press, 1992.

Gutman, Herbert G. *The Black Family in Slavery and Freedom, 1750–1925.* New York: Pantheon Books, 1976.

Hagstette, Todd. "Dueling and Identity: Constructions of Honor Violence in Nineteenth-Century Southern Letters." Ph.D. diss., University of South Carolina, 2010.

———. "Private vs. Public Honor in Wartime South Carolina: William Gilmore Simms in Lecture, Letter, and History." In *William Gilmore Simms's Unfinished Civil War: Consequences for a Southern Man of Letters*, edited by David Moltke-Hansen, 48–67. Columbia: University of South Carolina Press, 2013.

Hahn, Steven. "Honor and Patriarchy in the Old South." *American Quarterly* 36 (Spring 1984): 145–53.

Hale, Grace Elizabeth. *A Nation of Outsiders: How the White Middle Class Fell in Love with Rebellion in Postwar America*. New York: Oxford University Press, 2011.

Haliburton, Thomas C. *The Clockmaker; or, The Sayings and Doings of Samuel Slick of Slickville*. Halifax, Nova Scotia: Joseph Howe, 1836.

Hall, Kermit. "The Judiciary on Trial: State Constitutional Reform and the Rise of an Elected Judiciary, 1846–1860." *Historian* 44 (1983): 337–54.

Hallam, Henry. *A View of the State of Europe during the Middle Ages*. 2 vols. London: John Murray, 1818.

Halttunen, Karen. *Confidence Men and Painted Women: A Study of Middle-Class Culture in America, 1830–1870*. New Haven, Conn.: Yale University Press, 1982.

Hampton, Ann Fripp, ed. *A Divided Heart: Letters of Sally Baxter Hampton 1853–1862*. Columbia, S.C.: Phantom, 1994.

Handy, M. P. "Witchcraft among the Negroes." *Appleton's Journal: A Magazine of General Literature* 8 (1872): 666–67.

Hannah-Barksdale Family Papers. Library of Virginia, Richmond.

Hannity. Fox News, February 20, 2013.

Harding, Thomas S. *College Literary Societies: Their Contribution to Higher Education in the United States, 1815–1876*. New York: Pageant, 1971.

Hardwig, Bill. *Upon Provincialism: Southern Literature and National Periodical Culture, 1870–1900*. Charlottesville: University of Virginia Press, 2013.

Hardy, Stella Pickett. *Colonial Families of the Southern States of America*. New York: Tobias A. Wright, 1911.

Harland, Marion. *Marion Harland's Autobiography: The Story of a Long Life*. New York: Harper and Brothers, 1910.

Harris, Joel Chandler. *The Complete Tales of Uncle Remus*. Compiled by Richard Chase. With illustrations by Arthur Burdette Frost, Frederick Stuart Church, J. M. Condé, Edward Windsor Kemble, and William Holbrook Beard. Boston: Houghton Mifflin, 1955.

Hawkins, Wallace. *The Case of John C. Watrous, United States Judge for Texas: A Political Story of High Crimes and Misdemeanors*. Dallas: University Press, 1950.

Hawthorne, Julian. *Nathaniel Hawthorne and His Wife: A Biography*. 2 vols. Boston: James R. Osgood, 1885.

Hawthorne, Nathaniel. *The American Notebooks*. Edited by Claude M. Simpson. Columbus: Ohio State University Press, 1972.

———. "Biographical Sketch of Jonathan Cilley." *United States Magazine and Democratic Revew* 3 (September 1838): 66–76.

———. *Fanshawe*. In *The Blithedale Romance* and *Fanshawe*. Edited by William Charvat et al., 331–460. Columbus: Ohio State University Press, 1964.

———. *The House of the Seven Gables*. Edited by Robert S. Levine. New York: W. W. Norton, 2006.

Hawthorne, Nathaniel. *The Letters, 1813–1843*. Edited by Thomas Woodson et al. Columbus: Ohio State University Press, 1984.

———. *The Letters, 1843–1853*. Edited by Thomas Woodson et al. Columbus: Ohio State University Press, 1985.

———. *Miscellaneous Prose and Verse*. Edited by Thomas Woodson et al. Columbus: Ohio State University Press, 1994.

———. *The Scarlet Letter*. Edited by Nina Baym. New York: Penguin Books, 1983.

———. *Selected Tales and Sketches*. Edited by Michael J. Colacurcio. New York: Penguin Books, 1987.

Hay, Melba Porter. "Compromiser or Conspirator? Henry Clay and the Graves-Cilley Duel." In *A Mythic Land Apart: Reassessing Southerners and Their History*, edited by John David Smith and Thomas H. Appleton Jr., 57–79. Westport, Conn.: Greenwood, 1997.

Hayne, Isaac W. *Anniversary Address, on the Formation of Individual Character, and Causes Which Influence It; Delivered before the Erosophic Society of the University of Alabama, December 12, 1840*. Columbia, SC: A. S. Johnson, 1841.

Haynes, Stephen R. *Noah's Curse: The Biblical Justification of American Slavery*. New York: Oxford University Press, 2002.

Hazzard-Donald, Katrina. *Mojo Workin': The Old African American Hoodoo System*. Urbana: University of Illinois Press, 2013.

Headlee, Thomas Jefferson, Jr. *The Virginia State Court System, 1776–1870*. Richmond, VA: Virginia State Library, 1969.

Hemphill, C. Dallett. *Bowing to Necessity: A History of Manners in America, 1620–1860*. New York: Oxford University Press, 1999.

———. "Class, Gender, and the Regulation of Emotional Expression in Revolutionary Era Conduct Literature." In *An Emotional History of the United States*, edited by Peter N. Stearns and Jan Lewis, 33–51. New York: New York University Press, 1998.

Hemphill, Katie M. "'Driven to the Commission of This Crime': Women and Infanticide in Baltimore, 1835–1860." *Journal of the Early Republic* 32 (Fall 2012): 437–61.

Hendrix, Michael Patrick. *Down and Dirty: Archeology of the South Carolina Lowcountry*. Charleston, S.C.: History Press, 2006.

Henrico County, Minute Books, Library of Virginia, Richmond.

Henry, Patrick. *The Letters of Patrick Henry*. In *Official Letters of the Government of the State of Virginia*. Vol. 1. Richmond: Virginia State Library, 1926.

Herrington, Philip Mills. "Agricultural and Architectural Reform in the Antebellum South: Fruitland at Augusta, Georgia." *Journal of Southern History* 78 (2012): 855–86.

Hessinger, Rodney. *Seduced, Abandoned, and Reborn: Visions of Youth in Middle-Class America, 1780–1850*. Philadelphia: University of Pennsylvania Press, 2005.

Hettle, Wallace. *The Peculiar Democracy: Southern Democrats in Peace and Civil War*. Athens: University of Georgia Press, 2001.

Heyrman, Christine Leigh. *Southern Cross: The Beginnings of the Bible Belt*. Chapel Hill: University of North Carolina Press, 1988.

[Hines, David T.]. *The Life, Adventures, and Opinions of David Theo. Hines: Of South Carolina; Master of Arts, and Sometimes, Doctor of Medicine . . . in a Series of Letters to His Friends*. New York: Bradley and Clarke, 1840.

Historical Census Browser, University of Virginia, Geospatial and Statistical Data Center. 2004. http://fisher.lib.virginia.edu/collections/stats/histcensus/index.html (Accessed January 17, 2012).

History of Menard and Mason Counties, Illinois. Chicago: O. L. Baskin, 1879.

History of St. Clair County, Illinois: With Illustrations Descriptive of Its Scenery and Biographical Sketches of Some of Its Prominent Men and Pioneers. Philadelphia: Brink, McDonough, 1881.

Hobsbawm, Eric. *The Age of Revolution, 1789–1848.* New York: Vintage Books, 1996.

Hodes, Martha. *White Women, Black Men: Illicit Sex in the Nineteenth-Century South.* New Haven, Conn.: Yale University Press, 1997.

Hoffer, Williamjames Hull. *The Caning of Charles Sumner: Honor, Idealism, and the Origins of the Civil War.* Baltimore: Johns Hopkins University Press, 2010.

Hoganson, Kristin L. *Fighting for American Manhood: How Gender Politics Provoked the Spanish-American and Philippine-American Wars.* Yale Historical Publications. New Haven, Conn.: Yale University Press, 1998.

Holland, Barbara. *Gentlemen's Blood: A History of Dueling from Swords at Dawn to Pistols at Dusk.* New York: Bloomsburg, 2003.

Holway, Richard. *Becoming Achilles: Child Sacrifice, War, and Misrule in the Iliad and Beyond.* New York: Lexington Books, 2011.

Honderich, Ted. *Conservatism: Burke, Nozick, Bush, Blair?* London: Pluto, 2005.

Hooper, Johnson Jones. Adventures of Captain Simon Suggs, Late of the Tallapoosa Volunteers: Together with "Taking the Census" and Other Alabama Sketches. Reprinted, with an introduction by Johanna Nicol Shields. Tuscaloosa: University of Alabama Press, 1993.

Hooper, William. "The Discipline of the Heart, to Be Connected with the Culture of the Mind: A Discourse on Education, Delivered to the Students of the College, at Chapel Hill, North Carolina, August 22, 1830, and Published by Their Request." New York: Sleight and Robinson, 1830.

Horlick, Allan Stanley. *Country Boys and Merchant Princes: The Social Control of Young Men in New York.* Lewisburg, PA: Bucknell University Press, 1975.

Horowitz, Helen Lefkowitz. *Campus Life: Undergraduate Cultures from the End of the Eighteenth Century to the Present.* New York: Alfred A. Knopf, 1987.

———. *Rereading Sex: Battles over Sexual Knowledge and Suppression in Nineteenth-Century America.* New York: Vintage Books, 2003.

Horwitz, Robert B. *America's Right: Anti-establishment Conservatism from Goldwater to the Tea Party.* Malden, Mass.: Polity, 2013.

Houck, Louis. *History of Missouri from the Earliest Explorations and Settlements until the Admission of the State into the Union.* Vol. 3. Chicago: R. R. Donnelley and Sons, 1908.

Howard, A. E. Dick. *Commentaries on the Constitution of Virginia.* 2 vols. Charlottesville: University Press of Virginia, 1974.

Howe, Daniel Walker. *Making the American Self: Jonathan Edwards to Abraham Lincoln.* Oxford: Oxford University Press, 1997.

Hubbell, Jay. *The South in American Literature: 1607–1900.* Durham, N.C.: Duke University Press, 1954.

Hughes, Louis. *Thirty Years a Slave: From Bondage to Freedom; The Institution of Slavery as Seen on the Plantation and in the Home of the Planter.* Milwaukee: South Side Printing, 1897. Reprint, Detroit: Negro History Press, n.d.

Hulbert, Archer. *The Ohio River: A Course of Empire.* New York: G. P. Putnam's Sons, 1906.

Hundley, Daniel R. *Social Relations in Our Southern States.* Edited by William J. Cooper Jr. 1860. Reprint, Baton Rouge: Louisiana State University Press, 1979.

Hunt, Alan, and Gary Wickham. *Foucault and Law: Towards a Sociology of Law and Governance.* London: Pluto, 1994.

Huntington, B. W. "Individuality: An Address, Delivered before the Philomathic Society of the University of Alabama; At Its Twelfth Anniversary." Tuscaloosa, Ala.: M. D. J. Slade, 1845.

Hurst, J. Willard. *The Growth of American Law: The Law Makers.* Boston: Little, Brown, 1950.

Hurston, Zora Neale. "Hoodoo in America." *Journal of American Folk-Lore* 44 (1931): 317–417.

———. *Mules and Men.* In *Hurston: Folklore Memoirs, and Other Writings,* edited by Cheryl A. Wall. New York: Library of America, 1995.

Hyatt, Harry Middleton. *Hoodoo-Conjuration-Witchcraft-Rootwork.* 5 vols. Memoirs of the Alma Egan Hyatt Foundation. Hannibal, Mo.: Western, 1970–78.

Hyde William, and Howard Louis Conard, eds. *Encyclopedia of the History of Missouri: A Compendium of History and Biography for Ready Reference.* Vol. 1. New York: Southern History, 1899.

Iliffe, John. *Honour in African History.* New York: Cambridge University Press, 2005.

Independent Chronicle [Pa.].

Ingraham, Laura. *The Obama Diaries.* New York: Threshold Editions, 2010.

Isaac, Rhys. *The Transformation of Virginia, 1740–1790.* Chapel Hill: Omohundro Institute of Early American History and Culture; University of North Carolina Press, 1999.

Isenberg, Nancy. *Fallen Founder: The Life of Aaron Burr.* New York: Viking, 2007.

Ishkanian, Judith Mitchell. "Religion and Honor at Chapel Hill: The College Odyssey of William Sidney Mullins, 1840–42." Ph.D. diss., University of California, Santa Barbara, 1993.

Jabour, Anya. "Male Friendship and Masculinity in the Early National South: William Wirt and His Friends." *Journal of the Early Republic* 20, no. 1 (2000): 83–111.

———. "Masculinity and Adolescence in Antebellum America: Robert Wirt at West Point, 1820–1821." *Journal of Family History* 23 (October 1998): 393–416.

Jackson, Leon. "Jedidiah Morse and the Transformation of Print Culture in New England, 1784–1826." *Early American Literature* 34 (1999): 2–31.

———. "The Rights of Man and the Rites of Youth." In *The American College in the Nineteenth Century,* edited by Roger L. Geiger, 46–79. Nashville, Tenn.: Vanderbilt University Press, 2000.

Jacobs, Harriet A. *Incidents in the Life of a Slave Girl Written by Herself.* Edited by Jean Fagan Yellin. Cambridge, Mass.: Harvard University Press, 2000.

James, Edmund J. *The Territorial Records of Illinois.* Springfield, Ill.: Phillips Brothers, 1901.

James Henley Thornwell Papers, South Caroliniana Library, University of South Carolina, Columbia.

James Henry Hammond Papers. Library of Congress (LC).

James Lawrence Dusenbery Diary and Clipping, Southern Historical Collection, Manuscripts Department, University of North Carolina at Chapel Hill.

James McDowell, Joseph Johnson, Henry A. Wise, John Letcher. Executive papers. Library of Virginia, Richmond.

Jamison, David Flavel. *Bertrand du Guesclin et son époque.* Translated by J. Baissac. Paris: J. Rothschild, 1866.

———. *The Life and Times of Bertrand du Guesclin: A History of the Fourteenth Century.* 2 vols. Charleston: John Russell, 1864.

———. Review of Francois Guizot, *General History of Civilization in Europe. Southern Quarterly Review* 3, no. 5 (1843): 1–17.

Janney, Caroline E. *Remembering the Civil War: Reunion and the Limits of Reconciliation.* Chapel Hill: University of North Carolina Press, 2013.

Jefferson, Thomas. *Notes on the State of Virginia.* Chapel Hill: University of North Carolina Press, 1982.

[———]. *The Portable Thomas Jefferson.* Edited by Merrill D. Peterson. New York: Viking, 1975.

Jenkins, Howard, *Pennsylvania, Colonial and Federal: A History, 1842–1902.* Vol. 1. Philadelphia: Pennsylvania Historical Publishing Association, 1903.

Johnson, Bradley A. "'A Succinct and Formal Violence': The Function of the Duel in Southern Fiction, 1825–1950." Ph.D. diss., University of Connecticut, 2000.

Johnson, Lyman L. "Dangerous Words, Provocative Gestures, and Violent Acts." In *The Faces of Honor: Sex, Shame, and Violence in Colonial Latin America,* edited by Lyman L. Johnson and Sonya Lipsett-Rivera, 127–51. Albuquerque: University of New Mexico Press, 1998.

Johnson, Michael P. "Smothered Slave Infants: Were Slave Mothers at Fault?" *Journal of Southern History* 47 (November 1981): 493–520.

Johnson, Michael P., and James L. Roark. *Black Masters: A Free Family of Color in the Old South.* New York: W. W. Norton, 1984.

Johnson, Paul E. *A Shopkeeper's Millennium: Society and Revivals in Rochester, New York, 1815–1837.* New York: Hill and Wang, 1978.

Johnson, Rick. "A Noble and Dangerous Man." *Home Life* 63 (June 2009): 16–17.

Johnson, Walter. *River of Dark Dreams: Slavery and Empire in the Cotton Kingdom.* Cambridge, Mass.: Belknap Press of Harvard University Press, 2013.

Jones, Calvin. "An Address Delivered before the Philomatic Society at Its First Anniversary, February 9, 1833." Tuscaloosa, Ala.: Expositor Office, 1833.

Jones, Charles C. *The Religious Instruction of the Negroes: In the United States.* Savannah, Ga.: Thomas Purse, 1842.

Jones, David W. "Egalitarianism and Homosexuality: Connected or Autonomous Ideologies?" *Journal of Biblical Manhood and Womanhood* 8, no. 2 (Fall 2003): 5–19.

Jones, J. William. *Personal Reminiscences, Anecdotes, and Letters of Gen. Robert E. Lee.* New York: Appleton, 1875.

Jonesborough Whig [Tenn.].

Joseph Caldwell Papers, Southern Historical Collection, Manuscripts Department, University of North Carolina at Chapel Hill.

Journal of Biblical Manhood and Womanhood. 1998–2013.

Kabaservice, Geoffrey. *Rule and Ruin: The Downfall of Moderation and the Destruction of the Republican Party, from Eisenhower to the Tea Party.* New York: Oxford University Press, 2012.

Karcher, Carolyn L. *Shadow over the Promised Land: Slavery, Race, and Violence in Melville's America.* Baton Rouge: Louisiana State University Press, 1980.

Kasson, John F. *Rudeness and Civility: Manners in Nineteenth-Century Urban America.* New York: Hill and Wang, 1990.

Keetley, Dawn. "From Anger to Jealousy: Explaining Domestic Homicide in Antebellum America." *Journal of Social History* 42, no. 2 (2008): 269–97.

Kett, Joseph F. *Rites of Passage: Adolescence in America, 1790 to the Present.* New York: Basic Books, 1977.

Kibler, James Everett, Jr. Introduction to *Woodcraft; or, Hawks about the Dovecote,* by William Gilmore Simms, xxiii–xxxvi. Columbia: University of South Carolina Press, 2012. Originally published 1854.

Kibler, James Everett, Jr., and David Moltke-Hansen. "The Man of Letters as Critic." In *William Gilmore Simms's Selected Reviews on Literature and Civilization,* by William Gilmore Simms, 1–12. Columbia: University of South Carolina Press, 2014.

Kierner, Cynthia A. *Scandal at Bizarre: Rumor and Reputation in Jefferson's America.* Charlottesville: University of Virginia Press, 2004.

Kim, Janine Young. "The Rhetoric of Self-Defense." *Berkeley Journal of Criminal Law* 13 (2008): 261–305.

Kimmel, Michael S. *Manhood in America: A Cultural History.* New York: Free Press, 1996.

King, Wilma. "'Mad' Enough to Kill: Enslaved Women, Murder, and Southern Courts." *Journal of African American History* 92 (Winter 2007): 37–56.

———. *Stolen Childhood: Slave Youth in Nineteenth-Century America.* Bloomington: Indiana University Press, 1995.

Kinloch, George F. *To the Public [Correspondence concerning an Altercation between George F. Kinloch and George Rivers Walker], Charleston, SC 1878,* South Caroliniana Library, University of South Carolina, Columbia.

Kirk, Russell. *The Conservative Mind from Burke to Santayana.* 2nd rev. ed. Chicago: Regnery, 1953.

Knecht, R. J. "The Sword and the Pen: Blaise de Monluc and His *Commentaires.*" *Renaissance Studies* 9, no. 1 (1995): 104–18.

Knepper, George W., ed. *Travels in the Southland 1822–1823: The Journal of Lucius Verus Bierce.* Columbus: Ohio State University Press, 1966.

Krause, Sharon R. *Liberalism with Honor.* Cambridge, Mass.: Harvard University Press, 2002.

Kruse, Kevin. *White Flight and the Making of Modern Conservatism.* Princeton, N.J.: Princeton University Press, 2007.

Kuhlmann, Susan. *Knave, Fool, and Genius: The Confidence Man as He Appears in Nineteenth-Century American Fiction.* Chapel Hill: University of North Carolina Press, 1973.

Kuhn, Thomas S. *The Structure of Scientific Revolutions.* Chicago, IL: University of Chicago Press, 1996.

LaCroix, Alison L. "To Gain the Whole World and Lose His Own Soul: Nineteenth-Century American Dueling as Public Law and Private Code." *Hofstra Law Review* 33 (2004–5): 501–69.

A Lady of South Carolina. "Female Education: A Letter to the Editor." *The Orion, a Monthly Magazine of Literature and Art* 3, no. 2 (October 1843): 62.

Lamar, Lucius. *A Compilation of the Laws of the State of Georgia, Passed by the Legislature Since the Year 1810 to the Year 1819, Inclusive.* Augusta: T.S. Hannon, 1821.

Landers, Jane. "'In Consideration of Her Enormous Crime': Rape and Infanticide in Spanish St. Augustine." In *The Devil's Lane: Sex and Race in the Early South,* edited by Catherine Clinton and Michele Gillespie, 205–17. New York: Oxford University Press, 1997.

Landor, Walter Savage. *Count Julian: A Tragedy.* London: John Murray, 1812.

Larson, John Lauritz. *The Market Revolution in America: Liberty, Ambition, and the Eclipse of the Common Good.* Cambridge: Cambridge University Press, 2010.

Laws of the State of Mississippi: 1824–1838. Jackson, Miss.: 1838.

Laws of the State of New York Passed at the Twenty-Sixth Session of the Legislature Begun and Held at the City of Albany, the Twenty-Fifth Day of January, 1803. Albany, N.Y.: John Barber, 1803.

Laws of the State of New York. Albany, N.Y.: 1817, 1828.

Lee, Stephen D. "The First Step in the War." In *Battles and Leaders of the Civil War: Being for the Most Part Contributions by Union and Confederate Officers,* edited by Robert Underwood Johnson and Clarence Clough Buel, 74–81. New York: T. Yoseloff, 1956.

Le Goff, Jacques. *Time, Work, and Culture in the Middle Ages.* Chicago: University of Chicago Press, 1980.

Lenz, William E. *Fast Talk and Flush Times: The Confidence Man as a Literary Convention*. Columbia: University of Missouri Press, 1985.

Lerner, Gerda, ed. *Black Women in White America: A Documentary History*. New York: Pantheon, 1972.

Leverenz, David. *Honor Bound: Race and Shame in America*. New Brunswick: Rutgers University Press, 2012.

———. *Manhood and the American Renaissance*. Ithaca, N.Y.: Cornell University Press, 1989.

Levin, Mark R. *Ameritopia: The Unmaking of America*. New York: Threshold Editions, 2012.

Levine, Robert S. *Dislocating Race and Nation: Episodes in Nineteenth-Century American Literary Nationalism*. Chapel Hill: University of North Carolina Press, 2008.

Lewis, Charlene M. *Ladies and Gentlemen on Display: Planter Society at the Virginia Springs 1790–1860*. Charlottesville: University Press of Virginia, 2001.

Lewis, Henry W. "The Dugger-Dromgoole Duel." *North Carolina Historical Review* 34, no. 3 (1957): 327–45.

The Life and Adventures of Dr. David T. Hines: A Narrative of Thrilling Interest and Most Stirring Scenes of His Eventful Life. Charleston: J. B. Nixon, 1852.

The Life and Adventures of the Accomplished Forger and Swindler, Colonel Monroe Edwards. New York: H. Long, 1848.

Limbaugh, David. *Crimes against Liberty: An Indictment of President Barack Obama*. Washington, D.C.: Regnery, 2010.

Lindman, Janet Moore. "Acting the Manly Christian: White Evangelical Masculinity in Revolutionary Virginia." *William and Mary Quarterly* 57 (April 2000): 393–416.

Lippy, Charles H. *Do Real Men Pray? Images of the Christian Man and Male Spirituality in White Protestant America*. Knoxville: University of Tennessee Press, 2005.

Long, Carolyn Morrow. *Spiritual Merchants: Religion, Magic, and Commerce*. Knoxville: University of Tennessee Press, 2001.

Longstreet, A. B. *Georgia Scenes*. Introduction by James E. Kibler Jr. Nashville: J. S. Sanders, 1992.

Love, Harold. "Early Modern Print Culture: Assessing the Models." *Parergon* 20, no. 1 (2003): 45–64.

Loveland, Anne C. *Southern Evangelicals and the Social Order, 1800–1860*. Baton Rouge: Louisiana State University Press, 1980.

Lowe, Jessica K. "Guarding Republican Liberty: St. George Tucker and Judging in Federal Virginia." In *Signposts: New Directions in Southern Legal History*, edited by Sally E. Hadden and Patricia Hagler Minter, 111–33. Athens: University of Georgia Press, 2013.

Lucas, Mark. *The Southern Vision of Andrew Lytle*. Baton Rouge: Louisiana State University Press. 1986.

Lukasik, Christopher. *Discerning Characters: The Culture of Appearance in Early America*. Philadelphia: University of Pennsylvania Press, 2011.

Lystra, Karen. *Searching the Heart: Women, Men, and Romantic Love in Nineteenth-Century America*. New York: Oxford University Press, 1989.

Lytle, Andrew Nelson. "Life in the Cotton Belt." *New Republic* 67 (June 3, 1931): 77–78.

———. *The Long Night*. 1936. Reprinted, with an introduction by Frank L. Owsley Jr. Tuscaloosa: University of Alabama Press, 1988.

MacKethan, Lucinda. *The Dream of Arcady*. Baton Rouge: Louisiana State University Press, 1980.

[Mailles, Jacques de]. *The Right Joyous and Pleasant History of the Feasts, Gests, and Prowesses of the Chevalier Bayard, the Good Knight without Fear and without Reproach*. Translated by Sara Coleridge. 2 vols. London: John Murray, 1825.

Majewski, John D. *Modernizing a Slave Economy: the Economic Vision of the Confederate Nation.* Chapel Hill: University of North Carolina Press, 2009.

Malkin, Michelle. *Unhinged: Exposing Liberals Gone Wild.* Washington, D.C.: Regnery, 2005.

Mangan, J. A., and James Walvin. *Manliness and Morality: Middle-Class Masculinity in Britain and America, 1800–1940.* Manchester: Manchester University Press, 1987.

Mansfield, W. W. *A Digest of the Statutes of Arkansas.* Little Rock: Mitchell and Bettis, 1884.

Marsh, Fred T. "Mystery and Terror in Mr. Lytle's Novel of the South." *New York Times Book Review,* September 6, 1936, 9.

Marszalek, John F. *The Petticoat Affair: Manners, Mutiny, and Sex in Andrew Jackson's White House.* New York: Free Press, 1997.

Martin, Isabella D., and Myrta Lockett Avary. *A Diary from Dixie.* New York: D. Appleton, 1914.

Martin, Scott C. *Cultural Change and the Market Revolution in America, 1789–1860.* Lanham, Md.: Rowman and Littlefield, 2005.

Maxim, James R. *Belleville: The First One Hundred and Fifty Years.* Belleville, Ill.: Belleville Publishing, 1964.

Mayfield, John. *Counterfeit Gentlemen: Manhood and Humor in the Old South.* Gainesville: University Press of Florida, 2009.

———. "'The Soul of a Man!': William Gilmore Simms and the Myths of Southern Manhood." *Journal of the Early Republic* 15 (Fall 1995): 477–500.

McCardell, John. *The Idea of a Southern Nation: Southern Nationalists and Southern Nationalism, 1830–1860.* New York: W. W. Norton, 1979.

McCarty, Page. "Messrs. McCarty and Wise." *Campaign,* March 8, 1884, 2. http://virginiachronicle.com/cgi-bin/virginia?a=d&d=TC18840308.1.4# (accessed July 12, 2015).

McClay, Wilfred M. *The Masterless: Self and Society in Modern America.* Chapel Hill: University of North Carolina Press, 1994.

McConachie, Bruce. *Melodramatic Formations: American Theatre and Society, 1820–1870.* Iowa City: University of Iowa Press, 1992.

[McCord, David J.]. "Popular Education." *Southern Literary Journal and Monthly Magazine* 1 (1835): 177–86.

McCurry, Stephanie. *Masters of Small Worlds: Yeomen Households, Gender Relations, and the Political Culture of the Antebellum South Carolina Low Country.* New York: Oxford University Press, 1995.

McDonnell, Lawrence T. "Elizabethan Dreams, Victorian Nightmares: Antebellum South Carolina's Future through an English Looking Glass." In *The U.S. South and Europe: Transatlantic Relations in the Nineteenth and Twentieth Centuries,* edited by Cornelis A. van Minnen and Manfred Berg, 87–104. Lexington: University Press of Kentucky, 2013.

———. "Politics, Chess, Hats: The Microhistory of Disunion in Charleston, South Carolina." Ph.D. diss., University of Illinois at Urbana-Champaign, 2014.

McFall, Pearl Smith. *So Lives the Dream: History and Story of the Old Pendleton District, South Carolina, and the Establishment of Clemson College.* New York: Comet, 1953.

McKanna, Clare V. "Seeds of Destruction: Homicide, Race, and Justice in Omaha, 1880–1920." *Journal of American Ethnic History* 14 (1994): 65–90.

McLaren, John. *Dewigged, Bothered, and Bewildered: British Colonial Judges on Trial, 1800–1900.* Toronto: Osgoode Society, 2012.

McLaurin, Melton A. *Celia, a Slave.* Athens: University of Georgia Press, 1991. Reprint, New York: Perennial, 2002.

McNair, Glenn M. "Justice Bound: Aframericans, Crime, and Criminal Justice in Georgia, 1751–1865." Ph.D. diss., Emory University, 2001.

McNitt, V. V. *Chain of Error and the Mecklenburg Declaration of Independence: A New Study of Manuscripts, Their Use, Abuse, and Neglect.* New York: Hampden Hills, 1960.

McPherson, James. "Antebellum Southern Exceptionalism: A New Look at an Old Question." *Civil War History* 29 (1983): 230–44.

———. "Long-Legged Yankee Lies: The Southern Textbook Crusade." In *The Memory of the Civil War in American Culture,* edited by Alice Fahs and Joan Waugh, 64–78. Chapel Hill: University of North Carolina Press, 2004.

McReynolds, Edwin C. *Missouri: A History of the Crossroads State.* Norman: University of Oklahoma Press, 1975.

Mechanics' Free Press [Philadelphia, Pa.].

Meggs, Kale. *99 Nooses: Illinois Justice at the End of a Rope, 1779–1896.* Rockford, IL: Black Oak Media, 2012.

Meigs, Return J. and William F. Cooper. *The Code of Tennessee.* Nashville, Tenn.: E. G. Eastman, 1858.

Meisel, Martin. *Realisations: Narrative, Pictorial, and Theatrical Arts in Nineteenth-Century England.* Princeton, N.J.: Princeton: Princeton University Press, 1983.

Meleney, John C. *The Public Life of Aedanus Burke: Revolutionary Republican in Post-Revolutionary South Carolina.* Columbia: University of South Carolina Press, 1989.

Mellow, James R. *Nathaniel Hawthorne in His Times.* Boston: Houghton Mifflin, 1980.

Melville, Herman. *The Confidence-Man: His Masquerade.* New York: Dix, Edwards, 1857.

———. *Moby-Dick; or, The Whale.* New York: Harper and Brothers, 1851.

Memphis Daily Appeal [Tenn.].

Meriwether, Robert L. "Jamison, David Flavel." In *Dictionary of American Biography,* by American Council of Learned Societies, vol. 9, edited by Allen Johnson and Dumas Malone, 604–5. New York: Charles Scribner's Sons, 1936.

Michelet, Jules. *Histoire de France.* Vols. 1–6. Paris: Hachette, 1833–44.

Mickelsen, Berkeley, and Mickelsen, Alvera. "The Head of the Epistles." *Christianity Today* 25 (February 20, 1981): 20–23.

Miller, Edwin Haviland. *Salem Is My Dwelling Place: A Life of Nathaniel Hawthorne.* Iowa City: University of Iowa Press, 1991.

Miller, James David. *South by Southwest: Planter Emigration and Identity in the Slave South.* Charlottesville: University of Virginia Press, 2002.

Miller, John D. "A Sense of Things to Come: Redefining Gender and Promoting the Lost Cause in *The Sense of the Beautiful.*" In *William Gilmore Simms's Unfinished Civil War: Consequences for a Southern Man of Letters,* edited by David Moltke-Hansen, 212–23. Columbia: University of South Carolina Press, 2013.

Miller, Perry. *The Raven and the Whale: The War of Words and Wits in the Era of Poe and Melville.* New York: Harvest Books, 1956.

Miller, Stephen P. "The Persistence of Antiliberalism: Evangelicals and the Race Problem." In *American Evangelicalism and the 1960s,* edited by Axel R. Schäfer, 81–96. Madison: University of Wisconsin Press, 2013.

Miller, William Ian. *Humiliation, and Other Essays on Honor, Social Discomfort, and Violence.* Ithaca, N.Y.: Cornell University Press, 1993.

Miller's Weekly Messenger [Pendleton, S.C.].

Mills, Robert. *Statistics of South Carolina, Including a View of Its Natural, Civil, and Military History, General and Particular.* Charleston, S.C.: Hurlbut and Lloyd, 1826.

Millward, Jessica. "'As Cool as I Now Am': Identity, Abortion and Infanticide in the Slave South." M.A. thesis, University of California, Los Angeles, 1997.

Minor, Henry. *Reports of Cases Argued and Determined in the Supreme Court of Alabama.* New York: Collins and Hannay, 1830.

Minton, Amy K. R. "A Culture of Respectability: Southerners and Social Relations in Richmond, Virginia, 1820–1865." Ph.D. diss., University of Virginia, 2006.

Mississippi Free Trader and Natchez Daily Gazette [Miss.].

Moers, Ellen. *The Dandy: Brummel to Beerbohm.* New York: Viking, 1960.

Moltke-Hansen, David. "Between Plantation and Frontier: The South of William Gilmore Simms." In *William Gilmore Simms and the American Frontier,* edited by John Caldwell Guilds and Carolina Collins, 3–26. Athens: University of Georgia Press, 1997.

———. "The Critical Revolution and the Revolutionary Critic." In *William Gilmore Simms's Selected Reviews on Literature and Civilization,* by William Gilmore Simms, 197–214. Columbia: University of South Carolina Press, 2014.

———. "The Fictive Transformation of American Nationalism after Walter Scott." *Historically Speaking* 10, no. 3 (2009): 24–27.

———. Introduction to *Views and Reviews in American Literature, History, and Fiction,* by William Gilmore Simms, xxiii–xxxv. Columbia: University of South Carolina Press, 2013.

———. "Ordered Progress: The Historical Philosophy of William Gilmore Simms." In *"Long Years of Neglect": The Work and Reputation of William Gilmore Simms,* edited by John Caldwell Guilds, 126–47. Fayetteville: University of Arkansas Press, 1988.

———. Review of William Gilmore Simms, *The Life of the Chevalier Bayard . . . 1847. Simms Review* 21, no. 1/2 (2013): 111–14.

———. "Southern Literary Horizons in Young America: Imaginative Development of a Regional Geography." *Studies in the Literary Imagination* 42 (Spring 2009): 1–32.

———. "Turn Signals: Shifts in Values in Southern Life Writing." In *Dixie Redux: Essays in Honor of Sheldon Hackney,* edited by Raymond Arsenault and Orville Vernon Burton, 166–99. Montgomery: NewSouth Books, 2013.

———. "When History Failed: William Gilmore Simms's Artistic Negotiation of the Civil War's Consequences." In *William Gilmore Simms's Unfinished Civil War: Consequences for a Southern Man of Letters,* edited by David Moltke-Hansen, 3–31. Columbia: University of South Carolina Press, 2013.

———. "Why History Mattered: The Background of Ann Pamela Cunningham's Interest in the Preservation of Mount Vernon." *Furman Studies* 26 (December 1980): 34–42.

Montesquieu, Charles de. *The Spirit of the Laws.* Cambridge: Cambridge University Press, 1989.

Moore, Alex, ed. *Biographical Directory of the South Carolina House of Representatives, 1816–1828.* Vol. 5. Columbia: South Carolina Department of Archives and History, 1992.

Moore, Bartholomew F., and Asa Biggs. *Revised Code of North Carolina.* Boston: Little, Brown, 1855.

Moragne, William C. *An Address on the Character of the Scholar and the Gentleman, Delivered before the Young Men of the Presbyterian High Schools at Greenwood, Abbeville District, at the Close of the Examinations, July 28, 1853.* Anderson, S.C.: Advocate, 1853.

Morgan, Jennifer L. *Laboring Women: Reproduction and Gender in New World Slavery.* Philadelphia: University of Pennsylvania Press, 2004.

Morris, Christopher. *Becoming Southern: The Evolution of a Way of Life, Warren County and Vicksburg, Mississippi, 1760–1860*. New York: Oxford University Press, 1995.

———. "Within the Slave Cabin: Violence in Mississippi Slave Families." In *Over the Threshold: Intimate Violence in Early America*, edited by Christine Daniels and Michael V. Kennedy, 268–85. New York: Routledge, 1999.

Morris, Dick, and Eileen McGann. *2010: Take Back America; A Battle Plan*. New York: Harper, 2010.

Morrison, Betty L. *A Guide to Voodoo in New Orleans, 1820–1940*. Gretna, La.: Her Publishing, 1977.

Morrison, Toni. *Sula*. New York: Knopf, 1974.

Moses, John. *Illinois, Historical and Statistical: Comprising the Essential Facts of Its Planting and Growth as a Province, County, Territory, and State*. Vol. 2. Chicago: Fergus, 1892.

Muessig, Ulrike. "Superior Courts in Early-Modern France." In *Judges and Judging in the History of the Common Law and Civil Law*, edited by Paul Brand and Joshua Getzler, 209–33. Cambridge: Cambridge University Press, 2012.

Muhlenfeld, Elisabeth. *Mary Boykin Chesnut: A Biography*. Baton Rouge: Louisiana University Press, 1981.

Munford, George W. "Abstract from the Reports of the Clerks of the Courts of Appeals, and the Circuit Superior Courts of Law and Chancery, for the Year Ending August 30, 1845, Document 6." *Journal of the Virginia House of Delegates, 1845–1846*. Richmond, Va., 1846.

Murray, Charles. *Coming Apart: The State of White America, 1960–2010*. New York: Crown Forum, 2012.

Murray, Pauli. *Proud Shoes: The Story of an American Family*. New York: Harper and Brothers, 1956.

Nashville Union and American [Tenn.].

Natchez Courier [Miss.].

National Gazette [Philadelphia, Pa.].

Naylor, Gloria. *Mama Day*. New York: Ticknor and Fields, 1988.

Neely, Caroline Elizabeth. "'Dat's One Chile of Mine You Ain't Never Gonna Sell': Gynecological Resistance within the Plantation Community." M.A. thesis, Virginia Polytechnic Institute and State University, 2000.

"The Negro Cesar's Cure for Poison." *Massachusetts Magazine* 4 (1792): 103–4.

New England Galaxy [Boston, Mass.].

New England Weekly Review [Hartford, Conn.].

New Orleans Times-Picayune [La.].

New York Daily Tribune. Wednesday, July 20, 1859, 5. http://chroniclingamerica.loc.gov/lccn/sn83030213/1859-07020/ed-1/seq-5/#date1=1859&sort=relevance&rows=20&words=Aylett&searchType=basic&sequence=0&index=2&state=&date2=1859&proxtext=aylett&y=13&x=12&dateFilterType=yearRange&page=2 (accessed November 16, 2013).

New York Daily Tribune [N.Y.].

New York Herald [N.Y.].

New York Morning Herald [N.Y.].

New York Spectator [N.Y.].

New York Times [N.Y.].

New-York Journal [N.Y.].

Niles' National Register [Baltimore, Md.].

Nisbett, Richard E., and Dov Cohen. *Culture of Honor: The Psychology of Violence in the South.* Boulder, Colo.: Westview, 1996.

Nissenbaum, Stephen. *Sex, Diet, and Debility in Jacksonian America: Sylvester Graham and Health Reform.* Westport, Conn.: Greenwood, 1980.

Noll, Mark A. *America's God: From Jonathan Edwards to Abraham Lincoln.* New York: Oxford University Press, 2002.

North American and Daily Advertiser [Philadelphia, Pa.].

Novak, Steven J. *The Rights of Youth: American Colleges and Student Revolt, 1798–1815.* Cambridge, Mass.: Harvard University Press, 1977.

Oatley, Keith. *Emotions: A Brief History.* Blackwell Brief Histories of Psychology. Malden, Mass.: Blackwell, 2004.

O'Brien, Michael, ed. *All Clever Men Who Make Their Way: Critical Discourse in the Old South.* Athens: University of Georgia Press, 1992.

———. *Conjectures of Order: Intellectual Life and the American South, 1810–1860.* 2 Vols. Chapel Hill: University of North Carolina Press, 2004.

———, ed. *An Evening When Alone: Four Journals of Single Women in the South, 1827–1867.* Charlottesville, Va.: Published for the Southern Texts Society by the University Press of Virginia, 1993.

———. *Rethinking the South: Essays in Intellectual History.* Baltimore: Johns Hopkins University Press, 1988.

Olegario, Rowena. *A Culture of Credit: Embedding Trust and Transparency in American Business.* Cambridge, Mass.: Harvard University Press, 2006.

Oliphant, Mary C. Simms, et al. "Simms' Circle." In *The Letters of William Gilmore Simms,* by William Gilmore Simms, 1:xc–cxlix. Columbia: University of South Carolina Press, 1952.

Olsen, Christopher J. *Political Culture and Secession in Mississippi: Masculinity, Honor, and the Antiparty Tradition, 1830–1860.* New York: Oxford University Press, 2000.

O'Neill, Ann. "NRA's Marion Hammer Stands Her Ground," *CNN US,* April 15, 2012. http://www.cnn.com/2012/04/15/us/marion-hammer-profile (accessed August 9, 2013).

Ormond, John J., Arthur P. Bagby, and George Goldthwaite. *The Code of Alabama.* Montgomery, Ala.: Brittan and De Wolf, 1852.

O'Sullivan, John L. "Annexation." *United States Magazine and Democratic Review* 17 (July–August 1845): 5–10.

———. "The Martyrdom of Cilley." *United States Magazine and Democratic Review* 1 (March 1838): 493–508.

Osterweis, Rollin G. *Romanticism and Nationalism in the Old South.* Baton Rouge: Louisiana State University Press, 1949.

Owen, Thomas McAdory. *History of Alabama and Dictionary of Alabama Biography.* Vol. 4. Chicago: S. J. Clarke, 1921.

Ownby, Ted. *Subduing Satan: Religion, Recreation, and Manhood in the Rural South, 1865–1920.* Chapel Hill: University of North Carolina Press, 1990.

Pace, Robert F. *Halls of Honor: College Men in the Old South.* Baton Rouge: Louisiana State University Press, 2004.

Pace, Robert F., and Christopher A. Bjornsen. "Adolescent Honor and College Student Behavior in the Old South." *Southern Cultures* 6 (Fall 200): 9–28.

Page, Rosewell. *Thomas Nelson Page: A Memoir of a Virginia Gentleman.* Charles Scribner's Sons, 1923. Reprint, Port Washington, N.Y.: Kennikat, 1969.

Page, Thomas Nelson. *In Ole Virginia*. New York: Charles Scribner's Sons, 1887.

———. "Marse Chan." *In Ole Virginia*, 1–38. New York: Charles Scribner's Sons, 1922. Originally published 1887.

———. "The Old Virginia Lawyer." In *The Old South: Essays Social and Political*, 335–52. New York: Charles Scribner's Sons, 1906. Originally published 1892.

———. *Social Life in Old Virginia before the War*. 1892. Reprint, Sandwich, Mass.: Chapman Billies, 1994.

Palin, Sarah. *Going Rogue: An American Life*. New York: Harper, 2009.

Papers in Illinois History and Transactions for the Year, 1901. Springfield: Illinois State Journal Company, 1901.

Papers of the Gaston, Strait, Wylie, and Baskin Families, South Caroliniana Library, University of South Carolina, Columbia.

Parker, Christopher, and Matt A. Barreto. *Change They Can't Believe In: The Tea Party and Reactionary Politics in America*. Princeton, N.J.: Princeton University Press, 2013.

Patterson, Orlando. *Slavery and Social Death: A Comparative Study*. Cambridge, Mass.: Harvard University Press, 1982.

Patterson, Paige. "Letter from the President." *Southwestern News* 69 (Winter 2011): 5.

———. "Toward a Theology of Manhood." *Southwestern News* 69 (Winter 2011): 6–9.

Patton, John M., and Conway Robinson. *Code of Virginia: With the Declaration of Independence and Constitution of the United States; and the Declaration of Rights and Constitution of Virginia*. Richmond, Va.: W. F. Ritchie, 1849.

———. *Reports of the Revisors*. Richmond, VA: Samuel Shepherd, 1847–1849.

Pease, Jane H., and William H. Pease. *A Family of Women: The Carolina Petrigrus in Peace and War*. Chapel Hill: University of North Carolina Press, 1999.

———. *Ladies, Women, and Wenches: Choice and Constraint in Antebellum Charleston and Boston*. Chapel Hill: University of North Carolina Press, 1990.

Peltonen, Markku. *The Duel in Early Modern England: Civility, Politeness and Honour*. Cambridge: Cambridge University Press, 2003.

Pendleton Farmers' Society, Minutes, Typescript, 1824–25. Special Collections, Clemson University Library, Clemson, S.C.

Pendleton Farmers' Society. *Pendleton Farmers' Society*. Atlanta: Foote and Davies, 1908.

Pendleton Messenger [S.C.].

Penick, James L., Jr. *The Great Western Land Pirate: John A. Murrell in Legend and History*. Columbia: University of Missouri Press, 1981.

Pennsylvania Gazette [Pa.].

Pennsylvania Inquirer and Daily Courier [Philadelphia, Pa.].

Pensacola Gazette [Fla.].

Pepper, Simon. "Siege Law, Siege Ritual, and the Symbolism of City Walls in Renaissance Europe." In *City Walls: The Urban Enceinte in Global Perspective*, edited by James D. Tracy, 573–604. Cambridge: Cambridge University Press, 2000.

Peristiany, J. G., ed. *Honour and Shame: The Values of Mediterranean Society*. Chicago: University of Chicago Press, 1966.

Peristiany, J. G., and Julian Pitt-Rivers. "Introduction." In *Honor and Grace in Anthropology*, edited by J. G. Peristiany and Julian Pitt-Rivers. New York: Cambridge University Press, 1992.

Perkin, Harold J. *Origins of Modern English Society, 1780–1880*. London: Routledge and Kegan Paul, 1969.

Perosa, Sergio. *American Theories of the Novel: 1793–1903*. New York: New York University Press, 1983.

Persons, Stow. *The Decline of American Gentility*. New York: Columbia University Press, 1973.

Peter Cordes Porcher Papers, South Carolina Historical Society, Charleston.

Peterkin, Darryl Lynn. "'Lux, Libertas, and Learning': The First State University and the Transformation of North Carolina, 1789–1816." Ph.D. diss., Princeton University, 1995.

Peters, Richard. "Notices for a Young Farmer: Particularly One of Worn Lands; Being Some Rudiments for an Epitome of Good Husbandry; and Subjects Promotive of Its Prosperity." In *Memoirs of the Philadelphia Society for Promoting Agriculture: Containing Communications on Various Subjects in Husbandry and Rural Affairs*. Vol. 4. Philadelphia: Benjamin Warner, 1818, v–lii.

"Petition of James H. Gholson, January 25, 1847, Document 37." *Journal of the Virginia House of Delegates, 1846–1847*. Richmond, Va., 1847.

"Petition of Robert R. Collier, January 28, 1847, Document 40." *Journal of the Virginia House of Delegates, 1846–1847*. Richmond, Va. 1847.

Petitions and Schedules of Insolvent Debtors, Records of the Court of Common Pleas, Charleston County, South Carolina Department of Archives and History, Columbia, S.C.

Pettigrew, James Johnston. *Notes on Spain and the Spaniards, in the Summer of 1859, with a Glance at Sardinia*. 1861. Reprint, Columbia: University of South Carolina Press, 2010.

Pflugrad-Jackisch, Ami. *Brothers of a Vow: Secret Fraternal Orders and the Transformation of White Male Culture in Antebellum Virginia*. Athens: University of Georgia Press, 2010.

Philbrick, Francis S., ed. *The Laws of Illinois Territory, 1809–1818*. Springfield: Illinois State Historical Library, 1950.

———. *The Laws of Indiana Territory, 1801–1809*. Springfield: Illinois State Historical Library, 1930.

Phillips, Leon. *That Eaton Woman: In Defense of Peggy O'Neale Eaton*. New York: Crown, 1974.

Phillips, Sarah T. "Antebellum Agricultural Reform, Republican Ideology, and Sectional Tension." *Agricultural History* 74 (2000): 799–822.

Phillips, U. B. *Revised Statutes of Louisiana*. New Orleans: John Clairborne, 1856.

Piper, John, and Wayne Grudem, eds. *Recovering Biblical Manhood and Womanhood: A Response to Evangelical Feminism*. Rpt. ed. Wheaton, Ill.: Crossway, 2006.

Pitt-Rivers, Julian. "Honor." In *International Encyclopedia of the Social Sciences*, edited by David Sills, 503–11. New York: MacMillan Free Press, 1968.

———. "Honour and Social Status." In *Honour and Shame: The Values of Mediterranean Society*, edited by J. Peristiany, 19–77. Chicago: University of Chicago Press, 1966.

———. "Postscript: The Place of Grace in Anthropology." In *Honor and Grace in Anthropology*, edited by J. G. Peristiany and Julian Pitt-Rivers, 215–46. New York: Cambridge University Press, 1992.

Poe, Edgar A. "Raising the Wind [Diddling Considered as One of the Exact Sciences]." *Saturday Courier* [Philadelphia] 13.655 (October 14, 1843): 1.

Pollin, Burton R. "Poe's 'Diddling': The Source of Title and Tale." *Southern Literary Journal* 2 (1969): 106–11.

Pope, Nathaniel. *Laws of the Territory of Illinois*. Kaskaskia, Ill.: Matthew Duncan, 1815.

[Porcher, Frederick A.]. "Historical and Social Sketch of Craven County." *Southern Quarterly Review* 9 (1854): 377–428.

[———]. "The Conflict of Capital and Labour." *Russell's Magazine* 3 (1858): 289–98.

Porcher Family Collection, Southern Historical Collection, Manuscripts Department, Wilson Library, University of North Carolina, Chapel Hill.

Potter, David. "The Literary Society." In *History of Speech Education in America*, edited by Karl R. Wallace, 238–58. New York: Appleton-Century-Crofts, 1954.

Preston, Douglas, and Lincoln Child. *Cemetery Dance*. New York: Vision, 2009.

Prince, K. Stephen. "Marse Chan, New Southerner: or, Taking Thomas Nelson Page Seriously." In *Storytelling, History, and the Postmodern South*, edited by Jason Phillips. Baton Rouge: Louisiana State University Press, 2013: 88–104.

"Proceedings of the Select Committee Appointed to Investigate the Charges Preferred against Judge James H. Gholson." Library of Virginia, MS 4461.

Proctor, Nicholas W. *Bathed in Blood: Hunting and Mastery in the Old South*. Charlottesville: University Press of Virginia, 2002.

Providence Gazette [R.I.].

Public and General Statute Laws of the State of Illinois. Chicago: Stephen F. Gale, 1839.

Puckett, Newbell Niles. *Folk Beliefs of the Southern Negro*. Patterson Smith Reprint Series in Criminology, Law Enforcement, and Social Problems 22. Chapel Hill: University of North Carolina Press, 1926. Reprint, Montclair, NJ: Patterson Smith, 1968.

Puelo, Stephan. *The Caning: The Assault That Drove America to Civil War*. Yardley, PA: Westholme, 2012.

Quigley, Paul. *Shifting Grounds: Nationalism and the American South, 1848–1865*. New York: Oxford University Press, 2012.

Quist, John W. *Restless Visionaries: The Social Roots of Antebellum Reform in Alabama and Michigan*. Baton Rouge: Louisiana State University Press, 1998.

R., L., G., and A. "Conjure Doctors in the South." *Southern Workman* 7 (1878): 30–31.

Rable, George C. *God's Almost Chosen People: A Religious History of the American Civil War*. Chapel Hill: University of North Carolina Press, 2010.

Ramsey, David. *History of South Carolina from Its Settlement in 1700 to 1808*. Vol. 1. Newberry, S.C.: W. J. Duffie, 1858.

Rawick, George P., ed. *The American Slave: A Composite Autobiography*. Vol. 5. Westport, Conn.: Greenwood, 1972.

———. *The American Slave: A Composite Autobiography, Supplement, Series 1*. Vol. 6. Westport, Conn.: Greenwood, 1977.

Records of the Dialectic Society, University Archives, Manuscripts Department, Wilson Library, University of North Carolina at Chapel Hill.

Records of the Philanthropic Society, University Archives, Manuscripts Department, Wilson Library, University of North Carolina at Chapel Hill.

Reddy, William M. *The Navigation of Feeling: A Framework for the History of Emotions*. New York: Cambridge University Press, 2001.

Redpath, James. *The Roving Editor; or, Talks with Slaves in the Southern States*. New York: A. B. Burdick, 1859.

Reed, Ishmael. *Conjure: Selected Poems, 1963–1970*. Amherst: University of Massachusetts Press, 1972.

Rees, James. "The Bond-Jones Duel and the Shooting of Rice Jones by Dr. James Dunlap: What Really Happened in Kaskaskia, Indiana Territory on 8 August and 7 December 1808?" *Journal of the Illinois State Historical Society* 97, no. 4 (Winter 2004): 272–85.

Reese, Mary E. *Genealogy of the Reese Family in Wales and America, from Their Arrival in America to the Present Time.* Richmond, Va.: Whittet and Shepperson, 1903.

Regnery, Arthur. "Pillars of Conservatism." In *Big Tent: The Story of the Conservative Revolution—as Told by the Thinkers and Doers Who Made It Happen,* ed. Mallory Factor, loc. 468–746, Kindle edition. New York: Broadside Books, 2014.

Renfroe, J. J. D. *"The Battle Is God's": A Sermon Preached before Wilcox's Brigade, on Fast Day, the 21st August, 1863, near Orange Court-House, Va.* Richmond, Va.: Macfarlane and Fergusson, 1863.

Resolutions on Racial Reconciliation on the 150th Anniversary of the Southern Baptist Convention, June 1995. http://www.sbc.net/resolutions/amresolution.asp?id=899 (accessed March 30, 2013).

Revised Code of the Laws of Illinois. Vandalia, Ill.: Robert Blackwell, 1827.

Revised Code of the Laws of Mississippi, 1823. Natchez, Miss.: Francis Baker, 1824.

Revised Code of the Laws of Virginia. Richmond, Va.: Thomas Ritchie, 1819.

Revised Code of the Public General Laws of the State of Maryland. Baltimore: John Murphy, 1879.

Revised Code of the Statute Laws of the State of Mississippi. Jackson, Miss.: E. Barksdale, 1857.

Revised Code of the Statute Laws of the State of Mississippi. Jackson, Miss.: J. L. Power, 1880.

Revised Statutes of the Commonwealth of Massachusetts. Boston: Dutton and Wentworth, 1836.

Revised Statutes of the State of Illinois. Springfield, Ill.: William Walters, 1845.

Revised Statutes of the State of Indiana. Indianapolis: Douglass and Noel, 1838.

Revised Statutes of the State of Indiana. Indianapolis: Dowling and Cole, 1843.

Revised Statutes of the State of Missouri. St. Louis: Chambers and Knapp, 1845.

Revised Statutes of the State of Missouri. Jefferson City, Mo.: James Lusk, 1856.

Revised Statutes of the State of New-Jersey, Passed 1874. Trenton, N.J.: 1874–75.

Revised Statutes of the State of New York. Edited by Hiram Denion. Albany, N.Y.: Gould and Banks, 1852.

Revised Statutes of the State of North Carolina. Raleigh, N.C.: Turner and Hughes, 1837.

Revised Statutes of the State of South Carolina. Columbia, S.C.: Republican, 1873.

Reynolds, John. *The Pioneer History of Illinois: Containing the Discovery in 1673, and the History of the Country to the Year 1818, When the State Government Was Organized.* Chicago: Fergus, 1887.

R. G. Dun and Company Collection, Baker Library, Graduate School of Business Administration, Harvard University.

Rhodes, Jewell Parker. *Voodoo Dreams: A Novel of Marie Laveau.* New York: Picador USA, 1993.

Rice, Anne. *The Feast of All Saints.* New York: Ballantine, 1979.

Richmond Daily Dispatch [Va.].

Richmond Daily Dispatch [Va.]. July 27, 1859, 1. http://chroniclingamerica.loc.gov/lccn/sn84024738/1859-07-27/ed-1/seq1/#date1=1859&sort=relevance&rows=20&words=Aylett&searchType=basic&sequence=0&index=2&state=&date2=1859&proxtext=aylett&y=-221&x=-1140&dateFilterType=yearRange&page=1 (accessed October 4, 2013).

Richmond Daily Dispatch [Va.]. August 19, 1880, 1. http://chroniclingamerica.loc.gov/lccn/sn84024738/1880-08-19/ed-1/seq-1/#date1=1880&index=1&rows=20&words=Hobson+Wise+Wise%2FHobson&searchType=basic&sequence=0&state=&date2=1880&proxtext=wise+hobson&y=-221&x=-1103&dateFilterType=yearRange&page=1 (accessed December 14, 2013).

Richmond Daily Dispatch [Va.]. September 2, 1880, 1. http://chroniclingamerica.loc.gov/lccn/sn84024738/1859-07-27/ed-1/seq-1/#date1=1859&sort=relevance&rows=20&words=Aylett&search

Type=basic&sequence=0&index=2&state=&date2=1859&proxtext=aylett&y=-221&x=-1140&dateFilterType=yearRange&page=1 (accessed December 8, 2014).

Richmond Enquirer [Va.]. July 7, 1848.

Richmond Whig [Va.]. January 29, 1847.

Richmond Whig [Va.]. November 10, 1848.

Rittelmeyer, Helen. "The Smoker's Code." In *Proud to Be Right: Voices of the Next Conservative Generation,* ed. Jonah Goldberg, 172–79. New York: Harper, 2010.

Roberson, John R. "The Manuscript of Page's 'Marse Chan.'" *Studies in Bibliography* 9 (1957): 259–62.

Robert Francis Withers Allston Papers, South Caroliniana Library, University of South Carolina, Columbia.

Roberts and Hamiter. *The Criminal Laws of Arkansas.* Little Rock, Ark.: Brown, 1894.

Roberts, Kodi. "The Promise of Power: The Racial, Gender, and Economic Politics of Voodoo in New Orleans, 1881–1940." Ph.D. diss., University of Chicago, 2012.

Robson, David W. *Educating Republicans: The College in the Era of the American Revolution, 1750–1800.* Westport, Conn.: Greenwood, 1985.

"Rods." *Alabama Time-Piece.* March 11, 1898, 4.

Rogers, E. P. *Earnest Words to Young Men, in a Series of Discourses.* Charleston: Walker and James, 1851.

Rogers, Jeffery J. Introduction to *The Life of Chevalier Bayard,* by William Gilmore Simms, xxiii–xxxviii. 1847. Reprint, Columbia: University of South Carolina Press, 2013.

Rogers, Tommy W. "The Great Population Exodus from South Carolina, 1850–1860." *South Carolina Historical Magazine* 68, no. 1 (1967): 14–21.

Romine, Scott. *The Narrative Forms of Southern Community.* Baton Rouge: Louisiana State University Press, 1999.

Rosenwein, Barbara H. *Emotional Communities in the Early Middle Ages.* Ithaca, N.Y.: Cornell University Press, 2006.

———. "Worrying about Emotions in History." *American Historical Review* 107, no. 3 (2002): 821–45.

Rossiter, Clinton. *Conservatism in America: The Thankless Persuasion.* 2nd ed., rev. New York: Knopf, 1962.

Roth, Sarah N. "'The Blade Was in My Own Breast': Slave Infanticide in 1850s Fiction." *American Nineteenth Century History* 8 (June 2007): 169–85.

Rothman, Ellen K. *Hands and Hearts: A History of Courtship in America.* New York: Basic Books, 1984.

Rothman, Joshua D. *Flush Times and Fever Dreams: A Story of Capitalism and Slavery in the Age of Jackson* Athens: University of Georgia Press, 2012.

———. *Notorious in the Neighborhood: Sex and Families across the Color Line in Virginia, 1787–1861.* Chapel Hill: University of North Carolina Press, 2003.

Rotundo, E. Anthony. *American Manhood: Transformations in Masculinity from the Revolution to the Modern Era.* New York: Basic Books, 1993.

Rozbicki, Michal J. *The Complete Colonial Gentleman: Cultural Legitimacy in Plantation America.* Charlottesville: University Press of Virginia, 1998.

Ryan, Mary P. *Cradle of the Middle Class: The Family in Oneida County, New York, 1790–1865.* Cambridge: Cambridge University Press, 1981.

Sabine, Lorenzo. *The American Loyalists; or, Biographical Sketches of Adherents to the British Crown in the War of the Revolution.* Boston: Charles C. Little and James Brown, 1847.

———. *Notes on Duels and Duelling, Alphabetically Arranged, with a Preliminary Historical Essay.* Boston: Crosby, Nichols, 1855.

Salley, A. S. "Some Early Simons Records." *South Carolina Historical and Genealogical Magazine* 37, no. 4 (October 1936): 145–47.

Sampson, Robert D. *John L. O'Sullivan and His Times.* Kent, Ohio: Kent State University Press, 2003.

Samuel Cram Jackson Diary, South Caroliniana Library, University of South Carolina, Columbia.

Samuel Wells Leland Papers, South Caroliniana Library, University of South Carolina, Columbia.

Sandage, Scott. *Born Losers: A History of Failure in America.* Cambridge, Mass.: Harvard University Press, 2005.

Sargent, Greg. "What Coburn Really Said about Obama, Race, and Dependency." *Plum Line,* August 18, 2011. http://www.washingtonpost.com/blogs/plum-line/post/what-coburn-really-said-about-obama-race-and-dependency/2011/03/03/glQAdBYwNJ_blog.html (accessed August 9, 2013).

Savage, Michael. *Trickle Up Poverty: Stopping Obama's Attack on Our Borders, Economy, and Security.* New York: Harper, 2010.

Savannah Daily Morning News [Ga.].

Savitt, Todd L. *Medicine and Slavery: The Diseases and Health Care of Blacks in Antebellum Virginia.* 1978. Urbana: University of Illinois Press, 2002.

Saxon, Elizabeth Lyle. *A Southern Woman's War Time Reminiscences.* Memphis: Pilcher, 1905.

Scanzoni, Letha and Elizabeth Hardesty. *All That We're Meant to Be: A Biblical Approach to Women's Liberation.* Grand Rapids, MI: W.B. Eerdmans, 1992.

Schorsch, Peter. "Five Questions for Rep. Dennis Baxley." *SaintPetersBlog,* December 26, 2012. http://www.saintpetersblog.com/five-questions-for-rep-dennis-baxley-2 (accessed August 9, 2013).

Schultz, Harold S. *Nationalism and Sectionalism in South Carolina, 1852–1860: A Study of the Movement for Southern Independence.* Durham, N.C.: Duke University Press, 1950.

Schwalm, Leslie A. *A Hard Fight for We: Women's Transition from Slavery to Freedom in South Carolina.* Urbana: University of Illinois Press, 1997.

Schwartz, Lawrence H. *Creating Faulkner's Reputation.* Knoxville: University of Tennessee Press, 1988.

Schwartz, Marie Jenkins. *Born in Bondage: Growing Up Enslaved in the Antebellum South.* Cambridge, Mass.: Harvard University Press, 2000.

Scott, Sir Walter. "Essay on Chivalry." 1818. In *Essays on Chivalry, Romance, and the Drama.* London: Frederick Warne, 1887: 1–65.

———. *The Life of Napoleon Buonaparte, Emperor of the French: With a Preliminary View of the French Revolution.* 9 vols. London: Longman, Rees, Orme, Brown, and Green, 1827.

———. *The Vision of Don Roderick: A Poem.* Edinburgh: John Ballantyne, 1811.

Seavey, Todd. "Conservatism for Punks" In *Proud to Be Right: Voices of the Next Conservative Generation,* edited by Jonah Goldberg, 191–201. New York: Harper, 2010.

Seitz, Don C. *Famous American Duels: With Some Account of the Causes That Led Up to Them and the Men Engaged.* 1929. Freeport, N.Y.: Books for Libraries Press, 1966.

Sellers, Charles Grier. *The Market Revolution: Jacksonian America, 1815–1846.* New York: Oxford University Press, 1991.

Senior and Junior Orations, North Carolina Collection, Wilson Library, University of North Carolina at Chapel Hill.

Shear, Michael D. "N.R.A. Leader Denounces Obama's Call for Gun Control." *New York Times,* January 22, 2013, A15.

Shepard, E. Lee. *Judges of the Superior Courts of Virginia, 1776–1900.* Richmond: Virginia Historical Society.

Shields, David S. *Civil Tongues and Polite Letters in British America.* Chapel Hill: University of North Carolina Press, 1997.

Shields, Johanna Nicol. *Freedom in a Slave Society: Stories from the Antebellum South.* New York: Cambridge University Press, 2012.

Shillingsburg, Miriam J. "Simms's Failed Lecture Tour of 1856: The Mind of the North." In *"Long Years of Neglect": The Work and Reputation of William Gilmore Simms,* edited by John Caldwell Guilds, 183–201. Fayetteville: University of Arkansas Press, 1988.

Shugerman, Jed Handelsman. "Economic Crisis and the Rise of Judicial Elections and Judical Review." *Harvard Law Review* 132, no. 5 (2010): 1063–150.

Simms, Henry H. *The Rise of the Whigs in Virginia, 1824–1840.* Richmond, VA: William Byrd, 1929.

Simms, William Gilmore. "Bayard, the Chevalier; 'sans peur et sans reproche.'" *Southern and Western Monthly Magazine and Review* (Aug. 1845): 75–85 & (Sept. 1845): 193–200.

———. *The Book of My Lady: A Mélange.* Philadelphia: Kay and Biddle, 1833.

———. *The Cassique of Kiawah.* New York: Redfield, 1859.

———. "The Civil Warfare in the Carolinas and Georgia, during the Revolution." *Southern Literary Messenger* 12, no. 5–7 (1846): 257–65, 321–36, 385–400.

———. *Count Julian; or, The Last Days of the Goth; A Historical Romance.* Baltimore: William Taylor, 1845.

———. *The Damsel of Darien.* 2 vols. Philadelphia: Lea and Blanchard, 1839.

———. *Donna Florida: A Tale.* Charleston: Burgess and James, 1843.

———. *An Early and Strong Sympathy: The Indian Writings of William Gilmore Simms.* Edited by John C. Guilds and Charles Hudson. Columbia: University of South Carolina Press, 2007.

———. "The Epochs and Events of American History, as Suited to the Purposes of Art in Fiction." *Southern and Western* 2 (February 1845): 109–27; (March 1845): 182–91; (April 1845): 257–61; (June 1845): 385–92; (September 1845): 145–54.

———. *The History of South Carolina, from Its First European Discovery to Its Erection into a Republic: With a Supplementary Chronicle of Events to the Present Time.* Charleston, SC: S. Babcock and Co., 1840.

———. *The Letters of William Gilmore Simms.* 6 vols. Edited by Mary C. Simms Oliphant et al. Columbia: University of South Carolina Press, 1952–82. Vol. 6 reissued and supplemented in 2012.

———. *The Life of the Chevalier Bayard; "The Good Knight," "Sans peur et sans reproche."* New York: Harper and Brothers, 1847.

———. *The Life of Francis Marion.* New York: Henry G. Langley, 1844.

———. *The Lily and the Totem; or, The Huguenots in Florida.* New York: Baker and Scribner, 1850.

———. *Martin Faber, the Story of a Criminal; and Other Tales.* 2 vols. New York: Harper and Brothers, 1837.

———. *Pelayo: A Story of the Goth.* New York: Harper and Brothers, 1838.

———. *Self-Development: An Oration Delivered before the Literary Societies of Oglethorpe University; Georgia; November 10, 1847.* Milledgeville, GA: Thalian Society, 1847.

———. *The Social Principle.* Tuscaloosa, Ala.: Eurosophic Society, 1843.

———. *The Sources of American Independence.* Aiken, SC: Town Council, 1844.

———. *Vasconselos: A Romance of the New World.* New York: Redfield, 1853.

———. *The Vision of Cortes, Cain and Other Poems.* Charleston: James S. Burgess, 1829.

———. "The Voice of the Streamlet." *American Monthly Magazine* 5, no. 2 (1835): 81–88.

———. *The Yemassee: A Romance of Carolina.* New York: Redfield, 1853.

Simpson, R. W. *History of Old Pendleton District with a Genealogy of Leading Families of the District.* Anderson, S.C.: Oulla, 1913.

Singleton-Deveaux Family Papers, South Caroliniana Library, University of South Carolina, Columbia.

Sinha, Manisha. "The Caning of Charles Sumner: Slavery, Race, and Ideology in the Age of Civil War." *Journal of the Early Republic* 23, no. 2 (2003): 233–62.

Sismondi, Jean Charles Leonard Simonde de. *Histoire des Francais* [*History of the French*]. Paris: Treuttal et Wurtz, 1821–44.

Skocpol, Theda, and Vanessa Williamson. *The Tea Party and the Remaking of Republican Conservatism.* New York: Oxford University Press, 2012.

Sloan, David U. *Fogy Days, and Now; or, The World Has Changed.* Atlanta: Foote and Davies, 1891.

Smith, Alfred Glaze, Jr. *Economic Readjustment of an Old Cotton State: South Carolina, 1820–1860.* Columbia: University of South Carolina Press, 1958.

Smith, Jay M. *The Culture of Merit: Nobility, Royal Service, and the Making of Absolute Monarchy in France, 1600–1789.* Ann Arbor: University of Michigan Press, 1996.

Smith, Merril D. "'Unnatural Mothers': Infanticide, Motherhood, and Class in the Mid-Atlantic, 1730–1830." In *Over the Threshold: Intimate Violence in Early America,* edited by Christine Daniels and Michael V. Kennedy, 173–84. New York: Routledge, 1999.

Smith, Steven D. "Imagining the Swamp Fox: William Gilmore Simms and the National Memory of Francis Marion." In *William Gilmore Simms's Unfinished Civil War: Consequences for a Southern Man of Letters,* edited by David Moltke-Hansen, 32–47. Columbia: University of South Carolina Press, 2013.

Smith, Theophus H. *Conjuring Culture: Biblical Formations of Black America.* New York and Oxford: Oxford University Press, 1994.

Snider, William D. *Light on the Hill: A History of the University of North Carolina at Chapel Hill.* Chapel Hill: University of North Carolina Press, 1992.

Snyder, Jeffrey R. "A Nation of Cowards." In *Backward and Upward: The New Conservative Writing,* edited by David Brooks, 247–59. New York: Vintage, 1996.

"Some Conjure Doctors We Have Heard Of." *Southern Workman* 26 (1897): 37–38.

South Carolina Department of Archives and History (SCDAH).

South Carolina Gazette [Charleston, S.C.].

South Carolina Temperance Advocate [Columbia, S.C.].

Southern Chronicle [Camden, S.C.].

Southern Times and State Gazette [Columbia, S.C.].

Southey, Robert. "The Life of Bayard." In *Select Prose of Robert Southey,* edited by Jacob Zeitlin, 319–64. New York: Macmillan, 1916.

———. *Roderick, the Last of the Goths: A Tragic Poem.* 2 vols. London: Longman, Hurst, Rees, Orme, and Brown, 1814.

Sowell, Thomas. *A Conflict of Visions: Ideological Origins of Political Struggles.* Rev. ed. New York: Basic Books, 2007.

Spierenburg, Pieter. "Masculinity, Violence, and Honor: An Introduction." In *Men and Violence:*

Gender, Honor, and Rituals in Modern Europe and America, edited by Pieter Spierenburg, 1–29. Columbus: Ohio State University Press, 1998.

Stampp, Kenneth M. *The Peculiar Institution: Slavery in the Ante-bellum South.* New York: Alfred A. Knopf, 1956.

Standage, Tom. *The Turk: The Life and Times of the Famous Eighteenth-Century Chess-Playing Machine.* New York: Walker, 2002.

Stanton, Phoebe B. *The Gothic Revival and American Church Architecture: An Episode in Taste, 1840–1856.* Baltimore: Johns Hopkins University Press, 1968.

Stearns, Carol Zizowitz, and Peter N. Stearns. *Anger: The Struggle for Emotional Control in America's History.* Chicago: University of Chicago Press, 1986.

———. "Emotionology: Clarifying the History of Emotions and Emotional Standards." *American Historical Review* 90, no. 4 (1985): 813–36.

Stearns, Peter N. *Jealousy: The Evolution of an Emotion in American History.* New York: New York University Press, 1989.

Stearns, Peter N., and Jan Lewis, eds. *An Emotional History of the United States.* New York: New York University Press, 1998.

Steffen, Charles G. "In Search of the Good Overseer: The Failure of the Agricultural Reform Movement in Lowcountry South Carolina, 1821–1834." *The Journal of Southern History* 63 (Nov. 1997): 753–802.

Steiner, Roland. "Observations of the Practice of Conjuring in Georgia." *Journal of American Folk-Lore* 14 (1901): 173–80.

Stern, Julia A. *Mary Chesnut's Civil War Epic.* Chicago: University of Chicago Press, 2010.

Stevenson, Brenda E. *Life in Black and White: Family and Community in the Slave South.* New York: Oxford University Press, 1996.

Steward, Dick. *Duels and the Roots of Violence in Missouri.* Columbia: University of Missouri Press, 2000.

Stewart, Frank Henderson. *Honor.* Chicago: University of Chicago Press, 1994.

Stokes, Melvyn, and Stephen Conway, eds. *The Market Revolution in America: Social, Political, and Religious Expressions, 1800–1880.* Charlottesville: University Press of Virginia, 1996.

Stoney, Samuel G., ed. "Memoirs of Frederick Augustus Porcher." *South Carolina Historical Magazine* 47 (1946): 83–108.

Stowe, Steven M. *Intimacy and Power in the Old South: Ritual in the Lives of the Planters.* Baltimore: John Hopkins University Press, 1987.

Stuart, James. *Three Years in North America.* 2 vols. New York: Harper and Row, 1966.

Sue, Eugene, Jr. [pseud.]. *The Mysteries of Charleston: A Brief View of Matters and Things in General, the Internal Arrangements and Progressive Improvements, Past, Present, and Future, in the Great Metropolis of Charleston, with a Peep into the Various Ramifications of Society in Its Several Aspects, Moral, Social, Political, and Financial.* Charleston: Typographical Repository, 1846.

Sumterville Banner [S.C.].

Tate, Adam L. *Conservatism and Southern Intellectuals, 1789–1861.* Columbia: University of Missouri Press, 2005.

Thackeray, William M. *The Book of Snobs.* New York: D. Appleton, 1852.

Thomas, Emory M. *The Confederate Nation, 1861–1865.* New York: Harper and Row, 1979.

Thomas Miles Garrett Diary, Southern Historical Collection, Manuscripts Department, University of North Carolina at Chapel Hill.

Tise, Larry E. *Proslavery: A History of the Defense of Slavery in America, 1701–1840*. Athens: University of Georgia Press, 1987.

Tocqueville, Alexis de. *Democracy in America*. 1840. Translated by Arthur Goldhammer. New York: Library of America, 2004.

Tomlins, Christopher L. *Law, Labor, and Ideology in the Early American Republic*. Cambridge: Cambridge University Press, 1993.

Tomlinson, Stephen, and Kevin Windham. "Northern Piety and Southern Honor: Alva Woods and the Problem of Discipline at the University of Alabama, 1831–1837." *Perspectives on the History of Higher Education* 25 (2006): 1–42.

Transactions of the Illinois State Historical Society for the Year 1901. Springfield, Ill.: Phillips Brothers, 1901.

Trent, William Peterfield. *Robert E. Lee*. Boston: Small, Maynard, 1899.

Truman, Major Ben C. *Duelling in America*. San Diego: Joseph Tabler Books, 1993.

———. *The Field of Honor*. New York: Fords, Howard and Hulbert, 1884.

Trussel, James, and Richard Steckel. "The Age of Slaves at Menarche and Their First Birth." *Journal of Interdisciplinary History* 8 (Winter 1978): 477–505.

Twain, Mark. *Life on the Mississippi*. New York: Oxford University Press, 1996.

———. *A Yankee in King Arthur's Court*. New York: Charles L. Webster, 1889.

Tyler, Julia Gardiner. "To the Duchess of Sutherland and Ladies of England." *Southern Literary Messenger* 19 (February 1853): 120.

U.S. Congress. "Congressional Globe."

U.S. Government. *War of the Rebellion: A Compilation of the Official Records of the Union and Confederate Armies*. 128 vols. Washington, D.C.: U.S. Government Printing Office, 1880–1901.

United States Census, 1830, Lancaster District, S.C. National Archives and Records Administration, Microfilm Series: M-19, Roll 173.

Veblen, Thorstein. *The Theory of the Leisure Class*. N.p.: Oxford University Press, 2009.

Vermont Watchman and State Journal [Montpelier, Vt.].

Virginia Free Press [Charlestown, Va.].

Voskuil, Lynn M. *Acting Naturally: Victorian Theatricality and Authenticity*. Charlottesville: University Press of Virginia, 2004.

Wade, John Donald. "Sweet Are the Uses of Degeneracy." *Southern Review* 1 (1936): 449–66.

Wagoner, Jennings. "Honor and Dishonor at Mr. Jefferson's University: The Antebellum Years." *History of Education Quarterly* 26 (Summer 1986): 155–79.

Wakelyn, Jon L. "Antebellum College Life and the Relations between Fathers and Sons." In *The Web of Southern Social Relations: Women, Family, & Education*, edited by Walter J. Fraser, Jr., R. Frank Saunders, Jr., and Jon L. Wakelyn, 107–26. Athens: University of Georgia Press, 1985.

Walker, Alice. *The Third Life of Grange Copeland*. New York: Harcourt, Brace, Jovanovich, 1970.

Wall, Charles Coleman, Jr. "Students and Student Life at the University of Virginia, 1825 to 1861." Ph.D. diss., University of Virginia, 1978.

Ware, Henry, Jr. *The Law of Honor: A Discourse, Occasioned by the Recent Duel in Washington, Delivered March 4, 1838, in the Chapel of Harvard University, and in the West Church, Boston*. Cambridge, MA: Folsom, Wells, and Thurston, 1838.

Washington, Booker T. *Up from Slavery: An Autobiography*. Garden City, N.Y.: Doubleday, 1901. Retrieved from Documenting the American South, University Library, University of North Carolina at Chapel Hill, 1997. http://docsouth.unc.edu/fpn/washington/washing.html (accessed August 22, 2013).

Washington, Booker T., and W. E. B. Du Bois. *The Negro in the South: His Economic Progress in Relation to His Moral and Religious Development; Being the William Levi Bull Lectures for the Year 1907.* Philadelphia: George W. Jacobs, 1907. Retrieved from Project Gutenberg (EBook #35399).

Watson, Alan. *General Benjamin Smith: A Biography of the North Carolina Governor.* Jefferson, N.C.: McFarland, 2011.

Watson, Richie Devon. *Yeoman versus Cavalier: The Old Southwest's Fictional Road to Rebellion.* Baton Rouge: Louisiana State University Press, 1993.

Weaver, John C. *The Great Land Rush and the Making of the Modern World, 1650–1900.* Montreal: McGill Queens University Press, 2003.

Weber, Max. *Economy and Society: An Outline of Interpretive Sociology.* Vol. 2. Edited by Guenther Roth and Claus Wittich. Berkeley: University of California Press, 1978.

Weeks, Stephen B. "The Code in North Carolina: Contributions to the History of the Duello." *Magazine of American History* 26, no. 5 (December 1891): 443–56.

Weisenburger, Steven. *Modern Medea: A Family Story of Slavery and Child-Murder from the Old South.* New York: Hill and Wang, 1999.

Wells, Jonathan D. *The Origins of the Southern Middle Class, 1800–1861.* Chapel Hill: University of North Carolina Press, 2004.

Wells, Jonathan D., and Jennifer R. Green, eds. *The Southern Middle Class in the Long Nineteenth Century.* Baton Rouge: Louisiana State University Press, 2011.

Wesley, Timothy L. *The Politics of Faith during the Civil War.* Baton Rouge: Louisiana State University Press, 2013.

West, Stephen A. "From Yeoman to Redneck in Upstate South Carolina, 1850–1915." Ph.D. diss., Columbia University, 1998.

Whalen, Terence. "Poe's 'Diddling' and the Depression: Notes on the Sources of Swindling." *Studies in American Fiction* 23 (1995): 195–201.

"What Is the Future of Conservatism in the Wake of the 2012 Election?" *Commentary,* January 2013, 13–53.

Widmer, Edward L. *Young America: The Flowering of Democracy in New York City.* Oxford: Oxford University Press, 1999.

Wilcox, W. Bradford. *Soft Patriarchs, New Men: How Christianity Shapes Fathers and Husbands.* Chicago: University of Chicago Press, 2004.

Williams, Jack K. *Dueling in the Old South: Vignettes of Social History.* College Station: Texas A&M University Press, 1980.

Williams, Timothy J. *Intellectual Manhood: University, Self, and Society in the Antebellum South.* Chapel Hill: University of North Carolina Press, 2014.

Williams-Chesnut-Manning Collection (W-C-M Collection). South Caroliniana Library, University of South Carolina, Columbia.

William Sidney Mullins Diary, Southern Historical Collection, Manuscripts Department, University of North Carolina at Chapel Hill.

Willis, John C. "From the Dictates of Pride to the Paths of Righteousness: Slave Honor and Christianity in Antebellum Virginia." In *The Edge of the South: Life in Nineteenth-Century Virginia,* edited by Edward L. Ayers and John C. Willis, 37–55. Charlottesville: University Press of Virginia, 1991.

Willis, John Charles. "Behind 'Their Black Masks': Slave Honor in Antebellum Virginia." M.A. thesis, University of Virginia, 1987.

Wilson, Charles Reagan. *Baptized in Blood: The Religion of the Lost Cause, 1865–1920*. Athens: University of Georgia Press, 1980.

———. "'God's Project': The Southern Civil Religion, 1920–1980." In *Judgment & Grace in Dixie: Southern Faiths from Faulkner to Elvis*, ed. Charles Reagan Wilson, 18–36. Athens: University of Georgia Press, 1995.

Wilson, Edmund. "Tennessee Agrarians" *New Republic* 67 (July 29, 1931): 279–80.

Wilson, John Lyde. *The Code of Honor; or, Rules for the Government of Principals and Seconds in Dueling*. Charleston, S.C.: Thomas J. Eccles, 1838.

———. *The Code of Honor; or, Rules for the Government of Principals and Seconds in Duelling*. Charleston, S.C.: 1838). Reprinted in *Duelling in the Old South: Vignettes of Social History*, edited by Jack K. Williams, 87–104. College Station: Texas A&M University Press, 1980.

———. *The Code of Honor, or, Rules for the Government of Principals and Seconds in Duelling*. Charleston, S.C.: J. Phinney, 1858.

Wiltse, Charles M. *John C. Calhoun*. 3 vols. Indianapolis: Bobbs-Merrill, 1944–51.

Wineapple, Brenda. *Hawthorne: A Life*. New York: Alfred A. Knopf, 2003.

Wise, John Sergeant. *The End of an Era*. Boston: Houghton, Mifflin, 1899.

Wood, Gordon S. *The Americanization of Benjamin Franklin*. New York: Penguin, 2004.

Woodham-Smith, Cecil. *The Reason Why: The Story of the Fatal Charge of the Light Brigade*. London: Constable, 1953.

Woods, Michael E. "The Heart of the Sectional Conflict: Emotion, Politics, and the Coming of the American Civil War." Ph.D. diss., University of South Carolina, 2012.

———. "'The Indignation of Freedom-Loving People': The Caning of Charles Sumner and Emotion in Antebellum Politics." *Journal of Social History* 44, no. 3 (2011): 689–705.

Woodward, C. Vann, ed. *Mary Chestnut's Civil War*. New Haven, Conn.: Yale University Press, 1981.

Wright, Gavin. *The Political Economy of the Cotton South: Households, Markets, and Wealth in the Nineteenth Century*. New York: W. W. Norton, 1978.

Wyatt-Brown, Bertram. "Andrew Jackson's Honor." *Journal of the Early Republic* 17 (Spring 1997): 1–36.

———. "God and Dun and Bradstreet, 1841–1851." *Business History Review* 60, no. 4 (Winter 1966): 432–50.

———. *Hearts of Darkness: Wellsprings of a Southern Literary Tradition*. Baton Rouge: Louisiana State University Press, 2002.

———. *Honor and Violence in the Old South*. New York: Oxford University Press, 1986.

———. *The House of Percy: Honor, Melancholy and Imagination in a Southern Family*. New York: Oxford University Press, 1994.

———. "The Ideal Typology and Ante-bellum Southern History: Testing of a New Approach." *Societas* 5 (1975): 1–29.

———. "The Mask of Obedience: Male Slave Psychology in the Old South." *American Historical Review* 93 (December 1988): 1228–52.

———. *The Shaping of Southern Culture: Honor, Grace, and War, 1760s–1890s*. Chapel Hill: University of North Carolina Press, 2001.

———. *Southern Honor: Ethics and Behavior in the Old South*. New York: Oxford University Press, 1982.

———. *Southern Honor: Ethics and Behavior in the Old South*. 25th anniversary ed. New York: Oxford University Press, 2007.

———. *A Warring Nation: Honor, Race, and Humiliation in America and Abroad.* Charlottesville: University of Virginia Press, 2014.

———. *Yankee Saints and Southern Sinners.* Baton Rouge: Louisiana State University Press, 1985.

Yanuck, Julius. "The Garner Fugitive Slave Case." *Mississippi Valley Historical Review* 40 (June 1953): 47–66.

Young, Pearl J. "Religious Coming of Age among Students at Antebellum Georgia's Evangelical Colleges." M.A. thesis, Emory University, 2010.

CONTRIBUTORS

JEFFREY E. ANDERSON is Dr. William R. Hammond Professor of Liberal Arts at the University of Louisiana at Monroe. He is the author of *Conjure in African American Society* (2005), *Hoodoo, Voodoo, and Conjure: A Handbook* (2008), *The Voodoo Encyclopedia: Magic, Ritual, and Religion* (2015), and articles on related topics.

EDWARD L. AYERS is the Tucker-Boatwright Professor of Humanities and president emeritus at the University of Richmond. He is the author of several books, including *The Promise of the New South: Life after Reconstruction* and *In the Presence of Mine Enemies: Civil War in the Heart of America.*

DICKSON D. BRUCE JR. was professor of history at the University of California, Irvine. He authored eight books on such topics as religion, violence, African American literature, Southern culture, and the history of the early Republic. His book *The Kentucky Tragedy* blends social, legal, and literary aspects of a famous case of murder and suicide, and his *Violence and Culture in the Antebellum South* is a classic in its field.

EMILY S. BRUCE is a lecturer in residence in the Legal Studies Program at the University of California, Berkeley. She holds a J.D. from Stanford Law School and an A.B. in comparative literature from Princeton University.

MATTHEW A. BYRON is an assistant professor of history at Young Harris College. He is the author of several articles on dueling.

EDWARD R. CROWTHER is a professor of history at Adams State University. He is coeditor of *Between Fetters and Freedom* and the author of *Southern Evangelicals and the Coming of the Civil War* and many articles and reviews.

CHRISTOPHER MICHAEL CURTIS is a professor of history and Distinguished Faculty Research Fellow at Armstrong State University in Savannah, Georgia. He is the author of *Jefferson's Freeholders and the Politics of Ownership in the Old Dominion.*

BRENDA FAVERTY is an adjunct instructor at Kent State University. Her research has covered the subjects of southern antebellum women and the gendered aspects of honor.

JEFF FORRET is a professor of history at Lamar University in Beaumont, Texas. His has authored *Race Relations at the Margins: Slaves and Poor Whites in the Antebellum Southern Countryside* (2006), *Slavery in the United States* (2012), and *Slave against Slave: Plantation Violence in the Old South* (2015) and coedited *New Directions in Slavery Studies: Commodification, Community, and Comparison* (2015).

SARAH E. GARDNER is a professor of history and director of the Center for Southern Studies at Mercer University. She is the author of *Blood and Irony: Southern White Women's Narratives of the Civil War, 1861–1937* and of the forthcoming *Reviewing the South: The Literary Marketplace and the Creation of the Southern Renaissance,* on the literary marketplace and southern literature during the interwar years. She is currently working on a study of reading during the Civil War.

TODD HAGSTETTE is an assistant professor of English at University of South Carolina Aiken, former director of the *Simms Initiatives* for the South Carolinana Library, and founding director of the *Digital U.S. South* project for the USC Institute for Southern Studies. He is the author of several essays on William Gilmore Simms and southern honor and is the editor of the forthcoming *Reading William Gilmore Simms: Essays of Introduction to the Author's Canon.*

KATHLEEN M. HILLIARD is an associate professor of history at Iowa State University. She is author of *Masters, Slaves, and Exchange: Power's Purchase in the Old South* (2014). Her next book, *Bonds Burst Asunder: The Transformation of Southern Exchange in War and Freedom,* will examine the effects of the Civil War and emancipation on the exchange relations cultivated during slavery.

BRADLEY JOHNSON is a professor of English at Doane University in Crete, Nebraska. He has published articles on honor and violence in the works of Augusta Jane Evans Wilson and William Faulkner.

ANNA KOIVUSALO is a Ph.D. candidate at the University of Helsinki. She is preparing a doctoral dissertation on the connection of southern honor and emotions in the life and politics of James Chesnut Jr.

ROBERT S. LEVINE is Distinguished University Professor of English at the University of Maryland, College Park. He is the author of a number of books, including *Dislocating Race and Nation: Episodes in Nineteenth-Century American Literary Nationalism* and most recently, *The Lives of Frederick Douglass.* He is the general editor of *The Norton Anthology of American Literature.*

LAWRENCE T. MCDONNELL is an assistant professor of history at Iowa State University. He has published articles on slavery and social contradictions in the Old South and *Performing Disunion: The Coming of the Civil War in Charleston, South Carolina* (2017).

JOHN MAYFIELD is a professor of history at Samford University and a former Ford Foundation fellow. He is the author of articles on southern cultural and intellectual history, plus three books, including *The New Nation: 1800–1845* and, recently, *Counterfeit Gentlemen: Manhood and Humor in the Old South.*

DAVID MOLTKE-HANSEN spent thirty years developing historical collections and programs at the South Carolina Historical Society, the University of North Carolina at Chapel Hill, and the Historical Society of Pennsylvania before turning to full-time writing and editing. Author of fifty-plus essays and editor of nine volumes, primarily on aspects of southern intellectual and cultural history, he helped launch the *Simms Initiatives* at the University of South Carolina and cofounded Cambridge Studies on the American South.

AMANDA R. MUSHAL is an associate professor of history at The Citadel. Her work focuses on honor, credit reporting, and material culture in the commercial culture of antebellum South Carolina.

TIMOTHY J. WILLIAMS is a visiting assistant professor of history at the Robert D. Clark Honors College (University of Oregon). He is the author of *Intellectual Manhood: University, Self, and Society in the Antebellum South.*

INDEX